The Norton Reader

SEVENTH EDITION, SHORTER

W. W. NORTON & COMPANY, INC.
also publishes

THE NORTON ANTHOLOGY OF AMERICAN LITERATURE
edited by Nina Baym et al.

THE NORTON ANTHOLOGY OF CONTEMPORARY FICTION
edited by R. V. Cassill

THE NORTON ANTHOLOGY OF ENGLISH LITERATURE
edited by M. H. Abrams et al.

THE NORTON ANTHOLOGY OF LITERATURE BY WOMEN
edited by Sandra M. Gilbert and Susan Gubar

THE NORTON ANTHOLOGY OF MODERN POETRY
edited by Richard Ellmann and Robert O'Clair

THE NORTON ANTHOLOGY OF POETRY
edited by Arthur M. Eastman et al.

THE NORTON ANTHOLOGY OF SHORT FICTION
edited by R. V. Cassill

THE NORTON ANTHOLOGY OF WORLD MASTERPIECES
edited by Maynard Mack et al.

THE NORTON FACSIMILE OF
THE FIRST FOLIO OF SHAKESPEARE
prepared by Charlton Hinman

THE NORTON INTRODUCTION TO LITERATURE
edited by Carl E. Bain, Jerome Beaty, and J. Paul Hunter

and the

NORTON CRITICAL EDITIONS

The Norton Reader

An Anthology of Expository Prose

SEVENTH EDITION, SHORTER

Arthur M. Eastman, *General Editor*
VIRGINIA POLYTECHNIC INSTITUTE AND STATE UNIVERSITY

Caesar R. Blake
UNIVERSITY OF TORONTO

Hubert M. English, Jr.
UNIVERSITY OF MICHIGAN

Joan E. Hartman
COLLEGE OF STATEN ISLAND,
CITY UNIVERSITY OF NEW YORK

Alan B. Howes
UNIVERSITY OF MICHIGAN

Robert T. Lenaghan
UNIVERSITY OF MICHIGAN

Leo F. McNamara
UNIVERSITY OF MICHIGAN

James Rosier
UNIVERSITY OF PENNSYLVANIA

W·W·NORTON & COMPANY · *New York · London*

Published simultaneously in Canada by Penguin Books
Canada, Ltd., 2801 John Street, Markham, Ontario
L3R 1B4. Printed in the United States of America.

The text of this book is composed in Electra.
Composition by Vance Weaver Composition.
Manufacturing by R. R. Donnelley.
Book design by Antonina Krass.

Library of Congress Cataloging-in-Publication Data

The Norton reader. Shorter edn.

    Includes bibliographies and index.
    1. College readers. I. Eastman, Arthur M.,
1918-   . II. Blake, Caesar R. (Caesar Robert),
1925-   .
PE1122.N68   1988   808.88'8   87-24046

ISBN 0-393-95647-4

W. W. Norton & Company, Inc. 500 Fifth Avenue, New York, N.Y. 10110

W. W. Norton & Company Ltd., 37 Great Russell Street,
London WC1B 3NU

1 2 3 4 5 6 7 8 9 0

Contents

[*Entries marked with • are followed by questions.*]

EDUCATION

LANGUAGE AND COMMUNICATION

SIGNS OF THE TIMES

HUMAN NATURE

ETHICS

HISTORY

POLITICS AND GOVERNMENT

SCIENCE

LITERATURE AND THE ARTS

PHILOSOPHY AND RELIGION

Index of
Rhetorical Modes
and Strategies

RHETORICAL MODES

NARRATIVE

DESCRIPTION

EXPOSITION

RHETORICAL STRATEGIES

Title and Opening and Closing Paragraphs

Preface

Editors of texts that undergo repeated revision inevitably regard their latest effort as especially fine. Certainly the editors of this shorter seventh edition of *The Norton Reader* consider it the equal of its progenitors and possibly the best since the first edition of 1965. Its generous contents are varied in many ways—in length, style, tone, immediacy, difficulty, and subject; and period, nationality, age, and sex of the author. Seven essays, for example, are by Canadian authors, twenty-four by women. New and familiar essays by Native American, black, Asian American, and Chicano writers reflect the range of the *Reader.* All entries have been approved by at least three of the editors: quality has continued to be essential for inclusion.

Having satisfied the demands of most readers, two-thirds of the selections remain from earlier editions. It is a pleasure—simply to name selections from "Personal Report"—to print again old favorites by Dylan Thomas, Maya Angelou, Loren Eiseley, and E. B. White. It is no less a pleasure to introduce new selections that account for one-third of this edition. They come from such authors as Neil Postman, Nancy Sommers, Desmond Morris, and Ralph W. Conant. Further, inclusion of these new essayists points up a sharpened focus on modern and contemporary writing. Seventeen essays were published between 1900 and 1950, fifty-nine between 1950 and 1980, and thirty-one since 1980.

As heretofore, the essays are gathered into sections according to major fields of human concern, some of them familiar ground to students— "Personal Report," "Mind," "Education," "Language and Communication"—and others inviting ventures toward more specialized kinds of knowledge, such as "History," "Science," "Philosophy and Religion." Teachers familiar with earlier editions will, however, note important changes in the manner of presenting essays. The editors have sought a middle ground between anthologies that offer essays with little or no editorial help and others in which editorial advice overwhelms the readings. The editors, realizing that writing and reading can engage in dialogues to the benefit of both, have sought to stimulate such dialogues in several ways:

1. By increasing the number of essays for which study questions are provided.
2. By dividing these study questions into two complementary categories: "The Reader" and "The Writer." The first focuses on content and interpretation—in short, on meaning. The second focuses on means and ends, on the strategies of style, tone, and arrangement by which an author seeks to effect changes in the readers' mind.
3. By bringing to four the offerings of certain gifted essayists—E. B. White, Virginia Woolf, Lewis Thomas, and Joan Didion—so that students may discover how authors, like baseball pitchers, vary their delivery to suit the occasion. There are, too, other less frequent manifestations of the same voice employing in different essays different means for different ends: Benjamin Franklin and James Thurber, for example, or Wayne C. Booth, George Orwell, and Stephen Jay Gould.
4. By providing more cross-referencing questions that invite discrimination among the ways different authors treat related subjects—Loren Eiseley, E. B. White, Lewis Thomas, and Elisabeth Kübler-Ross on mortality, for example, or the paired essays, one by Virginia Woolf and one by Doris Lessing, entitled "My Father."
5. By providing a totally new introductory (rather than final) essay on reading and writing. The work of Robert E. Hosmer, Jr. of Mount Holyoke, it explicitly yet informally coaches young readers in analyzing the processes of writing and reasoned response.
6. By expanding the authors' biographies to help students determine the contexts from which writings emerge.
7. And by securing from Professor Hosmer a new teachers' *Guide*, one that treats the rhetoric and content of *all* essays in the *Reader*, focusing especially on the aforementioned quartets of essays by E. B. White, Virginia Woolf, Lewis Thomas, and Joan Didion.

Many of these improvements derive from suggestions from the field, and much of what remains does so because of support from teachers across the country. Among those whose aid it is a pleasure to acknowledge are the following: Christine Barkley, San Diego Mesa College; Ruth M. Bradley, Diablo Valley College; Roger D. Carlstrom, Yakima Valley Community College; Joseph J. Comprone, University of Louisville; Virginia Cooke, Simon Fraser University; Richard Hauer Costa, Texas A&M University; Carrol Daniels, Stephen F. Austin State University; Charles H. Daughaday, Murray State University; Wilfred O. Dietrich, Blinn College; J. L. Dillard, Northwestern State University of Louisiana; M. Elaine Dolan, Tulane University of Louisiana; Anita Gandolfo, West Virginia University; Marshall Gillaland, University of Saskatchewan; Frederick Goldberg, Clayton Junior College; Katherine K. Gottschalk, Cornell University; Theodore Haddin, University of Alabama in Birmingham; James Harrison, University of Guelph; Michael Hennessy,

Southwest Texas State University; Charles Hofmiller, University of Bridgeport; Elsie B. Holmes, Trinity University; M. Hoskinson, Los Angeles Pierce College; Patricia J. Howard, Baylor University; Susan Hunter, Harvey Mudd College; Joseph Johnson, Northwestern State University of Louisiana; Nancy Johnson, University of British Columbia; Paul Klemp, Oklahoma State University; John Lammers, University of Central Arkansas; Frank E. LaRosa, San Diego City College; Jane LeMoine, Florida Institute of Technology; Jonathan Loesberg, American University; Steve Lynn, University of South Carolina; Karen Lyons, University of Nebraska at Lincoln; Mary McBride, Texas Tech University; Paul J. McGinnis, California State University, Sacramento; Jay Macpherson, Victoria College, University of Toronto; Irene Makaryk, Université d'Ottawa; Sara Murray, University of Texas at San Antonio; J. Walter Nelson, Eastern Kentucky University; Karen C. Ogden, University of Manitoba; Walter O'Grady, University of Toronto; Herbert Perluck, Brooklyn College, City University of New York; Catherine Reyner, University of Missouri at Kansas City; Mary Beth Richards, University of Nebraska at Lincoln; Eleanor M. Robinson, Niagara County Community College; Robert Ross, Southern Methodist University; Dennis Rygiel, Auburn University; Gary D. Schmidt, Calvin College; H. W. Sheridan, Brown University; Sam Solecki, University of Toronto; H. M. Solomon, Auburn University; David E. Stacey, University of Louisville; Neal Steiger, University of Massachusetts—Amherst; Judith Stein, University of Maryland at College Park; Philip J. Tama, Marywood College; David Tangeman, Washburn University of Topeka; Eva Taube, Southwestern College; Mary Kay Temple, University of North Florida; Robert Wiltenburg, Washington University; L. Westervelt, University of Houston.

—Arthur M. Eastman

Notes on Reading and Writing

> Despair is no good—for the writer, for anyone. Only hope can carry us aloft, can keep us afloat. Only hope, and a certain faith that the incredible structure that has been fashioned by this most strange and ingenious of all mammals cannot end in ruin and disaster. This faith is a writer's faith, for writing itself is an act of faith, nothing else.
>
> —E. B. White, "The Faith of a Writer"

E. B. White's eloquent remarks, delivered on his receiving the National Medal for Literature in 1971, encourage all of us engaged in writing. His words provide a point of departure as we consider the whole project of reading and writing, and the role that *The Norton Reader* can play in enabling you to become a better writer. A *better* writer, for you can already write. That is not just to say that you know the language and some of the "mechanics," like exclamation points, periods, and paragraph indentions, needed to put your thoughts on paper. It also means that you know how to communicate your thoughts in writing, at least some of the time. Sometimes you know what you want to say, other times you do not; sometimes you can find the words to say exactly what you want to, other times you cannot; sometimes you are satisfied with what you have written, other times you are not. If you feel that these last remarks apply to you, do not despair—you are in the company of almost every writer, amateur and professional.

One of the first things to remember about writing derives from an awareness of what human beings are: limited, capable of mistakes, and constantly seeking to understand and express themselves. To recognize this is not to give way to despair; rather, it is to recognize two positive implications for you as a writer. First, your writing cannot be "perfect," and no one is asking you to write the perfect essay. Work toward

xxii NOTES ON READING AND WRITING

producing the best piece of writing you can deliver today, but do not be crippled by unrealistic expectations, your own or your instructor's. Second, because you are unique and your experiences and objectives are solely your own, you always have something to add to a text you have read, whether in thought, discussion, or writing.

Recognizing this should give you confidence. Writing, like many other human activities, goes hand in hand with self-confidence: if you think you can do it, you are halfway there. "Writing itself is an act of faith," primarily in yourself and your abilities, secondarily in language. If you remember how you learned to do certain things—prepare a meal, play a sport, pass an exam—you recall just how important self-confidence is. Of course, preparation and practice are equally important elements in any process. In the process of learning to write better, your preparation— reading, thinking, discussing—and your practice—writing, revising, editing—are essential. In addition, the work of your instructor and your classmates will be invaluable for you. They, too, are writers confronting the same problems that you confront.

The Norton Reader has been designed to play a significant part in that process. It offers a selection of well-written, thought-provoking essays for you to read, reflect on, discuss, and write about. These essays are here for you. The meaning of each essay does not reside "there" on the page, in the essay; nor does it reside solely in you. Furthermore, the essay does not mean whatever you want it to mean. Rather, meaning will emerge from the text and your response to it in that intervening distance between you and the printed page. The meaning that you derive will be tested, modified, rejected, or enhanced when you discuss your ideas in class and when you write. The remarks that follow may offer some helpful strategies as you work with the essays in this reader.

The Essay

It is far easier to say what the essay is *not* than to say what it is; it is not a poem or drama or catalogue or lab report or any one of a long list of other forms of writing we might cite. But definition by negation does not help much, nor does a definition such as Aldous Huxley's flippant "The essay is a literary device for saying almost everything about anything." One way to define the essay is to describe it as a "brief prose composition that attempts to make and develop an assertion in an engaging manner." It is worth pausing to consider the different elements of this definition. First, the essay is brief, perhaps only a few typed pages. Second, the essay is prose. Alexander Pope referred to his verse compositions, the "Essay on Criticism" and the "Essay on Man," as essays, but few writers since the eighteenth century have followed his example. Essays today are works of nonfiction in prose. Third, the essay writer attempts to develop an assertion, to make one point clearly and effectively. Finally, the word "essay," from the French noun *essai*, a "trial," reflects the view of Michel de Montaigne, a sixteenth-century French philosopher and creator of the "essai." Montaigne considered his essays attempts to respond to a wide variety of issues and events in a thoughtful, personal way.

One way to classify essays in general is to distinguish the formal essay from the informal essay. The formal essay most often presents a serious subject for a specialized audience; its author writes as an acknowledged authority whose purpose is to inform the reader; the tone of the formal essay tends to be impersonal. Nancy Sommers's "Revision Strategies of Student Writers and Experienced Adult Writers," Niccolò Machiavelli's "The Morals of the Prince," and Jean-Paul Sartre's "Existentialism" illustrate the formal essay. The informal essay, on the other hand, deals with events from everyday life and presents its subject matter for a general reader; its author is often a keen observer or participant who writes in a personal way. Examples of informal essays in *The Norton Reader* include Dylan Thomas's "Memories of Christmas," Daniel Mark Epstein's "The Case of Harry Houdini," and Phyllis Rose's "Shopping and Other Spiritual Adventures."

Every essay, whether formal or informal, focuses attention on a particular subject and seeks to make a definite point for a specific audience. It is a combination of objective elements and subjective responses. In writing essays in college, keep in mind the importance of balancing personal response with objective material. You limit the effectiveness of your writing when the reader is left with the impression that all you have written is opinion.

Rhetoric and the Modes of Essay Writing

When you hear someone's remarks dismissed as "mere rhetoric," you know that the term is less than glowing: the speaker or writer may have mastered the means of expression—style and delivery—but is found lacking in substance. Politicians often face this charge. Yet *rhetoric* also has positive meaning, for it refers to both knowledge and skill of strategies for effective communication. Aristotle's *Rhetoric* is the central document in the study of rhetoric. For Aristotle, rhetoric has mostly to do with persuasion, with inventing arguments, arranging evidence, and expressing ideas in aptly chosen language. For our purpose, rhetoric is the knowledge of the skills and strategies needed to communicate ideas, with grace and fluency, to a designated audience.

Rhetorical tradition provides a convenient way of distinguishing one type of essay from another. We can speak of four basic "modes" or types of essay writing: narrative, descriptive, expository, and argumentative.

Narrative essays, which relate an event or a series of events, demonstrate a particular dimension of the storyteller's art: creating a story from factual material. Unlike a short story or novel or fable, narrative essays deal exclusively with "real world" events. Descriptive essays create impressions that appeal to our senses. Expository essays offer explanations, most often by supplying substantial information presented in a logical manner. Among the most common forms of exposition, which can also be called analysis, are essays of comparison/contrast, classification, definition, process analysis, and causal analysis. Finally, argumentative essays seek to convince the reader of the correctness of a particular point of view. Strictly speaking, argument and persuasion are two different activities (argument appeals to reason and seeks assent; persuasion appeals to emotion and seeks action), but they are often combined in effective writing. Likewise, while it is possible to write an essay that is pure narrative or pure description or pure exposition, it is much more likely that you will mix modes in your own writing.

Writing as Process

The composing process involves all stages of your work, from the first ideas you have or notes you jot down through the presentation of the final copy. It extends well beyond the physical acts of putting pen to paper or hands to keyboard, for, in the process of composing—in reading, reflecting, discussing, and writing—you are actively involved in creating a text.

Consider the kinds of writing activities you might use in working on an essay: preliminary writing (notes, journal entries, freewriting); inventing a thesis and designing an essay (trial thesis statements and outlines); working up a draft; revising; editing the best draft for final copy. Seen in this way, writing is a process by and through which you can progress from tentative responses and jottings to a final draft worthy of submission.

Writing is also a cognitive process, a means by which you learn more about a particular subject, about other people, and about yourself. At no point will you or any writer know everything about a specific topic, but in most cases you will know more by the time you submit the final copy than you did when you invented your thesis or wrote your first draft. The status of writing as a cognitive process means two things for you. First, you can expect to learn from your writing. And second, you can be confident that your writing will improve with effort, for you and the essay are proceeding toward a goal.

Reading and Writing

Reading and writing might seem to be opposing activities. Careful reading calls for analysis, splitting a text apart in order to understand how it is constructed. Effective writing, on the other hand, demands synthesis, binding elements together so that they function as a whole. Yet reading and writing are complementary activities, for the better you understand how a given essay "works," the more you learn about how to make your own writing "work."

In considering anything you have read, you need to ask yourself two important questions, both of them posed by a distinguished teacher, Robert Scholes: What does this text mean? How does it mean? When you have finished reading, you will have some tentative responses; when you have discussed the reading in class, you will have clearer answers; and when you have written your essay, you will have significantly deepened your understanding of the text. Put another way, writing will complete the experience of reading.

How to Read: Some Practical Suggestions

A good understanding of any serious essay requires more than just one reading. You might adopt a three-part method for reading your assigned essays: first, an uninterrupted narrative reading to acquire a basic sense of the text (What does it mean?); then, a close, analytical, annotated reading to appreciate the structure and logic of the text (How does it mean?); finally, a "review reading" to synthesize your earlier readings. Because careful reading is analysis, you will want to be precise as you examine all the elements—even the title—of the essays you read.

As you read, annotate your text with a free but directed hand. Underline important ideas and essential terms; underline passages you do not understand; put question marks and comments in the margins. Imagine that you are in conversation with the writer and respond accordingly. If a particular idea strikes you as insightful, make a note. If the writer's thought seems unclear, note that you want to focus on it in your next reading or in discussion. Refer to your annotated text in class to remind you what ideas provoked you and where you had questions. Use your annotation to bring your personal perspective and experience to bear on what you read. This is an essential part of the composing process.

What to Look for When You Read

To get at the structure and substance of an essay, spend some time considering the following elements:

1. TITLE, AND OPENING AND CLOSING PARAGRAPHS
   Notice the title—it can be an important aspect of the essay, serving to catch the reader's interest and sometimes giving a clear indication of what the essay is about. Study the opening paragraph, a vital part of an

essay, one which establishes some common ground with the reader. The opening paragraph often articulates the thesis of the essay. Take a look at how Brent Staples in "Black Men and Public Space" and Betty Rollin in "Motherhood: Who Needs It?" startle the reader in their opening paragraphs. Consider the closing paragraph. It should reinforce the thesis and offer an assessment, an observation, or a prediction; it should leave the reader with something to think about. Look at the provocative closing paragraphs of "Decolonizing the Mind" by Ngũgĩ wa Thiong'o and "Shopping and Other Spiritual Adventures" by Phyllis Rose.

2. THESIS, DEVELOPMENT, AND SUPPORT

Examine the essay for a thesis statement, a sentence in which the writer takes a stand and indicates his or her central purpose. Sometimes, as in Judith Viorst's "Good as Guilt," the writer's thesis is explicitly stated. Other times, as in E. B. White's "Once More to the Lake," where there is probably no single sentence that will satisfactorily represent the entire essay, the writer implies it. In such cases the careful reader should be able to construct a thesis statement.

How does the writer develop the main idea of the essay? Sometimes a thesis will rest on assumptions, related ideas that the writer does not mention directly but expects the reader to understand or to agree to or, if the real purpose is deception, to overlook. Machiavelli, in "The Morals of the Prince," appears to assume that it is more important for a prince to stay in power than to be a "good" man. In considering what you read, always ask yourself: What assumptions has the writer made? Apply that question to Elisabeth Kübler-Ross's "On the Fear of Death" or Stephen Jay Gould's "The Terrifying Normalcy of AIDS."

How does the writer support the main idea of the essay? Determine what kinds of support have been enlisted. Factual evidence (material easily verifiable or attested to by reliable witnesses) or opinion? If opinion, whose? That of a recognized authority? Furthermore, consider whether or not the support is sufficient for the subject, purpose, and audience. Is the evidence appropriate and convincing? Evaluate the evidence Anthony Burgess draws on in his essay "Is America Falling Apart?"

3. ORGANIZATION

A well-written essay is clearly, logically, and carefully organized. Its skeletal structure can be discerned, removed, and examined. Think of this process as something like boning a fish: if the essay has been organized well, you should be able to delineate its structure as easily as you can separate the skeletal system from a freshly caught trout. As an exercise in discerning structure, see if you can "bone" George Orwell's "Shooting an Elephant" or Desmond Morris's "Territorial Behavior."

4. PERSONA

When you read an essay, you should be able to form an impression of the writer from the text. In response to choices of subject, purpose, and, most importantly, audience, the writer creates a particular image. Elements like tone, word choice, figures of speech, sentence complexity, and paragraph length—that is, the writer's "style"—create a persona. Your response to the writer's persona is of crucial importance, particularly in argument, where, if the writer fails to create a persona that is fair, knowledgeable, and trustworthy, the argument is lost. You should be able to characterize the writer's persona. One way to do this is to draw up a short list of adjectives that describe the voice you heard in the essay you read. Try this exercise on Margaret Atwood's "Writing the Male Character" or Eudora Welty's "One Writer's Beginnings."

Upon completion of your close reading, you should be able to summarize the essay as a whole, describe the strategies that the writer has used, and offer your view of the success or failure of the essay by pointing to specific elements in the text.

How to Write: Some Suggestions Based upon Reading

Through reading, you sharpen your sense of what a good essay is. You develop an awareness of the elements that determine its success or failure, taking into consideration title, opening and closing paragraphs, thesis, development and support, and persona. Now your work as a writer begins. The nine brief points that follow are suggestions for developing your understanding of writing.

1. Have something to say. You can know all the fine points of form and style, but unless you have discovered something to say, there is no sense in writing.
2. Know your subject. Review your annotated text and class notes.
3. Articulate your purpose. If it has not been assigned in class, determine it for yourself.
4. Develop a clear sense of your audience. Ask yourself two questions: For whom am I writing this? What must I do to communicate successfully with my reader? Develop a clear sense of your own voice—know your persona.
5. Once you have these four aspects defined, formulate a thesis statement that expresses the central idea of your essay. Use whatever method works for you—freewriting, brainstorming, cataloguing responses to what you have read—but put your thesis, however tentative, in writing.
6. Design your essay by drawing up an outline to guide its development.

7. Write a rough draft. Go ahead and write, no matter what you think of the quality. A first draft, however rough, gives you something to work with.

8 Revise the draft. "Re-see" your essay in light of its subject, purpose, and audience. Examine its design. Judge how effectively it supports its central thesis.

9. Edit your revised draft. Proofread your final essay.

—Robert E. Hosmer, Jr.,
Mount Holyoke College

The Norton Reader

SEVENTH EDITION, SHORTER

Personal Report

Dylan Thomas

MEMORIES OF CHRISTMAS

One Christmas was so much like another, in those years, around the sea-town corner now and out of all sound except the distant speaking of the voices I sometimes hear a moment before sleep, that I can never remember whether it snowed for six days and six nights when I was twelve or whether it snowed for twelve days and twelve nights when I was six; or whether the ice broke and the skating grocer vanished like a snowman through a white trap-door on that same Christmas Day that the mince-pies finished Uncle Arnold and we tobogganed down the seaward hill, all the afternoon, on the best tea-tray, and Mrs. Griffiths complained, and we threw a snowball at her niece, and my hands burned so, with the heat and the cold, when I held them in front of the fire, that I cried for twenty minutes and then had some jelly.

All the Christmases roll down the hill towards the Welsh-speaking sea, like a snowball growing whiter and bigger and rounder, like a cold and headlong moon bundling down the sky that was our street; and they stop at the rim of the ice-edged, fish-freezing waves, and I plunge my hands in the snow and bring out whatever I can find; holly or robins or pudding, squabbles and carols and oranges and tin whistles, and the fire in the front room, and bang go the crackers, and holy, holy, holy, ring the bells, and the glass bells shaking on the tree, and Mother Goose, and Struwelpeter[1] —oh! the baby-burning flames and the clacking scissorman!—Billy Bunter[2] and Black Beauty, Little Women and boys who have three helpings, Alice and Mrs. Potter's badgers,[3] penknives, teddy-bears—

1. The title character of *Struwelpeter (Slovenly Peter)*, or *Merry Tales and Funny Pictures*, a children's book originally in German, by Dr. Heinrich Hoffmann, containing gaily grim admonitory narratives in verse about little Pauline, for example, who played with matches and got burned up; or the little boy who sucked his thumbs until the tall scissorman cut them off.
2. The humorous fat boy in Frank Richards' tales of English school life.
3. Beatrix Potter, creator of *Peter Rabbit* and other animal tales for children, among them *The Tale of Mr. Tod*, a badger.

named after a Mr. Theodore Bear, their inventor, or father, who died recently in the United States—mouth-organs, tin-soldiers, and blanc-mange, and Auntie Bessie playing "Pop Goes the Weasel" and "Nuts in May" and "Oranges and Lemons" on the untuned piano in the parlor all through the thimble-hiding musical-chairing blind-man's-buffing party at the end of the never-to-be-forgotten day at the end of the un-remembered year.

In goes my hand into that wool-white bell-tongued ball of holidays resting at the margin of the carol-singing sea, and out come Mrs. Prothero and the firemen.

It was on the afternoon of the day of Christmas Eve, and I was in Mrs. Prothero's garden, waiting for cats, with her son Jim. It was snowing. It was always snowing at Christmas; December, in my memory, is white as Lapland, though there were no reindeers. But there were cats. Patient, cold, and callous, our hands wrapped in socks, we waited to snowball the cats. Sleek and long as jaguars and terrible-whiskered, spitting and snarling they would slink and sidle over the white back-garden walls, and the lynx-eyed hunters, Jim and I, fur-capped and moccasined trappers from Hudson's Bay off Eversley Road, would hurl our deadly snowballs at the green of their eyes. The wise cats never appeared. We were so still, Eskimo-footed arctic marksmen in the muffling silence of the eternal snows—eternal, ever since Wednesday—that we never heard Mrs. Prothero's first cry from her igloo at the bottom of the garden. Or, if we heard it at all, it was, to us, like the far-off challenge of our enemy and prey, the neighbor's Polar Cat. But soon the voice grew louder. "Fire!" cried Mrs. Prothero, and she beat the dinner-gong. And we ran down the garden, with the snowballs in our arms, towards the house, and smoke, indeed, was pouring out of the dining-room, and the gong was bombilat-ing, and Mrs. Prothero was announcing ruin like a town-crier in Pompeii. This was better than all the cats in Wales standing on the wall in a row. We bounded into the house, laden with snowballs, and stopped at the open door of the smoke-filled room. Something was burning all right; perhaps it was Mr. Prothero, who always slept there after midday dinner with a newspaper over his face; but he was standing in the middle of the room, saying "A fine Christmas!" and smacking at the smoke with a slipper.

"Call the fire-brigade," cried Mrs. Prothero as she beat the gong.

"They won't be there," said Mr. Prothero, "it's Christmas."

There was no fire to be seen, only clouds of smoke and Mr. Prothero standing in the middle of them, waving his slipper as though he were conducting.

"Do something," he said.

And we threw all our snowballs into the smoke—I think we missed Mr. Prothero—and ran out of the house to the telephone-box.

trudged uphill, into the cries of the dock-birds and the hooters of ships out in the white and whirling bay.

Bring out the tall tales now that we told by the fire as we roasted chestnuts and the gaslight bubbled low. Ghosts with their heads under their arms trailed their chains and said "whooo" like owls in the long nights when I dared not look over my shoulder; wild beasts lurked in the cubby-hole under the stairs where the gas-meter ticked. "Once upon a time," Jim said, "there were three boys, just like us, who got lost in the dark in the snow, near Bethesda Chapel, and this is what happened to them . . ." It was the most dreadful happening I had ever heard.

And I remember that we went singing carols once, a night or two before Christmas Eve, when there wasn't the shaving of a moon to light the secret, white-flying streets. At the end of a long road was a drive that led to a large house, and we stumbled up the darkness of the drive that night, each one of us afraid, each one holding a stone in his hand in case, and all of us too brave to say a word. The wind made through the drive-trees noises as of old and unpleasant and maybe web-footed men wheezing in caves. We reached the black bulk of the house.

"What shall we give them?" Dan whispered.

"'Hark the Herald'? 'Christmas comes but Once a Year'?"

"No," Jack said: "We'll sing 'Good King Wenceslas.' I'll count three."

One, two, three, and we began to sing, our voices high and seemingly distant in the snow-felted darkness round the house that was occupied by nobody we knew. We stood close together, near the dark door.

> Good King Wenceslas looked out
> On the Feast of Stephen.

And then a small, dry voice, like the voice of someone who has not spoken for a long time, suddenly joined our singing: a small, dry voice from the other side of the door: a small, dry voice through the keyhole. And when we stopped running we were outside our house; the front room was lovely and bright; the gramophone was playing; we saw the red and white balloons hanging from the gas-bracket; uncles and aunts sat by the fire; I thought I smelt our supper being fried in the kitchen. Everything was good again, and Christmas shone through all the familiar town.

"Perhaps it was a ghost," Jim said.

"Perhaps it was trolls," Dan said, who was always reading.

"Let's go in and see if there's any jelly left," Jack said. And we did that.

1945

Wallace Stegner

THE TOWN DUMP

The town dump of Whitemud, Saskatchewan, could only have been a few years old when I knew it, for the village was born in 1913 and I left there in 1919. But I remember the dump better than I remember most things in that town, better than I remember most of the people. I spent more time with it, for one thing; it has more poetry and excitement in it than people did.

It lay in the southeast corner of town, in a section that was always full of adventure for me. Just there the Whitemud River left the hills, bent a little south, and started its long traverse across the prairie and international boundary to join the Milk. For all I knew, it might have been on its way to join the Alph:[1] simply, before my eyes, it disappeared into strangeness and wonder.

Also, where it passed below the dumpground, it ran through willowed bottoms that were a favorite campsite for passing teamsters, gypsies, sometimes Indians. The very straw scattered around those camps, the ashes of those strangers' campfires, the manure of their teams and saddle horses, were hot with adventurous possibilities.

It was as an extension, a living suburb, as it were, of the dumpground that we most valued those camps. We scoured them for artifacts of their migrant tenants as if they had been archaeological sites full of the secrets of ancient civilizations. I remember toting around for weeks the broken cheek strap of a bridle. Somehow or other its buckle looked as if it had been fashioned in a far place, a place where they were accustomed to flatten the tongues of buckles for reasons that could only be exciting, and where they made a habit of plating the silver with some valuable alloy, probably silver. In places where the silver was worn away the buckle underneath shone dull yellow: probably gold.

It seemed that excitement liked that end of town better than our end. Once old Mrs. Gustafson, deeply religious and a little raddled in the head, went over there with a buckboard full of trash, and as she was driving home along the river she looked and saw a spent catfish, washed in from Cypress Lake or some other part of the watershed, floating on the yellow water. He was two feet long, his whiskers hung down, his fins and tail were limp. He was a kind of fish that no one had seen in the Whitemud in the three or four years of the town's life, and a kind that none of us children had ever seen anywhere. Mrs. Gustafson had never

1. The imaginary, mysterious river of Samuel Taylor Coleridge's poem "Kubla Khan."

6

seen one like him either; she perceived at once that he was the devil, and she whipped up the team and reported him at Hoffman's elevator.

We could hear her screeching as we legged it for the river to see for ourselves. Sure enough, there he was. He looked very tired, and he made no great effort to get away as we pushed out a half-sunken rowboat from below the flume, submerged it under him, and brought him ashore. When he died three days later we experimentally fed him to two half-wild cats, but they seemed to suffer no ill effects.

At that same end of town the irrigation flume crossed the river. It always seemed to me giddily high when I hung my chin over its plank edge and looked down, but it probably walked no more than twenty feet above the water on its spidery legs. Ordinarily in summer it carried about six or eight inches of smooth water, and under the glassy hurrying of the little boxed stream the planks were coated with deep sun-warmed moss as slick as frogs' eggs. A boy could sit in the flume with the water walling up against his back, and grab a cross brace above him, and pull, shooting himself sledlike ahead until he could reach the next brace for another pull and another slide, and so on across the river in four scoots.

After ten minutes in the flume he would come out wearing a dozen or more limber black leeches, and could sit in the green shade where darning needles flashed blue, and dragonflies hummed and darted and stopped, and skaters dimpled slack and eddy with their delicate transitory footprints, and there stretch the leeches out one by one while their sucking ends clung and clung, until at last, stretched far out, they let go with a tiny wet *puk* and snapped together like rubber bands. The smell of the river and the flume and the clay cutbanks and the bars of that part of the river was the smell of wolf willow.

But nothing in that end of town was as good as the dumpground that scattered along a little runoff coulee dipping down toward the river from the south bench. Through a historical process that went back, probably, to the roots of community sanitation and distaste for eyesores, but that in law dated from the Unincorporated Towns Ordinance of the territorial government, passed in 1888, the dump was one of the very first community enterprises, almost our town's first institution.

More than that, it contained relics of every individual who had ever lived there, and of every phase of the town's history.

The bedsprings on which the town's first child was begotten might be there; the skeleton of a boy's pet colt; two or three volumes of Shakespeare bought in haste and error from a peddler, later loaned in carelessness, soaked with water and chemicals in a house fire, and finally thrown out to flap their stained eloquence in the prairie wind.

Broken dishes, rusty tinware, spoons that had been used to mix paint; once a box of percussion caps, sign and symbol of the carelessness that most of those people felt about all matters of personal or public safety.

We put them on the railroad tracks and were anonymously denounced in the *Enterprise*. There were also old iron, old brass, for which we hunted assiduously, by night conning junkmen's catalogues and the pages of the *Enterprise* to find how much wartime value there might be in the geared insides of clocks or in a pound of tea lead[2] carefully wrapped in a ball whose weight astonished and delighted us. Sometimes the unimaginable outside world reached in and laid a finger on us. I recall that, aged no more than seven, I wrote a St. Louis junk house asking if they preferred their tea lead and tinfoil wrapped in balls, or whether they would rather have it pressed flat in sheets, and I got back a typewritten letter in a window envelope instructing me that they would be happy to have it in any way that was convenient for me. They added that they valued my business and were mine very truly. Dazed, I carried that windowed grandeur around in my pocket until I wore it out, and for months I saved the letter as a souvenir of the wondering time when something strange and distinguished had singled me out.

We hunted old bottles in the dump, bottles caked with dirt and filth, half buried, full of cobwebs, and we washed them out at the horse trough by the elevator, putting in a handful of shot along with the water to knock the dirt loose; and when we had shaken them until our arms were tired, we hauled them off in somebody's coaster wagon and turned them in at Bill Anderson's pool hall, where the smell of lemon pop was so sweet on the dark pool-hall air that I am sometimes awakened by it in the night, even yet.

Smashed wheels of wagons and buggies, tangles of rusty barbed wire, the collapsed perambulator that the French wife of one of the town's doctors had once pushed proudly up the planked sidewalks and along the ditchbank paths. A welter of foul-smelling feathers and coyote-scattered carrion which was all that remained of somebody's dream of a chicken ranch. The chickens had all got some mysterious pip at the same time, and died as one, and the dream lay out there with the rest of the town's history to rustle to the empty sky on the border of the hills.

There was melted glass in curious forms, and the half-melted office safe left from the burning of Bill Day's Hotel. On very lucky days we might find a piece of the lead casing that had enclosed the wires of the town's first telephone system. The casing was just the right size for rings, and so soft that it could be whittled with a jackknife. It was a material that might have made artists of us. If we had been Indians of fifty years before, that bright soft metal would have enlisted our maximum patience and craft and come out as ring and metal and amulet inscribed with the symbols of our observed world. Perhaps there were too many ready-made alternatives in the local drug, hardware, and general stores; perhaps our feeble

---

2. An alloy used for lining the chests in which tea was stored and transported.

artistic response was a measure of the insufficiency of the challenge we felt. In any case I do not remember that we did any more with the metal than to shape it into crude seal rings with our initials or pierced hearts carved in them; and these, though they served a purpose in juvenile courtship, stopped something short of art.

The dump held very little wood, for in that country anything burnable got burned. But it had plenty of old iron, furniture, papers, mattresses that were the delight of field mice, and jugs and demijohns that were sometimes their bane, for they crawled into the necks and drowned in the rain water or redeye that was inside.

If the history of our town was not exactly written, it was at least hinted, in the dump. I think I had a pretty sound notion even at eight or nine of how significant was that first institution of our forming Canadian civilization. For rummaging through its foul purlieus I had several times been surprised and shocked to find relics of my own life tossed out there to rot or blow away.

The volumes of Shakespeare belonged to a set that my father had bought before I was born. It had been carried through successive moves from town to town in the Dakotas, and from Dakota to Seattle, and from Seattle to Bellingham, and Bellingham to Redmond, and from Redmond back to Iowa, and from there to Saskatchewan. Then, stained in a stranger's house fire, these volumes had suffered from a house-cleaning impulse and been thrown away for me to stumble upon in the dump. One of the Cratchet girls had borrowed them, a hatchet-faced, thin, eager, transplanted Cockney girl with a frenzy, almost a hysteria, for reading. And yet somehow, through her hands, they found the dump, to become a symbol of how much was lost, how much thrown aside, how much carelessly or of necessity given up, in the making of a new country. We had so few books that I was familiar with them all, had handled them, looked at their pictures, perhaps even read them. They were the lares and penates, part of the skimpy impedimenta of household gods we had brought with us into Latium.[3] Finding those three thrown away was a little like finding my own name on a gravestone.

And yet not the blow that something else was, something that impressed me even more with the dump's close reflection of the town's intimate life. The colt whose picked skeleton lay out there was mine. He had been incurably crippled when dogs chased our mare, Daisy, the morning after she foaled. I had labored for months to make him well; had fed him by hand, curried him, exercised him, adjusted the iron braces that I had talked my father into having made. And I had not known that he would have to be destroyed. One weekend I turned him over to the

3. The region of Italy settled by the Trojans after their defeat by the Greeks in the Trojan War. Later, in Roman families, the lares and penates were the ancestral household gods; they came to embody the continuity of the family.

foreman of one of the ranches, presumably so that he could be cared for. A few days later I found his skinned body, with the braces still on his crippled front legs, lying on the dump.

Not even that, I think, cured me of going there, though our parents all forbade us on pain of cholera or worse to do so. The place fascinated us, as it should have. For this was the kitchen midden of all the civilization we knew; it gave us the most tantalizing glimpses into our lives as well as into those of the neighbors. It gave us an aesthetic distance from which to know ourselves.

The dump was our poetry and our history. We took it home with us by the wagonload, bringing back into town the things the town had used and thrown away. Some little part of what we gathered, mainly bottles, we managed to bring back to usefulness, but most of our gleanings we left lying around barn or attic or cellar until in some renewed fury of spring cleanup our families carted them off to the dump again, to be rescued and briefly treasured by some other boy with schemes for making them useful. Occasionally something we really valued with a passion was snatched from us in horror and returned at once. That happened to the mounted head of a white mountain goat, somebody's trophy from old times and the far Rocky Mountains, that I brought home one day in transports of delight. My mother took one look and discovered that his beard was full of moths.

I remember that goat; I regret him yet. Poetry is seldom useful, but always memorable. I think I learned more from the town dump than I learned from school: more about people, more about how life is lived, not elsewhere but here, not in other times but now. If I were a sociologist anxious to study in detail the life of any community, I would go very early to its refuse piles. For a community may be as well judged by what it throws away—what it has to throw away and what it chooses to—as by any other evidence. For whole civilizations we have sometimes no more of the poetry and little more of the history than this.

1959

THE READER

1. *Is Stegner's description of the dump and its surroundings vivid? Where does his writing directly appeal to the senses, and which senses are called into play?*

2. *Why does Stegner say (p. 9) that finding the three volumes of Shakespeare in the dump was "a little like finding my own name on a gravestone"? What is the purpose and effect of his allusion to Virgil's* Aeneid *in the sentence just before that?*

3. *Through what particular details does Stegner portray the dump as a record of his childhood? How is it shown to be also a record of the brief history of the town? In what respects does it more widely reflect and suggest European and American history and culture and, ultimately,*

the ancient past, the foundations of civilization?

THE WRITER

1. Stegner begins his reminiscence of the town dump by saying that it had *"poetry and excitement"* in it. In what ways does he seek to convey those qualities to the reader?
2. In his second paragraph, Stegner speaks of the Alph, the *"sacred river"* of Coleridge's poem *"Kubla Khan."* Why? How does allusion to that poem help him convey the strangeness and wonder he then felt?
3. In paragraphs 5–8, Stegner departs, as he had departed to a lesser degree in the two preceding paragraphs, from his description of the dump. Explain how that departure is justified and whether the writing there is appropriate to the essay as a whole.
4. Write an essay in which you deduce things about a person or a family from a room. You might use your room or an attic or a basement.

Maya Angelou

GRADUATION

The children in Stamps[1] trembled visibly with anticipation. Some adults were excited too, but to be certain the whole young population had come down with graduation epidemic. Large classes were graduating from both the grammar school and the high school. Even those who were years removed from their own day of glorious release were anxious to help with preparations as a kind of dry run. The junior students who were moving into the vacating classes' chairs were tradition-bound to show their talents for leadership and management. They strutted through the school and around the campus exerting pressure on the lower grades. Their authority was so new that occasionally if they pressed a little too hard it had to be overlooked. After all, next term was coming, and it never hurt a sixth grader to have a play sister in the eighth grade, or a tenth-year student to be able to call a twelfth grader Bubba. So all was endured in a spirit of shared understanding. But the graduating classes themselves were the nobility. Like travelers with exotic destinations on their minds, the graduates were remarkably forgetful. They came to school without their books, or tablets or even pencils. Volunteers fell over themselves to secure replacements for the missing equipment. When accepted, the willing workers might or might not be thanked, and

1. A town in Arkansas.

it was of no importance to the pregraduation rites. Even teachers were respectful of the now quiet and aging seniors, and tended to speak to them, if not as equals, as beings only slightly lower than themselves. After tests were returned and grades given, the student body, which acted like an extended family, knew who did well, who excelled, and what piteous ones had failed.

Unlike the white high school, Lafayette County Training School distinguished itself by having neither lawn, nor hedges, nor tennis court, nor climbing ivy. Its two buildings (main classrooms, the grade school and home economics) were set on a dirt hill with no fence to limit either its boundaries or those of bordering farms. There was a large expanse to the left of the school which was used alternately as a baseball diamond or basketball court. Rusty hoops on swaying poles represented the permanent recreational equipment, although bats and balls could be borrowed from the P.E. teacher if the borrower was qualified and if the diamond wasn't occupied.

Over this rocky area relieved by a few shady tall persimmon trees the graduating class walked. The girls often held hands and no longer bothered to speak to the lower students. There was a sadness about them, as if this old world was not their home and they were bound for higher ground. The boys, on the other hand, had become more friendly, more outgoing. A decided change from the closed attitude they projected while studying for finals. Now they seemed not ready to give up the old school, the familiar paths and classrooms. Only a small percentage would be continuing on to college—one of the South's A & M (agricultural and mechanical) schools, which trained Negro youths to be carpenters, farmers, handymen, masons, maids, cooks and baby nurses. Their future rode heavily on their shoulders, and blinded them to the collective joy that had pervaded the lives of the boys and girls in the grammar school graduating class.

Parents who could afford it had ordered new shoes and readymade clothes for themselves from Sears and Roebuck or Montgomery Ward. They also engaged the best seamstresses to make the floating graduating dresses and to cut down secondhand pants which would be pressed to a military slickness for the important event.

Oh, it was important, all right. Whitefolks would attend the ceremony, and two or three would speak of God and home, and the Southern way of life, and Mrs. Parsons, the principal's wife, would play the graduation march while the lower-grade graduates paraded down the aisles and took their seats below the platform. The high school seniors would wait in empty classrooms to make their dramatic entrance.

In the Store I was the person of the moment. The birthday girl. The center. Bailey[2] had graduated the year before, although to do so he had had to forfeit all pleasures to make up for his time lost in Baton Rouge.

My class was wearing butter-yellow piqué dresses, and Momma launched out on mine. She smocked the yoke into tiny crisscrossing puckers, then shirred the rest of the bodice. Her dark fingers ducked in and out of the lemony cloth as she embroidered raised daisies around the hem. Before she considered herself finished she had added a crocheted cuff on the puff sleeves, and a pointy crocheted collar.

I was going to be lovely. A walking model of all the various styles of fine hand sewing and it didn't worry me that I was only twelve years old and merely graduating from the eighth grade. Besides, many teachers in Arkansas Negro schools had only that diploma and were licensed to impart wisdom.

The days had become longer and more noticeable. The faded beige of former times had been replaced with strong and sure colors. I began to see my classmates' clothes, their skin tones, and the dust that waved off pussy willows. Clouds that lazed across the sky were objects of great concern to me. Their shiftier shapes might have held a message that in my new happiness and with a little bit of time I'd soon decipher. During that period I looked at the arch of heaven so religiously my neck kept a steady ache. I had taken to smiling more often, and my jaws hurt from the unaccustomed activity. Between the two physical sore spots, I suppose I could have been uncomfortable, but that was not the case. As a member of the winning team (the graduating class of 1940) I had outdistanced unpleasant sensations by miles. I was headed for the freedom of open fields.

Youth and social approval allied themselves with me and we trammeled memories of slights and insults. The wind of our swift passage remodeled my features. Lost tears were pounded to mud and then to dust. Years of withdrawal were brushed aside and left behind, as hanging ropes of parasitic moss.

My work alone had awarded me a top place and I was going to be one of the first called in the graduating ceremonies. On the classroom blackboard, as well as on the bulletin board in the auditorium, there were blue stars and white stars and red stars. No absences, no tardinesses, and my academic work was among the best of the year. I could say the preamble to the Constitution even faster than Bailey. We timed ourselves often: "WethepeopleoftheUnitedStatesinordertoformamoreperfectunion . . ." I had memorized the Presidents of the United States from Washington to Roosevelt in chronological as well as alphabetical order.

My hair pleased me too. Gradually the black mass had lengthened and thickened, so that it kept at last to its braided pattern, and I didn't have to

2. The author's brother.

yank my scalp off when I tried to comb it.

Louise and I had rehearsed the exercises until we tired out ourselves. Henry Reed was class valedictorian. He was a small, very black boy with hooded eyes, a long, broad nose and an oddly shaped head. I had admired him for years because each term he and I vied for the best grades in our class. Most often he bested me, but instead of being disappointed I was pleased that we shared top places between us. Like many Southern Black children, he lived with his grandmother, who was as strict as Momma and as kind as she knew how to be. He was courteous, respectful and soft-spoken to elders, but on the playground he chose to play the roughest games. I admired him. Anyone, I reckoned, sufficiently afraid or sufficiently dull could be polite. But to be able to operate at a top level with both adults and children was admirable.

His valedictory speech was entitled "To Be or Not to Be." The rigid tenth-grade teacher had helped him write it. He'd been working on the dramatic stresses for months.

The weeks until graduation were filled with heady activities. A group of small children were to be presented in a play about buttercups and daisies and bunny rabbits. They could be heard throughout the building practicing their hops and their little songs that sounded like silver bells. The older girls (nongraduates, of course) were assigned the task of making refreshments for the night's festivities. A tangy scent of ginger, cinnamon, nutmeg and chocolate wafted around the home economics building as the budding cooks made samples for themselves and their teachers.

In every corner of the workshop, axes and saws split fresh timber as the woodshop boys made sets and stage scenery. Only the graduates were left out of the general bustle. We were free to sit in the library at the back of the building or look in quite detachedly, naturally, on the measures being taken for our event.

Even the minister preached on graduation the Sunday before. His subject was, "Let your light so shine that men will see your good works and praise your Father, Who is in Heaven." Although the sermon was purported to be addressed to us, he used the occasion to speak to back-sliders, gamblers and general ne'er-do-wells. But since he had called our names at the beginning of the service we were mollified.

Among Negroes the tradition was to give presents to children going only from one grade to another. How much more important this was when the person was graduating at the top of the class. Uncle Willie and Momma had sent away for a Mickey Mouse watch like Bailey's. Louise gave me four embroidered handkerchiefs. (I gave her crocheted doilies.) Mrs. Sneed, the minister's wife, made me an undershirt to wear for graduation, and nearly every customer gave me a nickel or maybe even a dime with the instruction "Keep on moving to higher ground," or some such encouragement.

Amazingly the great day finally dawned and I was out of bed before I knew it. I threw open the back door to see it more clearly, but Momma said, "Sister, come away from that door and put your robe on."

I hoped the memory of that morning would never leave me. Sunlight was itself young, and the day had none of the insistence maturity would bring it in a few hours. In my robe and barefoot in the backyard, under cover of going to see about my new beans, I gave myself up to the gentle warmth and thanked God that no matter what evil I had done in my life He had allowed me to live to see this day. Somewhere in my fatalism I had expected to die, accidentally, and never have the chance to walk up the stairs in the auditorium and gracefully receive my hard-earned diploma. Out of God's merciful bosom I had won reprieve.

Bailey came out in his robe and gave me a box wrapped in Christmas paper. He said he had saved his money for months to pay for it. It felt like a box of chocolates, but I knew Bailey wouldn't save money to buy candy when we had all we could want under our noses.

He was as proud of the gift as I. It was a soft-leather-bound copy of a collection of poems by Edgar Allan Poe, or, as Bailey and I called him, "Eap." I turned to "Annabel Lee" and we walked up and down the garden rows, the cool dirt between our toes, reciting the beautifully sad lines.

Momma made a Sunday breakfast although it was only Friday. After we finished the blessing, I opened my eyes to find the watch on my plate. It was a dream of a day. Everything went smoothly and to my credit. I didn't have to be reminded or scolded for anything. Near evening I was too jittery to attend to chores, so Bailey volunteered to do all before his bath.

Days before, we had made a sign for the Store, and as we turned out the lights Momma hung the cardboard over the doorknob. It read clearly: CLOSED. GRADUATION.

My dress fitted perfectly and everyone said that I looked like a sunbeam in it. On the hill, going toward the school, Bailey walked behind with Uncle Willie, who muttered, "Go on, Ju." He wanted him to walk ahead with us because it embarrassed him to have to walk so slowly. Bailey said he'd let the ladies walk together, and the men would bring up the rear. We all laughed, nicely.

Little children dashed by out of the dark like fireflies. Their crepe-paper dresses and butterfly wings were not made for running and we heard more than one rip, dryly, and the regretful "uh uh" that followed.

The school blazed without gaiety. The windows seemed cold and unfriendly from the lower hill. A sense of ill-fated timing crept over me, and if Momma hadn't reached for my hand I would have drifted back to Bailey and Uncle Willie, and possibly beyond. She made a few slow jokes about my feet getting cold, and tugged me along to the now-strange building.

Around the front steps, assurance came back. There were my fellow "greats," the graduating class. Hair brushed back, legs oiled, new dresses and pressed pleats, fresh pocket handkerchiefs and little handbags, all homesewn. Oh, we were up to snuff, all right. I joined my comrades and didn't even see my family go in to find seats in the crowded auditorium.

The school band struck up a march and all classes filed in as had been rehearsed. We stood in front of our seats, as assigned, and on a signal from the choir director, we sat. No sooner had this been accomplished than the band started to play the national anthem. We rose again and sang the song, after which we recited the pledge of allegiance. We remained standing for a brief minute before the choir director and the principal signaled to us, rather desperately I thought, to take our seats. The command was so unusual that our carefully rehearsed and smooth-running machine was thrown off. For a full minute we fumbled for our chairs and bumped into each other awkwardly. Habits change or solidify under pressure, so in our state of nervous tension we had been ready to follow our usual assembly pattern: the American national anthem, then the pledge of allegiance, then the song every Black person I knew called the Negro National Anthem. All done in the same key, with the same passion and most often standing on the same foot.

Finding my seat at last, I was overcome with a presentiment of worse things to come. Something unrehearsed, unplanned, was going to happen, and we were going to be made to look bad. I distinctly remember being explicit in the choice of pronoun. It was "we," the graduating class, the unit, that concerned me then.

The principal welcomed "parents and friends" and asked the Baptist minister to lead us in prayer. His invocation was brief and punchy, and for a second I thought we were getting on the high road to right action. When the principal came back to the dais, however, his voice had changed. Sounds always affected me profoundly and the principal's voice was one of my favorites. During assembly it melted and lowed weakly into the audience. It had not been in my plan to listen to him, but my curiosity was piqued and I straightened up to give him my attention.

He was talking about Booker T. Washington, our "late great leader," who said we can be as close as the fingers on the hand, etc. . . . Then he said a few vague things about friendship and the friendship of kindly people to those less fortunate than themselves. With that his voice nearly faded, thin, away. Like a river diminishing to a stream and then to a trickle. But he cleared his throat and said, "Our speaker tonight, who is also our friend, came from Texarkana to deliver the commencement address, but due to the irregularity of the train schedule, he's going to, as they say, 'speak and run.'" He said that we understood and wanted the man to know that we were most grateful for the time he was able to give us and then something about how we were willing always to adjust to another's program, and without more ado—"I give you Mr. Edward Donleavy."

Not one but two white men came through the door off-stage. The shorter one walked to the speaker's platform, and the tall one moved to the center seat and sat down. But that was our principal's seat, and already occupied. The dislodged gentleman bounced around for a long breath or two before the Baptist minister gave him his chair, then with more dignity than the situation deserved, the minister walked off the stage.

Donleavy looked at the audience once (on reflection, I'm sure that he wanted only to reassure himself that we were really there), adjusted his glasses and began to read from a sheaf of papers.

He was glad "to be here and to see the work going on just as it was in the other schools."

At the first "Amen" from the audience I willed the offender to immediate death by choking on the word. But Amens and Yes, sir's began to fall around the room like rain through a ragged umbrella.

He told us of the wonderful changes we children in Stamps had in store. The Central School (naturally, the white school was Central) had already been granted improvements that would be in use in the fall. A well-known artist was coming from Little Rock to teach art to them. They were going to have the newest microscopes and chemistry equipment for their laboratory. Mr. Donleavy didn't leave us long in the dark over who made these improvements available to Central High. Nor were we to be ignored in the general betterment scheme he had in mind.

He said that he had pointed out to people at a very high level that one of the first-line football tacklers at Arkansas Agricultural and Mechanical College had graduated from good old Lafayette County Training School. Here fewer Amen's were heard. Those few that did break through lay dully in the air with the heaviness of habit.

He went on to praise us. He went on to say how he had bragged that "one of the best basketball players at Fisk sank his first ball right here at Lafayette County Training School."

The white kids were going to have a chance to become Galileos and Madame Curies and Edisons and Gauguins, and our boys (the girls weren't even in on it) would try to be Jesse Owenses and Joe Louises.

Owens and the Brown Bomber were great heroes in our world, but what school official in the white-goddom of Little Rock had the right to decide that those two men must be our only heroes? Who decided that for Henry Reed to become a scientist he had to work like George Washington Carver, as a bootblack, to buy a lousy microscope? Bailey was obviously always going to be too small to be an athlete, so which concrete angel glued to what country seat had decided that if my brother wanted to become a lawyer he had to first pay penance for his skin by picking cotton and hoeing corn and studying correspondence books at night for twenty years?

The man's dead words fell like bricks around the auditorium and too many settled in my belly. Constrained by hard-learned manners I couldn't look behind me, but to my left and right the proud graduating class of 1940 had dropped their heads. Every girl in my row had found something new to do with her handkerchief. Some folded the tiny squares into love knots, some into triangles, but most were wadding them, then pressing them flat on their yellow laps.

On the dais, the ancient tragedy was being replayed. Professor Parsons sat, a sculptor's reject, rigid. His large, heavy body seemed devoid of will or willingness, and his eyes said he was no longer with us. The other teachers examined the flag (which was draped stage right) or their notes, or the windows which opened on our now-famous playing diamond.

Graduation, the hush-hush magic time of frills and gifts and congratulations and diplomas, was finished for me before my name was called. The accomplishment was nothing. The meticulous maps, drawn in three colors of ink, learning and spelling decasyllabic words, memorizing the whole of *The Rape of Lucrece*[3]—it was for nothing. Donleavy had exposed us.

We were maids and farmers, handymen and washerwomen, and anything higher that we aspired to was farcical and presumptuous.

Then I wished that Gabriel Prosser and Nat Turner[4] had killed all whitefolks in their beds and that Abraham Lincoln had been assassinated before the signing of the Emancipation Proclamation, and that Harriet Tubman[5] had been killed by that blow on her head and Christopher Columbus had drowned in the *Santa Maria*.

It was awful to be a Negro and have no control over my life. It was brutal to be young and already trained to sit quietly and listen to charges brought against my color with no chance of defense. We should all be dead. I thought I should like to see us all dead, one on top of the other. A pyramid of flesh with the whitefolks on the bottom, as the broad base, then the Indians with their silly tomahawks and teepees and wigwams and treaties, the Negroes with their mops and recipes and cotton sacks and spirituals sticking out of their mouths. The Dutch children should all stumble in their wooden shoes and break their necks. The French should choke to death on the Louisiana Purchase (1803) while silkworms ate all the Chinese with their stupid pigtails. As a species, we were an abomination. All of us.

3. A narrative poem of 1,855 lines, by Shakespeare.
4. Leaders of Virginia slave rebellions in 1800 and 1831 respectively.
5. Nineteenth-century black abolitionist, a "conductor" on the Underground Railroad.

Donleavy was running for election, and assured our parents that if he won we could count on having the only colored paved playing field in that part of Arkansas. Also—he never looked up to acknowledge the grunts of acceptance—also, we were bound to get some new equipment for the home economics building and the workshop.

He finished, and since there was no need to give any more than the most perfunctory thank-you's, he nodded to the men on the stage, and the tall white man who was never introduced joined him at the door. They left with the attitude that now they were off to something really important. (The graduation ceremonies at Lafayette County Training School had been a mere preliminary.)

The ugliness they left was palpable. An uninvited guest who wouldn't leave. The choir was summoned and sang a modern arrangement of "Onward, Christian Soldiers," with new words pertaining to graduates seeking their place in the world. But it didn't work. Elouise, the daughter of the Baptist minister, recited "Invictus,"[6] and I could have cried at the impertinence of "I am the master of my fate, I am the captain of my soul."

My name had lost its ring of familiarity and I had to be nudged to go and receive my diploma. All my preparations had fled. I neither marched up to the stage like a conquering Amazon, nor did I look in the audience for Bailey's nod of approval. Marguerite Johnson, I heard the name again, my honors were read, there were noises in the audience of appreciation, and I took my place on the stage as rehearsed.

I thought about colors I hated: ecru, puce, lavender, beige and black.

There was shuffling and rustling around me, then Henry Reed was giving his valedictory address, "To Be or Not to Be." Hadn't he heard the whitefolks? We couldn't be, so the question was a waste of time. Henry's voice came out clear and strong. I feared to look at him. Hadn't he got the message? There was no "nobler in the mind" for Negroes because the world didn't think we had minds, and they let us know it. "Outrageous fortune"? Now, that was a joke. When the ceremony was over I had to tell Henry Reed some things. That is, if I still cared. Not "rub," Henry, "erase." "Ah, there's the erase." Us.

Henry had been a good student in elocution. His voice rose on tides of promise and fell on waves of warnings. The English teacher had helped him to create a sermon winging through Hamlet's soliloquy. To be a man, a doer, a builder, a leader, or to be a tool, an unfunny joke, a crusher of funky toadstools. I marveled that Henry could go through with the speech as if we had a choice.

I had been listening and silently rebutting each sentence with my eyes closed; then there was a hush, which in an audience warns that something unplanned is happening. I looked up and saw Henry Reed, the conserva-

6. An inspirational poem by the nineteenth-century poet William Ernest Henley, once very popular for occasions such as this one.

tive, the proper, the A student, turn his back to the audience and turn to us (the proud graduating class of 1940) and sing, nearly speaking,

> "Lift ev'ry voice and sing
> Till earth and heaven ring
> Ring with the harmonies of Liberty . . ."

It was the poem written by James Weldon Johnson. It was the music composed by J. Rosamond Johnson. It was the Negro national anthem. Out of habit we were singing it.

Our mothers and fathers stood in the dark hall and joined the hymn of encouragement. A kindergarten teacher led the small children onto the stage and the buttercups and daisies and bunny rabbits marked time and tried to follow:

> "Stony the road we trod
> Bitter the chastening rod
> Felt in the days when hope, unborn, had died.
> Yet with a steady beat
> Have not our weary feet
> Come to the place for which our fathers sighed?"

Each child I knew had learned that song with his ABC's and along with "Jesus Loves Me This I Know." But I personally had never heard it before. Never heard the words, despite the thousands of times I had sung them. Never thought they had anything to do with me.

On the other hand, the words of Patrick Henry had made such an impression on me that I had been able to stretch myself tall and trembling and say, "I know not what course others may take, but as for me, give me liberty or give me death."

And now I heard, really for the first time:

> "We have come over a way that with tears
> has been watered,
> We have come, treading our path through
> the blood of the slaughtered."

While echoes of the song shivered in the air, Henry Reed bowed his head, said "Thank you," and returned to his place in the line. The tears that slipped down many faces were not wiped away in shame.

We were on top again. As always, again. We survived. The depths had been icy and dark, but now a bright sun spoke to our souls. I was no longer simply a member of the proud graduating class of 1940; I was a proud member of the wonderful, beautiful Negro race.

Oh, Black known and unknown poets, how often have your auctioned pains sustained us? Who will compute the lonely nights made less lonely by your songs, or the empty pots made less tragic by your tales?

If we were a people much given to revealing secrets, we might raise monuments and sacrifice to the memories of our poets, but slavery cured us of that weakness. It may be enough, however, to have it said that we survive in exact relationship to the dedication of our poets (include preachers, musicians and blues singers).

1969

Hugh MacLennan

ON LIVING IN A COLD COUNTRY

I was twenty-one before I met a live writer; before I met, one might say, my fate. It was on my first voyage to England, where I was going to study: I had never been away from home before.

It is difficult for me to remember now how naïve I was then. I had worked and played hard, and had been equipping myself for twentieth-century life by studying Latin and Greek. I had never been outside the little province of Nova Scotia since the cessation of the period known to the psychologists as childhood amnesia (in my infancy, I'm told, I was in England for several months), and the polyglot passengers aboard that ship fascinated me, for the ship had sailed from New York and her ultimate destination was Antwerp. At Halifax, where I lived, she had stopped for half a day to take on two thousand barrels of apples, two elderly ladies, and myself.

Prowling about the ship after we got to sea, I had observed a sloppily dressed man of indeterminate age lounging in the smokeroof or brooding over the ocean with his elbows on the railing. I could not imagine what his profession was, but the cut of his suit was American—in those days even I could distinguish an American suit from an English one—and his face looked as though some things I had never heard of had sunk into it and stayed there. When he told me he was a writer, I was impressed. When he later informed me that he was engaged on a three-hundred-thousand-word novel about Lincoln, in three sections of equal length, and in three different styles, I was reverent.

"The first section will be in the style of Mark Twain," he explained. "Why? Because that is the only style that fits the mood of Lincoln's youth. The second section"—he paused and assessed me with giveaway, spaniel's eyes—"will be in the style of Henry James."

In those days I had heard of Henry James, but only barely.

"You see, Lincoln's middle period was one of doubts, hesitations, and parentheses. He was a Hamlet in Illinois. Shakespeare would have made a success of *Hamlet* if he had written it in novel form in the style of Henry

James."

The third section was to be written in the style of a writer I had not even heard about barely; it was to be written in the style of the last chapter of James Joyce's *Ulysses*.

"The choice is obvious," the writer explained. "Lincoln's third period was the presidency, and presidents, by the very nature of their jobs, can't think. They haven't the time. The stuff just pours through them."

I had never heard of this ship-met writer before, and perhaps I have already said enough to explain why I have never heard of him since. Yet he abides with me. I learned more from him about the trade of writing than I learned from any other teacher except Experience herself.

One night over his sixth drink he said that writing would be easy if it weren't for what he called "all the other things that went along with it," and that the chief of these other things were three insoluble problems. "Money," he said, "Women, and Liquor," and he pronounced each word as though a capital letter stood before it.

Much of what he had been saying had sounded strange to me, but this rang a familiar note. I admitted that my father had told me much the same thing the day before I sailed, but had not limited the three problems to writers. According to him, Money, Women, and Liquor were the three problems of every man who ever lived, nor were they (according to him) insoluble. With the first I was to be thrifty; the other two I was entirely to avoid.

The writer observed me gloomily: "If you take that advice, your Oedipus will be screaming before you're thirty."

I told him I had an *Oedipus* in my stateroom, and added guiltily that I ought to be studying it at that particular moment.

"My God," he said, "do you still think Oedipus is a play? But to get back—money you must have for obvious reasons, but too much is worse than too little. A high standard of living invariably produces a low standard of prose. But women and liquor, these are even more essential than money. They're necessary food for your subconscious. You need them to awaken your guilts." After ordering another drink, he sighed: "But the trouble with liquor is it's apt to leave you with nothing else *but* your subconscious. And alcoholic remorse, I'm sorry to say, is an uncreative remorse."

The next morning on deck he was obviously suffering from alcoholic remorse, and as we leaned on the railing and stared down at the yard-wide band of white brine seething along the vessel's flank, he told me he was feeling sorry for me.

"Because you want to be a writer," he said, "and you haven't a chance."

I felt myself flushing, for in those days I never told my love. I pretended that all I wished to be was a scholar.

"What gives you the idea I want to write?" I asked.

"When I meet a man I know will be no good for anything else, I always know he's going to get the bug sooner or later, and probably sooner."

"Well, supposing I do? Why do you say I haven't a chance?"

"You aren't decadent enough. In fact, you're not decadent at all, and as you're twenty-one already, I doubt if you'll become decadent in time for it to matter. Frankly, your country has ruined any chance you might ever have had of becoming a writer."

"What's my country to do with it?"

"It's a cold country. In the entire history of the human race, no important art has ever come out of a cold country."

"But Canada can also get very hot," I protested.

He shook his head. "No. Canada is a cold country because that's what the world believes it is. Wait till you begin talking to editors and you'll remember that I told you so."

Some twenty years later I was talking with an editor and I did remember that he had told me so. By that time I had been writing long enough to be acutely aware of the first of the Three Problems, and this editor belonged to a super-colossal magazine that paid super-colossal fees. I wanted one of those fees to finance six months' work on a novel. While we ate lunch, with a tableful of bilingual lawyers across the aisle discussing a case with Gallic gestures, the editor informed me that what he wanted was "a real, true-to-life piece on Canada." For a subject I could take my pick of Eskimos, trappers, Mounties, or husky dogs, and if I could manage to work all four of them into the same piece, it would be perfect, providing it met the literary standards of his magazine. While we talked, the temperature was ninety degrees, and the editor was feeling it, for he had come north clad in heavy worsteds. Mopping his forehead, he explained that this would be what he called a "duty-piece." His magazine sold several hundred thousand copies in Canada every month, and occasionally the management felt it a duty to print some Canadian material. I must have made a comment about there being no Eskimos, trappers, or husky dogs within fifteen hundred miles of where we were sitting, for he cut me short with a gesture.

"No, they're imperative. In an African duty-piece you stress the heat and the jungle. In an English duty-piece you stress how old everything is. A French duty-piece has got to be romantic, but at the same time we like an angle showing the French are also practical and getting themselves orientated to the up-to-date. But in a Canadian duty-piece you simply have to go heavy on the snow and the cold."

But to return to that morning at sea—for some reason my newly met American writer had taken an interest in me. After saying that he believed in Voltaire's[1] way of dealing with aspiring young authors ("If I had a son who wanted to write, I'd strangle him out of sheer good nature"), he asked me how I'd been living "up there," his notion of Canada being a red-painted roof on top of the North American house.

"Well actually," I told him, "and so much for your idea of my living in a cold country, for the past eleven years I've been living in a tent."

"In a *what?*"

"The first time in eleven years that I've slept between four walls was my first night aboard this ship. Well yes, I suppose it does sound a little odd."

"It sounds very odd." His eyes opened wide at me. "Indeed, it sounds so odd that it may indicate possibilities for you. Continue. Tell me about it."

So I told him.

In those days in Halifax the life was not much different from life in a village, even though we had the harbor, the university, the hospitals, the Government House,[2] the curfew gun on the Citadel, and the memory of the explosion which had smashed a third of the town a few years before. Behind every house was some sort of back yard—the word "yard" had probably reached us from New England Loyalists[3]—and most of these had a kitchen garden, a few fruit trees, and a one-horse stable which might or might not have been converted into a one-car garage. In the early 1920s there was still a faint smell of stable behind the houses and a reasonably strong smell of it in the streets. Each yard was separated from its neighbors by a rough board fence on the top of which prowling tomcats sat in the nights and howled at the female cats they knew were inside the houses.

In the summer of my eleventh year I went to a boys' camp where we slept under canvas, and when I returned to Halifax, the weather was so hot I could not sleep well indoors. Heat waves are rare in Nova Scotia, but when they come, the salt humidity sticks to your skin. My father reminded me of a little tent in the basement he had used years ago for fishing trips and he said it was probably moldy in spots. It was, but I got it out, pitched it in the back yard, installed a battered old hospital cot and a packing case to hold a saucer with a candle in it, and that night I slept beautifully. The next day I told my parents I intended to stay out in the tent until school began.

But when school began on the first of September it was still warm, so I decided to stay out until it got cold. Then in the first week of October the mornings were cool enough, but there was dew on the ripe apples and

1. Eighteenth-century French writer.
2. Official residence of the lieutenant governor of Nova Scotia.
3. Many of the New England colonists who remained loyal to the British crown during the American Revolution resettled in Nova Scotia and New Brunswick.

pears, and waking up in such air was a sensual experience as delicious as any I can remember. I told my parents I intended staying out until it got really cold. Three weeks later I woke to see the tent walls sagging and a foot of snow on the ground. Presumably this was really cold, but I told my parents I had slept so well I would stay out until it got impossibly cold.

It never did. The Canadian climate in the early 1920s had a mean average temperature three to four degrees lower than it has now, and this, meteorologists tell me, represents a substantial differential. Nowadays the temperature seldom drops below zero in Halifax, though the salt humidity of a Maritime climate makes zero feel as cold as twenty-five below on the prairies. But it often got below zero in Halifax when I was a boy, and one night in my first January in the tent the thermometer fell to seventeen below, and the trees cracked like guns in the frost. Once more I slept beautifully, and after that night I decided to remain outside indefinitely.

It seemed perfectly natural to do this. I used to wear in the winters two pairs of flannel pajamas, a pair of woolen socks, and a red beret. When I emerged from the back door in this regalia I carried a hot-water bottle (it was bad the night it broke) to warm the blankets before my own body-heat sustained a modest furnace inside of them. The only part of me that ever got cold in the tent was my nose. And here is an item for anyone who does not already know it: a cold nose is a better sedative than a quarter-grain Seconal.

Phenomena belonging to the science of physics became high poetry on the really cold nights. My breath made snow, real snow. As it issued warm from my nose and mouth, it mounted to the canvas under the ridge-pole and turned into a delicate cloud in the still, frigid air. When it congealed, it was converted into a filmy snowmist, which descended and settled on top of the bed. Once I woke with a bright orange sun flaring into the tent and found myself warm under a quarter-inch layer of the softest snow I ever saw, each crystal dancing in the eye of that Austerlitz sunrise.[4]

But congealed breath made another problem, an uncomfortable chin. In the vicinity of the mouth, when you sleep out in sub-zero weather, your breath does not turn into snow but into ice, and ice irritates the skin. Having been helpless all my adulthood in the presence of the most elementary technical problem, it gives me a certain satisfaction to relate how I dealt with this one when I was ten years old and resourceful. I asked my mother for an old sheet, cut it crosswise into strips a foot wide, and each night when I tucked myself in by candle light I laid this length of

4. That is, a dazzling sunrise, revealing all. The expression refers to the Battle of Austerlitz (1805), one of Napoleon's greatest victories: when the sun rose on the morning of the battle and dispersed the heavy mist, the enemy was revealed to have fallen into Napoleon's trap.

sheeting under my jaw. Whenever I woke with ice irritating me, I shifted
the sheeting to a dry place. After a while this routine became so automatic that I was unconscious of it.

A more serious problem was the one of waking up in the morning.

In those days my family kept a maid from Newfoundland called Sadie,
a fisherman's daughter from the little island of Ramea off the southern
coast of the Ancient Colony.[5] Ramea is barren, but the water surrounding it is so abundant in codfish that in Cabot's time the density of the cod
impeded the motion of his ships. Ramea's climate is a little milder than
Labrador's, but some of Sadie's tales of her experience of living in a cold
country made Halifax seem like a sultry port in a sugar island. Sometimes
the salt sea froze out a distance of two miles from the shore of Ramea, and
when this happened, if the fishermen wanted food, they had to haul their
dories over the treacherous, spongy, salt-water ice to deep water, and
then haul them back in the evening with the catch. More than one man
Sadie knew was drowned doing things like this. So to her, warmth was a
thing you hoarded. When her Newfoundland friends, seamen all, visited
her kitchen, the fog was so thick you could barely see through it, for while
the men smoked shag in cutty pipes, the stove glowed cherry-red as it
brewed the gallons of tea they drank. Happy in a hundred-degree temperature, the Newfoundlanders conversed in a dialect I could hardly understand, for the speech of their outports is the speech that was used by
common folk in western England in Shakespeare's time.

Newfoundlanders are polite people, and Sadie never said straight out
that I was crazy. But she did say it was no part of her duty to wade
through the snow of a zero morning in order to waken a small boy who
had a perfectly comfortable room indoors. My mother agreed with her;
indeed I suspect her of hoping that this would settle the matter, for she
knew I would never wake up in time for school if left to myself.

However, there was a chandler's shop along the Halifax waterfront
which boasted that it sold everything from a needle to an anchor, and
displayed in its window an anchor and a sailmaker's needle to prove it.
Thither I repaired one afternoon when school was out, and came home
lugging a four-pound gong of the kind they used to place on the outside of
school walls to ring in the children from recess. This gong I installed
inside the tent, and ran a cord from its clapper through a row of pulleys to
the kitchen window. After boring a hole through the window-frame, I
thrust the cord inside for Sadie to pull. And at seven-thirty the next
morning, pull she did—with the vigor of a fisher girl heaving on a
halyard.

The noise was appalling, for this was a gong which was meant to be

5. Newfoundland, the "Ancient Colony,"   mous Grand Banks fisheries. It became an
was probably first claimed for England in   English colony formally in 1583.
1497 by John Cabot, who discovered the fa-

audible for a quarter of a mile. I was out of the tent and inside the house before I was even awake. My father feared the police would intervene if the gong was used again. My mother, ever hopeful, telephoned the neighbours to apologize and to ask if they had been disturbed. She was told by all of them that they were delighted with the gong. They all got up at seven-thirty, and if they could be assured the gong would always ring, they would not have to worry about setting their own alarm clocks.

Now all the problems about sleeping in the tent were solved and I settled in for the years and the seasons that lay ahead. The little bells on the horses pulling milkmen's sleighs, jingling past on the street beyond the fence at six o'clock in the morning, used to reach through the walls of sleep like the bells of elfland. In the foggy springtimes I fell asleep with my ears filled with the groans, snores, and musical clangs of the fog signals and bell-buoys of Halifax harbor. When summer came, I often read by candlelight before falling asleep, and with the passage of seasons and years moved the passage of education and even of history.

I was sleeping in the tent when I learned how to translate the invaluable information that on the second day before the Kalends of June, Caesar moved his camp and marched his legions a distance of ten miles to a place where he made another camp. I was sleeping in the tent when, years later, I made my first acquaintance with communism in the form of Plato's *Republic*. I was in the tent the night when Lindbergh, after having spent the previous day flying over Nova Scotia, was dodging the ice-making clouds over the Atlantic. To the tent I returned at two o'clock in the morning the night Tunney beat Dempsey in Philadelphia, which also happened to be the first night I ever wore a dinner jacket or went to a Government House Ball.

Such was the story I told my writer-friend, and when I had finished I said: "So you see—it wasn't such a cold country after all."

He was silent a while, possibly engrossed in thoughts of Lincoln, probably worrying about his liver, and I felt embarrassed to have spoken so much about myself. But he seemed to have heard, for finally he turned and spoke.

"You'll never go back to that again, of course."

"I don't see why not."

"You must have slept without movement to have gotten away with it. If you'd moved in your sleep, you'd have disturbed the blankets and let in the cold."

"I did sleep without movement."

The spaniel eyes were prophetic: "Well, you have given me clear proof that your days of sleeping without movement are numbered. This avoidance of the house where your parents were sleeping, this compulsive crawling away from their vicinity and *into* that little tent in the back yard—if that doesn't indicate an Oedipus complex of magnitude, I don't

earth statement. So when I heard Eudora Welty was coming to the Northwest Writers Conference, nothing would do but that I get to talk to her.

I approached Redford and explained my problem. I wouldn't pay the ten dollar conference fee unless I got to talk alone with Eudora Welty. Redford promised to look into it for me. What a chance this seemed. Miss Welty might give some magic advice that would open my soul. Maybe she would say in a burst of insight (didn't all great writers have equally great bursts of insight?), "I can tell, Mr. Hugo, that you'll be a fine writer some day." Or maybe she'd advise me to go to Australia to broaden my base of experience. I would not have gone, but I would have considered it.

Had I ever met her I'm sure she would have said, though no doubt more graciously, what Roethke said two or three years later, "Get your fat ass to work." But I never did meet her. It turned out that she was in much demand and Redford couldn't guarantee a private audience with her though he could insure an audience with a very successful author, H. Reed Fulton. Ten dollars seemed high.

1986

THE READER

1. Does Hugo consider H. Reed Fulton a good writer? How do you know?
2. What does Hugo consider to be the only real reward of writing? Why might it be that this discovery came only after he concentrated all his efforts on poems instead of on stories?
3. What piece of advice do you suppose Hugo might give to aspiring writers?

THE WRITER

1. Do you see in the way his essay is written any indication that Hugo usually writes poems rather than stories?
2. Rewrite Hugo's essay in the style of H. Reed Fulton.
3. Write an essay comparing and contrasting Hugo's recollection of school with that given by Hans A. Schmitt in "January 30, 1933: A Memoir" (p. 33). Are German and American schools fundamentally different?

Hans A. Schmitt

JANUARY 30, 1933: A MEMOIR

I remember January 30, 1933. In Germany the next-to-last day of the first month is invariably unpleasant. If the sun should shine, in defiance of all metereological odds, it would illuminate a world lashed by crackling cold. If the clouds which rule the central European heavens from September to May claim this day as their own, as they generally do, then sleet or slushy brown snow covers the pavement. Children amble to school, and their elders walk purposefully to work, through a world suffused in a spectrum ranging from black to gray.

The best holidays of the year are over, and before every German schoolchild there stretches an expanse of dreary, homework-laden days before the academic term ends at Easter. It is the time when youngsters pray for an attack of influenza, or measles, in fact any affliction that promises to lighten life with an unscheduled holiday.

When I woke that morning, I felt the deep depression engendered by the approach of another day of educational misery: my geometry homework was only half done, the assigned passage in Ernest Lavisse's *Histoire de France* (simplified and expurgated beyond recognition) imperfectly understood. I was to face a scene with the German master for defiantly writing, once again, a composition in Latin rather than in German script. French irregular verbs were the only burden which the dismal morning found me ready to carry with a degree of authoritative ease. The day promised to be like any other day in school life, a day hardly worth living.

But wait! I swallowed and my head jerked upward, jolted by a sudden pain. Could it be? Eagerly I swallowed again. No doubt about it, my throat hurt. I repeated the process several times. I wanted to be sure that this was no dream. Evidence mounted: I had a sore throat. Lying back, I closed my eyes and prayed that the symptoms would not go away.

I remembered at once that the morning of a school day never found me well. I always had to wrestle with a powerful urge to go back to sleep. I always suffered from a matutinal heaviness of limb, coupled with slight dizziness. These were symptoms of chronic disaffection, the protests of a disconsolate soul. But the sore throat signaled a distempered body, and while the world of authority around me, my parents and my teachers, cared not about my psychic sufferings, it kept a 24-hour watch on my physical health. Every sport I enjoyed was proscribed as a source of potential injury. As soon as the daily rounds of school and chores had been completed and I seemed ready to claim a life of my own, other rules and curfews intervened. When I began the initiation into the mysteries of the English language in my fourth year of *Gymnasium*, "early to bed and early to rise makes a man healthy, wealthy and wise" was the first Anglo-Saxon maxim my classmates and I were forced to recite in unison. Duty without end promised a long, useful life, a gram of pleasure portended decay.

Now the time had come to turn the obstructive wisdom of my elders to my own advantage. Indifferent to suffering of my spirit, they would rise to the challenge of bodily disease.

I bolted out of bed to carry the day's first medical bulletin to my mother. By now it must have become clear that I was not looking for sympathy. The world in which I grew up gave none. It was divided by a two-party system which pitted the eternal majority of school and home against the child. Both harnessed me into a six-day curriculum of joyless obligations from which Sunday, punctuated by familial excursions on foot and indiscreet parental inquiries into scholastic progress, offered little relief. There was no escape, except vacation and illness, the latter afforded only after thorough tests by thermometer, careful examination of relevant sectors of the anatomy, and, in case of doubt, an earnest consultation with a third, part-time member of this grand coalition of adults, the family physician. These tests made up a daunting obstacle course, separating the claim of illness from its official recognition, but the defeats of life had not extinguished my will to tackle it once more.

"Open your mouth," my mother commanded. She peered intently down my throat. "Your throat is red," she announced. "I shall take your temperature." Under the covers I squeezed my thumbs between the second and third fingers of each hand, the German equivalent of keeping my fingers crossed. The first test had been passed.

German home medicine in those days decreed that body temperature be measured not by the easy introduction of the thermometer under the tongue, but by a far more degrading maneuver. Instead of sitting or lying on his back, the victim, in my case a pubescent boy of twelve, lay on his stomach waiting to learn whether submission to this indignity would turn out to be justified by the results.

Having thus impaled me, my mother hurried off to get my father's breakfast and supervise my younger brother's daily mobilization. She returned after half an hour and disclosed the thermometer reading: "You have a temperature. Cover up well and stay in bed. I shall call Dr. Wetzler." I pulled up my pajama trousers and slipped under the covers. Life had its moments, after all. January 30 would pass without geometry, without joining Caesar on his forays into Gaul. (Lavisse's summary was at least a kindlier guide than his Latin source, whose reading the modern language curriculum of my school spared me.) It would be a day of peace, spent alone, interrupted only by surreptitious reading of my latest favorite, a German translation of that congenial classic *Tom Sawyer*, the recent gift of an understanding friend of the family.

The morning passed gently in dozing, daydreaming, and reading. Whenever steps echoed outside my room, I deftly slipped *Tom Sawyer* under the mattress. The doctor appeared in time to confirm my mother's diagnosis and to prescribe that I stay in bed until the temperature was gone. On the other hand, he agreed that she should call the home of my friend Fritz, asking that he bring me the day's assignments, confirming that I was certainly not too ill to keep up with schoolwork.

At one-thirty Fritz duly appeared with a depressing list of new tasks. After my mother had left the room, not before warning him to keep his distance from my bed to avoid contamination, he leaned over with understandable unconcern and whispered excitedly:

"Do you know what I heard?"

"What?"

"Hitler has just become chancellor."

We always whispered. It was a convention of our age group, inured to live in constant opposition. Secretiveness was our way. We whispered to each other in class, when talking was naturally prohibited. We whispered in the schoolyard when exchanging a limited, unchanging repertory of anal and sexual jokes, or swapping derogatory remarks about teachers, parents, or other members of the adult world. Our existence was a furtive, resistant, sneaky microcosm of trivial secrets, our own only as long as it remained hidden from our elders.

"Is it true?" I asked.

"It went around school, and I saw storm troopers everywhere on my way home. Reif, the milkman, was in uniform today. You know, he wouldn't wear that get-up on his route unless it was safe."

Fritz was excited. Throughout the past year he had not passed a brownshirt on the street without sidling up to him, raising his hand, and whispering, "Heil Hitler." Sometimes his low voiced greeting had been noticed and returned, sometimes merely acknowledged with a condescending smile (the Nazis proclaimed their commitment to youth, but treated children no better than did other adults), sometimes disregarded. His father, with whom I seldom heard him exchange a friendly word and whom we avoided even more doggedly than we were wont to avoid fathers in general, was a Jewish lawyer whose sister had married a colonel in Germany's purportedly 100,000-man army. Fritz envied his cousins for having a father in uniform. He bragged about his uncle, and in our class he was the resident authority on Germany's glorious future in arms. We accepted his claim to being privy to all kinds of exciting martial secrets which his uncle, "who knew what was going on," supposedly passed on to him.

By the time my exultant friend left, the personal triumph with which the day had begun had soured. I, too, had an uncle who in my own mind

ment room. There he told the prisoner orderly to attend to the wound. While this was being done, the guard watched me closely for signs of pain but I was able to suppress them. As soon as the cutting was over, I started to leave. He showed surprise and asked why I didn't wait for further treatment. I said I had gotten the service I asked for, at which he told the orderly to make an exception and treat my hand. After I had left the room, he called me back and gave me a card entitling me to further treatment, and admittance to the clinic without inspection at the entrance.

* * *

Because my behavior did not correspond to what he expected of Jewish prisoners on the basis of his projection, he could not use his prepared defenses against being touched by the prisoner's plight. Since I did not act as the dangerous Jew was expected to, I did not activate the anxieties that went with his stereotype. Still he did not altogether trust me, so he continued to watch while I received treatment.

Throughout these dealings, the SS felt uneasy with me, though he did not unload on me the annoyance his uneasiness aroused. Perhaps he watched me closely because he expected that sooner or later I would slip up and behave the way his projected image of the Jew was expected to act. This would have meant that his delusional creation had become real.

1960

Joan Didion

ON GOING HOME

I am home for my daughter's first birthday. By "home" I do not mean the house in Los Angeles where my husband and I and the baby live, but the place where my family is, in the Central Valley of California. It is a vital although troublesome distinction. My husband likes my family but is uneasy in their house, because once there I fall into their ways, which are difficult, oblique, deliberately inarticulate, not my husband's ways. We live in dusty houses ("D-U-S-T," he once wrote with his finger on surfaces all over the house, but no one noticed it) filled with mementos quite without value to him (what could the Canton dessert plates mean to him? how could he have known about the assay scales, why should he care if he did know?), and we appear to talk exclusively about people we know who have been committed to mental hospitals, about people we know who have been booked on drunk-driving charges, and about property, particularly about property, land, price per acre and C-2 zoning and assessments and freeway access. My brother does not understand my husband's inability to perceive the advantage in the rather common real-estate transaction known as "sale-leaseback," and my husband in turn does not understand why so many of the people he hears about in my father's house have recently been committed to mental hospitals or booked on drunk-driving charges. Nor does he understand that when we talk about sale-leasebacks and right-of-way condemnations we are talking in code about the things we like best, the yellow fields and the cotton-woods and the rivers rising and falling and the mountain roads closing when the heavy snow comes in. We miss each other's points, have another drink and regard the fire. My brother refers to my husband, in his presence, as "Joan's husband." Marriage is the classic betrayal.

Or perhaps it is not any more. Sometimes I think that those of us who are now in our thirties were born into the last generation to carry the burden of "home," to find in family life the source of all tension and drama. I had by all objective accounts a "normal" and a "happy" family situation, and yet I was almost thirty years old before I could talk to my family on the telephone without crying after I had hung up. We did not fight. Nothing was wrong. And yet some nameless anxiety colored the emotional charges between me and the place that I came from. The question of whether or not you could go home again was a very real part of the sentimental and largely literary baggage with which we left home in the fifties; I suspect that it is irrelevant to the children born of the fragmentation after World War II. A few weeks ago in a San Francisco bar I saw a pretty young girl on crystal take off her clothes and dance for the cash prize in an "amateur-topless" contest. There was no particular sense of moment about this, none of the effect of romantic degradation, of "dark journey," for which my generation strived so assiduously. What sense could that girl possibly make of, say, *Long Day's Journey into Night?*[1] Who is beside the point?

That I am trapped in this particular irrelevancy is never more apparent to me than when I am home. Paralyzed by the neurotic lassitude engendered by meeting one's past at every turn, around every corner, inside every cupboard, I go aimlessly from room to room. I decide to meet it head-on and clean out a drawer, and I spread the contents on the bed. A bathing suit I wore the summer I was seventeen. A letter of rejection from *The Nation*, an aerial photograph of the site for a shopping center my father did not build in 1954. Three teacups hand-painted with cabbage roses and signed "E.M.," my grandmother's initials. There is no final solution for letters of rejection from *The Nation* and teacups hand-painted in 1900. Nor is there any answer to snapshots of one's grandfather as a young man on skis, surveying around Donner Pass in the year

1. A powerful domestic tragedy by the modern American playwright Eugene O'Neill, based on his early life.

1910. I smooth out the snapshot and look into his face, and do and do not see my own. I close the drawer, and have another cup of coffee with my mother. We get along very well, veterans of a guerrilla war we never understood.

Days pass. I see no one. I come to dread my husband's evening call, not only because he is full of news of what by now seems to me our remote life in Los Angeles, people he has seen, letters which require attention, but because he asks what I have been doing, suggests uneasily that I get out, drive to San Francisco or Berkeley. Instead I drive across the river to a family graveyard. It has been vandalized since my last visit and the monuments are broken, overturned in the dry grass. Because I once saw a rattlesnake in the grass I stay in the car and listen to a country-and-Western station. Later I drive with my father to a ranch he has in the foothills. The man who runs his cattle on it asks us to the roundup, a week from Sunday, and although I know that I will be in Los Angeles I say, in the oblique way my family talks, that I will come. Once home I mention the broken monuments in the graveyard. My mother shrugs.

I go to visit my great-aunts. A few of them think now that I am my cousin, or their daughter who died young. We recall an anecdote about a relative last seen in 1948, and they ask if I still like living in New York City. I have lived in Los Angeles for three years, but I say that I do. The baby is offered a horehound drop, and I am slipped a dollar bill "to buy a treat." Questions trail off, answers are abandoned, the baby plays with the dust motes in a shaft of afternoon sun.

It is time for the baby's birthday party: a white cake, strawberry-marshmallow ice cream, a bottle of champagne saved from another party. In the evening, after she has gone to sleep, I kneel beside the crib and touch her face, where it is pressed against the slats, with mine. She is an open and trusting child, unprepared for and unaccustomed to the ambushes of family life, and perhaps it is just as well that I can offer her little of that life. I would like to give her more. I would like to promise her that she will grow up with a sense of her cousins and of rivers and of her great-grandmother's teacups, would like to pledge her a picnic on a river with fried chicken and her hair uncombed, would like to give her home for her birthday, but we live differently now and I can promise her nothing like that. I give her a xylophone and a sundress from Madeira, and promise to tell her a funny story.

1967

THE READER

1. Does the author take a single attitude or several toward "home"? Try to specify the attitude or attitudes.
2. What does the author mean by "the ambushes of family life" (p. 42)?
3. Explain whether the essay gives you any clues as to why so much of the

talk at home is "about people we know who have been committed to mental hospitals, about people we know who have been booked on drunk-driving charges, and about property" (p. 40)?

4. In her concluding sentence, the author tells us she gives as birthday gifts to her daughter "a xylophone and a sundress from Madeira." Are these appropriate? Why or why not? Explain why she would like to give other gifts.

5. In "On Keeping a Notebook," Didion says that it is good to keep in touch with the people we used to be (p. 414). Is her account of this visit an effort to do that? Are there recalled phrases and observations in "On Going Home" like those she quotes from her notebooks, or does the different argument change the character of the phrases and observations she recalls?

THE WRITER

1. The author speaks of herself at home as "paralyzed by the neurotic lassitude engendered by meeting one's past at every turn" (p. 41). What details in the essay help explain that feeling?

2. If you have read or seen the play, explain the appropriateness of the author's reference (p. 41) to O'Neill's Long Day's Journey into Night.

3. Didion speaks of family life as "the source of all tension and drama." Point to details in the essay that illustrate that view. What kinds of details about her family might she have considered but rejected because they didn't advance that view or, indeed, contradicted it?

4. Write an essay about a trip you have made back to your home or back to a place you were once familiar with.

Joyce Maynard

FOUR GENERATIONS

My mother called last week to tell me that my grandmother is dying. She has refused an operation that would postpone, but not prevent, her death from pancreatic cancer. She can't eat, she has been hemorrhaging, and she has severe jaundice. "I always prided myself on being different," she told my mother. "Now I am different. I'm yellow."

My mother, telling me this news, began to cry. So I became the mother for a moment, reminding her, reasonably, that my grandmother is eighty-seven, she's had a full life, she has all her faculties, and no one who knows her could wish that she live long enough to lose them. Lately my mother has been finding notes in my grandmother's drawers at the nursing home, reminding her, "Joyce's husband's name is Steve. Their daughter is Audrey." In the last few years she hadn't had the strength to cook or

there at the edge of the concrete, contemplating the slug, I began to realize it was like standing on a shore where a different type of life creeps up and fumbles tentatively among the rocks and sea wrack. It knows its place and will only creep so far until something changes. Little by little as I stood there I began to see more of this shore that surrounds the place of man. I looked with sudden care and attention at things I had been running over thoughtlessly for years. I even waded out a short way into the grass and the wild-rose thickets to see more. A huge black-belted bee went droning by and there were some indistinct scurryings in the underbrush.

Then I came to a sign which informed me that this field was to be the site of a new Wanamaker suburban store. Thousands of obscure lives were about to perish, the spores of puffballs would go smoking off to new fields, and the bodies of little white-footed mice would be crunched under the inexorable wheels of the bulldozers. Life disappears or modifies its appearances so fast that everything takes on an aspect of illusion—a momentary fizzing and boiling with smoke rings, like pouring dissident chemicals into a retort. Here man was advancing, but in a few years his plaster and bricks would be disappearing once more into the insatiable maw of the clover. Being of an archaeological cast of mind, I thought of this fact with an obscure sense of satisfaction and waded back through the rose thickets to the concrete parking lot. As I did so, a mouse scurried ahead of me, frightened of my steps if not of that ominous Wanamaker sign. I saw him vanish in the general direction of my apartment house, his little body quivering with fear in the great open sun on the blazing concrete. Blinded and confused, he was running straight away from his field. In another week scores would follow him.

I forgot the episode then and went home to the quiet of my living room. It was not until a week later, letting myself into the apartment, that I realized I had a visitor. I am fond of plants and had several ferns standing on the floor in pots to avoid the noon glare by the south window.

As I snapped on the light and glanced carelessly around the room, I saw a little heap of earth on the carpet and a scrabble of pebbles that had been kicked merrily over the edge of one of the flower pots. To my astonishment I discovered a full-fledged burrow delving downward among the fern roots. I waited silently. The creature who had made the burrow did not appear. I remembered the wild field then, and the flight of the mice. No house mouse, no Mus domesticus, had kicked up this little heap of earth or sought refuge under a fern root in a flower pot. I thought of the desperate little creature I had seen fleeing from the wild-rose thicket. Through intricacies of pipes and attics, he, or one of his fellows, had climbed to this high green solitary room. I could visualize what had occurred. He had an image in his head, a world of seed pods and quiet, of green sheltering leaves in the dim light among the weed stems. It was the only world he knew and it was gone.

Somehow in his flight he had found his way to this room with drawn shades where no one would come till nightfall. And here he had smelled green leaves and run quickly up the flower pot to dabble his paws in common earth. He had even struggled half the afternoon to carry his burrow deeper and had failed. I examined the hole, but no whiskered twitching face appeared. He was gone. I gathered up the earth and refilled the burrow. I did not expect to find traces of him again.

Yet for three nights thereafter I came home to the darkened room and my ferns to find the dirt kicked gaily about the rug and the burrow reopened, though I was never able to catch the field mouse within it. I dropped a little food about the mouth of the burrow, but it was never touched. I looked under beds or sat reading with one ear cocked for rustlings in the ferns. It was all in vain; I never saw him. Probably he ended in a trap in some other tenant's room.

But before he disappeared I had come to look hopefully for his evening burrow. About my ferns there had begun to linger the insubstantial vapor of an autumn field, the distilled essence, as it were, of a mouse brain in exile from its home. It was a small dream, like our dreams, carried a long and weary journey along pipes and through spider webs, past holes over which loomed the shadows of waiting cats, and finally, desperately, into this room where he had played in the shuttered daylight for an hour among the green ferns on the floor. Every day these invisible dreams pass us on the street, or rise from beneath our feet, or look out upon us from beneath a bush.

Some years ago the old elevated railway in Philadelphia was torn down and replaced by a subway system. This ancient El with its barnlike stations containing nut-vending machines and scattered food scraps had, for generations, been the favorite feeding ground of flocks of pigeons, generally one flock to a station along the route of the El. Hundreds of pigeons were dependent upon the system. They flapped in and out of its stanchions and steel work or gathered in watchful little audiences about the feet of anyone who rattled the peanut-vending machines. They even watched people who jingled change in their hands, and prospected for food under the feet of the crowds who gathered between trains. Probably very few among the waiting people who tossed a crumb to an eager pigeon realized that this El was like a food-bearing river, and that the life which haunted its banks was dependent upon the running of the trains with their human freight.

I saw the river stop.

The time came when the underground tubes were ready; the traffic was transferred to a realm unreachable by pigeons. It was like a great river subsiding suddenly into desert sands. For a day, for two days, pigeons continued to circle over the El or stand close to the red vending

machines. They were patient birds, and surely this great river which had
flowed through the lives of unnumbered generations was merely suffering from some momentary drought.

They listened for the familiar vibrations that had always heralded an
approaching train; they flapped hopefully about the head of an occasional
workman walking along the steel runways. They passed from one empty
station to another, all the while growing hungrier. Finally they flew away.

I thought I had seen the last of them about the El, but there was a
revival and it provided a curious instance of the memory of living things
for a way of life or a locality that has long been cherished. Some weeks
after the El was abandoned workmen began to tear it down. I went to
work every morning by one particular station, and the time came when
the demolition crews reached this spot. Acetylene torches showered
passersby with sparks, pneumatic drills hammered at the base of the
structure, and a blind man who, like the pigeons, had clung with his cup
to a stairway leading to the change booth, was forced to give up his place.

It was then, strangely, momentarily, one morning that I witnessed the
return of a little band of the familiar pigeons. I even recognized one or
two members of the flock that had lived around this particular station
before they were dispersed into the streets. They flew bravely in and out
among the sparks and the hammers and the shouting workmen. They had
returned—and they had returned because the hubbub of the wreckers
had convinced them that the river was about to flow once more. For
several hours they flapped in and out through the empty windows,
nodding their heads and watching the fall of girders with attentive little
eyes. By the following morning the station was reduced to some burned-
off stanchions in the street. My bird friends had gone. It was plain,
however, that they retained a memory for an insubstantial structure now
compounded of air and time. Even the blind man clung to it. Someone
had provided him with a chair, and he sat at the same corner staring
sightlessly at an invisible stairway where, so far as he was concerned, the
crowds were still ascending to the trains.

I have said my life has been passed in the shade of a nonexistent tree, so
that such sights do not offend me. Prematurely I am one of the brown
wasps and I often sit with them in the great droning hive of the station,
dreaming sometimes of a certain tree. It was planted sixty years ago by a
boy with a bucket and a toy spade in a little Nebraska town. That boy was
myself. It was a cottonwood sapling and the boy remembered it because
of some words spoken by his father and because everyone died or moved
away who was supposed to wait and grow old under its shade. The boy
was passed from hand to hand, but the tree for some intangible reason
had taken root in his mind. It was under its branches that he sheltered; it
was from this tree that his memories, which are my memories, led away
into the world.

After sixty years the mood of the brown wasps grows heavier upon one. During a long inward struggle I thought it would do me good to go and look upon that actual tree. I found a rational excuse in which to clothe this madness. I purchased a ticket and at the end of two thousand miles I walked another mile to an address that was still the same. The house had not been altered.

I came close to the white picket fence and reluctantly, with great effort, looked down the long vista of the yard. There was nothing there to see. For sixty years that cottonwood had been growing in my mind. Season by season its seeds had been floating farther on the hot prairie winds. We had planted it lovingly there, my father and I, because he had a great hunger for soil and live things growing, and because none of these things had long been ours to protect. We had planted the little sapling and watered it faithfully, and I remembered that I had run out with my small bucket to drench its roots the day we moved away. And all the years since it had been growing in my mind, a huge tree that somehow stood for my father and the love I bore him. I took a grasp on the picket fence and forced myself to look again.

A boy with the hard bird eye of youth pedaled a tricycle slowly up beside me.

"What'cha lookin' at?" he asked curiously.

"A tree," I said.

"What for?" he said.

"It isn't there," I said, to myself mostly, and began to walk away at a pace just slow enough not to seem to be running.

"What isn't there?" the boy asked. I didn't answer. It was obvious I was attached by a thread to a thing that had never been there, or certainly not for long. Something that had to be held in the air, or sustained in the mind, because it was part of my orientation in the universe and I could not survive without it. There was more than an animal's attachment to a place. There was something else, the attachment of the spirit to a grouping of events in time; it was part of our morality.

So I had come home at last, driven by a memory in the brain as surely as the field mouse who had delved long ago into my flower pot or the pigeons flying forever amidst the rattle of nut-vending machines. These, the burrow under the greenery in my living room and the red-bellied bowls of peanuts now hovering in midair in the minds of pigeons, were all part of an elusive world that existed nowhere and yet everywhere. I looked once at the real world about me while the persistent boy pedaled at my heels.

It was without meaning, though my feet took a remembered path. In sixty years the house and street had rotted out of my mind. But the tree, the tree that no longer was, that had perished in its first season, bloomed on in my individual mind, unblemished as my father's words. "We'll plant a tree here, son, and we're not going to move any more. And when you're an old, old man you can sit under it and think how we planted it here, you and me, together."

I began to outpace the boy on the tricycle.

"Do you live here, Mister?" he shouted after me suspiciously. I took a firm grasp on airy nothing—to be precise, on the bole of a great tree. "I do," I said. I spoke for myself, one field mouse, and several pigeons. We were all out of touch but somehow permanent. It was the world that had changed.

1971

THE READER

1. Eiseley writes of old men in train stations, brown wasps, a field mouse, pigeons near the El, and his own return to his boyhood home in Nebraska. What do these matters have in common? Can you state the essay's theme?
2. In "Once More to the Lake" (p. 53), White describes his return to a lake he had known years earlier. What reflections arise in his mind on this occasion? Are they similar to, or different from, Eiseley's thoughts upon returning to his Nebraska home and the nonexistent tree?

THE WRITER

1. Some psychologists study animal behavior in order to learn about human behavior, but many of them write about animals in a very different fashion. Do you think that Eiseley's way of relating the behavior of animals to human behavior makes sense? If you are studying psychology, it might be interesting to compare a selection from your textbook with this essay.
2. Eiseley's essay contains sentences like "We cling to a time and place because without them man is lost, not only man but life" (p. 47) and "A boy with the hard bird eye of youth pedaled a tricycle slowly up beside me" (p. 51). What is the difference between these two kinds of sentences? Can you show how Eiseley manages to connect one kind with the other?
3. Write an essay comparing the theme or purpose of "The Brown Wasps" with that of Lorenz's "The Taming of the Shrew" (p. 543). Does Lorenz take a similar approach to his subject? Consider also the manner of the writing: how would you characterize it in each instance?

E. B. White

ONCE MORE TO THE LAKE

One summer, along about 1904, my father rented a camp on a lake in Maine and took us all there for the month of August. We all got ringworm from some kittens and had to rub Pond's Extract on our arms and legs night and morning, and my father rolled over in a canoe with all his clothes on; but outside of that the vacation was a success and from then on none of us ever thought there was any place in the world like that lake in Maine. We returned summer after summer—always on August 1st for one month. I have since become a salt-water man, but sometimes in summer there are days when the restlessness of the tides and the fearful cold of the sea water and the incessant wind which blows across the afternoon and into the evening make me wish for the placidity of a lake in the woods. A few weeks ago this feeling got so strong I bought myself a couple of bass hooks and a spinner and returned to the lake where we used to go, for a week's fishing and to revisit old haunts.

I took along my son, who had never had any fresh water up his nose and who had seen lily pads only from train windows. On the journey over to the lake I began to wonder what it would be like. I wondered how time would have marred this unique, this holy spot—the coves and streams, the hills that the sun set behind, the camps and the paths behind the camps. I was sure the tarred road would have found it out and I wondered in what other ways it would be desolated. It is strange how much you can remember about places like that once you allow your mind to return into the grooves which lead back. You remember one thing, and that suddenly reminds you of another thing. I guess I remembered clearest of all the early mornings, when the lake was cool and motionless, remembered how the bedroom smelled of the lumber it was made of and of the wet woods whose scent entered through the screen. The partitions in the camp were thin and did not extend clear to the top of the rooms, and as I was always the first up I would dress softly so as not to wake the others, and sneak out into the sweet outdoors and start out in the canoe, keeping close along the shore in the long shadows of the pines. I remembered being very careful never to rub my paddle against the gunwale for fear of disturbing the stillness of the cathedral.

The lake had never been what you would call a wild lake. There were cottages sprinkled around the shores, and it was in farming country although the shores of the lake were quite heavily wooded. Some of the cottages were owned by nearby farmers, and you would live at the shore and eat your meals at the farmhouse. That's what our family did. But although it wasn't wild, it was a fairly large and undisturbed lake and there were places in it which, to a child at least, seemed infinitely remote and primeval.

I was right about the tar: it led to within half a mile of the shore. But when I got back there, with my boy, and we settled into a camp near a farmhouse and into the kind of summertime I had known, I could tell that it was going to be pretty much the same as it had been before—I knew it, lying in bed the first morning, smelling the bedroom, and hearing the boy sneak quietly out and go off along the shore in a boat. I began to sustain the illusion that he was I, and therefore, by simple transposition, that I was my father. This sensation persisted, kept cropping up all the time we were there. It was not an entirely new feeling, but in this setting it grew much stronger. I seemed to be living a dual existence. I would be in the middle of some simple act, I would be picking up a bait box or laying down a table fork, or I would be saying something, and suddenly it would be not I but my father who was saying the words or making the gesture. It gave me a creepy sensation.

We went fishing the first morning. I felt the same damp moss covering the worms in the bait can, and saw the dragonfly alight on the tip of my rod as it hovered a few inches from the surface of the water. It was the arrival of this fly that convinced me beyond any doubt that everything was as it always had been, that the years were a mirage and there had been no years. The small waves were the same, chucking the rowboat under the chin as we fished at anchor, and the boat was the same boat, the same color green and the ribs broken in the same places, and under the floor-boards the same fresh-water leavings and débris—the dead helgramite,[1] the wisps of moss, the rusty discarded fishhook, the dried blood from yesterday's catch. We stared silently at the tips of our rods, at the dragonflies that came and went. I lowered the tip of mine into the water, tentatively, pensively dislodging the fly, which darted two feet away poised, darted two feet back, and came to rest again a little farther up the rod. There had been no years between the ducking of this dragonfly and the other one—the one that was part of memory. I looked at the boy, who was silently watching his fly, and it was my hands that held his rod, my eyes watching. I felt dizzy and didn't know which rod I was at the end of.

We caught two bass, hauling them in briskly as though they were mackerel, pulling them over the side of the boat in a businesslike manner without any landing net, and stunning them with a blow on the back of the head. When we got back for a swim before lunch, the lake was exactly where we had left it, the same number of inches from the dock, and there was only the merest suggestion of a breeze. This seemed an utterly enchanted sea, this lake you could leave to its own devices for a few hours

1. The nymph of the May-fly, used as bait.

and come back to, and find that it had not stirred, this constant and trustworthy body of water. In the shallows, the dark, water-soaked sticks and twigs, smooth and old, were undulating in clusters on the bottom against the clean ribbed sand, and the track of the mussel was plain. A school of minnows swam by, each minnow with its small individual shadow, doubling the attendance, so clear and sharp in the sunlight. Some of the other campers were in swimming, along the shore, one of them with a cake of soap, and the water felt thin and clear and unsubstantial. Over the years there had been this person with the cake of soap, this cultist, and here he was. There had been no years.

Up to the farmhouse to dinner through the teeming, dusty field, the road under our sneakers was only a two-track road. The middle track was missing, the one with the marks of the hooves and the splotches of dried, flaky manure. There had always been three tracks to choose from in choosing which track to walk in; now the choice was narrowed down to two. For a moment I missed terribly the middle alternative. But the way led past the tennis court, and something about the way it lay there in the sun reassured me; the tape had loosened along the backline, the alleys were green with plantains and other weeds, and the net (installed in June and removed in September) sagged in the dry noon, and the whole place steamed with midday heat and hunger and emptiness. There was a choice of pie for dessert, and one was blueberry and one was apple, and the waitresses were the same country girls, there having been no passage of time, only the illusion of it as in a dropped curtain—the waitresses were still fifteen; their hair had been washed, that was the only difference —they had been to the movies and seen the pretty girls with the clean hair.

Summertime, oh summertime, pattern of life indelible, the fade-proof lake, the woods unshatterable, the pasture with the sweetfern and the juniper forever and ever, summer without end; this was the background, and the life along the shore was the design, the cottagers with their innocent and tranquil design, their tiny docks with the flagpole and the American flag floating against the white clouds in the blue sky, the little paths over the roots of the trees leading from camp to camp and the paths leading back to the outhouses and the can of lime for sprinkling, and at the souvenir counters at the store the miniature birch-bark canoes and the post cards that showed things looking a little better than they looked. This was the American family at play, escaping the city heat, wondering whether the newcomers in the camp at the head of the cove were "common" or "nice," wondering whether it was true that the people who drove up for Sunday dinner at the farmhouse were turned away because there wasn't enough chicken.

It seemed to me, as I kept remembering all this, that those times and those summers had been infinitely precious and worth saving. There had been jollity and peace and goodness. The arriving (at the beginning of August) had been so big a business in itself, at the railway station the farm wagon drawn up, the first smell of the pine-laden air, the first glimpse of the smiling farmer, and the great importance of the trunks and your father's enormous authority in such matters, and the feel of the wagon under you for the long ten-mile haul, and at the top of the last long hill catching the first view of the lake after eleven months of not seeing this cherished body of water. The shouts and cries of the other campers when they saw you, and the trunks to be unpacked, to give up their rich burden. (Arriving was less exciting nowadays, when you sneaked up in your car and parked it under a tree near the camp and took out the bags and in five minutes it was all over, no fuss, no loud wonderful fuss about trunks.)

Peace and goodness and jollity. The only thing that was wrong now, really, was the sound of the place, an unfamiliar nervous sound of the outboard motors. This was the note that jarred, the one thing that would sometimes break the illusion and set the years moving. In those other summertimes all motors were inboard; and when they were at a little distance, the noise they made was a sedative, an ingredient of summer sleep. They were one-cylinder and two-cylinder engines, and some were make-and-break and some were jump-spark,[2] but they all made a sleepy sound across the lake. The one-lungers throbbed and fluttered, and the twin-cylinder ones purred and purred, and that was a quiet sound too. But now the campers all had outboards. In the daytime, in the hot mornings, these motors made a petulant, irritable sound; at night, in the still evening when the afterglow lit the water, they whined about one's ears like mosquitoes. My boy loved our rented outboard, and his great desire was to achieve singlehanded mastery over it, and authority, and he soon learned the trick of choking it a little (but not too much), and the adjustment of the needle valve. Watching him I would remember the things you could do with the old one-cylinder engine with the heavy flywheel, how you could have it eating out of your hand if you got really close to it spiritually. Motor boats in those days didn't have clutches, and you would make a landing by shutting off the motor at the proper time and coasting in with a dead rudder. But there was a way of reversing them, if you learned the trick, by cutting the switch and putting it on again exactly on the final dying revolution of the flywheel, so that it would kick back against compression and begin reversing. Approaching a dock in a strong following breeze, it was difficult to slow up sufficiently by the ordinary coasting method, and if a boy felt he had complete mastery over his motor, he was tempted to keep it running beyond its time and then reverse it a few feet from the dock. It took a cool nerve, because if

_____

2. Methods of ignition timing.

you threw the switch a twentieth of a second too soon you would catch the flywheel when it still had speed enough to go up past center, and the boat would leap ahead, charging bull-fashion at the dock.

We had a good week at the camp. The bass were biting well and the sun shone endlessly, day after day. We would be tired at night and lie down in the accumulated heat of the little bedrooms after the long hot day and the breeze would stir almost imperceptibly outside and the smell of the swamp drift in through the rusty screens. Sleep would come easily and in the morning the red squirrel would be on the roof, tapping out his gay routine. I kept remembering everything, lying in bed in the mornings —the small steamboat that had a long rounded stern like the lip of a Ubangi, and how quietly she ran on the moonlight sails, when the older boys played their mandolins and the girls sang and we ate doughnuts dipped in sugar, and how sweet the music was on the water in the shining night, and what it had felt like to think about girls then. After breakfast we would go up to the store and the things were in the same place—the minnows in a bottle, the plugs and spinners disarranged and pawed over by the youngsters from the boys' camp, the fig newtons and the Beeman's gum. Outside, the road was tarred and cars stood in front of the store. Inside, all was just as it had always been, except there was more Coca-Cola and not so much Moxie and root beer and birch beer and sarsaparilla. We would walk out with a bottle of pop apiece and sometimes the pop would backfire up our noses and hurt. We explored the streams, quietly, where the turtles slid off the sunny logs and dug their way into the soft bottom; and we lay on the town wharf and fed worms to the tame bass. Everywhere we went I had trouble making out which was I, the one walking at my side, the one walking in my pants.

One afternoon while we were there at that lake a thunderstorm came up. It was like the revival of an old melodrama that I had seen long ago with childish awe. The second-act climax of the drama of the electrical disturbance over a lake in America had not changed in any important respect. This was the big scene, still the big scene. The whole thing was so familiar, the first feeling of oppression and heat and a general air around camp of not wanting to go very far away. In midafternoon (it was all the same) a curious darkening of the sky, and a lull in everything that had made life tick; and then the way the boats suddenly swung the other way at their moorings with the coming of a breeze out of the new quarter, and the premonitory rumble. Then the kettle drum, then the snare, then the bass drum and cymbals, then crackling light against the dark, and the gods grinning and licking their chops in the hills. Afterward the calm, the rain steadily rustling in the calm lake, the return of light and hope and spirits, and the campers running out in joy and relief to go swimming in the rain, their bright cries perpetuating the deathless joke about how they were getting simply drenched, and the children screaming with delight at the new sensation of bathing in the rain, and the joke about getting drenched linking the generations in a strong indestructible chain. And the comedian who waded in carrying an umbrella.

When the others went swimming my son said he was going in too. He pulled his dripping trunks from the line where they had hung all through the shower, and wrung them out. Languidly, and with no thought of going in, I watched him, his hard little body, skinny and bare, saw him wince slightly as he pulled up around his vitals the small, soggy, icy garment. As he buckled the swollen belt suddenly my groin felt the chill of death.

1941

THE READER

1. White had not been back to the lake for many years. What bearing has this fact on the experience the essay describes?
2. How do the differences between boats of the past and boats of today relate to or support the point of the essay?
3. What is the meaning of White's last sentence? What relation has it to the sentence just preceding? How has White prepared us for this ending?
4. Read White's "Some Remarks on Humor" (p. 663). Is he writing humor in "Once More to the Lake"?

THE WRITER

1. What has guided White in his selection of the details he gives about the trip? Why, for example, does he talk about the road, the dragonfly, the bather with the cake of soap?
2. In "On Keeping a Notebook," Didion says that it is good to keep in touch with the people we used to be (p. 414). Is that what White is doing here?
3. Write an account of an experience, real or imagined, in which you return to a place you haven't seen for a while. Think about what point you wish to make through your narrative.

People, Places

Margaret Mead

HOME AND TRAVEL

For many people moving is one kind of thing and travel is something very different. Travel means going away from home and staying away from home; it is an antidote to the humdrum activities of everyday life, a prelude to a holiday one is entitled to enjoy after months of dullness. Moving means breaking up a home, sadly or joyfully breaking with the past; a happy venture or a hardship, something to be endured with good or ill grace.

For me, moving and staying at home, traveling and arriving, are all of a piece. The world is full of homes in which I have lived for a day, a month, a year, or much longer. How much I care about a home is not measured by the length of time I have lived there. One night in a room with a leaping fire may mean more to me than many months in a room without a fireplace, a room in which my life has been paced less excitingly.

From the time I can first remember, I knew that we had not always lived where we were living then—in Hammonton, New Jersey, where we had moved so that Mother could work on her doctoral thesis. I knew that I had spent my first summer at a resort called Lavallette, a place I did not visit again until I was seventeen, there to have the only authentic attack of homesickness I have ever had, brought on by the sound of the pounding surf. I knew also that we had lived on St. Marks Square, Philadelphia, because the next winter we lived near St. Marks Square and still knew people who lived there.

Every winter we went to live in or near Philadelphia so that Father would not have to travel too far or stay in the city on the nights that he lectured at the University. From the time I was seven years old, we went somewhere for the summer, too. So we moved four times a year, because for the fall and spring we returned to the house in Hammonton.

All the other houses were strange—houses that had to be made our own as quickly as possible so that they no longer would be strange. This did not mean that they were frightening, but only that we had to learn about every nook and corner, for otherwise it was hard to play hide-and-go-seek. As soon as we arrived, I ran ahead to find a room for myself as far away as possible from everyone else, preferably at the top of the house where I would always be warned by footsteps that someone was coming. After that, until we were settled in, I was busy exploring, making my own the new domain. Later, when I was about fourteen, I was in charge of unpacking, getting beds made, food in the icebox, and the lamps filled and lit before nightfall.

The next step was to explore the neighborhood. I had to find out what other children lived nearby and whether there were woods, wild flowers, tangles, or jungles—any hidden spot that could be turned into a miniature primeval forest where life could be quickly shaped to an imaginary world.

In Hammonton we had five whole acres, a good part of which was second-growth bush, studded with blueberries, which the little Italian children who were our neighbors picked and sold back to us. In Lansdowne and Swarthmore there were bits of woodlot. But in Philadelphia there was nothing, only stone walls of different heights on which to walk. Nothing, except for the winter when we lived at the edge of the park near the zoo.

However far away we moved and however often, we always came home again to Hammonton and the familiar and loved things that were too fragile to take with us—although Mother was very permissive about allowing us to carry along all the objects each of us wanted. In Hammonton there was the same blueberry thicket in which to wander along old paths and make new ones, the same surrey, which we hired from the livery stable, and the same door which was never opened—a second door on the front porch which was used only on one occasion, on the night the neighbors pounded on it to tell us that our chimney had caught fire.

There was the great tree from which a hornets' nest blew down in a storm. I had been dancing in the wind when it blew down and, still dancing, plunged my hands into it. I can still remember the wind but not the stings with which I was said to have been covered. There were the tall evergreen arborvitae that divided the lawn into little squares, where Grandma played games with us until one day she put her hand to her heart and then she did not play running games anymore. And outside the mock-orange hedge we once found faeces, and Mother said, in a tone of disgust close to horror, that they were human faeces.

There was the well with a pump that we used to prime with hot water, until one day my five-year-old brother and a desperado friend a year younger threw everything detachable down the well, and then it was never used again. There was an old dinghy in which we grew flowers until the boys tore it up. And once, when the barn had been reshingled and the old shingles had been piled in the barn for the winter, the two little boys threw all of them out. Grandma said it just showed how two children, each one quite good by himself, could get into mischief. You never could tell, when you put two children together, what the outcome would be. This enlarged my picture of what boys were like.

It was contrapuntal to an engraving in a homemade copper frame that stood on the mantelpiece. This showed a pair of children, a little girl diligently sewing a fine seam and a boy, beautiful and remote, simply sitting and looking out at the world. Long years later, the same picture provided the central image in a bitter little verse of feminine protest that I wrote when Edward Sapir[1] told me I would do better to stay at home and have children than to go off to the South Seas to study adolescent girls:

> Measure your thread and cut it
> To suit your little seam,
> Stitch the garment tightly, tightly,
> And leave no room for dream.
> . . .
> Head down, be not caught looking
> Where the restless wild geese fly.

There were treasures on Mother's dressing table, too—a Wedgwood pin dish, a little porcelain Mary and her lamb, the pale green, flowered top of a rose bowl that had broken, and Mother's silver-backed comb and brush and mirror. All these things held meaning for me. Each was—and still is—capable of evoking a rush of memories.

Taken altogether, the things that mattered a great deal to me when I was a child are very few when I compare them to the overloaded tables and overcrowded shelves through which children today have to thread their way. Only if they are very fortunate will they be able to weave together into memories the ill-assorted mass of gadgets, toys, and easily forgotten objects, objects without a past or a future, and piles of snapshots that will be replaced by new, brightly colored snapshots next year.

The difficulty, it seems to me, is not—as so many older people claim—that in the past life was simpler and there were fewer things, and so people were somehow better, as well as more frugal. It is, rather, that today's children have to find new ways of anchoring the changing moments of their lives, and they have to try to do this with very little help from their elders, who grew up in an extraordinarily different world. How many of the young people who are rebelling against the tyranny of things, who want to strip their lives down to the contents of a rucksack,

1. A well-known anthropologist and linguistics scholar.

can remember and name the things that lay on their mother's dressing table or can describe every toy and book they had as a child?

It has been found that when desperate, unhappy youngsters are preparing to break away from a disordered, drug-ridden commune in which they have been living for months, they first gather together in one spot their few possessions and introduce a semblance of order among them. The need to define who you are by the place in which you live remains intact, even when that place is defined by a single object, like the small blue vase that used to mean home to one of my friends, the daughter of a widowed trained nurse who continually moved from one place to another. The Bushmen of the Kalahari Desert often build no walls when they camp in the desert. They simply hollow out a small space in the sand. But then they bend a slender sapling into an arch to make a doorway, an entrance to a dwelling as sacrosanct from invasion as the walled estates of the wealthy are or as Makati, in Manila, is, where watchmen guard the rich against the poor.

I realized how few things are needed to make a "home" when I took my seven-year-old daughter on her first sea voyage. The ship—the *Marine Jumper,* an unrenovated troopship with iron decks—was crowded with over a thousand students. They were bunked below where the troops had slept, while Cathy and I shared one cabin with six other members of the staff. Cathy climbed into her upper berth, opened the little packages that had been given to her as going-away presents, and arranged them in a circle around her. Then she leaned over the side of the berth and said, "Now I am ready to see the ship."

Home, I learned, can be anywhere you make it. Home is also the place to which you come back again and again. The really poignant parting is the parting that may be forever. It is this sense that every sailing may be a point of no return that haunts the peoples of the Pacific islands. On the very day I arrived in Samoa, people began to ask, "When will you leave?" When I replied, "In a year," they sighed, "Alas, *talofai*"—our love to you —with the sadness of a thousand partings in their voices. Their islands were peopled by voyagers who set off on a short known journey and whose canoes were blown hundreds of miles off course. But even when a fishing canoe goes out there is a chance that it will upset on the dangerous reef and that someone will be drowned. The smallest journey may be forever.

I have seen something similar on the seacoast of Portugal, where every year for four hundred years fishermen set out in their frail boats for the fishing banks across the treacherous Atlantic and no one could tell when —or whether—they would return. Portugal is still a widow's walk. The old women, dressed in black, still seem to be looking out to sea for the men who disappeared into the distance and an unknown fate.

In all my years of field work, each place where I have lived has become home. Each small object I have brought with me, each arrangement on a shelf of tin cans holding beads or salt for trade or crayons for the children to draw with becomes the mark of home. When it is dismantled on the last morning—a morning that is marked by the greed of those who have little and hope for a share of whatever is left behind, as well as by the grief of feeling that someone is leaving forever—on that morning, I weep. I, too, know that this departure, unlike my forays from home as a child, is likely to be forever.

* * *

1972

THE READER

1. What is Mead's implied definition of home?
2. In Frost's poem "The Death of the Hired Man," a husband and a wife give two different definitions of home. The husband says: "Home is the place where, when you have to go there, / They have to take you in." The wife replies: "I should have called it / Something you somehow haven't to [i.e., don't have to] deserve." Explain which of these definitions you think comes closer to Mead's definition of home.
3. Mead had a long career as an anthropologist studying people of other, more primitive cultures. In this essay, is she looking at her own culture in ways that are similar to those she might adopt in looking at another culture? Explain.
4. Mead recounts an incident in which she was told it would be better if she stayed at home and had children, rather than going to the South Seas. Explain in what ways the poem she wrote is a reply.
5. Read Thomas's "Memories of Christmas" (p. 1) and White's "Once More to the Lake" (p. 53). In each case, explain whether the place described helps to "define" the author.

THE WRITER

1. Write about an object that has symbolic or nostalgic importance for you.
2. Describe the floor plan of the first home you can remember living in. What incidents do you associate with particular parts of the home?
3. Mead speaks of "the need to define who you are by the place in which you live." Write an essay explaining the extent to which the place in which you live can define who you are. What things can it tell about you? What things can't it tell about you?
4. Read Didion's "On Going Home" (p. 40). Then write a brief essay comparing and contrasting Didion's implied definition of home with Mead's.

Benjamin Stein

WHATEVER HAPPENED TO SMALL-TOWN AMERICA?

Jim Rockford, private detective in NBC-TV's popular *The Rockford Files,* is in trouble. He is driving along in rural northern California on routine detective business, when his car suddenly hits a big bump and is incapacitated. Rockford, who is used to life in Los Angeles, is frantic. There he is, in the middle of nowhere, without any means of getting out: no taxicabs, no rental cars, no buses, no limousine service, nothing.

Then salvation comes, in the form of a towtruck operator who just happens to be passing by. He offers to tow Rockford into the nearest town for repairs. By chance, the town is named "New Pastoria." Rockford grins with delight; he is back in the driver's seat. But then he gets a jolt—the towtruck driver wants $100 just to tow Rockford a few miles. There is no alternative, so Rockford agrees; at least he'll be able to leave soon. But while he is having lunch and waiting for the car to be fixed, Rockford learns that the repairs, which he thought would be minor, are going to cost over $1,500. Again, that jolt—he isn't in Los Angeles now, so he can't just go to Aamco and get another estimate. The situation is starting to become painful to Rockford—and to look familiar to veteran television viewers as well.

Naturally, the car can't be fixed until the next day. So Rockford is consigned to the local motel, where he soon finds himself in the arms of a seemingly confused but seductive teenybopper. Suddenly, someone bursts in and takes a compromising photograph; then while Rockford is still holding the supposedly shaken girl, a deputy sheriff comes roaring up, gun drawn, and threatens him. The deputy turns out to be the girl's fiancé, and he suspects that Rockford has been messing with his girl. Now hardened television watchers know for sure that they are about to see one of the few formula scenarios of the movies and television today—the nightmare descent of the innocent city dweller into the incomprehensibly wicked and evil depths of the countryside. It has been seen a hundred times before, with slight variations, and it is a story as familiar as the one about the rookie cop teamed up with the tough twenty-year veteran, or the murdered prostitute with the heart of gold.

This characterization of the small town as evil and threatening to innocent city dwellers is now a staple of contemporary American mass culture. But the small town wasn't always seen that way. Over a relatively brief time, cultural attitudes toward small towns have changed

result, when he gets the chance, he attacks the small town on television or in the movies.

No matter that statistics show that living in a small town is about seven times safer than living in a large city. A person whose sole source of knowledge about America came from watching television detective shows would think that driving outside a big city is comparable to jumping off a tall building. Any number of movies—*Deliverance, Macon County Line, The California Kid*—make the same point. The television shows and movies are not telling it "like it is"; instead they are giving us the point of view of a small and extremely powerful section of the American intellectual community—those who write for the mass visual media.

The Cultural Civil War

What is happening, as a consequence, is something unusual and re-markable. A national culture is making war upon a way of life that is still powerfully attractive and widely practiced in the safe country. To be specific, about half of all Americans still live in small towns and rural areas, and, more interestingly, about three out of four Americans sampled in a 1975 Gallup poll said they would prefer to live in a suburb or a small town, or on a farm. (Almost 25 percent chose a farm!) Thus feelings of affection for small towns run deep in America, and small-town life is treasured by millions of people. But in the mass culture of the country, a hatred for the small town is spewed out on television screens and movie screens every day.

So far as I know, this is a historical first. In many earlier societies, there had been a literature which belittled and criticized the small town and the rural way of life. But it was confined to small groups of the population. For the masses of the people, there was a folk tradition which glorified the rural and small-town way of life. Now that situation is turned around. Television and the movies are America's folk culture, and they have nothing but contempt for the way of life of a very large part of the folk.

In no time before the advent of television has a writer been able to reach so many people so quickly. Similarly, before the age of television, writers as a group were never able to circulate their opinions so widely in so short a space of time. What happened was the coincidence of a cultural event and an electronic event. The cultural event was rather complicated. It involved the emergence among television and movie writers of a predominantly left-wing, antiestablishment style of thought and view of the world—the result of a whole series of events that are too lengthy to enumerate (and which I do not fully understand), but are clearly apparent. Part of that worldview is an animus against small-town America. The electronic event was the growth of television; and entry to its ranks of writers, as for the movies, was decided on a strictly meritocratic basis. The result was that aggressive, striving people with a modicum of talent could become television and movie writers. Thus the medium and the message came together around the mid-1950s, although the two had been converging for some time before.

The consequence of this merger has been that the American people are told falsehoods about their country—untruths that those in control of writing for the media believe, or at any rate refuse to disbelieve. And the falsehoods have consequences.

The anti-small-town show makes the point clearly. Poll after poll has shown that Americans in cities fear crime more than anything else— even more than inflation. Statistics also show that the most frequently committed crime is simple mugging, and that the typical mugger is a teenage, minority-group male. And what people fear when they leave their cars and houses are precisely teenaged, minority-group youths.

But most writers of America cannot cope intellectually with the idea that some of those pitiful minorities, whom they were taught were oppressed and tormented, are now themselves tormenting others in turn. Many therefore take their own free-floating anxiety about crime and violence and move it to a place that is more comfortable for them—the small town, which they were taught to hate and fear. It is a complete reversal of reality to make the small town more dangerous than the big city, but it accords perfectly with these writers' view of reality—or what reality should be. (There are other examples of this inverted depiction of crime on television. For instance, if a crime is committed in the city, it is usually by a person who is either rich or insane. The real world, in which violent crimes are committed by people who are poor, vicious, and quite sane, rarely shows its head.)

The simple consequence of this distortion of reality is that people are misinformed. Far more serious and dangerous, however, is that people are taught to hate and fear their own culture. They are given additional reasons to detest a fundamental social unit of their country—the small town. This detestation leads like a stream, among many such streams that such writers and intellectuals have fashioned, into a mighty confluence of doubt of America by Americans. People are told that their culture is, at its root, sick, violent, and depraved, and this message gives them little confidence in the future of that culture. It also leads them to feel ashamed of their country and to believe that if their society is in decline, it deserves to be.

It is simply inconceivable that a medium capable of making a brand new deodorant number one in sales in only six months ("Try it under your own two arms—we're Sure") could not, after years of trying, make Americans feel ambivalent about small towns.

A Small-Town Revival?

And yet, the polls still show a strong attachment to the concept of small-town life. That, perhaps, is the result of some reality penetrating into the minds of people who watch television. Those people have been to small towns. The small towns are often pretty, clean, and quiet. No one hurt them or threatened them there. So the television shows make them feel ambivalent about the small town, but cannot destroy all feelings of affection. What the television shows and movies can do is create self-doubt and confusion. What would be terribly interesting would be the reactions of Americans to small towns if their views had not been affected by television shows and movies that are filled with negative images.

We may get to see just that. There are signs of a change in the attitude of the media toward small towns and rural America. Somewhere along the line, someone discovered that the hatred of small towns collided with the environmental issue. Suddenly, for the groups whose parents were taught that everything outside the city was the domain of the Klansman, the city and its pollution now became the enemy.

A new generation of ad men and women and music hucksters have come along who realized that when you call something "country" or "farm-fresh" or "natural," people think of it as lacking poisonous pollutants and additives. On the same shows where the small town is cruelly trapping the innocent city dweller, the commercials are showing how wonderful it is to live on a farm and get fresh food and have a fresh complexion, and how healthful it is to live in a small town where there is plenty of fresh air and hard work. People have begun to think that out in the country, there are not only fewer sulphur-dioxide emissions, but less meanness and tension. Television documentaries now tell about city people who are leading new lives in Vermont and Maine.

A generational clash is developing in the media. The people most in tune with the generation of the 1960s and 1970s know that, despite all the television shows, Ralph Nader has authoritatively told them that big cities are disgusting, unhealthy places—and they believe him. Such people are resuscitating the country image in those media forms which most quickly adapt to changing trends, music and advertising. On the radio air waves, country music expands to new stations at an almost geometric rate. It is customarily only a matter of time before such trends move to prime time and the silver screen.

But the writers who grew up without the environmental issue are still around, and are still powerful. Their world view has not changed and they are still grinding out the melodramas which make the small town eat dirt.

So a struggle in the media continues in which ground is gained and lost. The signs of how it will turn out are unclear, but they seem to indicate a small-town renascence. A recent phenomenon is the sudden emergence of pictures about small towns, particularly in the South, which are not slanderous and which are making big money, even in suburban markets. Think of Burt Reynolds and you can think of the cinematic genre referred to. The emergence of Nashville as a powerful media center is another sign of the regeneration of the image of the small town. It grows daily more powerful in both records and films, and it is the capital of small-town America (a fact which earned it an astonishingly crude slam in the movie which bears its name). Several new television shows are set in small towns—Sara, The Bionic Woman, and Mary Hartman, Mary Hartman—and the small towns are treated affectionately. Even a recent made-for-television movie adapted from the works of John O'Hara took a compassionate view of small-town life.

Still, these are just straws in the wind. The predominant theme in prime time and at the theater is still that small towns are places where bad things happen to innocent people. It is a view that is neither realistic nor helpful to America or to anyone in particular, but it reveals something about how the media and our culture are shaped.

1976

[*Benjamin Stein's article was challenged by the following letter. Stein's response to the letter is also given.*]

> Benjamin Stein's "Whatever Happened to Small-Town America?" [is] re-
> markable in its many inaccuracies—about Hollywood and its portrayal of
> small towns, and about small towns themselves. The conclusion of the article,
> that left-wing and liberal Jewish writers in Hollywood are subverting inno-
> cent (non-Jewish) moviegoers and television watchers, reminded me of simi-
> lar charges made fifty years ago by the right-wing opponents of Weimar
> democracy.[1]
>
> Admittedly, Mr. Stein never quite raises the religious issue; he says only
> that the "typical Hollywood writer, from my experience, is of an ethnic
> background from a large Eastern city—usually from Brooklyn." Perhaps he is
> right. Still, this does not prove the writers are liberal or left-wing, that they

---

1. In other words, the Nazi party.

were large donors to the McGovern and Hayden campaigns, or for that matter, that they are against small towns. More important, my impression (based on an inveterate reading of film and television credits) is that the Westerns, crime dramas, and adventure stories from which Mr. Stein draws most of his evidence are generally written by people whose names suggest they are neither ethnics nor from Brooklyn.

Mr. Stein is correct on one point: The media's love affair with the small-town pastoral has died down since World War II, even if it was never quite as passionate as Mr. Stein thinks. Still, the pastoral remains very much alive in television news features—for example, in Charles Kuralt's CBS news series, "On the Road."

Television's portrayal of small-town criminality, however, is more complex than Mr. Stein suggests. Hollywood writers are saying that crime is sometimes carried out and sometimes covered up by the power holders in small towns, and this process is immeasurably aided by the fact that they are friends, and often relatives. To me, these stories are mainly warnings against the pastoral myth, depicting the dark side of Gemeinschaft,[2] and suggesting that it can breed lawlessness and conspiracy as well as cohesion and warmth.

This theme is old as the hills, even in Hollywood, and it was probably first imported by the writers of Western movies, who were usually not from Brooklyn. Mr. Stein himself mentions the 1956 film *Bad Day at Black Rock,* but Will Wright's recent *Sixguns and Society* (University of California Press, 1975) indicates that the small-town society of the Western was almost always depicted as weak, thus creating the need for the outlaw-hero. In some films, such as *High Noon* (1952) and *Broken Arrow* (1950), the leaders of the small town even tried to have the hero killed because he was endangering its stability or other interests in his single-minded pursuit of morality.

Now that Westerns are passé, at least for the moment, their critique of small-town Gemeinschaft has been transferred to other television dramas and to contemporary hamlets—including "Fernwood, Ohio," where Mary Hartman lives and suffers. Although Mr. Stein sees *Mary Hartman, Mary Hartman* as a sign of a newly favorable attitude toward small towns on television, he evidently has not watched the series regularly. Otherwise he would know that while Mary Hartman may be a traditional small-town innocent, most of the townspeople—who cause suffering to her, her family, and her friends— are depicted as corrupt. Even so, "Fernwood, Ohio," is hardly a typical hamlet, since its major male characters all work on an assembly line.

Nor is television's current image of the small town pure fiction. Hollywood exaggerates empirical reality, as it exaggerates everything else, but the small towns are not as crime-free as Mr. Stein would like to believe. According to FBI Crime Reports, which divide America into "metropolitan areas," "other cities," and "rural areas," the "rural areas" have almost as high a violent-crime rate as "other cities," and keep up with them in rates of murder and

2. Community; the word was used by the Nazis to characterize the cultural and racial German elite, as opposed to minorities such as the Jews who were excluded from the community.

rape. To be sure, the rates are lower than those of large cities, and there is no street crime and mugging, but small town America is hardly peaceful. Moreover, a long list of journalistic and sociological studies, as well as naturalistic novels, have shown that the familial and friendship ties that typically characterize small-town life have cemented economic and political alliances that breed corruption and other forms of white-collar crime, and occasionally even murder. Rural political machines, for example, predated and have outlived their urban counterparts, and while the news media have not paid much attention to them, their deviations from legality differ little. In short, the media do not "detest a fundamental social unit," as Mr. Stein would have us believe, but only one of its faults.

I am also surprised that a viewer as experienced as Mr. Stein still believes that media fiction can alter basic attitudes and values. He admits himself that the media's portrayal of small-town criminality has not diminished the fondness many Americans feel toward the small town, but then goes on to say that "it is simply inconceivable that a medium capable of making a brand new deodorant number one in sales in only six months . . . could not, after years of trying, make Americans feel ambivalent about small towns." In fact, there is no evidence that the media are capable of making Americans feel such ambivalence—the ability to hype up deodorant sales proves nothing about attitudes. After all, when you sell patent medicines that at best offer symptomatic relief, it is not very difficult to persuade people to try a new one every so often with a catchy commercial.

In the end, Mr. Stein has the same view of the American public, whom he sees as being subverted by Hollywood, as that which he accuses the left-wing and liberal writers of having, those whom he imagines dominate television. He sees the television audience as a gullible mass whose culture is shaped by the media; consequently, he suggests that the continued fondness for small-town life "is, perhaps, the result of some reality penetrating into the minds of people who watch television." A curious phrase, but since Mr. Stein is out to expose a previously unrecognized menace, he must also invent a thickheaded populace for whom reality is only a sometime thing.

—Herbert J. Gans

[Benjamin Stein's reply:]

In my article, I tried to raise two points: 1) Movies and television programs typically picture small towns as evil, dangerous places; and 2) creative people involved in the making of these shows dislike and fear small towns, for largely political reasons.

Professor Gans apparently recognizes the first point, but believes that the trend began earlier than I said. That is possible, but his example, *High Noon* (1952), does not support his contention, since it was made twenty years after *I Am a Fugitive from a Chain Gang* (1932), which I cited as the first of the anti-small-town films.

That is a small point, however. If Professor Gans does not recognize that the animus against small towns has become a staple ingredient of television adventure dramas, he simply has not been watching television. If he does not acknowledge the movies' maltreatment of small towns, he simply has not been going to the movies.

The second point was, if anything, understated in my article. Since coming to Los Angeles I have interviewed many producers, directors, and writers concerning their political feelings. Without exception, they are fearful and worried about small towns, mainly because of the political views they see represented there.

Two examples make the point clearly. I asked Meta Rosenberg, an extremely intelligent woman who produces *The Rockford Files*, how she felt about small towns. She answered that they had some good points, but that they could easily become thoroughly corrupt, because there were no forces to dissipate corruption once it started. When I asked her if small towns were frightening, she thought for a moment and said, without prompting, "Jesus Christ, they did vote for Nixon."

When asked about small towns, Stanley Kramer, a producer-director with impressive credits (including *High Noon*), said, "Of course, they're reactionary, extremely reactionary. They pursue the clichés of America so strictly that they endanger America."

These comments are unusually succinct, but highly representative. I think it might be instructive for Professor Gans to spend some time in the dream factories to see how what goes in influences what comes out.

Jane Howard

POMP AND CIRCUMSTANCE IN GROUNDHOG HOLLOW

Every morning Matilda Titus Hastings fixes her husband, Wayne, a panful of biscuits and gravy to go with his specially fried eggs. Perhaps as a subtle consequence of this repeated alchemy, in the same way that dogs come to resemble their masters, Matilda looks something like a biscuit herself, wholesomely puffy. "Only one woman in Atkins, West Virginia," she likes to say, "is bigger than I am—the lady who runs the tavern."

But Tildy, as she is usually known except to the twelve who call her Mama and the three dozen or so to whom she is Granny, is not really all that fat. What she is is comfortable looking. Her hair, which never in her life has been cut, is pinned up in braids. "Before it got so thin," she says, "the braids were about as wide as my wrist."

She wears glasses for sewing, the only work for which she has ever been paid, and for reading, which is her furtive pleasure. (She reads on the sly, the way some people gamble.) Outside, on bright days, she puts on a homemade sunbonnet. Most of her dresses she makes herself, for about a dollar each, but once she spent sixteen dollars on a three-piece lace outfit. She owns two costume-jewelry pins. One, crown-shaped, is composed of the birthstones of her ten daughters and two sons. The other, made of coal, is shaped like West Virginia.

* * *

The Hastingses' two-story house is modest by many standards, but in West Virginia it is thought to be imposing. To get to that house you have to take a rough ride up Groundhog Hollow Road. The car bounces and jounces and rattles and shakes and so, if you are a passenger, do you. "I tell people that's how come I had so many girl babies," Tildy jokes during one such ride. "Going up and down this road all the time, I shook the balls off them."

Groundhog Hollow Road leads down a steep hill to Atkins, where the Hastingses shop. Turn right there and drive four miles and you will come to Rollo, where they get their mail. All around that region you will see cars with Kentucky and Virginia license plates, because both state borders are nearby. Medical facilities, however, are not. If something is wrong with the Hastingses' teeth, for example, they have to drive thirty-five miles to Welch. "There's supposed to be a dentist in War, sixteen miles over," says Tildy, "but seems like you never can find him in."

McDowell County, in which the Hastingses live, has been called the Coal Bin of America. Slag heaps in the wake of strip mines desecrate the lyrically lovely hillsides. Abandoned car hulks rot, with all deliberate speed, in stream beds. The best of the roads are poor. All change comes slowly. Incest is not unheard of—"They try to hush it up, but word gets around."—nor is illiteracy. "A lot of people," says Tildy, "have to have the postmistress read them their Black Lung checks." Ninety percent of the men in McDowell County who work or have worked in mines, including Wayne Hastings, suffer from silicosis.

Movie theaters and libraries are scarce, but churches abound. Just down the road from Groundhog Hollow, in Atkins, is a church whose members believe that the command given in Mark 16:18, "They shall take up serpents," must be followed literally. On Saturday evenings they really do handle real snakes. I wanted to visit this church the weekend I spent with the Hastingses; to me it sounded as exotic as a mosque. Wayne said we could, but first we would go to the Church of Christ, where he sometimes preaches. The service there lasted so long that by the time we got out the snake-handlers had gone home.

Tildy does not share her husband's enthusiasm for the Church of Christ, by which he is in fact ordained and to which he converted dramatically in 1953. Nothing can lure her away from the Jacob's Ladder Branch Church of the Old Hosanna Regular Primitive Baptist Association. She and Wayne can argue for hours about theology.

"It like to kill her daddy when Grace Ellen joined the Primitive Baptists," Tildy said of one of her daughters. "He said he'd rather see them dead than join my church. Several of the others joined his. On the surface you might think they cared more for their daddy than for me, because they make over him more. But they feared him, while I was more their friend. I'd stop them if they ever said anything disrespectful. I'd say 'That's your father, so don't you say that.'

"Wayne is interested in death and the hereafter," she says. "He believes in hell and damnation, everlasting fires. I'm interested in Christ and salvation. I believe we get our punishments and our blessings right here on earth. I can't believe I need to be water-baptized in total immersion to avoid eternal damnation. You should come here sometime the first Sunday in August, when we have, in my church, our old-time foot-washing.

"We wash each other's feet with two towels sewed together. Ladies wait on female members, men on men, and it doesn't matter whose feet we wash, because we all just love each other so much we want to be at each other's feet in humility. As we wash each other's feet, we keep on singing."

If you were setting Tildy's life to a musical score, you would draw from three sources: "Earnestly, Tenderly. Jesus Is Calling," "Turkey in the Straw," and "Pomp and Circumstance." Nothing in all the Hastings house is more arresting than the array in the living room of twelve high-school graduation pictures. Six graduates on top, six below, born between 1928 and 1947, each one dressed in cap and gown, some with diplomas clutched close to their cheeks.

The youngest of these children did not technically get a diploma but a certificate of attendance. "She had to fight to finish high school; she wanted so bad to have that picture up there with the others. Her I.Q. is 85, and she doesn't retain information. Wayne thought it was the teachers' fault; he thought they didn't try hard enough to pound the learning into her. In his own childhood, you see, people weren't retarded. They were crazy.

"But Wayne is as proud of those pictures as I am. He drives around even now, with all our children grown and gone, to visit the schoolrooms, or he tries to, anyway." In one schoolroom, a couple of years ago, a teacher told Wayne he could not pay an impromptu visit without special permission from the Board of Education. This hurt him. "If that ain't communism," he asked rhetorically, "could you tell me what is?"

Tildy herself, the second of nine children, only went as far as the eighth grade, because her father didn't believe in sending girls to high school. Sometimes, even when ice covered the ground, she would walk to school barefoot and contemplate stealing something from the country store so that she might be sent to reform school, "because at least it was a school.

"I was born in nineteen and eleven and raised up at the top of this same mountain," she says, "and I like to say my father moved just about every time the moon changed. We had a lot of superstitions in those days. If your nose itched, it meant somebody coming. If a rooster crowed on your porch before breakfast, you'd have company. If you stepped on a rusty nail, the thing to do was pull it out, rub it with bacon rind, and hang it on a hook. If you got a snake bite, you'd wrap the bite in black tape and try to kill the snake before it got to water—then the bite would heal."

From the moment she first saw Wayne Hastings, "I thought he was about the handsomest guy in the world. I was at a spring, dipping water, and he passed by and said, 'How do you do?' There was never another man in my life before and there hasn't been one since. Once I said I knew of two women around here who were decent, and someone said, 'Oh? Which two?' I said, 'Well, I know I am, and I'm pretty sure Mama is.' Mama was there, and she said, ''Pon my word, daughter, I am.'

"One night Wayne walked me home from a tent meeting and we started keeping company. He never proposed and I didn't, either. One day he said, 'I'm not going to walk this ridge so much.' I said, 'Oh? Why not?' He said, 'I'm going to make them come to see us.' He was twenty-two and I was seventeen when we got married on September nineteenth, nineteen and twenty-eight. It was a Wednesday, a popular day to be married in those times, and we never knew what a honeymoon was, except that somebody caught us a catfish so long it wouldn't lay flat in a three-dollar washtub.

"My mama warned me that Wayne was from a family that drank right much, and for a long time he did. He could be mean: he'd fuss at the children and once when he was cleaning onions with a butcher knife he looked at me and said, 'I ought to cut your throat.' I said, 'Go ahead, if you can,' and took off my glasses and stood right there, but he didn't. I left him once, over drinking, but I couldn't abandon the babies, so I came back. He never missed a day's work over it, and he was always a good provider. In October of nineteen and fifty-three he joined the church and never had a drop since, not even after the accident."

A rock "as big as a mattress on a bed" fell onto Wayne's spine inside the Island Creek Coal Company mine in 1959. "He was hunkered on his heels—they were blasting to get the coal out and he was shot fireman. Compared to what could have happened he was lucky. The hole he was caught in, they said, didn't look big enough for an eight-year-old child to survive in. And they weren't sure he would be able to walk at all, or have any use whatsoever of his sexual organs." A two-year period of rehabilitation at a United Mine Workers hospital in New Jersey restored partial use of the lower half of Wayne's body, but life has been difficult ever since then both for him and his wife.

"His morale was right bad after the accident. Once he said he felt so worthless we'd be better off without him, and he told me to get a divorce. I said, 'You can't drive me away—I don't want a divorce and you can't get one. When we were married I said it would be for life, and I've always held to that.' My one prayer is that I'll outlive him, so I can care for him as long as he lives. I don't think the children could cope with him. When I'm gone he subsists, but he never eats the right food, and he won't go visit his sisters. They offer to do for him, but he won't have it."

Tildy still likes to read visitors a letter she once received from her eighth child, Louella: "I think about when I was younger," Louella wrote, "maybe twenty or twenty-five years ago. I think about good things. I see the beauty of the mountains we lived in. All the fields cleared, with all the dandelions growing everywhere and the milkweeds and polk berries, the log house and the spring in the holler. Beautiful, beautiful sunshine everywhere. The cows, chickens, cats, and dogs. I don't believe the sun could shine any brighter than in the spring and fall as it did then. In spring everything seemed greener than green and in fall, everything red, yellow, and colors that can't be named. Hickory nuts and walnuts and squirrels. Watching the house being built was one long, beautiful movie."

Before they moved into their present house, in 1949, the Hastingses lived in a four-room log cabin half a mile or so down Groundhog Hollow. Before Wayne's illness there was no telephone; only since 1962 have they had indoor plumbing. Tildy can remember the first car she ever saw: "In nineteen and eighteen it sounded like a helicopter sounds now. When I heard it coming up the hill, I ran and hid." Not so long ago she herself washed on a board, cooked on a wood stove, and hand-ground entire 250-pound hogs, storing the meat in Mason jars.

Her babies were delivered in the old log cabin, with the help of a midwife. "When it was time, we'd send a neighbor boy over the mountain on a mule to fetch her, and she'd walk down with a bag that had in it a scale, a scissors, and a cord. Her fee was five dollars, and if she had to she'd stay around for a week at a time. She wasn't in any hurry to go. She was a wonderful woman, and I was blessed to sit by her bed and hold her hand when she left this world.

"If I had it to do over I'd have fewer children, because there isn't room enough in the world for everyone to have as many as I did, but I sure can't tell you which of them I'd give up. Without anesthetics it wasn't easy having them, but you just grit you teeth and bear it. Once I had six under the age of five, and when my youngest daughter was three months old my system wasn't too strong, and I almost had a nervous breakdown. If the company doctor hadn't got my tubes tied, I might have had more still. Wayne would divorce me if he heard me say so, but I feel more strongly about sterilization than abortions, though I think there are times when abortions should be permitted too."

Tildy tells of a doctor's visit to an equally fecund friend of hers. The doctor, calling on the woman in another old log cabin, suggested that properly timed cold baths might help to reduce chances of pregnancy. "Doctor," the woman asked him, "do you see that creek down there?" He saw it, a good 150 yards away. "Doctor, do you think I'm going to go down there four or five times a night to take a cold bath? Because, Doctor, if you do, you'd better think again."

Wayne and Tildy, like many American couples, have their failures in communication. "A lot of times I find out from other people what's going on with him," says Tildy. They have chronic disagreements, too. Wayne, for example, is still not persuaded that reading anything other than the Holy Scripture is a worthwhile activity. "Wayne says that reading costs money and that time spent reading could be better spent doing something different. But I've always read, all my life, and I'm not about to stop. I used to read to the kids, one on either knee, whether they wanted me to or not. Once, when I was missing my copies of *Life* magazine, I went to ask the postmistress how come they hadn't been coming, and she hinted that Wayne had them sent back. I said to him that if my magazine didn't come that next week, I'd go to the drugstore and buy a copy, so that was the end of that.

"But when the children were in school and he was working on the night shift, I'd read all the school books I missed as a child, and a novel a night. I've read *Franklin and Eleanor* and *My Life with Jackie* (I liked it but thought that author lady was very disloyal) and several of Taylor Cald-well's books and *Jane Eyre* and *I Know Why the Caged Bird Sings* and *Tap Roots*, a Civil War story that dealt with the Negro race, and a lot of Reader's Digest Condensed Books and *A Lion in the Streets* and *For Whom the Bell Tolls* and *Forever Amber* and another one I can't remember.

"I watch television some, but not as much as a lot of people do. Television's changed things a lot. Before television people used to be more friendlier, pay more attention, be more relaxed and settle-minded. Used to be whole families would come for a visit and stay overnight. Now sometimes weeks pass and nobody stops by here."

Not one of the Hastings children has settled in West Virginia: "They all went other places to find work, and they all found it too." It saddens the parents that none of the children wants to inherit the house they struggled so hard to build. "It's a dream," says Tildy, "but we'd like to make the house, after we pass on, into a home for wayward girls or old people or maybe disabled miners."

Most of the children live close enough, in neighboring states, to make occasional visits. Once in a while, in a masterful triumph of choreography, the whole family is reunited. On one such occasion somebody had made a sign which still hangs: OCCUPANCY BY MORE THAN 25 PERSONS IN THIS BATHROOM IS BOTH ILLEGAL AND UN-LAWFUL. And one July, when many of the dozen came home, they chipped in to buy their parents a new dinette set. "A couple of them took us down to the store in their car," Tildy remembers, "and when we drove back, they'd keep saying, 'Wonder if Santy Claus has been here?' When we got home, we saw the old chairs we'd been using out on the porch and the new set inside. Both our reclining chairs were gifts from the children too. Oh, we couldn't be more proud of them all."

Had she not had so many children, Tildy thinks she might have been a nurse or a writer. "I love to take care of people and I love to tell about people. You don't raise twelve children and help with a lot of grandchildren without doing a lot of nursing. I've helped in hospitals and had patients to ask me how long I've been in nursing. I delivered a baby one time in an emergency and helped with a lot of other deliveries. I put the first diaper on Clifford's wife's baby and the first diaper on Clifford's wife herself too.

"Once, out on Atkins mountain, a favorite uncle of mine had a stroke. I was out there caring for him when another daughter in Indiana was about to have surgery, and another one's babies were ill, and Wayne's mother had taken a turn for the worse. I debated which to go to: Grace Ellen or Velma Jean, and decided Velma Jean needed me worse. I stayed at the hospital a couple of nights and helped in the house, too. Wayne called and said Grace Ellen had to have brain surgery.

"Wilma, the one whose husband was in jail for being an alcoholic, she was about to go to the hospital for a baby. So I called her the next morning in Dayton, and the nurse said she was coming along fine. Wayne and I went to see Grace Ellen and found her mother-in-law already there. She said Grace Ellen was getting along all right, but Lord, how she looked. I got home Saturday evening, went to church Sunday morning, and on Monday morning went to Tennessee to get Wilma's boys. Tuesday morning I went to the hospital myself, from what I guess you might call an overdose of motherhood. I've had a heart condition, and spells off and on, ever since. I have to take it pretty easy these days.

"But there's lots of things I want to do. For one, I'd like right much to look into genealogy. They tell me my people go back to 1066, and that we're descended from a queen of England. I'd like to travel too, right much more than Wayne ever wanted to. It's hard for the kids to entertain their daddy when he and I come to visit. One thing he did like, when we went to Washington to see Louella, he liked the Wax Museum."

                                    * * *

"I don't think I can stay on the Mountain Artisans[1] board," Tildy said, "because of my health. But being *paid* to do the kind of work I've always done anyway since I was seven has given me a self-confidence I never had before. Somebody said the quilts we make aren't art, because we make them to a design and art's something there's only one of, but I said, 'What could be more artistic than something our grandmothers taught us how to do?'

"Besides, one year I earned $841, and some have made plenty more than that. For some, including me, it's the first money we ever made in our lives, and for others it's the only source of income at all. Not that I expect to be paid for all I do. I like working in the community too, trying to get school buses to go up into the hollers to get to the children, organizing a buyers' club, helping with Head Start, and helping with the old people too. Seems to me whatever more pleasure they can get, they sure do deserve it.

"Old women seem to me more lonely than old men, because old men can get together more, on street corners and in barber shops. Women are more sure of themselves than men, in this area anyway, but to me

1. A cooperative that marketed patchwork quilts and other products of West Virginia seamstresses.

women'll always be women, and they shouldn't try not to." Tildy put on a checkered sunbonnet and walked out her back door to look up over the hill. "But I don't think any person, male or female, should be a doormat," she went on. "I've heard married couples to say they've never had an argument in their lives. All I can say to that is they must be mighty meek and mild. I'm sure glad *I'm* not married to a man like that, and I'll bet the men wouldn't like it much either. I guess it works out about equal most of the time, but you could put it this way, if you understand what I mean: we make men *think* they run the show."

1973, 1982

Virginia Woolf

MY FATHER: LESLIE STEPHEN

By the time that his children were growing up, the great days of my father's life were over. His feats on the river and on the mountains had been won before they were born. Relics of them were to be found lying about the house—the silver cup on the study mantelpiece; the rusty alpenstocks that leaned against the bookcase in the corner; and to the end of his days he would speak of great climbers and explorers with a peculiar mixture of admiration and envy. But his own years of activity were over, and my father had to content himself with pottering about the Swiss valleys or taking a stroll across the Cornish moors.

That to potter and to stroll meant more on his lips than on other people's is becoming obvious now that some of his friends have given their own version of those expeditions. He would start off after breakfast alone, or with one companion. Shortly after dinner he would return. If the walk had been successful, he would have out his great map and commemorate a new short cut in red ink. And he was quite capable, it appears, of striding all day across the moors without speaking more than a word or two to his companion. By that time, too, he had written the *History of English Thought in the Eighteenth Century*, which is said by some to be his masterpiece; and the *Science of Ethics*—the book which interested him most; and *The Playground of Europe*, in which is to be found "The Sunset on Mont Blanc"—in his opinion the best thing he ever wrote. He still wrote daily and methodically, though never for long at a time.

In London he wrote in the large room with three long windows at the top of the house. He wrote lying almost recumbent in a low rocking chair which he tipped to and fro as he wrote, like a cradle, and as he wrote he smoked a short clay pipe, and he scattered books round him in a circle. The thud of a book dropped on the floor could be heard in the room beneath. And often as he mounted the stairs to his study with his firm, regular tread he would burst, not into song, for he was entirely unmusical, but into a strange rhythmical chant, for verse of all kinds, both "utter trash," as he called it, and the most sublime words of Milton and Wordsworth, stuck in his memory, and the act of walking or climbing seemed to inspire him to recite whichever it was that came uppermost or suited his mood.

But it was his dexterity with his fingers that delighted his children before they could potter along the lanes at his heels or read his books. He would twist a sheet of paper beneath a pair of scissors and out would drop an elephant, a stag, or a monkey, with trunks, horns, and tails delicately and exactly formed. Or, taking a pencil, he would draw beast after beast —an art that he practiced almost unconsciously as he read, so that the flyleaves of his books swarm with owls and donkeys as if to illustrate the "Oh, you ass!" or "Conceited dunce" that he was wont to scribble impatiently in the margin. Such brief comments, in which one may find the germ of the more temperate statements of his essays, recall some of the characteristics of his talk. He could be very silent, as his friends have testified. But his remarks, made suddenly in a low voice between the puffs of his pipe, were extremely effective. Sometimes with one word— but his one word was accompanied by a gesture of the hand—he would dispose of the tissue of exaggerations which his own sobriety seemed to provoke. "There are 40,000,000 unmarried women in London alone!" Lady Ritchie once informed him. "Oh, Annie, Annie!" my father exclaimed in tones of horrified but affectionate rebuke. But Lady Ritchie, as if she enjoyed being rebuked, would pile it up even higher next time she came.

The stories he told to amuse his children of adventures in the Alps— but accidents only happened, he would explain, if you were so foolish as to disobey your guides—or of those long walks, after one of which, from Cambridge to London on a hot day, "I drank, I am sorry to say, rather more than was good for me," were told very briefly, but with a curious power to impress the scene. The things that he did not say were always there in the background. So, too, though he seldom told anecdotes, and his memory for facts was bad, when he described a person—and he had known many people, both famous and obscure—he would convey exactly what he thought of him in two or three words. And what he thought might be the opposite of what other people thought. He had a way of upsetting established reputations and disregarding conventional values that could be disconcerting, and sometimes perhaps wounding, though no one was more respectful of any feeling that seemed to him genuine. But when, suddenly opening his bright blue eyes and rousing himself from what had seemed complete abstraction, he gave his opinion, it was difficult to disregard it. It was a habit, especially when deafness made him unaware that this opinion could be heard, that had its inconveniences.

"I am the most easily bored of men," he wrote, truthfully as usual; and when, as was inevitable in a large family, some visitor threatened to stay not merely for tea but also for dinner, my father would express his anguish at first by twisting and untwisting a certain lock of hair. Then he would burst out, half to himself, half to the powers above, but quite audibly, "Why can't he go? Why can't he go?" Yet such is the charm of simplicity—and did he not say, also truthfully, that "bores are the salt of the earth"?—that the bores seldom went, or, if they did, forgave him and came again.

Too much, perhaps, has been said of his silence; too much stress has been laid upon his reserve. He loved clear thinking; he hated sentimentality and gush; but this by no means meant that he was cold and unemotional, perpetually critical and condemnatory in daily life. On the contrary, it was his power of feeling strongly and of expressing his feeling with vigor that made him sometimes so alarming as a companion. A lady, for instance, complained of the wet summer that was spoiling her tour in Cornwall. But to my father, though he never called himself a democrat, the rain meant that the corn was being laid; some poor man was being ruined; and the energy with which he expressed his sympathy—not with the lady—left her discomfited. He had something of the same respect for farmers and fishermen that he had for climbers and explorers. So, too, he talked little of patriotism, but during the South African War—and all wars were hateful to him—he lay awake thinking that he heard the guns on the battlefield. Again, neither his reason nor his cold common sense helped to convince him that a child could be late for dinner without having been maimed or killed in an accident. And not all his mathematics together with a bank balance which he insisted must be ample in the extreme could persuade him, when it came to signing a check, that the whole family was not "shooting Niagara to ruin,"[1] as he put it. The pictures that he would draw of old age and the bankruptcy court, of ruined men of letters who have to support large families in small houses at Wimbledon (he owned a very small house at Wimbledon), might have convinced those who complain of his understatements that hyperbole was well within his reach had he chosen.

Yet the unreasonable mood was superficial, as the rapidity with which it vanished would prove. The checkbook was shut; Wimbledon and the workhouse were forgotten. Some thought of a humorous kind made him chuckle. Taking his hat and his stick, calling for his dog and his daughter, he would stride off into Kensington Gardens, where he had walked as a

1. The reference is to going over Niagara Falls in a boat.

little boy, where his brother Fitzjames and he had made beautiful bows to young Queen Victoria and she had swept them a curtsy; and so, round the Serpentine, to Hyde Park Corner, where he had once saluted the great Duke himself; and so home. He was not then in the least "alarming"; he was very simple, very confiding; and his silence, though one might last unbroken from the Round Pond to the Marble Arch, was curiously full of meaning, as if he were thinking half aloud, about poetry and philosophy and people he had known.

He himself was the most abstemious of men. He smoked a pipe perpetually, but never a cigar. He wore his clothes until they were too shabby to be tolerable; and he held old-fashioned and rather puritanical views as to the vice of luxury and the sin of idleness. The relations between parents and children today have a freedom that would have been impossible with my father. He expected a certain standard of behavior, even of ceremony, in family life. Yet if freedom means the right to think one's own thoughts and to follow one's own pursuits, then no one respected and indeed insisted upon freedom more completely than he did. His sons, with the exception of the Army and Navy, should follow whatever professions they chose; his daughters, though he cared little enough for the higher education of women, should have the same liberty. If at one moment he rebuked a daughter sharply for smoking a cigarette —smoking was not in his opinion a nice habit in the other sex—she had only to ask him if she might become a painter, and he assured her that so long as she took her work seriously he would give her all the help he could. He had no special love for painting; but he kept his word. Freedom of that sort was worth thousands of cigarettes.

It was the same with the perhaps more difficult problem of literature. Even today there may be parents who would doubt the wisdom of allowing a girl of fifteen the free run of a large and quite unexpurgated library. But my father allowed it. There were certain facts—very briefly, very shyly he referred to them. Yet "Read what you like," he said, and all his books, "mangy and worthless," as he called them, but certainly they were many and various, were to be had without asking. To read what one liked because one liked it, never to pretend to admire what one did not— that was his only lesson in the art of reading. To write in the fewest possible words, as clearly as possible, exactly what one meant—that was his only lesson in the art of writing. All the rest must be learned for oneself. Yet a child must have been childish in the extreme not to feel that such was the teaching of a man of great learning and wide experience, though he would never impose his own views or parade his own knowledge. For, as his tailor remarked when he saw my father walk past his shop up Bond Street, "There goes a gentleman that wears good clothes without knowing it."

In those last years, grown solitary and very deaf, he would sometimes call himself a failure as a writer; he had been "jack of all trades, and master of none." But whether he failed or succeeded as a writer, it is permissible to believe that he left a distinct impression of himself on the minds of his friends. Meredith[2] saw him as "Phoebus Apollo turned fasting friar" in his earlier days; Thomas Hardy, years later, looked at the "spare and desolate figure" of the Schreckhorn[3] and thought of

> him,
> Who scaled its horn with ventured life and limb,
> Drawn on by vague imaginings, maybe,
> Of semblance to his personality
> In its quaint glooms, keen lights, and rugged trim.

But the praise he would have valued most, for though he was an agnostic nobody believed more profoundly in the worth of human relationships, was Meredith's tribute after his death: "He was the one man to my knowledge worthy to have married your mother." And Lowell,[4] when he called him "L.S., the most lovable of men," has best described the quality that makes him, after all these years, unforgettable.

1950[5]

2. George Meredith (1828–1909), English novelist and poet.
3. One of the peaks in the Swiss Alps.
4. James Russell Lowell, nineteenth-century American poet, essayist, and editor.
5. Published posthumously.

THE READER

1. *What are the basic qualities Woolf admires, as revealed in this selection?*
2. *Would you like to have been Leslie Stephen's son or daughter? Why, or why not?*
3. *In some of her other work, Woolf shows a deep and sensitive concern for women's experience and awareness. Do you find a feminist awareness here? In what way?*
4. *In her novel* To the Lighthouse, *Woolf creates the fictional character of Mr. Ramsay from recollections of her father. Compare the characterization in her essay with this passage from the novel: "What he said was true. It was always true. He was incapable of untruth; never tampered with a fact; never altered a disagreeable word to suit the pleasure or convenience of any mortal being, least of all of his own children, who, sprung from his loins, should be aware from childhood that life is difficult; facts uncompromising; and the passage to that fabled land where our brightest hopes are extinguished, our frail barks founder in darkness (here Mr. Ramsay would straighten his back and narrow his little blue eyes upon the horizon), one that needs, above all, courage, truth, and the power to endure."* (To the Lighthouse, Harcourt, Brace & World, 1927; © 1955 Leonard Woolf, pp. 10–11.)

THE WRITER

1. *Giving praise can be a difficult rhetorical and social undertaking. How*

does Woolf avoid the pitfalls or try to? Compare Lessing's "My Father" (below) to this selection. Does Lessing take similar risks?
2. *Does Woolf's portrait of her father conform to her criteria for such writing as she defines them in "The New Biography" (p. 420)?*
3. *What are the main currents of the Stephens' family life as revealed here? Since any such description must be selective, what does Woolf leave out? Do the omissions detract from her essay? If you think so, say why.*
4. *If you didn't know that Leslie Stephen was Woolf's father, could you deduce that fact from the way she writes about him? Why, or why not?*
5. *Write a sketch about a father, real or fictional, adopting a tone similar to Woolf's in this sketch.*

Doris Lessing

MY FATHER

We use our parents like recurring dreams, to be entered into when needed; they are always there for love or for hate; but it occurs to me that I was not always there for my father. I've written about him before, but novels, stories, don't have to be "true." Writing this article is difficult because it has to be "true." I knew him when his best years were over.

There are photographs of him. The largest is of an officer in the 1914–18 war. A new uniform—buttoned, badged, strapped, tabbed—confines a handsome, dark young man who holds himself stiffly to confront what he certainly thought of as his duty. His eyes are steady, serious, and responsible, and show no signs of what he became later. A photograph at sixteen is of a dark, introspective youth with the same intent eyes. But it is his mouth you notice—a heavily-jutting upper lip contradicts the rest of a regular face. His moustache was to hide it: "Had to do something—a damned fleshy mouth. Always made me uncomfortable, that mouth of mine."

Earlier a baby (eyes already alert) appears in a lace waterfall that cascades from the pillowy bosom of a fat, plain woman to her feet. It is the face of a head cook. "Lord, but my mother was a practical female—almost as bad as you!" as he used to say, or throw at my mother in moments of exasperation. Beside her stands, or droops, arms dangling, his father, the source of the dark, arresting eyes, but otherwise masked by a long beard.

The birth certificate says: Born 3rd August, 1886, Walton Villa, Creffield Road, S. Mary at the Wall, R.S.D. Name, Alfred Cook. Name and surname of Father: Alfred Cook Tayler. Name and maiden name of Mother: Caroline May Batley. Rank or Profession: Bank Clerk.

Colchester, Essex.

They were very poor. Clothes and boots were a problem. They "made their own amusements." Books were mostly the Bible and *The Pilgrim's Progress*.[1] Every Saturday night they bathed in a hipbath in front of the kitchen fire. No servants. Church three times on Sundays. "Lord, when I think of those Sundays! I dreaded them all week, like a nightmare coming at you full tilt and no escape." But he rabbited with ferrets along the lanes and fields, bird-nested, stole fruit, picked nuts and mushrooms, paid visits to the blacksmith and the mill and rode a farmer's carthorse.

They ate economically, but when he got diabetes in his forties and subsisted on lean meat and lettuce leaves, he remembered suet puddings, treacle puddings, raisin and currant puddings, steak and kidney puddings, bread and butter pudding, "batter cooked in the gravy with the meat," potato cake, plum cake, butter cake, porridge with treacle, fruit tarts and pies, brawn, pig's trotters and pig's cheek and home-smoked ham and sausages. And "lashings of fresh butter and cream and eggs." He wondered if this diet had produced the diabetes, but said it was worth it.

There was an elder brother described by my father as: "Too damned clever by half. One of those quick, clever brains. Now I've always had a slow brain, but I get there in the end, damn it!"

The brothers went to a local school and the elder did well, but my father was beaten for being slow. They both became bank clerks in, I think, the Westminster Bank, and one must have found it congenial, for he became a manager, the "rich brother," who had cars and even a yacht. But my father did not like it, though he was conscientious. For instance, he changed his writing, letter by letter, because a senior criticised it. I never saw his unregenerate hand, but the one he created was elegant, spiky, careful. Did this mean he created a new personality for himself, hiding one he did not like, as he hid his "damned fleshy mouth"? I don't know.

Nor do I know when he left home to live in Luton, or why. He found family life too narrow? A safe guess—he found everything too narrow. His mother was too down-to-earth? He had to get away from his clever elder brother?

Being a young man in Luton was the best part of his life. It ended in 1914, so he had a decade of happiness. His reminiscences of it were all of pleasure, the delight of physical movement, of dancing in particular. All his girls were "a beautiful dancer, light as a feather." He played billiards and ping-pong (both for his country); he swam, boated, played cricket and football,[2] went to picnics and horse races, sang at musical evenings. One family of a mother and two daughters treated him "like a son only

1. An allegory of Christian's progress toward heaven through a world filled with tempters, by the seventeenth-century writer John Bunyan.

2. Soccer.

better. I didn't know whether I was in love with the mother or the daughters, but oh I did love going there; we had such good times." He was engaged to one daughter, then, for a time, to the other. An engagement was broken off because she was rude to a waiter. "I could not marry a woman who allowed herself to insult someone who was defenceless." He used to say to my wryly smiling mother: "Just as well I didn't marry either of *them*; they would never have stuck it out the way you have, old girl."

Just before he died he told me he had dreamed he was standing in a kitchen on a very high mountain holding X in his arms. "Ah, yes, that's what I've missed in my life. Now don't you let yourself be cheated out of life by the old dears. They take all the colour out of everything if you let them."

But in that decade—"I'd walk 10, 15 miles to a dance two or three times a week and think nothing of it. Then I'd dance every dance and walk home again over the fields. Sometimes it was moonlight, but I liked the snow best, all crisp and fresh. I loved walking back and getting into my digs[3] just as the sun was rising. My little dog was so happy to see me, and I'd feed her, and make myself porridge and tea, then I'd wash and shave and go off to work."

The boy who was beaten at school, who went too much to church, who carried the fear of poverty all his life, but who nevertheless was filled with the memories of country pleasures; the young bank clerk who worked such long hours for so little money, but who danced, sang, played, flirted —this naturally vigorous, sensuous being was killed in 1914, 1915, 1916. I think the best of my father died in that war, that his spirit was crippled by it. The people I've met, particularly the women, who knew him young, speak of his high spirits, his energy, his enjoyment of life. Also of his kindness, his compassion and—a word that keeps recurring—his wisdom. "Even when he was just a boy he understood things that you'd think even an old man would find it easy to condemn." I do not think these people would have easily recognised the ill, irritable, abstracted, hypochondriac man I knew.

He "joined up" as an ordinary soldier out of a characteristically quirky scruple: it wasn't right to enjoy officers' privileges when the Tommies[4] had such a bad time. But he could not stick the communal latrines, the obligatory drinking, the collective visits to brothels, the jokes about girls. So next time he was offered a commission he took it.

His childhood and young man's memories, kept fluid, were added to, grew, as living memories do. But his war memories were congealed in stories that he told again and again, with the same words and gestures, in stereotyped phrases. They were anonymous, general, as if they had come

---

3. Lodgings.   4. Foot soldiers.

out of a communal war memoir. He met a German in no-man's-land, but both slowly lowered their rifles and smiled and walked away. The Tommies were the salt of the earth, the British fighting men the best in the world. He had never known such comradeship. A certain brutal officer was shot in a sortie by his men, but the other officers, recognising rough justice, said nothing. He had known men intimately who saw the Angels at Mons.[5] He wished he could force all the generals on both sides into the trenches for just one day, to see what the common soldiers endured—that would have ended the war at once.

There was an undercurrent of memories, dreams, and emotions much deeper, more personal. This dark region in him, fate-ruled, where nothing was true but horror, was expressed inarticulately, in brief, bitter exclamations or phrases of rage, incredulity, betrayal. The men who went to fight in that war believed it when they said it was to end war. My father believed it. And he was never able to reconcile his belief in his country with his anger at the cynicism of its leaders. And the anger, the sense of betrayal, strengthened as he grew old and ill.

But in 1914 he was naïve, the German atrocities in Belgium inflamed him, and he enlisted out of idealism, although he knew he would have a hard time. He knew because a fortuneteller told him. (He could be described as uncritically superstitious or as psychically gifted.) He would be in great danger twice, yet not die—he was being protected by a famous soldier who was his ancestor. "And sure enough, later I heard from the Little Aunties that the church records showed we were descended the backstairs way from the Duke of Wellington, or was it Marlborough? Damn it, I forget. But one of them would be beside me all through the war, she said." (He was romantic, not only about this solicitous ghost, but also about being a descendant of the Huguenots, on the strength of the "e" in Tayler; and about "the wild blood" in his veins from a great uncle who, sent unjustly to prison for smuggling, came out of a ten-year sentence and earned it, very efficiently, along the coasts of Cornwall until he died.)

The luckiest thing that ever happened to my father, he said, was getting his leg shattered by shrapnel ten days before Passchendaele.[6] His whole company was killed. He knew he was going to be wounded because of the fortuneteller, who had said he would know. "I did not understand what she meant, but both times in the trenches, first when my appendix burst and I nearly died, and then just before Passchendaele, I felt for some days as if a thick, black velvet pall was settled over me. I can't tell you what it was like. Oh, it was awful, awful, and the second time it was so bad I wrote to the old people and told them I was going to

5. An apparition that appeared during a World War I battle.
6. A prolonged and futile battle of World War I, in which British and Commonwealth forces sustained massive casualties.

be killed."

His leg was cut off at mid-thigh, he was shell-shocked, he was very ill for many months, with a prolonged depression afterwards. "You should always remember that sometimes people are all seething underneath. You don't know what terrible things people have to fight against. You should look at a person's eyes, that's how you tell. . . . When I was like that, after I lost my leg, I went to a nice doctor man and said I was going mad, but he said, don't worry, everyone locks up things like that. You don't know—horrible, horrible, awful things. I was afraid of myself, of what I used to dream. I wasn't myself at all."

In the Royal Free Hospital was my mother, Sister McVeagh. He married his nurse which, as they both said often enough (though in different tones of voice), was just as well. That was 1919. He could not face being a bank clerk in England, he said, not after the trenches. Besides, England was too narrow and conventional. Besides, the civilians did not know what the soldiers had suffered, they didn't want to know, and now it wasn't done even to remember "The Great Unmentionable." He went off to the Imperial Bank of Persia, in which country I was born.

The house was beautiful, with great stone-floored high-ceilinged rooms whose windows showed ranges of snow-streaked mountains. The gardens were full of roses, jasmine, pomegranates, walnuts. Kermanshah he spoke of with liking, but soon they went to Teheran, populous with "Embassy people," and my gregarious mother created a lively social life about which he was irritable even in recollection.

Irritableness—that note was first struck here, about Persia. He did not like, he said, "the graft and the corruption." But here it is time to try and describe something difficult—how a man's good qualities can also be his bad ones, or if not bad, a danger to him.

My father was honourable—he always knew exactly what that word meant. He had integrity. His "one does not do that sort of thing," his "no, it is not right," sounded throughout my childhood and were final for all of us. I am sure it was true he wanted to leave Persia because of "the corruption." But it was also because he was already unconsciously longing for something freer, because as a bank official he could not let go into the dream-logged personality that was waiting for him. And later in Rhodesia, too, what was best in him was also what prevented him from shaking away the shadows: it was always in the name of honesty or decency that he refused to take this step or that out of the slow decay of the family's fortunes.

In 1925 there was leave from Persia. That year in London there was an Empire Exhibition, and on the Southern Rhodesian stand some very fine maize cobs and a poster saying that fortunes could be made on maize at

25/-[7] a bag. So on an impulse, turning his back forever on England, washing his hands of the corruption of the East, my father collected all his capital, £800, I think, while my mother packed curtains from Liberty's, clothes from Harrods, visiting cards, a piano, Persian rugs, a governess and two small children.

Soon, there was my father in a cigar-shaped house of thatch and mud on the top of a kopje[8] that overlooked in all directions a great system of mountains, rivers, valleys, while overhead the sky arched from horizon to empty horizon. This was a couple of hundred miles south from the Zambesi, a hundred or so west from Mozambique, in the district of Banket, so called because certain of its reefs were of the same formation as those called *banket* on the Rand. Lomagundi—gold country, tobacco country, maize country—wild, almost empty. (The Africans had been turned off it into reserves.) Our neighbours were four, five, seven miles off. In front of the house . . . no neighbours, nothing; no farms, just wild bush with two rivers but no fences to the mountains seven miles away. And beyond these mountains and bush again to the Portuguese border,[9] over which "our boys" used to escape when wanted by the police for pass or other offences.

And then? There was bad luck. For instance, the price of maize dropped from 25/- to 9/- a bag. The seasons were bad, prices bad, crops failed. This was the sort of thing that made it impossible for him ever to "get off the farm," which, he agreed with my mother, was what he most wanted to do.

It was an absurd country, he said. A man could "own" a farm for years that was totally mortgaged to the Government and run from the Land Bank, meanwhile employing half-a-hundred Africans at 12/- a month and none of them knew how to do a day's work. Why, two farm labourers from Europe could do in a day what twenty of these ignorant black savages would take a week to do. (Yet he was proud that he had a name as a just employer, that he gave "a square deal.") Things got worse. A fortuneteller had told him that her heart ached when she saw the misery ahead for my father: this was the misery.

But it was my mother who suffered. After a period of neurotic illness, which was a protest against her situation, she became brave and resourceful. But she never saw that her husband was not living in a real world, that he had made a captive of her common sense. We were always about to "get off the farm." A miracle would do it—a sweepstake, a goldmine, a legacy. And then? What a question! We would go to England where life would be normal with people coming in for musical evenings and nice supper parties at the Trocadero after a show. Poor

7. Twenty-five shillings. A shilling was then worth about twenty-five cents.
8. Small hill. The term is South African Dutch.
9. That is, the border of Mozambique, then a Portuguese possession.

woman, for the twenty years we were on the farm, she waited for when life would begin for her and for her children, for she never understood that what was a calamity for her was for them a blessing.

Meanwhile my father sank towards his death (at 61). Everything changed in him. He had been a dandy and fastidious, now he hated to change out of shabby khaki. He had been sociable, now he was misan-thropic. His body's disorders—soon diabetes and all kinds of stomach ailments—dominated him. He was brave about his wooden leg, and even went down mine shafts and climbed trees with it, but he walked clumsily and it irked him badly. He greyed fast, and slept more in the day, but would be awake half the night pondering about. . . .

It could be gold divining. For ten years he experimented on private theories to do with the attractions and repulsions of metals. His whole soul went into it but his theories were wrong or he was unlucky—after all, if he had found a mine he would have had to leave the farm. It could be the relation between the minerals of the earth and of the moon; his decision to make infusions of all the plants on the farm and drink them himself in the interests of science; the criminal folly of the British Government in not realising that the Germans and the Russians were conspiring as Anti-Christ to . . . the inevitability of war because no one would listen to Churchill, but it would be all right because God (by then he was a British Israelite[1]) had destined Britain to rule the world; a prophecy said 10 million dead would surround Jerusalem—how would the corpses be cleared away?; people who wished to abolish flogging should be flogged; the natives understood nothing but a good beating; hanging must not be abolished because the Old Testament said "an eye for an eye and a tooth for a tooth. . . ."

Yet, as this side of him darkened, so that it seemed all his thoughts were of violence, illness, war, still no one dared to make an unkind comment in his presence or to gossip. Criticism of people, particularly of women, made him more and more uncomfortable till at last he burst out with: "It's all very well, but no one has the right to say that about another person."

In Africa, when the sun goes down, the stars spring up, all of them in their expected places, glittering and moving. In the rainy season, the sky flashed and thundered. In the dry season, the great dark hollow of night was lit by veld fires: the mountains burned through September and October in chains of red fire. Every night my father took out his chair to watch the sky and the mountains, smoking, silent, a thin shabby fly-away figure under the stars. "Makes you think—there are so many worlds up there, wouldn't really matter if we did blow ourselves up—plenty more

---

1. A reference to the contention that the English-speaking peoples are the descend-ants of the "ten tribes" of Israel, deported by Sargon of Assyria on the fall of Samaria in 721 B.C.

where we came from."

The Second World War, so long foreseen by him, was a bad time. His son was in the Navy and in danger, and his daughter a sorrow to him. He became very ill. More and more often it was necessary to drive him into Salisbury with him in a coma, or in danger of one, on the back seat. My mother moved him into a pretty little suburban house in town near the hospitals, where he took to his bed and a couple of years later died. For the most part he was unconscious under drugs. When awake he talked obsessively (a tongue licking a nagging sore place) about "the old war." Or he remembered his youth. "I've been dreaming—Lord, to see those horses come lickety-split down the course with their necks stretched out and the sun on their coats and everyone shouting. . . . I've been dreaming how I walked along the river in the mist as the sun was rising. . . . Lord, lord, lord, what a time that was, what good times we all had then, before the old war."

1974

THE READER

1. *Find facts about Lessing's father that are repeated or referred to more than once. Why does she repeat them?*
2. *Lessing says that it was difficult for her to write about her father because she "knew him when his best years were over." What other things about those "best years" might she have wanted to know that she apparently didn't?*

THE WRITER

1. *Lessing says that "writing this article is difficult because it has to be 'true.'" Why does she put quotation marks around "true"? Why would it be more difficult to write something that has to be "true" than, as she says, stories that "don't have to be 'true'"? How has she tried to make this sketch "true"? How well do you think she has succeeded?*
2. *If a stranger were writing about Lessing's father but had the same facts available, might the account differ in any ways? Explain.*
3. *If you wrote a sketch of a father after reading Woolf's "My Father: Leslie Stephen" (p. 83), write another sketch about the same or a different father, adopting a tone similar to Lessing's.*

Daniel Mark Epstein

THE CASE OF HARRY HOUDINI

When my grandfather was a boy he saw the wild-haired magician escape from a riveted boiler. He would remember that image as long as he lived, and how Harry Houdini, the rabbi's son, defeated the German Imperial Police at the beginning of the twentieth century. Hearing those tales and others even more incredible, sixty years after the magician's death we cannot help but wonder: What did the historical Houdini *really* do? And how on earth did he do it?

The newspaper accounts are voluminous, and consistent. The mere cataloguing of Houdini's escapes soon grows tedious, which they were not, to be sure, in the flesh. But quickly: the police stripped him naked and searched him thoroughly before binding his wrists and ankles with five pairs of irons. Then they would slam him into a cell and turn the key of a three-bond burglar-proof lock. He escaped, hundreds of times, from the most secure prisons in the world. He hung upside down in a strait-jacket from the tallest buildings in America, and escaped in full view of the populace. He was chained hand and foot and nailed into a packing case weighted with lead; the packing case was dropped from a tugboat into New York's East River and ninety seconds later Houdini surfaced. The packing case was hauled up intact, with the manacles inside, still fastened. He was sealed into a paper bag and got out without disturbing the seal. He was sewn into a huge football, into the belly of a whale, and escaped. In California he was buried six feet underground, and clawed his way out. He did this, he did that. These are facts that cannot be exaggerated, for they were conceived as exaggerations. We know he did these things beccause his actions were more public than the proceedings of Congress, and most of them he performed over and over, so no one would miss the point.

How did he do such things? For all rational people who are curious, sixty years after the magician's death, there is good news and bad news. The good news is that we know how the vast majority of Houdini's tricks were done, and the explanations are as fascinating as the mystery was. Much of our knowledge comes from the magician's writings, for Houdini kept ahead of his imitators by exposing his cast-off tricks. We have additional information from technicians and theater historians. No magician will reveal Houdini's secrets—their code forbids it. But so much controversy has arisen concerning his powers—so much conjecture they may have been supernatural—that extraordinary measures have been taken to assure us Houdini was a *mortal* genius. Many secrets have leaked out, and others have been discovered from examining the props. So at last we know more about Houdini's technique than any other magician's.

The disturbing news is that, sixty years after his last performance, some of his more spectacular escapes remain unexplained. And while magicians such as Doug Henning are bound not to expose their colleagues, they are free to admit what mystifies them. They know how Houdini walked through the brick wall at Hammerstein's Roof Garden, in 1914, but they do not know how he made the elephant disappear in 1918. This trick he performed only for a few months in New York. And when people asked him why he did not continue he told them that Teddy Roosevelt, a great hunter, had begged him to stop before he exhausted the world's supply of pachyderms.

But before we grapple with the mysteries, let us begin with what we can understand. Let us begin with my grandfather's favorite story, the case of Harry Houdini versus the German Police. Houdini's first tour of Europe depended upon the good will and cooperation of the law. When he arrived in London in 1900 the twenty-six-year-old magician did not have a single booking. His news clippings eventually inspired an English agent, who had Houdini manacled to a pillar in Scotland Yard. Seeing that Houdini was securely fastened, Superintendent Melville of the Criminal Investigation Department said he would return in a couple of hours, when the escapist had worn himself out. By the time Melville got to the door the magician was free to open it for him.

The publicity surrounding his escape from the most prestigious police force in the world opened up many another door for the young magician. Booked at the Alhambra Theater in London, he performed his "Challenge" handcuff act, which had made him famous on the vaudeville circuit. After some card tricks and standard illusions, Houdini would stand before the proscenium and challenge the world to restrain him with ropes, straitjackets, handcuffs, whatever they could bring on, from lock-shops, prisons, and museums. A single failure might have ruined him. There is no evidence that he ever failed, though in several cases he nearly died from the effort required to escape from sadistic shackles. The "Challenge" act filled the Alhambra Theater for two months. Houdini might have stayed there if Germany had not already booked him; the Germans could hardly wait to get a look at Houdini.

As he had done in America and England, Houdini began his tour of Germany with a visit to police headquarters. The Dresden officers were not enthusiastic, yet they could hardly refuse the magician's invitation to lock him up. That might suggest a crisis of confidence. And like their colleagues the world over, the Dresden police viewed Houdini's news clippings as so much paper in the balance with their locks and chains. Of course the Dresden police had no more success than those of Kansas City, or San Francisco, or Scotland Yard. Their manacles were paper to him.

The police chief reluctantly signed the certificate Houdini demanded, but the newspapers gave him little coverage.

So on his opening night at Dresden's Central Theatre, Houdini arranged to be fettered in the leg irons and manacles of the Mathildegasse Prison. Some of the locks weighed forty pounds. The audience, packed to the walls, went wild over his escape, and the fact that he spoke their language further endeared him. If anything could have held him captive it would have been the adoring burghers of Dresden, who mobbed the theater for weeks. The manager wanted to buy out Houdini's contract with the Wintergarten of Berlin, so as to hold him over in Dresden, but the people of Berlin could not wait to see the magician.

Houdini arrived in Berlin in October of 1900. The first thing he did was march into the police station, strip stark naked, and challenge the jailors. They could not hold him. This time Count von Windheim, the highest ranking policeman in Germany, signed the certificate of Houdini's escape. The Wintergarten was overrun. The management appealed to the theater of Houdini's next engagement, in Vienna, so they might hold him over an extra month in Berlin. The Viennese finally yielded, demanding an indemnity equal to Houdini's salary for one month. When the magician, at long last, opened at the Olympic Theater in Paris, in December of 1901, he was the highest paid foreign entertainer in French history.

But meanwhile there was big trouble brewing in Germany. It seems the police there had little sense of humor about Houdini's peculiar gifts, and the Jew had quickly exhausted what little there was. In Dortmund he escaped from the irons that had bound Glowisky, a notorious murderer, beheaded three days before. At Hanover the police chief, Count von Schwerin, plotted to disgrace Houdini, challenging him to escape from a special straitjacket reinforced with thick leather. Houdini agonized for one and a half hours while von Schwerin looked on, his jubilant smile melting in wonder, then rage, as the magician worked himself free.

The cumulative anger of the German police went public in July of 1901. Inspector Werner Graff witnessed Houdini's escape from all the manacles at the Cologne police station and vowed to end the humiliation. It was not a simple matter of pride. Graff, along with von Schwerin and other officials, feared Houdini was weakening their authority and inviting jailbreaks, if not other kinds of antisocial behavior. So Graff wrote a letter to Cologne's newspaper, the *Rheinische Zeitung*. The letter stated that Houdini had escaped from simple restraints at the police headquarters, by trickery; but his publicity boasted he could escape from restraints *of any kind*. Such a claim, Graff wrote, was a lie, and Houdini ought to be prosecuted for fraud.

Though he knew the letter was nonsense the magician could not ignore it, for it was dangerous nonsense. If the police began calling him a fraud in every town he visited, Houdini would lose his audience. So he demanded that Graff apologize and the newspaper publish a retraction. Graff refused, and other German dailies reprinted his letter. Should Harry Houdini sue the German policeman for libel? Consider the circumstances. Germany, even in 1901, was one of the most authoritarian states in the world. Houdini was an American, a Jew who embarrassed the police. A libel case against Graff would turn upon the magician's claim that he could escape from any restraint, and the courtroom would become an international theater. There a German judge and jury would try his skill, and, should they find it wanting, Houdini would be washed up, exiled to play beer halls and dime museums. Only an artist with colossal pride and total confidence in his methods would act as Houdini did. He hired the most prominent trial lawyer in Cologne, and ordered him to sue Werner Graff and the Imperial Police of Germany for criminal libel.

There was standing room only in the Cologne Schöffengericht. The judge allowed Werner Graff to seek out the most stubborn locks and chains he could find, and tangle Houdini in them, in full view of everyone. Here was a hitch, for Houdini did not wish to show the crowd his technique. He asked the judge to clear the courtroom, and in the ensuing turmoil the magician released himself so quickly no one knew how he had done it. The Schöffengericht fined the astonished policeman and ordered a public apology. So Graff's lawyer appealed the case.

Two months later Graff was better prepared. In the Strafkammer, or court of appeals, he presented thirty letters from legal authorities declaring that the escape artist could not justify his advertisements. And Graff had a shiny new pair of handcuffs. The premier locksmith of Germany had engineered the cuffs especially for the occasion. Werner Graff explained to the judge that the lock, once closed, could never be opened, even with its own key. Let Houdini try to get out of these.

This time the court permitted Houdini to work in privacy, and a guard led the magician to an adjacent chamber. Everyone else settled down for a long wait, in a chatter of anticipation. They were interrupted four minutes later by the entrance of Houdini, who tossed the manacles on the judge's bench. So the Strafkammer upheld the lower court's decision, as did the Oberlandesgericht in a "paper" appeal. The court fined Werner Graff thirty marks and ordered him to pay for the trials as well as a published apology. Houdini's next poster showed him in evening dress, his hands manacled, standing before the judge, jurors, and a battery of mustachioed policemen. Looking down on the scene is a bust of the Kaiser against a crimson background, and a scroll that reads: "The Imperial Police of Cologne slandered Harry Houdini . . . were compelled to advertise 'An Honorary Apology' and pay costs of the trials. By command of Kaiser Wilhelm II, Emperor of Germany."

Now this is surely a wondrous tale, like something out of the Arabian Nights, and it will seem no less wonderful when we understand the technique that made it come true. In 1901, when Houdini took on the Imperial Police, he was not whistling in the dark. By the time he left America at the end of the nineteenth century he had dissected every kind of lock he could find in the New World, and whatever he could import from the old one. Arriving in London Houdini could write that there were only a few kinds of British handcuffs, "seven or eight at the utmost," and these were some of the simplest he had ever seen. He searched the markets, antique shops, and locksmiths, buying up all the European locks he could find so he could dismantle and study them.

Then during his Berlin engagement he worked up to ten hours a day at Mueller's locksmith on the Mittelstrasse, studying restraints. He was the Bobby Fischer of locks. With a chessmaster's foresight Houdini devised a set of picks to release every lock in existence, as well as any he could imagine. Such tireless ingenuity produced the incandescent light bulb and the atom bomb. Houdini's creation of a theatrical metaphor made a comparable impact on the human spirit. He had a message which he delivered so forcefully it goes without mentioning in theater courses: humankind cannot be held in chains. The European middle class had reached an impressionable age, and the meaning of Houdini's theater was not lost upon them. Nor was he mistaken by the aristocracy, who stayed away in droves. The spectacle of this American Jew bursting from chains by dint of ingenuity did not amuse the rich. They wanted desperately to demythologize him.

It was not about to happen in the German courtroom. When Werner Graff snapped the "new" handcuffs on Houdini, they were not strange to the magician. He had already invented them, so to speak, as well as the pick to open them, and the pick was in his pocket. Only a locksmith whose knowledge surpassed Houdini's could stop him; diligent study assured him that, as of 1901, there could be no such locksmith on the face of the earth.

What else can we understand about the methods of Harry Houdini, born Ehrich Weiss? We know he was a superbly conditioned athlete who did not smoke or take a drop of alcohol. His straitjacket escapes he performed in full view of the world so they could see it was by main force and flexibility that he freed himself. He may or may not have been able to dislocate his shoulders at will—he said he could, and it seems no more marvelous than certain other skills he demonstrated. Friends reported that his toes could untie knots most of us could not manage with our fingers. And routinely the magician would hold his breath for as long as four minutes to work underwater escapes. To cheapen the supernatural claims of the fakir Rahman Bey, Houdini remained underwater in an iron box for ninety minutes, as against the Egyptian's sixty. Examining Houdini, a physician testified that the fifty-year-old wizard had halved his blood pressure while doubling his pulse. Of course, more wonderful than any of these skills was the courage allowing him to employ them, in predicaments where any normal person would panic.

These things are known about Houdini. The same tireless ingenuity, when applied to locks and jails, packing cases and riveted boilers; the same athletic prowess, when applied at the bottom of the East River, or while dangling from a rope attached to the cornice of the Sun Building in Baltimore—these talents account for the vast majority of Houdini's exploits. As we have mentioned, theater historians, notably Raymund Fitzsimons in his *Death and the Magician*, have carefully exposed Houdini's ingenuity, knowing that nothing can tarnish the miracle of the man's existence. Their accounts are technical and we need not dwell on them, except to say they *mostly* support Houdini's oath that his effects were achieved by natural, or mechanical means. The Houdini problem arises from certain outrageous effects no one has ever been able to explain, though capable technicians have been trying for more than sixty years.

Let us briefly recall those effects. We have mentioned the Disappearing Elephant. On January 7, 1918, Houdini had a ten-thousand-pound elephant led onto the bright stage of the Hippodrome in New York City. A trainer marched the elephant around a cabinet large enough for an elephant, proving there was space behind. There was no trapdoor in the floor of the Hippodrome, and the elephant could not fly. Houdini ushered the pachyderm into the cabinet and closed the curtains. Then he opened them, and where the elephant had stood there was nothing but empty space. Houdini went on with his program, which might have been making the Hippodrome disappear, for all the audience knew. A reporter for the *Brooklyn Eagle* noted: "The program says that the elephant vanished into thin air. The trick is performed fifteen feet from the backdrop and the cabinet is slightly elevated. That explanation is as good as any." After Houdini stopped making elephants disappear, nineteen weeks later, the trick would never be precisely duplicated.

That is the single "conventional" illusion of Houdini's repertoire that remains unexplained. He was not the greatest illusionist of his time, though he was among them. His expertise was the "escape" act, that specialty of magic furthest removed from theater, for its challenges are quite real and sometimes beyond the magician's control. It was the escapes, as his wife later wrote, that were truly dangerous, and Houdini privately admitted some anxieties about them. Give a wizard twenty years to build a cabinet which snuffs an elephant, and you will applaud his cleverness if he succeeds, in the controlled environment of his theater. But surrender the same man, stark naked, to the Russian police, who stake their honor upon detaining him in a convict van, and you may well suspect the intercession of angels should he get out.

And that is exactly what Houdini did, in one of the strangest and most celebrated escapes of his career. Strange, because it was Houdini's habit to escape only from barred jail cells where the locks were within easy reach, and then only after inspection, so he might hide picks in crannies, or excuse himself if he foresaw failure. But the Siberian Transport Cell made his blood boil. On May 11, 1903, the chief of the Russian secret police searched the naked Houdini inside and out. The revolt of 1905 was in its planning stages and the Imperial Police were understandably touchy. The magician's wrists were padlocked and his ankles fettered before the police locked him into the *carette*. Mounted on a wagon, the zinc-lined steel cell stood in the prison courtyard in view of chief Lebedoeff, his staff, and a number of civilians. Twenty-eight minutes later Houdini was walking around the courtyard, stretching. Nobody saw him get out, but he was out. The police ran to the door of the *carette*. The door was still locked and the shackles lay on the floor of the undamaged van. The police were so furious they would not sign the certificate of escape, but so many people had witnessed the event that the news was soon being shouted all over Moscow. Doug Henning has written: "It remains one of his escapes about which the real method is pure conjecture."

In the Houdini Museum at Niagara Falls, Canada, you may view the famous Mirror Handcuffs. If you are a scholar you can inspect them. In March of 1904 the London *Daily Mirror* discovered a blacksmith who had been working for five years to build a set of handcuffs no mortal man could pick. Examining the cuffs, the best locksmiths in London agreed they had never seen such an ingenious mechanism. The newspaper challenged Houdini to escape from them. On March 17, before a house of four thousand in the London Hippodrome, a journalist fastened the cuffs on Houdini's wrists and turned the key six times. The magician retired to his cabinet onstage, and the band struck up a march. He did not emerge for twenty minutes. When he did, it was to hold the lock up to the light. Remember that most "Challenge" handcuffs were regulation, and familiar to Houdini. He studied the lock in the light, and then went back into the cabinet, as the band played a waltz.

Ten minutes later Houdini stuck his head out, asking if he could have a cushion to kneel on. He was denied. After almost an hour Houdini came out of the cabinet again, obviously worn out, and his audience groaned. He wanted the handcuffs to be unlocked for a moment so he could take off his coat, as he was sweating profusely. The journalist denied the request, since Houdini had never before seen the handcuffs unlocked, and that might give him an advantage. Whereupon Houdini, in full view of the four thousand, extracted a penknife from his pocket and opened it with his teeth. Turning the coat inside out over his head, he shredded it loose with the penknife, and returned to the cabinet. Someone called out that Houdini had been handcuffed for more than an hour. As the band played on, the journalists of the London *Daily Mirror* could taste the greatest scoop of the twentieth century. But ten minutes later there was a cry from the cabinet and Houdini leapt out of it, free, waving the handcuffs high in the air. While the crowd roared, several men from the audience carried Houdini on their shoulders around the theater. He was crying as if his heart would break.

For all his other talents Houdini was a notoriously wooden actor, and we may assume the rare tears were altogether real, the product of an uncounterfeitable emotion. It is as if the man himself had been overwhelmed by his escape. Eighty years of technological progress have shed no light upon it. We know how Houdini got out of other handcuffs, but not these. As far as anyone can tell, the Mirror Handcuffs remain as the blacksmith described them—a set of handcuffs no mortal man could pick. One is tempted to dismiss the whole affair as mass hypnosis.

In the same Canadian museum you may view the Chinese Water Torture Cell, in which the magician was hung upside down, in water, his ankles padlocked to the riveted roof. His escape from this cell was the crowning achievement of his stage career, and though he performed it on tour during the last ten years of his life, no one has the slightest notion how he did it. The gifted Doug Henning revived the act in 1975, on television. But he would be the first to tell you his was *not* Houdini's version, but his own, and he would not do it onstage before a live audience seven nights a week, with matinees on Wednesday and Saturday, because the trick would be unspeakably dangerous even if he could perform it there. When Houdini died he willed the contraption to his brother Hardeen, a fine magician in his own right. But Hardeen would not get in it either, and the instructions were to be burned upon his death. Again, as with the Vanishing Elephant, we are reviewing a stage illusion under controlled conditions, and may bow to a master's technical superiority, without fretting that he has used supernatural powers.

But the Mirror Handcuffs and the Siberian Van Escape are troublesome, as are certain of Houdini's escapes from reinforced straitjackets, and packing cases underwater. So is the fact that he was buried six feet underground, and clawed his way out. He only tried it once, and nearly died in the struggle, but the feat was attested, and you do not need a degree in physics to know it is as preposterous as rising from the dead. The weight of the earth is so crushing you could not lift it in the open air. Try doing this with no oxygen. The maestro himself misjudged the weight, and, realizing his folly, tried to signal his crew when the grave was not yet full. They could not hear him and kept right on shoveling as fast as they could, so as not to keep him waiting. Then they stood back, to watch. A while later they saw his bleeding hands appear above the ground.

If we find Houdini's record unsettling, imagine what our grandparents must have thought of him. They knew almost nothing of his technique. Where we remain troubled by a few of his illusions and escapes, our ancestors were horrified by most of them. The European journalists thought he was some kind of hobgoblin, a shapeshifter who could crawl through keyholes, or dematerialize and reappear at will. One can hardly blame them. Despite his constant reassurances that his effects were technical, and natural, the practical-minded layman could not believe it, and even fellow magicians were disturbed by his behavior.

So we come to the central issue in the case of Harry Houdini. It is an issue he carefully avoided in public, while studying it diligently in private. To wit: Can a magician, by the ultimate perfection of a technique, generate a force which, at critical moments, will achieve a supernatural result? Houdini's writings show this was the abiding concern of his intellectual life. It is, of course, the essential mystery of classical magic since before the Babylonians. Yet it remained a private and professional concern until Houdini's career forced it upon the public.

With the same determination that opened the world's locks, Houdini searched for an answer. His own technique was so highly evolved that its practice might have satisfied him, but his curiosity was unquenchable. He amassed the world's largest collection of books pertaining to magic and the occult, and no less a scholar than Edmund Wilson honored Houdini's authority. The son of a rabbi, Houdini pursued his studies with rabbinic thoroughness. And, from the beginning of his career, he sought out the living legends of magic and badgered them in retirement, sometimes with tragicomic results.

As far back as 1895 it seemed to Houdini something peculiar was going on when he performed the Metamorphosis with his wife Bess. You have probably seen this classic illusion. Two friends of mine once acted it in my living room, as a birthday present. When the Houdinis performed the Metamorphosis, Bess whould handcuff Harry, tie him in a sack, and lock him in a trunk. She would draw a curtain hiding the trunk and then it would open, showing Houdini free upon the stage. Where was Bess? Inside the trunk, inside the sack, handcuffed—there was Bess. The method of this trick is only mysterious if you cannot pay for it. But the Houdinis' *timing* of the Metamorphosis got very mysterious indeed. They polished the act until it happened in less than three seconds—three rather blurred seconds in their own minds, to be sure. Believe me, you cannot get *into* the trunk in less than three seconds. So when the Houdinis had done the trick they were often as stunned as their audience. It seemed a sure case of technique unleashing a supernatural force. Perplexed, Houdini planned to interview Hermann the Great, the preeminent conjuror in America in 1895, and ask Hermann what was up. But Hermann died as Houdini was about to ask him the question.

And Houdini shadowed the marvelous Harry Kellar, cross-examining him, and Alexander Heimburger, and the decrepit Ira Davenport, who had been a medium as well as a magician. But the great magicians flatly denied the psychic possibility, and Davenport would not answer to Houdini's satisfaction. In 1903 he discovered that Wiljalba Frikell, a seemingly mythic wizard of the nineteenth century, was still alive, in retirement near Dresden. When the ancient mage would not acknowledge his letters, Houdini grew convinced Wiljalba Frikell was the man to answer his question. He took the train to Dresden and knocked on Frikell's door. His wife sent Houdini away. On the road in Germany and Russia, Houdini continued to send letters and gifts to Frikell. And at last, six months after he had been turned away from Frikell's door, the reclusive magician agreed to see him.

Houdini rang the doorbell at 2:00 P.M. on October 8, 1903, the exact hour of his appointment. The door swung open. An hour earlier Wiljalba Frikell had dressed in his best suit, and laid out his scrapbooks, programs, and medals for Houdini to view. Houdini excitedly followed Frikell's wife into the room where the master sat surrounded by the mementos of his glorious career. But he would not be answering any of the questions that buzzed in Houdini's brain. The old man was stone dead.

Throughout his life Houdini categorically denied that any of his effects were achieved by supernatural means. He crusaded against mediums, clairvoyants, and all who claimed psychic power, advertising that he would reproduce any of their manifestations by mechanical means. In the face of spiritualists who accused *him* of being a physical medium, he protested that all his escapes and illusions were tricks. He was probably telling the truth, as he understood it. But Rabbi Drachman, who spoke at Houdini's funeral, and had been in a position to receive confidences, said: "Houdini possessed a wondrous power that he never understood, and which he never revealed to anyone in life."

Houdini was not Solomon; he was a vaudeville specialist. If he ever experienced a psychic power it surely humbled his understanding. And to admit such a power, in his position, would have been a monumental stupidity. Why? If for no other reason, Talmudic law forbids the performance of miracles, and Houdini was the obedient son of Rabbi Weiss. Also, in case he should forget the Jewish law, it is strictly against the magician's code to claim a supernatural power, for reasons impossible to ignore. Mediums made such claims, at their own risk. Two of the more famous mediums of the nineteenth century, Ira and William Davenport, achieved manifestations similar to Houdini's. Audiences in Liverpool, Leeds, and Paris rioted, stormed the stage, and ran the mediums out of town, crying their performances were an outrage against God and a danger to man. Whether or not the acts were supernatural is beside the point—billing them as such was bad business, and hazardous to life and limb. Yet the Davenports were no more than a sideshow, compared to Houdini. The man was blinding. There had not been such a public display of apparent miracles in nearly two thousand years. Had the Jew so much as hinted his powers were spiritual he might have expected no better treatment than the renegade Hebrew of Nazareth.

Houdini was the self-proclaimed avatar of nothing but good old American know-how, and that is how he wished to be remembered. His wife of thirty years, Beatrice Houdini (known as "Bess"), was loyal to him in this, as in all other things. Pestered for revelations about Houdini's magic long after his death, the widow swore by her husband's account. But against her best intentions, Bess clouded the issue by saying just a little more than was necessary. It was in a letter to Sir Arthur Conan Doyle, who had been a close friend of hers and Houdini's.

The friendship was an odd one. The author of Sherlock Holmes believed in Spiritualism, and championed the séance with all the fervor with which Houdini opposed it. There were two great mysteries in Doyle's life: the powers of Sherlock Holmes and Harry Houdini. Doyle knew the Houdinis intimately, and nothing the magician said could shake Sir Arthur's conviction that certain of Houdini's escapes were supernatural. Doyle never stopped trying to get Houdini to confess. In 1922 it was more than a personal issue. The séance had become big business in America, with millions of bereaved relatives paying to communicate with their dear departed. Spiritualism was a home-grown, persuasive religious movement, a bizarre reaction to American science and pragmatism. The great critic Edmund Wilson, who admired Houdini and understood his gifts, recognized that the magician had appeared at a critical moment in the history of Spiritualism. Houdini was the only man living who had the authority, and the competence, to expose the predatory mediums, and his success was decisive.

Yet Houdini's lecture-demonstrations, and exposures of false mediums, only fueled Doyle's suspicions that his friend was the real thing, a physical medium. In all fairness, Sir Arthur Conan Doyle was a credulous old gentleman, who knew nothing of Houdini's techniques. But his instinct was sound. Two months after Houdini died, Sir Arthur wrote to Bess in despair of ever learning the truth from the magician's lips, and she wrote Doyle a long letter. What concerns us here are a few sentences which, coming from the woman who shared his life and work, and maintained her loyalty to Houdini alive and dead, we must regard as altogether startling.

> I will never be offended by anything you say for him or about him, but that he possessed psychic powers—he never knew it. As I told Lady Doyle often he

would get a difficult lock, I stood by the cabinet and I would hear him say, "This is beyond me," and after many minutes when the audience became restless I nervously would say "Harry, if there is anything in this belief in Spiritism,—why don't you call on them to assist you," and before many minutes had passed Houdini had mastered the lock.

We never attributed this to psychic help. We just knew that that particular instrument was the one to open that lock, and so did all his tricks.

The tone of this letter penned so soon after her husband's death is somber throughout, painfully sincere. This was not a subject for levity, this being the central issue in the life of Harry Houdini. So what on earth is Bess trying to tell Sir Arthur when she testifies to the invocation of spirits in one sentence, and repudiates psychic help in the next? What kind of double-talk is this, when the widow refers to the summoning of spiritual aid as "that particular instrument," as if a spirit were no different from any other skeleton key? It sounds like sheer euphemism; it sounds like the Houdinis' lifetime of work had uncovered a power so terrifying they would not admit it to each other, let alone the world. Would that Albert Einstein had been so discreet in 1905.

So what if Harry Houdini, once in a while, "spirited" himself out of a Siberian Van, or a pair of Mirror Handcuffs, or a packing case at the bottom of the East River? It is perhaps no more remarkable than that an American Jew won a verdict against the German Police for criminal libel in 1901, or reversed a religious movement in America in 1922. Houdini died in Detroit on Halloween in 1926, of acute appendicitis. He was born in Budapest on March 24, 1874, but told the world he was born in Appleton, Wisconsin on April 6. Not until after World War II did Americans discover that their greatest magician was an alien. Houdini's work was no more miraculous than his life. His life was no more miraculous than the opening and closing of a flower.

1986

THE READER

1. Do you find the figure of Houdini appealing, attractive, as Epstein presents him? What do you take to be the outstanding qualities of his character?

2. How important to this account of Houdini is the fact that he was a Jew? What are some of the implications here of that fact? What might Epstein be saying (even if unexpressed) in his account of the confrontations between Houdini and the German police?

3. What, according to Epstein, was the message to mankind of Houdini's career? What details in the essay exemplify that message?

THE WRITER

1. At several points in his account of Houdini, Epstein creates an effect of

suspense. How does he manage that effect? What purposes does it serve?

2. *Epstein's account of Houdini leaves some unanswered questions. What are they? Why are they unanswered? Would it be a better account if there were no questions left unanswered? Do you see any connection between the fact of unanswered questions and the theme of the essay?*

Mind

Robertson Davies

A FEW KIND WORDS FOR SUPERSTITION

In grave discussions of "the renaissance of the irrational" in our time, superstition does not figure largely as a serious challenge to reason or science. Parapsychology, UFO's, miracle cures, transcendental meditation and all the paths to instant enlightenment are condemned, but superstition is merely deplored. Is it because it has an unacknowledged hold on so many of us?

Few people will admit to being superstitious; it implies naïveté or ignorance. But I live in the middle of a large university, and I see superstition in its four manifestations, alive and flourishing among people who are indisputably rational and learned.

You did not know that superstition takes four forms? Theologians assure us that it does. First is what they call Vain Observances, such as not walking under a ladder, and that kind of thing. Yet I saw a deeply learned professor of anthropology, who had spilled some salt, throwing a pinch of it over his left shoulder; when I asked him why, he replied, with a wink, that it was "to hit the Devil in the eye." I did not question him further about his belief in the Devil: but I noticed that he did not smile until I asked him what he was doing.

The second form is Divination, or consulting oracles. Another learned professor I know, who would scorn to settle a problem by tossing a coin (which is a humble appeal to Fate to declare itself), told me quite seriously that he had resolved a matter related to university affairs by consulting the *I Ching*.[1] And why not? There are thousands of people on this continent who appeal to the *I Ching*, and their general level of education seems to absolve them of superstition. Almost, but not quite.

---

1. A Chinese work of divination.

The *I Ching*, to the embarrassment of rationalists, often gives excellent advice.

The third form is Idolatry, and universities can show plenty of that. If you have ever supervised a large examination room, you know how many jujus, lucky coins and other bringers of luck are placed on the desks of the candidates. Modest idolatry, but what else can you call it?

The fourth form is Improper Worship of the True God. A while ago, I learned that every day, for several days, a ½ bill (in Canada we have ½ bills, regarded by some people as unlucky) had been tucked under a candlestick on the altar of a college chapel. Investigation revealed that an engineering student, worried about a girl, thought that bribery of the Deity might help. When I talked with him, he did not think he was pricing God cheap, because he could afford no more. A reasonable argument, but perhaps God was proud that week, for the scientific oracle went against him.

Superstition seems to run, a submerged river of crude religion, below the surface of human consciousness. It has done so for as long as we have any chronicle of human behavior, and although I cannot prove it, I doubt if it is more prevalent today than it has always been. Superstition, the theologians tell us, comes from the Latin *superstitio*, meaning to stand in terror of the Deity. Most people keep their terror within bounds, but they cannot root it out, nor do they seem to want to do so.

The more the teaching of formal religion declines, or takes a sociological form, the less God appears to great numbers of people as a God of Love, resuming his older form of a watchful, minatory power, to be placated and cajoled. Superstition makes its appearance, apparently unbidden, very early in life, when children fear that stepping on cracks in the sidewalk will bring ill fortune. It may persist even among the greatly learned and devout, as in the case of Dr. Samuel Johnson, who felt it necessary to touch posts that he passed in the street. The psychoanalysts have their explanation, but calling a superstition a compulsion neurosis does not banish it.

Many superstitions are so widespread and so old that they must have risen from a depth of the human mind that is indifferent to race or creed. Orthodox Jews place a charm on their doorposts; so do (or did) the Chinese. Some peoples of Middle Europe believe that when a man sneezes, his soul, for that moment, is absent from his body, and they hasten to bless him, lest the soul be seized by the Devil. How did the Melanesians come by the same idea? Superstition seems to have a link with some body of belief that far antedates the religions we know— religions which have no place for such comforting little ceremonies and charities.

People who like disagreeable historical comparisons recall that when Rome was in decline, superstition proliferated wildly, and that something of the same sort is happening in our Western world today. They point to the popularity of astrology, and it is true that sober newspapers that would scorn to deal in love philters carry astrology columns and the fashion magazines count them among their most popular features. But when has astrology not been popular? No use saying science discredits it. When has the heart of man given a damn for science?

Superstition in general is linked to man's yearning to know his fate, and to have some hand in deciding it. When my mother was a child, she innocently joined her Roman Catholic friends in killing spiders on July 11, until she learned that this was done to ensure heavy rain the day following, the anniversary of the Battle of Boyne, when the Orangemen[2] would hold their parade. I knew an Italian, a good scientist, who watched every morning before leaving his house, so that the first person he met would not be a priest or a nun, as this would certainly bring bad luck.

I am not one to stand aloof from the rest of humanity in this matter, for when I was a university student, a gypsy woman with a child in her arms used to appear every year at examination time, and ask a shilling[3] of anyone who touched the Lucky Baby; that swarthy infant cost me four shillings altogether, and I never failed an examination. Of course, I did it merely for the joke—or so I thought then. Now, I am humbler.

1978

2. Protestant Irish. The Battle of the Boyne (1690), the final and decisive defeat of the forces of British Catholicism, made Protestantism secure as the official religion of Great Britain.
3. Then about twenty-five cents.

THE READER

1. What is Davies's definition of superstition?
2. Can superstition exist without religion? In what ways can it substitute for religion?

THE WRITER

1. There is a certain quaintness about the names for the four forms of superstition. Why do you think Davies chose such names? Does his division of superstition into these four forms serve to clarify the nature or function of superstitions you know about?
2. Write an essay describing the nature and function of a superstition you know about. In his conclusion, Davies suggests two perspectives on the subject—a joking one and the later, "humbler" one. Which comes more naturally to you as the point of view in your essay? Or do you have a different perspective?

Benjamin Franklin

THE CONVENIENCE OF BEING "REASONABLE"

I believe I have omitted mentioning that, in my first voyage from Boston, being becalmed off Block Island, our people set about catching cod, and hauled up a great many. Hitherto I had stuck to my resolution of not eating animal food, and on this occasion I considered, with my master Tryon,[1] the taking every fish as a kind of unprovoked murder, since none of them had, or ever could do us any injury that might justify the slaughter. All this seemed very reasonable. But I had formerly been a great lover of fish, and, when this came hot out of the frying-pan, it smelled admirably well. I balanced some time between principle and inclination, till I recollected that, when the fish were opened, I saw smaller fish taken out of their stomachs; then thought I, "if you eat one another, I don't see why we mayn't eat you." So I dined upon cod very heartily, and continued to eat with other people, returning only now and then occasionally to a vegetable diet. So convenient a thing it is to be a *reasonable creature*, since it enables one to find or make a reason for everything one has a mind to do.

1791

1. "When about 16 years of age, I happened to meet with a book written by one [Thomas] Tryon [The Way to Health, Wealth, and Happiness, 1682] recommending a vegetable diet. I determined to go into it. * * * My refusing to eat flesh occasioned an inconveniency, and I was frequently chid for my singularity" [Franklin, Autobiography].

William Golding

THINKING AS A HOBBY

While I was still a boy, I came to the conclusion that there were three grades of thinking; and since I was later to claim thinking as my hobby, I came to an even stranger conclusion—namely, that I myself could not think at all.

I must have been an unsatisfactory child for grownups to deal with. I remember how incomprehensible they appeared to me at first, but not, of course, how I appeared to them. It was the headmaster of my grammar school who first brought the subject of thinking before me—though neither in the way, nor with the result he intended. He had some statuettes in his study. They stood on a high cupboard behind his desk. One was a lady wearing nothing but a bath towel. She seemed frozen in an eternal panic lest the bath towel slip down any farther; and since she had no arms, she was in an unfortunate position to pull the towel up again. Next to her, crouched the statuette of a leopard, ready to spring down at the top drawer of a filing cabinet labeled A-AH. My innocence interpreted this as the victim's last, despairing cry. Beyond the leopard was a naked, muscular gentleman, who sat, looking down, with his chin on his fist and his elbow on his knee. He seemed utterly miserable.

Some time later, I learned about these statuettes. The headmaster had placed them where they would face delinquent children, because they symbolized to him the whole of life. The naked lady was the Venus of Milo. She was Love. She was not worried about the towel. She was just busy being beautiful. The leopard was Nature, and he was being natural. The naked, muscular gentleman was not miserable. He was Rodin's Thinker, an image of pure thought. It is easy to buy small plaster models of what you think life is like.

I had better explain that I was a frequent visitor to the headmaster's study, because of the latest thing I had done or left undone. As we now say, I was not integrated. I was, if anything, disintegrated; and I was puzzled. Grownups never made sense. Whenever I found myself in a penal position before the headmaster's desk, with the statuettes glimmering whitely above him, I would sink my head, clasp my hands behind my back and writhe one shoe over the other.

The headmaster would look opaquely at me through flashing spectacles.

"What are we going to do with you?"

Well, what were they going to do with me? I would writhe my shoe some more and stare down at the worn rug.

"Look up, boy! Can't you look up?"

Then I would look up at the cupboard, where the naked lady was frozen in her panic and the muscular gentleman contemplated the hindquarters of the leopard in endless gloom. I had nothing to say to the headmaster. His spectacles caught the light so that you could see nothing human behind them. There was no possibility of communication.

"Don't you ever think at all?"

No, I didn't think, wasn't thinking, couldn't think—I was simply waiting in anguish for the interview to stop.

"Then you'd better learn—hadn't you?"

On one occasion the headmaster leaped to his feet, reached up and plonked Rodin's masterpiece on the desk before me.

"That's what a man looks like when he's really thinking."

I surveyed the gentleman without interest or comprehension.

"Go back to your class."

Clearly there was something missing in me. Nature had endowed the rest of the human race with a sixth sense and left me out. This must be so, I mused, on my way back to the class, since whether I had broken a window, or failed to remember Boyle's Law, or been late for school, my teachers produced me one, adult answer: "Why can't you think?"

As I saw the case, I had broken the window because I had tried to hit Jack Arney with a cricket ball and missed him; I could not remember Boyle's Law because I had never bothered to learn it; and I was late for school because I preferred looking over the bridge into the river. In fact, I was wicked. Were my teachers, perhaps, so good that they could not understand the depths of my depravity? Were they clear, untormented people who could direct their every action by this mysterious business of thinking? The whole thing was incomprehensible. In my earlier years, I found even the statuette of the Thinker confusing. I did not believe any of my teachers were naked, ever. Like someone born deaf, but bitterly determined to find out about sound, I watched my teachers to find out about thought.

There was Mr. Houghton. He was always telling me to think. With a modest satisfaction, he would tell me that he had thought a bit himself. Then why did he spend so much time drinking? Or was there more sense in drinking than there appeared to be? But if not, and if drinking were in fact ruinous to health—and Mr. Houghton was ruined, there was no doubt about that—why was he always talking about the clean life and the virtues of fresh air? He would spread his arms wide with the action of a man who habitually spent his time striding along mountain ridges.

"Open air does me good, boys—I know it!"

Sometimes, exalted by his own oratory, he would leap from his desk and hustle us outside into a hideous wind.

"Now, boys! Deep breaths! Feel it right down inside you—huge draughts of God's good air!"

He would stand before us, rejoicing in his perfect health, an open-air man. He would put his hands on his waist and take a tremendous breath. You could hear the wind, trapped in the cavern of his chest and struggling with all the unnatural impediments. His body would reel with shock and his ruined face go white at the unaccustomed visitation. He would stagger back to his desk and collapse there, useless for the rest of the morning.

Mr. Houghton was given to high-minded monologues about the good life, sexless and full of duty. Yet in the middle of one of these monologues, if a girl passed the window, tapping along on her neat little feet, he would interrupt his discourse, his neck would turn of itself and he would watch her out of sight. In this instance, he seemed to me ruled not by thought but by an invisible and irresistible spring in his nape.

His neck was an object of great interest to me. Normally it bulged a bit over his collar. But Mr. Houghton had fought in the First World War alongside both Americans and French, and had come—by who knows what illogic?—to a settled detestation of both countries. If either country happened to be prominent in current affairs, no argument could make Mr. Houghton think well of it. He would bang the desk, his neck would bulge still further and go red. "You can say what you like," he would cry, "but I've thought about this—and I know what I think!"

Mr. Houghton thought with his neck.

There was Miss Parsons. She assured us that her dearest wish was our welfare, but I knew even then, with the mysterious clairvoyance of childhood, that what she wanted most was the husband she never got. There was Mr. Hands—and so on.

I have dealt at length with my teachers because this was my introduction to the nature of what is commonly called thought. Through them I discovered that thought is often full of unconscious prejudice, ignorance and hypocrisy. It will lecture on disinterested purity while its neck is being remorselessly twisted toward a skirt. Technically, it is about as proficient as most businessmen's golf, as honest as most politicians' intentions, or—to come near my own preoccupation—as coherent as most books that get written. It is what I came to call grade-three thinking, though more properly, it is feeling, rather than thought.

True, often there is a kind of innocence in prejudices, but in those days I viewed grade-three thinking with an intolerant contempt and an incautious mockery. I delighted to confront a pious lady who hated the Germans with the proposition that we should love our enemies. She taught me a great truth in dealing with grade-three thinkers; because of her, I no longer dismiss lightly a mental process which for nine-tenths of the population is the nearest they will ever get to thought. They have immense solidarity. We had better respect them, for we are outnumbered and surrounded. A crowd of grade-three thinkers, all shouting the same thing, all warming their hands at the fire of their own prejudices, will not thank you for pointing out the contradictions in their beliefs. Man is a gregarious animal, and enjoys agreement as cows will graze all the same way on the side of a hill.

Grade-two thinking is the detection of contradictions. I reached grade two when I trapped the poor, pious lady. Grade-two thinkers do not stampede easily, though often they fall into the other fault and lap behind. Grade-two thinking is a withdrawal, with eyes and ears open. It became my hobby and brought satisfaction and loneliness in either hand. For grade-two thinking destroys without having the power to create. It set me watching the crowds cheering His Majesty and King and asking myself what all the fuss was about, without giving me anything positive to put in the place of that heady patriotism. But there were compensations. To hear people justify their habit of hunting foxes and tearing them to pieces by claiming that the foxes liked it. To hear our Prime Minister talk about the great benefit we conferred on India by jailing people like Pandit Nehru and Gandhi. To hear American politicians talk about peace in one sentence and refuse to join the League of Nations in the next. Yes, there were moments of delight.

But I was growing toward adolescence and had to admit that Mr. Houghton was not the only one with an irresistible spring in his neck. I, too, felt the compulsive hand of nature and began to find that pointing out contradiction could be costly as well as fun. There was Ruth, for example, a serious and attractive girl. I was an atheist at the time. Grade-two thinking is a menace to religion and knocks down sects like skittles. I put myself in a position to be converted by her with an hypocrisy worthy of grade three. She was a Methodist—or at least, her parents were, and Ruth had to follow suit. But, alas, instead of relying on the Holy Spirit to convert me, Ruth was foolish enough to open her pretty mouth in argument. She claimed that the Bible (King James Version) was literally inspired. I countered by saying that the Catholics believed in the literal inspiration of Saint Jerome's *Vulgate*,[1] and the two books were different. Argument flagged.

At last she remarked that there were an awful lot of Methodists, and they couldn't be wrong, could they—not all those millions? That was too easy, said I restively (for the nearer you were to Ruth, the nicer she was to be near to) since there were more Roman Catholics than Methodists anyway; and they couldn't be wrong, could they—not all those hundreds of millions? An awful flicker of doubt appeared in her eyes. I slid my arm around her waist and murmured breathlessly that if we were counting heads, the Buddhists were the boys for my money. But Ruth had *really* wanted to do me good, because I was so nice. She fled. The combination of my arm and those countless Buddhists was too much for her.

That night her father visited my father and left, red-cheeked and indignant. I was given the third degree to find out what had happened. It was lucky we were both of us only fourteen. I lost Ruth and gained an undeserved reputation as a potential libertine.

So grade-two thinking could be dangerous. It was in this knowledge, at the age of fifteen, that I remember making a comment from the heights of grade two, on the limitations of grade three. One evening I found myself alone in the school hall, preparing it for a party. The door of the headmaster's study was open. I went in. The headmaster had ceased to thump Rodin's Thinker down on the desk as an example to the young. Perhaps he had not found any more candidates, but the statuettes were still there, glimmering and gathering dust on top of the cupboard. I stood on a chair and rearranged them. I stood Venus in her bath towel on the filing

---

1. The Latin Bible as revised in the fourth century A.D. by Jerome and used thereafter as the authoritative text for Roman Catholic ritual.

cabinet, so that now the top drawer caught its breath in a gasp of sexy excitement. "A-ah!" The portentous Thinker I placed on the edge of the cupboard so that he looked down at the bath towel and waited for it to slip.

Grade-two thinking, though it filled life with fun and excitement, did not make for content. To find out the deficiencies of our elders bolsters the young ego but does not make for personal security. I found that grade two was not only the power to point out contradictions. It took the swimmer some distance from the shore and left him there, out of his depth. I decided that Pontius Pilate was a typical grade-two thinker. "What is truth?" he said, a very common grade-two thought, but one that is used always as the end of an argument instead of the beginning. There is still a higher grade of thought which says, "What is truth?" and sets out to find it.

But these grade-one thinkers were few and far between. They did not visit my grammar school in the flesh though they were there in books. I aspired to them, partly because I was ambitious and partly because I now saw my hobby as an unsatisfactory thing if it went no further. If you set out to climb a mountain, however high you climb, you have failed if you cannot reach the top.

I *did* meet an undeniably grade-one thinker in my first year at Oxford. I was looking over a small bridge in Magdalen Deer Park, and a tiny mustached and hatted figure came and stood by my side. He was a German who had just fled from the Nazis to Oxford as a temporary refuge. His name was Einstein.

But Professor Einstein knew no English at that time and I knew only two words of German. I beamed at him, trying wordlessly to convey by my bearing all the affection and respect that the English felt for him. It is possible—and I have to make the admission—that I felt here were two grade-one thinkers standing side by side; yet I doubt if my face conveyed more than a formless awe. I would have given my Greek and Latin and French and a good slice of my English for enough German to communicate. But we were divided; he was as inscrutable as my headmaster. For perhaps five minutes we stood together on the bridge, undeniable grade-one thinker and breathless aspirant. With true greatness, Professor Einstein realized that my contact was better than none. He pointed to a trout wavering in midstream.

He spoke: *"Fisch."*

My brain reeled. Here I was, mingling with the great, and yet helpless as the veriest grade-three thinker. Desperately I sought for some sign by which I might convey that I, too, revered pure reason. I nodded vehemently. In a brilliant flash I used up half of my German vocabulary.

"Fisch. Ja Ja."

For perhaps another five minutes we stood side by side. Then Professor Einstein, his whole figure still conveying good will and amiability, drifted away out of sight.

I, too, would be a grade-one thinker. I was irreverent at the best of times. Political and religious systems, social customs, loyalties and traditions, they all came tumbling down like so many rotten apples off a tree. This was a fine hobby and a sensible substitute for cricket, since you could play it all the year round. I came up in the end with what must always remain the justification for grade-one thinking, its sign, seal and charter. I devised a coherent system for living. It was a moral system, which was wholly logical. Of course, as I readily admitted, conversion of the world to my way of thinking might be difficult, since my system did away with a number of trifles, such as big business, centralized government, armies, marriage. . . .

It was Ruth all over again. I had some very good friends who stood by me, and still do. But my acquaintances vanished, taking the girls with them. Young women seemed oddly contented with the world as it was. They valued the meaningless ceremony with a ring. Young men, while willing to concede the chaining sordidness of marriage, were hesitant about abandoning the organizations which they hoped would give them a career. A young man on the first rung of the Royal Navy, while perfectly agreeable to doing away with big business and marriage, got as rednecked as Mr. Houghton when I proposed a world without any battleships in it.

Had the game gone too far? Was it a game any longer? In those prewar days, I stood to lose a great deal, for the sake of a hobby.

Now you are expecting me to describe how I saw the folly of my ways and came back to the warm nest, where prejudices are so often called loyalties, where pointless actions are hallowed into custom by repetition, where we are content to say we think when all we do is feel.

But you would be wrong. I dropped my hobby and turned professional.

If I were to go back to the headmaster's study and find the dusty statuettes still there, I would arrange them differently. I would dust Venus and put her aside, for I have come to love her and know her for the fair thing she is. But I would put the Thinker, sunk in his desperate thought, where there were shadows before him—and at his back, I would put the leopard, crouched and ready to spring.

                                                                    1961

THE READER

1. *It has been said: "Third-rate thinkers think like everybody else because everybody else thinks the same way. Second-rate thinkers think differently from everybody else because everybody else thinks the same way. First-rate thinkers think." Does this saying correspond to Golding's message? Would you modify it in any way in light of what he*

writes?

2. *What are the special attractions and what are the penalties of grade-three thinking? Grade-two? Grade-one?*

3. *Are Golding's three categories all-encompassing? If so, how? If not, what additional ones would you add?*

4. *Are Golding's categories useful for assessing the value of a person's statements? Choose several selections in this book, and examine them by Golding's implied criteria.*

THE WRITER

1. *Why does Golding, at the end of his essay, return to the three statuettes? Have the statuettes anything to do with the three kinds of thinking described in the essay? Why would Golding rearrange the statuettes as he does in the final paragraph?*

2. *Why does Golding include the anecdote about Einstein? Does it have any bearing upon his account of the three categories of thinking?*

3. *One would not usually consider thinking a "hobby." Why does Golding do so? Write an essay on something else not usually considered a hobby, using the title "_____ as a Hobby."*

4. *Golding is the author of* Lord of the Flies. *If you have read that novel, write an essay attempting to relate his depiction of characters and events to the three categories of thinking.*

Carl Sagan

THE ABSTRACTIONS OF BEASTS

"Beasts abstract not," announced John Locke, expressing mankind's prevailing opinion throughout recorded history: Bishop Berkeley[1] had, however, a sardonic rejoinder: "If the fact that brutes abstract not be made the distinguishing property of that sort of animal, I fear a great many of those that pass for men must be reckoned into their numbers." Abstract thought, at least in its more subtle varieties, is not an invariable accompaniment of everyday life for the average man. Could abstract thought be a matter not of kind but of degree? Could other animals be capable of abstract thought but more rarely or less deeply than humans?

We have the impression that other animals are not very intelligent. But have we examined the possibility of animal intelligence carefully enough, or, as in François Truffaut's poignant film *The Wild Child*, do we simply equate the absence of our style of expression of intelligence

1. John Locke, English philosopher, author of *An Essay Concerning Human Understanding* (1690); Bishop George Berkeley, Irish philosopher, author of *A Treatise Concerning the Principles of Human Knowledge* (1710).

with the absence of intelligence? In discussing communication with the animals, the French philosopher Montaigne remarked, "The defect that hinders communication betwixt them and us, why may it not be on our part as well as theirs?"

There is, of course, a considerable body of anecdotal information suggesting chimpanzee intelligence. The first serious study of the behavior of simians—including their behavior in the wild—was made in Indonesia by Alfred Russel Wallace, the co-discoverer of evolution by natural selection. Wallace concluded that a baby orangutan he studied behaved "exactly like a human child in similar circumstances." In fact, "orangutan" is a Malay phrase meaning not ape but "man of the woods." Teuber recounted many stories told by his parents, pioneer German ethologists who founded and operated the first research station devoted to chimpanzee behavior on Tenerife in the Canary Islands early in the second decade of this century. It was here that Wolfgang Kohler performed his famous studies of Sultan, a chimpanzee "genius" who was able to connect two rods in order to reach an otherwise inaccessible banana. On Tenerife, also, two chimpanzees were observed maltreating a chicken: One would extend some food to the fowl, encouraging it to approach; whereupon the other would thrust at it with a piece of wire it had concealed behind its back. The chicken would retreat but soon allow itself to approach once again—and be beaten once again. Here is a fine combination of behavior sometimes thought to be uniquely human: cooperation, planning a future course of action, deception and cruelty. It also reveals that chickens have a very low capacity for avoidance learning.

Until a few years ago, the most extensive attempt to communicate with chimpanzees went something like this: A newborn chimp was taken into a household with a newborn baby, and both would be raised together —twin cribs, twin bassinets, twin high chairs, twin potties, twin diaper pails, twin babypowder cans. At the end of three years, the young chimp had, of course, far outstripped the young human in manual dexterity, running, leaping, climbing and other motor skills. But while the child was happily babbling away, the chimp could say only, and with enormous difficulty, "Mama," "Papa," and "cup." From this it was widely concluded that in language, reasoning and other higher mental functions, chimpanzees were only minimally competent: "Beasts abstract not."

But in thinking over these experiments, two psychologists, Beatrice and Robert Gardner, at the University of Nevada, realized that the pharynx and larynx of the chimp are not suited for human speech. Human beings exhibit a curious multiple use of the mouth for eating, breathing and communicating. In insects such as crickets, which call to one another by rubbing their legs, these three functions are performed by completely separate organ systems. Human spoken language seems to be adventitious. The exploitation of organ systems with other functions for communication in humans is also indicative of the comparatively recent evolution of our linguistic abilities. It might be, the Gardners reasoned, that chimpanzees have substantial language abilities which could not be expressed because of the limitations of their anatomy. Was there any symbolic language, they asked, that could employ the strengths rather than the weaknesses of chimpanzee anatomy?

The Gardners hit upon a brilliant idea: Teach a chimpanzee American sign language, known by its acronym Ameslan, and sometimes as "American deaf and dumb language" (the "dumb" refers, of course, to the inability to speak and not to any failure of intelligence). It is ideally suited to the immense manual dexterity of the chimpanzee. It also may have all the crucial design features of verbal languages.

There is by now a vast library of described and filmed conversations, employing Ameslan and other gestural languages, with Washoe, Lucy, Lana and other chimpanzees studied by the Gardners and others. Not only are there chimpanzees with working vocabularies of 100 to 200 words; they are also able to distinguish among nontrivially different grammatical patterns and syntaxes. What is more, they have been remarkably inventive in the construction of new words and phrases.

On seeing for the first time a duck land quacking in a pond, Washoe gestured "waterbird," which is the same phrase used in English and other languages, but which Washoe invented for the occasion. Having never seen a spherical fruit other than an apple, but knowing the signs for the principal colors, Lana, upon spying a technician eating an orange, signed "orange apple." After tasting a watermelon, Lucy described it as "candy drink" or "drink fruit," which is essentially the same word form as the English "water melon." But after she had burned her mouth on her first radish, Lucy forever after described them as "cry hurt food." A small doll placed unexpectedly in Washoe's cup elicited the response "Baby in my drink." When Washoe soiled, particularly clothing or furniture, she was taught the sign "dirty," which she then extrapolated as a general term of abuse. A rhesus monkey that evoked her displeasure was repeatedly signed at: "Dirty monkey, dirty monkey, dirty monkey." Occasionally Washoe would say things like "Dirty Jack, gimme drink." Lana, in a moment of creative annoyance, called her trainer "You green shit." Chimpanzees have invented swear words. Washoe also seems to have a sort of sense of humor; once, when riding on her trainer's shoulders and, perhaps inadvertently, wetting him, she signed: "Funny, funny."

Lucy was eventually able to distinguish clearly the meanings of the phrases "Roger tickle Lucy" and "Lucy tickle Roger," both of which activities she enjoyed with gusto. Likewise, Lana extrapolated from "Tim groom Lana" to "Lana groom Tim." Washoe was observed "reading" a magazine—i.e., slowly turning the pages, peering intently at the pictures and making, to no one in particular, an appropriate sign, such as "cat" when viewing a photograph of a tiger, and "drink" when examining a Vermouth advertisement. Having learned the sign "open" with a door, Washoe extended the concept to a briefcase. She also attempted to converse in Ameslan with the laboratory cat, who turned out to be the only illiterate in the facility. Having acquired this marvelous method of communication, Washoe may have been surprised that the cat was not also competent in Ameslan. And when one day Jane, Lucy's foster mother, left the laboratory, Lucy gazed after her and signed: "Cry me. Me cry."

Boyce Rensberger is a sensitive and gifted reporter for the New York Times whose parents could neither speak nor hear, although he is in both respects normal. His first language, however, was Ameslan. He had been abroad on a European assignment for the Times for some years. On his return to the United States, one of his first domestic duties was to look into the Gardners' experiments with Washoe. After some little time with the chimpanzee, Rensberger reported, "Suddenly I realized I was conversing with a member of another species in my native tongue." The use of the word tongue is, of course, figurative: it is built deeply into the structure of the language (a word that also means "tongue"). In fact, Rensberger was conversing with a member of another species in his native "hand." And it is just this transition from tongue to hand that has permitted humans to regain the ability—lost, according to Josephus,[2] since Eden—to communicate with the animals.

In addition to Ameslan, chimpanzees and other nonhuman primates are being taught a variety of other gestural languages. At the Yerkes Regional Primate Research Center in Atlanta, Georgia, they are learning a specific computer language called (by the humans, not the chimps) "Yerkish." The computer records all of its subjects' conversations, even during the night when no humans are in attendance; and from its ministrations we have learned that chimpanzees prefer jazz to rock and movies about chimpanzees to movies about human beings. Lana had, by January 1976, viewed The Developmental Anatomy of the Chimpanzee 245 times. She would undoubtedly appreciate a larger film library.

* * * The machine provides for many of Lana's needs, but not all. Sometimes, in the middle of the night, she forlornly types out: "Please, machine, tickle Lana." More elaborate requests and commentaries, each requiring a creative use of a set grammatical form, have been developed subsequently.

Lana monitors her sentences on a computer display, and erases those with grammatical errors. Once, in the midst of Lana's construction of an elaborate sentence, her trainer mischievously and repeatedly interposed,

2. First-century Jewish general and historian.

from his separate computer console, a word that made nonsense of Lana's sentence. She gazed at her computer display, spied her trainer at his console, and composed a new sentence: "Please, Tim, leave room." Just as Washoe and Lucy can be said to speak, Lana can be said to write.

At an early stage in the development of Washoe's verbal abilities, Jacob Bronowski and a colleague wrote a scientific paper denying the significance of Washoe's use of gestural language because, in the limited data available to Bronowski, Washoe neither inquired nor negated. But later observations showed that Washoe and other chimpanzees were perfectly able both to ask questions and to deny assertions put to them. And it is difficult to see any significant difference in quality between chimpanzee use of gestural language and the use of ordinary speech by children in a manner that we unhesitatingly attribute to intelligence. In reading Bronowski's paper I cannot help but feel that a little pinch of human chauvinsim has crept in, an echo of Locke's "Beasts abstract not." In 1949, the American anthropologist Leslie White stated unequivocally: "Human behavior is symbolic behavior; symbolic behavior is human behavior." What would White have made of Washoe, Lucy and Lana?

These findings on chimpanzee language and intelligence have an intriguing bearing on "Rubicon" arguments[3]—the contention that the total brain mass, or at least the ratio of brain to body mass, is a useful index of intelligence. Against this point of view it was once argued that the lower range of the brain masses of microcephalic humans overlaps the upper range of brain masses of adult chimpanzees and gorillas; and yet, it was said, microcephalics have some, although severely impaired, use of language—while the apes have none. But in only relatively few cases are microcephalics capable of human speech. One of the best behavioral descriptions of microcephalics was written by a Russian physician, S. Korsakov, who in 1893 observed a female microcephalic named "Masha." She could understand a very few questions and commands and could occasionally reminisce on her childhood. She sometimes chattered away, but there was little coherence to what she uttered. Korsakov characterized her speech as having "an extreme poverty of logical associations." As an example of her poorly adapted and automaton-like intelligence, Korsakov described her eating habits. When food was present on the table, Masha would eat. But if the food was abruptly removed in the midst of a meal, she would behave as if the meal had ended, thanking those in charge and piously blessing herself. If the food were returned, she would eat again. The pattern apparently was subject to

3. Those assuming a definitive boundary between different kinds of intelligence. The allusion is to the river Rubicon, in ancient times the boundary between Rome and its "barbaric" Germanic provinces.

indefinite repetition. My own impression is that Lucy or Washoe would be a far more interesting dinner companion than Masha, and that the comparison of microcephalic humans with normal apes is not inconsistent with some sort of "Rubicon" of intelligence. Of course, both the quality and the quantity of neural connections are probably vital for the sorts of intelligence that we can easily recognize.

Recent experiments performed by James Dewson of the Stanford University School of Medicine and his colleagues give some physiological support to the idea of language centers in the simian neocortex—in particular, like humans, in the left hemisphere. Monkeys were trained to press a green light when they heard a hiss and a red light when they heard a tone. Some seconds after a sound was heard, the red or the green light would appear at some unpredictable position—different each time—on the control panel. The monkey pressed the appropriate light and, in the case of a correct guess, was rewarded with a pellet of food. Then the time interval between hearing the sound and seeing the light was increased up to twenty seconds. In order to be rewarded, the monkeys now had to remember for twenty seconds which noise they had heard. Dewson's team then surgically excised part of the so-called auditory association cortex from the left hemisphere of the neocortex in the temporal lobe. When retested, the monkeys had very poor recall of which sound they were then hearing. After less than a second they could not recall whether it was a hiss or a tone. The removal of a comparable part of the temporal lobe from the right hemisphere produced no effect whatever on this task. "It looks," Dewson was reported to say, "as if we removed the structure in the monkeys' brains that may be analogous to human language centers." Similar studies on rhesus monkeys, but using visual rather than auditory stimuli, seem to show no evidence of a difference between the hemispheres of the neocortex.

Because adult chimpanzees are generally thought (at least by zookeepers) to be too dangerous to retain in a home or home environment, Washoe and other verbally accomplished chimpanzees have been involuntarily "retired" soon after reaching puberty. Thus we do not yet have experience with the adult language abilities of monkeys and apes. One of the most intriguing questions is whether a verbally accomplished chimpanzee mother will be able to communicate language to her offspring. It seems very likely that this should be possible and that a community of chimps initially competent in gestural language could pass down the language to subsequent generations.

Where such communication is essential for survival, there is already some evidence that apes transmit extragenetic or cultural information. Jane Goodall observed baby chimps in the wild emulating the behavior of their mothers and learning the reasonably complex task of finding an appropriate twig and using it to prod into a termite's nest so as to acquire some of these tasty delicacies.

Differences in group behavior—something that it is very tempting to call cultural differences—have been reported among chimpanzees, baboons, macaques and many other primates. For example, one group of monkeys may know how to eat bird's eggs, while an adjacent band of precisely the same species may not. Such primates have a few dozen sounds or cries, which are used for intra-group communication, with such meanings as "Flee; here is a predator." But the sound of the cries differs somewhat from group to group: there are regional accents.

An even more striking experiment was performed accidentally by Japanese primatologists attempting to relieve an overpopulation and hunger problem in a community of macaques on an island in south Japan. The anthropologists threw grains of wheat on a sandy beach. Now it is very difficult to separate wheat grains one by one from sand grains; such an effort might even expend more energy than eating the collected wheat would provide. But one brilliant macaque, Imo, perhaps by accident or out of pique, threw handfuls of the mixture into the water. Wheat floats; sand sinks, a fact that Imo clearly noted. Through the sifting process she was able to eat well (on a diet of soggy wheat, to be sure). While older macaques, set in their ways, ignored her, the younger monkeys appeared to grasp the importance of her discovery, and imitate it. In the next generation, the practice was more widespread; today all macaques on the island are competent at water sifting, an example of a cultural tradition among the monkeys.

Earlier studies on Takasakiyama, a mountain in northeast Kyushu inhabited by macaques, show a similar pattern in cultural evolution. Visitors to Takasakiyama threw caramels wrapped in paper to the monkeys—a common practice in Japanese zoos, but one the Takasakiyama macaques had never before encountered. In the course of play, some young monkeys discovered how to unwrap the caramels and eat them. The habit was passed on successively to their playmates, their mothers, the dominant males (who among the macaques act as babysitters for the very young) and finally to the subadult males, who were at the furthest social remove from the monkey children. The process of acculturation took more than three years. In natural primate communities, the existing nonverbal communications are so rich that there is little pressure for the development of a more elaborate gestural language. But if gestural language were necessary for chimpanzee survival, there can be little doubt that it would be transmitted culturally down through the generations.

I would expect a significant development and elaboration of language in only a few generations if all the chimps unable to communicate were to die or fail to reproduce. Basic English corresponds to about 1,000 words. Chimpanzees are already accomplished in vocabularies exceeding 10 percent of that number. Although a few years ago it would have seemed the most implausible science fiction, it does not appear to me out of the question that, after a few generations in such a verbal chimpanzee community, there might emerge the memoirs of the natural history and mental life of a chimpanzee, published in English or Japanese (with perhaps an "as told to" after the by-line).

If chimpanzees have consciousness, if they are capable of abstractions, do they not have what until now has been described as "human rights"? How smart does a chimpanzee have to be before killing him constitutes murder? What further properties must he show before religious missionaries must consider him worthy of attempts at conversion?

I recently was escorted through a large primate research laboratory by its director. We approached a long corridor lined, to the vanishing point as in a perspective drawing, with caged chimpanzees. They were one, two or three to a cage, and I am sure the accommodations were exemplary as far as such institutions (or for that matter traditional zoos) go. As we approached the nearest cage, its two inmates bared their teeth and with incredible accuracy let fly great sweeping arcs of spittle, fairly drenching the lightweight suit of the facility's director. They then uttered a staccato of short shrieks, which echoed down the corridor to be repeated and amplified by other caged chimps, who had certainly not seen us, until the corridor fairly shook with the screeching and banging and rattling of bars. The director informed me that not only spit is apt to fly in such a situation; and at his urging we retreated.

I was powerfully reminded of those American motion pictures of the 1930s and '40s, set in some vast and dehumanized state or federal penitentiary, in which the prisoners banged their eating utensils against the bars at the appearance of the tyrannical warden. These chimps are healthy and well-fed. If they are "only" animals, if they are beasts which abstract not, then my comparison is a piece of sentimental foolishness. But chimpanzees can abstract. Like other mammals, they are capable of strong emotions. They have certainly committed no crimes. I do not claim to have the answer, but I think it is certainly worthwhile to raise the question: Why, exactly, all over the civilized world, in virtually every major city, are apes in prison?

For all we know, occasional viable crosses between humans and chimpanzees are possible. The natural experiment must have been tried very infrequently, at least recently. If such off-spring are ever produced, what will their legal status be? The cognitive abilities of chimpanzees force us, I think, to raise searching questions about the boundaries of the community of beings to which special ethical considerations are due, and can, I hope, help to extend our ethical perspectives downward through the taxa on Earth and upwards to extraterrestial organisms, if they exist.

* * *

Neil Postman

CONFUSING LEVELS OF ABSTRACTION

Many years ago, mathematicians and logicians were confounded by a certain paradox for which their intellectual habits could produce no solutions. The paradox, which had been known about for centuries, is easily stated in the following way: A Cretan says, "All Cretans are liars." If the statement is true, then it is also false (because at least one Cretan, the speaker, has told the truth). We have a proposition, in other words, that is both true and false at the same time, which is terrifying to mathematicians and logicians. Bertrand Russell and Alfred North Whitehead solved this paradox in their great work, published in 1913, *Principia Mathematica.* They called their solution The Theory of Logical Types, and it, also, may be easily stated: A class of things must not be considered a member of that class. Or, to quote Russell and Whitehead, "Whatever involves *all* of a collection must not be one of that collection." And so, a particular statement by one Cretan about all of the statements made by Cretans is not itself to be considered part of what he is talking about. It is of a different logical type, a different order of things. To confuse them would be like confusing the word finger with a finger itself, so that if I asked you to count the number of fingers on your hand, you would (if you were confused) say six—five fingers plus the name of the class of things.

To take another example: There is no paradox in the statement "Never say never" because the first *never* is not at the same level of abstraction as the second, the first *never* referring to all statements, the second to particular ones.

Now, all of this has made mathematicians and logicians reasonably happy, but what about the rest of us? If does not happen very often, not even on the isle of Crete, that a Cretan will approach anybody and announce, "All Cretans are liars." And as for fingers, not even a deranged logician will say he has six fingers on each hand—five plus the class of things. And yet, for all that, The Theory of Logical Types has some practical implications for reducing our stupid and crazy talk. For one thing, it provides us with a certain awareness of the different types of statements we customarily make. For example, we make statements about things and processes in the world, such as, "The temperature is now ninety degrees." And we make statements about our *reactions* to things and processes in the world, such as, "It is hot." If you think that those two statements are virtually the same, you are on a path that is

127

bound to lead to some interesting stupid talk. Whether or not a thermometer registers ninety degrees is an issue that can be settled by
anyone who knows how to read a thermometer. But whether or not
something is "hot" depends on who is being heated. To a Laplander, a
temperature of fifty-eight degrees may be "hot," to a South African it
may be "cold." The statement "It is hot (or cold)" is a statement about
what is going on inside one's body. The statement "The temperature is
now ninety degress (or fifty-eight degrees)" is a statement about what is
going on outside one's body. Alfred Korzybski[1] provided us with two
terms which are useful in talking about these different types of statements: *Extensional* statements are those which try to point to observable
processes that are occurring outside our skins. *Intensional* statements are
those which point to processes occurring inside our skins.

This distinction is by no means trivial. As I mentioned earlier, more
than a few arguments and misunderstandings are generated by people
who have confused the two types of statements and who, therefore, look
in the wrong direction for verification of what they are saying. I can never
prove to a Laplander that fifty-eight degrees is "cool," but I can prove to
him that it is fifty-eight degrees. In other words, there is no paradox in
two different people's concluding that the weather is both "hot" and
"cold" at the same time. As long as they know that each of them is talking
about a different reality, their conversation can proceed in a fairly orderly
way.

In addition to the differing "horizontal" directions of our statements
(inside and outside), there are differing "vertical" directions of our statements. For example, assuming you and I are talking about some event
that has occurred, and that we are trying to describe it "objectively," we
may still differ in the degree of specificity of our sentences. I may say,
"Two vehicles collided." And you may say, "Two Chevy Impalas collided." We are both being extensional in our remarks, but you have
included more details than I and, to that extent, come closer to depicting
"reality." We may say that my level of abstraction is higher than yours.
And as a general rule, the higher the level of abstraction, the less able it is
to denote the color and texture and uniqueness of specific realities. I do
not say—please note—the less "true" it is. The statement "$E = mc^2$," I
am told, is about as "true" as a statement can be, but it is at such a high
level of abstraction—it leaves out so many details—as to be virtually
useless to all but a select few who use it for specialized purposes. Einstein
himself remarked that the more "true" mathematics is, the less it has to
do with reality. Nowhere can this be seen more clearly than in our

---

1.   American   scientist   and   writer   science of general semantics, the study of
(1879–1950), born in Poland, founder of the   how language conveys meaning.

attempts to apply statistical statements to "real" situations. There is, for example, an apocryphal story about a pregnant woman (let us call her Mrs. Green) who went to see her obstetrician in a state of agitation bordering on hysteria. She had read in a magazine that one out of every five babies born in the world is Chinese. She already had given birth to four children and feared that her next would be a victim of the inexorable laws of statistics. The point is that the statement "one out of every five babies in the world is Chinese" is "true," but it is at such a high level of abstraction that it bears no relation to the realities of any *particular* person. It is of a different logical type from any statement made about Mrs. Green's situation and what she, in particular, might expect.

Mrs. Green's problem is apocryphal, but her confusion is not. There are plenty of people who worry themselves to death because they have discovered that they are "below average" in some respect. And there is no shortage of people who falsely assess their own expectations and, indeed, merit, because they have determined they are "above average." For example, a person whose IQ score is "above average" ought not to assume that he or she will have a better chance of understanding a certain situation than a person whose IQ score is "below average." For one thing, a score on a test is a highly abstract statement in itself. For another, a statement about one's score in relation to a thousand other scores is a further abstraction—so far removed from one's performance in a particular situation as to be meaningless. The point is that statistical language of even the most rudimentary sort leaves out so many details that it is, almost literally, not about anything. There is nothing "personal" about it, and therefore it is best to regard it as being of a different logical type from statements about what is actually happening to people.

Generalizations about groups of people present a similar problem. It may be "true," for example, that Jews, as a class of people, have a higher income than Italians, but it does not follow that Al Schwartz, in particular, earns more than Dominick Alfieri, in particular. One of the roots of what may be called prejudice lies somewhere in our confusion over what may be "true" in a general sense and what may be "true" in a particular sense.

The Theory of Logical Types, then, is useful in helping us to sort out our different modalities of talk. There are statements about what we observe and statements about how we feel and statements about our statements (of which self-reflexiveness is an example) and statements about how we classify things—in a phrase, statements about different orders of "reality."

It does not always matter, of course, that we be aware of these distinctions. No one is more obnoxious than the fanatical semanticist who insists upon straightening everyone out even though they have no wish to be straightened. But, obviously, there are many situations in which people descend into argument, confusion, or despair because they are not aware of the differing types of statements being made. In these cases, knowledge of logical types, levels of abstraction, and extensionality-intensionality can be very useful.

But there is still another application to all of this that is even more useful. I am referring to our efforts at solving problems. The basic distinction that is required here is between "first-order" thinking and "second-order" thinking. (I am lifting these terms from a remarkable book, Change, by Paul Watzlawick, John Weakland, and Richard Fisch, in which the authors explain, in great detail, how to apply The Theory of Logical Types to the resolution of practical human problems.) The difference between first- and second-order thinking is a difference in the level of abstraction at which we perceive a problem. When we try to solve a problem through first-order thinking, we work within the framework of the system, accepting the assumptions on which the system is based. For instance, suppose you were given this problem to solve: Here is a number, VI. By the addition of one line, can you make it into a seven? The answer is simple enough—VII. First-order perceptions are entirely adequate for such a problem. But now suppose you are given the following problem: Here is a number, IX. By the addition of one line, can you make it into a six? This problem does not yield to first-order thinking. If you try to solve it by rearranging the elements of the system, you will not come up with a solution. But if you go to another level of abstraction, if you step outside the system, so to speak, an answer suggests itself: SIX. People who cannot solve this problem have usually failed for the following reasons: They assume that IX is a Roman number, and only a Roman number. They assume that the answer must, therefore, be expressed in a Roman number. And they assume that "a line" must be a straight line. In other words, they have "framed" the problem in a certain way and have tried to solve it by staying within that frame. Second-order thinking means going outside the "frame" of a problem and drawing on resources not contained in the original "frame."

There are several different names for second-order thinking. Some have referred to it simply as "creative thinking." The authors of Change call it "reframing." Edward de Bono calls it lateral thinking, of which he gives the following example:

> There is made in Switzerland a pear brandy in which a whole pear is to be seen within the bottle. How did the pear get into the bottle? The usual guess is that the bottle neck has been closed after the pear has been put into the bottle. Others guess that the bottom of the bottle was added after the pear was inside. It is always assumed that since the pear is a fully grown pear that it must have been placed in the bottle as a fully grown pear. In fact if a branch bearing a tiny bud was inserted through the neck of the bottle then the pear

would actually grow within the bottle and there would be no question of how it got inside.

(Lateral Thinking, pp. 93 and 94)

One must grant that problems about Roman numbers and pears in bottles are not of the type which ordinarily worry poeple. But the process by which they are solved—going to another level of perception—can be of substantial practical value. For example, in some New York City public schools, the teachers have a great deal of trouble keeping their students inside the classrooms. Students wander through the hallways during class time, sometimes running, fighting, and screaming, which is not only dangerous but also distracting to those inside the classrooms. Now, if you assume that a classroom is the only place where learning can occur and that those who are not in their classrooms are a "problem," you will spend all your energy trying to get the problems to go where the solution is. You will threaten, plead, and even call the police, none of which works very well. But suppose you "reframe" the problem. Suppose, for example, you say that the issue is not how to get the students into a room but how to get them to learn something. All sorts of possibilities will now become available. In one New York City school, the assistant principal came up with this solution: She announced that the school was instituting a radical educational plan, known as "the open hall policy." The plan made *staying in the halls* a legitimate educational activity. A few teachers were made available to talk with students about a variety of subjects, and thus the halls *became* the classroom. The screaming, running, and fighting stopped, and I have been told on good authority that other principals now visit this school to observe this startling educational innovation.

To take another example, in *Change*, Watzlawick and his associates suggest that people suffering from insomnia will often choose the worst possible path to sleep. They will tell themselves that their problem is "to get to sleep." But since sleep must come spontaneously or it does not come, to work at getting to sleep will defeat its purpose. They recommend a little reverse English: Tell yourself that your problem is to stay awake, and try to do so.

Another example: The New York State Thruway Authority faced the problem of an excessive number of speed-limit violations. They could have, at great expense, hired more troopers to track down the violators. Instead, they raised the speed limit, and thus eliminated much of the problem, with no increase in the accident rate.

The point of all this is that a great deal of stupid talk can be eliminated if we can get beyond and outside of our own assumptions. We too often become tyrannized by the way we have framed a certain situation; that is, we allow a set of words and sentences to define for us the level of perception at which we will view a matter. But if we change our words, we may change the matter. And, therefore, the solution.

1976

THE READER

1. Postman shows several implications of The Theory of Logical Types. What are these? Do you find them of value for practical thinking? Can you think of further implications and uses?
2. What point is exemplified by Postman's discussion of the difference between saying "The temperature is now ninety degrees" and "It is hot" (pp. 127–128)?
3. At the close of his essay, Postman offers several instances of creative solutions to practical problems arrived at by the application of second-order thinking (pp. 130–131). Do the solutions seem satisfactory to you? What assumptions underlie his judgment that these are good solutions to the problems posed?
4. What similarities do you find between Postman's discussion of different orders of abstraction and the discussion in Golding's "Thinking as a Hobby" (p. 112)? Are there important differences between them?

THE WRITER

1. Postman says (p. 130) that in many situations "people descend into argument, confusion, or despair because they are not aware of the differing types of statements being made." Has this ever happened to you? Have you ever known anyone who seemed to delight in using "logic" to confuse and confound you? Write an account of your personal experience in one such situation or with one such logic-mongering acquaintance.
2. Why does Postman include in his essay a discussion of the use and misuse of statistics? Consider the following (actual) newspaper headline: "Study shows half of U.S. population below average intelligence." Survey one issue of a newspaper for all instances of stories or analyses based on statistical material, and write a report of your findings.
3. In grappling with a vexing problem, have you ever experienced the sudden finding of a solution that seemed to result from a shift from first- to second-order thinking? Write an account of it, tracing as carefully as you can the precise sequence of details in the process.
4. Write an essay comparing and contrasting Postman's discussion of first- and second-order thinking with Bronowski's discussion of imagination (p. 133) or Asimov's discussion of the "eureka" phenomenon (p. 140).

Jacob Bronowski

THE REACH OF IMAGINATION

For three thousand years, poets have been enchanted and moved and perplexed by the power of their own imagination. In a short and summary essay I can hope at most to lift one small corner of that mystery; and yet it is a critical corner. I shall ask, What goes on in the mind when we imagine? You will hear from me that one answer to this question is fairly specific: which is to say, that we can describe the working of the imagination. And when we describe it as I shall do, it becomes plain that imagination is a specifically *human* gift. To imagine is the characteristic act, not of the poet's mind, or the painter's, or the scientist's, but of the mind of man.

My stress here on the word *human* implies that there is a clear difference in this between the actions of men and those of other animals. Let me then start with a classical experiment with animals and children which Walter Hunter thought out in Chicago about 1910. That was the time when scientists were agog with the success of Ivan Pavlov in forming and changing the reflex actions of dogs, which Pavlov had first announced in 1903. Pavlov had been given a Nobel prize the next year, in 1904; although in fairness I should say that the award did not cite his work on the conditioned reflex, but on the digestive gland.

Hunter duly trained some dogs and other animals on Pavlov's lines. They were taught that when a light came on over one of three tunnels out of their cage, that tunnel would be open; they could escape down it, and were rewarded with food if they did. But once he had fixed that conditioned reflex, Hunter added to it a deeper idea: he gave the mechanical experiment a new dimension, literally—the dimension of time. Now he no longer let the dog go to the lighted tunnel at once; instead, he put out the light, and then kept the dog waiting a little while before he let him go. In this way Hunter timed how long an animal can remember where he has last seen the signal light to his escape route.

The results were and are staggering. A dog or a rat forgets which one of three tunnels has been lit up within a matter of seconds—in Hunter's experiment, ten seconds at most. If you want such an animal to do much better than this, you must make the task much simpler: you must face him with only two tunnels to choose from. Even so, the best that Hunter could do was to have a dog remember for five minutes which one of two tunnels had been lit up.

I am not quoting these times as if they were exact and universal: they surely are not. Hunter's experiment, more than fifty years old now, had many faults of detail. For example, there were too few animals, they were oddly picked, and they did not all behave consistently. It may be unfair to test a dog for what he *saw*, when he commonly follows his nose rather than his eyes. It may be unfair to test any animal in the unnatural setting of a laboratory cage. And there are higher animals, such as chimpanzees and other primates, which certainly have longer memories than the animals that Hunter tried.

Yet when all these provisos have been made (and met, by more modern experiments) the facts are still startling and characteristic. An animal cannot recall a signal from the past for even a short fraction of the time that a man can—for even a short fraction of the time that a child can. Hunter made comparable tests with six-year-old children, and found, of course, that they were incomparably better than the best of his animals. There is a striking and basic difference between a man's ability to imagine something that he saw or experienced, and an animal's failure.

Animals make up for this by other and extraordinary gifts. The salmon and the carrier pigeon can find their way home as we cannot: they have, as it were, a practical memory that man cannot match. But their actions always depend on some form of habit: on instinct or on learning, which reproduce by rote a train of known responses. They do not depend, as human memory does, on calling to mind the recollection of absent things.

Where is it that the animal falls short? We get a clue to the answer, I think, when Hunter tells us how the animals in his experiment tried to fix their recollection. They most often pointed themselves at the light before it went out, as some gun dogs point rigidly at the game they scent —and get the name *pointer* from the posture. The animal makes ready to act by building the signal into its action. There is a primitive imagery in its stance, it seems to me; it is as if the animal were trying to fix the light on its mind by fixing it in its body. And indeed, how else can a dog mark and (as it were) name one of three tunnels, when he has no such words as *left* and *right*, and no such numbers as *one, two, three?* The directed gesture of attention and readiness is perhaps the only symbolic device that the dog commands to hold on to the past, and thereby to guide himself into the future.

I used the verb *to imagine* a moment ago, and now I have some ground for giving it a meaning. *To imagine* means to make images and to move them about inside one's head in new arrangements. When you and I recall the past, we imagine it in this direct and homely sense. The tool that puts the human mind ahead of the animal is imagery. For us, memory does not demand the preoccupation that it demands in animals, and it lasts immensely longer, because we fix it in images or other substitute symbols. With the same symbolic vocabulary we spell out the future—not one but many futures, which we weigh one against another.

I am using the word *image* in a wide meaning, which does not restrict it to the mind's eye as a visual organ. An image in my usage is what Charles Peirce called a sign, without regard for its sensory quality. Peirce distinguished between different forms of signs, but there is no reason to make his distinction here, for the imagination works equally with them all, and that is why I call them all images.

Indeed, the most important images for human beings are simply words, which are abstract symbols. Animals do not have words, in our sense: there is no specific center for language in the brain of any animal, as there is in the human being. In this respect at least we know that the human imagination depends on a configuration in the brain that has only evolved in the last one or two million years. In the same period, evolution has greatly enlarged the front lobes in the human brain, which govern the sense of the past and the future; and it is a fair guess that they are probably the seat of our other images. (Part of the evidence for this guess is that damage to the front lobes in primates reduces them to the state of Hunter's animals.) If the guess turns out to be right, we shall know why man has come to look like a highbrow or an egghead: because otherwise there would not be room in his head for his imagination.

The images play out for us events which are not present to our senses, and thereby guard the past and create the future—a future that does not yet exist, and may never come to exist in that form. By contrast, the lack of symbolic ideas, or their rudimentary poverty, cuts off an animal from the past and the future alike, and imprisons him in the present. Of all the distinctions between man and animal, the characteristic gift which makes us human is the power to work with symbolic images: the gift of imagination.

This is really a remarkable finding. When Philip Sidney in 1580 defended poets (and all unconventional thinkers) from the Puritan charge that they were liars, he said that a maker must imagine things that are not. Halfway between Sidney and us, William Blake said, "What is now proved was once only imagined." About the same time, in 1796, Samuel Taylor Coleridge for the first time distinguished between the passive fancy and the active imagination, "the living Power and prime Agent of all human Perception." Now we see that they were right, and precisely right: the human gift is the gift of imagination—and that is not just a literary phrase.

Nor is it just a literary gift; it is, I repeat, characteristically human. Almost everything that we do that is worth doing is done in the first place in the mind's eye. The richness of human life is that we have many lives; we live the events that do not happen (and some that cannot) as vividly as those that do; and if thereby we die a thousand deaths, that is the price we pay for living a thousand lives. (A cat, of course, has only nine.) Literature is alive to us because we live its images, but so is any play of the mind—so is chess: the lines of play that we foresee and try in our heads and dismiss are as much a part of the game as the moves that we make. John Keats said that the unheard melodies are sweeter, and all chess players sadly recall that the combinations that they planned and which never came to be played were the best.

I make this point to remind you, insistently, that imagination is the manipulation of images in one's head; and that the rational manipulation belongs to that, as well as the literary and artistic manipulation. When a child begins to play games with things that stand for other things, with chairs or chessmen, he enters the gateway to reason and imagination together. For the human reason discovers new relations between things not by deduction, but by that unpredictable blend of speculation and insight that scientists call induction, which—like other forms of imagination—cannot be formalized. We see it at work when Walter Hunter inquires into a child's memory, as much as when Blake and Coleridge do. Only a restless and original mind would have asked Hunter's questions and could have conceived his experiments, in a science that was dominated by Pavlov's reflex arcs and was heading toward the behaviorism of John Watson.[1]

Let me find a spectacular example for you from history. What is the most famous experiment that you had described to you as a child? I will hazard that it is the experiment that Galileo is said to have made in Sidney's age, in Pisa about 1590, by dropping two unequal balls from the Leaning Tower. There, we say, is a man in the modern mold, a man after our own hearts: he insisted on questioning the authority of Aristotle and St. Thomas Aquinas, and seeing with his own eyes whether (as they said) the heavy ball would reach the ground before the light one. Seeing is believing.

Yet seeing is also imagining. Galileo did challenge the authority of Aristotle, and he did look at his mechanics. But the eye that Galileo used was the mind's eye. He did not drop balls from the Leaning Tower of Pisa —and if he had, he would have got a very doubtful answer. Instead, Galileo made an imaginary experiment in his head, which I will describe as he did years later in the book he wrote after the Holy Office silenced him: the Discorsi . . . intorno a due nuove scienze,[2] which was smuggled out to be printed in the Netherlands in 1638.

Suppose, said Galileo, that you drop two unequal balls from the tower at the same time. And suppose that Aristotle is right—suppose that the heavy ball falls faster, so that it steadily gains on the light ball, and hits the ground first. Very well. Now imagine the same experiment done

1. Watson, a forerunner of B. F. Skinner, argued that all human behavior consists of conditioned reflexes in response to environmental stimuli.
2. Treatise . . . on Two New Sciences. In 1630,

after publishing his heretical theory that the earth moves around the sun, Galileo was forced by the Inquisition to recant it under threat of torture.

again, with only one difference: this time the two unequal balls are joined by a string between them. The heavy ball will again move ahead, but now the light ball holds it back and acts as a drag or brake. So the light ball will be speeded up and the heavy ball will be slowed down; they must reach the ground together because they are tied together, but they cannot reach the ground as quickly as the heavy ball alone. Yet the string between them has turned the two balls into a single mass which is heavier than either ball—and surely (according to Aristotle) this mass should therefore move faster than either ball? Galileo's imaginary experiment has uncovered a contradiction; he says trenchantly, "You see how, from your assumption that a heavier body falls more rapidly than a lighter one, I infer that a (still) heavier body falls more slowly." There is only one way out of the contradiction: the heavy ball and the light ball must fall at the same rate, so that they go on falling at the same rate when they are tied together.

This argument is not conclusive, for nature might be more subtle (when the two balls are joined) than Galileo has allowed. And yet it is something more important: it is suggestive, it is stimulating, it opens a new view—in a word, it is imaginative. It cannot be settled without an actual experiment, because nothing that we imagine can become knowledge until we have translated it into, and backed it by, real experience. The test of imagination is experience. But then, that is as true of literature and the arts as it is of science. In science, the imaginary experiment is tested by confronting it with physical experience; and in literature, the imaginative conception is tested by confronting it with human experience. The superficial speculation in science is dismissed because it is found to falsify nature; and the shallow work of art is discarded because it is found to be untrue to our own nature. So when Ella Wheeler Wilcox died in 1919, more people were reading her verses than Shakespeare's; yet in a few years her work was dead. It had been buried by its poverty of emotion and its trivialness of thought: which is to say that it had been proved to be as false to the nature of man as, say, Jean Baptiste Lamarck and Trofim Lysenko[3] were false to the nature of inheritance. The strength of the imagination, its enriching power and excitement, lies in its interplay with reality—physical and emotional.

I doubt if there is much to choose here between science and the arts: the imagination is not much more free, and not much less free, in one than in the other. All great scientists have used their imagination freely, and let it ride them to outrageous conclusions without crying "Halt!" Albert Einstein fiddled with imaginary experiments from boyhood, and

3. Lamarck was a French biologist (1744-1829) who held that characteristics acquired by experience were biologically transmittable. Lysenko is a Russian biologist (1898-) who has held that hereditary properties of organisms could be changed by manipulating the environment.

was wonderfully ignorant of the facts that they were supposed to bear on. When he wrote the first of his beautiful papers on the random movement of atoms, he did not know that the Brownian motion which it predicted could be seen in any laboratory. He was sixteen when he invented the paradox that he resolved ten years later, in 1905, in the theory of relativity, and it bulked much larger in his mind than the experiment of Albert Michelson and Edward Morley[4] which had upset every other physicist since 1881. All his life Einstein loved to make up teasing puzzles like Galileo's, about falling lifts and the detection of gravity; and they carry the nub of the problems of general relativity on which he was working.

Indeed, it could not be otherwise. The power that man has over nature and himself, and that a dog lacks, lies in his command of imaginary experience. He alone has the symbols which fix the past and play with the future, possible and impossible. In the Renaissance, the symbolism of memory was thought to be mystical, and devices that were invented as mnemonics (by Giordano Bruno, for example, and by Robert Fludd) were interpreted as magic signs. The symbol is the tool which gives man his power, and it is the same tool whether the symbols are images or words, mathematical signs or mesons. And the symbols have a reach and a roundness that goes beyond their literal and practical meaning. They are the rich concepts under which the mind gathers many particulars into one name, and many instances into one general induction. When a man says left and right, he is outdistancing the dog not only in looking for a light; he is setting in train all the shifts of meaning, the overtones and the ambiguities, between gauche and adroit and dexterous, between sinister and the sense of right. When a man counts one, two, three, he is not only doing mathematics; he is on the path to the mysticism of numbers in Pythagoras and Vitruvius and Kepler, to the Trinity and the signs of the Zodiac.

I have described imagination as the ability to make images and to move them about inside one's head in new arrangements. This is the faculty that is specifically human, and it is the common root from which science and literature both spring and grow and flourish together. For they do flourish (and languish) together; the great ages of science are the great ages of all the arts, because in them powerful minds have taken fire from one another, breathless and higgledy-piggledy, without asking too nicely whether they ought to tie their imagination to falling balls or a haunted island. Galileo and Shakespeare, who were born in the same year, grew into greatness in the same age; when Galileo was looking through his

4. Physicists had believed space to be filled with an ether which made possible the propagation of light and magnetism; the Michelson-Morley experiment proved this untrue. Einstein, an outsider, always claimed not to have heard of the experiment until after he published his special theory of relativity, which not only accounted for the Michelson-Morley findings but resolved such paradoxes as the impossibility of distinguishing qualitatively between gravity and the pull caused by the acceleration of an elevator, or lift.

telescope at the moon, Shakespeare was writing *The Tempest* and all Europe was in ferment, from Johannes Kepler to Peter Paul Rubens, and from the first table of logarithms by John Napier to the Authorized Version of the Bible.

Let me end with a last and spirited example of the common inspiration of literature and science, because it is as much alive today as it was three hundred years ago. What I have in mind is man's ageless fantasy, to fly to the moon. I do not display this to you as a high scientific enterprise; on the contrary, I think we have more important discoveries to make here on earth than wait for us, beckoning, at the horned surface of the moon. Yet I cannot belittle the fascination which that ice-blue journey has had for the imagination of men, long before it drew us to our television screens to watch the tumbling astronauts. Plutarch and Lucian, Ariosto and Ben Jonson wrote about it, before the days of Jules Verne and H. G. Wells and science fiction. The seventeenth century was heady with new dreams and fables about voyages to the moon. Kepler wrote one full of deep scientific ideas, which (alas) simply got his mother accused of witchcraft. In England, Francis Godwin wrote a wild and splendid work, *The Man in the Moone,* and the astronomer John Wilkins wrote a wild and learned one, *The Discovery of a New World.* They did not draw a line between science and fancy; for example, they all tried to guess just where in the journey the earth's gravity would stop. Only Kepler understood that gravity has no boundary, and put a law to it—which happened to be the wrong law.

All this was a few years before Isaac Newton was born, and it was all in his head that day in 1666 when he sat in his mother's garden, a young man of twenty-three, and thought about the reach of gravity. This was how he came to conceive his brilliant image, that the moon is like a ball which has been thrown so hard that it falls exactly as fast as the horizon, all the way round the earth. The image will do for any satellite, and Newton modestly calculated how long therefore an astronaut would take to fall round the earth once. He made it ninety minutes, and we have all seen now that he was right; but Newton had no way to check that. Instead he went on to calculate how long in that case the distant moon would take to round the earth, if indeed it behaves like a thrown ball that falls in the earth's gravity, and if gravity obeyed a law of inverse squares. He found that the answer would be twenty-eight days.

In that telling figure, the imagination that day chimed with nature, and made a harmony. We shall hear an echo of that harmony on the day when we land on the moon, because it will be not a technical but an imaginative triumph, that reaches back to the beginning of modern science and literature both. All great acts of imagination are like this, in the arts and in science, and convince us because they fill out reality with a deeper sense of rightness. We start with the simplest vocabulary of images, with

left and right and one, two, three, and before we know how it happened
the words and the numbers have conspired to make a match with nature:
we catch in them the pattern of mind and matter as one.

1967

THE READER

1. *How does the Hunter experiment provide Bronowski with the ground
   for defining the imagination?*
2. *On p. 135, Bronowski attributes the imagination to a "configuration"
   in the brain.* Configuration *seems vague here. What else shows uncertainty about exactly what happens in the brain? Does this uncertainty
   compromise the argument of this essay?*

THE WRITER

1. *Bronowski discusses the work of Galileo and Newton in the middle
   and at the end of his essay. What use does he make of their work? Does
   it justify placing them in the central and final positions?*
2. *What function is given to the mind by the title metaphor of reaching
   (later extended to symbols on p. 134)? What words does Bronowski use
   to indicate the objects reached for? What is the significance of his
   selecting these words?*
3. *Bronowski says that "seeing is also imagining." Write a brief essay
   exploring that assertion.*

Isaac Asimov

THE EUREKA PHENOMENON

In the old days, when I was writing a great deal of fiction, there would
come, once in a while, moments when I was stymied. Suddenly, I would
find I had written myself into a hole and could see no way out. To take
care of that, I developed a technique which invariably worked.

It was simply this—I went to the movies. Not just any movie. I had to
pick a movie which was loaded with action but which made no demands
on the intellect. As I watched, I did my best to avoid any conscious
thinking concerning my problem, and when I came out of the movie I
knew exactly what I would have to do to put the story back on the track.

It never failed.

In fact, when I was working on my doctoral dissertation, too many
years ago, I suddenly came across a flaw in my logic that I had not noticed
before and that knocked out everything I had done. In utter panic, I made
my way to a Bob Hope movie—and came out with the necessary change

in point of view.

It is my belief, you see, that thinking is a double phenomenon like breathing.

You can control breathing by deliberate voluntary action: you can breathe deeply and quickly, or you can hold your breath altogether, regardless of the body's needs at the time. This, however, doesn't work well for very long. Your chest muscles grow tired, your body clamors for more oxygen, or less, and you relax. The automatic involuntary control of breathing takes over, adjusts it to the body's needs and unless you have some respiratory disorder, you can forget about the whole thing.

Well, you can think by deliberate voluntary action, too, and I don't think it is much more efficient on the whole than voluntary breath control is. You can deliberately force your mind through channels of deductions and associations in search of a solution to some problem and before long you have dug mental furrows for yourself and find yourself circling round and round the same limited pathways. If those pathways yield no solution, no amount of further conscious thought will help.

On the other hand, if you let go, then the thinking process comes under automatic involuntary control and is more apt to take new pathways and make erratic associations you would not think of consciously. The solution will then come while you *think* you are *not* thinking.

The trouble is, though, that conscious thought involves no muscular action and so there is no sensation of physical weariness that would force you to quit. What's more, the panic of necessity tends to force you to go on uselessly, with each added bit of useless effort adding to the panic in a vicious cycle.

It is my feeling that it helps to relax, deliberately, by subjecting your mind to material complicated enough to occupy the voluntary faculty of thought, but superficial enough not to engage the deeper involuntary one. In my case, it is an action movie; in your case, it might be something else.

I suspect it is the involuntary faculty of thought that gives rise to what we call "a flash of intuition," something that I imagine must be merely the result of unnoticed thinking.

Perhaps the most famous flash of intuition in the history of science took place in the city of Syracuse in third-century B.C. Sicily. Bear with me and I will tell you the story—

About 250 B.C., the city of Syracuse was experiencing a kind of Golden Age. It was under the protection of the rising power of Rome, but it retained a king of its own and considerable self-government; it was prosperous; and it had a flourishing intellectual life.

The king was Hieron II, and he had commissioned a new golden crown from a goldsmith, to whom he had given an ingot of gold as raw material.

Hieron, being a practical man, had carefully weighed the ingot and then weighed the crown he received back. The two weights were precisely equal. Good deal!

But then he sat and thought for a while. Suppose the goldsmith had subtracted a little bit of the gold, not too much, and had substituted an equal weight of the considerably less valuable copper. The resulting alloy would still have the appearance of pure gold, but the goldsmith would be plus a quantity of gold over and above his fee. He would be buying gold with copper, so to speak, and Hieron would be neatly cheated.

Hieron didn't like the thought of being cheated any more than you or I would, but he didn't know how to find out for sure if he had been. He could scarcely punish the goldsmith on mere suspicion. What to do?

Fortunately, Hieron had an advantage few rulers in the history of the world could boast. He had a relative of considerable talent. The relative was named Archimedes and he probably had the greatest intellect the world was to see prior to the birth of Newton.

Archimedes was called in and was posed the problem. He had to determine whether the crown Hieron showed him was pure gold, or was gold to which a small but significant quantity of copper had been added.

If we were to reconstruct Archimedes' reasoning, it might go as follows. Gold was the densest known substance (at that time). Its density in modern terms is 19.3 grams per cubic centimeter. This means that a given weight of gold takes up less volume than the same weight of anything else! In fact, a given weight of pure gold takes up less volume than the same weight of any kind of impure gold.

The density of copper is 8.92 grams per cubic centimeter, just about half that of gold. If we consider 100 grams of pure gold, for instance, it is easy to calculate it to have a volume of 5.18 cubic centimeters. But suppose that 100 grams of what looked like pure gold was really only 90 grams of gold and 10 grams of copper. The 90 grams of gold would have a volume of 4.66 cubic centimeters, while the 10 grams of copper would have a volume of 1.12 cubic centimeters; for a total value of 5.78 cubic centimeters.

The difference between 5.18 cubic centimeters and 5.78 cubic centimeters is quite a noticeable one, and would instantly tell if the crown were of pure gold, or if it contained 10 per cent copper (with the missing 10 per cent of gold tucked neatly in the goldsmith's strongbox).

All one had to do, then, was measure the volume of the crown and compare it with the volume of the same weight of pure gold.

The mathematics of the time made it easy to measure the volume of many simple shapes: a cube, a sphere, a cone, a cylinder, any flattened object of simple regular shape and known thickness, and so on.

We can imagine Archimedes saying, "All that is necessary, sire, is to pound that crown flat, shape it into a square of uniform thickness, and then I can have the answer for you in a moment."

Whereupon Hieron must certainly have snatched the crown away and said, "No such thing. I can do that much without you; I've studied the principles of mathematics, too. This crown is a highly satisfactory work of art and I won't have it damaged. Just calculate its volume without in any way altering it."

But Greek mathematics had no way of determining the volume of anything with a shape as irregular as the crown, since integral calculus had not yet been invented (and wouldn't be for two thousand years, almost). Archimedes would have had to say, "There is no known way, sire, to carry through a non-destructive determination of volume."

"Then think of one," said Hieron testily.

And Archimedes must have set about thinking of one, and gotten nowhere. Nobody knows how long he thought, or how hard, or what hypotheses he considered and discarded, or any of the details.

What we do know is that, worn out with thinking, Archimedes decided to visit the public baths and relax. I think we are quite safe in saying that Archimedes had no intention of taking his problem to the baths with him. It would be ridiculous to imagine he would, for the public baths of a Greek metropolis weren't intended for that sort of thing.

The Greek baths were a place for relaxation. Half the social aristocracy of the town would be there and there was a great deal more to do than wash. One steamed one's self, got a massage, exercised, and engaged in general socializing. We can be sure that Archimedes intended to forget the stupid crown for a while.

One can envisage him engaging in light talk, discussing the latest news from Alexandria and Carthage, the latest scandals in town, the latest funny jokes at the expense of the country-squire Romans—and then he lowered himself into a nice hot bath which some bumbling attendant had filled too full.

The water in the bath slopped over as Archimedes got in. Did Archimedes notice that at once, or did he sigh, sink back, and paddle his feet awhile before noting the water-slop. I guess the latter. But, whether soon or late, he noticed, and that one fact, added to all the chains of reasoning his brain had been working on during the period of relaxation when it was unhampered by the comparative stupidities (even in Archimedes) of voluntary thought, gave Archimedes his answer in one blinding flash of insight.

Jumping out of the bath, he proceeded to run home at top speed through the streets of Syracuse. He did *not* bother to put on his clothes. The thought of Archimedes running naked through Syracuse has titillated dozens of generations of youngsters who have heard this story, but I must explain that the ancient Greeks were quite lighthearted in their attitude toward nudity. They thought no more of seeing a naked man on the streets of Syracuse, than we would on the Broadway stage.

And as he ran, Archimedes shouted over and over, "I've got it! I've got it!" Of course, knowing no English, he was compelled to shout it in Greek, so it came out, "*Eureka! Eureka!*"

Archimedes' solution was so simple that anyone could understand it— once Archimedes explained it.

If an object that is not affected by water in any way, is immersed in water, it is bound to displace an amount of water equal to its own volume, since two objects cannot occupy the same space at the same time.

Suppose, then, you had a vessel large enough to hold the crown and suppose it had a small overflow spout set into the middle of its side. And suppose further that the vessel was filled with water exactly to the spout, so that if the water level were raised a bit higher, however slightly, some would overflow.

Next, suppose that you carefully lower the crown into the water. The water level would rise by an amount equal to the volume of the crown, and that volume of water would pour out the overflow and be caught in a small vessel. Next, a lump of gold, known to be pure and exactly equal in weight to the crown, is also immersed in the water and again the level rises and the overflow is caught in a second vessel.

If the crown were pure gold, the overflow would be exactly the same in each case, and the volume of water caught in the two small vessels would be equal. If, however, the crown were of alloy, it would produce a larger overflow than the pure gold would and this would be easily noticeable.

What's more, the crown would in no way be harmed, defaced, or even as much as scratched. More important, Archimedes had discovered the "principle of buoyancy."

And was the crown pure gold? I've heard that it turned out to be alloy and that the goldsmith was executed, but I wouldn't swear to it.

How often does this "Eureka phenomenon" happen? How often is there this flash of deep insight during a moment of relaxation, this triumphant cry of "I've got it! I've got it!" which must surely be a moment of the purest ecstasy this sorry world can afford?

I wish there were some way we could tell. I suspect that in the history of science it happens *often*; I suspect that very few significant discoveries are made by the pure technique of voluntary thought; I suspect that voluntary thought may possibly prepare the ground (if even that), but that the final touch, the real inspiration, comes when thinking is under involuntary control.

But the world is in a conspiracy to hide the fact. Scientists are wedded to reason, to the meticulous working out of consequences from assumptions to the careful organization of experiments designed to check those consequences. If a certain line of experiments ends nowhere, it is omitted from the final report. If an inspired guess turns out to be correct, it is *not* reported as an inspired guess. Instead, a solid line of voluntary thought is invented after the fact to lead up to the thought, and that is what is inserted in the final report.

The result is that anyone reading scientific papers would swear that *nothing* took place but voluntary thought maintaining a steady clumping stride from origin to destination, and that just can't be true.

It's such a shame. Not only does it deprive science of much of its glamour (how much of the dramatic story in Watson's *Double Helix* do you suppose got into the final reports announcing the great discovery of the structure of DNA?[1]), but it hands over the important process of "insight," "inspiration," "revelation" to the mystic.

The scientist actually becomes ashamed of having what we might call a revelation, as though to have one is to betray reason—when actually what we call revelation in a man who has devoted his life to reasoned thought, is after all merely reasoned thought that is not under voluntary control.

Only once in a while in modern times do we ever get a glimpse into the workings of involuntary reasoning, and when we do, it is always fascinating. Consider, for instance, the case of Friedrich August Kekule von Stradonitz.

In Kekule's time, a century and a quarter ago, a subject of great interest to chemists was the structure of organic molecules (those associated with living tissue). Inorganic molecules were generally simple in the sense that they were made up of few atoms. Water molecules, for instance, are made up of two atoms of hydrogen and one of oxygen (H_2O). Molecules of ordinary salt are made up of one atom of sodium and one of chlorine ($NaCl$), and so on.

Organic molecules, on the other hand, often contained a large number of atoms. Ethyl alcohol molecules have two carbon atoms, six hydrogen atoms, and an oxygen atom (C_2H_6O); the molecule of ordinary cane sugar is $C_{12}H_{22}O_{11}$, and other molecules are even more complex.

Then, too, it is sufficient, in the case of inorganic molecules generally, merely to know the kinds and numbers of atoms in the molecule; in organic molecules, more is necessary. Thus, dimethyl ether has the formula C_2H_6O, just as ethyl alcohol does, and yet the two are quite different in properties. Apparently, the atoms are arranged differently within the molecules—but how to determine the arrangements?

In 1852, an English chemist, Edward Frankland, had noticed that the atoms of a particular element tended to combine with a fixed number of

1. I'll tell you, in case you're curious. None! [Asimov's note]. How Francis Crick and James Watson discovered the molecular structure of this vital substance is told in Watson's autobiographical book, *The Double Helix*.

other atoms. This combining number was called "valence." Kekule in
1858 reduced this notion to a system. The carbon atom, he decided (on
the basis of plenty of chemical evidence) had a valence of four; the
hydrogen atom, a valence of one; and the oxygen atom, a valence of two
(and so on).

Why not represent the atoms as their symbols plus a number of
attached dashes, that number being equal to the valence. Such atoms
could then be put together as though they were so many Tinker Toy
units and "structural formulas" could be built up.

It was possible to reason out that the structural formula of ethyl alcohol
was

$$
\begin{array}{ccc}
H & H & \\
| & | & \\
H-C-C-O-H, \\
| & | & \\
H & H &
\end{array}
$$

while that of dimethyl ether was

$$
\begin{array}{ccc}
H & & H \\
| & & | \\
H-C-O-C-H. \\
| & & | \\
H & & H
\end{array}
$$

In each case, there were two carbon atoms, each with four dashes
attached; six hydrogen atoms, each with one dash attached; and an
oxygen atom with two dashes attached. The molecules were built up of
the same components, but in different arrangements.

Kekule's theory worked beautifully. It has been immensely deepened
and elaborated since his day, but you can still find structures very much
like Kekule's Tinker Toy formulas in any modern chemical textbook.
They represent oversimplifications of the true situation, but they remain
extremely useful in practice even so.

The Kekule structures were applied to many organic molecules in the
years after 1858 and the similarities and contrasts in the structures neatly
matched similarities and contrasts in properties. The key to the rationalization of organic chemistry had, it seemed, been found.

Yet there was one disturbing fact. The well-known chemical benzene
wouldn't fit. It was known to have a molecule made up of equal numbers
of carbon and hydrogen atoms. Its molecular weight was known to be 78
and a single carbon-hydrogen combination had a weight of 13. Therefore, the benzene molecule had to contain six carbon-hydrogen combina-

tions and its formula had to be C_6H_6.

But that meant trouble. By the Kekule formulas, the hydrocarbons (molecules made up of carbon and hydrogen atoms only) could easily be envisioned as chains of carbon atoms with hydrogen atoms attached. If all the valences of the carbon atoms were filled with hydrogen atoms, as in "hexane," whose molecule looks like this—

$$
\begin{array}{ccccccc}
H & H & H & H & H & H \\
| & | & | & | & | & | \\
H-C-C-C-C-C-C-H \\
| & | & | & | & | & | \\
H & H & H & H & H & H
\end{array}
$$

the compound is said to be saturated. Such saturated hydrocarbons were found to have very little tendency to react with other substances.

If some of the valences were not filled, unused bonds were added to those connecting the carbon atoms. Double bonds were formed as in "hexene"—

$$
\begin{array}{ccccccc}
H & H & H & H & H & H \\
| & | & | & | & | & | \\
H-C-C-C=C-C-C-H \\
| & | & & & | & | \\
H & H & & & H & H
\end{array}
$$

Hexene is unsaturated, for that double bond has a tendency to open up and add other atoms. Hexene is chemically active.

When six carbons are present in a molecule, it takes fourteen hydrogen atoms to occupy all the valence bonds and make it inert—as in hexane. In hexene, on the other hand, there are only twelve hydrogens. If there were still fewer hydrogen atoms, there would be more than one double bond; there might even be triple bonds, and the compound would be still more active than hexene.

Yet benzene, which is C_6H_6 and has eight fewer hydrogen atoms than hexane, is *less* active than hexene, which has only two fewer hydrogen atoms than hexane. In fact, benzene is even less active than hexane itself. The six hydrogen atoms in the benzene molecule seem to satisfy the six carbon atoms to a greater extent than do the fourteen hydrogen atoms in hexane.

For heaven's sake, why?

This might seem unimportant. The Kekule formulas were so beautifully suitable in the case of so many compounds that one might simply dismiss benzene as an exception to the general rule.

Science, however, is not English grammar. You can't just categorize something as an exception. If the exception doesn't fit into the general system, then the general system must be wrong.

Or, take the more positive approach. An exception can often be made to fit into a general system, provided the general system is broadened. Such broadening generally represents a great advance and for this reason, exceptions ought to be paid great attention.

For some seven years, Kekule faced the problem of benzene and tried to puzzle out how a chain of six carbon atoms could be completely satisfied with as few as six hydrogen atoms in benzene and yet be left unsatisfied with twelve hydrogen atoms in hexene.

Nothing came to him!

And then one day in 1865 (he tells the story himself) he was in Ghent, Belgium, and in order to get to some destination, he boarded a public bus. He was tired and, undoubtedly, the droning beat of the horses' hooves on the cobblestones, lulled him. He fell into a comatose half-sleep.

In that sleep, he seemed to see a vision of atoms attaching themselves to each other in chains that moved about. (Why not? It was the sort of thing that constantly occupied his waking thoughts.) But then one chain twisted in such a way that head and tail joined, forming a ring—and Kekule woke with a start.

To himself, he must surely have shouted "Eureka," for indeed he had it. The six carbon atoms of benzene formed a ring and not a chain, so that the structural formula looked like this:

To be sure, there were still three double bonds, so you might think the molecule had to be very active—but now there was a difference. Atoms in a ring might be expected to have different properties from those in a chain and double bonds in one case might not have the properties of those in the other. At least, chemists could work on that assumption and see if it involved them in contradictions.

It didn't. The assumption worked excellently well. It turned out that organic molecules could be divided into two groups: aromatic and aliphatic. The former had the benzene ring (or certain other similar rings) as part of the structure and the latter did not. Allowing for different properties within each group, the Kekule structures worked very well.

For nearly seventy years, Kekule's vision held good in the hard field of actual chemical techniques, guiding the chemist through the jungle of reactions that led to the synthesis of more and more molecules. Then, in 1932, Linus Pauling applied quantum mechanics to chemical structure with sufficient subtlety to explain just why the benzene ring was so special and what had proven correct in practice proved correct in theory as well.

Other cases? Certainly.

In 1764, the Scottish engineer James Watt was working as an instrument maker for the University of Glasgow. The university gave him a model of a Newcomen steam engine, which didn't work well, and asked him to fix it. Watt fixed it without trouble, but even when it worked perfectly, it didn't work well. It was far too inefficient and consumed incredible quantities of fuel. Was there a way to improve that?

Thought didn't help; but a peaceful, relaxed walk on a Sunday afternoon did. Watt returned with the key notion in mind of using two separate chambers, one for steam only and one for cold water only, so that the same chamber did not have to be constantly cooled and reheated to the infinite waste of fuel.

The Irish mathematician William Rowan Hamilton worked up a theory of "quaternions" in 1843 but couldn't complete that theory until he grasped the fact that there were conditions under which $p \times q$ was not equal to $q \times p$. The necessary thought came to him in a flash one time when he was walking to town with his wife.

The German physiologist Otto Loewi was working on the mechanism of nerve action, in particular, on the chemicals produced by nerve endings. He awoke at 3 A.M. one night in 1921 with a perfectly clear notion of the type of experiment he would have to run to settle a key point that was puzzling him. He wrote it down and went back to sleep. When he woke in the morning, he found he couldn't remember what his inspiration had been. He remembered he had written it down, but he couldn't read his writing.

The next night, he woke again at 3 A.M. with the clear thought once more in mind. This time, he didn't fool around. He got up, dressed himself, went straight to the laboratory and began work. By 5 A.M. he had proved his point and the consequences of his findings became important enough in later years so that in 1936 he received a share in the Nobel prize in medicine and physiology.

How very often this sort of thing must happen, and what a shame that scientists are so devoted to their belief in conscious thought that they so consistently obscure the actual methods by which they obtain their results.

1971

THE READER

1. Does Asimov argue that science ought to abandon reasoned thought in favor of intuition?
2. Is cultivation of "the Eureka phenomenon" encouraged in any of the science courses you may have taken or are now taking? Why, or why not?
3. In the preceding essay, Bronowski discusses imagination and science. Are there points on which Asimov and Bronowski would seem to be in agreement concerning science?

THE WRITER

1. What does Asimov find wrong about scientific reports as they are customarily written? Do you agree? If scientific writing were not strictly reasonable, wouldn't there be a danger of misrepresenting science?
2. Have you ever experienced anything like "the Eureka phenomenon" Asimov describes? If so, write an account of what happened. Tell what your feelings were when the phenomenon occurred. Did you ever report the discovery in just that way to any one else (to a teacher, for example)? If so, what was the other person's response?

Education

Education

John Holt

HOW TEACHERS MAKE CHILDREN
HATE READING

When I was teaching English at the Colorado Rocky Mountain School, I used to ask my students the kinds of questions that English teachers usually ask about reading assignments—questions designed to bring out the points that *I* had decided *they* should know. They, on their part, would try to get me to give them hints and clues as to what I wanted. It was a game of wits. I never gave my students an opportunity to say what they really thought about a book.

I gave vocabulary drills and quizzes too. I told my students that every time they came upon a word in their book they did not understand, they were to look it up in the dictionary. I even devised special kinds of vocabulary tests, allowing them to use their books to see how the words were used. But looking back, I realize that these tests, along with many of my methods, were foolish.

My sister was the first person who made me question my conventional ideas about teaching English. She had a son in the seventh grade in a fairly good public school. His teacher had asked the class to read Cooper's *The Deerslayer*. The choice was bad enough in itself; whether looking at man or nature, Cooper was superficial, inaccurate and sentimental, and his writing is ponderous and ornate. But to make matters worse, this teacher had decided to give the book the microscope and x-ray treatment. He made the students look up and memorize not only the definitions but the derivations of every big word that came along—and there were plenty. Every chapter was followed by close questioning and testing to make sure the students "understood" everything.

Being then, as I said, conventional, I began to defend the teacher, who was a good friend of mine, against my sister's criticisms. The argument soon grew hot. What was wrong with making sure that children understood everything they read? My sister answered that until this year her boy had always loved reading, and had read a lot on his own; now he had stopped. (He was not really to start again for many years.)

Still I persisted. If children didn't look up the words they didn't know, how would they ever learn them? My sister said, "Don't be silly! when you were little you had a huge vocabulary, and were always reading very grown-up books. When did you ever look up a word in a dictionary?"

She had me. I don't know that we had a dictionary at home; if we did, I didn't use it. I don't use one today. In my life I doubt that I have looked up as many as fifty words, perhaps not even half that.

Since then I have talked about this with a number of teachers. More than once I have said, "According to tests, educated and literate people like you have a vocabulary of about twenty-five thousand words. How many of these did you learn by looking them up in a dictionary?" They usually are startled. Few claim to have looked up even as many as a thousand. How did they learn the rest?

They learned them just as they learned to talk—by meeting words over and over again, in different contexts, until they saw how they fitted.

Unfortunately, we English teachers are easily hung up on this matter of understanding. Why should children understand everything they read? Why should anyone? Does anyone? I don't, and I never did. I was always reading books that teachers would have said were "too hard" for me, books full of words I didn't know. That's how I got to be a good reader. When about ten, I read all the D'Artagnan stories and loved them. It didn't trouble me in the least that I didn't know why France was at war with England or who was quarreling with whom in the French court or why the Musketeers should always be at odds with Cardinal Richelieu's men. I didn't even know who the Cardinal was, except that he was a dangerous and powerful man that my friends had to watch out for. This was all I needed to know.

Having said this, I will now say that I think a big, unabridged dictionary is a fine thing to have in any home or classroom. No book is more fun to browse around in—*if* you're not made to. Children, depending on their age, will find many pleasant and interesting things to do with a big dictionary. They can look up funny-sounding words, which they like, or words that nobody else in the class has ever heard of, which they like, or long words, which they like, or forbidden words, which they like best of all. At a certain age, and particularly with a little encouragement from parents or teachers, they may become very interested in where words came from and when they came into the language and how their meanings have changed over the years. But exploring for the fun of it is very different from looking up words out of your reading because you're going to get into trouble with your teacher if you don't.

While teaching fifth grade two years or so after the argument with my sister, I began to think again about reading. The children in my class were supposed to fill out a card—just the title and author and a one-sentence summary—for every book they read. I was not running a competition to see which child could read the most books, a competition that almost always leads to cheating. I just wanted to know what the children were reading. After a while it became clear that many of these very bright kids, from highly literate and even literary backgrounds, read very few books and deeply disliked reading. Why should this be?

At this time I was coming to realize, as I described in my book *How Children Fail*, that for most children school was a place of danger, and their main business in school was staying out of danger as much as possible. I now began to see also that books were among the most dangerous things in school.

From the very beginning of school we make books and reading a constant source of possible failure and public humiliation. When children are little we make them read aloud, before the teacher and other children, so that we can be sure they "know" all the words they are reading. This means that when they don't know a word, they are going to make a mistake, right in front of everyone. Instantly they are made to realize that they have done something wrong. Perhaps some of the other children will begin to wave their hands and say, "Ooooh! O-o-o-oh!" Perhaps they will just giggle, or nudge each other, or make a face. Perhaps the teacher will say, "Are you sure?" or ask someone else what he thinks. Or perhaps, if the teacher is kindly, she will just smile a sweet, sad smile—often one of the most painful punishments a child can suffer in school. In any case, the child who has made the mistake knows he has made it, and feels foolish, stupid, and ashamed, just as any of us would in his shoes.

Before long many children associate books and reading with mistakes, real or feared, and penalties and humiliation. This may not seem sensible, but it is natural. Mark Twain once said that a cat that sat on a hot stove lid would never sit on one again—but it would never sit on a cold one either. As true of children as of cats. If they, so to speak, sit on a hot book a few times, if books cause them humiliation and pain, they are likely to decide that the safest thing to do is to leave all books alone.

After having taught fifth-grade classes for four years I felt quite sure of this theory. In my next class were many children who had had great trouble with schoolwork, particularly reading. I decided to try at all costs to rid them of their fear and dislike of books, and to get them to read oftener and more adventurously.

One day soon after school had started, I said to them, "Now I'm going to say something about reading that you have probably never heard a teacher say before. I would like you to read a lot of books this year, but I want you to read them only for pleasure. I am not going to ask you questions to find out whether you understand the books or not. If you understand enough of a book to enjoy it and want to go on reading it, that's enough for me. Also I'm not going to ask you what words mean.

"Finally," I said, "I don't want you to feel that just because you start a book, you have to finish it. Give an author thirty or forty pages or so to get his story going. Then if you don't like the characters and don't care what happens to them, close the book, put it away, and get another. I don't care whether the books are easy or hard, short or long, as long as you enjoy them. Furthermore I'm putting all this in a letter to your parents, so they won't feel they have to quiz and heckle you about books at home."

The children sat stunned and silent. Was this a teacher talking? One girl, who had just come to us from a school where she had had a very hard time, and who proved to be one of the most interesting, lively, and intelligent children I have ever known, looked at me steadily for a long time after I had finished. Then, still looking at me, she said slowly and solemnly, "Mr. Holt, do you really mean that?" I said just as solemnly, "I mean every word of it."

Apparently she decided to believe me. The first book she read was Dr. Seuss's *How the Grinch Stole Christmas*, not a hard book even for most third graders. For a while she read a number of books on this level. Perhaps she was clearing up some confusion about reading that her teachers, in their hurry to get her up to "grade level," had never given her enough time to clear up. After she had been in the class six weeks or so and we had become good friends, I very tentatively suggested that, since she was a skillful rider and loved horses, she might like to read *National Velvet*. I made my sell as soft as possible, saying only that it was about a girl who loved and rode horses, and that if she didn't like it, she could put it back. She tried it, and though she must have found it quite a bit harder than what she had been reading, finished it and liked it very much.

During the spring she really astonished me, however. One day, in one of our many free periods, she was reading at her desk. From a glimpse of the illustrations I thought I knew what the book was. I said to myself, "It can't be," and went to take a closer look. Sure enough, she was reading *Moby Dick*, in the edition with woodcuts by Rockwell Kent. When I came close to her desk she looked up. I said, "Are you really reading that?" She said she was. I said, "Do you like it?" She said, "Oh, yes, it's neat!" I said, "Don't you find parts of it rather heavy going?" She answered "Oh, sure, but I just skip over those parts and go on to the next good part."

This is exactly what reading should be and in school so seldom is—an exciting, joyous adventure. Find something, dive into it, take the good parts, skip the bad parts, get what you can out of it, go on to something else. How different is our mean-spirited, picky insistence that every child get every last little scrap of "understanding" that can be dug out of a book.

For teachers who really enjoy doing it, and will do it with gusto, reading aloud is a very good idea. I have found that not just fifth graders but even ninth and eleventh graders enjoy it. Jack London's "To Build a Fire" is a good read-aloud story. So are ghost stories, and "August Heat," by W. F. Harvey, and "The Monkey's Paw," by W. W. Jacobs, are among the best. Shirley Jackson's "The Lottery" is sure-fire, and will raise all kinds of questions for discussion and argument. Because of a TV program they had seen and that excited them, I once started reading my fifth graders William Golding's Lord of the Flies, thinking to read only a few chapters, but they made me read it to the end.

In my early fifth-grade classes the children usually were of high IQ, came from literate backgrounds and were generally felt to be succeeding in school. Yet it was astonishingly hard for most of those children to express themselves in speech or in writing. I have known a number of five-year-olds who were considerably more articulate than most of the fifth graders I have known in school. Asked to speak, my fifth graders were covered with embarrassment; many refused altogether. Asked to write, they would sit for minutes on end, staring at the paper. It was hard for most of them to get down a half page of writing, even on what seemed to be interesting topics or topics they chose themselves.

In desperation I hit on a device that I named the Composition Derby. I divided the class into teams, and told them that when I said, "Go," they were to start writing something. It could be about anything they wanted, but it had to be about something—they couldn't just write "dog dog dog dog" on the paper. It could be true stories, descriptions of people or places or events, wishes, made-up stories, dreams—anything they liked. Spelling didn't count, so they didn't have to worry about it. When I said, "Stop," they were to stop and count up the words they had written. The team that wrote the most words would win the derby.

It was a success in many ways and for many reasons. The first surprise was that the two children who consistently wrote the most words were two of the least successful students in the class. They were bright, but they had always had a very hard time in school. Both were very bad spellers, and worrying about this had slowed down their writing without improving their spelling. When they were free of this worry and could let themselves go, they found hidden and unsuspected talents.

One of the two, a very driven and anxious little boy, used to write long

adventures, or misadventures, in which I was the central character—
"The Day Mr. Holt Went to Jail," "The Day Mr. Holt Fell Into the
Hole," "The Day Mr. Holt Got Run Over," and so on. These were very
funny, and the class enjoyed hearing me read them aloud. One day I asked
the class to write a derby on a topic I would give them. They groaned;
they liked picking their own. "Wait till you hear it," I said. "It's 'The Day
the School Burned Down.'"

With a shout of approval and joy they went to work, and wrote
furiously for 20 minutes or more, laughing and chuckling as they wrote.
The papers were all much alike; in them the children danced around the
burning building, throwing in books and driving me and the other
teachers back in when we tried to escape.

In our first derby the class wrote an average of about ten words a
minute; after a few months their average was over 20. Some of the slower
writers tripled their output. Even the slowest, one of whom was the best
student in the class, were writing 15 words a minute. More important,
almost all the children enjoyed the derbies and wrote interesting things.

Some time later I learned that Professor S. I. Hayakawa, teaching
freshman English, had invented a better technique. Every day in class he
asked his students to write without stopping for about half an hour. They
could write on whatever topic or topics they chose, but the important
thing was not to stop. If they ran dry, they were to copy their last
sentence over and over again until new ideas came. Usually they came
before the sentence had been copied once. I use this idea in my own
classes, and call this kind of paper a Non-Stop. Sometimes I ask students
to write a Non-Stop on an assigned topic, more often on anything they
choose. Once in a while I ask them to count up how many words they
have written, though I rarely ask them to tell me; it is for their own
information. Sometimes these papers are to be handed in; often they are
what I call private papers, for the students' eyes alone.

The private paper has proved very useful. In the first place, in any
English class—certainly any large English class—if the amount the students write is limited by what the teacher can find time to correct, or
even to read, the students will not write nearly enough. The only remedy
is to have them write a great deal that the teacher does not read. In the
second place, students writing for themselves will write about many
things that they would never write on a paper to be handed in, once they
have learned (sometimes it takes a while) that the teacher means what he
says about the papers' being private. This is important, not just because
it enables them to get things off their chest, but also because they are
most likely to write well, and to pay attention to how they write, when
they are writing about something important to them.

Some English teachers, when they first hear about private papers, object that students do not benefit from writing papers unless the papers are corrected. I disagree for several reasons. First, most students, particularly poor students, do not read the corrections on their papers; it is boring, even painful. Second, even when they do read these corrections, they do not get much help from them, do not build the teacher's suggestions into their writing. This is true even when they really believe the teacher knows what he is talking about.

Third, and most important, we learn to write by writing, not by reading other people's ideas about writing. What most students need above all else is practice in writing, and particularly in writing about things that matter to them, so that they will begin to feel the satisfaction that comes from getting important thoughts down in words and will care about stating these thoughts forcefully and clearly.

Teachers of English—or, as some schools say (ugh!), Language Arts— spend a lot of time and effort on spelling. Most of it is wasted; it does little good, and often more harm than good. We should ask ourselves, "How do good spellers spell? What do they do when they are not sure which spelling of a word is right?" I have asked this of a number of good spellers. Their answer never varies. They do not rush for a dictionary or rack their brains trying to remember some rules. They write down the word both ways, or several ways, look at them and pick the one that looks best. Usually they are right.

Good spellers know what words look like and even, in their writing muscles, feel like. They have a good set of word images in their minds, and are willing to trust these images. The things we do to "teach" spelling to children do little to develop these skills or talents, and much to destroy them or prevent them from developing.

The first and worst thing we do is to make children anxious about spelling. We treat a misspelled word like a crime and penalize the misspeller severely; many teachers talk of making children develop a "spelling conscience," and fail otherwise excellent papers because of a few spelling mistakes. This is self-defeating. When we are anxious, we don't perceive clearly or remember what we once perceived. Everyone knows how hard it is to recall even simple things when under emotional pressure; the harder we rack our brains, the less easy it is to find what we are looking for. If we are anxious enough, we will not trust the messages that memory sends us. Many children spell badly because although their first hunches about how to spell a word may be correct, they are afraid to trust them. I have often seen on children's papers a word correctly spelled, then crossed out and misspelled.

There are some tricks that might help children get sharper word images. Some teachers may be using them. One is the trick of air writing; that is, of "writing" a word in the air with a finger and "seeing" the image so formed. I did this quite a bit with fifth graders, using either the air or the top of a desk, on which their fingers left no mark. Many of them were tremendously excited by this. I can still hear them saying, "There's nothing there, but I can see it!" It seemed like black magic. I remember that when I was little I loved to write in the air. It was effortless, voluptuous, satisfying, and it was fun to see the word appear in the air. I used to write "Money Money Money," not so much because I didn't have any as because I liked the way it felt, particularly that y at the end, with its swooping tail.

Another thing to help sharpen children's image-making machinery is taking very quick looks at words—or other things. The conventional machine for doing this is the tachistoscope. But these are expensive, so expensive that most children can have few chances to use them, if any at all. With some three-by-five and four-by-eight file cards you can get the same effect. On the little cards you put the words or the pictures that the child is going to look at. You hold the larger card over the card to be read, uncover it for a split second with a quick wrist motion, then cover it up again. Thus you have a tachistoscope that costs one cent and that any child can work by himself.

Once when substituting in a first-grade class, I thought that the children, who were just beginning to read and write, might enjoy some of the kind of free, nonstop writing that my fifth graders had. One day about 40 minutes before lunch, I asked them all to take pencil and paper and start writing about anything they wanted to. They seemed to like the idea, but right away one child said anxiously, "Suppose we can't spell a word."

"Don't worry about it," I said. "Just spell it the best way you can."

A heavy silence settled on the room. All I could see were still pencils and anxious faces. This was clearly not the right approach. So I said, "All right, I'll tell you what we'll do. Any time you want to know how to spell a word, tell me and I'll write it on the board."

They breathed a sigh of relief and went to work. Soon requests for words were coming fast; as soon as I wrote one, someone asked me another. By lunchtime, when most of the children were still busily writing, the board was full. What was interesting was that most of the words they had asked for were much longer and more complicated than anything in their reading books or workbooks. Freed from worry about spelling, they were willing to use the most difficult and interesting words that they knew.

The words were still on the board when we began school next day. Before I began to erase them, I said to the children, "Listen, everyone. I have to erase these words, but before I do, just out of curiosity, I'd like to see if you remember some of them."

The result was surprising. I had expected that the child who had asked for and used a word might remember it, but I did not think many others would. But many of the children still knew many of the words. How had they learned them? I suppose each time I wrote a word on the board a number of children had looked up, relaxed yet curious, just to see what the word looked like, and these images and the sound of my voice saying the word had stuck in their minds until the next day. This, it seems to me, is how children may best learn to write and spell.

What can a parent do if a school, or a teacher, is spoiling the language for a child by teaching it in some tired way? First, try to get them to change or at least let them know you are eager for a change. Talk to other parents; push some of these ideas in the PTA; talk to the English department at the school; talk to the child's own teacher. Many teachers and schools want to know what the parents want.

If the school or teacher cannot be persuaded, then what? Perhaps all you can do is try not to let your child become too bored or discouraged or worried by what is happening in school. Help him meet the school's demands, foolish though they may seem, and try to provide more interesting alternatives at home—plenty of books and conversation, and a serious and respectful audience when a child wants to talk. Nothing that ever happened to me in English classes at school was as helpful to me as the long conversations I used to have every summer with my uncle, who made me feel that the difference in our ages was not important and that he was really interested in what I had to say.

At the end of her freshman year in college a girl I know wrote home to her mother, "Hooray! Hooray! Just think—I never have to take English any more!" But this girl had always been an excellent English student, had always loved books, writing, ideas. It seems unnecessary and foolish and wrong that English teachers should so often take what should be the most flexible, exciting, and creative of all school courses and make it into something that most children can hardly wait to see the last of. Let's hope that we can and soon will begin to do much better.

1967

THE READER

1. *What are the major indictments Holt makes against conventional teaching methods? What alternatives does he propose?*
2. *Booth discusses various metaphors (including man as machine and man as animal) that underline different theories of education ("Is There Any Knowledge That a Man Must Have?" p. 196). How would Holt respond to these metaphors? If Holt were to construct a metaphor of his own, what might it be?*
3. *Is the kind of teaching that Holt describes likely to lead to students' having the knowledge that Booth believes essential?*

THE WRITER

1. Here are two accounts of a young boy's going to school, the second a summary or précis of the first. Determine what has been removed from the original in the summary. Then write a short comparison of original and summary from Holt's educational point of view, as it can be inferred from his essay.

His days were rich in formal experience. Wearing overalls and an old sweater (the accepted uniform of the private seminary), he sallied forth at morn accompanied by a nurse or a parent and walked (or was pulled) two blocks to a corner where the school bus made a flag stop. This flashy vehicle was as punctual as death: seeing us waiting at the cold curb, it would sweep to a halt, open its mouth, suck the boy in, and spring away with an angry growl. It was a good deal like a train picking up a bag of mail. At school the scholar was worked on for six or seven hours by half a dozen teachers and a nurse, and was revived on orange juice in midmorning. In a cinder court he played games supervised by an athletic instructor, and in a cafeteria he ate lunch worked out by a dietitian.

—E. B. White, "Education"

His days followed a set routine. He wore overalls and an old sweater, as everyone else did in his school. In the morning, a parent or nurse walked the two blocks with him to the corner where he met the school bus. The bus was always on time. During the six or seven hours of the school day, he had six teachers. The school also employed a nurse and a dietitian. Games were supervised. The children ate in the cafeteria. Orange juice was served during the morning session.

—End-of-year examinations in English for college-bound students, grades 9–12, Commission on English

2. Holt uses some unconventional methods to teach students to read and to enjoy reading. Write about a teacher whose methods brought a subject or an idea to life for you. What are the qualities that distinguish a good teacher?

Barbara Ehrenreich

COLLEGE TODAY: TUNE IN, DROP OUT, AND TAKE THE CASH

I would do anything to keep my kids from going to college. It's not just that the cost of tuition is now about the same as a good-size endowment; I am afraid of what will happen to them there. A recent news story described an apparently brilliant college senior who was abandoning her plans for medical school because a medical career couldn't give her "a sufficient return on her investment." Now I would have thought that the practice of medicine—supplemented, perhaps, with a little unnecessary surgery—could support even the most gluttonous standard of living. But no, this young woman will soon be forgetting her organic chemistry, her calculus, her Western Civ, to make a quick killing in finance.

I've heard worse stories, too, like the case of one local boy—a decent, likable kid who went off to college with his hair up in orange spikes, an earring in one ear and a longstanding commitment to the legalization of marijuana and came back for Thanskgiving wearing a Le Tigre shirt and talking about stock options. So it is with deep foreboding that I look at my own children, so unspoiled, so dashing in their little New Wave outfits, so ignorant of the rudiments of capital accumulation. Anything could happen in college. I tell them: "You could fall in with the wrong crowd. You could meet some boy who'd want to take you up to his room and show you his portfolio. Some cynical upper classman could come along and offer you a debenture or a soybean future or whatever, and I hope I don't have to tell you what that could lead to."

Even if college were free I would be opposed to it these days, but the fact that we are expected to pay to have our children transformed into preppies or worse only heightens my antagonism. Between the coming cutbacks in financial aid and the continuing increases in tuition, I will have passed the point of total destitution well before my youngest one's graduation. And I have no reason to believe I will be invited to that event either, because no up-and-coming young man will want his frat brothers to know that his mother is a bag lady. When I think of myself rooting through public trash cans while my children are off on some bucolic campus learning to hold their liquor along with future stockbrokers and purveyors of military hardware, then I too must wonder what constitutes a sufficient return on an investment.

I began to discourage them from college at a very early age. While other children were spending their pre-K years practicing taking the S.A.T.'s in crayon, I encouraged mine to hang out in the kitchen and express themselves in Play-Doh. There were no computer summer camps for my children, no interviews at academically renowned nursery schools. As soon as they could read—an achievement I delayed as long as possible by promising I would still be reading aloud to them until they were 35 or so—I left brochures around the house describing the local college of cosmetology and various correspondence schools advertised on matchbooks. At P.T.A. meetings, while the other mothers clamored for more homework and basics, I ran a lonely campaign for a two-hour recess and an afternoon cookie break. Now that we're in the teen and preteen years, they do sometimes sneak off to their rooms to study, but I can usually distract them with offers of a lift, one way, to the shopping mall.

As they've gotten older and smarter, I've also had to come up with ever more ingenious arguments against college. I tell them that the first thing they will learn from studying the liberal arts is that hardly any of the Great Persons of history were college graduates. It wasn't Marcus Aurelius, Ph.D., or Catherine de' Medici, M.B.A.[1] In fact many of the truly stellar figures, like Joan of Arc and Thomas Edison, were, if I remember right, grade school dropouts; and much of Western philosophy consists of the offhand remarks of carpenters, stonemasons and unemployable misfits. I tell them also about the many members of our own extended family who have never been to college and are perfectly content to be bartenders, telephone operators, factory operatives and the like. And of course I tell them about the many other family members who have been to college and are therefore somewhat less content to be bartenders, telephone operators, etc.

It is not that I'm opposed to learning or even to the learned professions. On the contrary, I am proud that my children are dedicated readers and will be prouder still if they eventually take up some honorable intellectual endeavor, such as philosophy, history, poetry or pure science. But I also know that the job market for, say, historians is very similar to what it is for blacksmiths, so that if you intend to devote your life to the study of 17th-century social movements or the Peloponnesian War,[2] it is a good idea to start by learning to drive a cab. Hence, I tell my son, who shows some promise as a classicist, to avoid Dartmouth where (as I know from a

---

1. Marcus Aurelius: Roman philosopher (A.D. 121–180); Catherine de' Medici: Italian who became queen of France (1519–89).

2. A war involving Athens and other Greek states, 431–404 B.C.

recent book on the subject) he might be drawn into an unsavory right-wing student group, and to keep away from Princeton, where he would have to be interviewed extensively before he could even eat dinner, and to apply himself instead to a study of a Manhattan street map. Anything he wishes to know about Virgil or Hesiod[3] he can find out from a tape deck installed just under the meter.

I suspect that other parents will soon see the wisdom of having their children skip college and go straight on to their careers. If, for example, a son is interested in something that has no market value, such as the liberal arts, the social sciences and many of the natural ones, he should be encouraged to become a busboy at once, without squandering his parents' life savings.

If, on the other hand, a child is drawn to a more highly regarded occupation, like currency speculation, she should be sent into it straight from high school and before her mind is beclouded with the existential dilemmas, habits of critical inquiry and other possible byproducts of higher education. For example, the parents of that young woman who switched from premed to finance should have taken her aside right after her high school prom and handed her the $60,000 or so they were planning to spend on college tuition. "Here, sweetie," they might have said. "It's yours to invest in something that pays better than calculus or chemistry. Just try to get 15 percent on the dollar."

The colleges will soon have to close, of course, and the professors—many of whom are already reduced to wearing second-hand denims and accepting tips from students—will join the best of their former students as janitors or key-punch operators. It will probably not be any harder than it is now to get an education, however. If you want to know about cosmology or French literature or some other recondite field, you'll always be able to ask a cabdriver.

1985

3. Virgil: Roman poet (70–19 B.C.); Hesiod: Greek poet (eighth century B.C.).

James Thurber

UNIVERSITY DAYS

I passed all the other courses that I took at my university, but I could never pass botany. This was because all botany students had to spend several hours a week in a laboratory looking through a microscope at plant cells, and I could never see through a microscope. I never once saw a cell through a microscope. This used to enrage my instructor. He would wander around the laboratory pleased with the progress all the students were making in drawing the involved and, so I am told, interesting structure of flower cells, until he came to me. I would just be standing there. "I can't see anything," I would say. He would begin patiently enough, explaining how anybody can see through a microscope, but he would always end up in a fury, claiming that I could *too* see through a microscope but just pretended that I couldn't. "It takes away from the beauty of flowers anyway," I used to tell him. "We are not concerned with beauty in this course," he would say. "We are concerned solely with what I may call the *mechanics* of flars." "Well," I'd say, "I can't see anything." "Try it just once again," he'd say, and I would put my eye to the microscope and see nothing at all, except now and again a nebulous milky substance—a phenomenon of maladjustment. You were supposed to see a vivid, restless clockwork of sharply defined plant cells. "I see what looks like a lot of milk," I would tell him. This, he claimed, was the result of my not having adjusted the microscope properly, so he would readjust it for me, or rather, for himself. And I would look again and see milk.

I finally took a deferred pass, as they called it, and waited a year and tried again. (You had to pass one of the biological sciences or you couldn't graduate.) The professor had come back from vacation brown as a berry, bright-eyed, and eager to explain cell-structure again to his classes. "Well," he said to me, cheerily, when we met in the first laboratory hour of the semester, "we're going to see cells this time, aren't we?" "Yes, sir," I said. Students to right of me and to left of me and in front of me were seeing cells; what's more, they were quietly drawing pictures of them in their notebooks. Of course, I didn't see anything.

"We'll try it," the professor said to me, grimly, "with every adjustment of the microscope known to man. As God is my witness, I'll arrange this glass so that you see cells through it or I'll give up teaching. In twenty-two years of botany, I—" He cut off abruptly for he was beginning to quiver all over, like Lionel Barrymore,[1] and he genuinely wished to hold onto his temper; his scenes with me had taken a great deal out of him.

1. Famed American actor (1878–1954), especially noted for elderly roles.

So we tried it with every adjustment of the microscope known to man. With only one of them did I see anything but blackness or the familiar lacteal opacity, and that time I saw, to my pleasure and amazement, a variegated constellation of flecks, specks, and dots. These I hastily drew. The instructor, noting my activity, came back from an adjoining desk, a smile on his lips and his eyebrows high in hope. He looked at my cell drawing. "What's that?" he demanded, with a hint of a squeal in his voice. "That's what I saw," I said. "You didn't, you didn't, you *didn't*!" he screamed, losing control of his temper instantly, and he bent over and squinted into the microscope. His head snapped up. "That's your eye!" he shouted. "You've fixed the lens so that it reflects! You've drawn your eye!"

Another course that I didn't like, but somehow managed to pass, was economics. I went to that class straight from the botany class, which didn't help me any in understanding either subject. I used to get them mixed up. But not as mixed up as another student in my economics class who came there direct from a physics laboratory. He was a tackle on the football team, named Bolenciecwcz. At that time Ohio State University had one of the best football teams in the country, and Bolenciecwcz was one of its outstanding stars. In order to be eligible to play it was necessary for him to keep up in his studies, a very difficult matter, for while he was not dumber than an ox he was not any smarter. Most of his professors were lenient and helped him along. None gave him more hints in answering questions or asked him simpler ones than the economics professor, a thin, timid man named Bassum. One day when we were on the subject of transportation and distribution, it came Bolenciecwcz's turn to answer a question. "Name one means of transportation," the professor said to him. No light came into the big tackle's eyes. "Just any means of transportation," said the professor. Bolenciecwcz sat staring at him. "That is," pursued the professor, "any medium, agency, or method of going from one place to another." Bolenciecwcz had the look of a man who is being led into a trap. "You may choose among steam, horsedrawn, or electrically propelled vehicles," said the instructor. "I might suggest the one which we commonly take in making long journeys across land." There was a profound silence in which everybody stirred uneasily, including Bolenciecwcz and Mr. Bassum, Mr. Bassum abruptly broke this silence in an amazing manner. "Choo-choo-choo," he said, in a low voice, and turned instantly scarlet. He glanced appealingly around the room. All of us, of course, shared Mr. Bassum's desire that Bolenciecwcz should stay abreast of the class in economics, for the Illinois game, one of the hardest and most important of the season, was only a week off. "Toot, toot, too-tooooooot!" some student with a deep voice moaned, and we all looked encouragingly at Bolenciecwcz. Somebody else gave a fine imitation of a locomotive letting off steam. Mr. Bassum himself rounded off the little show. "Ding, dong, ding, dong," he said, hopefully. Bolenciecwcz was staring at the floor now, trying to think, his great brow furrowed, his huge hands rubbing together, his face red.

"How did you come to college this year, Mr. Bolenciecwcz?" asked the professor. "*Chuffa* chuffa, *chuffa* chuffa."

"M'father sent me," said the football player.

"What on?" asked Bassum.

"I git an 'lowance," said the tackle, in a low, husky voice, obviously embarrassed.

"No, no," said Bassum. "Name a means of transportation. What did you *ride* here on?"

"Train," said Bolenciecwcz.

"Quite right," said the professor. "Now, Mr. Nugent, will you tell us—"

If I went through anguish in botany and economics—for different reasons—gymnasium work was even worse. I don't even like to think about it. They wouldn't let you play games or join in the exercises with your glasses on and I couldn't see with mine off. I bumped into professors, horizontal bars, agricultural students, and swinging iron rings. Not being able to see, I could take it but I couldn't dish it out. Also, in order to pass gymnasium (and you had to pass it to graduate) you had to learn to swim if you didn't know how. I didn't like the swimming pool, I didn't like swimming, and I didn't like the swimming instructor, and after all these years I still don't. I never swam but I passed my gym work anyway, by having another student give my gymnasium number (978) and swim across the pool in my place. He was a quiet, amiable blond youth, number 473, and he would have seen through a microscope for me if we could have got away with it, but we couldn't get away with it. Another thing I didn't like about gymnasium work was that they made you strip the day you registered. It is impossible for me to be happy when I am stripped and being asked a lot of questions. Still, I did better than a lanky agricultural student who was cross-examined just before I was. They asked each student what college he was in—that is, whether Arts, Engineering, Commerce, or Agriculture. "What college are you in?" the instructor snapped at the youth in front of me. "Ohio State University," he said promptly.

It wasn't that agricultural student but it was another a whole lot like him who decided to take up journalism, possibly on the ground that when farming went to hell he could fall back on newspaper work. He didn't realize, of course, that that would be very much like falling back full-length on a kit of carpenter's tools. Haskins didn't seem cut out for journalism, being too embarrassed to talk to anybody and unable to use a typewriter, but the editor of the college paper assigned him to the cow barns, the sheep house, the horse pavilion, and the animal husbandry department generally. This was a genuinely big "beat," for it took up five times as much ground and got ten times as great a legislative appropriation as the College of Liberal Arts. The agricultural student knew animals, but nevertheless his stories were dull and colorlessly written. He took all afternoon on each of them, on account of having to hunt for each letter on the typewriter. Once in a while he had to ask somebody to help him hunt. "C" and "L," in particular, were hard letters for him to find. His editor finally got pretty much annoyed at the farmer-journalist because his pieces were so uninteresting. "See here, Haskins," he snapped at him one day, "why is it we never have anything hot from you on the horse pavilion? Here we have two hundred head of horses on this campus —more than any other university in the Western Conference[2] except Purdue—and yet you never get any real lowdown on them. Now shoot over to the horse barns and dig up something lively." Haskins shambled out and came back in about an hour; he said he had something. "Well, start it off snappily," said the editor. "Something people will read." Haskins set to work and in a couple of hours brought a sheet of typewritten paper to the desk; it was a two-hundred-word story about some disease that had broken out among the horses. Its opening sentence was simple but arresting. It read: "Who has noticed the sores on the tops of the horses in the animal husbandry building?"

Ohio State was a land grant university and therefore two years of military drill was compulsory. We drilled with old Springfield rifles and studied the tactics of the Civil War even though the World War was going on at the time. At 11 o'clock each morning thousands of freshmen and sophomores used to deploy over the campus, moodily creeping up on the old chemistry building. It was good training for the kind of warfare that was waged at Shiloh[3] but it had no connection with what was going on in Europe. Some people used to think there was German money behind it, but they didn't dare say so or they would have been thrown in jail as German spies. It was a period of muddy thought and marked, I believe, the decline of higher education in the Middle West.

As a soldier I was never any good at all. Most of the cadets were glumly indifferent soldiers, but I was no good at all. Once General Littlefield, who was commandant of the cadet corps, popped up in front of me during regimental drill and snapped, "You are the main trouble with this university!" I think he meant that my type was the main trouble with the university but he may have meant me individually. I was mediocre at drill, certainly—that is, until my senior year. By that time I had drilled longer than anybody else in the Western Conference, having failed at military at the end of each preceding year so that I had to do it all over again. I was the only senior still in uniform. The uniform which, when

2. The Big Ten.
3. In southwestern Tennessee, site of 1862 Union victory.

new, had made me look like an interurban railway conductor, now that it had become faded and too tight made me look like Bert Williams in his bellboy act.[4] This had a definitely bad effect on my morale. Even so, I had become by sheer practice little short of wonderful at squad maneuvers.

One day General Littlefield picked our company out of the whole regiment and tried to get it mixed up by putting it through one movement after another as fast as we could execute them: squads right, squads left, squads on right into line, squads right about, squads left front into line, etc. In about three minutes one hundred and nine men were marching in one direction and I was marching away from them at an angle of forty degrees, all alone. "Company, halt!" shouted General Littlefield. "That man is the only man who has it right!" I was made a corporal for my achievement.

The next day General Littlefield summoned me to his office. He was swatting flies when I went in. I was silent and he was silent too, for a long time, I don't think he remembered me or why he had sent for me, but he didn't want to admit it. He swatted some more flies, keeping his eyes on them narrowly before he let go with the swatter. "Button up your coat!" he snapped. Looking back on it now I can see that he meant me although he was looking at a fly, but I just stood there. Another fly came to rest on a paper in front of the general and began rubbing its hind legs together. The general lifted the swatter cautiously. I moved restlessly and the fly flew away. "You startled him!" barked General Littlefield, looking at me severely. I said I was sorry. "That won't help the situation!" snapped the General, with cold military logic. I didn't see what I could do except offer to chase some more flies toward his desk, but I didn't say anything. He stared out the window at the faraway figures of co-eds crossing the campus toward the library. Finally, he told me I could go. So I went. He either didn't know which cadet I was or else he forgot what he wanted to see me about. It may have been that he wished to apologize for having called me the main trouble with the university; or maybe he had decided to compliment me on my brilliant drilling of the day before and then at the last minute decided not to. I don't know. I don't think about it much any more.

1933

4. Popular vaudeville comedian.

THE READER

1. On the basis of this essay, what do you think Thurber's definition or description of an ideal college education would be?
2. In "Examsmanship and the Liberal Arts" (p. 177), Perry distinguishes between two kinds of knowledge: "cow" and "bull." Read or review the Perry essay, and then determine, judging by Thurber's essay, which kind of knowledge seems to have been in greater demand at

Thurber's university.
3. In *"Some Remarks on Humor"* (p. 663), White says about humorists: "Humorists fatten on trouble.... You find them wrestling with foreign languages, fighting folding ironing boards and swollen drainpipes, suffering the terrible discomfort of tight boots.... They pour out their sorrows profitably, in a form that is not quite fiction nor quite fact either. Beneath the sparkling surface of these dilemmas flows the strong tide of human woe." Discuss the validity of White's assertion, and test it by applying it to Thurber's essay.

THE WRITER

1. Why did Thurber pick these particular incidents of his college career to write about? What do they have in common?
2. Take one of the incidents in the essay, and analyze how Thurber describes it. What do you think he may have added to or subtracted from what actually happened? Take a similar incident (real or imagined), and, in a brief essay, try to treat it the way Thurber treats his incidents.

William Zinsser

COLLEGE PRESSURES

Dear Carlos: I desperately need a dean's excuse for my chem midterm which will begin in about 1 hour. All I can say is that I totally blew it this week. I've fallen incredibly, inconceivably behind.

Carlos: Help! I'm anxious to hear from you. I'll be in my room and won't leave it until I hear from you. Tomorrow is the last day for . . .

Carlos: I left town because I started bugging out again. I stayed up all night to finish a take-home make-up exam & am typing it to hand in on the 10th. It was due on the 5th. P.S. I'm going to the dentist. Pain is pretty bad.

Carlos: Probably by Friday I'll be able to get back to my studies. Right now I'm going to take a long walk. This whole thing has taken a lot out of me.

Carlos: I'm really up the proverbial creek. The problem is I really *bombed* the history final. Since I need that course for my major I . . .

Carlos: Here follows a tale of woe. I went home this weekend, had to help my Mom, & caught a fever so didn't have much time to study. My professor . . .

Carlos: Aargh! Trouble. Nothing original but everything's piling up at once. To be brief, my job interview . . .

Hey Carlos, good news! I've got mononucleosis.

Who are these wretched supplicants, scribbling notes so laden with anxiety, seeking such miracles of postponement and balm? They are men and women who belong to Branford College, one of the twelve residential colleges at Yale University, and the messages are just a few of the hundreds that they left for their dean, Carlos Hortas—often slipped under his door at 4 A.M.—last year.

But students like the ones who wrote those notes can also be found on campuses from coast to coast—especially in New England and at many other private colleges across the country that have high academic standards and highly motivated students. Nobody could doubt that the notes are real. In their urgency and their gallows humor they are authentic voices of a generation that is panicky to succeed.

My own connection with the message writers is that I am master of Branford College. I live in its Gothic quadrangle and know the students well. (We have 485 of them.) I am privy to their hopes and fears—and also to their stereo music and their piercing cries in the dead of night ("Does anybody ca-a-are?"). If they went to Carlos to ask how to get through tomorrow, they come to me to ask how to get through the rest of their lives.

Mainly I try to remind them that the road ahead is a long one and that it will have more unexpected turns than they think. There will be plenty of time to change jobs, change careers, change whole attitudes and approaches. They don't want to hear such liberating news. They want a map—right now—that they can follow unswervingly to career security, financial security. Social Security and, presumably, a prepaid grave.

What I wish for all students is some release from the clammy grip of the future. I wish them a chance to savor each segment of their education as an experience in itself and not as a grim preparation for the next step. I wish them the right to experiment, to trip and fall, to learn that defeat is as instructive as victory and is not the end of the world.

My wish, of course, is naïve. One of the few rights that America does not proclaim is the right to fail. Achievement is the national god, venerated in our media—the million-dollar athlete, the wealthy executive—and glorified in our praise of possessions. In the presence of such a potent state religion, the young are growing up old.

I see four kinds of pressure working on college students today: economic pressure, parental pressure, peer pressure, and self-induced pressure. It is easy to look around for villains—to blame the colleges for charging too much money, the professors for assigning too much work, the parents for pushing their children too far, the students for driving themselves too hard. But there are no villains; only victims.

"In the late 1960s," one dean told me, "the typical question that I got from students was 'Why is there so much suffering in the world?' or 'How can I make a contribution?' Today it's 'Do you think it would look better for getting into law school if I did a double major in history and political science, or just majored in one of them?'" Many other deans confirmed this pattern. One said: "They're trying to find an edge—the intangible something that will look better on paper if two students are about equal."

Note the emphasis on looking better. The transcript has become a sacred document, the passport to security. How one appears on paper is more important than how one appears in person. A is for Admirable and B is for Borderline, even though, in Yale's official system of grading, A means "excellent" and B means "very good." Today, looking very good is no longer good enough, especially for students who hope to go on to law school or medical school. They know that entrance into the better schools will be an entrance into the better law firms and better medical practices where they will make a lot of money. They also know that the odds are harsh, Yale Law School, for instance, matriculates 170 students from an applicant pool of 3,700; Harvard enrolls 550 from a pool of 7,000.

It's all very well for those of us who write letters of recommendation for our students to stress the qualities of humanity that will make them good lawyers or doctors. And it's nice to think that admission officers are really reading our letters and looking for the extra dimension of commitment or concern. Still, it would be hard for a student not to visualize these officers shuffling so many transcripts studded with As that they regard a B as positively shameful.

The pressure is almost as heavy on students who just want to graduate and get a job. Long gone are the days of the "gentleman's C," when students journeyed through college with a certain relaxation, sampling a wide variety of courses—music, art, philosophy, classics, anthropology, poetry, religion—that would send them out as liberally educated men and women. If I were an employer I would rather employ graduates who have this range and curiosity than those who narrowly pursued safe subjects and high grades. I know countless students whose inquiring minds exhilarate me. I like to hear the play of their ideas. I don't know if they are getting As or Cs, and I don't care. I also like them as people. The country needs them, and they will find satisfying jobs. I tell them to relax. They can't.

Nor can I blame them. They live in a brutal economy. Tuition, room, and board at most private colleges now comes to at least $7,000, not counting books and fees. This might seem to suggest that the colleges are getting rich. But they are equally battered by inflation. Tuition covers only 60 percent of what it costs to educate a student, and ordinarily the remainder comes from what colleges receive in endowments, grants, and gifts. Now the remainder keeps being swallowed by the cruel costs—

higher every year—of just opening the doors. Heating oil is up. Insurance is up. Postage is up. Health-premium costs are up. Everything is up. Deficits are up. We are witnessing in America the creation of a brotherhood of paupers—colleges, parents, and students, joined by the common bond of debt.

Today it is not unusual for a student, even if he works part time at college and full time during the summer, to accrue $5,000 in loans after four years—loans that he must start to repay within one year after graduation. Exhorted at commencement to go forth into the world, he is already behind as he goes forth. How could he not feel under pressure throughout college to prepare for this day of reckoning? I have used "he," incidentally, only for brevity. Women at Yale are under no less pressure to justify their expensive education to themselves, their parents, and society. In fact, they are probably under more pressure. For although they leave college superbly equipped to bring fresh leadership to traditionally male jobs, society hasn't yet caught up with this fact.

Along with economic pressure goes parental pressure. Inevitably, the two are deeply intertwined.

I see many students taking pre-medical courses with joyless tenacity. They go off to their labs as if they were going to the dentist. It saddens me because I know them in other corners of their life as cheerful people.

"Do you want to go to medical school?" I ask them.

"I guess so," they say, without conviction, or "Not really."

"Then why are you going?"

"Well, my parents want me to be a doctor. They're paying all this money and . . ."

Poor students, poor parents. They are caught in one of the oldest webs of love and duty and guilt. The parents mean well; they are trying to steer their sons and daughters toward a secure future. But the sons and daughters want to major in history or classics or philosophy—subjects with no "practical" value. Where's the payoff on the humanities? It's not easy to persuade such loving parents that the humanities do indeed pay off. The intellectual faculties developed by studying subjects like history and classics—an ability to synthesize and relate, to weigh cause and effect, to see events in perspective—are just the faculties that make creative leaders in business or almost any general field. Still, many fathers would rather put their money on courses that point toward a specific profession —courses that are pre-law, pre-medical, pre-business, or, as I sometimes heard it put, "pre-rich."

But the pressure on students is severe. They are truly torn. One part of them feels obligated to fulfill their parents' expectations; after all, their parents are older and presumably wiser. Another part tells them that the expectations that are right for their parents are not right for them.

I know a student who wants to be an artist. She is very obviously an artist and will be a good one—she has already had several modest local exhibits. Meanwhile she is growing as a well-rounded person and taking humanistic subjects that will enrich the inner resources out of which her art will grow. But her father is strongly opposed. He thinks that an artist is a "dumb" thing to be. The student vacillates and tries to please everybody. She keeps up with her art somewhat furtively and takes some of the "dumb" courses her father wants her to take—at least they are dumb courses for her. She is a free spirit on a campus of tense students—no small achievement in itself—and she deserves to follow her muse.

Peer pressure and self-induced pressure are also intertwined, and they begin almost at the beginning of freshman year.

"I had a freshman student I'll call Linda," one dean told me, "who came in and said she was under terrible pressure because her roommate, Barbara, was much brighter and studied all the time. I couldn't tell her that Barbara had come in two hours earlier to say the same thing about Linda."

The story is almost funny—except that it's not. It's symptomatic of all the pressures put together. When every student thinks every other student is working harder and doing better, the only solution is to study harder still. I see students going off to the library every night after dinner and coming back when it closes at midnight. I wish they would sometimes forget about their peers and go to a movie. I hear the clacking of typewriters in the hours before dawn. I see the tension in their eyes when exams are approaching and papers are due: *"Will I get everything done?"*

Probably they won't. They will get sick. They will get "blocked." They will sleep. They will oversleep. They will bug out. *Hey Carlos, help!*

Part of the problem is that they do more than they are expected to do. A professor will assign five-page papers. Several students will start writing ten-page papers to impress him. Then more students will write ten-page papers, and a few will raise the ante to fifteen. Pity the poor student who is still just doing the assignment.

Once you have twenty or thirty percent of the student population deliberately overexerting," one dean points out, "it's bad for everybody. When a teacher gets more and more effort from his class, the student who is doing normal work can be perceived as not doing well. The tactic works, psychologically."

Why can't the professor just cut back and not accept longer papers? He can, and he probably will. But by then the term will be half over and the damage done. Grade fever is highly contagious and not easily reversed. Besides, the professor's main concern is with his course. He knows his students only in relation to the course and doesn't know that they are also overexerting in their other courses. Nor is it really his business. He didn't sign up for dealing with the student as a whole person and with all the emotional baggage the student brought along from home. That's what deans, masters, chaplains, and psychiatrists are for.

To some extent this is nothing new: a certain number of professors have always been self-contained islands of scholarship and shyness, more comfortable with books than with people. But the new pauperism has widened the gap still further, for professors who actually like to spend time with students don't have as much time to spend. They also are overexerting. If they are young, they are busy trying to publish in order not to perish, hanging by their finger nails onto a shrinking profession. If they are old and tenured, they are buried under the duties of administering departments—as departmental chairmen or members of committees —that have been thinned out by the budgetary axe.

Ultimately it will be the students' own business to break the circles in which they are trapped. They are too young to be prisoners of their parents' dreams and their classmates' fears. They must be jolted into believing in themselves as unique men and women who have the power to shape their own future.

"Violence is being done to the undergraduate experience," says Carlos Hortas. "College should be open-ended: at the end it should open many, many roads. Instead, students are choosing their goal in advance, and their choices narrow as they go along. It's almost as if they think that the country has been codified in the type of jobs that exist—that they've got to fit into certain slots. Therefore, fit into the best-paying slot.

"They ought to take chances. Not taking chances will lead to a life of colorless mediocrity. They'll be comfortable. But something in the spirit will be missing."

I have painted too drab a portrait of today's students, making them seem a solemn lot. That is only half of their story; if they were so dreary I wouldn't so thoroughly enjoy their company. The other half is that they are easy to like. They are quick to laugh and to offer friendship. They are not introverts. They are unusually kind and are more considerate of one another than any student generation I have known.

Nor are they so obsessed with their studies that they avoid sports and extracurricular activities. On the contrary, they juggle their crowded hours to play on a variety of teams, perform with musical and dramatic groups, and write for campus publications. But this in turn is one more cause of anxiety. There are too many choices. Academically, they have 1,300 courses to select from; outside class they have to decide how much spare time they can spare and how to spend it.

This means that they engage in fewer extracurricular pursuits than their predecessors did. If they want to row on the crew and play in the symphony they will eliminate one; in the '60s they would have done both. They also tend to choose activities that are self-limiting. Drama, for instance, is flourishing in all twelve of Yale's residential colleges as it never has before. Students hurl themselves into these productions—as actors, directors, carpenters, and technicians—with a dedication to create the best possible play, knowing that the day will come when the run will end and they can get back to their studies.

They also can't afford to be the willing slave of organizations like the *Yale Daily News*. Last spring at the one-hundredth anniversary banquet of that paper—whose past chairmen include such once and future kings as Potter Stewart, Kingman Brewster, and William F. Buckley, Jr.—much was made of the fact that the editorial staff used to be small and totally committed and that "newsies" routinely worked fifty hours a week. In effect they belonged to a club; Newsies is how they defined themselves at Yale. Today's student will write one or two articles a week, when he can, and he defines himself as a student. I've never heard the word Newsie except at the banquet.

If I have described the modern undergraduate primarily as a driven creature who is largely ignoring the blithe spirit inside who keeps trying to come out and play, it's because that's where the crunch is, not only at Yale but throughout American education. It's why I think we should all be worried about the values that are nurturing a generation so fearful of risk and so goal-obsessed at such an early age.

I tell students that there is no one "right" way to get ahead—that each of them is a different person, starting from a different point and bound for a different destination. I tell them that change is a tonic and that all the slots are not codified nor the frontiers closed. One of my ways of telling them is to invite men and women who have achieved success outside the academic world to come and talk informally with my students during the year. They are heads of companies or ad agencies, editors of magazines, politicians, public officials, television magnates, labor leaders, business executives, Broadway producers, artists, writers, economists, photographers, scientists, historians—a mixed bag of achievers.

I ask them to say a few words about how they got started. The students assume that they started in their present profession and knew all along that it was what they wanted to do. Luckily for me, most of them got into their field by a circuitous route, to their surprise, after many detours. The students are startled. They can hardly conceive of a career that was not pre-planned. They can hardly imagine allowing the hand of God or chance to nudge them down some unforeseen trail.

1979

THE READER

1. On p. 170, Zinsser names four kinds of pressure on college students. Are there others? Are they equally strong? What counterpressures

176 WILLIAM ZINSSER

exist? What would be necessary for a state of equilibrium? Would those changes or that state be desirable?

2. *In his fifth paragraph, Zinsser says he wishes "for all students . . . some release from the clammy grip of the future" so that they could both "savor each segment of their education" and "learn that defeat is as instructive as victory." Are these two compatible? Which is more important, savoring each segment of one's education or learning from defeat? How would a college program designed to fulfill either or both of these two functions differ from that of the average college or from the one you are pursuing?*

THE WRITER

1. *By beginning with quotations from student notes to the counseling dean, Zinsser seeks to establish the problem of college pressures as a concrete personal reality; then he seeks to generalize, using those personal statements to represent also the situation of other students at other colleges. Does this plan work? What makes the statements sound authentic or inauthentic?*

2. *In describing the four kinds of pressure, Zinsser has to make transitions. One of these ("Along with economic pressure . . . " [p. 172] is loose. Could it be tightened? Should it be? What about the others? What are the logical relations among the four kinds of pressure?*

3. *On p. 175, Zinsser refers to "the blithe spirit" inside the "driven" college student. Gaylin, in "What You See Is the Real You" (p. 386), rejects such analyses. Which view do you find more persuasive? Why?*

4. *In the New York Times for May 14, 1970, Fred Hechinger reported an apparent increase in cheating by college students and pointed out that, historically, cheating occurs when grades are used to determine success in competition for economic and social rewards. He then concluded that some people are wondering if this process is not damaging the colleges, if "the economic and political system is improperly exploiting the educational system." By making "system" the subject of the clause, he avoided having to say who in particular is responsible for the problem. Write an essay in which you show who is responsible, or show that the problem doesn't exist at present or isn't important, or redefine the problem to lead to different conclusions.*

5. *Write an essay on one of these topics:*
   a) The Value of Failure
   b) The Necessity for Pressures
   c) Ways to Eliminate Pressures
   d) An Alternative to Grading
   Then write a paragraph rebutting the point of view in your essay. Which seems more effective to you? Why?

William G. Perry, Jr.

EXAMSMANSHIP AND THE LIBERAL ARTS:
A STUDY IN EDUCATIONAL EPISTEMOLOGY

"But sir, I don't think I really deserve it, it was mostly bull, really." This disclaimer from a student whose examination we have awarded a straight "A" is wondrously depressing. Alfred North Whitehead invented its only possible rejoinder: "Yes sir, what you wrote is nonsense, utter nonsense. But ah! Sir! It's the right *kind* of nonsense!"

Bull, in this university,[1] is customarily a source of laughter, or a problem in ethics. I shall step a little out of fashion to use the subject as a take-off point for a study in comparative epistemology. The phenomenon of bull, in all the honor and opprobrium with which it is regarded by students and faculty, says something, I think, about our theories of knowledge. So too, the grades which we assign on examinations communicate to students what these theories may be.

We do not have to be out-and-out logical-positivists[2] to suppose that we have something to learn about "what we think knowledge is" by having a good look at "what we do when we go about measuring it." We know the straight "A" examination when we see it, of course, and we have reason to hope that the student will understand why his work receives our recognition. He doesn't always. And those who receive lesser honor? Perhaps an understanding of certain anomalies in our customs of grading good bull will explain the students' confusion.

I must beg patience, then, both of the reader's humor and of his morals. Not that I ask him to suspend his sense of humor but that I shall ask him to go beyond it. In a great university the picture of a bright student attempting to outwit his professor while his professor takes pride in not being outwitted is certainly ridiculous. I shall report just such a scene, for its implications bear upon my point. Its comedy need not present a serious obstacle to thought.

As for the ethics of bull, I must ask for a suspension of judgment. I wish that students could suspend theirs. Unlike humor, moral commitment is hard to think beyond. Too early a moral judgment is precisely what stands between many able students and a liberal education. The stunning realization that the Harvard Faculty will often accept, as evidence of knowledge, the cerebrations of a student who has little data at his

---

1. Harvard.
2. Members of a contemporary school of philosophy which sees philosophy as an activity rather than a body of knowledge, and concerns itself not with abstract notions of what a thing is but with empirical observation of what it does.

177

disposal, confronts every student with an ethical dilemma. For some it forms an academic focus for what used to be thought of as "adolescent disillusion." It is irrelevant that rumor inflates the phenomenon to mythical proportions. The students know that beneath the myth there remains a solid and haunting reality. The moral "bind" consequent on this awareness appears most poignantly in serious students who are reluctant to concede the competitive advantage to the bullster and who yet feel a deep personal shame when, having succumbed to "temptation," they themselves receive a high grade for work they consider "dishonest."

I have spent many hours with students caught in this unwelcome bitterness. These hours lend an urgency to my theme. I have found that students have been able to come to terms with the ethical problem, to the extent that it is real, only after a refined study of the true nature of bull and its relation to "knowledge." I shall submit grounds for my suspicion that we can be found guilty of sharing the students' confusion of moral and epistemological issues.

I

I present as my "premise," then, an amoral *fabliau*. Its hero-villain is the Abominable Mr. Metzger '47. Since I celebrate his virtuosity, I regret giving him a pseudonym, but the peculiar style of his bravado requires me to honor also his modesty. Bull in pure form is rare; there is usually some contamination by data. The community has reason to be grateful to Mr. Metzger for having created an instance of laboratory purity, free from any adulteration by matter. The more credit is due him, I think, because his act was free from premeditation, deliberation, or hope of personal gain.

Mr. Metzger stood one rainy November day in the lobby of Memorial Hall. A junior, concentrating in mathematics, he was fond of diverting himself by taking part in the drama, a penchant which may have had some influence on the events of the next hour. He was waiting to take part in a rehearsal in Sanders Theatre, but, as sometimes happens, no other players appeared. Perhaps the rehearsal had been canceled without his knowledge? He decided to wait another five minutes.

Students, meanwhile, were filing into the Great Hall opposite, and taking seats at the testing tables. Spying a friend crossing the lobby toward the Great Hall's door, Metzger greeted him and extended appropriate condolences. He inquired, too, what course his friend was being tested in. "Oh, Soc. Sci. something-or-other." "What's it all about?" asked Metzger, and this, as Homer remarked of Patroclus, was the beginning of evil for him.

"It's about Modern Perspectives on Man and Society and All That," said his friend. "Pretty interesting, really."

"Always wanted to take a course like that," said Metzger. "Any good reading?"

"Yeah, great. There's this book"—his friend did not have time to finish.

"Take your seats please" said a stern voice beside them. The idle conversation had somehow taken the two friends to one of the tables in the Great Hall. Both students automatically obeyed; the proctor put blue-books before them; another proctor presented them with copies of the printed hour-test.

Mr. Metzger remembered afterwards a brief misgiving that was suddenly overwhelmed by a surge of curiosity and puckish glee. He wrote "George Smith" on the blue book, opened it, and addressed the first question.

I must pause to exonerate the Management. The Faculty has a rule that no student may attend an examination in a course in which he is not enrolled. To the wisdom of this rule the outcome of this deplorable story stands witness. The Registrar, charged with the enforcement of the rule, has developed an organization with procedures which are certainly the finest to be devised. In November, however, class rosters are still shaky, and on this particular day another student, named Smith, was absent. As for the culprit, we can reduce his guilt no further than to suppose that he was ignorant of the rule, or, in the face of the momentous challenge before him, forgetful.

We need not be distracted by Metzger's performance on the "objective" or "spot" questions on the test. His D on these sections can be explained by those versed in the theory of probability. Our interest focuses on the quality of his essay. It appears that when Metzger's friend picked up his own blue book a few days later, he found himself in company with a large proportion of his section in having received on the essay a C. When he quietly picked up "George Smith's" blue book to return it to Metzger, he observed that the grade for the essay was A. In the margin was a note in the section man's hand. It read "Excellent work. Could you have pinned these observations down a bit more closely? Compare . . . in . . . pp. . . . ."

Such news could hardly be kept quiet. There was a leak, and the whole scandal broke on the front page of Tuesday's Crimson. With the press Metzger was modest, as becomes a hero. He said that there had been nothing to it at all, really. The essay question had offered a choice of two books, Margaret Mead's And Keep Your Powder Dry or Geoffrey Gorer's The American People. Metzger reported that having read neither of them, he had chosen the second "because the title gave me some notion as to what the book might be about." On the test, two critical comments were offered on each book, one favorable, one unfavorable. The students were asked to "discuss." Metzger conceded that he had played safe in throwing his lot with the more laudatory of the two comments, "but I did not forget to be balanced."

I do not have Mr. Metzger's essay before me except in vivid memory. As I recall, he took his first cue from the name Geoffrey, and committed his strategy to the premise that Gorer was born into an "Anglo-Saxon" culture, probably English, but certainly "English speaking." Having heard that Margaret Mead was a social anthropologist, he inferred that Gorer was the same. He then entered upon his essay, centering his inquiry upon what he supposed might be the problems inherent in an anthropologist's observation of a culture which was his own, or nearly his own. Drawing in part from memories of table-talk on cultural relativity[3] and in part from creative logic, he rang changes on the relation of observer to observed, and assessed the kind and degree of objectivity which might accrue to an observer through training as an anthropologist. He concluded that the book in question did in fact contribute a considerable range of "'objective', and even 'fresh'," insights into the nature of our culture. "At the same time," he warned, "these observations must be understood within the context of their generation by a person only partly freed from his embeddedness in the culture he is observing, and limited in his capacity to transcend those particular tendencies and biases which he has himself developed as a personality in his interraction with this culture since his birth. In this sense the book portrays as much the character of Geoffrey Gorer as it analyzes that of the American people." It is my regretable duty to report that at this moment of triumph Mr. Metzger was carried away by the temptations of parody and added, "We are thus much the richer."

In any case, this was the essay for which Metzger received his honor grade and his public acclaim. He was now, of course, in serious trouble with the authorities.

I shall leave him for the moment to the mercy of the Administrative Board of Harvard College and turn the reader's attention to the section man who ascribed the grade. He was in much worse trouble. All the consternation in his immediate area of the Faculty and all the glee in other areas fell upon his unprotected head. I shall now undertake his defense.

I do so not simply because I was acquainted with him and feel a respect for his intelligence; I believe in the justice of his grade! Well, perhaps "justice" is the wrong word in a situation so manifestly absurd. This is more a case in "equity." That is, the grade is equitable if we accept other aspects of the situation which are equally absurd. My proposition is this: if we accept as valid those C grades which were accorded students who, like Metzger's friend, demonstrated a thorough familiarity with the details of the book without relating their critique to the methodological

---

3. "An important part of Harvard's education takes place during meals in the Houses."   An Official Publication [Perry's note]. The Houses are residences for upperclassmen.

problems of social anthropology, then "George Smith" deserved not only the same, but better.

The reader may protest that the C's given to students who showed evidence only of diligence were indeed not valid and that both these students and "George Smith" should have received E's. To give the diligent E is of course not in accord with custom. I shall take up this matter later. For now, were I to allow the protest, I could only restate my thesis: that "George Smith's" E would, in a college of liberal arts, be properly a "better" E.

At this point I need a short-hand. It is a curious fact that there is no academic slang for the presentation of evidence of diligence alone. "Parroting" won't do; it is possible to "parrot" bull. I must beg the reader's pardon, and, for reasons almost too obvious to bear, suggest "cow."

Stated as nouns, the concepts look simple enough:

> cow (pure): data, however relevant, without relevancies.
> bull (pure): relevancies, however relevant, without data.

The reader can see all too clearly where this simplicity would lead. I can assure him that I would not have imposed on him this way were I aiming to say that knowledge in this university is definable as some neuter compromise between cow and bull, some infertile hermaphrodite. This is precisely what many diligent students seem to believe: that what they must learn to do is to "find the right mean" between "amounts" of detail and "amounts" of generalities. Of course this is not the point at all. The problem is not quantitative, nor does its solution lie on a continuum between the particular and the general. Cow and bull are not poles of a single dimension. A clear notion of what they really are is essential to my inquiry, and for heuristic purposes I wish to observe them further in the celibate state.

When the pure concepts are translated into verbs, their complexities become apparent in the assumptions and purposes of the students as they write:

To cow (v. *intrans.*) or the act of cowing:
   To list data (or perform operations) without awareness of, or comment upon, the contexts, frames of reference, or points of observation which determine the origin, nature, and meaning of the data (or procedures). To write on the assumption that "a fact is a fact." To present evidence of hard work as a substitute for understanding, without any intent to deceive.

To bull (v. *intrans.*) or the act of bulling:
   To discourse upon the contexts, frames of reference and points of observation which would determine the origin, nature, and meaning of data if one had any. To present evidence of an understanding of form in the hope that the reader may be deceived into supposing a familiarity with content.

At the level of conscious intent, it is evident that cowing is more moral, or less immoral, than bulling. To speculate about unconscious intent would be either an injustice or a needless elaboration of my theme. It is enough that the impression left by cow is one of earnestness, diligence, and painful naiveté. The grader may feel disappointment or even irritation, but these feelings are usually balanced by pity, compassion, and a reluctance to hit a man when he's both down and moral. He may feel some challenge to his teaching, but none whatever to his one-ups-manship. He writes in the margin: "See me."

We are now in a position to understand the anomaly of custom: As instructors, we always assign bull an E, *when we detect it*; whereas we usually give cow a C, *even though it is always obvious*.

After all, we did not ask to be confronted with a choice between morals and understanding (or did we?). We evince a charming humanity, I think, in our decision to grade in favor of morals and pathos. "I simply *can't* give this student an E after he has *worked* so hard." At the same time we tacitly express our respect for the bullster's strength. We recognize a colleague. If he knows so well how to dish it out, we can be sure that he can also take it.

Of course it is just possible that we carry with us, perhaps from our own school-days, an assumption that if a student is willing to work hard and collect "good hard facts" he can always be taught to understand their relevance, whereas a student who has caught onto the forms of relevance without working at all is a lost scholar.

But this is not in accord with our experience.

It is not in accord either, as far as I can see, with the stated values of a liberal education. If a liberal education should teach students "how to think," not only in their own fields but in fields outside their own—that is, to understand "how the other fellow orders knowledge," then bulling, even in its purest form, expresses an important part of what a pluralist university holds dear, surely a more important part than the collecting of "facts that are facts" which schoolboys learn to do. Here then, good bull appears not as ignorance at all but as an aspect of knowledge. It is both relevant and "true." In a university setting good bull is therefore of more value than "facts," which, without a frame of reference, are not even "true" at all.

Perhaps this value accounts for the final anomaly: as instructors, we are inclined to reward bull highly, *where we do not detect its intent*, to the consternation of the bullster's acquaintances. And often we do not examine the matter too closely. After a long evening of reading blue books full of cow, the sudden meeting with a student who at least understands the problems of one's field provides a lift like a draught of refreshing wine, and a strong disposition toward trust.

This was, then, the sense of confidence that came to our unfortunate section man as he read "George Smith's" sympathetic considerations.

II

In my own years of watching over students' shoulders as they work, I have come to believe that this feeling of trust has a firmer basis than the confidence generated by evidence of diligence alone. I believe that the theory of a liberal education holds. Students who have dared to understand man's real relation to his knowledge have shown themselves to be in a strong position to learn content rapidly and meaningfully, and to retain it. I have learned to be less concerned about the education of a student who has come to understand the nature of man's knowledge, even though he has not yet committed himself to hard work, than I am about the education of the student who, after one or two terms at Harvard, is working desperately hard and still believes that collected "facts" constitute knowledge. The latter, when I try to explain to him, too often understands me to be saying that he "doesn't *put in enough generalities.*" Surely he has "put in *enough* facts."

I have come to see such quantitative statements as expressions of an entire, coherent epistemology. In grammar school the student is taught that Columbus discovered America in 1492. The more such items he gets "right" on a given test the more he is credited with "knowing." From years of this sort of thing it is not unnatural to develop the conviction that knowledge consists of the accretion of hard facts by hard work.

The student learns that the more facts and procedures he can get "right" in a given course, the better will be his grade. The more courses he takes, the more subjects he has "had," the more credits he accumulates, the more diplomas he will get, until, after graduate school, he will emerge with his doctorate, a member of the community of scholars.

The foundation of this entire life is the proposition that a fact is a fact. The necessary correlate of this proposition is that a fact is either right or wrong. This implies that the standard against which the rightness or wrongness of a fact may be judged exists *someplace*—perhaps graven upon a tablet in a Platonic world[4] outside and above *this* cave of tears. In grammar school it is evident that the tablets which enshrine the spelling of a word or the answer to an arithmetic problem are visible to my teacher who need only compare my offerings to it. In high school I observe that my English teachers disagree. This can only mean that the tablets in such matters as the goodness of a poem are distant and obscured by clouds. They surely exist. The pleasing of befuddled English teachers degenerates into assessing their prejudices, a game in which I have no protection against my competitors more glib of tongue. I respect only my science teachers, authorities who *really know*. Later I learn from

---

4. That is, a world of ideal forms, of which this world is but the distorted image. See Plato's "Allegory of the Cave," p. 1111.

them that "this is only what we think *now*." But eventually, surely. . . .
Into this epistemology of education, apparently shared by teachers in
such terms as "credits," "semester hours" and "years of French" the
student may invest his ideals, his drive, his competitiveness, his safety,
his self-esteem, and even his love.

College raises other questions: by whose calendar is it proper to say
that Columbus discovered America in 1492? How, when and by whom
was the year 1 established in this calendar? What of other calendars? In
view of the evidence for Leif Ericson's previous visit (and the American
Indians), what historical ethnocentrism is suggested by the use of the
word "discover" in this sentence? As for Leif Ericson, in accord with
what assumptions do you order the evidence?

These questions and their answers are not "more" knowledge. They
are devastation. I do not need to elaborate upon the epistemology, or
rather epistemologies, they imply. A fact has become at last "an observation or an operation performed in a frame of reference." A liberal education is founded in an awareness of frame of reference even in the most
immediate and empirical examination of data. Its acquirement involves
relinquishing hope of absolutes and of the protection they afford against
doubt and the glib-tongued competitor. It demands an ever widening
sophistication about systems of thought and observation. It leads, not
away from, but *through* the arts of gamesmanship to a new trust.

This trust is in the value and integrity of systems, their varied character, and the way their apparently incompatible metaphors enlighten,
from complementary facets, the particulars of human experience. As one
student said to me: "I used to be cynical about intellectual games. Now I
want to know them thoroughly. You see I came to realize that it was only
when I knew the rules of the game cold that I could tell whether what I
was saying was tripe."

We too often think of the bullster as cynical. He can be, and not always
in a light-hearted way. We have failed to observe that there can lie
behind cow the potential of a deeper and more dangerous despair. The
moralism of sheer work and obedience can be an ethic that, unwilling to
face a despair of its ends, glorifies its means. The implicit refusal to
consider the relativity of both ends and means leaves the operator in an
unconsidered proprietary absolutism. History bears witness that in the
pinches this moral superiority has no recourse to negotiation, only to
force.

A liberal education proposes that man's hope lies elsewhere: in the
negotiability that can arise from an understanding of the integrity of
systems and of their origins in man's address to his universe. The prereq-
uisite is the courage to accept such a definition of knowledge. From then
on, of course, there is nothing incompatible between such an epistemology and hard work. Rather the contrary.

I can now at last let bull and cow get together. The reader knows best how a productive wedding is arranged in his own field. This is the nuptial he celebrates with a straight A on examinations. The masculine context must embrace the feminine particular, though itself "born of woman." Such a union is knowledge itself, and it alone can generate new contexts and new data which can unite in their turn to form new knowledge.

In this happy setting we can congratulate in particular the Natural Sciences, long thought to be barren ground to the bullster. I have indeed drawn my examples of bull from the Social Sciences, and by analogy from the Humanities. Essay-writing in these fields has long been thought to nurture the art of bull to its prime. I feel, however, that the Natural Sciences have no reason to feel slighted. It is perhaps no accident that Metzger was a mathematician. As part of my researches for this paper, furthermore, a student of considerable talent has recently honored me with an impressive analysis of the art of amassing "partial credits" on examinations in advanced physics. Though beyond me in some respects, his presentation confirmed my impression that instructors of Physics frequently honor on examinations operations structurally similar to those requisite in a good essay.

The very qualities that make the Natural Sciences fields of delight for the eager gamesman have been essential to their marvelous fertility.

III

As priests of these mysteries, how can we make our rites more precisely expressive? The student who merely cows robs himself, without knowing it, of his education and his soul. The student who only bulls robs himself, as he knows full well, of the joys of inductive discovery—that is, of engagement. The introduction of frames of reference in the new curricula of Mathematics and Physics in the schools is a hopeful experiment. We do not know yet how much of these potent revelations the very young can stand, but I suspect they may rejoice in them more than we have supposed. I can't believe they have never wondered about Leif Ericson and that word "discovered," or even about 1492. They have simply been too wise to inquire.

Increasingly in recent years better students in the better high schools and preparatory schools are being allowed to inquire. In fact they appear to be receiving both encouragement and training in their inquiry. I have the evidence before me.

Each year for the past five years all freshmen entering Harvard and Radcliffe have been asked in freshman week to "grade" two essays answering an examination question in History. They are then asked to give their reasons for their grades. One essay, filled with dates, is 99% cow. The other, with hardly a date in it, is a good essay, easily mistaken for bull. The "official" grades of these essays are, for the first (alas!) C "because he has worked so hard," and for the second (soundly, I think) B. Each year a larger majority of freshmen evaluate these essays as would the majority of the faculty, and for the faculty's reasons, and each year a smaller minority give the higher honor to the essay offering data alone. Most interesting, a larger number of students each year, while not over-rating the second essay, award the first the straight E appropriate to it in a college of liberal arts.

For us who must grade such students in a university, these develop-ments imply a new urgency, did we not feel it already. Through our grades we describe for the students, in the showdown, what we believe about the nature of knowledge. The subtleties of bull are not peripheral to our academic concerns. That they penetrate to the center of our care is evident in our feelings when a student whose good work we have awarded a high grade reveals to us that he does not feel he deserves it. Whether he disqualifies himself because "there's too much bull in it," or worse because "I really don't think I've worked that hard," he presents a serious educational problem. Many students feel this sleaziness; only a few reveal it to us.

We can hardly allow a mistaken sense of fraudulence to undermine our students' achievements. We must lead students beyond their concept of bull so that they may honor relevancies that are really relevant. We can willingly acknowledge that, in lieu of the date 1492, a consideration of calendars and of the word "discovered," may well be offered with intent to deceive. We must insist that this does not make such considerations intrinsically immoral, and that, contrariwise, the date 1492 may be no substitute for them. Most of all, we must convey the impression that we grade understanding qua understanding. To be convincing, I suppose we must concede to ourselves in advance that a bright student's understand-ing is understanding even if he achieved it by osmosis rather than by hard work in our course.

These are delicate matters. As for cow, its complexities are not what need concern us. Unlike good bull, it does not represent partial knowl-edge at all. It belongs to a different theory of knowledge entirely. In our theories of knowledge it represents total ignorance, or worse yet, a knowledge downright inimical to understanding. I even go so far as to propose that we award no more C's for cow. To do so is rarely, I feel, the act of mercy it seems. Mercy lies in clarity.

The reader may be afflicted by a lingering curiosity about the fate of Mr. Metzger. I hasten to reassure him. The Administrative Board of Harvard College, whatever its satanic reputations, is a benign body. Its members, to be sure, were on the spot. They delighted in Metzger's exploit, but they were responsible to the Faculty's rule. The hero stood in danger of probation. The debate was painful. Suddenly one member, of a refined legalistic sensibility, observed that the rule applied specifically to "examinations" and that the occasion had been simply an hour-test. Mr. Metzger was merely "admonished."

1963

THE READER

1. Perry speaks several times of "good bull." Explain what "bad bull" would be in Perry's view, and give an example of it.
2. Perry points out the essential inaccuracy of such a supposedly simple statement of fact as "Columbus discovered America in 1492." Analyze one or two other such commonly accepted statements of fact in the same way Perry does.
3. Perry says that the ideal is "a productive wedding" between bull and cow. Find another essay in this book that you think represents such a "productive wedding," and explain how the author has brought that wedding about.

THE WRITER

1. Near the beginning of his essay, Perry says that he must "beg patience . . . both of the reader's humor and of his morals" (p. 177). Why does he find this necessary, and what assumptions does he make about his readers?
2. What tone does Perry adopt in his essay? Explain how the indicated words in these phrases contribute to Perry's creation of a tone appropriate to his thesis: (1) "the stunning realization that the Harvard Faculty will often accept, as evidence of knowledge, the cerebrations of a student who has little data at his disposal"; (2) "the peculiar style of his bravado requires me to honor also his modesty"; (3) "Bull in pure form is rare; there is usually some contamination by data"; (4) "some neuter compromise between cow and bull, some infertile hermaphrodite." Find and comment on other examples that help to define the tone of the essay.
3. In "Education by Poetry" (p. 630), Frost talks about the importance of metaphor in a liberal education. Write an essay relating Frost's remarks about metaphor to Perry's remarks about the place of bull and cow in a liberal education.

Lewis Thomas

HUMANITIES AND SCIENCE

Lord Kelvin was one of the great British physicists of the late nine-teenth century, an extraordinarily influential figure in his time, and in some ways a paradigm of conventional, established scientific leadership. He did a lot of good and useful things, but once or twice he, like Homer, nodded. The instances are worth recalling today, for we have nodders among our scientific eminences still, from time to time, needing to have their elbows shaken.

On one occasion, Kelvin made a speech on the overarching importance of numbers. He maintained that no observation of nature was worth paying serious attention to unless it could be stated in precisely quantita-tive terms. The numbers were the final and only test, not only of truth but about meaning as well. He said, "When you can measure what you are speaking about, and express it in numbers, you know something about it. But when you cannot—your knowledge is of a meagre and unsatisfactory kind."

But, as at least one subsequent event showed, Kelvin may have had things exactly the wrong way round. The task of converting observations into numbers is the hardest of all, the last task rather than the first thing to be done, and it can be done only when you have learned, beforehand, a great deal about the observations themselves. You can, to be sure, achieve a very deep understanding of nature by quantitative measure-ment, but you must know what you are talking about before you can begin applying the numbers for making predictions. In Kelvin's case, the problem at hand was the age of the earth and solar sytem. Using what was then known about the sources of energy and the loss of energy from the physics of that day, he calculated that neither the earth nor the sun were [sic] older than several hundred million years. This caused a considerable stir in biological and geological circles, especially among the evolution-ists. Darwin himself was distressed by the numbers; the time was much too short for the theory of evolution. Kelvin's figures were described by Darwin as one of his "sorest troubles."

T. H. Huxley had long been aware of the risks involved in premature extrapolations from mathematical treatment of biological problems. He said, in an 1869 speech to the Geological Society concerning numbers, "This seems to be one of the many cases in which the admitted accuracy of mathematical processes is allowed to throw a wholly inadmissible appearance of authority over the results obtained by them.... As the grandest mill in the world will not extract wheat flour from peascods, so pages of formulas will not get a definite result out of loose data."

The trouble was that the world of physics had not moved fast enough to allow for Kelvin's assumptions. Nuclear fusion and fission had not yet been dreamed of, and the true age of the earth could not even be guessed from the data in hand. It was not yet the time for mathematics in this subject.

There have been other examples, since those days, of the folly of using numbers and calculations uncritically. Kelvin's own strong conviction that science could not be genuine science without measuring things was catching. People in other fields of endeavor, hankering to turn their disciplines into exact sciences, beset by what has since been called "physics envy," set about converting whatever they knew into numbers and thence into equations with predictive pretensions. We have it with us still, in economics, sociology, psychology, history, even, I fear, in English-literature criticism and linguistics, and it frequently works, when it works at all, with indifferent success. The risks of untoward social consequences in work of this kind are considerable. It is as important— and as hard—to learn *when* to use mathematics as *how* to use it, and this matter should remain high on the agenda of consideration for education in the social and behavioral sciences.

Of course, Kelvin's difficulty with the age of the earth was an exceptional, almost isolated instance of failure in quantitative measurement in nineteenth-century physics. The instruments devised for approaching nature by way of physics became increasingly precise and powerful, carrying the field through electromagnetic theory, triumph after triumph, and setting the stage for the great revolution of twentieth-century physics. There is no doubt about it: measurement works when the instruments work, and when you have a fairly clear idea of what it is that is being measured, and when you know what to do with the numbers when they tumble out. The system for gaining information and comprehension about nature works so well, indeed, that it carries another hazard: the risk of convincing yourself that you know everything.

Kelvin himself fell into this trap toward the end of the century. (I don't mean to keep picking on Kelvin, who was a very great scientist; it is just that he happened to say a couple of things I find useful for this discussion.) He stated, in a summary of the achievements of nineteenth-century physics, that it was an almost completed science; virtually everything that needed knowing about the material universe had been learned; there were still a few anomalies and inconsistencies in electromagnetic theory, a few loose ends to be tidied up, but this would be done within the next several years. Physics, in these terms, was not a field any longer likely to attract, as it previously had, the brightest and most imaginative young brains. The most interesting part of the work had already been done. Then, within the next decade, came radiation, Planck, the quantum,

Einstein, Rutherford, Bohr, and all the rest—quantum mechanics—and the whole field turned over and became a brand-new sort of human endeavor, still now, in the view of many physicists, almost a full century later, a field only at its beginnings.

But even today, despite the amazements that are turning up in physics each year, despite the jumps taken from the smallest parts of nature—particle physics—to the largest of all—the cosmos itself—the impression of science that the public gains is rather like the impression left in the nineteenth-century public mind by Kelvin. Science, in this view, is first of all a matter of simply getting all the numbers together. The numbers are sitting out there in nature, waiting to be found, sorted and totted up. If only they had enough robots and enough computers, the scientists could go off to the beach and wait for their papers to be written for them. Second of all, what we know about nature today is pretty much the whole story: we are very nearly home and dry. From here on, it is largely a problem of tying up loose ends, tidying nature up, getting the files in order. The only real surprises for the future—and it is about those that the public is becoming more concerned and apprehensive—are the technological applications that the scientists may be cooking up from today's knowledge.

I suggest that the scientific community is to blame. If there are disagreements between the world of the humanities and the scientific enterprise as to the place and importance of science in a liberal-arts education, and the role of science in twentieth-century culture, I believe that the scientists are themselves responsible for a general misunderstanding of what they are really up to.

Over the past half century, we have been teaching the sciences as though they were the same academic collection of cut-and-dried subjects as always, and—here is what has really gone wrong—as though they would always be the same. The teaching of today's biology, for example, is pretty much the same kind of exercise as the teaching of Latin was when I was in high school long ago. First of all, the fundamentals, the underlying laws, the essential grammar, and then the reading of texts. Once mastered, that is that: Latin is Latin and forever after will be Latin. And biology is precisely biology, a vast array of hard facts to be learned as fundamentals, followed by a reading of the texts.

Moreover, we have been teaching science as though its facts were somehow superior to the facts in all other scholarly disciplines, more fundamental, more solid, less subject to subjectivism, immutable. English literature is not just one way of thinking, it is all sorts of ways. Poetry is a moving target. The facts that underlie art, architecture, and music are not really hard facts, and you can change them any way you like by arguing about them, but science is treated as an altogether different kind of learning: an unambiguous, unalterable, and endlessly useful display of data needing only to be packaged and installed somewhere in one's temporal lobe in order to achieve a full understanding of the natural world.

And it is, of course, not like this at all. In real life, every field of science that I can think of is incomplete, and most of them—whatever the record of accomplishment over the past two hundred years—are still in the earliest stage of their starting point. In the fields I know best, among the life sciences, it is required that the most expert and sophisticated minds be capable of changing those minds, often with a great lurch, every few years. In some branches of biology the mind-changing is occurring with accelerating velocities. The next week's issue of any scientific journal can turn a whole field upside down, shaking out any number of immutable ideas and installing new bodies of dogma, and this is happening all the time. It is an almost everyday event in physics, in chemistry, in materials research, in neurobiology, in genetics, in immunology. The hard facts tend to soften overnight, melt away, and vanish under the pressure of new hard facts, and the interpretations of what appear to be the most solid aspects of nature are subject to change, now more than at any other time in history. The conclusions reached in science are always, when looked at closely, far more provisional and tentative than are most of the assumptions arrived at by our colleagues in the humanities.

The running battle now in progress between the sociobiologists and the antisociobiologists is a marvel for students to behold, close up. To observe, in open-mouthed astonishment, the polarized extremes, one group of highly intelligent, beautifully trained, knowledgeable, and imaginative scientists maintaining that all sorts of behavior, animal and human, are governed exclusively by genes, and another group of equally talented scientists saying precisely the opposite and asserting that all behavior is set and determined by the environment, or by culture, and both sides brawling in the pages of periodicals such as *The New York Review of Books,* is an educational experience that no college student should be allowed to miss. The essential lesson to be learned has nothing to do with the relative validity of the facts underlying the argument, it is the argument itself that is the education: we do not yet know enough to settle such questions.

It is true that any given moment there is the appearance of satisfaction, even self-satisfaction, within every scientific discipline. On any Tuesday morning, if asked, a good working scientist will gladly tell you that the affairs of the field are nicely in order, that things are finally looking clear and making sense, and all is well. But come back again, on another Tuesday, and he may let you know that the roof has just fallen in on his life's work, that all the old ideas—last week's ideas in some cases—are no longer good ideas, that something strange has happened.

It is the very strangeness of nature that makes science engrossing. That ought to be at the center of science teaching. There are more than seven-times-seven types of ambiguity in science, awaiting analysis. The poetry of Wallace Stevens is crystal-clear alongside the genetic code.

I prefer to turn things around in order to make precisely the opposite case. Science, especially twentieth-century science, has provided us with a glimpse of something we never really knew before, the revelation of human ignorance. We have been used to the belief, down one century after another, that we more or less comprehend everything bar one or two mysteries like the mental processes of our gods. Every age, not just the eighteenth century, regarded itself as the Age of Reason, and we have never lacked for explanations of the world and its ways. Now, we are being brought up short, and this has been the work of science. We have a wilderness of mystery to make our way through in the centuries ahead, and we will need science for this but not science alone. Science will, in its own time, produce the data and some of the meaning in the data, but never the full meaning. For getting a full grasp, for perceiving real significance when significance is at hand, we shall need minds at work from all sorts of brains outside the fields of science, most of all the brains of poets, of course, but also those of artists, musicians, philosophers, historians, writers in general.

It is primarily because of this need that I would press for changes in the way science is taught. There is a need to teach the young people who will be doing the science themselves, but this will always be a small minority among us. There is a deeper need to teach science to those who will be needed for thinking about it, and this means pretty nearly everyone else, in hopes that a few of these people—a much smaller minority than the scientific community and probably a lot harder to find—will, in the thinking, be able to imagine new levels of meaning that are likely to be lost on the rest of us.

In addition, it is time to develop a new group of professional thinkers, perhaps a somewhat larger group than the working scientists, who can create a discipline of scientific criticism. We have had good luck so far in the emergence of a few people ranking as philosophers of science and historians and journalists of science, and I hope more of these will be coming along, but we have not yet seen a Ruskin or a Leavis or an Edmund Wilson. Science needs critics of this sort, but the public at large needs them more urgently.

I suggest that the introductory courses in science, at all levels from grade school through college, be radically revised. Leave the fundamentals, the so-called basics, aside for a while, and concentrate the attention of all students on the things that are *not* known. You cannot possibly teach quantum mechanics without mathematics, to be sure, but you can describe the strangeness of the world opened up by quantum theory. Let it be known, early on, that there are deep mysteries, and profound paradoxes, revealed in their distant outlines, by the quantum. Let it be known that these can be appraoched more closely, and puzzled over, once the language of mathematics has been sufficiently mastered.

Teach at the outset, before any of the fundamentals, the still imponderable puzzles of cosmology. Let it be known, as clearly as possible, by the youngest minds, that there are some things going on in the universe that lie beyond comprehension, and make it plain how little is known.

Do not teach that biology is a useful and perhaps profitable science; that can come later. Teach instead that there are structures squirming inside all our cells, providing all the energy for living, that are essentially foreign creatures, brought in for symbiotic living a billion or so years ago, the lineal descendants of bacteria. Teach that we do not have the ghost of an idea how they got there, where they came from, or how they evolved to their present structure and function. The details of oxidative phosphorylation[1] and photosynthesis can come later.

Teach ecology early on. Let it be understood that the earth's life is a system of interliving, interdependent creatures, and that we do not understand at all how it works. The earth's environment, from the range of atmospheric gases to the chemical constituents of the sea, has been held in an almost unbelievably improbable state of regulated balance since life began, and the regulation of stability and balance is accomplished solely by the life itself, like the internal environment of an immense organism, and we do not know how *that* one works, even less what it means. Teach that.

Go easy, I suggest, on the promises sometimes freely offered by science. Technology relies and depends on science these days, more than ever before, but technology is nothing like the first justification for doing research, nor is it necessarily an essential product to be expected from science. Public decisions about what to have in the way of technology are totally different problems from decisions about science, and the two enterprises should not be tangled together. The central task of science is to arrive, stage by stage, at a clearer comprehension of nature, but this does not mean, as it is sometimes claimed to mean, a search for mastery over nature. Science may provide us, one day, with a better understanding of ourselves, but never, I hope, with a set of technologies for doing something or other to improve ourselves. I am made nervous by assertions that human consciousness will someday be unraveled by research, laid out for close scrutiny like the workings of a computer, and then, *and then*! I hope with some fervor that we can learn a lot more than we now know about the human mind, and I see no reason why this strange puzzle should remain forever and entirely beyond us. But I would be deeply disturbed by any prospect that we might use the new knowledge in order

---

1. "A vital process of intracellular respiration" (*American Heritage Dictionary*).

to begin doing something about it, to improve it, say. This is a different matter from searching for information to use against schizophrenia or dementia, where we are badly in need of technologies, indeed likely one day to be sunk without them. But the ordinary, everyday, more or less normal human mind is too marvelous an instrument ever to be tampered with by anyone, science or no science.

The education of humanists cannot be regarded as complete, or even adequate, without exposure in some depth to where things stand in the various branches of science, and particularly, as I have said, in the areas of our ignorance. This does not mean that I know how to go about doing it, nor am I unaware of the difficulties involved. Physics professors, most of them, look with revulsion on assignments to teach their subject to poets. Biologists, caught up by the enchantment of their new power, armed with flawless instruments to tell the nucleotide sequences of the entire human genome, nearly matching the physicists in the precision of their measurements of living processes, will resist the prospect of broad survey courses; each biology professor will demand that any student in his path must master every fine detail within that professor's research program. The liberal-arts faculties, for their part, will continue to view the scientists with suspicion and apprehension. "What do the scientists want?" asked a Cambridge professor in Francis Cornford's wonderful *Microcosmographia Academica*. "Everything that's going," was the quick answer. That was back in 1912, and universities haven't much changed.

The worst thing that has happened to science education is that the great fun has gone out of it. A very large number of good students look at it as slogging work to be got through on the way to medical school. Others look closely at the premedical students themselves, embattled and bleeding for grades and class standing, and are turned off. Very few see science as the high adventure it really is, the wildest of all explorations ever undertaken by human beings, the chance to catch close views of things never seen before, the shrewdest maneuver for discovering how the world works. Instead, they become baffled early on, and they are misled into thinking that bafflement is simply the result of not having learned all the facts. They are not told, as they should be told, that everyone else—from the professor in his endowed chair down to the platoons of postdoctoral students in the laboratory all night—is baffled as well. Every important scientific advance that has come in looking like an answer has turned, sooner or later—usually sooner—into a question. And the game is just beginning.

An appreciation of what is happening in science today, and of how great a distance lies ahead for exploring, ought to be one of the rewards of a liberal-arts education. It ought to be a good in itself, not something to be acquired on the way to a professional career but part of the cast of thought needed for getting into the kind of century that is now just down the road. Part of the intellectual equipment of an educated person, however his or her time is to be spent, ought to be a feel for the queernesses of nature, the inexplicable things.

And maybe, just maybe, a new set of courses dealing systematically with ignorance in science might take hold. The scientists might discover in it a new and subversive technique for catching the attention of students driven by curiosity, delighted and surprised to learn that science is exactly as Bush described it: an "endless frontier." The humanists, for their part, might take considerable satisfaction watching their scientific colleagues confess openly to not knowing everything about everything. And the poets, on whose shoulders the future rests, might, late nights, thinking things over, begin to see some meanings that elude the rest of us. It is worth a try.

1983

THE READER

1. What does Thomas believe that scientists "are really up to"?
2. What, in Thomas's view, is the relationship between science and technology? The differences? Why is it important that science and technology be distinguished?
3. Thomas describes the battle between the sociobiologists and the antisociobiologists, and says, "it is the argument itself that is the education" (p. 191). Take Wilson's "The Superorganism" (p. 520) as an example of sociobiology. How do you think Wilson would react to Thomas's assertion?
4. Does Thomas imply that there are often things wrong about the way the humanities are usually taught? Have you been taught that English literature is "one way of thinking," or have you been taught to regard poetry as a "moving target" (p. 190)?

THE WRITER

1. Thomas's essay implies that science and the humanities have more in common than is customarily supposed. What details in the discussion lead to that implication?
2. Write a brief essay supporting or denying Thomas's assertion that "the conclusions reached in science are always . . . far more provisional and tentative than are most of the assumptions arrived at . . . in the humanities."
3. Thomas suggests that "a new set of courses dealing systematically with ignorance in science might take hold." Write a brief description of one such course. Then compare it with some courses it might replace, coming to some conclusion as to which might be more valuable for you.
4. Write a definition of "the scientific method," as you take that term to be commonly understood. Then write a critique of that definition as Thomas's view might suggest.
5. Here Thomas is dealing with a subject that is sweeping and important

and in "Notes on Punctuation" (p. 217) with one that is restricted and minor. Describe the personality Thomas presents to you here and then the one he presents in "Notes on Puctuation." Are they similar? Different? Do they overlap? Is his analysis in "On Magic in Medicine" (p. 370) consistent with this personality or these personalities?

Wayne C. Booth

IS THERE ANY KNOWLEDGE THAT A MAN *MUST* HAVE?

Everyone lives on the assumption that a great deal of knowledge is not worth bothering about; though we all know that what looks trivial in one man's hands may turn out to be earth-shaking in another's, we simply cannot know very much, compared with what might be known, and we must therefore choose. What is shocking is not the act of choice which we all commit openly but the claim that some choices are wrong. Especially shocking is the claim implied by my title: There is some knowledge that a man *must* have.

There clearly is no such thing, if by knowledge we mean mere acquaintance with this or that thing, fact, concept, literary work, or scientific law. When C. P. Snow and F. R. Leavis exchanged blows on whether knowledge of Shakespeare is more important than knowledge of the second law of thermodynamics, they were both, it seemed to me, much too ready to assume as indispensable what a great many wise and good men have quite obviously got along without. And it is not only nonprofessionals who can survive in happy ignorance of this or that bit of lore. I suspect that many successful scientists (in biology, say) have lost whatever hold they might once have had on the second law; I know that a great many literary scholars survive and even flourish without knowing certain "indispensable" classics. We all get along without vast loads of learning that other men take as necessary marks of an educated man. If we once begin to "reason the need" we will find, like Lear, that "our basest beggars/Are in the poorest thing superfluous." Indeed, we can survive, in a manner of speaking, even in the modern world, with little more than the bare literacy necessary to tell the "off" buttons from the "on."

Herbert Spencer would remind us at this point that we are interpreting *need* as if it were entirely a question of private survival. Though he talks about what a man must know to stay alive, he is more interested, in his defense of science, in what a *society* must know to survive: "Is there any knowledge that *man* must have?"—not a man; but *man*. This question is put to us much more acutely in our time than it was in Spencer's, and it is by no means as easy to argue now as it was then that the knowledge needed for man's survival is scientific knowledge. The threats of atomic annihilation, of engulfing population growth, of depleted air, water, and food must obviously be met, if man is to survive, and in meeting them man will, it is true, need more and more scientific knowledge; but it is not at all clear that more and more scientific knowledge will by itself suffice. Even so, a modern Herbert Spencer might well argue that a conference like this one, with its emphasis on the individual and his cognitive needs, is simply repeating the mistakes of the classical tradition. The knowledge most worth having would be, from his point of view, that of how to pull mankind through the next century or so without absolute self-destruc-tion. The precise proportions of different kinds of knowledge—physical, biological, political, ethical, psychological, historical, or whatever— would be different from those prescribed in Spencer's essay, but the nature of the search would be precisely the same.

We can admit the relevance of this emphasis on social utility and at the same time argue that our business here is with other matters entirely. If the only knowledge a man *must* have is how to cross the street without getting knocked down—or, in other words, how to navigate the centuries without blowing himself up—then we may as well close the conference and go home. We may as well also roll up the college and mail it to a research institute, because almost any place that is not cluttered up with notions of liberal education will be able to discover and transmit practical bits of survival-lore better than we can. Our problem of survival is a rather different one, thrust at us as soon as we change our title slightly once again to "Is there any knowledge (other than the knowledge for survival) that a man must have?" That slight shift opens a new perspec-tive on the problem, because the question of what it is to be a man, of what it is to be fully human, is the question at the heart of liberal education.

To be human, to be human, to be fully human. What does it mean? What is required? Immediately, we start feeling nervous again. Is the speaker suggesting that some of us are not fully human *yet?* Here come those hierarchies again. Surely in our pluralistic society we can admit an unlimited number of legitimate ways to be a man, without prescribing some outmoded aristocratic code!

Who—or what—is the creature we would educate? Our answer will determine our answers to educational questions, and it is therefore, I think, worth far more vigorous effort than it usually receives. I find it convenient, and only slightly unfair, to classify the educational talk I encounter these days under four notions of man, three of them metaphorical, only one literal. Though nobody's position, I suppose, fits my types neatly, some educators talk as if they were programming machines, some talk as if they were conditioning rats, some talk as if they were training ants to take a position in the anthill, and some—precious few—talk as if they thought of themselves as men dealing with men.

One traditional division of the human soul, you will remember, was into three parts: the vegetable, the animal, and the rational. Nobody, so far as I know, has devised an educational program treating students as vegetables, though one runs into the analogy used negatively in academic sermons from time to time. Similarly, no one ever really says that men are ants, though there is a marvelous passage in Kwame Nkrumah's autobiography in which he meditates longingly on the order and pure functionality of an anthill.[1] Educators do talk of men as machines or as animals, but of course they always point out that men are much more complicated than any other known animals or machines. My point here is not so much to attack any one of these metaphors—dangerous as I think they are—but to describe briefly what answers to our question each of them might suggest.

Ever since Descartes, La Mettrie,[2] and others explicitly called a man a machine, the metaphor has been a dominant one in educational thinking. Some have thought of man as a very complex machine, needing very elaborate programming; others have thought of him as a very simple machine, requiring little more than a systematic pattern of stimuli to produce foretellable responses. I heard a psychologist recently repeat the old behaviorist claim (first made by John B. Watson, I believe) that if you would give him complete control over any normal child's life from birth, he could turn that child into a great musician or a great mathematician or a great poet—you name it and he could produce it. On being pressed, the professor admitted that this claim was only "in theory," because we don't yet have the necessary knowledge. When I pushed further by asking why he was so confident in advance of experimental proof, it became clear that his faith in the fundamental metaphor of man as a programmable machine was unshakable.

When the notion of man as machine was first advanced, the machine was a very simple collection of pulleys and billiard balls and levers. Such original simplicities have been badly battered by our growing awareness both of how complex real machines can be and of how much more complex man is than any known machine. Modern notions of stimulus-response patterns are immeasurably more complicated than anything Descartes imagined, because we are now aware of the fantastic variety of

1. Nkrumah was the first premier of the African republic of Ghana; he was ultimately deposed in a coup and went to live in China.
2. René Descartes (1596–1650), French philosopher and mathematician; Julian Offray de La Mettrie (1709–1751), French physician and philosopher.

stimuli that the man-machine is subject to and of the even more fantastic complexity of the responding circuits.

But whether the machine is simple or complex, the educational task for those who think of man under this metaphor is to program the mechanism so that it will produce the results that we have foreordained. We do not simply fill the little pitchers, like Mr. Gradgrind in Dickens' *Hard Times;*[3] we are much too sophisticated to want only undigested "pourback," as he might have called his product. But we still program the information channels so that the proper if-loops and do-loops will be followed and the right feedback produced. The "programming" can be done by human teachers, of course, and not only by machines; but it is not surprising that those whose thinking is dominated by this metaphor tend to discover that machines are better teachers than men. The more ambitious programmers do not hesitate to claim that they can teach both thought and creativity in this way. But I have yet to see a program that can deal effectively with any subject that cannot be reduced to simple yes and no answers, that is, to answers that are known in advance by the programmer and can thus be fixed for all time.

We can assume that subtler machines will be invented that can engage in simulated dialogue with the pupil, and perhaps even recognize when a particularly bright pupil has discovered something new that refutes the program. But even the subtlest teaching machine imaginable will still be subject, one must assume, to a final limitation: it can teach only what a machine can "learn." For those who believe that man is literally nothing but a very complicated machine, this is not in fact a limitation; machines will ultimately be able to duplicate all mental processes, thus "learning" everything learnable, and they will be able in consequence to teach everything.

I doubt this claim for many reasons, and I am glad to find the testimony of Norbert Wiener, the first and best known cyberneticist, to the effect that there will always remain a radical gap between computers and the human mind. But "ultimately" is a long way off, and I am not so much concerned with whether ultimately man's mind will closely resemble some ultimately inventable machine as I am with the effects, here and now, of thinking about men under the analogy with machines of today. Let me simply close this section with an illustration of how the mechanistic model can permeate our thought in destructive ways. Ask yourselves what picture of creature-to-be-educated emerges from this professor of teacher education:

> To implement the TEAM Project new curriculum proposal . . . our first concerns are with instructional systems, materials to feed the system, and

---

3. Thomas Gradgrind thought of his students as "little pitchers . . . who were to be filled so full of facts."

personnel to operate the system. We have defined an instructional system as
the optimal blending of the demands of content, communication, and learning. While numerous models have been developed, our simplified model of
an instructional system would look like Figure 2. . . . We look at the process of
communication—communicating content to produce learning—as something involving the senses: . . . [aural, oral, tactile, visual]. And I think in
teacher education we had better think of the communications aspect of the
instructional system as a package that includes the teacher, textbook, new
media, classroom, and environment. To integrate these elements to more
effectively transmit content into permanent learning, new and better instructional materials are needed and a new focus on the teacher of teachers is
required. The teacher of teachers must: (1) examine critically the content of
traditional courses in relation to desired behavioral outcomes; (2) become
more sophisticated in the techniques of communicating course content; and
(3) learn to work in concert with media specialists to develop the materials
and procedures requisite to the efficient instructional system. And if the
media specialist were to be charged with the efficient operation of the system,
his upgrading would demand a broad-based "media generalist" orientation.

I submit that the author of this passage was thinking of human beings
as stimulus-response systems on the simplest possible model, and that he
was thinking of the purpose of education as the transfer of information
from one machine to another. Though he would certainly deny it if we
asked him, he has come to think about the human mind so habitually in
the mechanistic mode that he doesn't even know he's doing it.[4]

But it is time to move from the machine metaphor to animal metaphors. They are closely related, of course, because everybody who believes that man is a machine also believes that animals are machines, only
simpler ones. But many people who would resist the word "machine" do
tend to analogize man to one or another characteristic of animals. Since
man is obviously an animal in one sense, he can be studied as an animal,
and he can be taught as an animal is taught. Most of the fundamental
research in learning theory underlying the use of teaching machines has
been done, in fact, on animals like rats and pigeons. You can teach
pigeons to play Ping-Pong rather quickly by rewarding every gesture
they make that moves them toward success in the game and refusing to
reward those gestures that you want to efface. Though everybody admits
that human beings are more complicated than rats and pigeons, just as
everyone admits that human beings are more complicated than computers, the basic picture of the animal as a collection of drives or instincts, "conditioned" to learn according to rewards or punishments, has
underlain much modern educational theory.

---

4. I am not of course suggesting that any use
of teaching machines implies a mechanistic
reduction of persons to machines; programmers rightly point out that machines can free
teachers from the mechanical and save time
for the personal [Booth's note].

The notion of the human being as a collection of drives different from animal drives only in being more complex carries with it implications for education planners. If you and I are motivated only by sex or hunger or more complex drives like desire for power or for ego-satisfaction, then of course all education depends on the provision of satisfactions along our route to knowledge. If our teachers can just program carrots along the path at the proper distance, we donkey-headed students will plod along the path from carrot to carrot and end up as educated men.

I cannot take time here to deal with this view adequately, but it seems to me that it is highly questionable even about animals themselves. What kind of thing, really, is a rat or a monkey? The question of whether animals have souls has been debated actively for at least nine centuries; now psychologists find themselves dealing with the same question under another guise: What are these little creatures that we kill so blithely for the sake of knowledge? What are these strangely resistant little bundles of energy that will prefer—as experiments with rats have shown—a complicated interesting maze without food to a dull one *with* food?

There are, in fact, many experiments by now showing that at the very least we must postulate, for animals, a strong independent drive for mastery of the environment or satisfaction of curiosity about it. All the more advanced animals will learn to push levers that produce interesting results—clicks or bells or flashing lights or sliding panels—when no other reward is offered. It seems clear that even to be a fulfilled animal, as it were, something more than "animal satisfaction" is needed!

I am reminded here of the experiments on mother-love in monkeys reported by Harry F. Harlow in the *Scientific American* some years ago. Harlow called his article "Love in Infant Monkeys," and the subtitle of his article read, "Affection in infants was long thought to be generated by the satisfactions of feeding. Studies of young rhesus monkeys now indicate that love derives mainly from close bodily contact." The experiment consisted of giving infant monkeys a choice between a plain wire figure that offered the infant milk and a terry-cloth covered figure without milk. There was a pathetic picture of an infant clinging to the terry-cloth figure, and a caption that read "The infants spent most of their time clinging to the soft cloth 'mother' even when nursing bottles were attached to the wire mother." The article concluded—rather prematurely, I thought—that "contact comfort" had been shown to be a "prime requisite in the formation of an infant's love for its mother," that the act of nursing had been shown to be unimportant if not totally irrelevant in forming such love (though it was evident to any reader, even at the time, that no genuine "act of nursing" had figured in the experiment at all), and that "our investigations have established a secure experimental approach to this realm of dramatic and subtle emotional relationships." The only real problem, Harlow said, was the availability of enough infant monkeys for experiment.

Now I would not want to underrate the importance of Harlow's demonstration to the scientific community that monkeys do not live by bread alone. But I think that most scientists and humanists reading the article would have been struck by two things. The first is the automatic assumption that the way to study a subject like love is to break it down into its component parts; nobody looking at that little monkey clinging to the terry-cloth could possibly have said, "This is love," unless he had been blinded by a hidden conviction that love in animals is—must be—a mere cumulative result of a collection of drive satisfactions. This assumption is given quite plainly in Harlow's concluding sentence: "Finally with such techniques established, there appears to be no reason why we cannot at some future time investigate the fundamental neurophysiological and biochemical variables underlying affection and love." For Harlow monkeys (and people) seem to be mere collections of neurophysiological and biochemical variables, and love will be best explained when we can explain the genesis of each of its parts. The second striking point is that for Harlow animals do not matter, except as they are useful for experiment. If he had felt that they mattered, he might have noticed the look on his infant's face—a look that predicted for me, and for other readers of the *Scientific American* I've talked with, that these monkeys were doomed.

And indeed they were. A year or so later another article appeared, reporting Harlow's astonished discovery that all of the little monkeys on which he had earlier experimented had turned out to be incurably psychotic. Not a single monkey could mate, not a single monkey could play, not a single monkey could in fact become anything more than the twisted half-creatures that Harlow's deprivations had made of them. Harlow's new discovery was that monkeys needed close association with their peers during infancy and that such association was even more important to their development than genuine mothering. There was no sign that Harlow had learned any fundamental lessons from his earlier gross mistakes; he had landed nicely on his feet, still convinced that the way to study love is to break it down into its component parts and that the way to study animals is to maim them or reduce them to something less than themselves. As Robert White says, summarizing his reasons for rejecting similar methods in studying human infancy, it is too often assumed that the scientific way is to analyze behavior until one can find a small enough unit to allow for detailed research, but in the process "very vital common properties" are lost from view.

I cite Harlow's two reports not, of course, to attack animal experimentation—though I must confess that I am horrified by much that goes on in its name—nor to claim that animals are more like human beings than they are. Rather, I want simply to suggest that the danger of thinking of men as animals is heightened if the animals we think of are reduced to machines on a simple model.

The effects of reducing education to conditioning can be seen throughout America today. Usually they appear in subtle forms, disguised with the language of personalism; you will look a long time before you find anyone (except a very few Skinnerians) saying that he thinks of education as exactly like conditioning pigeons. But there are plenty of honest, blunt folk around to let the cat out of the bag—like the author of an article this year in *College Composition and Communications*: "The Use of a Multiple Response Device in the Teaching of Remedial English." The author claimed to have evidence that if you give each student four buttons to be pushed on multiple-choice questions, with all the buttons wired into a lighted grid at the front of the room, the resulting "instantaneous feedback"—every child learning immediately whether he agrees with the rest of the class—speeds up the learning of grammatical rules considerably over the usual workbook procedures. I daresay it does—but meanwhile what has happened to education? Or take the author of an article on "Procedures and Techniques of Teaching," who wrote as follows: "If we expect students to learn skills, they have to practice, but practice doesn't make perfect. Practice works if the learner *learns the results* of his practice, i.e., if he receives feedback. Feedback is most effective when it is contiguous to the response being learned. One of the chief advantages of teaching machines is that the learner finds out quickly whether his response is right or wrong . . . [Pressey] has published the results of an extensive program of research with tests that students score for themselves by punching alternatives until they hit the correct one. . . . [Thus] teaching machines or workbooks have many theoretical advantages over lecturing or other conventional methods of instruction." But according to what theory, one must ask, *do* systematic feedback mechanisms, perfected to whatever degree, have "theoretical advantages" over human contact? Whatever else can be said for such a theory, it will be based on the simplest of comparisons with animal learning. Unfortunately, the author goes on, experimental evidence is on the whole rather discouraging: "Experiments at the Systems Development Corporation . . . suggest that teaching incorporating . . . human characteristics is more effective than the typical fixed-sequence machines. (In this experiment instead of using teaching machines to simulate human teachers, the experimenters used humans to simulate teaching machines!)"

So far I have dealt with analogies for man that apply only to individuals. My third analogy turns to the picture of men in groups, and it is given to me partly by discussions of education, like those of Admiral Rickover, that see it simply as filling society's needs. I know of only one prominent

educator who has publicly praised the anthill as a model for the kind of
society a university should serve—a society of specialists each trained to
do his part. But the notion pervades many of the defenses of the emerging
multiversities.[5]

If knowledge is needed to enable men to function as units in society,
and if the health of society is taken as the purpose of their existence, then
there is nothing wrong in training the ants to fill their niches; it would be
wrong not to. "Education is our first line of defense—make it strong," so
reads the title of the first chapter of Admiral Rickover's book, *Education
and Freedom* (New York: Dutton, 1959). "We must upgrade our schools"
in order to "guarantee the future prosperity and freedom of the Republic." You can tell whether the ant-analogy is dominating a man's thinking
by a simple test of how he orders his ends and means. In Admiral
Rickover's statement, the schools must be upgraded in order to guarantee future prosperity, that is, we improve education for the sake of some
presumed social good.

I seldom find anyone putting it the other way round: we must guarantee prosperity so that we can improve the schools, and the reason we
want to improve the schools is that we want to insure the development of
certain kinds of persons, both as teachers and as students. You cannot
even say what I just said so long as you are really thinking of ants and
anthills. Ants are not ends in themselves, ultimately more valuable than
the hills they live in (I *think* they are not; maybe to themselves, or in the
eyes of God, even ants are ultimate, self-justifying ends). At least from
our point of view, ants are expendable, or to put it another way, their
society is more beautiful, more interesting, more admirable than they
are. And I would want to argue that too many people think of human
beings in the same way when they think of educating them. The Communists make this quite explicit: the ends of Communist society justify
whatever distortion or destruction of individual purposes is necessary to
achieve them; men are educated for the state, not for their own well-
being. They are basically political animals, not in the Aristotelian sense
that they require society if they are to achieve their full natures and thus
their own special, human kind of happiness, but in the sense that they
exist, like ants, for the sake of the body politic.

If the social order is the final justification of what we do in education,
then a certain attitude toward teaching and research will result: all of us
little workmen, down inside the anthill, will go on happily contributing
our tiny bit to the total scheme without worrying much about larger
questions of the why and wherefore. I know a graduate student who says
that she sometimes sees her graduate professors as an army of tiny

5. A 1960s term for the gargantuan universities which often set government and corporate research, and the training of graduate
students to do that research, above undergraduate education.

industrious miners at the bottom of a vast mine, chipping away at the edges and shipping their bits of knowledge up to the surface, blindly hoping that someone up there will know what to do with it all. An order is received for such-and-such new organic compounds; society needs them. Another order is received for an atomic bomb; it is needed, and it is therefore produced. Often no orders come down, but the chipping goes on anyway, and the shipments are made, because everyone knows that the health of the mine depends on a certain tonnage of specialized knowledge each working day.

We have learned lately that "they" are going to establish a great new atom-smasher, perhaps near Chicago. The atom-smasher will employ two thousand scientists and technicians. I look out at you here, knowing that some of you are physics majors, and I wonder whether any of you will ultimately be employed in that new installation, and if you are, whether it will be as an ant or as a human being. Which it will be must depend not on your ultimate employers but on yourself and on what happens to your education between now and then: if you have been given nothing but training to be that ultimate unit in that ultimate system, only a miracle can save you from formic dissolution of your human lineaments.

But it is long past time for me to turn from these negative, truncated portraits of what man really is not and attempt to say what he is. And here we encounter a difficulty that I find very curious. You will note that each of these metaphors has reduced man to something less than man, or at least to a partial aspect of man. It is easy to say that man is not a machine, though he is in some limited respects organized like a machine and even to some degree "programmable." It is also easy to say that man is not simply a complicated rat or monkey, though he is in some ways like rats and monkeys. Nor is man an ant, though he lives and must function in a complicated social milieu. All these metaphors break down not because they are flatly false but because they are metaphors, and any metaphorical definition is inevitably misleading. The ones I have been dealing with are especially misleading, because in every case they have reduced something more complex to something much less complex. But even if we were to analogize man to something more complex, say, the universe, we would be dissatisfied. What we want is some notion of what man really *is*, so that we will know what or whom we are trying to educate.

And here it is that we discover something very important about man, something that even the least religious person must find himself mystified by: man is the one "thing" we know that is completely resistant to our efforts at metaphor or analogy or image-making. What seems to be the most important literal characteristic of man is his resistance to definitions in terms of anything else. If you call me a machine, even a very

complicated machine, I know that you deny what I care most about, my
selfhood, my sense of being a person, my consciousness, my conviction of
freedom and dignity, my awareness of love, my laughter. Machines have
none of these things, and even if we were generous to their prospects, and
imagined machines immeasurably superior to the most complicated ones
now in existence, we would still feel an infinite gap between them and
what we know to be a basic truth about ourselves: machines are expendable, ultimately expendable, and men are mysteriously ends in themselves.

I hear people deny this, but when they do they always argue for their
position by claiming marvelous feats of super-machine calculation that
machines can now do or will someday be able to do. But that is not the
point; of course machines can outcalculate us. The question to ask is
entirely a different one: Will they ever outlove us, outlive us, outvalue
us? Do we build machines because machines are good things in themselves? Do we nurture them for their own good, as we nurture our
children? An obvious way to test our sense of worth in men and machines
is to ask ourselves whether we would ever campaign to liberate the poor
downtrodden machines who have been enslaved. Shall we form a National Association for the Advancement of Machinery? Will anyone ever
feel a smidgeon of moral indignation because this or that piece of machinery is not given equal rights before the law? Or put it another way: Does
anyone value Gemini[6] more than the twins? There may be men now
alive who would rather "destruct," as we say, the pilot than the experimental rocket, but most of us still believe that the human being in the
space ship is more important than the space ship.

When college students protest the so-called depersonalization of education, what they mean, finally, is not simply that they want to meet their
professors socially or that they want small classes or that they do not want
to be dealt with by IBM machines. All these things are but symptoms of a
deeper sense of a violation of their literal reality as persons, ends in
themselves rather than mere expendable things. Similarly, the current
deep-spirited revolt against racial and economic injustice seems to me
best explained as a sudden assertion that people, of whatever color or
class, are not reducible to social conveniences. When you organize your
labor force or your educational system as if men were mere social conveniences, "human resources," as we say, contributors to the gross national
product, you violate something that we all know, in a form of knowledge
much deeper than our knowledge of the times tables or the second law of
thermodynamics: those field hands, those children crowded into the
deadening classroom, those men laboring without dignity in the city
anthills are *men*, creatures whose worth is mysteriously more than any

6. Here referring not to the astrological sign but to the space rockets.

description of it we might make in justifying what we do to them.

Ants, rats, and machines can all learn a great deal. Taken together, they "know" a very great part of what our schools and colleges are now designed to teach. But is there any kind of knowledge that a creature must have to qualify as a man? Is there any part of the educational task that is demanded of us by virtue of our claim to educate this curious entity, this *person* that cannot be reduced to mechanism or animality alone?

You will not be surprised, by now, to have me sound, in my answer, terribly traditional, not to say square: the education that a *man* must have is what has traditionally been called liberal education. The knowledge it yields is the knowledge or capacity or power of how to act freely as a man. That's why we call liberal education liberal: it is intended to liberate from whatever it is that makes animals act like animals and machines act like machines.

I'll return in a moment to what it means to act freely as a man. But we are already in a position to say something about what knowledge a man must have—he must first of all be able to learn for himself. If he cannot learn for himself, he is enslaved by his teachers' ideas, or by the ideas of his more persuasive contemporaries, or by machines programmed by other men. He may have what we call a good formal education, yet still be totally bound by whatever opinions happen to have come his way in attractive garb. One wonders how many of our graduates have learned how to take hold of a subject and "work it up," so that they can make themselves experts on what other men have concluded. In some ways this is not a very demanding goal, and it is certainly not very exciting. It says nothing about that popular concept, creativity, or about imagination or originality. All it says is that anyone who is dependent on his teachers *is* dependent, not free, and that anyone who knows how to learn for himself is less like animals and machines than anyone who does not know how to learn for himself.

We see already that a college is not being merely capricious or arbitrary when it insists that some kinds of learning are more important than some others. The world is overflowing with interesting subjects and valuable skills, but surely any college worth the name will put first things first: it will try to insure, as one inescapable goal, that every graduate can dig out from the printed page what he needs to know. And it will not let the desire to tamp in additional tidbits of knowledge, however delicious, interfere with training minds for whom a formal teacher is no longer required.

To put our first goal in this way raises some real problems that we cannot solve. Obviously no college can produce self-learners in very many subjects. Are we not lucky if a graduate can learn for himself even in one field, now that knowledge in all areas has advanced as far as it has? Surely we cannot expect our graduates to reach a stage of independence in mathematics and physics, in political science and psychology, in philosophy and English, and in all the other nice subjects that one would like to master.

Rather than answer this objection right away, let me make things even more difficult by saying that it is not enough to learn how to learn. The man who cannot *think* for himself, going beyond what other men have learned or thought, is still enslaved to other men's ideas. Obviously the goal of learning to think is even more difficult than the goal of learning to learn. But difficult as it is we must add it to our list. It is simply not enough to be able to get up a subject on one's own, like a good encyclopedia employee, even though any college would take pride if all its graduates could do so. To be fully human means in part to think one's own thoughts, to reach a point at which, whether one's ideas are different from or similar to other men's, they are truly one's own.

The art of asking oneself critical questions that lead either to new answers or to genuine revitalizing of old answers, the art of making thought live anew in each new generation, may not be entirely amenable to instruction. But it is a necessary art nonetheless, for any man who wants to be free. It is an art that all philosophers have tried to pursue, and many of them have given direct guidance in how to pursue it. Needless to say, it is an art the pursuit of which is never fully completed. No one thinks for himself very much of the time or in very many subjects. Yet the habitual effort to ask the right critical questions and to apply rigorous tests to our hunches is a clearer mark than any other of an educated man.

But again we stumble upon the question, "Learn to think about *what?*" The modern world presents us with innumerable subjects to think about. Does it matter whether anyone achieves this rare and difficult point in more than one subject? And if not, won't the best education simply be the one that brings a man into mastery of a narrow specialty as soon as possible, so that he can learn to think for himself as soon as possible? Even at best most of us are enslaved to opinions provided for us by experts in *most* fields. So far, it might be argued, I still have not shown that there is any kind of knowledge that a man must have, only that there are certain skills that he must be able to exercise in at least one field.

To provide a proper grounding for my answer to that objection would require far more time than I have left, and I'm not at all sure that I could do so even with all the time in the world. The question of whether it is possible to maintain a human stance toward any more than a tiny fraction of modern knowledge is not clearly answerable at this stage in our history. It will be answered, if at all, only when men have learned how to store and retrieve all "machinable" knowledge, freeing themselves for distinctively human tasks. But in the meantime, I find myself unable to surrender, as it were, three distinct kinds of knowledge that seem to me indispensable to being human.

To be a man, a man must first know something about his own nature and his place in Nature, with a capital N—something about the truth of things, as men used to say in the old-fashioned days before the word "truth" was banned from academia. Machines are not curious, so far as I can judge; animals are, but presumably they never go, in their philosophies, even at the furthest, beyond a kind of solipsistic existentialism. But in science, in philosophy (ancient and modern), in theology, in psychology and anthropology, and in literature (of some kinds), we are presented with accounts of our universe and of our place in it that as men we can respond to in only one manly way: by thinking about them, by speculating and testing our speculations.

We know before we start that our thought is doomed to incompleteness and error and downright chanciness. Even the most rigorously scientific view will be changed, we know, within a decade, or perhaps even by tomorrow. But to refuse the effort to understand is to resign from the human race; the unexamined life can no doubt be worth living in other respects—after all, it is no mean thing to be a vegetable, an oak tree, an elephant, or a lion.[7] But a man, a man will want to see, in this speculative domain, beyond his next dinner.

By putting it in this way, I think we can avoid the claim that to be a man I must have studied any one field—philosophy, science, theology. But to be a man, *I must speculate,* and I must learn how to test my speculations so that they are not simply capricious, unchecked by other men's speculations. A college education, surely, should throw every student into a regular torrent of speculation, and it should school him to recognize the different standards of validation proper to different kinds of claims to truth. You cannot distinguish a man who in this respect is educated from other men by whether or not he believes in God, or in UFO's. But you can tell an educated man by the way he takes hold of the question of whether God exists, or whether UFO's are from Mars. Do you know your own reasons for your beliefs, or do you absorb your beliefs from whatever happens to be in your environment, like plankton taking in nourishment?

Second, the man who has not learned how to make the great human achievements in the arts his own, who does not know what it means to *earn* a great novel or symphony or painting for himself, is enslaved either to caprice or to other men's testimony or to a life of ugliness. You will notice that as I turn thus to "beauty"—another old-fashioned term—I do

7. Here Booth echoes the assertion of Socrates, defending his practice of probing students' conventional beliefs, that the unexamined life is not worth living.

not say that a man must know how to prove what is beautiful or how to discourse on aesthetics. Such speculative activities are pleasant and worthwhile in themselves, but they belong in my first domain. Here we are asking that a man be educated to the experience of beauty; speculation about it can then follow. My point is simply that a man is less than a man if he cannot respond to the art made by his fellow man.

Again I have tried to put the standard in a way that allows for the impossibility of any one man's achieving independent responses in very many arts. Some would argue that education should insure some minimal human competence in all of the arts, or at least in music, painting, and literature. I suppose I would be satisfied if all of our graduates had been "hooked" by at least one art, hooked so deeply that they could never get free. As in the domain of speculation, we could say that the more types of distinctively human activity a man can master, the better, but we are today talking about floors, not ceilings, and I shall simply rest content with saying that to be a man, a man must know artistic beauty, in some form, and know it in the way that beauty can be known. (The distinction between natural and man-made beauty might give me trouble if you pushed me on it here, but let me just say, dogmatically, that I would not be satisfied simply to know natural beauty—women and sunsets, say—as a substitute for art.)

Finally, the man who has not learned anything about how to understand his own intentions and to make them effective in the world, who has not, through experience and books, learned something about what is possible and what impossible, what desirable and what undesirable, will be enslaved by the political and social intentions of other men, benign or malign. The domain of practical wisdom is at least as complex and troublesome as the other two, and at the same time it is even more self-evidently indispensable. How should a man live? How should a society be run? What direction should a university take in 1966? For that matter what should be the proportion, in a good university, of inquiry into truth, beauty, and "goodness"? What kind of knowledge of self or of society is pertinent to living the life proper to a man? In short, the very question of this conference falls within this final domain: What knowledge, if any, is most worthy of pursuit? You cannot distinguish the men from the boys according to any one set of conclusions, but you can recognize a man, in this domain, simply by discovering whether he can think for himself about practical questions, with some degree of freedom from blind psychological or political or economic compulsions. Ernest Hemingway tells somewhere of a man who had "moved one dollar's width to the [political] right for every dollar that he'd ever earned." Perhaps no man ever achieves the opposite extreme, complete freedom in his choices from irrelevant compulsions. But all of us who believe in education believe that it is possible for any man, through study and conscientious thought, to school his choices—that is, to free them through coming to understand the forces working on them.

Even from this brief discussion of the three domains, I think we are put in a position to see how it can be said that there is some knowledge that a man must have. The line I have been pursuing will not lead to a list of great books, or even to a list of indispensable departments in a university. Nor will it lead, in any clear-cut fashion, to a pattern of requirements in each of the divisions. Truth, beauty, and goodness (or "right choice") are relevant to study in every division within the university; the humanities, for example, have no corner on beauty or imagination or art, and the sciences have no corner on speculative truth. What is more, a man can be ignorant even of Shakespeare, Aristotle, Beethoven, and Einstein, and be a man for a' that—*if* he has learned how to think his own thoughts, experience beauty for himself, and choose his own actions.

It is not the business of a college to determine or limit what a man will know; if it tries to, he will properly resent its impositions, perhaps immediately, perhaps ten years later when the imposed information is outmoded. But I think that it *is* the business of a college to help teach a man how to use his mind for himself, in at least the three directions I have suggested * * * To think for oneself is, as we all know, hard enough. To design a program and assemble faculty to assist rather than hinder students in their efforts to think for themselves is even harder. But in an age that is oppressed by huge accumulations of unassimilated knowledge, the task of discovering what it means to educate a man is perhaps more important than ever before.

1967

Language and Communication

Ralph Waldo Emerson

THE LANGUAGE OF THE STREET

The language of the street is always strong. What can describe the folly and emptiness of scolding like the word *jawing*? I feel too the force of the double negative, though clean contrary to our grammar rules. And I confess to some pleasure from the stinging rhetoric of a rattling oath in the mouths of truckmen and teamsters. How laconic and brisk it is by the side of a page of the *North American Review*. Cut these words and they would bleed; they are vascular and alive; they walk and run. Moreover they who speak them have this elegancy, that they do not trip in their speech. It is a shower of bullets, whilst Cambridge men and Yale men correct themselves and begin again at every half sentence.

1840   1914

THE READER

1. Analyze a paragraph from each of the following writers in the terms of this one: Lincoln (pp. 255, 504) and White (pp. 514, 663).
2. Emerson uses specific examples of people who used "the language of the street" in his time. What examples might he use if he were writing today?

THE WRITER

1. How would you characterize Emerson's own language in this piece?
2. Write two brief descriptions of the same person, scene, or event, one using the language of the street and one using more formal language.

Wallace Stegner

GOOD-BYE TO ALL T - - T!

Not everyone who laments what contemporary novelists have done to
the sex act objects to the act itself, or to its mention. Some want it valued
higher than fiction seems to value it; they want the word "climax" to
retain some of its literary meaning. Likewise, not everyone who has come
to doubt the contemporary freedom of language objects to strong language in itself. Some of us object precisely because we value it.

I acknowledge that I have used four-letter words familiarly all my life,
and have put them into books with some sense that I was insisting on the
proper freedom of the artist. I have applauded the extinction of those d- -
- -d emasculations of the Genteel Tradition and the intrusion into serious fiction of honest words with honest meanings and emphasis. I have
wished, with D. H. Lawrence, for the courage to say shit before a lady,
and have sometimes had my wish.

Words are not obscene: naming things is a legitimate verbal act. And
"frank" does not mean "vulgar," any more than "improper" means
"dirty." What vulgar does mean is "common"; what improper means is
"unsuitable." Under the right circumstances, any word is proper. But
when any sort of word, especially a word hitherto taboo and therefore
noticeable, is scattered across a page like chocolate chips through a
tollhouse cookie, a real impropriety occurs. The sin is not the use of an
"obscene" word; it is the use of a loaded word in the wrong place or in the
wrong quantity. It is the sin of false emphasis, which is not a moral but a
literary lapse, related to sentimentality. It is the sin of advertisers who so
plaster a highway with neon signs that you can't find the bar or liquor
store you're looking for. Like any excess, it quickly becomes comic.

If I habitually say shit before a lady, what do I say before a flat tire at the
rush hour in Times Square or on the San Francisco Bay Bridge? What do
I say before a revelation of the inequity of the universe? And what if the
lady takes the bit in her teeth and says shit before *me*?

I have been a teacher of writing for many years and have watched this
problem since it was no bigger than a man's hand. It used to be that with
some Howellsian notion of the young-girl audience one tried to protect
tender female members of a mixed class from the coarse language of
males trying to show off. Some years ago Frank O'Connor and I agreed on
a system. Since we had no intention whatever of restricting students'
choice of subject or language, and no desire to expurgate or bowdlerize
while reading their stuff aloud for discussion, but at the same time had to
deal with these young girls of an age our daughters might have been, we

213

announced that any stuff so strong that it would embarrass us to read it aloud could be read by its own author.

It was no deterrent at all, but an invitation, and not only to coarse males. For clinical sexual observation, for full acceptance of the natural functions, for discrimination in the selection of graffiti, for boldness in the use of words that it should take courage to say before a lady, give me a sophomore girl every time. Her strength is as the strength of ten, for she assumes that if one shocker out of her pretty mouth is piquant, fifty will be literature. And so do a lot of her literary idols.

Some acts like some words, were never meant to be casual. That is why houses contain bedrooms and bathrooms. Profanity and so-called obscenities are literary resources, verbal ways of rendering strong emotion. They are not meant to occur every ten seconds, any more than—Norman Mailer to the contrary notwithstanding—orgasms are.

So I am not going to say shit before any more ladies. I am going to hunt words that have not lost their sting, and it may be I shall have to go back to gentility to find them. Pleasant though it is to know that finally a writer can make use of any word that fits his occasion, I am going to investigate the possibilities latent in restraint.

I remember my uncle, a farmer who had used four-letter words ten to the sentence ever since he learned to talk. One day he came too near the circular saw and cut half his fingers off. While we stared in horror, he stood watching the bright arterial blood pump from his ruined hand. Then he spoke, and he did not speak loud. "Aw, the dickens," he said.

I think he understood, better than some sophomore girls and better than some novelists, the nature of emphasis.

1965

John Leo

JOURNALESE FOR THE LAY READER

Journalese, the native tongue of newsgatherers and pundits, retains a faint similarity to English but is actually closer to Latin. Like Latin, it is primarily a written language, prized for its incantatory powers, and is best learned early, while the mind is still supple. Every cub reporter, for instance, knows that fires rage out of control, minor mischief is perpetrated by Vandals (never Visigoths, Franks, or a single Vandal working alone) and key labor accords are hammered out by weary negotiators in marathon, round-the-clock bargaining sessions, thus narrowly averting threatened walkouts. The discipline required for a winter storm report is awesome. The first reference to seasonal precipitation is "snow," followed by "the white stuff," then either "it" or "the flakes," but not both. The word snow may be used once again toward the end of the report, directly after discussion of ice-slicked roads and the grim highway toll.

Every so often, an inexperienced reporter attempts to describe a dwelling as "attractive" or "impressive." This is incorrect. In journalese, all homes are either modest or stately. When confronted with a truly ramshackle fixer-upper, knowing scribes will deflect attention to the surrounding area, describing the residence as "off the beaten track" or "in a developing area," that is, a slum. Distaste for the suburbs is conveyed by mentioning "trimmed lawns and neat flower beds," thus artfully suggesting both compulsiveness and a high level of intolerance for life in its hearty, untrimmed state.

Journalese is rich in mystic nouns: gentrification, quichification, greenmail, dealignment, watershed elections and apron strings (the political coattails of a female candidate). But students of the language agree that adjectives do most of the work, smuggling in actual information under the guise of normal journalism. Thus the use of soft-spoken (mousy), loyal (dumb), high-minded (inept), hardworking (plodding), self-made (crooked) and pragmatic (totally immoral). A person who is dangerous as well as immoral can be described as a fierce competitor or gut fighter, and a meddler who cannot leave his subordinates alone is a hands-on executive. When strung together properly, apparently innocent modifiers can acquire megaton force. For instance, a journalist may write, "A private, deliberate man, Frobisher dislikes small talk, but can be charming when he wants to." In translation this means, "An antisocial, sullen plodder, Frobisher is obnoxious and about as articulate as a canteloupe." The familiar phrase "can be charming" is as central to good journalese as "affordable" is to automobile ads and "excellence" is to education reports. It indicates that Frobisher's charm production is a rare result of mighty exertion, yet it manages to end the revelation about his dismal character on an upbeat note.

"Spry" refers to any senior citizen who is not in a wheelchair or a coma, and "stereotype" introduces the discussion of something entirely obvious that the writer wishes to disparage, as in "the stereotype that boys like to play with trucks and girls like to play with dolls." "Life-style" has made the transition from psychobabble to journalese. Though often misused to indicate gays, joggers, wheat-germ consumers and other defiant minorities, it actually refers to any practice that makes the normal citizen's hair stand on end. The fellow who tortures iguanas in his basement has a life-style. The rest of us merely have lives.

Many terms in journalese come from sportswriting. "A complex, sensitive man" (lunatic) and "ebullient" (space cadet) were developed by baseball writers. When baseball players of the 1940s and 1950s were

fined for the usual excesses with women and booze, the writers faithfully
reported that the penalties were for "nightclubbing." Nowadays the vast
consumption of controlled and uncontrolled substances would be covered by circumlocutions like "he works hard and he plays hard." Sports-
writers also taught journalese users how to recast a boring story with
exciting verbiage. Hence all the crucial issues, dramatic confrontations
and stunning breakthroughs. "Arguably" is the most useful adverb on
the excitement frontier, because it introduces a sweeping factoid that no
one will be able to check: "Frobisher is arguably the richest Rotarian
living west of the Susquehanna."

Often English words mean exactly the opposite in journalese. "Multitalented" means "untalented" and is used to identify entertainers who
have great pep and perspire a lot but do nothing particularly well.
"Community" means non-community, as in the intelligence community,
the gay community or the journalese-speaking community. Under this
usage, everyone shooting everyone else in and around Beirut, say, could
be fairly referred to as the Lebanese community.

"Middle America" has disappeared from political journalese, for the
simple reason that in the Age of Reagan, America is all middle, with no
edges. Similarly, yesterday's "radical right-winger" is today's "mainstream Republican," while "unabashed" now modifies "liberal" instead
of "conservative." Yet most political journalese is timeless. A "savvy
political pro" is anyone who has lived through two or more Administrations and can still get a table in a decent restaurant. An elder stateman is
an out-of-office politician who is senile, and a neoliberal is any Democrat
under 45 with blow-dried hair. All seasoned reporters (old-timers) know
that when two or more political appointees are fired on the same day,
they need only check their calendars before tapping out "Bloody
Wednesday" or "the Thursday Early-Afternoon Massacre." Political
journalese has a number of famed option plays. One man's squealer is
another's whistle blower, and Frobisher's magnificent five-point agenda
can also be described as a shopping list, or worse, a wish list.

One inflexible rule of journalese is that American assassins must have
three names: John Wilkes Booth, Lee Harvey Oswald, James Earl Ray,
Mark David Chapman. This courtesy of a resonant three-part moniker is
also applied to other dangerous folk. This is why the "subway vigilante"
is "Bernhard Hugo Goetz" to many journalists who consider him a
monster, and just plain "Bernhard Goetz" to almost everyone else.
Another rule of the language is that euphemisms for "fat" are understood
too quickly by the public and are therefore in constant need of replacement. "Jolly," "Rubenesque" and the like have long been abandoned. A
Washington writer scored by praising a woman's "Wagnerian good
looks," which is far more polite than saying she is not bad looking for a
massive Brünnhilde. The disinfecting compliment is particularly deft. As

all practitioners know, a corrective lurch toward balance is the hallmark of good journalese. After all, journalism is a crucially important field that attracts high-minded, multitalented professionals, arguably the finest in the land.

1985

THE READER

1. What are the major characteristics of journalese? What purposes does it serve?
2. Read Orwell's "Politics and the English Language" (p. 241). How does Orwell's tone differ from Leo's? What might Orwell say about Leo's essay?
3. What is Leo doing in his last sentence?

THE WRITER

1. What techniques does Leo use in giving his definition of journalese?
2. How does Leo's use of humor contribute to the effectiveness of his essay?
3. Write a brief sketch of a person or an account of an event. Then rewrite it in journalese as Leo defines and describes it. What are the differences?

Lewis Thomas

NOTES ON PUNCTUATION

There are no precise rules about punctuation (Fowler[1] lays out some general advice (as best he can under the complex circumstances of English prose (he points out, for example, that we possess only four stops (the comma, the semicolon, the colon and the period (the question mark and exclamation point are not, strictly speaking, stops; they are indicators of tone (oddly enough, the Greeks employed the semicolon for their question mark (it produces a strange sensation to read a Greek sentence which is a straightforward question: Why weepest thou; (instead of Why weepest thou? (and, of course, there are parentheses (which are surely a kind of punctuation making this whole much more complicated by having to count up the left-handed parentheses in order to be sure of closing with the right number (but if the parentheses were left out, with nothing to work with but the stops, we would have considerably more flexibility in the deploying of layers of meaning than if we tried to

1. H. W. Fowler, author of *Modern English Usage* (1926, revised 1965 by Sir Ernest Gowers), a standard reference work.

separate all the clauses by physical barriers (and in the latter case, while we might have more precision and exactitude for our meaning, we would lose the essential flavor of language, which is its wonderful ambiguity)))))))))))).

The commas are the most useful and usable of all the stops. It is highly important to put them in place as you go along. If you try to come back after doing a paragraph and stick them in the various spots that tempt you you will discover that they tend to swarm like minnows into all sorts of crevices whose existence you hadn't realized and before you know it the whole long sentence becomes immobilized and lashed up squirming in commas. Better to use them sparingly, and with affection, precisely when the need for each one arises, nicely, by itself.

I have grown fond of semicolons in recent years. The semicolon tells you that there is still some question about the preceding full sentence; something needs to be added; it reminds you sometimes of the Greek usage. It is almost always a greater pleasure to come across a semicolon than a period. The period tells you that that is that; if you didn't get all the meaning you wanted or expected, anyway you got all the writer intended to parcel out and now you have to move along. But with a semicolon there you get a pleasant little feeling of expectancy; there is more to come; read on; it will get clearer.

Colons are a lot less attractive, for several reasons: firstly, they give you the feeling of being rather ordered around, or at least having your nose pointed in a direction you might not be inclined to take if left to yourself, and, secondly, you suspect you're in for one of those sentences that will be labeling the points to be made: firstly, secondly and so forth, with the implication that you haven't sense enough to keep track of a sequence of notions without having them numbered. Also, many writers use this system loosely and incompletely, starting out with number one and number two as though counting off on their fingers but then going on and on without the succession of labels you've been led to expect, leaving you floundering about searching for the ninethly or seventeenthly that ought to be there but isn't.

Exclamation points are the most irritating of all. Look! they say, look at what I just said! How amazing is my thought! It is like being forced to watch someone else's small child jumping up and down crazily in the center of the living room shouting to attract attention. If a sentence really has something of importance to say, something quite remarkable, it doesn't need a mark to point it out. And if it is really, after all, a banal sentence needing more zing, the exclamation point simply emphasizes its banality!

Quotation marks should be used honestly and sparingly, when there is a genuine quotation at hand, and it is necessary to be very rigorous about the words enclosed by the marks. If something is to be quoted, the *exact* words must be used. If part of it must be left out because of space limitations, it is good manners to insert three dots to indicate the omission, but it is unethical to do this if it means connecting two thoughts which the original author did not intend to have tied together. Above all, quotation marks should not be used for ideas that you'd like to disown, things in the air so to speak. Nor should they be put in place around clichés; if you want to use a cliché you must take full responsibility for it yourself and not try to job it off on anon., or on society. The most objectionable misuse of quotation marks, but one which illustrates the dangers of misuse in ordinary prose, is seen in advertising, especially in advertisements for small restaurants, for example "just around the corner," or "a good place to eat." No single, identifiable, citable person ever really said, for the record, "just around the corner," much less "a good place to eat," least likely of all for restaurants of the type that use this type of prose.

The dash is a handy device, informal and essentially playful, telling you that you're about to take off on a different tack but still in some way connected with the present course—only you have to remember that the dash is there, and either put a second dash at the end of the notion to let the reader know that he's back on course, or else end the sentence, as here, with a period.

The greatest danger in punctuation is for poetry. Here it is necessary to be as economical and parsimonious with commas and periods as with the words themselves, and any marks that seem to carry their own subtle meanings, like dashes and little rows of periods, even semicolons and question marks, should be left out altogether rather than inserted to clog up the thing with ambiguity. A single exclamation point in a poem, no matter what else the poem has to say, is enough to destroy the whole work.

The things I like best in T. S. Eliot's poetry, especially in the *Four Quartets*, are the semicolons. You cannot hear them, but they are there, laying out the connections between the images and the ideas. Sometimes you get a glimpse of a semicolon coming, a few lines farther on, and it is like climbing a steep path through woods and seeing a wooden bench just at a bend in the road ahead, a place where you can expect to sit for a moment, catching your breath.

Commas can't do this sort of thing; they can only tell you how the different parts of a complicated thought are to be fitted together, but you can't sit, not even take a breath, just because of a comma,

1979

THE READER

1. Compare Thomas's statements about the various punctuation marks with a handbook's rules on the subject. How do they differ? Do they

make any of the same points?

2. Compare the punctuation in two or more of the pieces in "An Album of Styles" (p. 253). You might look particularly at the selections by Bacon, Thurber, and White before making your choices.

3. Gertrude Stein once said: "There are two different ways of thinking about colons and semi-colons you can think of them as commas and as such they are purely servile or you can think of them as periods and then using them can make you feel adventurous." What might Thomas's comment on Stein's statement be?

THE WRITER

1. How soon in this essay do you realize that Thomas is playing a kind of game with the reader? Why doesn't he tell you at the beginning what he is going to do?

2. Here Thomas deals with a restricted, minor subject and, in "Humanities and Science" (p. 188), with one that is sweeping and important. Describe the personality he presents to you here and then the one he presents in "Humanities and Science." Are they similar? Different? Do they overlap? Is his analysis in "On Magic in Medicine" (p. 370) consistent with this personality or these personalities?

3. The first paragraph in Thomas's essay is a single sentence. Rewrite the paragraph so that it is several sentences. What changes in punctuation did you make?

4. Write a short essay on "My Encounters with Punctuation" or "The Semicolon and I."

Wayne C. Booth

BORING FROM WITHIN: THE ART OF THE FRESHMAN ESSAY[1]

Last week I had for about the hundredth time an experience that always disturbs me. Riding on a train, I found myself talking with my seat-mate, who asked me what I did for a living. "I teach English." Do you have any trouble predicting his response? His face fell, and he groaned, "Oh, dear, I'll have to watch my language." In my experience there are only two other possible reactions. The first is even less inspiriting: "I hated English in school; it was my worst subject." The second, so rare as to make an honest English teacher almost burst into tears of gratitude when it occurs, is an animated conversation about literature, or ideas, or

1. Adapted by Mr. Booth from a speech delivered in May 1963 to the Illinois Council of College Teachers of English.

the American language—the kind of conversation that shows a continuing respect for "English" as something more than being sure about *who*
and *whom*, *lie* and *lay*.

Unless the people you meet are a good deal more tactful or better liars
than the ones I meet, you've had the two less favorable experiences many
times. And it takes no master analyst to figure out why so many of our
fellow citizens think of us as unfriendly policemen: it is because too many
of us have seen ourselves as unfriendly policemen. I know of a high school
English class in Indiana in which the students are explicitly told that
their paper grades will not be affected by anything they say; required to
write a paper a week, they are graded simply on the number of spelling
and grammatical errors. What is more, they are given a standard form for
their papers: each paper is to have three paragraphs, a beginning, a
middle, and an end—or is it an introduction, a body, and a conclusion?
The theory seems to be that if the student is not troubled about having to
say anything, or about discovering a good way of saying it, he can then
concentrate on the truly important matter of avoiding mistakes.

What's wrong with such assignments? What's wrong with getting the
problem of correctness focused sharply enough so that we can really work
on it? After all, we do have the job of teaching correct English, don't we?
We can't possibly teach our hordes of students to be colorful writers, but
by golly, we can beat the bad grammar out of them. Leaving aside the
obvious fact that we *can't* beat the bad grammar out of them, not by
direct assault, let's think a bit about what that kind of assignment does to
the poor teacher who gives it. Those papers must be read, by someone,
and unless the teacher has more trained assistance than you and I have,
she's the victim. She can't help being bored silly by her own paper-
reading, and we all know what an evening of being bored by a class's
papers does to our attitude toward that class the next day. The old
formula of John Dewey was that any teaching that bores the student is
likely to fail. The formula was subject to abuse, quite obviously, since
interest in itself is only one of many tests of adequate teaching. A safer
formula, though perhaps also subject to abuse, might be: Any teaching
that bores the teacher is sure to fail. And I am haunted by the picture of
that poor woman in Indiana, week after week reading batches of papers
written by students who have been told that nothing they say can
possibly affect her opinion of those papers. Could any hell imagined by
Dante or Jean-Paul Sartre[2] match this self-inflicted futility?

I call it self-inflicted, as if it were a simple matter to avoid receiving
papers that bore us. But unfortunately it is not. It may be a simple matter
to avoid the *total* meaninglessness that the students must give that

2. Booth refers to the elaborately described
hell of the *Inferno*, by the fourteenth-century
Italian poet Dante Alighieri, and to the banal
locked room in which the characters of Sartre's *No Exit* discover that hell is "other people."

Indiana teacher, but we all know that it is no easy matter to produce interesting papers; our pet cures for boredom never work as well as they ought to. Every beginning teacher learns quickly and painfully that nothing works with all students, and that on bad days even the most promising ideas work with nobody.

As I try to sort out the various possible cures for those batches of boredom—in ink, double-spaced, on one side of the sheet, only, please—I find them falling into three groups: efforts to give the students a sharper sense of writing to an audience, efforts to give them some substance to express, and efforts to improve their habits of observation and of approach to their task—what might be called improving their mental personalities.

This classification, both obvious and unoriginal, is a useful one not only because it covers—at least I hope it does—all of our efforts to improve what our students can do but also because it reminds us that no one of the three is likely to work unless it is related to each of the others. In fact each of the three types of cure—"develop an awareness of audience," "give them something to say," and "enliven their writing personalities"—threatens us with characteristic dangers and distortions; all three together are indispensable to any lasting cure.

Perhaps the most obvious omission in that Indiana teacher's assignments is all sense of an audience to be persuaded, of a serious rhetorical purpose to be achieved. One tempting cure for this omission is to teach them to put a controversial edge on what they say. So we ask them to write a three-page paper arguing that China should be allowed into the UN or that women are superior to men or that American colleges are failing in their historic task. Then we are surprised when the papers turn out to be as boring as ever. The papers on Red China are full of abstract pomposities that the students themselves obviously do not understand or care about, since they have gleaned them in a desperate dash through the most readily available sources listed in the *Readers' Guide*. Except for the rare student who has some political background and awareness, and who thus might have written on the subject anyway, they manage to convey little more than their resentment at the assignment and their boredom in carrying it out. One of the worst batches of papers I ever read came out of a good idea we had at Earlham College for getting the whole student body involved in controversial discussion about world affairs. We required them to read Barbara Ward's *Five Ideas that Change the World*; we even had Lady Jackson[3] come to the campus and talk to everyone about her concern for the backward nations. The papers, to our surprise, were a discouraging business. We found ourselves in desperation collecting the boners that are always a sure sign, when present in great numbers,

3. Barbara Ward.

that students are thoroughly disengaged. "I think altruism is all right, so long as we practice it in our own interest." "I would be willing to die for anything fatal." "It sure is a doggie dog world."

It is obvious what had gone wrong: though we had ostensibly given the student a writing purpose, it had not become *his* purpose, and he was really no better off, perhaps worse, than if we had him writing about, say, piccolos or pizza. We might be tempted in revulsion from such overly ambitious failures to search for controversy in the students' own mundane lives. This may be a good move, but we should not be surprised when the papers on "Let's clean up the campus" or "Why must we have traffic fatalities?" turn out to be just as empty as the papers on the UN or the Congo. They may have more exclamation points and underlined adjectives, but they will not interest any teacher who would like to read papers for his own pleasure or edification. "People often fail to realize that nearly 40,000 people are killed on our highways each year. Must this carnage continue?" Well, I suppose it must, until people who write about it learn to see it with their own eyes, and hearts, instead of through a haze of cliché. The truth is that to make students assume a controversial pose before they have any genuine substance to be controversial about is to encourage dishonesty and slovenliness, and to ensure our own boredom. It may very well lead them into the kind of commercial concern for the audience which makes almost every *Reader's Digest* article intelligible to everyone over the chronological age of ten and boring to everyone over the mental age of fifteen. *Newsweek* magazine recently had a readability survey conducted on itself. It was found to be readable by the average twelfth grader, unlike *Time*, which is readable by the average eleventh grader. The editors were advised, and I understand are taking the advice, that by improving their "readability" by one year they could improve their circulation by several hundred thousand. Whether they will thereby lop off a few thousand adult readers in the process was not reported.

The only protection from this destructive type of concern for the audience is the control of substance, of having something solid to say. Our students bore us, even when they take a seemingly lively controversial tone, because they have nothing to say, to us or to anybody else. If and when they discover something to say, they will no longer bore us, and our comments will no longer bore them. Having something to say, they will be interested in learning how to say it better. Having something to say, they can be taught how to give a properly controversial edge to what will by its nature be controversial—nothing, after all, is worth saying that everybody agrees on already.

When we think of providing substance, we are perhaps tempted first to find some way of filling students' minds with a goodly store of general ideas, available on demand. This temptation is not necessarily a bad one.

After all, if we think of the adult writers who interest us, most of them have such a store; they have read and thought about man's major problems, and they have opinions and arguments ready to hand about how men ought to live, how society ought to be run, how literature ought to be written. Edmund Wilson, for example, one of the most consistently interesting men alive, seems to have an inexhaustible flow of reasoned opinions on any subject that comes before him. Obviously our students are not going to interest us until they too have some ideas.

But it is not easy to impart ideas. It is not even easy to impart opinions, though a popular teacher can usually manage to get students to parrot his views. But ideas—that is, opinions backed with genuine reasoning—are extremely difficult to develop. If they were not, we wouldn't have a problem in the first place; we could simply send our students off with an assignment to prove their conviction that God does or does not exist or that the American high school system is the best on God's earth, and the interesting arguments would flow.

There is, in fact, no short cut to the development of reasoned ideas. Years and years of daily contact with the world of ideas are required before the child can be expected to begin formulating his own ideas and his own reasons. And for the most part the capacity to handle abstract ideas comes fairly late. I recently saw a paper of a bright high school sophomore, from a good private school, relating the economic growth of China and India to their political development and relative supply of natural resources. It was a terrible paper; the student's hatred of the subject, his sense of frustration in trying to invent generalizations about processes that were still too big for him, showed in every line. The child's parent told me that when the paper was returned by the geography teacher, he had pencilled on the top of one page, "Why do you mix so many bad ideas with your good ones?" The son was almost in tears, his father told me, with anger and helplessness. "He talks as if I'd put bad ideas in on purpose. *I* don't know a bad idea from a good one on this subject."

Yet with all this said, I am still convinced that general ideas are not only a resource but also a duty that cannot be dodged just because it is a dangerous one. There is nothing we touch, as English teachers, that is immune to being tainted by our touch; all the difference lies in how we go about it.

Ideas are a resource because adolescents are surprisingly responsive to any real encouragement to think for themselves, *if* methods of forced feeding are avoided. The seventeen-year-old who has been given nothing but commonplaces and clichés all his life and who finally discovers a teacher with ideas of his own may have his life changed, and, as I shall say in my final point, when his life is changed his writing is changed. Perhaps some of you can remember, as I can, a first experience with a teacher who could think for himself. I can remember going home from a conversation with my high school chemistry teacher and audibly vowing to myself: "Someday I'm going to be able to think for myself like that." There was nothing especially unconventional about Luther Gidding's ideas—at least I can remember few of them now. But what I cannot forget is the way he had with an idea, the genuine curiosity with which he approached it, the pause while he gave his little thoughtful cough, and then the bulldog tenacity with which he would argue it through. And I am convinced that though he never required me to write a line, he did more to improve my writing during the high school years than all of my English teachers put together. The diary I kept to record my sessions with him, never read by anyone, was the best possible writing practice.

If ideas, in this sense of speculation backed up with an attempt to think about things rigorously and constructively, are a great and often neglected resource, they are also our civic responsibility—a far more serious responsibility than our duty to teach spelling and grammar. It is a commonplace to say that democracy depends for its survival on an informed citizenry, but we all know that mere information is not what we are talking about when we say such things. What we mean is that democracy depends on a citizenry that can reason for themselves, on men who know whether a case has been proved, or at least made probable. Democracy depends, if you will forgive some truisms for a moment, on free choices, and choices cannot be in any sense free if they are made blind: free choice is, in fact, choice that is based on knowledge—not just opinions, but knowledge in the sense of reasoned opinion. And if that half of our population who do not go beyond high school do not learn from us how to put two and two together and how to test the efforts of others to do so, and if the colleges continue to fail with most of the other half, we are doomed to become even more sheeplike, as a nation, than we are already.

Papers about ideas written by sheep are boring; papers written by thinking boys and girls are interesting. The problem is always to find ideas at a level that will allow the student to *reason*, that is, to provide support for his ideas, rather than merely assert them in half-baked form. And this means something that is all too often forgotten by the most ambitious teachers—namely, that whatever ideas the student writes about must somehow be connected with his own experience. Teaching machines will never be able to teach the kind of writing we all want, precisely because no machine can ever know which general ideas relate, for a given student, to some meaningful experience. In the same class we'll have one student for whom philosophical and religious ideas are meaningful, another who can talk with confidence about entropy and the second law of thermodynamics, a third who can write about social justice, and a fourth who can discuss the phony world of Holden Caulfield.[4] Each of them can do a good job on his own subject, because he has as part of his equipment a growing awareness of how conclusions in that subject are related to the steps of argument that support conclusions. Ideally, each of these students ought to have the personal attention of a tutor for an hour or so each week, someone who can help him sharpen those connections, and not force him to write on topics not yet appropriate to his interests or experience. But when these four are in a class of thirty or forty others, taught by a teacher who has three or four other similar sections, we all know what happens: the teacher is forced by his circumstances to provide some sort of mold into which all of the students can be poured. Although he is still better able to adapt to individual differences than a machine, he is unfortunately subject to boredom and fatigue, as a machine would not be. Instead of being the philosopher, scientist, political analyst, and literary critic that these four students require him to be, teaching them and learning from them at the same time, the teacher is almost inevitably tempted to force them all to write about the ideas he himself knows best. The result is that at least three of the four must write out of ignorance.

Now clearly the best way out of this impasse would be for legislatures and school boards and college presidents to recognize the teaching of English for what it is: the most demanding of all teaching jobs, justifying the smallest sections and the lightest course loads. No composition teacher can possibly concentrate on finding special interests, making imaginative assignments, and testing the effectiveness and cogency of papers if he has more than seventy-five students at a time; the really desirable limit would be about forty-five—three sections of fifteen students each. Nobody would ever expect a piano teacher, who has no themes to read, to handle the great masses of pupils that we handle. Everyone recognizes that for all other technical skills individual attention is required. Yet for this, the most delicate of all skills, the one requiring the most subtle interrelationships of training, character, and experience, we fling students and teachers into hopelessly impersonal patterns.

But if I'm not careful I'll find myself saying that our pupils bore us because the superintendents and college presidents hire us to be bored. Administrative neglect and misallocation of educational funds are basic to our problem, and we should let the citizenry know of the scandal on every occasion. But meanwhile, back at the ranch, we are faced with the situation as it now is: we must find some way to train a people to write responsibly even though the people, as represented, don't want this service sufficiently to pay for it.

The tone of political exhortation into which I have now fallen leads me

4. The hero of *The Catcher in the Rye*, by J. D. Salinger.

to one natural large source of ideas as we try to encourage writing that is not just lively and controversial but informed and genuinely persuasive. For many students there is obviously more potential interest in social problems and forces, political controversy, and the processes of everyday living around them than in more general ideas. The four students I described a moment ago, students who can say something about philosophy, science, general political theory, or literary criticism, are rare. But most students, including these four, can in theory at least be interested in meaningful argument about social problems in which they are personally involved.

As a profession we have tried, over the past several decades, a variety of approaches attempting to capitalize on such interests. Papers on corruption in TV, arguments about race relations, analyses of distortions in advertising, descriptions of mass communication—these have been combined in various quantities with traditional subjects like grammar, rhetoric, and literature. The "communications" movement, which looked so powerful only a few years ago and which now seems almost dead, had at its heart a perfectly respectable notion, a notion not much different from the one I'm working with today: get them to write about something they know about, and make sure that they see their writing as an act of communication, not as a meaningless exercise. And what better material than other acts of communication.

The dangers of such an approach are by now sufficiently understood. As subject matter for the English course, current "communications media" can at best provide only a supplement to literature and analysis of ideas. But they can be a valuable supplement. Analysis in class of the appeals buried in a New Yorker or Life advertisement followed by a writing assignment requiring similar analyses can be a far more interesting introduction to the intricacies of style than assignments out of a language text on levels of usage or emotion-charged adjectives. Analysis of a Time magazine account, purporting to be objective news but in actual fact a highly emotional editorial, can be not only a valuable experience in itself, but it can lead to papers in which the students do say something to us. Stylistic analysis of the treatment of the same news events by two newspapers or weeklies of different editorial policy can lead to an intellectual awakening of great importance, and thus to papers that will not, cannot, bore the teacher. But this will happen only if the students' critical powers are genuinely developed. It will not do simply to teach the instructor's own prejudices.

There was a time in decades not long past when many of the most lively English teachers thought of their job as primarily to serve as handmaids to liberalism. I had one teacher in college who confessed to me that his overriding purpose was to get students to read and believe The Nation rather than the editorials of their daily paper. I suppose that his approach was not entirely valueless. It seems preferable to the effort to be noncontroversial that marks too many English teachers in the '60's, and at least it stirred some of us out of our dogmatic slumbers. But unfortunately it did nothing whatever about teaching us to think critically. Though we graduated from his course at least aware—as many college graduates do not seem to be today—that you can't believe anything you read in the daily press until you have analyzed it and related it to your past experience and to other accounts, it failed to teach us that you can't believe what you read in The Nation either. It left the job undone of training our ability to think, because it concentrated too heavily on our opinions. The result was, as I remember, that my own papers in that course were generally regurgitated liberalism. I was excited by them, and that was something. But I can't believe that the instructor found reading them anything other than a chore. There was nothing in them that came from my own experience, my own notions of what would constitute evidence for my conclusions. There I was, in Utah in the depths of the depression, writing about the Okies when I could have been writing about the impoverished farmers all around me. I wrote about race relations in the south without ever having talked with a Negro in my life and without recognizing that the bootblack I occasionally saw in Salt Lake City in the Hotel Utah was in any way related to the problem of race relations.

The third element that accounts for our boring papers is the lack of character and personality in the writer. My life, my observations, my insights were not included in those papers on the Okies and race relations and the New Deal. Every opinion was derivative, every observation second-hand. I had no real opinions of my own, and my eyes were not open wide enough for me to make first-hand observations on the world around me. What I wrote was therefore characterless, without true personality, though often full of personal pronouns. My opinions had been changed, my self had not. The style was the boy, the opinionated, immature, uninformed boy; whether my teacher knew it or not—and apparently he did not—his real job was to make a man of me if he wanted me to write like a man.

Putting the difficulty in this way naturally leads me to what perhaps many of you have been impatient about from the beginning. Are not the narrative arts, both as encountered in great literature and as practiced by the students themselves, the best road to the infusion of individuality that no good writing can lack? Would not a real look at the life of that bootblack, and an attempt to deal with him in narrative, have led to a more interesting paper than all of my generalized attacks on the prejudiced southerners?

I think it would, but once again I am almost more conscious of the dangers of the cure than of the advantages. As soon as we make our

general rule something like, "Have the students write a personal narrative on what they know about, what they can see and feel at first hand,"
we have opened the floodgates for those dreadful assignments that we all
find ourselves using, even though we know better: "My Summer Vacation," "Catching My First Fish," and "Our Trip to the Seattle World's
Fair." Here are personal experiences that call for personal observation
and narration. What's wrong with them?

Quite simply, they invite triviality, superficiality, puerility. Our students have been writing essays on such non-subjects all their lives, and
until they have developed some sort of critical vision, some way of
looking at the world they passed through on their vacations or fishing
trips, they are going to feed us the same old bromides that have always
won their passing grades. "My Summer Vacation" is an invitation to a
grocery list of items, because it implies no audience, no point to be made,
no point of view, no character in the speaker. A bright student will make
something of such an invitation, by dramatizing the comic family quarrel
that developed two days out, or by comparing his view of the American
motel system with Nabokov's in *Lolita*, or by remembering the types of
people seen in the campgrounds. If he had his own eyes and ears open he
might have seen, in a men's room in Grand Canyon last summer, a
camper with a very thick French accent trying to convert a Brooklyn Jew
into believing the story of the Mormon gold plates.[5] Or he could have
heard, at Mesa Verde, a young park ranger, left behind toward the end of
the season by all of the experienced rangers, struggling ungrammatically
through a set speech on the geology of the area and finally breaking down
in embarrassment over his lack of education. Such an episode, really *seen*,
could be used narratively to say something to other high school students
about what education really is.

But mere narration can be in itself just as dull as the most abstract
theorizing about the nature of the universe or the most derivative opin-
ion-mongering about politics. Even relatively skilful narration, used too
obviously as a gimmick to catch interest, with no real relation to the
subject, can be as dull as the most abstract pomposities. We all know the
student papers that begin like *Reader's Digest* articles, with stereotyped
narration that makes one doubt the event itself: "On a dark night last
January, two teen agers were seen etc., etc." One can open any issue of
Time and find this so-called narrative interest plastered throughout.
From the March 29 issue I find, among many others, the following bits of
fantasy: #1: "A Bolivian father sadly surveyed his nation's seven universities, then made up his mind. 'I don't want my son mixed up in politics.' . . . So saying, he sent his son off to West Germany to college." So
writing, the author sends me into hysterical laughter: the quote is phony,

5. Bearing, according to Mormon tradition,   the prophet Joseph Smith in upstate New
the Book of Mormon, divinely revealed to   York in 1827.

made up for the occasion to disguise the generality of the news item. #2: "Around 12:30 P.M. every Monday and Friday, an aging Cubana Airlines turbo-prop Britannia whistles to a halt at Mexico City's International Airport. Squads of police stand by. All passengers . . . without diplomatic or Mexican passports are photographed and questioned. . . . They always dodge questions. 'Why are you here? Where are you going?' ask the Mexicans. 'None of your business,' answer the secretive travelers." "Why should I go on reading?" ask I. #3: "At 6:30 one morning early this month, a phone shrilled in the small office off the bedroom of Egypt's President. . . Nasser. [All early morning phones "shrill" for *Time*.] Already awake, he lifted the receiver to hear exciting news: a military coup had just been launched against the anti-Nasser government of Syria. The phone rang again. It was the Minister of Culture. . . . How should Radio Cairo handle the Syrian crisis? 'Support the rebels,' snapped Nasser." Oh lucky reporter, I sigh, to have such an efficient wiretapping service. #4: "In South Korea last week, a farmer named Song Kyu Il traveled all the way from the southern provinces to parade before Seoul's Duk Soo Palace with a placard scrawled in his own blood. . . . Farmer Song was thrown in jail, along with some 200 other demonstrators." That's the last we hear of Song, who is invented as an individual for this opening and then dropped. #5: "Defense Secretary Robert McNamara last spring stood beside President Kennedy on the tenth-deck bridge of the nuclear-powered carrier *Enterprise*. For as the eye could see, other U.S. ships deployed over the Atlantic seascape." Well, maybe. But for as far as the eye can see, the narrative clichés are piled, rank on rank. At 12:00 midnight last Thursday a gaunt, harried English professor could be seen hunched over his typewriter, a pile of *Time* magazines beside him on the floor. "What," he murmured to himself, sadly, "Whatever can we do about this trashy imitation of narration?"

Fortunately there is something we can do, and it is directly within our province. We can subject our students to models of genuine narration, with the sharp observation and penetrating critical judgment that underlies all good story telling, whether reportorial or fictional.

> It is a truth universally acknowledged, that a single man in possession of a good fortune must be in want of a wife.
> However little known the feelings or views of such a man may be on his first entering a neighborhood, this truth is so well fixed in the minds of the surrounding families, that he is considered as the rightful property of someone or other of their daughters.
> "My dear Mr. Bennet," said his lady to him one day, "have you heard that Netherfield Park is let at last?"

And already we have a strong personal tone established, a tone of mocking irony which leaves Jane Austen's Mrs. Bennet revealed before us as the grasping, silly gossip she is. Or try this one:

> I am an American, Chicago-born—Chicago, that somber city—and go at
> things as I have taught myself, free-style, and will make the record in my own
> way: first to knock, first admitted; sometimes an innocent knock, sometimes a
> not so innocent. But a man's character is his fate, says Heraclitus, and in the
> end there isn't any way to disguise the nature of the knocks by acoustical work
> on the door or gloving the knuckles.
>
> Everybody knows there is no fineness or accuracy of suppression; if you
> hold down one thing you hold down the adjoining.
>
> My own parents were not much to me, though I cared for my mother. She
> was simple-minded, and what I learned from her was not what she taught. . . .

Do you catch the accent of Saul Bellow here, beneath the accent of his
Augie March? You do, of course, but the students, many of them, do not.
How do you know, they will ask, that Jane Austen is being ironic? How do
you know, they ask again, that Augie is being characterized by his author
through what he says? In teaching them how we know, in exposing them
to the great narrative voices, ancient and modern, and in teaching them
to hear these voices accurately, we are, of course, trying to change their
lives, to make them new, to raise their perceptions to a new level
altogether. Nobody can really catch these accents who has not grown up
sufficiently to see through cheap substitutes. Or, to put it another way, a
steady exposure to such voices is the very thing that will produce the
maturity that alone can make our students ashamed of beclouded, commercial, borrowed spectacles for viewing the world.

It is true that exposure to good fiction will not in itself transform our
students into good writers. Even the best-read student still needs endless
hours and years of practice, with rigorous criticism. Fiction will not do
the job of discipline in reasoned argument and of practice in developing
habits of addressing a living audience. But in the great fiction they will
learn what it means to look at something with full attention, what it
means to see beneath the surface of society's platitudes. If we then give
them practice in writing about things close to the home base of their own
honest observations, constantly stretching their powers of generalization
and argument but never allowing them to drift into pompous inanities or
empty controversiality, we may have that rare but wonderful pleasure of
witnessing the miracle: a man and a style where before there was only a
bag of wind or a bundle of received opinions. Even when, as with most of
our students, no miracles occur, we can hope for papers that we can enjoy
reading. And as a final bonus, we might hope that when our students
encounter someone on a train who says that he teaches English, their
automatic response may be something other than looks of pity or, cries of
mock alarm.

1963

THE READER

1. What steps are necessary before an "opinion" can become a "reasoned opinion"? Select some subject on which you have a strong opinion, and decide whether it is a reasoned opinion.
2. Booth characterizes the writing in the Reader's Digest and Time (p. 223). What does he feel the two magazines have in common? Analyze an article from either one of these magazines to see how accurate Booth's characterization is.

THE WRITER

1. Booth is writing for an audience of English teachers. In what ways might the essay differ if he were writing for an audience of students?
2. On p. 226, Booth says he has "now fallen" into a "tone of political exhortation." (Tone may be defined as the reflection in language of the attitude a writer takes toward his or her subject or audience or both.) What other "tones" are there in the essay? Why does Booth find it necessary to vary the tone?
3. Write an account of the process you went through in writing some paper recently or the process you typically go through in writing a paper. Then, in a paragraph or two, tell what you think Booth's comments on your process of writing might be.

Nancy Sommers

REVISION STRATEGIES OF STUDENT WRITERS AND EXPERIENCED ADULT WRITERS

Although various aspects of the writing process have been studied extensively of late, research on revision has been notably absent. * * * Dissatisfied with * * * the lack of attention to the process of revision, I conducted a series of studies over the past three years which examined the revision processes of student writers and experienced writers to see what role revision played in their writing processes. In the course of my work the revision process was redefined as *a sequence of changes in a composition—changes which are initiated by cues and occur continually throughout the writing of a work.*

Methodology

I used a case study approach. The student writers were twenty freshmen at Boston University and the University of Oklahoma with SAT verbal scores ranging from 450–600 in their first semester of composition. The twenty experienced adult writers from Boston and Oklahoma City included journalists, editors, and academics. To refer to the two groups, I use the terms *student writers* and *experienced writers* because the principal difference between these two groups is the amount of experience they have had in writing.

Each writer wrote three essays, expressive, explanatory, and persuasive, and rewrote each essay twice, producing nine written products in draft and final form. Each writer was interviewed three times after the final revision of each essay. And each writer suggested revisions for a composition written by an anonymous author. Thus extensive written and spoken documents were obtained from each writer.

The essays were analyzed by counting and categorizing the changes made. Four revision operations were identified: deletion, substitution, addition, and reordering. And four levels of changes were identified: word, phrase, sentence, theme (the extended statement of one idea). A coding system was developed for identifying the frequency of revision by level and operation. In addition, transcripts of the interviews in which the writers interpreted their revisions were used to develop what was called a *scale of concerns* for each writer. This scale enabled me to codify what were the writer's primary concerns, secondary concerns, tertiary concerns, and whether the writers used the same scale of concerns when revising the second or third drafts as they used in revising the first draft.

Revision Strategies of Student Writers

Most of the students I studied did not use the terms *revision* or *rewriting*. In fact, they did not seem comfortable using the word *revision* and explained that revision was not a word they used, but the word their teachers used. Instead, most of the students had developed various functional terms to describe the type of changes they made. The following are samples of these definitions:

Scratch Out and Do Over Again: "I say scratch out and do over, and that means what it says. Scratching out and cutting out. I read what I have written and I cross out a word and put another word in; a more decent word or a better word. Then if there is somewhere to use a sentence that I have crossed out, I will put it there."

Reviewing: "Reviewing means just using better words and eliminating words that are not needed. I go over and change words around."

Reviewing: "I just review every word and make sure that everything is worded right. I see if I am rambling; I see if I can put a better word in or leave one out. Usually when I read what I have written, I say to myself, 'that word is so bland or so trite,' and then I go and get my thesaurus."

Redoing: "Redoing means cleaning up the paper and crossing out. It is looking at something and saying, no that has to go, or no, that is not right."

Marking Out: "I don't use the word rewriting because I only write one draft and the changes that I make are made on top of the draft. The changes that I make are usually just marking out words and putting different ones in."

Slashing and Throwing Out: "I throw things out and say they are not good. I like to write like Fitzgerald did by inspiration, and if I feel inspired then I don't need to slash and throw much out."

The predominant concern in these definitions is vocabulary. The students understand the revision process as a rewording activity. They do so because they perceive words as the unit of written discourse. That is, they concentrate on particular words apart from their role in the text. Thus one student quoted above thinks in terms of dictionaries, and, following the eighteenth century theory of words parodied in *Gulliver's Travels*,[1] he imagines a load of things carried about to be exchanged. Lexical changes are the major revision activities of the students because economy is their goal. They are governed, like the linear model itself, by the Law of Occam's razor[2] that prohibits logically needless repetition: redundancy and superfluity. Nothing governs speech more than such superfluities; speech constantly repeats itself precisely because spoken words, as Barthes writes, are expendable in the cause of communication.[3] The aim of revision according to the students' own description is therefore to clean up speech; the redundancy of speech is unnecessary in writing, their logic suggests, because writing, unlike speech, can be reread. Thus one student said, "Redoing means cleaning up the paper and crossing out." The remarkable contradiction of cleaning by marking might, indeed, stand for student revision as I have encountered it.

The students place a symbolic importance on their selection and rejection of words as the determiners of success or failure for their compositions. When revising, they primarily ask themselves: can I find a better word or phrase? A more impressive, not so cliched, or less humdrum word? Am I repeating the same word or phrase too often? They approach the revision process with what could be labeled as a "thesaurus philosophy of writing"; the students consider the thesaurus a harvest of lexical substitutions and believe that most problems in their essays can be solved by rewording. What is revealed in the students' use of the thesaurus is a governing attitude toward their writing: that the meaning

1. In Part 3 of Jonathan Swift's work.
2. A principle of parsimony formulated by the English philosopher William of Occam or Ockham (?1300–?49) that entities should not be multiplied unnecessarily—i.e., the simplest of competing theories should be preferred to more complex ones, and explanations of unknown phenomena should be sought in the known.
3. Sommers, in a portion of the essay omitted, cites Roland Barthes's "Writers, Intellectuals, Teachers," in *Image-Music-Text*, trans. Stephen Heath (New York: Hill and Wang, 1977).

to be communicated is already there, already finished, already produced, ready to be communicated, and all that is necessary is a better word "rightly worded." One student defined revision as "redoing": "redoing" meant "just using better words and eliminating words that are not needed." For the students, writing is translating: the thought to the page, the language of speech to the more formal language of prose, the word to its synonym. Whatever is translated, an original text already exists for students, one which need not be discovered or acted upon, but simply communicated.[4]

The students list repetition as one of the elements they most worry about. This cue signals to them that they need to eliminate the repetition either by substituting or deleting words or phrases. Repetition occurs, in lage part, because student writing imitates—transcribes—speech: atten- tion to repetitious words is a manner of cleaning speech. Without a sense of the developmental possibilities of revision (and writing in general) students seek, on the authority of many textbooks, simply to clean up their language and prepare to type. What is curious, however, is that students are aware of lexical repetition, but not conceptual repetition. They only notice the repetition if they can "hear" it; they do not diag- nose lexical repetition as symptomatic of problems on a deeper level. By rewording their sentences to avoid the lexical repetition, the students solve the immediate problem, but blind themselves to problems on a textual level; although they are using different words, they are sometimes merely restating the same idea with different words. Such blindness, as I discovered with student writers, is the inability to "see" revision as a process: the inability to "re-view" their work again, as it were, with different eyes, and to start over.

The revision strategies described above are consistent with the stu- dents' understanding of the revision process as requiring lexical changes but not semantic changes. For the students, the extent to which they revise is a function of their level of inspiration. In fact, they use the word *inspiration* to describe the ease or difficulty with which their essay is written, and the extent to which the essay needs to be revised. If students feel inspired, if the writing comes easily, and if they don't get stuck on individual words or phrases, then they say that they cannot see any reason to revise. Because students do not see revision as an acitivity in which they modify and develop perspectives and ideas, they feel that if they know what they want to say, then there is little reason for making revisions.

The only modification of ideas in the students' essays occurred when they tried out two or three introductory paragraphs. This results, in part, because the students have been taught in another version of the linear

4. Nancy Sommers and Ronald Schleifer, "Means and Ends: Some Assumptions of Student Writers," *Composition and Teach- ing*, [II (1981)] [author's note].

model of composing to use a thesis statement as a controlling device in their introductory paragraphs. Since they write their introductions and their thesis statements even before they have really discovered what they want to say, their early close attention to the thesis statement, and more generally the linear model, function to restrict and circumscribe not only the development of their ideas, but also their ability to change the direction of these ideas.

Too often as composition teachers we conclude that students do not willingly revise. The evidence from my research suggests that it is not that students are unwilling to revise, but rather that they do what they have been taught to do in a consistently narrow and predictable way. On every occasion when I asked students why they hadn't made any more changes, they essentially replied, "I knew something larger was wrong, but I didn't think it would help to move words around." The students have strategies for handling words and phrases and their strategies helped them on a word or sentence level. What they lack, however, is a set of strategies to help them identify the "something larger" that they sensed was wrong and work from there. The students do not have strategies for handling the whole essay. They lack procedures or heuristics to help them reorder lines of reasoning or ask questions about their purposes and readers. The students view their compositions in a linear way as a series of parts. Even such potentially useful concepts as "unity" or "form" are reduced to the rule that a composition, if it is to have form, must have an introduction, a body, and a conclusion, or the sum total of the necessary parts.

The students decide to stop revising when they decide that they have not violated any of the rules for revising. These rules, such as "Never begin a sentence with a conjunction" or "Never end a sentence with a preposition," are lexically cued and rigidly applied. In general, students will subordinate the demands of the specific problems of their text to the demands of the rules. Changes are made in compliance with abstract rules about the product, rules that quite often do not apply to the specific problems in the text. These revision strategies are teacher-based, directed towards a teacher-reader who expects compliance with rules—with pre-existing "conceptions"—and who will only examine parts of the composition (writing comments about those parts in the margins of their essays) and will cite any violations of rules in those parts. At best the students see their writing altogether passively through the eyes of former teachers or their surrogates, the textbooks, and are bound to the rules which they have been taught.

Revision Strategies of Experienced Writers

One aim of my research has been to contrast how student writers define revision with how a group of experienced writers define their revision processes. Here is a sampling of the definitions from the experienced writers:

> *Rewriting:* "It is a matter of looking at the kernel of what I have written, the content, and then thinking about it, responding to it, making decisions, and actually restructuring it."

> *Rewriting:* "I rewrite as I write. It is hard to tell what is a first draft because it is not determined by time. In one draft, I might cross out three pages, write two, cross out a fourth, rewrite it, and call it a draft. I am constantly writing and rewriting. I can only conceptualize so much in my first draft—only so much information can be held in my head at one time; my rewriting efforts are a reflection of how much information I can encompass at one time. There are levels and agenda which I have to attend to in each draft."

> *Rewriting:* "Rewriting means on one level, finding the argument, and on another level, language changes to make the argument more effective. Most of the time I feel as if I can go on rewriting forever. There is always one part of a piece that I could keep working on. It is always difficult to know at what point to abandon a piece of writing. I like this idea that a piece of writing is never finished, just abandoned.

> *Rewriting:* My first draft is usually very scattered. In rewriting, I find the line of argument. After the argument is resolved, I am much more interested in word choice and phrasing."

> *Revising:* "My cardinal rule in revising is never to fall in love with what I have written in a first or second draft. An idea, sentence, or even a phrase that looks catchy, I don't trust. Part of this idea is to wait a while. I am much more in love with something after I have written it than I am a day or two later. It is much easier to change anything with time."

> *Revising:* "It means taking apart what I have written and putting it back together again. I ask major theoretical questions of my ideas, respond to those questions, and think of proportion and structure, and try to find a controlling metaphor. I find out which ideas can be developed and which should be dropped. I am constantly chiseling and changing as I revise."

The experienced writers describe their primary objective when revising as finding the form or shape of their argument. Although the metaphors vary, the experienced writers often use structural expressions such as "finding a framework," "a pattern," or "a design" for their argument. When questioned about this emphasis, the experienced writers responded that since their first drafts are usually scattered attempts to define their territory, their objective in the second draft is to begin observing general patterns of development and deciding what should be included and what excluded. One writer explained, "I have learned from experience that I need to keep writing a first draft until I figure out what I want to say. Then in a second draft, I begin to see the structure of an argument and how all the various sub-arguments which are buried beneath the sruface of all those sentences are related." What is described here is a process in which the writer is both agent and vehicle. "Writing," says Barthes, unlike speech, "develops like a seed, not a line,"[5] and like a seed it confuses beginning and end, conception and production. Thus, the experienced writers say their drafts are "not determined by time," that rewriting is a "constant process," that they feel as if (they) "can go on forever." Revising confuses the beginning and end, the agent and vehicle; it confuses, in order to find, the line of argument.

After a concern for form, the experienced writers have a second objective: a concern for their readership. In this way, "production" precedes "conception." The experienced writers imagine a reader (reading their product) whose existence and whose expectations influence their revision process. They have abstracted the standards of a reader and this reader seems to be partially a reflection of themselves and functions as a critical and productive collaborator—a collaborator who has yet to love their work. The anticipation of a reader's judgment causes a feeling of dissonance when the writer recognizes incongruities between intention and execution, and requires these writers to make revisions on all levels. Such a reader gives them just what the students lacked: new eyes to "re-view" their work. The experienced writers believe that they have learned the causes and conditions, the product, which will influence their reader, and their revision strategies are geared towards creating these causes and conditions. They demonstrate a complex understanding of which examples, sentences, or phrases should be included or excluded. For example, one experienced writer decided to delete public examples and add private examples when writing about the energy crisis because "private examples would be less controversial and thus more persuasive." Another writer revised his transitional sentences because "some kinds of transitions are more easily recognized as transitions than others." These examples represent the type of strategic attempts these experienced writers use to manipulate the conventions of discourse in order to communicate to their reader.

But these revision strategies are a process of more than communication; they are part of the process of *discovering meaning* altogether. Here we can see the importance of dissonance; at the heart of revision is the process by which writers recognize and resolve the dissonance they sense in their writing. Ferdinand de Saussure has argued that meaning is differential or "diacritical," based on differences between terms rather than "essential" or inherent qualities of terms. "Phonemes," he said, "are characterized, not as one might think, by their own positive quality but

5. "Writing Degree Zero," in *Writing Degree Zero and Elements of Semiology*, trans.   Annette Lavers and Colin Smith (New York: Hill and Wang, 1968), p. 20 [author's note].

simply by the fact that they are distinct."[6] In fact, Saussure bases his entire *Course in General Linguistics* on these differences, and such differences are dissonant; like musical dissonances which gain their significance from their relationship to the "key" of the composition which itself is determined by the whole langue, specific language (parole) gains its meaning from the system of language (langue) of which it is a manifestation and part. The musical composition—a "composition" of parts—creates its "key" as in an over-all structure which determines the value (meaning) of its parts. The analogy with music is readily seen in the compositions of experienced writers: both sorts of composition are based precisely on those structures experienced writers seek in their writing. It is this complicated relationship between the parts and the whole in the work of experienced writers which destroys the linear model; writing cannot develop "like a line" because each addition or deletion is a reordering of the whole. Explicating Saussure, Jonathan Culler asserts that "meaning depends on difference of meaning."[7] But student writers constantly struggle to bring their essays into congruence with a predefined meaning. The experienced writers do the opposite: they seek to discover (to create) meaning in the engagement with their writing, in revision. They seek to emphasize and exploit the lack of clarity, the differences of meaning, the dissonance, that writing as opposed to speech allows in the possibility of revision. Writing has spatial and temporal features not apparent in speech—words are recorded in space and fixed in time—which is why writing is susceptible to reordering and later addition. Such features make possible the dissonance that both provokes revision and promises, from itself, new meaning.

For the experienced writers the heaviest concentration of changes is on the sentence level, and the changes are predominantly by addition and deletion. But, unlike the students, experienced writers make changes on all levels and use all revision operations. Moreover, the operations the students fail to use—reordering and addition—seem to require a theory of the revision process as a totality—a theory which, in fact, encompasses the *whole* of the composition. Unlike the students, the experienced writers possess a nonlinear theory in which a sense of the whole writing both precedes and grows out of an examination of the parts. As we saw, one writer said he needed "a first draft to figure out what to say," and "a second draft to see the structure of an argument buried beneath the surface." Such a "theory" is both theoretical and strategical; once again, strategy and theory are conflated in ways that are literally impossible for the linear model. Writing appears to be more like a seed than a line.

Two elements of the experienced writers' theory of the revision pro-

6. *Course in General Linguistics*, trans. Wade Baskin (New York: [McGraw-Hill,] 1966), p. 119 [author's note].

7. Jonathan Culler, *Saussure* (Penguin Modern Masters Series; London: Penguin Books, 1976), p. 70 [author's note].

cess are the adoption of a holistic perspective and the perception that revision is a recursive process. The writers ask: what does my essay as a *whole* need for form, balance, rhythm, or communication. Details are added, dropped, substituted, or reordered according to their sense of what the essay needs for emphasis and proportion. This sense, however, is constantly in flux as ideas are developed and modified; it is constantly "re-viewed" in relation to the parts. As their ideas change, revision becomes an attempt to make their writing consonant with that changing vision.

The experienced writers see their revision process as a recursive process—a process with significant recurring activities—with different levels of attention and different agenda for each cycle. During the first revision cycle their attention is primarily directed towards narrowing the topic and delimiting their ideas. At this point, they are not as concerned as they are later about vocabulary and style. The experienced writers explained that they get closer to their meaning by not limiting themselves too early to lexical concerns. As one writer commented to explain her revision process, a comment inspired by the summer 1977 New York power failure: "I feel like Con Edison cutting off certain states to keep the generators going. In first and second drafts, I try to cut off as much as I can of my editing generator, and in a third draft, I try to cut off some of my idea generators, so I can make sure that I will actually finish the essay." Although the experienced writers describe their revision process as a series of different levels or cycles, it is inaccurate to assume that they have only one objective for each cycle and that each cycle can be defined by a different objective. The same objectives and sub-processes are present in each cycle, but in different proportions. Even though these experienced writers place the predominant weight upon finding the form of their argument during the first cycle, other concerns exist as well. Conversely, during the later cycles, when the experienced writers' primary attention is focused upon stylistic concerns, they are still attuned, although in a reduced way, to the form of the argument. Since writers are limited in what they can attend to during each cycle (understandings are temporal), revision strategies help balance competing demands on attention. Thus, writers can concentrate on more than one objective at a time by developing strategies to sort out and organize their different concerns in successive cycles of revision.

It is a sense of writing as discovery—a repeated process of beginning over again, starting out new—that the students failed to have. I have used the notion of dissonance because such dissonance, the incongruities between intention and execution, governs both writing and meaning. Students do not see the incongruities. They need to rely on their own internalized sense of good writing and to see their writing with their "own" eyes. Seeing in revision—seeing beyond hearing—is at the root of the word *revision* and the process itself; current dicta on revising blind our students to what is actually involved in revision. In fact, they blind them to what constitutes good writing altogether. Good writing disturbs: it creates dissonance. Students need to seek the dissonance of discovery, utilizing in their writing, as the experienced writers do, the very difference between writing and speech—the possibility of revision.[8]

1980

8. *Acknowledgement*: The author wishes to express her gratitude to Professor William Smith, University of Pittsburgh, for his vital assistance with the research reported in this article and to Patrick Hays, her husband, for extensive discussions and critical help [author's note].

George Orwell

POLITICS AND THE ENGLISH LANGUAGE

Most people who bother with the matter at all would admit that the English language is in a bad way, but it is generally assumed that we cannot by conscious action do anything about it. Our civilization is decadent and our language—so the argument runs—must inevitably share in the general collapse. It follows that any struggle against the abuse of language is a sentimental archaism, like preferring candles to electric light or hansom cabs to aeroplanes. Underneath this lies the half-conscious belief that language is a natural growth and not an instrument which we shape for our own purposes.

Now, it is clear that the decline of a language must ultimately have political and economic causes: it is not due simply to the bad influence of this or that individual writer. But an effect can become a cause, reinforcing the original cause and producing the same effect in an intensified form, and so on indefinitely. A man may take to drink because he feels himself to be a failure, and then fail all the more completely because he drinks. It is rather the same thing that is happening to the English language. It becomes ugly and inaccurate because our thoughts are foolish, but the slovenliness of our language makes it easier for us to have foolish thoughts. The point is that the process is reversible. Modern English, especially written English, is full of bad habits which spread by imitation and which can be avoided if one is willing to take the necessary trouble. If one gets rid of these habits one can think more clearly, and to think clearly is a necessary first step towards political regeneration: so that the fight against bad English is not frivolous and is not the exclusive concern of professional writers. I will come back to this presently, and I hope that by that time the meaning of what I have said here will have become clearer. Meanwhile, here are five specimens of the English language as it is now habitually written.

These five passages have not been picked out because they are especially bad—I could have quoted far worse if I had chosen—but because they illustrate various of the mental vices from which we now suffer. They are a little below the average, but are fairly representative samples. I number them so that I can refer back to them when necessary:

> "(1) I am not, indeed, sure whether it is not true to say that the Milton who once seemed not unlike a seventeenth-century Shelley had not become, out of an experience ever more bitter in each year, more alien [sic] to the founder of that Jesuit sect which nothing could induce him to tolerate."
> Professor Harold Laski (Essay in *Freedom of Expression*).

> "(2) Above all, we cannot play ducks and drakes with a native battery of idioms which prescribes such egregious collocations of vocables as the Basic *put up with* for *tolerate* or *put at a loss* for *bewilder*."
> Professor Lancelot Hogben (*Interglossa*).

> "(3) On the one side we have the free personality: by definition it is not neurotic, for it has neither conflict nor dream. Its desires, such as they are, are transparent, for they are just what institutional approval keeps in the forefront of consciousness; another institutional pattern would alter their number and intensity; there is little in them that is natural, irreducible, or culturally dangerous. But *on the other side*, the social bond itself is nothing but the mutual reflection of these self-secure integrities. Recall the definition of love. Is not this the very picture of a small academic? Where is there a place in this hall of mirrors for either personality or fraternity?"
> Essay on psychology in *Politics* (New York).

> "(4) All the 'best people' from the gentlemen's clubs, and all the frantic fascist captains, united in common hatred of Socialism and bestial horror of the rising tide of the mass revolutionary movement, have turned to acts of provocation, to foul incendiarism, to medieval legends of poisoned wells, to legalize their own destruction of proletarian organizations, and rouse the agitated petty-bourgeoisie to chauvinistic fervour on behalf of the fight against the revolutionary way out of the crisis."
> Communist pamphlet.

> "(5) If a new spirit *is* to be infused into this old country, there is one thorny and contentious reform which must be tackled, and that is the humanization and galvanization of the B.B.C. Timidity here will bespeak cancer and atrophy of the soul. The heart of Britain may be sound and of strong beat, for instance, but the British lion's roar at present is like that of Bottom in Shakespeare's *Midsummer Night's Dream*—as gentle as any sucking dove. A virile new Britain cannot continue indefinitely to be traduced in the eyes or rather ears, of the world by the effete languors of Langham Place, brazenly masquerading as 'standard English'. When the Voice of Britain is heard at

nine o'clock, better far and infinitely less ludicrous to hear aitches honestly dropped than the present priggish, inflated, inhibited, school-ma'amish arch braying of blameless bashful mewing maidens!"

Letter in Tribune.

Each of these passages has faults of its own, but, quite apart from avoidable ugliness, two qualities are common to all of them. The first is staleness of imagery: the other is lack of precision. The writer either has a meaning and cannot express it, or he inadvertently says something else, or he is almost indifferent as to whether his words mean anything or not. This mixture of vagueness and sheer incompetence is the most marked characteristic of modern English prose, and especially of any kind of political writing. As soon as certain topics are raised, the concrete melts into the abstract and no one seems able to think of turns of speech that are not hackneyed: prose consists less and less of *words* chosen for the sake of their meaning, and more and more of *phrases* tacked together like the sections of a prefabricated hen-house. I list below, with notes and examples, various of the tricks by means of which the work of prose-construction is habitually dodged:

Dying Metaphors

A newly invented metaphor assists thought by evoking a visual image, while on the other hand a metaphor which is technically "dead" (e.g. *iron resolution*) has in effect reverted to being an ordinary word and can generally be used without loss of vividness. But in between these two classes there is a huge dump of worn-out metaphors which have lost all evocative power and are merely used because they save people the trouble of inventing phrases for themselves. Examples are: *Ring the changes on, take up the cudgels for, toe the line, ride roughshod over, stand shoulder to shoulder with, play into the hands of, no axe to grind, grist to the mill, fishing in troubled waters, on the order of the day, Achilles' heel, swan song, hotbed.* Many of these are used without knowledge of their meaning (what is a "rift," for instance?), and incompatible metaphors are frequently mixed, a sure sign that the writer is not interested in what he is saying. Some metaphors now current have been twisted out of their original meaning without those who use them even being aware of the fact. For example, *toe the line* is sometimes written *tow the line.* Another example is *the hammer and the anvil,* now always used with the implication that the anvil gets the worst of it. In real life it is always the anvil that breaks the hammer, never the other way about: a writer who stopped to think what he was saying would be aware of this, and would avoid perverting the original phrase.

Operators or Verbal False Limbs

These save the trouble of picking out appropriate verbs and nouns, and at the same time pad each sentence with extra syllables which give it an appearance of symmetry. Characteristic phrases are: *render inoperative, militate against, make contact with, be subjected to, give rise to, give grounds for, have the effect of, play a leading part (role) in, make itself felt, take effect, exhibit a tendency to, serve the purpose of,* etc., etc. The keynote is the elimination of simple verbs. Instead of being a single word, such as *break, stop, spoil, mend, kill,* a verb becomes a *phrase,* made up of a noun or adjective tacked on to some general-purposes verb such as *prove, serve, form, play, render.* In addition, the passive voice is wherever possible used in preference to the active, and noun constructions are used instead of gerunds (*by examination of* instead of *by examining*). The range of verbs is further cut down by means of the *-ize* and *de-* formation, and the banal statements are given an appearance of profundity by means of the *not un-* formation. Simple conjunctions and prepositions are replaced by such phrases as *with respect to, having regard to, the fact that, by dint of, in view of, in the interests of, on the hypothesis that;* and the ends of sentences are saved from anticlimax by such resounding commonplaces as *greatly to be desired, cannot be left out of account, a development to be expected in the near future, deserving of serious consideration, brought to a satisfactory conclusion,* and so on and so forth.

Pretentious Diction

Words like *phenomenon, element, individual* (as noun), *objective, categorical, effective, virtual, basic, primary, promote, constitute, exhibit, exploit, utilize, eliminate, liquidate,* are used to dress up simple statements and give an air of scientific impartiality to biased judgments. Adjectives like *epoch-making, epic, historic, unforgettable, triumphant, age-old, inevitable, inexorable, veritable,* are used to dignify the sordid processes of international politics, while writing that aims at glorifying war usually takes on an archaic colour, its characteristic words being: *realm, throne, chariot, mailed fist, trident, sword, shield, buckler, banner, jackboot, clarion.* Foreign words and expressions such as *cul de sac, ancien régime, deus ex machina, mutatis mutandis, status quo, gleichschaltung, weltanschauung,* are used to give an air of culture and elegance. Except for the useful abbreviations *i.e., e.g.,* and *etc.,* there is no real need for any of the hundreds of foreign phrases now current in English. Bad writers, and especially scientific, political and sociological writers, are nearly always haunted by the notion that Latin or Greek words are grander than Saxon ones, and unnecessary words like *expedite, ameliorate, predict, extrane-*

ous, deracinated, clandestine, subaqueous and hundreds of others constantly gain ground from their Anglo-Saxon opposite numbers.[1] The jargon peculiar to Marxist writing (*hyena, hangman, cannibal, petty bourgeois, these gentry, lacquey, flunkey, mad dog, White Guard,* etc.) consists largely of words and phrases translated from Russian, German or French; but the normal way of coining a new word is to use a Latin or Greek root with the appropriate affix and, where necessary, the *-ize* formation. It is often easier to make up words of this kind (*deregionalize, impermissible, extramarital, nonfragmentatory* and so forth) than to think up the English words that will cover one's meaning. The result, in general, is an increase in slovenliness and vagueness.

Meaningless Words

In certain kinds of writing, particularly in art criticism and literary criticism, it is normal to come across long passages which are almost completely lacking in meaning.[2] Words like *romantic, plastic, values, human, dead, sentimental, natural, vitality,* as used in art criticism, are strictly meaningless in the sense that they not only do not point to any discoverable object, but are hardly ever expected to do so by the reader. When one critic writes, "The outstanding feature of Mr. X's work is its living quality", while another writes, "The immediately striking thing about Mr. X's work is its peculiar deadness", the reader accepts this as a simple difference of opinion. If words like *black* and *white* were involved, instead of the jargon words *dead* and *living,* he would see at once that language was being used in an improper way. Many political words are similarly abused. The word *Fascism* has now no meaning except in so far as it signifies "something not desirable." The words *democracy, socialism, freedom, patriotic, realistic, justice,* have each of them several different meanings which cannot be reconciled with one another. In the case of a word like *democracy,* not only is there no agreed definition, but the attempt to make one is resisted from all sides. It is almost universally felt that when we call a country democratic we are praising it: consequently the defenders of every kind of régime claim that it is a democracy, and fear that they might have to stop using the word if it were tied down to

1. An interesting illustration of this is the way in which the English flower names which were in use till very recently are being ousted by Greek ones, *snapdragon* becoming *antirrhinum, forget-me-not* becoming *myosotis,* etc. It is hard to see any practical reason for this change of fashion: it is probably due to an instinctive turning-away from the more homely word and a vague feeling that the Greek word is scientific [Orwell's note].

2. Example: "Comfort's catholicity of perception and image, strangely Whitmanesque in range, almost the exact opposite in aesthetic compulsion, continues to evoke that trembling atmospheric accumulative hinting at a cruel, an inexorably serene timelessness ... Wrey Gardiner scores by aiming at simple bull's-eyes with precision. Only they are not so simple, and through this contented sadness- runs more than the surface bittersweet of resignation" (*Poetry Quarterly*) [Orwell's note].

any one meaning. Words of this kind are often used in a consciously dishonest way. That is, the person who uses them has his own private definition, but allows his hearer to think he means something quite different. Statements like *Marshal Pétain was a true patriot, The Soviet Press is the freest in the world, The Catholic Church is opposed to persecution*, are almost always made with intent to deceive. Other words used in variable meanings, in most cases more or less dishonestly, are: *class, totalitarian, science, progressive, reactionary, bourgeois, equality.*

Now that I have made this catalogue of swindles and perversions, let me give another example of the kind of writing that they lead to. This time it must of its nature be an imaginary one. I am going to translate a passage of good English into modern English of the worst sort. Here is a well-known verse from *Ecclesiastes:*

> "I returned and saw under the sun, that the race is not to the swift, nor the battle to the strong, neither yet bread to the wise, nor yet riches to men of understanding, nor yet favour to men of skill; but time and chance happeneth to them all."

Here it is in modern English:

> "Objective consideration of contemporary phenomena compels the conclusion that success or failure in competitive activities exhibits no tendency to be commensurate with innate capacity, but that a considerable element of the unpredictable must invariably be taken into account."

This is a parody, but not a very gross one. Exhibit (3), above, for instance, contains several patches of the same kind of English. It will be seen that I have not made a full translation. The beginning and ending of the sentence follow the original meaning fairly closely, but in the middle the concrete illustrations—race, battle, bread—dissolve into the vague phrase "success or failure in competitive activities." This had to be so, because no modern writer of the kind I am discussing—no one capable of using phrases like "objective consideration of contemporary phenomena"—would ever tabulate his thoughts in that precise and detailed way. The whole tendency of modern prose is away from concreteness. Now analyse these two sentences a little more closely. The first contains forty-nine words but only sixty syllables, and all its words are those of everyday life. The second contains thirty-eight words of ninety syllables: eighteen of its words are from Latin roots, and one from Greek. The first sentence contains six vivid images, and only one phrase ("time and chance") that could be called vague. The second contains not a single fresh, arresting phrase, and in spite of its ninety syllables it gives only a shortened version of the meaning contained in the first. Yet without a doubt it is the second kind of sentence that is gaining ground in modern English. I do not want to exaggerate. This kind of writing is not yet universal, and outcrops of simplicity will occur here and there in the worst-written page. Still, if you or I were told to write a few lines on the uncertainty of human fortunes, we should probably come much nearer to my imaginary sentence than to the one from *Ecclesiastes*.

As I have tried to show, modern writing at its worst does not consist in picking out words for the sake of their meaning and inventing images in order to make the meaning clearer. It consists in gumming together long strips of words which have already been set in order by someone else, and making the results presentable by sheer humbug. The attraction of this way of writing is that it is easy. It is easier—even quicker, once you have the habit—to say *In my opinion it is a not unjustifiable assumption that* than to say *I think*. If you use ready-made phrases, you not only don't have to hunt about for words; you also don't have to bother with the rhythms of your sentences, since these phrases are generally so arranged as to be more or less euphonious. When you are composing in a hurry—when you are dictating to a stenographer, for instance, or making a public speech—it is natural to fall into a pretentious, Latinized style. Tags like *a consideration which we should do well to bear in mind* or *a conclusion to which all of us would readily assent* will save many a sentence from coming down with a bump. By using stale metaphors, similes and idioms, you save much mental effort, at the cost of leaving your meaning vague, not only for your reader but for yourself. This is the significance of mixed metaphors. The sole aim of a metaphor is to call up a visual image. When these images clash—as in *The Fascist octopus has sung its swan song, the jackboot is thrown into the melting pot*—it can be taken as certain that the writer is not seeing a mental image of the objects he is naming; in other words he is not really thinking. Look again at the examples I gave at the beginning of this essay. Professor Laski (1) uses five negatives in fifty-three words. One of these is superfluous, making nonsense of the whole passage, and in addition there is the slip *alien* for akin, making further nonsense, and several avoidable pieces of clumsiness which increase the general vagueness. Professor Hogben (2) plays ducks and drakes with a battery which is able to write prescriptions, and, while disapproving of the everyday phrase *put up with*, is unwilling to look *egregious* up in the dictionary and see what it means. (3), if one takes an uncharitable attitude towards it, is simply meaningless: probably one could work out its intended meaning by reading the whole of the article in which it occurs. In (4), the writer knows more or less what he wants to say, but an accumulation of stale phrases chokes him like tea leaves blocking a sink. In (5), words and meaning have almost parted company. People who write in this manner usually have a general emotional meaning—they dislike one thing and want to express solidarity with another—but they are not interested in the detail of what they are saying. A scrupulous writer, in every sentence that he writes, will ask himself at least four questions, thus: What am I trying to say? What words will express it? What image or idiom will make it clearer? Is this image fresh enough to have an effect? And he will probably ask himself two more: Could I put it more shortly? Have I said anything that is avoidably ugly? But you are not obliged to go to all this trouble. You can shirk it by simply throwing your mind open and letting the ready-made phrases come crowding in. They will construct your sentences for you—even think your thoughts for you, to a certain extent—and at need they will perform the important service of partially concealing your meaning even from yourself. It is at this point that the special connection between politics and the debasement of language becomes clear.

In our time it is broadly true that political writing is bad writing. Where it is not true, it will generally be found that the writer is some kind of rebel, expressing his private opinions and not a "party line." Orthodoxy, of whatever colour, seems to demand a lifeless, imitative style. The political dialects to be found in pamphlets, leading articles, manifestos, White Papers and the speeches of under-secretaries do, of course, vary from party to party, but they are all alike in that one almost never finds in them a fresh, vivid, home-made turn of speech. When one watches some tired hack on the platform mechanically repeating the familiar phrases—*bestial atrocities, iron heel, bloodstained tyranny, free peoples of the world, stand shoulder to shoulder*—one often has a curious feeling that one is not watching a live human being but some kind of dummy: a feeling which suddenly becomes stronger at moments when the light catches the speaker's spectacles and turns them into blank discs which seem to have no eyes behind them. And this is not altogether fanciful. A speaker who uses that kind of phraseology has gone some distance towards turning himself into a machine. The appropriate noises are coming out of his larynx, but his brain is not involved as it would be if he were choosing his words for himself. If the speech he is making is one that he is accustomed to make over and over again, he may be almost unconscious of what he is saying, as one is when one utters the responses in church. And this reduced state of consciousness, if not indispensable, is at any rate favourable to political conformity.

In our time, political speech and writing are largely the defence of the indefensible. Things like the continuance of British rule in India, the Russian purges and deportations, the dropping of the atom bombs on Japan, can indeed be defended, but only by arguments which are too brutal for most people to face, and which do not square with the professed aims of political parties. Thus political language has to consist largely of euphemism, question-begging and sheer cloudy vagueness. Defenceless villages are bombarded from the air, the inhabitants driven out into the countryside, the cattle machine-gunned, the huts set on fire with incendiary bullets: this is called *pacification*. Millions of peasants are robbed of their farms and sent trudging along the roads with no more than they can carry: this is called *transfer of population* or *rectification of frontiers*. People are imprisoned for years without trial, or shot in the back of the neck or sent to die of scurvy in Arctic lumber camps: this is called *elimination of unreliable elements*. Such phraseology is needed if one wants to name things without calling up mental pictures of them. Consider for instance some comfortable English professor defending Russian totalitarianism. He cannot say outright, "I believe in killing off your opponents when you can get good results by doing so." Probably, therefore, he will say something like this:

"While freely conceding that the Soviet régime exhibits certain features which the humanitarian may be inclined to deplore, we must, I think, agree that a certain curtailment of the right to political opposition is an unavoidable concomitant of transitional periods, and that the rigors which the Russian people have been called upon to undergo have been amply justified in the sphere of concrete achievement."

The inflated style is itself a kind of euphemism. A mass of Latin words falls upon the facts like soft snow, blurring the outlines and covering up all the details. The great enemy of clear language is insincerity. When there is a gap between one's real and one's declared aims, one turns as it were instinctively to long words and exhausted idioms, like a cuttlefish squirting out ink. In our age there is no such thing as "keeping out of politics." All issues are political issues, and politics itself is a mass of lies, evasions, folly, hatred and schizophrenia. When the general atmosphere is bad, language must suffer. I should expect to find—this is a guess which I have not sufficient knowledge to verify—that the German, Russian and Italian languages have all deteriorated in the last ten or fifteen years, as a result of dictatorship.

But if thought corrupts language, language can also corrupt thought. A bad usage can spread by tradition and imitation, even among people who should and do know better. The debased language that I have been discussing is in some ways very convenient. Phrases like *a not unjustifiable assumption, leaves much to be desired, would serve no good purpose, a consideration which we should do well to bear in mind*, are a continuous temptation, a packet of aspirins always at one's elbow. Look back through this essay, and for certain you will find that I have again and again committed the very faults I am protesting against. By this morning's post I have received a pamphlet dealing with conditions in Germany. The author tells me that he "felt impelled" to write it. I open it at random, and here is almost the first sentence that I see: "(The Allies) have an opportunity not only of achieving a radical transformation of Germany's social and political structure in such a way as to avoid a nationalistic reaction in Germany itself, but at the same time of laying the foundations of a cooperative and unified Europe." You see, he "feels impelled" to write—

feels, presumably, that he has something new to say—and yet his words, like cavalry horses answering the bugle, group themselves automatically into the familiar dreary pattern. This invasion of one's mind by ready-made phrases (*lay the foundations, achieve a radical transformation*) can only be prevented if one is constantly on guard against them, and every such phrase anaesthetizes a portion of one's brain.

I said earlier that the decadence of our language is probably curable. Those who deny this would argue, if they produced an argument at all, that language merely reflects existing social conditions, and that we cannot influence its development by any direct tinkering with words and constructions. So far as the general tone or spirit of a language goes, this may be true, but it is not true in detail. Silly words and expressions have often disappeared, not through any evolutionary process but owing to the conscious action of a minority. Two recent examples were *explore every avenue* and *leave no stone unturned*, which were killed by the jeers of a few journalists. There is a long list of flyblown metaphors which could similarly be got rid of if enough people would interest themselves in the job; and it should also be possible to laugh the *not un-* formation out of existence,[3] to reduce the amount of Latin and Greek in the average sentence, to drive out foreign phrases and strayed scientific words, and, in general, to make pretentiousness unfashionable. But all these are minor points. The defence of the English language implies more than this, and perhaps it is best to start by saying what it does *not* imply.

To begin with it has nothing to do with archaism, with the salvaging of obsolete words and turns of speech, or with the setting up of a "standard English" which must never be departed from. On the contrary, it is especially concerned with the scrapping of every word or idiom which has outworn its usefulness. It has nothing to do with correct grammar and syntax, which are of no importance so long as one makes one's meaning clear, or with the avoidance of Americanisms, or with having what is called a "good prose style." On the other hand it is not concerned with fake simplicity and the attempt to make written English colloquial. Nor does it even imply in every case preferring the Saxon word to the Latin one, though it does imply using the fewest and shortest words that will cover one's meaning. What is above all needed is to let the meaning choose the word, and not the other way about. In prose, the worst thing one can do with words is to surrender to them. When you think of a concrete object, you think wordlessly, and then, if you want to describe the thing you have been visualizing you probably hunt about till you find the exact words that seem to fit. When you think of something abstract you are more inclined to use words from the start, and unless you make a conscious effort to prevent it, the existing dialect will come rushing in

3. One can cure oneself of the *not un*-formation by memorizing this sentence: *A not un-* *black dog was chasing a not unsmall rabbit across a not ungreen field* [Orwell's note].

and do the job for you, at the expense of blurring or even changing your meaning. Probably it is better to put off using words as long as possible and get one's meaning as clear as one can through pictures or sensations. Afterwards one can choose—not simply *accept*—the phrases that will best cover the meaning, and then switch round and decide what impression one's words are likely to make on another person. This last effort of the mind cuts out all stale or mixed images, all prefabricated phrases, needless repetitions, and humbug and vagueness generally. But one can often be in doubt about the effect of a word or a phrase, and one needs rules that one can rely on when instinct fails. I think the following rules will cover most cases:

> (i) Never use a metaphor, simile or other figure of speech which you are used to seeing in print.
> (ii) Never use a long word where a short one will do.
> (iii) If it is possible to cut a word out, always cut it out.
> (iv) Never use the passive where you can use the active.
> (v) Never use a foreign phrase, a scientific word or a jargon word if you can think of an everyday English equivalent.
> (vi) Break any of these rules sooner than say anything outright barbarous.

These rules sound elementary, and so they are, but they demand a deep change of attitude in anyone who has grown used to writing in the style now fashionable. One could keep all of them and still write bad English, but one could not write the kind of stuff that I quoted in those five specimens at the beginning of this article.

I have not here been considering the literary use of language, but merely language as an instrument for expressing and not for concealing or preventing thought. Stuart Chase and others have come near to claiming that all abstract words are meaningless, and have used this as a pretext for advocating a kind of political quietism. Since you don't know what Fascism is, how can you struggle against Fascism? One need not swallow such absurdities as this, but one ought to recognize that the present political chaos is connected with the decay of language, and that one can probably bring about some improvement by starting at the verbal end. If you simplify your English, you are freed from the worst follies of orthodoxy. You cannot speak any of the necessary dialects, and when you make a stupid remark its stupidity will be obvious, even to yourself. Political language—and with variations this is true of all political parties, from Conservatives to Anarchists—is designed to make lies sound truthful and murder respectable, and to give an appearance of solidity to pure wind. One cannot change this all in a moment, but one can at least change one's own habits, and from time to time one can even, if one jeers loudly enough, send some worn-out and useless phrase—some jackboot, Achilles' heel, hotbed, melting pot, acid test, veritable inferno or other lump of verbal refuse—into the dustbin where it belongs.

1946

THE READER

1. What is Orwell's pivotal point? Where is it best stated?
2. Discuss Orwell's assertion that "the decline of a language must ultimately have political and economic causes." Is this "clear," as he claims?
3. Orwell suggests that if you look back through his essay, you will find that he has "again and again committed the very faults" he is protesting against. Is this true? If it is, does it affect the validity of his major points?

THE WRITER

1. How can you be sure that a metaphor is dying, rather than alive or dead? Is Orwell's test of seeing it often in print a sufficient one? Can you defend any of his examples of dying metaphors as necessary or useful additions to our vocabularies?
2. Orwell gives a list of questions for the writer to ask himself (pp. 247–248) and a list of rules for the writer to follow (p. 251). Why does he consider it necessary to give both kinds of advice? How much do the two overlap? Are both consistent with Orwell's major ideas expressed elsewhere in the essay? Does his injunction to "break any of these rules sooner than say anything outright barbarous" beg the question?
3. Words create a personality or confer a character. Write a brief essay describing the personality that would be created by following Orwell's six rules. Show that character in action.

An Album of Styles

Francis Bacon: OF REVENGE

Revenge is a kind of wild justice; which the more man's nature runs to, the more ought law to weed it out. For as for the first wrong, it doth but offend the law; but the revenge of that wrong putteth the law out of office. Certainly, in taking revenge, a man is but even with his enemy; but in passing it over, he is superior; for it is a prince's part to pardon. And Salomon, I am sure, saith, *It is the glory of a man to pass by an offence*. That which is past is gone, and irrevocable; and wise men have enough to do with things present and to come: therefore they do but trifle with themselves, that labour in past matters. There is no man doth a wrong for the wrong's sake; but thereby to purchase himself profit, or pleasure, or honour, or the like. Therefore why should I be angry with a man for loving himself better than me? And if any man should do wrong merely out of ill nature, why, yet it is but like the thorn or briar, which prick and scratch, because they can do no other. The most tolerable sort of revenge is for those wrongs which there is no law to remedy; but then let a man take heed the revenge be such as there is no law to punish; else a man's enemy is still beforehand, and it is two for one. Some, when they take revenge, are desirous the party should know whence it cometh: this is the more generous. For the delight seemeth to be not so much in doing the hurt as in making the party repent: but base and crafty cowards are like the arrow that flieth in the dark. Cosmus, duke of Florence, had a desperate saying against perfidious or neglecting friends, as if those wrongs were unpardonable: *You shall read* (saith he) *that we are commanded to forgive our enemies; but you never read that we are commanded to forgive our friends*. But yet the spirit of Job was in a better tune: *Shall we* (saith he) *take good at God's hands, and not be content to take evil also?* And so of friends in a proportion. This is certain, that a man that studieth revenge keeps his own wounds green, which otherwise would heal and do well. Public revenges are for the most part fortunate; as that for the death of Caesar; for the death of Pertinax;[1] for the death of Henry the third of France;[2] and many more. But in private revenges it is not so. Nay rather, vindictive persons live the life of witches; who as they are mischievous, so end they infortunate.

1625

1. Publius Helvius Pertinax became Emperor of Rome in 193 and was assassinated three months after his accession to the throne by a soldier in his praetorian Guard.
2. King of France 1574–1589; assassinated during the Siege of Paris.

John Donne: MEN ARE SLEEPING PRISONERS

We are all conceived in close prison; in our Mothers wombs, we are close prisoners all; when we are born, we are born but to the liberty of the house;[1] prisoners still, though within larger walls; and then all our life is but a going out to the place of execution, to death. Now was there ever any man seen to sleep in the cart, between Newgate, and Tyburn?[2] Between the prison and the place of execution, does any man sleep? And we sleep all the way; from the womb to the grave we are never thoroughly awake; but pass on with such dreams, and imaginations as these, I may live as well, as another, and why should I die, rather than another? But awake, and tell me, says this text *Quis homo?*[3] Who is that other that thou talkest of? *What man is he that liveth, and shall not see death?*

1640

1. Donne distinguishes between a prisoner confined to a cell and one given somewhat more liberty.
2. London prisoners were taken in carts from Newgate prison to nearby Tyburn for execution.
3. "Who [is] the man?"

Abraham Lincoln: The Gettysburg Address

Four score and seven years ago our fathers brought forth on this continent, a new nation, conceived in Liberty, and dedicated to the proposition that all men are created equal.

Now we are engaged in a great civil war, testing whether that nation, or any nation so conceived and so dedicated, can long endure. We are met on a great battle-field of that war. We have come to dedicate a portion of that field, as a final resting place for those who here gave their lives that that nation might live. It is altogether fitting and proper that we should do this.

But, in a larger sense, we can not dedicate—we can not consecrate—we can not hallow—this ground. The brave men, living and dead, who struggled here, have consecrated it, far above our poor power to add or detract. The world will little note, nor long remember what we say here, but it can never forget what they did here. It is for us the living, rather, to be dedicated here to the unfinished work which they who fought here have thus far so nobly advanced. It is rather for us to be here dedicated to the great task remaining before us—that from these honored dead we take increased devotion to that cause for which they gave the last full measure of devotion—that we here highly resolve that these dead shall not have died in vain—that this nation, under God, shall have a new birth of freedom—and that government of the people, by the people, for the people, shall not perish from the earth.

1863

Anonymous: No Dawn to the East

My sun is set. My day is done. Darkness is stealing over me. Before I lie down to rise no more I will speak to my people. Hear me, for this is not the time to tell a lie. The Great Spirit made us, and gave us this land we live in. He gave us the buffalo, antelope, and deer for food and clothing. Our hunting grounds stretched from the Mississippi to the great mountains. We were free as the winds and heard no man's commands. We fought our enemies, and feasted our friends. Our braves drove away all who would take our game. They captured women and horses from our foes. Our children were many and our herds were large. Our old men talked with spirits and made good medicine. Our young men hunted and made love to the girls. Where the tipi was, there we stayed, and no house imprisoned us. No one said, "To this line is my land, to that is yours." Then the white man came to our hunting grounds, a stranger. We gave him meat and presents, and told him go in peace. He looked on our women and stayed to live in our tipis. His fellows came to build their roads across our hunting grounds. He brought among us the mysterious iron that shoots. He brought with him the magic water that makes men foolish. With his trinkets and beads he even bought the girl I loved. I said, "The white man is not a friend, let us kill him." But their numbers were greater than blades of grass. They took away the buffalo and shot down our best warriors. They took away our lands and surrounded us by fences. Their soldiers camped outside with cannon to shoot us down. They wiped the trails of our people from the face of the prairies. They forced our children to forsake the ways of their fathers. When I turn to the east I see no dawn. When I turn to the west the approaching night hides all.

c. 1870

Ernest Hemingway: FROM A FAREWELL TO ARMS

* * * I was always embarrassed by the words sacred, glorious, and sacrifice and the expression in vain. We had heard them, sometimes standing in the rain almost out of earshot, so that only the shouted words came through, and had read them, on proclamations that were slapped up by billposters over other proclamations, now for a long time, and I had seen nothing sacred, and the things that were glorious had no glory and the sacrifices were like the stockyards at Chicago if nothing was done with the meat except to bury it. There were many words that you could not stand to hear and finally only the names of places had dignity. Certain numbers were the same way and certain dates and these with the names of places were all you could say and have them mean anything. Abstract words such as glory, honor, courage, or hallow were obscene beside the concrete names of villages, the numbers of roads, the names of rivers, the numbers of regiments and the dates.

1929

Virgina Woolf: WHAT THE NOVELIST GIVES US

It is simple enough to say that since books have classes—fiction, biography, poetry—we should separate them and take from each what it is right that each should give us. Yet few people ask from books what books can give us. Most commonly we come to books with blurred and divided minds, asking of fiction that it shall be true, of poetry that it shall be false, of biography that it shall be flattering, of history that it shall enforce our own prejudices. If we could banish all such preconceptions when we read, that would be an admirable beginning. Do not dictate to your author; try to become him. Be his fellow-worker and accomplice. If you hang back, and reserve and criticize at first, you are preventing yourself from getting the fullest possible value from what you read. But if you open your mind as widely as possible, then signs and hints of almost imperceptible fineness, from the twist and turn of the first sentences, will bring you into the presence of a human being unlike any other. Steep yourself in this, acquaint yourself with this, and soon you will find that your author is giving you, or attempting to give you, something far more definite. The thirty-two chapters of a novel—if we consider how to read a novel first—are an attempt to make something as formed and controlled as a building: but words are more impalpable than bricks; reading is a longer and more complicated process than seeing. Perhaps the quickest way to understand the elements of what a novelist is doing is not to read, but to write; to make your own experiment with the dangers and difficulties of words. Recall, then, some event that has left a distinct impression on you—how at the corner of the street, perhaps, you passed two people talking. A tree shook; an electric light danced; the tone of the talk was comic, but also tragic; a whole vision, an entire conception, seemed contained in that moment.

But when you attempt to reconstruct it in words, you will find that it breaks into a thousand conflicting impressions. Some must be subdued; others emphasized; in the process you will lose, probably, all grasp upon the emotion itself. Then turn from your blurred and littered pages to the opening pages of some great novelist—Defoe, Jane Austen, Hardy. Now you will be better able to appreciate their mastery. It is not merely that we are in the presence of a different person—Defoe, Jane Austen, or Thomas Hardy—but that we are living in a different world. Here, in *Robinson Crusoe*, we are trudging a plain high road; one thing happens after another; the fact and the order of the fact is enough. But if the open air and adventure mean everything to Defoe they mean nothing to Jane

Austen. Hers is the drawing-room, and people talking, and by the many mirrors of their talk revealing their characters. And if, when we have accustomed ourselves to the drawing-room and its reflections, we turn to Hardy, we are once more spun around. The moors are round us and the stars are above our heads. The other side of the mind is now exposed— the dark side that comes uppermost in solitude, not the light side that shows in company. Our relations are not towards people, but towards Nature and destiny. Yet different as these worlds are, each is consistent with itself. The maker of each is careful to observe the laws of his own perspective, and however great a strain they may put upon us they will never confuse us, as lesser writers so frequently do, by introducing two different kinds of reality into the same book. Thus to go from one great novelist to another—from Jane Austen to Hardy, from Peacock to Trol-lope, from Scott to Meredith—is to be wrenched and uprooted; to be thrown this way and then that. To read a novel is a difficult and complex art. You must be capable not only of great finesse of perception, but of great boldness of imagination if you are going to make use of all that the novelist—the great artist—gives you.

1932

E. B. White: PROGRESS AND CHANGE

In resenting progress and change, a man lays himself open to censure. I suppose the explanation of anyone's defending anything as rudimentary and cramped as a Pullman berth is that such things are associated with an earlier period in one's life and that this period in retrospect seems a happy one. People who favor progress and improvements are apt to be people who have had a tough enough time without any extra inconven-ience. Reactionaries who pout at innovations are apt to be well-heeled sentimentalists who had the breaks. Yet for all that, there is always a subtle danger in life's refinements, a dim degeneracy in progress. I have just been refining the room in which I sit, yet I sometimes doubt that a writer should refine or improve his workroom by so much as a dictionary: one thing leads to another and the first thing you know he has a stuffed chair and is fast asleep in it. Half a man's life is devoted to what he calls improvements, yet the original had some quality which is lost in the process. There was a fine natural spring of water on this place when I bought it. Our drinking water had to be lugged in a pail, from a wet glade of alder and tamarack. I visited the spring often in those first years, and had friends there—a frog, a woodcock, and an eel which had churned its way all the way up through the pasture creek to enjoy the luxury of pure water. In the normal course of development, the spring was rocked up, fitted with a concrete curb, a copper pipe, and an electric pump. I have visited it only once or twice since. This year my only gesture was the purely perfunctory one of sending a sample to the state bureau of health for analysis. I felt cheap, as though I were smelling an old friend's breath.

1938

William Faulkner: NOBEL PRIZE AWARD SPEECH

I feel that this award was not made to me as a man but to my work—a life's work in the agony and sweat of the human spirit, not for glory and least of all for profit, but to create out of the materials of the human spirit something which did not exist before. So this award is only mine in trust. It will not be difficult to find a dedication for the money part of it commensurate with the purpose and significance of its origin. But I would like to do the same with the acclaim too, by using this moment as a pinnacle from which I might be listened to by the young men and women already dedicated to the same anguish and travail, among whom is already that one who will some day stand here where I am standing.

Our tragedy today is a general and universal physical fear so long sustained by now that we can even bear it. There are no longer problems of the spirit. There is only the question: When will I be blown up? Because of this, the young man or woman writing today has forgotten the problems of the human heart in conflict with itself which alone can make good writing because only that is worth writing about, worth the agony and the sweat.

He must learn them again. He must teach himself that the basest of all things is to be afraid; and, teaching himself that, forget it forever, leaving no room in his workshop for anything but the old verities and truths of the heart, the old universal truths lacking which any story is ephemeral and doomed—love and honor and pity and pride and compassion and sacrifice. Until he does so, he labors under a curse. He writes not of love but of lust, of defeats in which nobody loses anything of value, of victories without hope and, worst of all, without pity or compassion. His griefs grieve on no universal bones leaving no scars. He writes not of the heart but of the glands.

Until he relearns these things, he will write as though he stood alone and watched the end of man. I decline to accept the end of man. It is easy enough to say that man is immortal simply because he will endure; that when the last ding-dong of doom has clanged and faded from the last worthless rock hanging tideless in the last red and dying evening, that even then there will still be one more sound: that of his puny inexhaustible voice, still talking. I refuse to accept this. I believe that man will not merely endure: he will prevail. He is immortal, not because he alone among creatures has an inexhaustible voice but because he has a soul, a spirit capable of compassion and sacrifice and endurance. The poet's, the writer's, duty is to write about these things. It is his privilege to help man endure by lifting his heart, by reminding him of the courage and honor and hope and pride and compassion and pity and sacrifice which have been the glory of his past. The poet's voice need not merely be the record of man, it can be one of the props, the pillars to help him endure and prevail.

1949

James Thurber: A DOG'S EYE VIEW OF MAN

If Man has benefited immeasurably by his association with the dog, what, you may ask, has the dog got out of it? His scroll has, of course, been heavily charged with punishments: he has known the muzzle, the leash, and the tether; he has suffered the indignities of the show bench, the tin can on the tail, the ribbon in the hair; his love life with the other sex of his species has been regulated by the frigid hand of authority, his digestion ruined by the macaroons and marshmallows of doting women. The list of his woes could be continued indefinitely. But he has also had his fun, for he has been privileged to live with and study at close range the only creature with reason, the most unreasonable of creatures.

The dog has got more fun out of Man than Man has got out of the dog, for the clearly demonstrable reason that Man is the more laughable of the two animals. The dog has long been bemused by the singular activities and the curious practices of men, cocking his head inquiringly to one side, intently watching and listening to the strangest goings-on in the world. He has seen men sing together and fight one another in the same evening. He has watched them go to bed when it is time to get up, and get up when it is time to go to bed. He has observed them destroying the soil in vast areas, and nurturing it in small patches. He has stood by while men built strong and solid houses for rest and quiet, and then filled them with lights and bells and machinery. His sensitive nose, which can detect what's cooking in the next township, has caught at one and the same time the bewildering smells of the hospital and the munitions factory. He has seen men raise up great cities to heaven and then blow them to hell.

1955

John Updike: BEER CAN

This seems to be an era of gratuitous inventions and negative improvements. Consider the beer can. It was beautiful—as beautiful as the clothespin, as inevitable as the wine bottle, as dignified and reassuring as the fire hydrant. A tranquil cylinder of delightfully resonant metal, it could be opened in an instant, requiring only the application of a handy gadget freely dispensed by every grocer. Who can forget the small, symmetrical thrill of those two triangular punctures, the dainty *pffff*, the little crest of suds that foamed eagerly in the exultation of release? Now we are given, instead, a top beetling with an ugly, shmoo-shaped "tab," which, after fiercely resisting the tugging, bleeding fingers of the thirsty man, threatens his lips with a dangerous and hideous hole. However, we have discovered a way to thwart Progress, usually so unthwartable. *Turn the beer can upside down and open the bottom.* The bottom is still the way the top used to be. True, this operation gives the beer an unsettling jolt, and the sight of a consistently inverted beer can might make people edgy, not to say queasy. But the latter difficulty could be eliminated if manufacturers would design cans that looked the same whichever end was up, like playing cards. What we need is Progress with an escape hatch.

1964

Signs of the Times

Anthony Burgess

IS AMERICA FALLING APART?

I am back in Bracciano, a castellated town about 13 miles north of Rome, after a year in New Jersey. I find the Italian Government still unstable, gasoline more expensive than anywhere in the world, butchers and bank clerks and tobacconists (which also means saltsellers) ready to go on strike at the drop of a *cappello*,[1] neo-Fascists at their dirty work, the hammer and sickle painted on the rumps of public statues, a thousand-lire note (officially worth about $1.63) shrunk to the slightness of a dollar bill.

Nevertheless, it's delightful to be back. People are underpaid but they go through an act of liking their work, the open markets are luscious with esculent color, the community is more important than the state, the human condition is humorously accepted. The *tramontana*[2] blows viciously today, and there's no central heating to turn on, but it will be pleasant when the wind drops. The two television channels are inadequate, but next Wednesday's rerun of an old Western, with Gary Cooper coming into a saloon saying "*Ciao, ragazzi*,"[3] is something to look forward to. Manifold consumption isn't important here. The quality of life has nothing to do with the quantity of brand names. What matters is talk, family, cheap wine in the open air, the wresting of minimal sweetness out of the long-known bitterness of living. I was spoiled in New Jersey. The Italian for *spoiled* is *viziato*, cognate with *vitiated*, which has to do with vice.

Spoiled? Well, yes. I never had to shiver by a fire that wouldn't draw, or go without canned kraut juice or wild rice. America made me develop new appetites in order to make proper use of the supermarket. A charac-

---

1. Hat.
2. North wind.

3. "Howdy, boys," in Italian.

ter in Evelyn Waugh's *Put Out More Flags* said that the difference between prewar and postwar life was that, prewar, if one thing went wrong the day was ruined; postwar, if one thing went right the day would be made. America is a prewar country, psychologically unprepared for one thing to go wrong. Now everything seems to be going wrong. Hence the neurosis, despair, the Kafka feeling that the whole marvelous fabric of American life is coming apart at the seams. Italy is used to everything going wrong. This is what the human condition is about.

Let me stay for a while on this subject of consumption. American individualism, on the face of it an admirable philosophy, wishes to manifest itself in independence of the community. You don't share things in common; you have your own things. A family's strength is signalized by its possessions. Herein lies a paradox. For the desire for possessions must eventually mean dependence on possessions. Freedom is slavery. Once let the acquisitive instinct burgeon (enough flour for the winter, not just for the week), and there are ruggedly individual forces only too ready to make it come to full and monstrous blossom. New appetites are invented; what to the European are bizarre luxuries become, to the American, plain necessities.

During my year's stay in New Jersey I let my appetites flower into full Americanism except for one thing. I did not possess an automobile. This self-elected deprivation was a way into the nastier side of the consumer society. Where private ownership prevails, public amenities decay or are prevented from coming into being. The wretched run-down rail services of America are something I try, vainly, to forget. The nightmare of filth, outside and in, that enfolds the trip from Springfield, Mass., to Grand Central Station would not be accepted in backward Europe. But far worse is the nightmare of travel in and around Los Angeles, where public transport does not exist and people are literally choking to death in their exhaust fumes. This is part of the price of the metaphysic of individual ownership.

But if the car owner can ignore the lack of public transport, he can hardly ignore the decay of services in general. His car needs mechanics, and mechanics grow more expensive and less efficient. The gadgets in the home are cheaper to replace than repair. The more efficiently self-contained the home, primary fortress of independence, seems to be, the more dependent it is on the great impersonal corporations, as well as a diminishing army of servitors. Skills at the lowest level have to be wooed slavishly and exorbitantly rewarded. Plumbers will not come. Nor, at the higher level, will doctors. And doctors and dentists, in a nation committed to maiming itself with sugar and cholesterol, know their scarcity value and behave accordingly.

Americans are at last realizing that the acquisition of goods is not the

whole of life. Consumption, on one level, is turning insipid, especially as
the quality of the artifacts themselves seems to be deteriorating. Planned
obsolescence is not conducive to pride in workmanship. On another
level, consumption is turning sour. There is a growing guilt about the
masses of discarded junk—rusting automobiles and refrigerators and
washing machines and dehumidifiers—that it is uneconomical to recycle.
Indestructible plastic hasn't even the grace to undergo chemical change.
America, the world's biggest consumer, is the world's biggest polluter.
Awareness of this is a kind of redemptive grace, but it doesn't appreciably lead to repentance and a revolution in consumer habits. Citizens of
Los Angeles are horrified by that daily pall of golden smog, but they don't
noticeably clamor for a decrease in the number of owner-vehicles. There
is no worse neurosis than that which derives from a consciousness of guilt
and an inability to reform.

America is anachronistic in so many ways, and not least in its clinging
to a belief—now known to be unviable—in the capacity of the individual
citizen to do everything for himself. Americans are admirable in their
distrust of the corporate state—they have fought both Fascism and
Communism—but they forget that there is a use for everything, even the
loathesome bureaucratic machine. America needs a measure of socialization, as Britain needed it. Things—especially those we need most—don't
always pay their way, and it is here that the state must enter, dismissing
the profit element. Part of the present American neurosis, again, springs
from awareness of this but inability to do anything about practical
implementation. Perhaps only a country full of bombed cities feels capable of this kind of social revolution.

It would be supererogatory for me to list those areas in which thoughtful Americans feel that collapse is coming. It is enough for me to concentrate on what, during my New Jersey stay, impinged on my own life.
Education, for instance, since I have a 6-year-old son to be brought up.
America has always despised its teachers and, as a consequence, it has
been granted the teachers it deserves. The quality of first-grade education that my son received, in a New Jersey town noted for the excellence
of its public schools, could not, I suppose, be faulted on the level of
dogged conscientiousness. The principal had read all the right pedagogic
books, and was ready to quote these in the footnotes to his circular
exhortations to parents. The teachers worked rigidly from the approved
rigidly programed primers, ensuring that school textbook publication
remains the big business it is.

But there seemed to be no spark; no daring, no madness, no readiness
to engage the individual child's mind as anything other than raw material
for statistical reductions. The fear of being unorthodox is rooted in the
American teacher's soul: you can be fired for treading the path of experi-

mental enterprise. In England, teachers cannot be fired, except for raping girl students and getting boy students drunk. In consequence, there is the kind of security that breeds eccentric genius, the capacity for firing mad enthusiasms.

I know that American technical genius, and most of all the moon landings, seems to give the lie to too summary a condemnation of the educational system, but there is more to education than the segmental equipping of the mind. There is that transmission of the value of the past as a force still miraculously fertile and moving—mostly absent from American education at all levels.

Of course, America was built on a rejection of the past. Even the basic Christianity which was brought to the continent in 1620 was of a novel and bizarre kind that would have nothing to do with the great rank river of belief that produced Dante and Michelangelo. America as a nation has never been able to settle to a common belief more sophisticated than the dangerous naiveté of the Declaration of Independence. "Life, liberty and the pursuit of happiness," indeed. And now America, filling in the vacuum left by the liquefied British Empire, has the task of telling the rest of the world that there's something better than Communism. The something better can only be money-making and consumption for its own sake. In the name of this ghastly creed the jungles must be defoliated.[3]

No wonder the guilt of the thoughtful Americans I met in Princeton and New York and, indeed, all over the Union tended to express itself as an extravagant masochism, a desire for flagellation. Americans want to take on all the blame they can find, gluttons for punishment. "What do Europeans really think of us?" is a common question at parties. The expected answer is: "They think you're a load of decadent, gross-lipped, potbellied, callous, overbearing neoimperialists." Then the head can be bowed and the chest smitten: "Nostra culpa, nostra maxima culpa. . . ."[4] But the fact is that such an answer, however much desired, would not be an honest one. Europeans think more highly of Americans now than they ever did. Let me try to explain why.

When Europe, after millennia of war, rapine, slavery, famine, intolerance, had sunk to the level of a sewer, America became the golden dream, the Eden where innocence could be recovered. Original sin was the monopoly of that dirty continent over there; in America man could glow in an aura of natural goodness, driven along his shining path by divine reason. The Declaration of Independence itself is a monument to reason.

3. That is, in order to deny the enemy protective cover—a part of American strategy during the Vietnam war.
4. "Through our fault, through our most grievous fault," a modification of *Mea culpa, mea maxima culpa* ("Through my fault . . ."), part of the act of confession in the Roman Catholic church.

Progress was possible, and the wrongs committed against the Indians, the wildlife, the land itself, could be explained away in terms of the rational control of environment necessary for the building of a New Jerusalem.[5] Right and wrong made up the moral dichotomy; evil—that great eternal inextirpable entity—had no place in America.

At last, with the Vietnam war and especially the Mylai horror,[6] Americans are beginning to realize that they are subject to original sin as much as Europeans are. Some things—the massive crime figures, for instance—can now be explained only in terms of absolute evil. Europe, which has long known about evil and learned to live with it (*live* is *evil* spelled backwards), is now grimly pleased to find that America is becoming like Europe. America is no longer Europe's daughter nor her rich step-mother: she is Europe's sister. The agony that America is undergoing is not to be associated with breakdown so much as with the parturition of self-knowledge.

It has been assumed by many that the youth of America has been in the vanguard of the discovery of both the disease and the cure. The various copping-out movements, however, from the Beats on, have committed the gross error of assuming that original sin rested with their elders, their rulers, and that they themselves could manifest their essential innocence by building little neo-Edens. The drug culture could confirm that the paradisal vision was available to all who sought it. But instant ecstasy has to be purchased, like any other commodity, and, in economic terms, that passive life of pure being involves parasitism. Practically all of the crime I encountered in New York—directly or through report—was a preying of the opium-eaters on the working community. There has to be a snake in paradise. You can't escape the heritage of human evil by building com-munes, usually on an agronomic ignorance that, intended to be a rejec-tion of inherited knowledge, that suspect property of the elders, does violence to life. The American young are well-meaning but misguided, and must not themselves be taken as guides.

The guides, as always, lie among the writers and artists. And Ameri-cans ought to note that, however things may seem to be falling apart, arts and the humane scholarship are flourishing here, as they are not, for instance, in England. I'm not suggesting that Bellow, Mailer, Roth and the rest have the task of finding a solution to the American mess, but they can at least clarify its nature and show how it relates to the human condition in general. Literature, that most directly human of the arts, often reacts magnificently to an ambience of unease or apparent break-down. The Elizabethans,[7] to whose era we look back as to an irrecovera-

---

5. The holy city described by John in Revela-tion xxi, here a figurative expression for a perfected society.
6. A massacre by American troops of over a hundred Vietnamese civilians in the village of Mylai.
7. The British during the reign of Elizabeth I, 1558–1603.

ble Golden Age, were far more conscious than modern Americans of the chaos and corruption and incompetence of the state. Shakespeare's period was one of poverty, unemployment, ghastly inflation, violence in the streets. Twenty-six years after his death there was a bloody civil war, followed by a dictatorship of religious fanatics, followed by a calm respite in which the seeds of a revolution were sown. England survived. America will survive.

I'm not suggesting that Americans sit back and wait for a transient period of mistrust and despair to resolve itself, like a disease, through the unconscious healing forces which lie deep in organic nature. Man, as Thornton Wilder showed in *The Skin of Our Teeth*,[8] always comes through—though sometimes only just. Americans living here and now have a right to an improvement in the quality of their lives, and they themselves, not the remote governors, must do something about it. It is not right that men and women should fear to go on the streets at night, and that they should sometimes fear the police as much as the criminals, both of whom sometimes look like mirror images of each other. I have had too much evidence, in my year in New Jersey, of the police behaving like the "Fascist pigs" of the revolutionary press. There are too many guns about, and the disarming of the police should be a natural aspect of the disarming of the entire citizenry.

American politics, at both the state and the Federal levels, is too much concerned with the protection of large fortunes, America being the only example in history of a genuine timocracy. The wealth qualification for the aspiring politician is taken for granted; a governmental system dedicated to the promotion of personal wealth in a few selected areas will never act for the public good. The time has come, nevertheless, for citizens to demand, from their government, a measure of socialization—the provision of amenities for the many, of which adequate state pensions and sickness benefits, as well as nationalized transport, should be priorities.

As for those remoter solutions to the American nightmare—only an aspect, after all, of the human nightmare—an Englishman must be diffident about suggesting that America made her biggest mistake in becoming America—meaning a revolutionary republic based on a romantic view of human nature. To reject a limited monarchy in favor of an absolute one (which is, after all, what the American Presidency is) argues a trust in the disinterestedness of an elected ruler which is, of course, no more than a reflection of belief in the innate goodness of man—so long as he happens to be American man. The American Constitution is out of date. Republics tend to corruption. Canada and Australia have their own

8. American play depicting man's tragicomic struggle for survival from prehistoric times to the present.

problems, but they are happier countries than America.

This *Angst*[9] about America coming apart at the seams, which apparently is shared by nearly 50 per cent of the entire American population, is something to rejoice about. A sense of sin is always admirable, though it must not be allowed to become neurotic. If electric systems break down and gadgets disintegrate, it doesn't matter much. There is always wine to be drunk by candlelight, uniced. If America's position as a world power collapses, and the Union dissolves into independent states, there is still the life of the family or the individual to be lived. England has survived her own dissolution as an imperial power, and Englishmen seem to be happy enough. But I ask the reader to note that I, an Englishman, no longer live in England, and I can't spend more than six months at a stretch in Italy—or any other European country, for that matter. I come to America as to a country more stimulating than depressing. The future of mankind is being worked out there on a scale typically American— vast, dramatic, almost apocalyptical. I brave the brutality and the guilt in order to be in on the scene. I shall be back.

1971

9. Anxiety.

THE READER

1. *Burgess wrote this piece in 1971. If he were writing it today, what might he want to leave out, add, or modify?*
2. *Burgess says that in the school his son attended, there was "no readiness to engage the individual child's mind as anything other than raw material for statistical reductions." Can you recall incidents from your early schooldays that would either support or counter Burgess's criticism of American education?*

THE WRITER

1. *Burgess writes as a visitor to America but a native of Great Britain. How might his account have differed if he had been an American?*
2. *Burgess's observation about the Italian word for* spoiled *implies a concern for etymology and precision of language. Is there evidence of that concern in his choice of English words?*
3. *Write your own brief characterization of one area of American life that Burgess talks about. How does your view differ from Burgess's?*
4. *Burgess refers to "the dangerous naiveté of the Declaration of Independence." Study the Declaration (p. 510), and write a brief argument either for considering it as a "naive" piece of writing or not.*

Phyllis Rose

SHOPPING AND OTHER SPIRITUAL ADVENTURES

Last year a new Waldbaum's Food Mart opened in the shopping mall on Route 66. It belongs to the new generation of superdupermarkets open 24 hours that have computerized checkout. I went to see the place as soon as it opened and I was impressed. There was trail mix in Lucite bins. There was freshly made pasta. There were coffee beans, 4 kinds of tahini, 10 kinds of herb teas, raw shrimp in shells and cooked shelled shrimp, fresh-squeezed orange juice. Every sophistication known to the big city, even goat's cheese covered with ash, was now available in Middletown, Conn. People raced from the warehouse aisle to the bagel bin to the coffee beans to the fresh fish market, exclaiming at all the new things. Many of us felt elevated, graced, complimented by the presence of this food palace in our town.

This is the wonderful egalitarianism of American business. Was it Andy Warhol[1] who said that the nice thing about Coke is, no can is any better or worse than any other? Some people may find it dull to cross the country and find the same chain stores with the same merchandise from coast to coast, but it means that my town is as good as yours, my shopping mall as important as yours, equally filled with wonders.

Imagine what people ate during the winter as little as 75 years ago. They ate food that was local, long-lasting and dull, like acorn squash, turnips and cabbage. Walk into an American supermarket in February and the world lies before you: grapes, melons, artichokes, fennel, lettuce, peppers, pistachios, dates, even strawberries, to say nothing of ice cream. Have you ever considered what a triumph of civilization it is to be able to buy a pound of chicken livers? If you lived on a farm and had to kill a chicken when you wanted to eat one, you wouldn't ever accumulate a pound of chicken livers.

Another wonder of Middletown is Caldor, the discount department store. Here is man's plenty: tennis racquets, pantyhose, luggage, glassware, records, toothpaste, Timex watches, Cadbury's chocolate, corn poppers, hair dryers, warm-up suits, car wax, light bulbs, television sets. All good quality at low prices with exchanges cheerfully made on defective goods. There are worse rules to live by. I feel good about America whenever I walk into this store, which is almost every midwinter Sunday

1. Andy Warhol: American pop artist (?1930–87) who often used repeated images.

afternoon, when life elsewhere has closed down. I go to Caldor the way English people go to pubs: out of sociability. To get away from my house. To widen my horizons. For culture's sake. Caldor provides me too with a welcome sense of seasonal change. When the first outdoor grills and lawn furniture appear there, it's as exciting a sign of spring as the first crocus or robin.

Someone told me about a Soviet émigré who practices English by declaiming, at random, sentences that catch his fancy. One of his favorites is, "Fifty percent off all items today only." Refugees from Communist countries appreciate our supermarkets and discount department stores for the wonders they are. An Eastern European scientist visiting Middletown wept when she first saw the meat counter at Waldbaum's. On the other hand, before her year in America was up, her pleasure turned sour. She wanted everything she saw. Her approach to consumer goods was insufficiently abstract, too materialistic. We Americans are beyond a simple, possessive materialism. We're used to abundance and the possibility of possessing things. The things, and the possibility of possessing them, will still be there next week, next year. So today we can walk the aisles calmly.

It is a misunderstanding of the American retail store to think we go there necessarily to buy. Some of us shop. There's a difference. Shopping has many purposes, the least interesting of which is to acquire new articles. We shop to cheer ourselves up. We shop to practice decision-making. We shop to be useful and productive members of our class and society. We shop to remind ourselves how much is available to us. We shop to remind ourselves how much is to be striven for. We shop to assert our superiority to the material objects that spread themselves before us.

Shopping's function as a form of therapy is widely appreciated. You don't really need, let's say, another sweater. You need the feeling of power that comes with buying or not buying it. You need the feeling that someone wants something you have—even if it's just your money. To get the benefit of shopping, you needn't actually purchase the sweater, any more than you have to marry every man you flirt with. In fact, window-shopping, like flirting, can be more rewarding, the same high without the distressing commitment, the material encumbrance. The purest form of shopping is provided by garage sales. A connoisseur goes out with no goal in mind, open to whatever may come his or her way, secure that it will cost very little. Minimum expense, maximum experience. Perfect shopping.

I try to think of the opposite, a kind of shopping in which the object is all-important, the pleasure of shopping at a minimum. For example, the purchase of blue jeans. I buy new blue jeans as seldom as possible because the experience is so humiliating. For every pair that looks good on me, 15 look grotesque. But even shopping for blue jeans at Bob's Surplus on

Main Street—no frills, bare-bones shopping—is an event in the life of the spirit. Once again I have to come to terms with the fact that I will never look good in Levi's. Much as I want to be mainstream, I never will be.

In fact, I'm doubly an oddball, neither Misses nor Junior, but Misses Petite. I look in the mirror, I acknowledge the disparity between myself and the ideal, I resign myself to making the best of it: I will buy the Lee's Misses Petite. Shopping is a time of reflection, assessment, spiritual self-discipline.

It is appropriate, I think, that Bob's Surplus has a communal dressing room. I used to shop only in places where I could count on a private dressing room with a mirror inside. My impulse then was to hide my weaknesses. Now I believe in sharing them. There are other women in the dressing room at Bob's Surplus trying on blue jeans who look as bad as I do. We take comfort from one another. Sometimes a woman will ask me which of two items looks better. I always give a definite answer. It's the least I can do. I figure we are all in this together, and I emerge from the dressing room not only with a new pair of jeans but with a renewed sense of belonging to a human community.

When a Solzhenitsyn[2] rants about American materialism, I have to look at my digital Timex and check what year this is. Materialism? Like conformism, a hot moral issue of the 50's, but not now. How to spread the goods, maybe. Whether the goods are the Good, no. Solzhenitsyn, like the visiting scientist who wept at the beauty of Waldbaum's meat counter but came to covet everything she saw, takes American materialism too materialistically. He doesn't see its spiritual side. Caldor, Waldbaum's, Bob' Surplus—these, perhaps, are our cathedrals.

1984

2. Alexandr I. Solzhenitsyn: Russian novelist and émigré (1918–   ).

THE READER

1. What, according to Rose, is the spiritual significance of shopping (as opposed to buying things)? How does shopping nourish and enhance the spirit?
2. What is Solzhenitsyn's error and the mistake made by the visiting scientist who wept at the meat counter?
3. It is often said that Americans are "too materialistic." Would Rose agree? Why, or why not? Do you think Americans might be too spiritual?

THE WRITER

1. What is the tone of Rose's article? Does it have a single dominant tone, or are there several tones? What particular elements in the article provide evidence for your answer?
2. Describe Rose's intended audience, specifying details in the article

from which you infer that audience.
3. *"Caldor, Waldbaum's, Bob's Surplus—these, perhaps, are our cathedrals." Write an essay testing this suggestion. Choose a particular store and a particular cathedral with which you are familiar. Do you find more resemblances or contrasts?*

Ian Frazier

JUST A COUNTRY BOY

If you think that when you look at me you're looking at rock, rhythm and blues, jazz, classical, or pop, then you are wrong, because I am country from my head down to my boots. If you're looking at me, then by definition you are looking at country. When I was in my early teens, the great Hank Williams[1] told me, "Son, you ain't country unless you've looked at a lot of miles over the back end of a mule." Unfortunately, because of conflicts in my schedule at the time, I did not have a chance to look at as many miles over the back end of a mule as I would have liked to. Hank, however, made some excellent videotapes of miles with the back end of a mule in the foreground, and I spent countless hours screening those tapes.

Excuse me. That's my phone.

Sorry. That was the lonesome highway calling me. It calls me just about every day at this time. Just about every day, I get calls from the lonesome highway, the gentle Southern summer breezes, my Smoky Mountain memories, and that lonesome freight-train whistle's whine. If I'm not in, they leave messages. I don't mind all these calls, because they remind me that I'm just a country boy and that's all I'll ever be. (Although sometimes that lonesome freight-train whistle's whine can be a little irritating. I pick up the phone and all I hear is this whine.)

I like it when the lonesome highway calls, because for a long time it has been my only friend. I don't know exactly why I always keep moving on down the road. One reason might be that I've got a different girl in every town you can name. There's a Cajun[2] Queen down in Baton Rouge who usually tries to avoid me. And in North Dallas there's a rich man's daughter who says she doesn't like me that much. In old San Antone there's a dark-eyed señorita who didn't have a very good time with me, while up in Memphis there are several Tennessee belles whose feelings toward me are lukewarm at best. I tell them all the same thing: "I am not

---

1. Hank Williams: leading country-music singer, musician, and composer (1923–1953).

2. Louisianian descended from Acadian French-speaking ancestors.

the kind of man to hang around with any one woman for too long, because I am always chasing rainbows. So please bear that in mind." That is not an easy thing to tell someone (particularly if you have to yell it through her locked door), but I know myself well enough to say that it is nothing more or less than the simple truth.

I am country today, and I was country this time last year—I have photographs to prove it. I was country back before Hollywood brought Texas to New York and imitation cowboys turned up all over the Sunset Strip. I was country in '80, '79, '78, '77, '76—it doesn't matter how far back you want to go. I was country when country wasn't cool. In fact, I was country back when it was forbidden by law in most states and the federal government turned a blind eye to this blatant violation of the rights of its people. I was country back when if you were intelligent enough to buy beer and you tried to be country you could be fined, or even imprisoned. Now it is hard to believe that such times ever existed.

My daddy was just a simple backwoods art director (B.F.A., Rhode Island School of Design) out of Checotah, Oklahoma. He raised me right. He insisted that I spend at least three hours out of every day honky-tonking, and he was very strict. I had to bring him bar tabs from as many places as I could, to prove I had really bar-hopped. He also made me practice cheating and slipping around behind my wife's back. Of course, I was much too young to be married, so we pretended I was married to Yeller, my dog. Then I would go over to our neighbor's yard and sweet-talk their dog, Blue. "What part of heaven did you fall from, angel?" I'd say. "No, no, no!" Daddy would holler. "Say it like you mean it! Put some ol' country sorghum in your voice!"[3] And he'd make me try it again and again, until I finally had Yeller howling with jealousy. At that time, I have to admit, I hated my daddy for being so hard on me, but now I understand what he was doing, and I thank him for it.

Many of the experiences of my life were like that; I did not understand at the time that they were molding me into pure country, which is what I am today. Like when I went to tennis camp with Bob Wills and several of the Texas Playboys. Or the time I made a snow sculpture with Ernest Tubb. Or the time I went on a two-month tour of the canals of Europe with Jimmie Rodgers, the Singing Brakeman.[4] Each of these experiences taught me a little bit more about what country really means.

So when people who don't have the benefit of similar experiences ask me "What is country?" I don't know what to tell them. Country is so many things. It's knowing how to find the country station on your radio

3. I.e., be sweetly sentimental ("sorghum": a sweet syrup made from sorgo).
4. Bob Wills and the Texas Playboys: Western swing band popular in the 1930s; Ernest Tubb (b. 1914): Texas balladeer who intro- duced the electric guitar to country-Western mainstream; Jimmie (James Charles) Rodgers (1897–1933): early and influential star of "hillbilly" music known for his "blue yodels" and sentimental songs.

dial. It's watching the TV pages to see when the next country-music awards show is on. It's knowing the location of the aisle labeled "Country" at your record store . . . It's all these things, and yet, somehow, it's more. It's ineffable, really. And when my friends, all of them country "kickers" like myself, and I watch people who just plain *ain't* country trying to pretend they are—when we watch them fumble with their radios searching for a country station—well, then we just smile. Because if you're not country, then there's nothing you can do about it. Because real, down-home country is something that comes from the heart. Because there is no way if you aren't country that you can ever possibly become country—certainly not without working at it for, at the very least, seven to ten years.

1986

John McMurtry

KILL 'EM! CRUSH 'EM! EAT 'EM RAW!

A few months ago my neck got a hard crick in it. I couldn't turn my head; to look left or right I'd have to turn my whole body. But I'd had cricks in my neck since I started playing grade-school football and hockey, so I just ignored it. Then I began to notice that when I reached for any sort of large book (which I do pretty often as a philosophy teacher at the University of Guelph) I had trouble lifting it with one hand. I was losing the strength in my left arm, and I had such a steady pain in my back I often had to stretch out on the floor of the room I was in to relieve the pressure.

A few weeks later I mentioned to my brother, an orthopedic surgeon, that I'd lost the power in my arm since my neck began to hurt. Twenty-four hours later I was in a Toronto hospital not sure whether I might end up with a wasted upper limb. Apparently the steady pounding I had received playing college and professional football in the late Fifties and early Sixties had driven my head into my backbone so that the discs had crumpled together at the neck—"acute herniation"—and had cut the nerves to my left arm like a pinched telephone wire (without nerve stimulation, of course, the muscles atrophy, leaving the arm crippled). So I spent my Christmas holidays in the hospital in heavy traction and much of the next three months with my neck in a brace. Today most of the pain has gone, and I've recovered most of the strength in my arm. But from time to time I still have to don the brace, and surgery remains a possibility.

Not much of this will surprise anyone who knows football. It is a sport in which body wreckage is one of the leading conventions. A few days after I went into hospital for that crick in my neck, another brother, an outstanding football player in college, was undergoing spinal surgery in the same hospital two floors above me. In his case it was a lower, more massive herniation, which every now and again buckled him so that he was unable to lift himself off his back for days at a time. By the time he entered the hospital for surgery he had already spent several months in bed. The operation was successful, but, as in all such cases, it will take him a year to recover fully.

These aren't isolated experiences. Just about anybody who has ever played football for any length of time, in high school, college or one of the professional leagues, has suffered for it later physically.

Indeed, it is arguable that body shattering is the very *point* of football, as killing and maiming are of war. (In the United States, for example, the game results in 15 to 20 deaths a year and about 50,000 major operations on knees alone.) To grasp some of the more conspicuous similarities between football and war, it is instructive to listen to the imperatives most frequently issued to the players by their coaches, teammates and fans. "Hurt'em!" "Level'em!" "Kill'em!" "Take'em apart!" Or watch for the plays that are most enthusiastically applauded by the fans. Where someone is "smeared," "knocked silly," "creamed," "nailed," "broken in two," or even "crucified." (One of my coaches when I played corner linebacker with the Calgary Stampeders in 1961 elaborated, often very inventively, on this language of destruction: admonishing us to "unjoin" the opponent, "make 'im remember you" and "stomp 'im like a bug.") Just as in hockey, where a fight will bring fans to their feet more often than a skillful play, so in football the mouth waters most of all for the really crippling block or tackle. For the kill. Thus the good teams are "hungry," the best players are "mean," and "casualties" are as much a part of the game as they are of a war.

The family resemblance between football and war is, indeed, striking. Their languages are similar: "field general," "long bomb," "blitz," "take a shot," "front line," "pursuit," "good hit," "the draft" and so on. Their principles and practices are alike: mass hysteria, the art of intimidation, absolute command and total obedience, territorial aggression, censorship, inflated insignia and propaganda, blackboard maneuvers and strategies, drills, uniforms, formations, marching bands and training camps. And the virtues they celebrate are almost identical: hyper-aggressiveness, coolness under fire and suicidal bravery. All this has been implicitly recognized by such jock-loving Americans as media stars General Patton and President Nixon, who have talked about war as a football game. Patton wanted to make his Second World War tank men look like football players. And Nixon, as we know, was fond of comparing attacks on Vietnam to football plays and drawing coachly diagrams on a black-board for TV war fans.

One difference between war and football, though, is that there is little or no protest against football. Perhaps the most extraordinary thing about the game is that the systematic infliction of injuries excites in people not concern, as would be the case if they were sustained at, say, a rock festival, but a collective rejoicing and euphoria. Players and fans alike revel in the spectacle of a combatant felled into semiconsciousness, "blindsided," "clotheslined" or "decapitated." I can remember, in fact, being chided by a coach in pro ball for not "getting my hat" injuriously into a player who was already lying helpless on the ground. (On another occasion, after the Stampeders had traded the celebrated Joe Kapp to BC, we were playing the Lions in Vancouver and Kapp was forced on one play to run with the ball. He was coming "down the chute," his bad knee wobbling uncertainly, so I simply dropped on him like a blanket. After I returned to the bench I was reproved for not exploiting the opportunity to unhinge his bad knee.)

After every game, of course, the papers are full of reports on the day's injuries, a sort of post-battle "body count," and the respective teams go to work with doctors and trainers, tape, whirlpool baths, cortisone and morphine to patch and deaden the wounds before the next game. Then the whole drama is reenacted—injured athletes held together by adhesive, braces and drugs—and the days following it are filled with even more feverish activity to put on the show yet again at the end of the next week. (I remember being so taped up in college that I earned the nickname "mummy.") The team that survives this merry-go-round spectacle of skilled masochism with the fewest incapacitating injuries usually wins. It is a sort of victory by ordeal: "We hurt them more than they hurt us."

My own initiation into this brutal circus was typical. I loved the game from the moment I could run with a ball. Played shoeless on a green open field with no one keeping score and in a spirit of reckless abandon and laughter, it's a very different sport. Almost no one gets hurt and it's rugged, open and exciting (it still is for me). But then, like everything else, it starts to be regulated and institutionalized by adult authorities. And the fun is over.

So it was as I began the long march through organized football. Now there was a coach and elders to make it clear by their behavior that beating other people was the only thing to celebrate and that trying to shake someone up every play was the only thing to be really proud of. Now there were severe rule enforcers, audiences, formally recorded victors and losers, and heavy equipment to permit crippling bodily moves and collisions (according to one American survey, more than 80% of all football injuries occur to fully equipped players). And now there was the official "given" that the only way to keep playing was to wear suffocating armor, to play to defeat, to follow orders silently and to renounce spontaneity for joyless drill. The game had been, in short, ruined. But because I loved to play and play skillfully, I stayed. And progressively and inexorably, as I moved through high school, college and pro leagues, my body was dismantled. Piece by piece.

I started off with torn ligaments in my knee at 13. Then, as the organization and the competition increased, the injuries came faster and harder. Broken nose (three times), broken jaw (fractured in the first half and dismissed as a "bad wisdom tooth," so I played with it for the rest of the game), ripped knee ligaments again. Torn ligaments in one ankle and a fracture in the other (which I remember feeling relieved about because it meant I could honorably stop drill-blocking a 270-pound defensive end). Repeated rib fractures and cartilage tears (usually carried, again, through the remainder of the game). More dislocations of the left shoulder than I can remember (the last one I played with because, as the Calgary Stampeder doctor said, it "couldn't be damaged any more"). Occasional broken or dislocated fingers and toes. Chronically hurt lower back (I still can't lift with it or change a tire without worrying about folding). Separated right shoulder (as with many other injuries, like badly bruised hips and legs, needled with morphine for the games). And so on. The last pro grame I played—against Winnipeg Blue Bombers in the Western finals in 1961—I had a recently dislocated left shoulder, a more recently wrenched right shoulder and a chronic pain center in one leg. I was so tied up with soreness I couldn't drive my car to the airport. But it never occurred to me or anyone else that I miss a play as a corner linebacker.

By the end of my football career, I had learned that physical injury—giving it and taking it—is the real currency of the sport. And that in the final analysis the "winner" is the man who can hit to kill even if only half his limbs are working. In brief, a warrior game with a warrior ethos into which (like almost everyone else I played with) my original boyish enthusiasm had been relentlessly taunted and conditioned.

In thinking back on how all this happened, though, I can pick out no villains. As with the social system as a whole, the game has a life of its own. Everyone grows up inside it, accepts it and fulfills its dictates as obediently as helots. Far from ever questioning the principles of the activity, people simply concentrate on executing these principles more aggressively than anybody around them. The result is a group of people who, as the leagues become of a higher and higher class, are progressively insensitive to the possibility that things could be otherwise. Thus, in football, anyone who might question the wisdom or enjoyment of putting on heavy equipment on a hot day and running full speed at someone else with the intention of knocking him senseless would be regarded simply as not really a devoted athlete and probably "chicken." The choice is made straightforward. Either you, too, do your very utmost to efficiently smash and be smashed, or you admit incompetence or cowardice and quit. Since neither of these admissions is very pleasant, people generally keep any doubts they have to themselves and carry on.

Of course, it would be a mistake to suppose that there is more blind acceptance of brutal practices in organized football than elsewhere. On the contrary, a recent Harvard study has approvingly argued that football's characteristics of "impersonal acceptance of inflicted injury," an overriding "organization goal," the "ability to turn oneself on and off" and being, above all, "out to win" are of "inestimable value" to big corporations. Clearly, our sort of football is no sicker than the rest of our society. Even its organized destruction of physical well-being is not anomalous. A very large part of our wealth, work and time is, after all, spent in systematically destroying and harming human life. Manufacturing, selling and using weapons that tear opponents to pieces. Making ever bigger and faster predator-named cars with which to kill and injure one another by the million every year. And devoting our very lives to outgunning one another for power in an ever more destructive rat race. Yet all these practices are accepted without question by most people, even zealously defended and honored. Competitive, organized injuring is integral to our way of life, and football is simply one of the more intelligible mirrors of the whole process: a sort of colorful morality play showing us how exciting and rewarding it is to Smash Thy Neighbor.

Now it is fashionable to rationalize our collaboration in all this by arguing that, well, man *likes* to fight and injure his fellows and such games as football should be encouraged to discharge this original-sin urge into less harmful channels than, say, war. Public-show football, this line goes, plays the same sort of cathartic role as Aristotle said stage tragedy does: without real blood (or not much), it releases players and audience from unhealthy feelings stored up inside them.

As an ex-player in the seasonal coast-to-coast drama, I see little to recommend such a view. What organized football did to me was make me *suppress* my natural urges and re-express them in an alienating, vicious form. Spontaneous desires for free bodily exuberance and fraternization with competitors were shamed and forced under ("If it ain't hurtin' it ain't helpin' ") and in their place were demanded armored mechanical moves and cool hatred of all opposition. Endless authoritarian drill and dressing-room harangues (ever wonder why competing teams can't prepare for a game in the same dressing room?) were the kinds of mechanisms employed to reconstruct joyful energies into mean and alien shapes. I am quite certain that everyone else around me was being similarly forced into this heavily equipped military precision and angry antagonism, because there was always a mutinous attitude about full-dress practices, and everybody (the pros included) had to concentrate incredibly hard for days to whip themselves into just one hour's hostility a week against another club. The players never speak of these things, of course, because everyone is so anxious to appear tough.

The claim that men like seriously to battle one another to some sort of finish is a myth. It only endures because it wears one of the oldest and most propagandized of masks—the romantic combatant. I sometimes wonder whether the violence all around us doesn't depend for its survival on the existence and preservation of this tough-guy disguise.

As for the effect of organized football on the spectator, the fan is not released from supposed feelings of violent aggression by watching his athletic heroes perform it so much as encouraged in the view that people-smashing is an admirable mode of self-expression. The most savage attackers, after all, are, by general agreement, the most efficient and worthy players of all (the biggest applause I ever received as a football player occurred when I ran over people or slammed them so hard they couldn't get up). Such circumstances can hardly be said to lessen the spectators' martial tendencies. Indeed it seems likely that the whole show just further develops and titillates the North American addiction for violent self-assertion.... Perhaps, as well, it helps explain why the greater the zeal of U.S. political leaders as football fans (Johnson, Nixon, Agnew), the more enthusiastic the commitment to hard-line politics. At any rate there seems to be a strong correlation between people who relish tough football and people who relish intimidating and beating the hell out of commies, hippies, protest marchers and other opposition groups.

Watching well-advertised strong men knock other people round, make them hurt, is in the end like other tastes. It does not weaken with feeding and variation in form. It grows.

I got out of football in 1962. I had asked to be traded after Calgary had offered me a $25-a-week-plus-commissions off-season job as a clothing-store salesman. ("Dear Mr. Finks:" I wrote. [Jim Finks was then the Stampeders' general manager.] "Somehow I do not think the dialectical subtleties of Hegel, Marx and Plato would be suitably oriented amidst the environmental stimuli of jockey shorts and herringbone suits. I hope you make a profitable sale or trade of my contract to the East.") So the Stampeders traded me to Montreal. In a preseason intersquad game with the Alouettes I ripped the cartilages in my ribs on the hardest block I'd ever thrown. I had trouble breathing and I had to shuffle-walk with my torso on a tilt. The doctor in the local hospital said three weeks rest, the coach said scrimmage in two days. Three days later I was back home reading philosophy.

1971

THE READER

1. What relationship does McMurtry see between football and war? Do you find his suggestion persuasive?

2. *Does football, in McMurtry's view, provide for participants and spectators a harmless release of potentially harmful tensions and impulses, like "letting off steam"? Do you agree with McMurtry's view?*

3. *McMurtry says he can "pick out no villains" for the damage football does to its players. Do you agree? Explain.*

4. *To what extent is what McMurtry says of football true of any other sport?*

5. *What relationships does McMurtry see between football and society at large? Do his comparisons make sense to you?*

THE WRITER

1. *Is McMurtry's essay mainly about his personal experiences in football? What effect is produced by his recounting his experiences in detail?*

2. *What evidence in the essay, if any, do you find to show that McMurtry is not a "team player"? If he is not a "team player," would that account for the fact that he finds so much to criticize about football and about society?*

3. *McMurtry says that "our sort of football is no sicker than the rest of our society." Write a brief argument supporting or denying that view.*

4. *Write an essay drawing connections between "real life" and some kind of game or play familiar to you. Does this illuminate any social arrangements, help you to see them in a new light? How far can you truthfully generalize?*

Herb Goldberg

IN HARNESS: THE MALE CONDITION

Most men live in harness. Richard was one of them. Typically he had no awareness of how his male harness was choking him until his personal and professional life and his body had nearly fallen apart.

Up to that time he had experienced only occasional short bouts of depression that a drink would bring him out of. For Richard it all crashed at an early age, when he was thirty-three. He came for psychotherapy with resistance, but at the instruction of his physician. He had a bad ulcer, was losing weight, and, in spite of repeated warnings that it could kill him, he was drinking heavily.

His personal life was also in serious trouble. He had recently lost his job as a disc jockey on a major radio station because he'd been arrested for drunk driving. He had totaled his car against a tree and the newspapers had a picture of it on the front page. Shortly thereafter his wife moved out, taking with her their eight-year-old daughter. She left at the advice of friends who knew that he had become violent twice that year while drunk.

As he began to talk about himself it became clear that he had been securely fitted into his male harness early in his teens. In high school he was already quite tall and stronger than most. He was therefore urged to go out for basketball, which he did, and he got lots of attention for it.

He had a deep, resonant voice that he had carefully cultivated. He was told that he should go into radio announcing and dramatics, so he got into all the high school plays. In college he majored in theater arts.

In his senior year in college he dated one of the most beautiful and sought-after girls in the junior class. His peer group envied him, which reassured Richard that he had a good thing going. So he married Joanna a year after graduating and took a job with a small radio station in Fresno, California. During the next ten years he played out the male role; he fathered a child and fought his way up in a very competitive profession.

It wasn't until things had fallen apart that he even let himself know that he had any feelings of his own, and in therapy he began to see why it had been so necessary to keep his feelings buried. They were confusing and frightening.

More than anything else, there was a hypersensitive concern over what others thought about him as a "man." As other suppressed feelings began to surface they surprised him. He realized how he had hated the pressures of being a college basketball player. The preoccupation with being good and winning had distorted his life in college.

Though he had been to bed with many girls before marriage and even a few afterward, he acknowledged that rarely was it a genuine turn-on for him. He liked the feeling of being able to seduce a girl but the experience itself was rarely satisfying, so he would begin the hunt for another as soon as he succeeded with one. "Some of those girls were a nightmare," he said, "I would have been much happier without them. But I was caught in the bag of proving myself and I couldn't seem to control it."

The obsessive preoccupation in high school and college with cultivating a deep, resonant "masculine" voice he realized was similar to the obsession some women have with their figures. Though he thought he had enjoyed the attention he got being on stage, he acknowledged that he had really disliked being an entertainer, or "court jester," as he put it.

When he thought about how he had gotten married he became particularly uncomfortable. "I was really bored with Joanna after the first month of dating but I couldn't admit it to myself because I thought I had a great thing going. I married her because I figured if I didn't one of the other guys would. I couldn't let that happen."

Richard had to get sick in his harness and nearly be destroyed by role-playing masculinity before he could allow himself to be a person with his own feelings, rather than just a hollow male image. Had it not been for a bleeding ulcer he might have postponed looking at himself for many years more.

Like many men, Richard had been a zombie, a daytime sleepwalker. Worse still, he had been a highly "successful" zombie, which made it so difficult for him to risk change. Our culture is saturated with successful male zombies, businessmen zombies, golf zombies, sports car zombies, playboy zombies, etc. They are playing by the rules of the male game plan. They have lost touch with, or are running away from, their feelings and awareness of themselves as people. They have confused their social masks for their essence and they are destroying themselves while fulfilling the traditional definitions of masculine-appropriate behavior. They set their life sails by these role definitions. They are the heroes, the studs, the providers, the warriors, the empire builders, the fearless ones. Their reality is always approached through these veils of gender expectations.

When something goes seriously wrong, they discover that they are shadows to themselves as well as to others. They are unknown because they have been so busy manipulating and masking themselves in order to maintain and garner more status that a genuine encounter with another person would threaten them, causing them to flee or to react with extreme defensiveness.

Men evaluate each other and are evaluated by many women largely by the degree to which they approximate the ideal masculine model. Women have rightfully lashed out against being placed into a mold and being related to as a sex object. Many women have described their roles in marriage as a form of socially approved prostitution. They assert that they are selling themselves out for an unfulfilling portion of supposed security. For psychologically defensive reasons the male has not yet come to see himself as a prostitute, day in and day out, both in and out of the marriage relationship.

The male's inherent survival instincts have been stunted by the seemingly more powerful drive to maintain his masculine image. He would, for example, rather die in the battle than risk living in a different way and being called a "coward" or "not a man." He would rather die at his desk prematurely than free himself from his compulsive patterns and pursuits. As a recently published study concluded, "A surprising number of men approaching senior citizenship say they would rather die than be buried in retirement."

The male in our culture is at a growth impasse. He won't move—not because he is protecting his cherished central place in the sun, but because he can't move. He is a cardboard Goliath precariously balanced and on the verge of toppling over if he is pushed even ever so slightly out of his well-worn path. He lacks the fluidity of the female who can readily move between the traditional definitions of male or female behavior and roles. She can be wife and mother or a business executive. She can dress in typically feminine fashion or adopt the male styles. She will be loved for having "feminine" interests such as needlework or cooking, or she will be admired for sharing with the male in his "masculine" interests. That will make her a "man's woman." She can be sexually assertive or sexually passive. Meanwhile, the male is rigidly caught in his masculine pose and, in many subtle and direct ways, he is severely punished when he steps out of it.

Unlike some of the problems of women, the problems of men are not readily changed through legislation. The male has no apparent and clearly defined targets against which he can vent his rage. Yet he is oppressed by the cultural pressures that have denied him his feelings, by the mythology of the woman and the distorted and self-destructive way he sees and relates to her, by the urgency for him to "act like a man" which blocks his ability to respond to his inner promptings both emotionally and physiologically, and by a generalized self-hate that causes him to feel comfortable only when he is functioning well in harness, or when he lives for joy and for personal growth.

The prevalent "enlightened" male's reaction to the women's liberation movement bears testimony to his inability to mobilize himself on his own behalf. He has responded to feminist assertions by donning sack cloth, sprinkling himself with ashes, and flagellating himself—accusing himself of the very things she is accusing him of. An article entitled, "You've Come a Long Way, Buddy," perhaps best illustrates the male self-hating attitude. In it, the writer said,

> The members of the men's liberation movement are . . . a kind of embarrassing vanguard, the first men anywhere on record to take a political stand based on the idea that what the women are saying is right—men are a bunch of lazy, selfish, horny, unhappy oppressors.

Many other undoubtedly well-intentioned writers on the male condition have also taken a basically guilt- and shame-oriented approach to the male, alternately scolding him, warning him, and preaching to him that he better change and not be a male chauvinist pig anymore. During many years of practice as a psychotherapist, I have never seen a person grow or change in a self-constructive, meaningful way when he was motivated by guilt, shame, or self-hate. That manner of approach smacks of old-time religion and degrades the male by ignoring the complexity of the binds and repressions that are his emotional heritage.

Precisely because the tenor and mood of the male liberation efforts so far have been one of self-accusation, self-hate, and a repetition of feminist assertions, I believe it is doomed to failure in its present form. It is buying the myth that the male is culturally favored—a notion that is clung to despite the fact that every critical statistic in the area of longevity, disease, suicide, crime, accidents, childhood emotional disorders, alcoholism, and drug addiction shows a disproportionately higher male rate.

Many men who join male liberation groups do so to please or impress their women or to learn how to deal with and hold onto their recently liberated wives or girlfriends. Once in a male liberation group they intellectualize their feelings and reactions into lifelessness. In addition, the men tend to put each other down for thinking like "typical male chauvinists" or using words like "broad," "chick," "dike," etc. They have introjected the voices of their feminist accusers and the result is an atmosphere that is joyless, self-righteous, cautious, and lacking in a vitalizing energy. A new, more subtle kind of competitiveness pervades the atmosphere: the competition to be the least competitive and most free of the stereotyped version of male chauvinism.

The women's liberation movement did not effect its astounding impact via self-hate, guilt, or the desire to placate the male. Instead it has been energized by anger and outrage. Neither will the male change in any meaningful way until he experiences his underlying rage toward the endless, impossible binds under which he lives, the rigid definitions of his role, the endless pressure to be all things to all people, and the guilt-oriented, self-denying way he has traditionally related to women, to his feelings, and to his needs.

Because it is so heavily repressed, male rage only manifests itself indirectly and in hidden ways. Presently it is taking the form of emotional detachment, interpersonal withdrawal, and passivity in relationship to women. The male has pulled himself inward in order to deny his anger and to protect himself and others from his buried cascade of resentment and fury. Pathetic, intellectualized attempts not to be a male chauvinist pig will never do the job.

There is also a commonly expressed notion that men will somehow be freed as a by-product of the feminist movement. This is a comforting fantasy for the male but I see no basis for it becoming a reality. It simply disguises the fear of actively determining his own change. Indeed, by responding inertly and passively, the male will be moved, but not in a meaningful and productive direction. If there is to be a constructive change for the male he will have to chart his own way, develop his own style and experience his own anxieties, fear, and rage because *this time mommy won't do it!*

Recently, I asked a number of men to write to me about how they see their condition and what liberation would mean to them. A sense of suffocation and confusion was almost always present.

A forty-six-year-old businessman wrote: "From what do I need to be liberated? I'm too old and tired to worry about myself. I know that I'm only a high-grade mediocrity. I've come to accept a life where the dreams are now all revealed as unreality. I don't know how my role or my son's role should change. If I knew I suppose it would be in any way that would make my wife happier and less of a shrew."

A thirty-nine-year-old carpenter discussing the "joys" of working responded: "I contend that the times in which it is fun and rewarding in a healthy way have been fairly limited. Most of the time it has been a question of running in fear of failure." Referring to his relationships, he continued. "There is another aspect of women's and men's lib that I haven't experienced extensively. This is the creation of close friendships outside of the marriage. My past experiences have been stressful to the point where I am very careful to limit any such contact. What's the fear? I didn't like the sense of insecurity developed by my wife and the internal stresses that I felt. It created guilt feelings."

A fifty-seven-year-old college professor expressed it this way: "Yes, there's a need for male lib and hardly anyone writes about it the way it really is, though a few make jokes. My gut reaction, which is what you asked for, is that men—the famous male chauvinist pigs who neglect their wives, underpay their women employees, and rule the world—are literally slaves. They're out there picking that cotton, sweating, swearing, taking lashes from the boss, working fifty hours a week to support themselves and the plantation, only then to come back to the house to do another twenty hours a week rinsing dishes, toting trash bags, writing checks, and acting as butlers at the parties. It's true of young husbands and middle-aged husbands. Young bachelors may have a nice deal for a couple of years after graduating, but I've forgotten, and I'll never again be young! Old men. Some have it sweet, some have it sour.

"Man's role—how has it affected my life? At thirty-five, I chose to emphasize family togetherness and income and neglect my profession if necessary. At fifty-seven, I see no reward for time spent with and for the family, in terms of love or appreciation. I see a thousand punishments for neglecting my profession. I'm just tired and have come close to just walking away from it and starting over; just research, publish, teach, administer, play tennis, and travel. Why haven't I? Guilt. And love. And fear of loneliness. How should the man's role in my family change? I really don't know how it can, but I'd like a lot more time to do my thing."

The most remarkable and significant aspect of the feminist movement to date has been woman's daring willingness to own up to her resistances and resentment toward her time-honored, sanctified roles of wife and even mother. The male, however, has yet to fully realize, acknowledge, and rebel against the distress and stifling aspects of many of the roles he plays—from good husband, to good daddy, to good provider, to good lover, etc. Because of the inner pressure to constantly affirm his dominance and masculinity, he continues to act as if he can stand up under, fulfill, and even enjoy all the expectations placed on him no matter how contradictory and devitalizing they are.

It's time to remove the disguises of privilege and reveal the male condition for what it really is.

1976

THE READER

1. *Describing what happens to men who try to understand women's liberation by joining a group of their own, Goldberg says that "once in a male liberation group [men] intellectualize their feelings and reactions into lifelessness" (p. 284). What other paths to understanding do men have open to them? Do liberated women pose a threat to men and their images?*

2. *Rollin, in "Motherhood: Who Needs It?" (p. 292), talks about extinguishing the "Motherhood Myth" to encourage women to discover and be themselves. What does Goldberg imply about extinguishing fatherhood? How do these two ideas differ? Which would have a greater impact on society?*

3. *Compare the approach to human personality taken by Goldberg with that of Gaylin, also a psychotherapist, in "What You See Is the Real You" (p. 386). Do they seem to agree on the nature of human personality? Explain.*

THE WRITER

1. *From what sort of evidence or experience does Goldberg draw his conclusions? Do the men who seek help from a psychotherapist represent a good cross section of all males? What biases might be encountered in such a group of subjects?*

2. *Write a brief essay comparing Goldberg's conception of the male in harness with Perelman's idea of machismo (p. 287). Are the two talking about similar things? Is it true, as Goldberg states, that "the male in our culture is at a growth impasse" (p. 282)?*

3. *Construct a dialogue in which Goldberg's "harnessed" man and a liberated woman discuss birth control, the proper role of parents, platonic relationships between men and women, or some similar topic.*

S. J. Perelman

THE MACHISMO MYSTIQUE

It was 3 P.M., that climactic midafternoon moment toward which every gallant worthy of the name bends his energies, and I'd done all the preparatory work time and an unencumbered credit card could accomplish. I had stoked my Chilean vis-à-vis with three vodka martinis, half a gallon of Sancerre, and two balloons of Armagnac until her eyes were veritable liquid pools. Under my bold, not to say outrageous, compliments her damask skin and the alabaster column of her throat glowed like a lovely pink pearl; her hair, black as the raven's wing, shimmered in the reflection of the boudoir lamp shading our discreet banquette; and every now and again as my knee nudged hers under the table, my affinity's magnificent bosom heaved uncontrollably. I had glissed through all those earnest confidences that begin, "You know, I've never said this to anyone before," to, "Look, I'm not very articulate, but I feel that in these parlous times, it behooves us all to reach out, to cling to another lonely person— do you know what I mean?" Suddenly I had the feeling that she knew what I meant, all right. In a swift glance, I encompassed the small chic restaurant whence all but we had fled—its idle barman and the maître d'hôtel stifling a yawn—and I struck.

"Listen," I said as if inspired. "This friend of mine, the Marquis de Cad, who has a wonderful collection of African sculpture, was called away to Cleveland, and I promised to stop by his flat and dust it. Why don't we pick up a bottle of lemon oil . . ."

Inamorata threw back her sleek head and shouted with laughter. "Stop, querido,"[1] she implored. "You're ruining my mascara. Such machismo— who would have expected it from a shrimp like you?"

Quicker than any hidalgo of Old Spain to erase an insult, I sprang up prepared to plunge my poniard into her bosom (a striking demonstration of the maxim that man kills that which he most loves). Unfortunately, I had left my poniard at home on the bureau and was wearing only a tie-tack that could never penetrate anyone so thick-skinned. Nonetheless, I made the hussy smart for her insolence. "Let me tell you something, Chubby," I rasped. "Never underestimate the American male. I may not dance the mambo or reek of garlic, but I'm just as feisty as those caballeros of yours below the Rio Grande. Remember that our first colonial flag in Kentucky, the Dark and Bloody Ground, portrayed a coiled rattlesnake over the legend, 'Don't Tread on Me.'"

"Big deal," she scoffed. "Do you want an example of real machismo—

1. Beloved.

the kind of masculinity Latin-American men are capable of? Tell them to bring me another Armagnac."

Downcast at the realization that our matinee had blown out the back, I sullenly acceded. The story as she related it dealt with a bar in Guatemala City called *Mi apuesta* (The Wager) after a bet once made there. Two young bloods or *machos*, it appeared, had swaggered in one evening, stiff with conceit and supremely self-confident, arrogant as a pair of fighting cocks. Lounging at the bar over a glass of manzanilla, one of them remarked to the other, "*Te apuesto que no eres bastante macho para matar al primero que entre*" (I wager you're not man enough to kill the first hombre who comes in).

The other sneered thinly. "No?" he said. "I bet you fifty *centavos* I will."

The bet was covered, whereupon the challenged party extracted a Beretta from his waistband, and a moment later, as a totally inoffensive stranger stepped through the saloon door, a bullet drilled him through the heart.

"*Madre de Dios*," I exclaimed, shocked. "What happened to the assassin?"

"*Niente*," said Inamorata calmly. "The judge gave him a three months' suspended sentence on the ground that the crime was in no way premeditated."

Needless to say, whenever Inamorata rang up after our abortive meeting and besought me to lunch her again, I showed her a clean pair of heels. (They were two fellows who dispensed towels at the Luxor Baths; they pursued her madly, and I hope with more success than I had.) At any rate, in pondering the whole business of *machismo*, of male bravado and excessive manliness, it occurred to me that I had met quite a few *machos* in my time, both in the entertainment world and belles-lettres. The one I remember most vividly in the former was a Hollywood screenwriter—a big redheaded blowhard I'll call Rick Ferret. A Montanan who claimed to have grown up on the range, Ferret was forever beating his gums about his amatory exploits; by his own blushing admission, he was Casanova reborn, the swordsman supreme, the reincarnation of Don Juan. According to him, women in every walk of life—society leaders and shopgirls, leading ladies and vendeuses—fell in windrows in his path, and though it was obvious to his auditors at the Brown Derby that he dealt in quantity rather than quality, the references he dropped to his nuclear power and durability left us pale with jealousy.

One evening, I attended a party at his house in Laurel Canyon. Living with him at the time was a lady named Susie, quite well-endowed and with a rather sharp tongue. So late was the hour when the bash ended that the two insisted I stay over, and the next morning, while I was adjusting my false lashes, Ferret entered the bathroom and proceeded to take a shower. Just as he was snorting and puffing like a grampus, I chanced to observe a quite formidable scar on his *Sitzfleisch*. With an apology for the personal nature of the question, I asked if it was a war wound of some kind.

"Yes, in a way," he said carelessly, turning off the taps. "There's quite a story attached to it." He opened the door of the bathroom to disperse the steam, and I glimpsed his Susie breakfasting in bed a few feet distant. "The fact is," he went on, "it happened some years ago down on the south fork of the Brazos while I was rounding up some mavericks. This gang of rustlers from Durango way cut into the herd, and I took after them hell for leather. Well, the greasers were spoiling for action, and they got it." He chuckled. "Before I could yank out my six-guns, they creased me here, but I managed to rub out the whole dad-blamed lot."

"Oh, for God's sake, Ferret," I heard Susie's voice croak from the bedroom. "You know perfectly well you had a boil lanced on your tail only last Tuesday."

The two most celebrated *machos* I ever knew, I suppose, were Ernest Hemingway—unquestionably the holder of the black belt in the Anglo-Saxon world—and Mike Todd, who, to pilfer a phrase from Marcel Proust, might aptly be termed the Sweet Cheat Gone. My go-around with Hemingway took place in the winter of 1954, directly after his two widely publicized plane crashes in East Africa. He was borne into the New Stanley Hotel in Nairobi in a somewhat disoriented state, suffering a double concussion, a smashed kidney, and alarming symptoms of *folie de grandeur*.[2] I turned up there two days later from Uganda with fourteen women comprising the first American all-girl safari (quite another story), and since my room was adjacent to his, saw a good bit of him thereafter. What with his tribulations and frequent infusions of hooch, Papa was inclined to ramble somewhat, and it was not always easy to follow the thread of his discourse. Once in a while, though, the clouds dissipated, and we were able to chat about mutual friends in the Montparnasse of the 'twenties. It was on such an occasion, one night, that he told me an anecdote that stunningly dramatized his *machismo*.

It concerned a period when he used to box at Stillman's Gymnasium in New York, a favorite haunt of enthusiasts of what is termed the manly art. His adversaries, Hemingway blushingly admitted, never matched his own speed and strength, but one of them improved so under his tutelage that occasionally the pair had a tolerable scrimmage. Thinking to intensify it, Hemingway suggested they discard their gloves and fight bareknuckle. This, too, while diverting, soon palled, but at last he had an inspiration.

"The room we boxed in," Hemingway explained, "had these rows of

2. Delusions of grandeur.

pipes running along the walls—you know, like backstage in a theater? Well, we flooded the place with steam, so thickly that it looked like a pea-soup fog in London. Then we started charging each other like a couple of rhinos. Butting our heads together and roaring like crazy. God, it was terrific—you could hear the impact of bone on bone, and we bled like stuck pigs. Of course, that made the footwork a bit more difficult, slipping and sliding all over, but it sure heightened the fun. Man, those were the days. You had to have real *cojones*[3] to stand up to it."

The same hormonal doodads were imperative in order to cope with Mike Todd and his vagaries. Todd's *machismo* was that common form that afflicts all undersized men—megalomania. He freely identified himself with Napoleon, P. T. Barnum, and Carl Laemmle, Junior, not to mention the Roman emperors of the decline. Whereas the latter, however, believed in giving the populace bread and circuses, Todd gave them circuses and kept the bread. Rarely if ever has there been anyone more unwilling to fork over what he owed to those actors, writers, and technicians who aided him in his grandiloquent projects of stage and screen. The little corpuscle, in short, believed in flaunting money where it made the most impression—at Deauville, Monaco, and the gaming tables of Las Vegas. In this respect, he was a true *macho*. My sole souvenir of our frenetic association is a replica of the carpetbag Phileas Fogg carried on his celebrated journey, a thousand of which Todd distributed in lordly fashion to Broadway companions, investors, accountants, dentists, and other sycophants. But surely, his admirers have since queried me, I must have been awed by his tremendous vitality; Only in part, I respond: *Moi-même*, I prefer the anthropoid apes. The gibbon swings farther, the chimpanzee's reflexes are quicker, the orangutan can scratch faster, and the gorilla—my particular love object—has been known to crunch a Stillson wrench in his teeth.

Of such literary *machos* was the late Robert Ruark, who of course patterned himself on Hemingway. Their careers afford ample demonstration of my two favorite maxims: a) that the gaudier the patter, the cheaper the scribe, and b) that easy writing makes hard reading. The legend of Ruark's fatal charisma with women still gives one a pain in the posterior when recounted, and his press interviews, studded with reference to the millions of words he merchandised, act as a tourniquet on bleeders like myself who labor over a postcard. Even John O'Hara, somewhat more talented, was not above buttonholing acquaintances and boasting that he had written this or that deathless vignette in three quarters of an hour. It is interesting, by the way, that Scott Fitzgerald, with whom O'Hara was given to comparing himself, never made any

3. Testicles.

claims to his own facility when I knew him in Hollywood. On the contrary, both he and Nathanael West were continually obsessed by delusions of their inadequacy with sex and their small literary output.

Looking back over a long and mottled career, I think the best illustration of real *machismo* I ever beheld took place on the terrace of the Café du Dôme in Paris in 1927. I was seated there at dusk one day with a fellow journalist when an enormous yellow Hispano-Suiza landaulet driven by a chauffeur drew up at the curb. From it emerged a tall and beautiful, exquisitely clad lady, followed by another even more photogenic—both clearly high-fashion mannequins. Reaching into the tonneau, they brought forth a wizened homunculus with a yellow face resembling Earl Sande, the celebrated jockey. Hooking their arms through his, they assisted him to a table farther down the terrace. I turned to my *copain* with my eyebrows raised, searching for some explanation of the phenomenon. A slow smile overspread his countenance, and he held his hands apart as does one when asked to steady a skein of wool.

That's *machismo*, sweetheart.

1975

THE READER

1. Perelman says his next-to-last paragraph contains his "best illustration of real machismo." Explain why you agree or disagree.
2. Perelman implies that machismo attitudes are reflected in language. Find examples from contemporary newspapers or magazines.

THE WRITER

1. Write your own definition of machismo, basing it on Perelman's examples.
2. Toward the end of his essay, Perelman talks about writers who boast about how fast and how much they write. Why do you think Perelman includes these examples? Explain whether they are a part of his definition of machismo or merely analogous to it.
3. Perelman has a very distinctive style. Try to determine what its characteristics are by rewriting one of his paragraphs in a more neutral style.
4. Describe an incident (either actual or invented) that illustrates machismo. Then change the incident so that it no longer illustrates machismo. Explain whether the changes involve (a) changes in people, (b) changes in circumstances or social customs, or (c) changes in both. What conclusions can you draw about whether machismo is a part of human nature or is culturally conditioned?

Betty Rollin

MOTHERHOOD: WHO NEEDS IT?

Motherhood is in trouble, and it ought to be. A rude question is long overdue: Who needs it? The answer used to be (1) society and (2) women. But now, with the impending horrors of overpopulation, society desperately *doesn't* need it. And women don't need it either. Thanks to the Motherhood Myth—the idea that having babies is something that all normal women instinctively want and need and will enjoy doing—they just *think* they do.

The notion that the maternal wish and the activity of mothering are instinctive or biologically predestined is baloney. Try asking most sociologists, psychologists, psychoanalysts, biologists—many of whom are mothers—about motherhood being instinctive: it's like asking department store presidents if their Santa Clauses are real. "Motherhood— instinctive?" shouts distinguished sociologist/author Dr. Jessie Bernard. "Biological destiny? Forget biology! If it were biology, people would die from not doing it."

"Women don't need to be mothers any more than they need spaghetti," says Dr. Richard Rabkin, a New York psychiatrist. "But if you're in a world where everyone is eating spaghetti, thinking they need it and want it, you will think so too. Romance has really contaminated science. So-called instincts have to do with stimulation. They are not things that well up inside of you."

"When a woman says with feeling that she craved her baby from within, she is putting into biological language what is psychological," says University of Michigan psychoanalyst and motherhood-researcher Dr. Frederick Wyatt. "There are no instincts," says Dr. William Goode, president-elect of the American Sociological Association. "There are reflexes, like eye-blinking, and drives, like sex. There is no innate drive for children. Otherwise, the enormous cultural pressures that there are to reproduce wouldn't exist. There are no cultural pressures to sell you on getting your hand out of the fire."

There are, to be sure, biologists and others who go on about biological destiny, that is, the innate or instinctive goal of motherhood. (At the turn of the century, even good old capitalism was explained by a theorist as "the *instinct* of acquisitiveness.") And many psychoanalysts will hold the Freudian view that women feel so rotten about not having a penis that they are necessarily propelled into the child-wish to replace the missing organ. Psychoanalysts also make much of the psychological need to repeat what one's parent of the same sex has done. Since every woman has a mother, it is considered normal to wish to imitate one's mother by being a mother.

There is, surely, a wish to pass on love if one has received it, but to insist women must pass it on in the same way is like insisting that every man whose father is a gardener has to be a gardener. One dissenting psychoanalyst says, simply, "There is a wish to comply with one's biology, yes, but we needn't and sometimes we shouldn't." (Interestingly, the woman who has been the greatest contributor to child therapy and who has probably given more to children than anyone alive is Dr. Anna Freud, Freud's magnificent daughter, who is not a mother.)

Anyway, what an expert cast of hundreds is telling us is, simply, that biological *possibility* and desire are not the same as biological *need*. Women have childbearing equipment. To choose not to use the equipment is no more blocking what is instinctive than it is for a man who, muscles or no, chooses not to be a weight lifter.

So much for the wish. What about the "instinctive" *activity* of mothering? One animal study shows that when a young member of a species is put in a cage, say, with an older member of the same species, the latter will act in a protective, "maternal" way. But that goes for both males and females who have been "mothered" themselves. And studies indicate that a human baby will also respond to whoever is around playing mother —even if it's father. Margaret Mead and many others frequently point out that mothering can be a fine occupation, if you want it, for either sex. Another experiment with monkeys who were brought up without mothers found them lacking in maternal behavior toward their own offspring. A similar study showed that monkeys brought up without other monkeys of the opposite sex had no interest in mating—all of which suggests that both mothering and mating behavior are learned, not instinctual. And, to turn the cart (or the baby carriage) around, baby ducks who lovingly follow their mothers seemed, in the mother's absence, to just as lovingly follow wooden ducks or even vacuum cleaners.

If motherhood isn't instinctive, when and why, then, was the Motherhood Myth born? Until recently, the entire question of maternal motivation was academic. Sex, like it or not, meant babies. Not that there haven't always been a lot of interesting contraceptive tries. But until the creation of the diaphragm in the 1880's, the birth of babies was largely unavoidable. And, generally speaking, nobody really seemed to mind. For one thing, people tend to be sort of good sports about what seems to be inevitable. For another, in the past, the population needed beefing up. Mortality rates were high, and agricultural cultures, particularly, have always needed children to help out. So because it "just happened" and because it was needed, motherhood was assumed to be innate.

Originally, it was the word of God that got the ball rolling with "Be fruitful and multiply," a practical suggestion, since the only people around then were Adam and Eve. But in no time, supermoralists like St. Augustine changed the tone of the message: "Intercourse, even with one's legitimate wife, is unlawful and wicked where the conception of the offspring is prevented," he, we assume, thundered. And the Roman Catholic position was thus cemented. So then and now, procreation took on a curious value among people who viewed (and view) the pleasures of sex as sinful. One could partake in the sinful pleasure, but feel vindicated by the ensuing birth. Motherhood cleaned up sex. Also, it cleaned up women, who have always been considered somewhat evil, because of Eve's transgression ("... but the woman was deceived and became a transgressor. Yet woman will be saved through bearing children ...," I Timothy, 2:14-15), and somewhat dirty because of menstruation.

And so, based on need, inevitability, and pragmatic fantasy—the Myth *worked*, from society's point of view—the Myth grew like corn in Kansas. And society reinforced it with both laws and propaganda—laws that made woman a chattel, denied her education and personal mobility, and madonna propaganda that she was beautiful and wonderful doing it and it was all beautiful and wonderful to do. (One rarely sees a madonna washing dishes.)

In fact, the Myth persisted—breaking some kind of record for long-lasting fallacies—until something like yesterday. For as the truth about the Myth trickled in—as women's rights increased, as women gradually got the message that it was certainly possible for them to do most things that men did, that they live longer, that their brains were not tinier—then, finally, when the really big news rolled in, that they could *choose* whether or not to be mothers—what happened? The Motherhood Myth soared higher than ever. As Betty Friedan made oh-so-clear in *The Feminine Mystique*, the '40's and '50's produced a group of ladies who not only had babies as if they were going out of style (maybe they were) but, as never before, they turned motherhood into a cult. First, they wallowed in the aesthetics of it all—natural childbirth and nursing became maternal musts. Like heavy-bellied ostriches, they grounded their heads in the sands of motherhood, only coming up for air to say how utterly happy and fulfilled they were. But, as Mrs. Friedan says only too plainly, they weren't. The Myth galloped on, moreover, long after making babies had turned from practical asset to liability for both individual parents *and* society. With the average cost of a middle-class child figured conservatively at $30,000 (not including college), any parent knows that the only people who benefit economically from children are manufacturers of consumer goods. Hence all those gooey motherhood commercials. And the Myth gathered momentum long after sheer numbers, while not yet extinguishing us, have made us intensely uncomfortable. Almost all of our societal problems, from minor discomforts like traffic to major ones like hunger, the population people keep reminding us, have to do with there being too many people. And who suffers most? The kids who have been so mindlessly brought into the world, that's who. They are the ones who have to cope with all of the difficult and dehumanizing conditions brought on by overpopulation. They are the ones who have to cope with the psychological nausea of feeling unneeded by society. That's not the only reason for drugs, but, surely, it's a leading contender.

Unfortunately, the population curbers are tripped up by a romantic, stubborn, ideological hurdle. How can birth-control programs really be effective as long as the concept of glorious motherhood remains unchanged? (Even poor old Planned Parenthood has to euphemize—why not Planned Unparenthood?) Particularly among the poor, motherhood is one of the few inherently positive institutions that are accessible. As Berkeley demographer Judith Blake points out, "Poverty-oriented birth control programs do not make sense as a welfare measure . . . as long as existing pronatalist policies . . . encourage mating, pregnancy, and the care, support, and rearing of children." Or, she might have added, as long as the less-than-idyllic child-rearing part of motherhood remains "in small print."

Sure, motherhood gets dumped on sometimes: Philip Wylie's Momism[1] got going in the '40's and Philip Roth's *Portnoy's Complaint* did its best to turn rancid the chicken-soup concept of Jewish motherhood. But these are viewed as the sour cries of a black humorist here, a malcontent there. Everyone shudders, laughs, but it's like the mouse and the elephant joke. Still, the Myth persists. Last April, a Brooklyn woman was indicted on charges of manslaughter and negligent homicide—eleven children died in a fire in a building she owned and criminally neglected— "But," sputtered her lawyer, "my client, Mrs. Breslow, is a mother, a grandmother, and a great-grandmother!"

Most remarkably, the Motherhood Myth persists in the face of the most overwhelming maternal unhappiness and incompetence. If reproduction were merely superfluous and expensive, if the experience were as rich and rewarding as the cliché would have us believe, if it were a predominantly joyous trip for everyone riding—mother, father, child— then the going everybody-should-have-two-children plan would suffice. Certainly, there are a lot of joyous mothers, and their children and (sometimes, not necessarily) their husbands reflect their joy. But a lot of evidence suggests that for more women than anyone wants to admit, motherhood can be miserable. ("If it weren't," says one psychiatrist wryly, "the world wouldn't be in the mess it's in.")

There is a remarkable statistical finding from a recent study of Dr. Bernard's, comparing the mental illness and unhappiness of married mothers and single women. The latter group, it turned out, was both

1. Philip Wylie's *A Generation of Vipers* (1942) blamed many of the ills of American society on dominating mothers.

markedly less sick and overtly more happy. Of course, it's not easy to measure slippery attitudes like happiness. "Many women have achieved a kind of reconciliation—a conformity," says Dr. Bernard,

> that they interpret as happiness. Since feminine happiness is supposed to lie in devoting one's life to one's husband and children, they do that; so *ipso facto*, they assume they are happy. And for many women, untrained for independence and "processed" for motherhood, they find their state far preferable to the alternatives, which don't really exist.

Also, unhappy mothers are often loath to admit it. For one thing, if in society's view not to be a mother is to be a freak, not to be a blissful mother is to be a witch. Besides, unlike a disappointing marriage, disappointing motherhood cannot be terminated by divorce. Of course, none of that stops such a woman from expressing her dissatisfaction in a variety of ways. Again, it is not only she who suffers but her husband and children as well. Enter the harridan housewife, the carping shrew. The realities of motherhood can turn women into terrible people. And, judging from the 50,000 cases of child abuse in the U.S. each year, some are worse than terrible.

In some cases, the unpleasing realities of motherhood begin even before the beginning. In *Her Infinite Variety*, Morton Hunt describes young married women pregnant for the first time as "very likely to be frightened and depressed, masking these feelings in order not to be considered contemptible. The arrival of pregnancy interrupts a pleasant dream of motherhood and awakens them to the realization that they have too little money, or not enough space, or unresolved marital problems. . . ."

The following are random quotes from interviews with some mothers in Ann Arbor, Mich., who described themselves as reasonably happy. They all had positive things to say about their children, although when asked about the best moment of their day, they *all* confessed it was when the children were in bed. Here is the rest:

> Suddenly I had to devote myself to the child totally. I was under the illusion that the baby was going to fit into my life, and I found that I had to switch my life and my schedule to fit *him*. You think, "I'm in love, I'll get married, and we'll have a baby." First there's two, then three, it's simple and romantic. You don't even think about the work. . . .

> You never get away from the responsibility. Even when you leave the children with a sitter, you are not out from under the pressure of the responsibility. . . .

> I hate ironing their pants and doing their underwear, and they never put their clothes in the laundry basket. . . . As they get older, they make less demands on our time because they're in school, but the demands are greater

in forming their values. . . . Best moment of the day is when all the children are in bed. . . . The worst time of the day is 4 P.M., when you have to get dinner started, the kids are tired, hungry and crabby—everybody wants to talk to you about *their* day . . . your day is only half over.

Once a mother, the responsibility and concern for my children became so encompassing. . . . It took a great deal of will to keep up other parts of my personality. . . . To me, motherhood gets harder as they get older because you have less control. . . . In an abstract sense, I'd have several. . . . In the non-abstract, I would not have any . . . .

I had anticipated that the baby would sleep and eat, sleep and eat. Instead, the experience was overwhelming. I really had not thought particularly about what motherhood would mean in a realistic sense. I want to do *other* things, like to become involved in things that are worthwhile—I don't mean women's clubs—but I don't have the physical energy to go out in the evenings. I feel like I'm missing something . . . the experience of being somewhere with people and having them talking about something—something that's going on in the world.

Every grownup person expects to pay a price for his pleasures, but seldom is the price as vast as the one endured "however happily" by most mothers. We have mentioned the literal cost factor. But what does that mean? For middle-class American women, it means a life style with severe and usually unimagined limitations; i.e., life in the suburbs, because who can afford three bedrooms in the city? And what do suburbs mean? For women, suburbs mean other women and children and leftover peanut-butter sandwiches and car pools and seldom-seen husbands. Even the Feminine Mystiqueniks—the housewives who finally admitted that their lives behind brooms (OK, electric brooms) were driving them crazy —were loath to trace their predicament to their children. But it is simply a fact that a childless married woman has no child-work and little house-work. She can live in a city, or, if she still chooses the suburbs or the country, she can leave on the commuter train with her husband if she wants to. Even the most ardent job-seeking mother will find little in the way of great opportunities in Scarsdale.[2] Besides, by the time she wakes up, she usually lacks both the preparation for the outside world and the self-confidence to get it. You will say there are plenty of city-dwelling working mothers. But most of those women do additional-funds-for-the-family kind of work, not the interesting career kind that takes plugging during childbearing years.

Nor is it a bed of petunias for the mother who does make it professionally. Says writer critic Marya Mannes:

If the creative woman has children, she must pay for this indulgence with a long burden of guilt, for her life will be split three ways between them and her

2. A wealthy suburb of New York City.

husband and her work.... No woman with any heart can compose a paragraph when her child is in trouble.... The creative woman has no wife to
protect her from intrusion. A man at his desk in a room with closed door is a
man at work. A woman at a desk in any room is available.

Speaking of jobs, do remember that mothering, salary or not, is a job.
Even those who can afford nurses to handle the nitty-gritty still need to
put out emotionally. "Well-cared-for" neurotic rich kids are not exactly
unknown in our society. One of the more absurd aspects of the Myth is
the underlying assumption that, since most women are biologically
equipped to bear children, they are psychologically, mentally, emotionally, and technically equipped (or interested) to rear them. Never mind
happiness. To assume that such an exacting, consuming, and important
task is something almost all women are equipped to do is far more
dangerous and ridiculous than assuming that everyone with vocal chords
should seek a career in the opera.

A major expectation of the Myth is that children make a not-so-hot
marriage hotter, or a hot marriage, hotter still. Yet almost every available
study indicates that childless marriages are far happier. One of the
biggest, of 850 couples, was conducted by Dr. Harold Feldman of Cornell
University, who states his finding in no uncertain terms: "Those couples
with children had a significantly lower level of marital satisfaction than
did those without children." Some of the reasons are obvious. Even the
most adorable children make for additional demands, complications, and
hardships in the lives of even the most loving parents. If a woman feels
disappointed and trapped in her mother role, it is bound to affect her
marriage in any number of ways: she may take out her frustrations
directly on her husband, or she may count on him too heavily for what
she feels she is missing in her daily life.

"... You begin to grow away from your husband," says one of the
Michigan ladies. "He's working on his career and you're working on your
family. But you both must gear your lives to the children. You do things
the children enjoy, more than things you might enjoy." More subtle and
possibly more serious is what motherhood may do to a woman's sexuality.
Often when the stork flies in, sexuality flies out. Both in the emotional
minds of some women *and* in the minds of their husbands, when a woman
becomes a mother, she stops being a woman. It's not only that motherhood may destroy her physical attractiveness, but its madonna concept
may destroy her *feelings* of sexuality.

And what of the payoff? Usually, even the most self-sacrificing of
maternal self-sacrificers expects a little something back. Gratified parents are not unknown to the Western world, but there are probably at
least just as many who feel, to put it crudely, shortchanged. The experi-

ment mentioned earlier—where the baby ducks followed vacuum clean-ers instead of their mothers—indicates that what passes for love from baby to mother is merely a rudimentary kind of object attachment. Without necessarily feeling like a Hoover, a lot of women become disheartened because babies and children are not only not interesting to talk to (not everyone thrills at the wonders of da-da-ma-ma talk) but they are generally not empathetic, considerate people. Even the nicest chil-dren are not capable of empathy, surely a major ingredient of love, until they are much older. Sometimes they're never capable of it. Dr. Wyatt says that often, in later years particularly, when most of the "returns" are in, it is the "good mother" who suffers most of all. It is then she must face a reality: The child—the appendage with her genes—is not an appen-dage, but a separate person. What's more, he or she may be a separate person who doesn't even like her—or whom she doesn't really like.

So if the music is lousy, how come everyone's dancing? Because the motherhood minuet is taught freely from birth, and whether or not she has rhythm or likes the music, every woman is expected to do it. Indeed, she wants to do it. Little girls start learning what to want—and what to be —when they are still in their cribs. Dr. Miriam Keiffer, a young social psychologist at Bensalem, the Experimental College of Fordham Univer-sity, points to studies showing that

> at six months of age, mothers are already treating their baby girls and boys quite differently. For instance, mothers have been found to touch, comfort, and talk to their females more. If these differences can be found at such an early stage, it's not surprising that the end product is as different as it is. What is surprising is that men and women are, in so many ways, similar.

Some people point to the way little girls play with dolls as proof of their innate motherliness. But remember, little girls are given dolls. When Margaret Mead presented some dolls to New Guinea children, it was the boys, not the girls, who wanted to play with them, which they did by crooning lullabies and rocking them in the most maternal fashion.

By the time they reach adolescence, most girls, unconsciously or not, have learned enough about role definition to qualify for a master's de-gree. In general, the lesson has been that no matter what kind of career thoughts one may entertain, one must, first and foremost, be a wife and mother. A girl's mother is usually her first teacher. As Dr. Goode says, "A woman is not only taught by society to have a child; she is taught to have a child who will have a child." A woman who has hung her life on the Motherhood Myth will almost always reinforce her young married daughter's early training by pushing for grandchildren. Prospective grandmothers are not the only ones. Husbands, too, can be effective sellers. After all, they have the Fatherhood Myth to cope with. A married man is supposed to have children. Often, particularly among Latins, children are a sign of potency. They help him assure the world—and himself—that he is the big man he is supposed to be. Plus, children give him both immortality (whatever that means) and possibly the chance to become more in his lifetime through the accomplishments of his children, particularly his son. (Sometimes it's important, however, for the son to do better, but not *too* much better.)

Friends, too, can be counted on as myth-pushers. Naturally one wants to do what one's friends do. One study, by the way, found a correlation between a woman's fertility and that of her three closest friends. The negative sell comes into play here, too. We have seen what the concept of non-mother means (cold, selfish, unwomanly, abnormal). In practice, particularly in the suburbs, it can mean, simply, exclusion—both from child-centered activities (that is, most activities) and child-centered conversations (that is, most conversations). It can also mean being the butt of a lot of unfunny jokes. ("Whaddya waiting for? An immaculate conception? Ha ha.") Worst of all, it can mean being an object of pity.

In case she's escaped all those pressures (that is, if she was brought up in a cave), a young married woman often wants a baby just so that she'll (1) have something to do (motherhood is better than clerk/typist, which is often the only kind of job she can get, since little more has been expected of her and, besides, her boss also expects her to leave and be a mother); (2) have something to hug and possess, to be needed by and have power over; and (3) have something to be—e.g., a baby's mother. Motherhood affords an instant identity. First, through wifehood, you are somebody's wife; then you are somebody's mother. Both give not only identity and activity, but status and stardom of a kind. During pregnancy, a woman can look forward to the kind of attention and pampering she may not ever have gotten or may never otherwise get. Some women consider birth the biggest accomplishment of their lives, which may be interpreted as saying not much for the rest of their lives. As Dr. Goode says, "It's like the gambler who may know the roulette wheel is crooked, but it's the only game in town." Also, with motherhood, the feeling of accomplishment is immediate. It is really much faster and easier to make a baby than paint a painting, or write a book, or get to the point of accomplishment in a job. It is also easier in a way to shift focus from self-development to child development—particularly since, for women, self-development is considered selfish. Even unwed mothers may achieve a feeling of this kind. (As we have seen, little thought is given to the aftermath.) And, again, since so many women are underdeveloped as people, they feel that, besides children, they have little else to give—to themselves, their husbands, to their world.

You may ask why then, when the realities do start pouring in, does a woman want to have a second, third, even fourth child? OK, (1) just because reality is pouring in doesn't mean she wants to *face* it. A new baby can help bring back some of the old illusions. Says psychoanalyst Dr. Natalie Shainess, "She may view each successive child as a knight in armor that will rescue her from being a 'bad unhappy mother.'" (2) Next on the horror list of having no children, is having one. It suffices to say that only children are not only OK, they even have a high rate of exceptionality. (3) Both parents usually want at least one child of each sex. The husband, for reasons discussed earlier, probably wants a son. (4) The more children one has, the more of an excuse one has not to develop in any other way.

What's the point? A world without children? Of course not. Nothing could be worse or more unlikely. No matter what anyone says in *Look* or anywhere else, motherhood isn't about to go out like a blown bulb, and who says it should? Only the Myth must go out, and now it seems to be dimming.

The younger-generation females who have been reared on the Myth have not rejected it totally, but at least they recognize it can be more loving to children not to have them. And at least they speak of adopting children instead of bearing them. Moreover, since the new nonbreeders are "less hung-up" on ownership, they seem to recognize that if you dig loving children, you don't necessarily have to own one. The end of the Motherhood Myth might make available more loving women (and men!) for those children who already exist.

When motherhood is no longer culturally compulsory, there will, certainly, be less of it. Women are now beginning to think and do more about development of self, of their individual resources. Far from being selfish, such development is probably our only hope. That means more alternatives for women. And more alternatives mean more selective, better, happier, motherhood—and childhood and husbandhood (or manhood) and peoplehood. It is not a question of whether or not children are sweet and marvelous to have and rear; the question is, even if that's so, whether or not one wants to pay the price for it. It doesn't make sense any more to pretend that women need babies, when what they really need is themselves. If God were still speaking to us in a voice we could hear, even He would probably say, "Be fruitful. Don't multiply."

1970

Joan Didion

SALVADOR

The three-year-old El Salvador International Airport is glassy and white and splendidly isolated, conceived during the waning of the Molina "National Transformation" as convenient less to the capital (San Salvador is forty miles away, until recently a drive of several hours) than to a central hallucination of the Molina and Romero[1] regimes, the projected beach resorts, the Hyatt, the Pacific Paradise, tennis, golf, water-skiing, condos, Costa del Sol; the visionary invention of a tourist industry in yet another republic where the leading natural cause of death is gastrointestinal infection. In the general absence of tourists these hotels have since been abandoned, ghost resorts on the empty Pacific beaches, and to land at this airport built to service them is to plunge directly into a state in which no ground is solid, no depth of field reliable, no perception so definite that it might not dissolve into its reverse.

The only logic is that of acquiescence. Immigration is negotiated in a thicket of automatic weapons, but by whose authority the weapons are brandished (Army or National Guard or National Police or Customs Police or Treasury Police or one of a continuing proliferation of other shadowy and overlapping forces) is a blurred point. Eye contact is avoided. Documents are scrutinized upside down. Once clear of the airport, on the new highway that slices through green hills rendered phosphorescent by the cloud cover of the tropical rainy season, one sees mainly underfed cattle and mongrel dogs and armored vehicles, vans and trucks and Cherokee Chiefs fitted with reinforced steel and bulletproof Plexiglas an inch thick. Such vehicles are a fixed feature of local life, and are popularly associated with disappearance and death. There was the Cherokee Chief seen following the Dutch television crew killed in Chalatenango province in March of 1982. There was the red Toyota three-quarter-ton pickup sighted near the van driven by the four American-Catholic workers on the night they were killed in 1980. There were, in the late spring and summer of 1982, the three Toyota panel trucks, one yellow, one blue, and one green, none bearing plates, reported present at each of the mass detentions (a "detention" is another fixed feature of local life, and often precedes a "disappearance") in the Amatepec district of San Salvador. These are the details—the models and the colors of armored vehicles, the makes and calibers of weapons, the particular methods of dismemberment and decapitation used in particular instances—on

1. Arturo Armando Molina and Carlos Humberto Romero: presidents of El Salvador 1972–77 and 1977–79, respectively.

which the visitor to Salvador learns immediately to concentrate, to the exclusion of past or future concerns, as in a prolonged amnesiac fugue. * * *

Terror is the given of the place. Black-and-white police cars cruise in pairs, each with the barrel of a rifle extruding from an open window. Roadblocks materialize at random, soldiers fanning out from trucks and taking positions, fingers always on triggers, safeties clicking on and off. Aim is taken as if to pass the time. Every morning *El Diario de Hoy* and *La Prensa Gráfica* carry cautionary stories. *"Una madre y sus dos hijos fueron asesinados con arma cortante (corvo) por ocho sujetos desconocidos el lunes en la noche"*: A mother and her two sons hacked to death in their beds by eight *desconocidos*, unknown men. The same morning's paper: the unidentified body of a young man, strangled, found on the shoulder of a road. Same morning, different story: the unidentified bodies of three young men, found on another road, their faces partially destroyed by bayonets, one face carved to represent a cross.

It is largely from these reports in the newspapers that the United States embassy compiles its body counts, which are transmitted to Washington in a weekly dispatch referred to by embassy people as "the grim-gram." These counts are presented in a kind of tortured code that fails to obscure what is taken for granted in El Salvador, that government forces do most of the killing. In a January 15 1982 memo to Washington, for example, the embassy issued a "guarded" breakdown on its count of 6,909 "reported" political murders between September 16 1980 and September 15 1981. Of these 6,909, according to the memo, 922 were "believed committed by security forces," 952 "believed committed by leftist terrorists," 136 "believed committed by rightist terrorists," and 4,889 "committed by unknown assailants," the famous *desconocidos* favored by those San Salvador newspapers still publishing. (The figures actually add up not to 6,909 but to 6,899, leaving ten in a kind of official limbo.) The memo continued:

> 'The uncertainty involved here can be seen in the fact that responsibility cannot be fixed in the majority of cases. We note, however, that it is generally believed in El Salvador that a large number of the unexplained killings are carried out by the security forces, officially or unofficially. The Embassy is aware of dramatic claims that have been made by one interest group or another in which the security forces figure as the primary agents of murder here. El Salvador's tangled web of attack and vengeance, traditional criminal violence and political mayhem make this an impossible charge to sustain. In saying this, however, we make no attempt to lighten the responsibility for the deaths of many hundreds, and perhaps thousands, which can be attributed to the security forces. . . . "

The body count kept by what is generally referred to in San Salvador as "the Human Rights Commission" is higher than the embassy's, and documented periodically by a photographer who goes out looking for bodies. These bodies he photographs are often broken into unnatural positions, and the faces to which the bodies are attached (when they are attached) are equally unnatural, sometimes unrecognizable as human faces, obliterated by acid or beaten to a mash of misplaced ears and teeth or slashed ear to ear and invaded by insects. *"Encontrado en Antiguo Cuscatlán el día 25 de Marzo 1982: camison de dormir celeste,"* the typed caption reads on one photograph: found in Antiguo Cuscatlán March 25 1982 wearing a sky-blue nightshirt. The captions are laconic. Found in Soyapango May 21 1982. Found in Mejicanos June 11 1982. Found at El Playón May 30, 1982, white shirt, purple pants, black shoes.

The photograph accompanying that last caption shows a body with no eyes, because the vultures got to it before the photographer did. There is a special kind of practical information that the visitor to El Salvador acquires immediately, the way visitors to other places acquire information about the currency rates, the hours for the museums. In El Salvador one learns that vultures go first for the soft tissue, for the eyes, the exposed genitalia, the open mouth. One learns that an open mouth can be used to make a specific point, can be stuffed with something emblematic; stuffed, say, with a penis, or if the point has to do with land title, stuffed with some of the dirt in question. One learns that hair deteriorates less rapidly than flesh, and that a skull surrounded by a perfect corona of hair is a not uncommon sight in the body dumps.

All forensic photographs induce in the viewer a certain protective numbness, but dissociation is more difficult here. In the first place these are not, technically, "forensic" photographs, since the evidence they document will never be presented in a court of law. In the second place the disfigurement is too routine. The locations are too near, the dates too recent. There is the presence of the relatives of the disappeared: the women who sit every day in this cramped office on the grounds of the archdiocese, waiting to look at the spiral-bound photo albums in which the photographs are kept. These albums have plastic covers bearing soft-focus color photographs of young Americans in dating situation (strolling through autumn foliage on one album, recumbent in a field of daisies on another), and the women, looking for the bodies of their husbands and brothers and sisters and children, pass them from hand to hand without comment or expression.

> "One of the more shadowy elements of the violent scene here [is] the death squad. Existence of these groups has long been disputed, but not by many Salvadorans. . . . Who constitutes the death squads is yet another difficult question. We do not believe that these squads exist as permanent formations but rather as ad hoc vigilante groups that coalesce according to perceived need. Membership is also uncertain, but in addition to civilians we believe

that both on- and off-duty members of the security forces are participants. This was unofficially confirmed by right-wing spokesman Maj. Roberto D'Aubuisson who stated in an interview in early 1981 that security force members utilize the guise of the death squad when a potentially embarrassing or odious task needs to be performed."
   —From the confidential but later declassified January 15, 1982 memo previously cited, drafted for the State Department by the political section at the embassy in San Salvador.

The dead and pieces of the dead turn up in El Savador everywhere, every day, as taken for granted as in a nightmare, or a horror movie. Vultures of course suggest the presence of a body. A knot of children on the street suggests the presence of a body. Bodies turn up in the brush of vacant lots, in the garbage thrown down ravines in the richest districts, in public rest rooms, in bus stations. Some are dropped in Lake Ilopango, a few miles east of the city, and wash up near the lakeside cottages and clubs frequented by what remains in San Salvador of the sporting bourgeoisie. Some still turn up in El Playón, the lunar lava field of rotting human flesh visible at one time or another on every television screen in America but characterized in June of 1982 in the El Salvador News Gazette, an English-language weekly edited by an American named Mario Rosenthal, as an "uncorroborated story . . . dredged up from the files of leftist propaganda." Others turn up at Puerta del Diablo, above Parque Balboa, a national Turicentro described as recently as the April–July 1982 issue of Aboard TACA, the magazine provided passengers on the national airline of El Salvador, as "offering excellent subjects for color photography."
   I drove up to Puerta del Diablo one morning in June of 1982, past the Casa Presidencial and the camouflaged watch towers and heavy concentrations of troops and arms south of town, on up a narrow road narrowed further by landslides and deep crevices in the roadbed, a drive so insistently premonitory that after a while I began to hope that I would pass Puerta del Diablo without knowing it, just miss it, write it off, turn around and go back. There was however no way of missing it. Puerta del Diablo is a "view site" in an older and distinctly literary tradition, nature as lesson, an immense cleft rock through which half of El Salvador seems framed, a site so romantic and "mystical," so theatrically sacrificial in aspect, that it might be a cosmic parody of nineteenth-century landscape painting. The place presents itself as pathetic fallacy:[2] the sky "broods," the stones "weep," a constant seepage of water weighting the ferns and moss. The foliage is thick and slick with moisture. The only sound is a steady buzz, I believe of cicadas.
   Body dumps are seen in El Salvador as a kind of visitors' must-do,

2. Attributing human traits and feelings to nature.

difficult but worth the detour. "Of course you have seen El Playón," an aide to President Alvaro Magaña said to me one day, and proceeded to discuss the site geologically, as evidence of the country's geothermal resources. He made no mention of the bodies. I was unsure if he was sounding me out or simply found the geothermal aspect of overriding interest. One difference between El Playón and Puerta del Diablo is that most bodies at El Playón appear to have been killed somewhere else, and then dumped; at Puerta del Diablo the executions are believed to occur in place, at the top, and the bodies thrown over. Sometimes reporters will speak of wanting to spend the night at Puerta del Diablo, in order to document the actual execution, but at the time I was in Salvador no one had.

The aftermath, the daylight aspect, is well documented. "Nothing fresh today, I hear," an embassy officer said when I mentioned that I had visited Puerta del Diablo. "Were there any on top?" someone else asked. "There were supposed to have been three on top yesterday." The point about whether or not there had been any on top was that usually it was necessary to go down to see bodies. The way down is hard. Slabs of stone, slippery with moss, are set into the vertiginous cliff, and it is down this cliff that one begins the descent to the bodies, or what is left of the bodies, pecked and maggoty masses of flesh, bone, hair. On some days there have been helicopters circling, tracking those making the descent. Other days there have been militia at the top, in the clearing where the road seems to run out, but on the morning I was there the only people on top were a man and a woman and three small children, who played in the wet grass while the woman started and stopped a Toyota pickup. She appeared to be learning how to drive. She drove forward and then back toward the edge, apparently following the man's signals, over and over again.

We did not speak, and it was only later, down the mountain and back in the land of the provisionally living, that it occurred to me that there was a definite question about why a man and a woman might choose a well-known body dump for a driving lesson. This was one of a number of occasions, during the two weeks my husband and I spent in El Salvador, on which I came to understand, in a way I had not understood before, the exact mechanism of terror.

Whenever I had nothing better to do in San Salvador I would walk up in the leafy stillness of the San Benito and Escalón districts, where the hush at midday is broken only by the occasional crackle of a walkie-talkie, the click of metal moving on a weapon. I recall a day in San Benito when I opened my bag to check an address, and heard the clicking of metal on metal all up and down the street. On the whole no one walks up here, and pools of blossoms lie undisturbed on the sidewalks. Most of the houses in San Benito are more recent than those in Escalón, less idiosyncratic and probably smarter, but the most striking architectural features in both districts are not the houses but their walls, walls built upon walls, walls stripped of the usual copa de oro[3] and bougainvillea, walls that reflect successive generations of violence: the original stone, the additonal five or six or ten feet of brick, and finally the barbed wire, sometimes concertina, sometimes electrified; walls with watch towers, gun ports, closed-circuit television cameras, walls now reaching twenty and thirty feet.

San Benito and Escalón appear on the embassy security maps as districts of relatively few "incidents," but they remain districts in which a certain oppressive uneasiness prevails. In the first place there are always "incidents"—detentions and deaths and disappearances—in the *barrancas*, the ravines lined with shanties that fall down behind the houses with the walls and the guards and the walkie-talkies; one day in Escalón I was introduced to a woman who kept the lean-to that served as a grocery in a *barranca* just above the Hotel Sheraton. She was sticking prices on bars of Camay and Johnson's baby soap, stopping occasionally to sell a plastic bag or two filled with crushed ice and Coca-Cola, and all the while she talked in a low voice about her fear, about her eighteen-year-old son, about the boys who had been taken out and shot on successive nights recently in a neighboring *barranca*.

In the second place there is, in Escalón, the presence of the Sheraton itself, a hotel that has figured rather too prominently in certain local stories involving the disappearance and death of Americans. The Sheraton always seems brighter and more mildly festive than either the Camino Real or the Presidente, with children in the pool and flowers and pretty women in pastel dresses, but there are usually several bullet-proofed Cherokee Chiefs in the parking area, and the men drinking in the lobby often carry the little zippered purses that in San Salvador suggest not passports or credit cards but Browning 9-mm. pistols.

It was at the Sheraton that one of the few American *desaparecidos*,[4] a young free-lance writer named John Sullivan, was last seen in December of 1980. It was also at the Sheraton, after eleven on the evening of January 3 1981, that the two American advisers on agrarian reform, Michael Hammer and Mark Pearlman, were killed, along with the Salvadoran director of the Institute for Agrarian Transformation, José Rodolfo Viera. The three were drinking coffee in a dining room of the lobby, and whoever killed them used an Ingram MAC-10, without sound suppressor, and then walked out through the lobby, unapprehended. The Sheraton has even turned up in the investigation into the December 1980 deaths of the four American churchwomen, Sisters Ita Ford and Maura Clarke, the two Maryknoll nuns; Sister Dorothy Kazel, the Ursuline nun; and Jean Donovan, the lay volunteer. In *Justice in El Salvador: A Case*

3. Cupflower (literally, cup of gold).   4. Missing (i.e., abducted) persons.

Study, prepared and released in July of 1982 in New York by the Lawyers' Committee for International Human Rights, there appears this note:

> "On December 19, 1980, the [Duarte government's] Special Investigative Commission reported that 'a red Toyota ¾-ton pickup was seen leaving (the crime scene) at about 11:00 P.M. on December 2' and that 'a red splotch on the burned van' of the churchwomen was being checked to determine whether the paint splotch 'could be the result of a collision between that van and the red Toyota pickup.' By February 1981, the Maryknoll Sisters' Office of Social Concerns, which has been actively monitoring the investigation, received word from a source which it considered reliable that the FBI had matched the red splotch on the burned van with a red Toyota pickup belonging to the Sheraton hotel in San Salvador. . . . Subsequent to the FBI's alleged matching of the paint splotch and a Sheraton truck, the State Department has claimed, in a communication with the families of the churchwomen, that 'the FBI could not determine the source of the paint scraping.'"

There is also mention in this study of a young Salvadoran businessman named Hans Christ (his father was a German who arrived in El Salvador at the end of World War II), a part owner of the Sheraton. Hans Christ lives now in Miami, and that his name should have even come up in the Maryknoll investigation made many people uncomfortable, because it was Hans Christ, along with his brother-in-law, Ricardo Sol Meza, who, in April of 1981, was first charged with the murders of Michael Hammer and Mark Pearlman and José Rodolfo Viera at the Sheraton. These charges were later dropped, and were followed by a series of other charges, arrests, releases, expressions of "dismay" and "incredulity" from the American embassy, and even, in the fall of 1982, confessions to the killings from two former National Guard corporals, who testified that Hans Christ had led them through the lobby and pointed out the victims. Hans Christ and Ricardo Sol Meza have said that the dropped case against them was a government frame-up, and that they were only having drinks at the Sheraton the night of the killings, with a National Guard intelligence officer. It was logical for Hans Christ and Ricardo Sol Meza to have drinks at the Sheraton because they both had interests in the hotel, and Ricardo Sol Meza had just opened a roller disco, since closed, off the lobby into which the killers walked that night. The killers were described by witnesses as well dressed, their faces covered. The room from which they walked was at the time I was in San Salvador no longer a restaurant, but the marks left by the bullets were still visible, on the wall facing the door.

Whenever I had occasion to visit the Sheraton I was apprehensive, and this apprehension came to color the entire Escalón district for me, even its lower reaches, where there were people and movies and restaurants. I recall being struck by it on the canopied porch of a restaurant near the Mexican embassy, on an evening when rain or sabotage or habit had blacked out the city and I became abruptly aware, in the light cast by a passing car, of two human shadows, silhouettes illuminated by the headlights and then invisible again. One shadow sat behind the smoked glass windows of a Cherokee Chief parked at the curb in front of the restaurant; the other crouched between the pumps at the Esso station next door, carrying a rifle. It seemed to me unencouraging that my husband and I were the only people seated on the porch. In the absence of the headlights the candle on our table provided the only light, and I fought the impulse to blow it out. We continued talking carefully. Nothing came of this, but I did not forget the sensation of having been in a single instant demoralized, undone, humiliated by fear, which is what I meant when I said that I came to understand in El Salvador the mechanism of terror. * * *

1983

THE READER

1. *In the first paragraph of her essay, Didion refers to "a central hallucination of the Molina and Romero regimes." Why does she use the word "hallucination"?*
2. *How does Didion feel about the things she sees and experiences? How does she convey those feelings?*
3. *Didion says she "came to understand ... the exact mechanism of terror." What is that mechanism?*
4. *In her other essays included in this book, Didion is vitally interested in what she and others thought and felt. Is that interest apparent in this essay? In "On Going Home" (p. 40), she speaks of her mother and herself as "veterans of a guerrilla war we never understood" and of "the ambushes of daily life." Do these metaphors shed any light on her interest in "Salvador"?*

THE WRITER

1. *Why does Didion find it necessary to explain the significance of some of the words she uses, such as "logic ... of acquiescence," "detention," "disappearance"? Find other similar terms in her essay that she has had to define.*
2. *Look closely at the third paragraph of Didion's essay. Why does she make "police cars," "roadblocks" and "aim" the subjects of her second, third, and fourth sentences? Why does she use so many past participles ("hacked," "strangled," "found," "destroyed," "carved") in the last three sentences of the paragraph?*
3. *In "How Bad Do You Want to Get to Danang?" (p. 405), Herr describes the terror of experiences in the Vietnam War. Write a brief comparison of the terror Herr describes with the "mechanism of terror" described by Didion.*

Jonathan Schell

THE DESTRUCTIVE POWER OF A ONE-MEGATON BOMB ON NEW YORK CITY

* * *

One way to begin to grasp the destructive power of present-day nuclear weapons is to describe the consequences of the detonation of a one-megaton bomb, which possesses eighty times the explosive power of the Hiroshima bomb, on a large city, such as New York. Burst some eighty-five hundred feet above the Empire State Building, a one-megaton bomb would gut or flatten almost every building between Battery Park and 125th Street, or within a radius of four and four-tenths miles, or in an area of sixty-one square miles, and would heavily damage buildings between the northern tip of Staten Island and the George Washington Bridge, or within a radius of about eight miles, or in an area of about two hundred square miles. A conventional explosive delivers a swift shock, like a slap, to whatever it hits, but the blast wave of a sizable nuclear weapon endures for several seconds and "can surround and destroy whole buildings" (Glasstone).[1] People, of course, would be picked up and hurled away from the blast along with the rest of the debris. Within the sixty-one square miles, the walls, roofs, and floors of any buildings that had not been flattened would be collapsed, and the people and furniture inside would be swept down onto the street. (Technically, this zone would be hit by various overpressures of at least five pounds per square inch. Overpressure is defined as the pressure in excess of normal atmospheric pressure.) As far away as ten miles from ground zero, pieces of glass and other sharp objects would be hurled about by the blast wave at lethal velocities. In Hiroshima, where buildings were low and, outside the center of the city, were often constructed of light materials, injuries from falling buildings were often minor. But in New York, where the buildings are tall and are constructed of heavy materials, the physical collapse of the city would certainly kill millions of people. The streets of New York are narrow ravines running between the high walls of the city's buildings. In a nuclear attack, the walls would fall and the ravines would fill up. The people in the buildings would fall to the street with the debris of the buildings, and the people in the street would be crushed by this avalanche of people and buildings. At a distance of two miles or so from ground zero, winds would reach four hundred miles an hour, and another two miles away they would reach a hundred and eighty miles an hour. Meanwhile, the fireball would be growing, until it was more than a

---

1. Samuel Glasstone, editor with Philip Dolan of *Effects of Nuclear Weapons*.

mile wide, and rocketing upward, to a height of over six miles. For ten seconds, it would broil the city below. Anyone caught in the open within nine miles of ground zero would receive third-degree burns and would probably be killed; closer to the explosion, people would be charred and killed instantly. From Greenwich Village up to Central Park, the heat would be great enough to melt metal and glass. Readily inflammable materials, such as newspapers and dry leaves, would ignite in all five boroughs (though in only a small part of Staten Island) and west to the Passaic River, in New Jersey, within a radius of about nine and a half miles from ground zero, thereby creating an area of more than two hundred and eighty square miles in which mass fires were likely to break out.

If it were possible (as it would not be) for someone to stand at Fifth Avenue and Seventy-second Street (about two miles from ground zero) without being instantly killed, he would see the following sequence of events. A dazzling white light from the fireball would illumine the scene, continuing for perhaps thirty seconds. Simultaneously, searing heat would ignite everything flammable and start to melt windows, cars, buses, lampposts, and everything else made of metal or glass. People in the street would immediately catch fire, and would shortly be reduced to heavily charred corpses. About five seconds after the light appeared, the blast wave would strike, laden with the debris of a now nonexistent midtown. Some buildings might be crushed, as though a giant fist had squeezed them on all sides, and others might be picked up off their foundations and whirled uptown with the other debris. On the far side of Central Park, the West Side skyline would fall from south to north. The four-hundred-mile-an-hour wind would blow from south to north, die down after a few seconds, and then blow in the reverse direction with diminished intensity. While these things were happening, the fireball would be burning in the sky for the ten seconds of the thermal pulse. Soon huge, thick clouds of dust and smoke would envelop the scene, and as the mushroom cloud rushed overhead (it would have a diameter of about twelve miles) the light from the sun would be blotted out, and day would turn to night. Within minutes, fires, ignited both by the thermal pulse and by broken gas mains, tanks of gas and oil, and the like, would begin to spread in the darkness, and a strong, steady wind would begin to blow in the direction of the blast. As at Hiroshima, a whirlwind might be produced, which would sweep through the ruins, and radioactive rain, generated under the meteorological conditions created by the blast, might fall. Before long, the individual fires would coalesce into a mass fire, which, depending largely on the winds, would become either a conflagration or a firestorm. In a conflagration, prevailing winds spread a wall of fire as far as there is any combustible material to sustain it; in a firestorm, a vertical updraft caused by the fire itself sucks the surrounding air in toward a central point, and the fires therefore converge in a single fire of extreme heat. A mass fire of either kind renders shelters useless by burning up all the oxygen in the air and creating toxic gases, so that anyone inside the shelters is asphyxiated, and also by heating the ground to such high temperatures that the shelters turn, in effect, into ovens, cremating the people inside them. In Dresden, several days after the firestorm raised there by Allied conventional bombing, the interiors of some bomb shelters were still so hot that when they were opened the inrushing air caused the contents to burst into flame. Only those who had fled their shelters when the bombing started had any chance of surviving. (It is difficult to predict in a particular situation which form the fires will take. In actual experience, Hiroshima suffered a firestorm and Nagasaki suffered a conflagration.)

In this vast theatre of physical effects, all the scenes of agony and death that took place at Hiroshima would again take place, but now involving millions of people rather than hundreds of thousands. Like the people of Hiroshima, the people of New York would be burned, battered, crushed, and irradiated in every conceivable way. The city and its people would be mingled in a smoldering heap. And then, as the fires started, the survivors (most of whom would be on the periphery of the explosion) would be driven to abandon to the flames those family members and other people who were unable to flee, or else to die with them. Before long, while the ruins burned, the processions of injured, mute people would begin their slow progress out of the outskirts of the devastated zone. However, this time a much smaller proportion of the population than at Hiroshima would have a chance of escaping. In general, as the size of the area of devastation increases, the possibilities for escape decrease. When the devastated area is relatively small, as it was at Hiroshima, people who are not incapacitated will have a good chance of escaping to safety before the fires coalesce into a mass fire. But when the devastated area is great, as it would be after the detonation of a megaton bomb, and fires are springing up at a distance of nine and a half miles from ground zero, and when what used to be the streets are piled high with burning rubble, and the day (if the attack occurs in the daytime) has grown impenetrably dark, there is little chance that anyone who is not on the very edge of the devastated area will be able to make his way to safety. In New York, most people would die wherever the blast found them, or not very far from there.

If instead of being burst in the air the bomb were burst on or near the ground in the vicinity of the Empire State Building, the overpressure would be very much greater near the center of the blast area but the range hit by a minimum of five pounds per square inch of overpressure would be less. The range of the thermal pulse would be about the same as that of the air burst. The fireball would be almost two miles across, and would engulf midtown Manhattan from Greenwich Village nearly to Central Park. Very little is known about what would happen to a city that was inside a fireball, but one would expect a good deal of what was there to be first pulverized and then melted or vaporized. Any human beings in the area would be reduced to smoke and ashes; they would simply disappear. A crater roughly three blocks in diameter and two hundred feet deep would open up. In addition, heavy radioactive fallout would be created as dust and debris from the city rose with the mushroom cloud and then fell back to the ground. Fallout would begin to drop almost immediately, contaminating the ground beneath the cloud with levels of radiation many times lethal doses, and quickly killing anyone who might have survived the blast wave and the thermal pulse and might now be attempting an escape; it is difficult to believe that there would be appreciable survival of the people of the city after a megaton ground burst. And for the next twenty-four hours or so more fallout would descend downwind from the blast, in a plume whose direction and length would depend on the speed and the direction of the wind that happened to be blowing at the time of the attack. If the wind was blowing at fifteen miles an hour, fallout of lethal intensity would descend in a plume about a hundred and fifty miles long and as much as fifteen miles wide. Fallout that was sublethal but could still cause serious illness would extend another hundred and fifty miles downwind. Exposure to radioactivity in human beings is measured in units called rems—an acronym for "roentgen equivalent in man." The roentgen is a standard measurement of gamma- and X-ray radiation, and the expression "equivalent in man" indicates that an adjustment has been made to take into account the differences in the degree of biological damage that is caused by radiation of different types. Many of the kinds of harm done to human beings by radiation—for example, the incidence of cancer and of genetic damage—depend on the dose accumulated over many years; but radiation sickness, capable of causing death, results from an "acute" dose, received in a period of anything from a few seconds to several days. Because almost ninety per cent of the so-called "infinite-time dose" of radiation from fallout—that is, the dose from a given quantity of fallout that one would receive if one lived for many thousands of years—is emitted in the first week, the one-week accumulated dose is often used as a convenient measure for calculating the immediate harm from fallout. Doses in the thousands of rems, which could be expected throughout the city, would attack the central nervous system and would bring about death within a few hours. Doses of around a thousand rems, which would be delivered some tens of miles downwind from the blast, would kill within two weeks everyone who was exposed to them. Doses of around five hundred rems, which would be delivered as far as a hundred and fifty miles downwind (given a wind speed of fifteen miles per hour), would kill half of all exposed able-bodied young adults. At this level of exposure, radiation sickness proceeds in the three stages observed at Hiroshima. The plume of lethal fallout could descend, depending on the direction of the wind, on other parts of New York State and parts of New Jersey, Pennsylvania, Delaware, Maryland, Connecticut, Massachusetts, Rhode Island, Vermont, and New Hampshire, killing additional millions of people. The circumstances in heavily contaminated areas, in which millions of people were all declining together, over a period of weeks, toward painful deaths, are ones that, like so many of the consequences of nuclear explosions, have never been experienced.

A description of the effects of a one-megaton bomb on New York City gives some notion of the meaning in human terms of a megaton of nuclear explosive power, but a weapon that is more likely to be used against New York is the twenty-megaton bomb, which has one thousand six hundred times the yield of the Hiroshima bomb. The Soviet Union is estimated to have at least a hundred and thirteen twenty-megaton bombs in its nuclear arsenal, carried by Bear intercontinental bombers. In addition, some of the Soviet SS-18 missiles are capable of carrying bombs of this size, although the actual yields are not known. Since the explosive power of the twenty-megaton bombs greatly exceeds the amount necessary to destroy most military targets, it is reasonable to suppose that they are meant for use against large cities. If a twenty-megaton bomb were airburst over the Empire State Building at an altitude of thirty thousand feet, the zone gutted or flattened by the blast wave would have a radius of twelve miles and an area of more than four hundred and fifty square miles, reaching from the middle of Staten Island to the northern edge of the Bronx, the eastern edge of Queens, and well into New Jersey, and the zone of heavy damage from the blast wave (the zone hit by a minimum of two pounds of overpressure per square inch) would have a radius of twenty-one and a half miles, or an area of one thousand four hundred and fifty square miles, reaching to the southernmost tip of Staten Island, north as far as southern Rockland County, east into Nassau County, and west to Morris County, New Jersey. The fireball would be about four and a half miles in diameter and would radiate the thermal pulse for some twenty seconds. People caught in the open twenty-three miles away from ground zero, in Long Island, New Jersey, and southern New York State, would be burned to death. People hundreds of miles away who looked at the burst would be temporarily blinded and would risk permanent eye injury. (After the test of a fifteen-megaton bomb on Bikini Atoll, in the South Pacific, in March of 1954, small animals were found to have suffered retinal burns at a distance of three hundred and forty-five miles.) The mushroom cloud would be seventy miles in diameter. New York City and its suburbs would be transformed into a lifeless, flat, scorched desert in a few seconds.

If a twenty-megaton bomb were ground-burst on the Empire State Building, the range of severe blast damage would, as with the one-megaton ground blast, be reduced, but the fireball, which would be almost six miles in diameter, would cover Manhattan from Wall Street to northern Central Park and also parts of New Jersey, Brooklyn, and Queens, and everyone within it would be instantly killed, with most of them physically disappearing. Fallout would again be generated, this time covering thousands of square miles with lethal intensities of radiation. A fair portion of New York City and its incinerated population, now radioactive dust, would have risen into the mushroom cloud and would now be descending on the surrounding territory. On one of the few occasions when local fallout was generated by a test explosion in the multi-megaton range, the fifteen-megaton bomb tested on Bikini Atoll, which was exploded seven feet above the surface of a coral reef, "caused substantial contamination over an area of more than seven thousand square miles," according to Glasstone. If, as seems likely, a twenty-megaton bomb ground-burst on New York would produce at least a comparable amount of fallout, and if the wind carried the fallout onto populated areas, then this one bomb would probably doom upward of twenty million people, or almost ten per cent of the population of the United States.

* * *

1982

Brent Staples

BLACK MEN AND PUBLIC SPACE

My first victim was a woman—white, well dressed, probably in her early twenties. I came upon her late one evening on a deserted street in Hyde Park, a relatively affluent neighborhood in an otherwise mean, impoverished section of Chicago. As I swung onto the avenue behind her, there seemed to be a discreet, uninflammatory distance between us. Not so. She cast back a worried glance. To her, the youngish black man—a broad six feet two inches with a beard and billowing hair, both hands shoved into the pockets of a bulky military jacket—seemed menacingly close. After a few more quick glimpses, she picked up her pace and was soon running in earnest. Within seconds she disappeared into a cross street.

That was more than a decade ago, I was twenty-two years old, a graduate student newly arrived at the University of Chicago. It was in the

echo of that terrified woman's footfalls that I first began to know the
unwieldy inheritance I'd come into—the ability to alter public space in
ugly ways. It was clear that she thought herself the quarry of a mugger, a
rapist, or worse. Suffering a bout of insomnia, however, I was stalking
sleep, not defenseless wayfarers. As a softy who is scarcely able to take a
knife to a raw chicken—let alone hold one to a person's throat—I was
surprised, embarrassed, and dismayed all at once. Her flight made me feel
like an accomplice in tyranny. It also made it clear that I was indistinguishable from the muggers who occasionally seeped into the area from
the surrounding ghetto. That first encounter, and those that followed,
signified that a vast, unnerving gulf lay between nighttime pedestrians—
particularly women—and me. And I soon gathered that being perceived
as dangerous is a hazard in itself. I only needed to turn a corner into a
dicey situation, or crowd some frightened, armed person in a foyer
somewhere, or make an errant move after being pulled over by a policeman. Where fear and weapons meet—and they often do in urban America—there is always the possibility of death.

In that first year, my first away from my hometown, I was to become
thoroughly familiar with the language of fear. At dark, shadowy intersec-
tions, I could cross in front of a car stopped at a traffic light and elicit the
thunk, thunk, thunk, thunk of the driver—black, white, male, or female—
hammering down the door locks. On less traveled streets after dark, I
grew accustomed to but never comfortable with people crossing to the
other side of the street rather than pass me. Then there were the standard
unpleasantries with policemen, doormen, bouncers, cabdrivers, and
others whose business it is to screen out troublesome individuals before
there is any nastiness.

I moved to New York nearly two years ago and I have remained an avid
night walker. In central Manhattan, the near-constant crowd cover mini-
mizes tense one-on-one street encounters. Elsewhere—in SoHo, for example, where sidewalks are narrow and tightly spaced buildings shut out
the sky—things can get very taut indeed.

After dark, on the warrenlike streets of Brooklyn where I live, I often
see women who fear the worst from me. They seem to have set their faces
on neutral, and with their purse straps strung across their chests bando-
lier-style, they forge ahead as though bracing themselves against being
tackled. I understand, of course, that the danger they perceive is not a
hallucination. Women are particularly vulnerable to street violence, and
young black males are drastically overrepresented among the perpetrators of that violence. Yet these truths are no solace against the kind of
alienation that comes of being ever the suspect, a fearsome entity with
whom pedestrians avoid making eye contact.

It is not altogether clear to me how I reached the ripe old age of twenty-
two without being conscious of the lethality nighttime pedestrians attrib-

uted to me. Perhaps it was because in Chester, Pennsylvania, the small, angry industrial town where I came of age in the 1960s, I was scarcely noticeable against a backdrop of gang warfare, street knifings, and murders. I grew up one of the good boys, had perhaps a half-dozen fistfights. In retrospect, my shyness of combat has clear sources.

As a boy, I saw countless tough guys locked away; I have since buried several, too. They were babies, really—a teenage cousin, a brother of twenty-two, a childhood friend in his mid-twenties—all gone down in episodes of bravado played out in the streets. I came to doubt the virtues of intimidation early on. I chose, perhaps unconsciously, to remain a shadow—timid, but a survivor.

The fearsomeness mistakenly attributed to me in public places often has a perilous flavor. The most frightening of these confusions occurred in the late 1970s and early 1980s, when I worked as a journalist in Chicago. One day, rushing into the office of a magazine I was writing for with a deadline story in hand, I was mistaken for a burglar. The office manager called security and, with an ad hoc[1] posse, pursued me through the labyrinthine halls, nearly to my editor's door. I had no way of proving who I was. I could only move briskly toward the company of someone who knew me.

Another time I was on assignment for a local paper and killing time before an interview. I entered a jewelry store on the city's affluent Near North Side. The proprietor excused herself and returned with an enormous red Doberman pinscher straining at the end of a leash. She stood, the dog extended toward me, silent to my questions, her eyes bulging nearly out of her head. I took a cursory look around, nodded, and bade her good night.

Relatively speaking, however, I never fared as badly as another black male journalist. He went to nearby Waukegan, Illinois, a couple of summers ago to work on a story about a murderer who was born there. Mistaking the reporter for the killer, police officers hauled him from his car at gunpoint and but for his press credentials would probably have tried to book him. Such episodes are not uncommon. Black men trade tales like this all the time.

Over the years, I learned to smother the rage I felt at so often being taken for a criminal. Not to do so would surely have led to madness. I now take precautions to make myself less threatening. I move about with care, particularly late in the evening. I give a wide berth to nervous people on subway platforms during the wee hours, particularly when I have exchanged business clothes for jeans. If I happen to be entering a building behind some people who appear skittish, I may walk by, letting them clear the lobby before I return, so as not to seem to be following them. I

1. "Ad hoc": for a particular purpose.

have been calm and extremely congenial on those rare occasions when I've been pulled over by the police.

And on late-evening constitutionals I employ what has proved to be an excellent tension-reducing measure: I whistle melodies from Beethoven and Vivaldi and the more popular classical composers. Even steely New Yorkers hunching toward nighttime destinations seem to relax, and occasionally they even join in the tune. Virtually everybody seems to sense that a mugger wouldn't be warbling bright, sunny selections from Vivaldi's *Four Seasons*.[2] It is my equivalent of the cowbell that hikers wear when they know they are in bear country.

1986

2. Work by eighteenth-century composer Antonio Vivaldi celebrating the seasons.

THE READER

1. In his essay, Staples writes of situations correctly perceived as danger-ous and situations misperceived as dangerous. Give specific instances of each. How are they related?
2. Staples shows that his personal background and experiences led him to see things in a particular way. To what degree is that particular way idiosyncratic—specific to him? To what degree is that particular way expressive of general truth—experience common to all or most persons?

THE WRITER

1. Does Staples take a humorous approach to his subject at certain points in the essay? If so, does this distract from or contribute to the serious-ness of the matter? Explain.
2. Is the concluding sentence an effective close? Draw out its implica-tions, showing how these relate to the details of his discussion.
3. Do you have perceptions and apprehensions similar to or largely different from those described by Staples? Write an essay on this topic, placing yourself in familiar or in unusual surroundings.

Garrison Keillor

THE TOWER PROJECT

Many of our personnel, conscious of the uncertainties of the construction business, have voiced concern relative to their future employment with the Company. What lies ahead on our horizon, they wonder, of the magnitude of the Fred M. and Ida S. Freebold Performing Arts Center, the Tannersfield Freeway Overpass, and other works that have put us in the construction forefront? They recall the cancellation in mid-contract of the Vietnam Parking Lot project, and they ask, "Will the Super-Tall Tower project, too, go down the drain, with a resultant loss of jobs and Company position in the building field?"

The Company believes such will not be the case. While we aren't putting all our "eggs" on one tower and are keeping an eye on the Los Angeles–Honolulu Bridge option and the proposed Lake Michigan Floating Airport, we feel that the Super-Tall Tower has achieved priority status in Washington, and all phases of research and development, land clearance, and counter-resistance are moving forward in expectation of final approval.

As for the Tower critics, they are few in number, and there isn't one of their objections that we haven't answered. Let's look at the record. Their favorite line is "Why build a Super-Tall Tower when money is so urgently needed for cancer and poverty?" With all due respect to the unwell or impoverished person and his or her family, we state our case as follows:

First, Tower construction will create a hundred thousand new jobs, not only in the Babel area and the Greater Southwest but also in other places where the bricks and slime will be made by subcontractors.

Second, because it will be the world's tallest tower, we will be able to see more from it than from any existing tower.

Third, we have reason to believe the Chinese are well along in the development of *their* tower. If we don't wish to abdicate tower leadership to Communist nations, however friendly at the moment, we can't afford to slow down now. To do so would mean the waste of all the money spent on tower research so far and would set back American tower technology for decades to come. Thus, our national prestige is at stake—not merely national pride but the confidence in our ability to rise toward the heavens. When a nation turns away from the sky and looks at its feet, it begins to die as a civilization. Man has long dreamed of building a tall tower from which he could look out and see many interesting and unusual things. Most Americans, we believe, share this dream.

320   GARRISON KEILLOR

Fourth, environmentalist groups have predicted various disastrous effects from the Tower—that the humming noise of its high-speed elevator will be "unbearable" to the passengers and to nearby residents, that its height will confuse migrating birds, that its long shadow will anger the sun, and so forth. The Company's research laboratory has engaged in a crash program that has already achieved a significant degree of hum reduction; at the same time, our engineers are quick to point out that since no elevator now in service can approach the speed and accompanying hum projected for the Tower elevator, there is no viable data on which to base the entire concept of an "unbearable" hum. Such a determination must wait until the completion of the Tower. In any event, the hum may serve to warn off approaching birds. As for the sun, we feel that, with certain sacrifices, this problem can be taken care of.

1982

THE READER

1. Is "The Tower Project" a fable? If so, what is the moral?
2. What can you infer about the nature of "the Company" from this document?
3. What specific objections to the Tower are put forward by environmentalists and other critics? How seriously are we to take each of these objections? How adequately are the objections answered by "the Company"?
4. It is said that the Tower will be constructed of "bricks and slime." Is slime usually used as a building material? How are we to understand the meaning of the word in this context?
5. Read the passage from Genesis 11:1-9 below. What relevance does it have to Keillor's piece?

GENESIS 11:1-9

And the whole earth was of one language, and of one speech.

2 And it came to pass, as they journeyed from the east, that they found a plain in the land of Shī'när; and they dwelt there.

3 And they said one to another, Go to, let us make brick, and burn them throughly. And they had brick for stone, and slime had they for morter.

4 And they said, Go to, let us build us a city and a tower, whose top may reach unto heaven; and let us make us a name, lest we be scattered abroad upon the face of the whole earth.

5 And the LORD came down to see the city and the tower, which the children of men builded.

6 And the LORD said, Behold, the people is one, and they have all one language; and this they begin to do: and now nothing will be restrained from them, which they have imagined to do.

7 Go to, let us go down, and there confound their language, that they may not understand one another's speech.

8 So the LORD scattered them abroad from thence upon the face of all the earth: and they left off to build the city.

9 Therefore is the name of it called Babel; because the LORD did there confound the language of all the earth: and from thence did the LORD scatter them abroad upon the face of all the earth.

THE WRITER

1. Explain the effect produced by Keillor's choice of words in these phrases or sentences: (1) "all phases of research and development, land clearance, and counter-resistance are moving forward"; (2) "Let's look at the record"; (3) "With all due respect to the unwell or impoverished person and his or her family"; (4) "Man has long dreamed of building a tall tower from which he could look out and see many interesting and unusual things"; (5) "there is no viable data on which to base the entire concept of an 'unbearable' hum."
2. In "A Modest Proposal" (p. 489), Swift gives you various clues that he is not to be taken literally. Does Keillor give clues similar to Swift's or different from Swift's?
3. What is Keillor's attitude toward business or large companies? Toward politicians? Toward environmentalists? Explain how you know.
4. Write a brief essay, using as here the tone, diction, and style of a writer employed by the Company, to draw out the implications of the concluding sentence and to set forth in detail the Company's proposal for taking care of the problem.
5. Take an incident from history or mythology, and use an updated version of it to make some satirical point(s).

Human Nature

Robert Finch

VERY LIKE A WHALE

One day last week at sunset I went back to Corporation Beach in Dennis[1] to see what traces, if any, might be left of the great, dead finback whale that had washed up there several weeks before. The beach was not as hospitable as it had been that sunny Saturday morning after Thanksgiving when thousands of us streamed over the sand to gaze and look. A few cars were parked in the lot, but these kept their inhabitants. Bundled up against a sharp wind, I set off along the twelve-foot swath of trampled beach grass, a raw highway made in a few hours by ten thousand feet that day.

I came to the spot where the whale had beached and marveled that such a magnitude of flesh could have been there one day and gone the next. But the carcass had been hauled off and the tide had smoothed and licked clean whatever vestiges had remained. The cold, salt wind had lifted from the sands the last trace of that pervasive stench of decay that clung to our clothes for days, and now blew clean and sharp into my nostrils.

The only sign that anything unusual had been there was that the beach was a little too clean, not quite so pebbly and littered as the surrounding areas, as the grass above a new grave is always fresher and greener. What had so manifestly occupied this space a short while ago was now utterly gone. And yet the whale still lay heavily on my mind; a question lingered, like a persistent odor in the air. And its dark shape, though now sunken somewhere beneath the waves, still loomed before me, beckoning, asking something.

What was it? What had we seen? Even the several thousand of us that

1. Village on Cape Cod.

managed to get down to the beach before it was closed off did not see much. Whales, dead or alive, are protected these days under the Federal Marine Mammals Act, and shortly after we arrived, local police kept anyone from actually touching the whale. I could hardly regret this, since in the past beached whales, still alive, have had cigarettes put out in their eyes and bits of flesh hacked off with pocket knives by souvenir seekers. And so, kept at a distance, we looked on while the specialists worked, white-coated, plastic-gloved autopsists from the New England Aquarium, hacking open the thick hide with carving knives and plumbing its depth for samples to be shipped to Canada for analysis and determination of causes of death. What was it they were pulling out? What fetid mystery would they pluck from that huge coffin of dead flesh? We would have to trust them for the answer.

But as the crowds continued to grow around the whale's body like flies around carrion, the question seemed to me, and still seems, not so much why did the whale die, as why had we come to see it? What made this dark bulk such a human magnet, spilling us over onto private lawns and fields? I watched electricians and oil truck drivers pulling their vehicles off the road and clambering down to the beach. Women in high heels and pearls, on their way to Filene's,[2] stumbled through the loose sand to gaze at a corpse. The normal human pattern was broken and a carnival atmosphere was created, appropriate enough in the literal sense of "a farewell to the flesh." But there was also a sense of pilgrimage in those trekking across the beach, an obligation to view such a thing. But for what? Are we really such novices to death? Or so reverent toward it?

I could understand my own semiprofessional interest in the whale, but what had drawn these hordes? There are some obvious answers, of course: a break in the dull routine, "something different." An old human desire to associate ourselves with great and extraordinary events. We placed children and sweethearts in front of the corpse and clicked cameras. "Ruthie and the whale." "Having a whale of a time on Cape Cod."

Curiosity, the simplest answer, doesn't really answer anything. What, after all, did we learn by being there? We were more like children at a zoo, pointing and poking, or Indians on a pristine beach, gazing in innocent wonder at strange European ships come ashore. Yet, as the biologists looted it with vials and plastic bags and the press captured it on film, the spectators also tried to make something of the whale. Circling around it as though for some hold on its slippery bulk, we grappled it with metaphors, lashed similes around its immense girth. It lay upside down, overturned "like a trailer truck." Its black skin was cracked and peeling, red underneath, "like a used tire." The distended, corrugated lower jaw, "a giant accordion," was afloat with the gas of putrefaction and, when

2. Department store in Boston.

pushed, oscillated slowly "like an enormous waterbed." Like our primitive ancestors, we still tend to make images to try to comprehend the unknown.

But what were we looking at? Or more to the point, from what perspective were we looking at it? What did we see in it that might tell us why we had come? A male finback whale—*Balaenoptera physalus*—a baleen cetacean. The second largest creature ever to live on earth. An intelligent and complex mammal. A cause for conservationists. A remarkably adapted swimming and eating machine. Perfume, pet food, engineering oil. A magnificent scientific specimen. A tourist attraction. A media event, a "day to remember." A health menace, a "possible carrier of a communicable disease." A municipal headache and a navigational hazard. Material for an essay.

On the whale's own hide seemed to be written its life history, which we could remark but not read. The right fluke was almost entirely gone, lost in some distant accident or battle and now healed over with a white scar. The red eye, unexpectedly small and mammalian, gazed out at us with fiery blankness. Like the glacial scratches sometimes found on our boulders, there were strange marks or grooves in the skin around the anal area, perhaps caused by scraping the ocean bottom.

Yet we could not seem to scratch its surface. The whale—dead, immobile, in full view—nonetheless shifted kaleidoscopically before our eyes. The following morning it was gone, efficiently and sanitarily removed, like the week's garbage. What was it we saw? I have a theory, though probably (as they say in New England) it hardly does.

There is a tendency these days to defend whales and other endangered animals by pointing out their similarities to human beings. Cetaceans, we are told, are very intelligent. They possess a highly complex language and have developed sophisticated communications systems that transmit over long distances. They form family groups, develop social structures and personal relationships, and express loyalty and affection toward one another. Much of their behavior seems to be recreational: they sing, they play. And so on.

These are not sentimental claims. Whales apparently do these things, at least as far as our sketchy information about their habits warrants such interpretations. And for my money, any argument that helps to preserve these magnificent creatures can't be all bad.

I take exception to this approach not because it is wrong, but because it is wrongheaded and misleading. It is exclusive, anthropocentric, and does not recognize nature in its own right. It implies that whales and other creatures have value only insofar as they reflect man himself and conform to his ideas of beauty and achievement. This attitude is not really far removed from that of the whalers themselves. To consume whales solely for their nourishment of human values is only a step from consuming

them for meat and corset staves. It is not only presumptuous and patron-
izing, but it is misleading and does both whales and men a grave disservice. Whales have an inalienable right to exist, not because they
resemble man or because they are useful to him, but simply because they
do exist, because they have a proven fitness to the exactitudes of being on
a global scale matched by few other species. If they deserve our admiration and respect, it is because, as Henry Beston put it, "They are other
nations, caught with ourselves in the net of life and time, fellow prisoners
of the splendour and travail of life."

But that still doesn't explain the throngs who came pell-mell to stare
and conjecture at the dead whale that washed up at Corporation Beach
and dominated it for a day like some extravagant *memento mori*. Surely
we were not flattering ourselves, consciously or unconsciously, with any
human comparisons to that rotting hulk. Nor was there much, in its
degenerate state, that it had to teach us. And yet we came—why?

The answer may be so obvious that we have ceased to recognize it.
Man, I believe, has a crying need to confront otherness in the universe.
Call it nature, wilderness, the "great outdoors," or what you will—we
crave to look out and behold something other than our own human faces
staring back at us, expectantly and increasingly frustrated. What the
human spirit wants, as Robert Frost said, "Is not its own love back in
copy-speech, / But counter-love, original reponse."

This sense of otherness is, I feel, as necessary a requirement to our
personalities as food and warmth are to our bodies. Just as an individual,
cut off from human contact and stimulation, may atrophy and die of
loneliness and neglect, so mankind is today in a similar, though more
subtle, danger of cutting himself off from the natural world he shares with
all creatures. If our physical survival depends upon our devising a proper
use of earth's materials and produce, our growth as a species depends
equally upon our establishing a vital and generative relationship with
what surrounds us.

We need plants, animals, weather, unfettered shores and unbroken
woodland, not merely for a stable and healthy environment, but as an
antidote to introversion, a preventive against human inbreeding. Here in
particular, in the splendor of natural life, we have an extraordinary
reservoir of the Cape's untapped possibilities and modes of being, ways
of experiencing life, of knowing wind and wave. After all, how many
neighborhoods have whales wash up in their backyards? To confine this
world in zoos or in exclusive human terms does injustice not only to
nature, but to ourselves as well.

Ever since his beginnings, when primitive man adopted totems and
animal spirits to himself and assumed their shapes in ritual dance, *Homo
sapiens* has been a superbly imitative animal. He has looked out across
the fields and seen and learned. Somewhere along the line, though, he

decided that nature was his enemy, not his ally, and needed to be confined and controlled. He abstracted nature and lost sight of it. Only now are we slowly realizing that nature can be confined only by narrowing our own concepts of it, which in turn narrows us. That is why we came to see the whale.

We substitute human myth for natural reality and wonder why we starve for nourishment. "Your Cape" becomes "your Mall," as the local radio jingle has it. Thoreau's "huge and real Cape Cod . . . a wild, rank place with no flattery in it," becomes the Chamber of Commerce's "Rural Seaside Charm"—until forty tons of dead flesh wash ashore and give the lie to such thin, flattering conceptions, flesh whose stench is still the stench of life that stirs us to reaction and response. That is why we came to see the whale. Its mute, immobile bulk represented that ultimate, unknowable otherness that we both seek and recoil from, and shouted at us louder than the policeman's bullhorn that the universe is fraught, not merely with response or indifference, but incarnate assertion.

Later that day the Dennis Board of Health declared the whale carcass to be a "health menace" and warned us off the beach. A health menace? More likely an intoxicating, if strong, medicine that might literally bring us to our senses.

But if those of us in the crowd failed to grasp the whale that day, others did not have much better luck. Even in death the whale escaped us: the tissue samples taken in the autopsy proved insufficient for analysis and the biologists concluded, "We will never know why the whale died." The carcass, being towed tail-first by a Coast Guard cutter for a final dumping beyond Provincetown, snapped a six-inch hawser. Eluding further attempts to reattach it, it finally sank from sight. Even our powers of disposal, it seemed, were questioned that day.

And so, while we are left on shore with the memory of a deflated and stinking carcass and of bullhorns that blared and scattered us like flies, somewhere out beyond the rolled waters and the shining winter sun, the whale sings its own death in matchless, sirenian strains.

1981

THE READER

1. What is Finch's basis for a whale's "inalienable right" to exist? Does the AIDS virus have the same right?
2. Why does the whale provide a confrontation with otherness (p. 325)? Presumably the trampled grass did not and a dead gull would not. Why?
3. Explain Finch's irony in the last two paragraphs. He spoke earlier (p. 323) of grappling the whale with metaphors. What is an example in the last paragraph? What is the relation between the irony and the metaphors?

THE WRITER

1. *Finch's strategy might be described as question-and-deferred-answer. Does deferring the answer help make confronting otherness a better answer than curiosity?*
2. *Find some places where Finch might seem condescending to the people who came to see the whale. What, if anything, does he do to check that condescension?*
3. *Rewrite the last paragraph without metaphors.*
4. *Write a paragraph explaining the difference referred to in "The Reader," question 2 (above).*

Barbara Garson

WHISTLE WHILE YOU WORK

At the Bumble Bee seafood plant in Oregon I talked to a tuna cleaner named Starlein. Her job was to pull the veins of dark meat (cat food) from the skinned white loins of tuna.

"The loins come past me on a moving belt," she explained. "I put the clean loins on the second belt and the cat food on the third belt and I save my bones." [The supervisor later checked her output by counting the bones.]

Do you talk a lot to the other women?" I asked.

"Not really," she answered.

"What do you do all day?"

"I daydream."

"What do you daydream about?"

"About sex."

At this point her boyfriend apologized proudly. "I guess that's my fault," he grinned.

"No it's not you," she said. "It's the tuna fish."

I wondered what she meant.

"Well first it's the smell. You've got that certain smell in your nose all day.... It's not like out here. [Starlein and I and the boyfriend were talking in the smelly cannery yard.] Your own fish next to you is sweet.... But it's mostly *handling* the loins. Not the touch itself, because we wear gloves. But the soft colors. The reds, the whites, and the purples. The most exciting thing is the dark meat. It comes in streaks. It's red-brown and you have to pull it out with your knife. You pile it next to your loin and it's crumbly and dark red and moist like earth.

"You're supposed to put the cat food on the belt as you finish each loin.

But I hold it to make as big a pile of dark meat as I can."

Starlein was new at the cannery then. The next time I met her the tuna cleaning process had lost some of its sensual allure.

"I still try to see how much cat food I can collect but it's just for the size of the pile now."

At a Ping-Pong factory in Rhode Island I talked to a girl whose job was to stack Ping-Pong paddles into piles of fifty.

"Maybe it wouldn't have been so bad if I could have seen all the piles I stacked at the end of the day. But they were taking them down as fast as I was piling them up. That was the worst part of the job."

At the same Ping-Pong plant a Haitian box assembler amused himself by doing the job with his eyes closed. He was very proud of the fact that if the foreman passed behind him he could not tell the difference.

Many assembly-line workers deliberately slow their pace from time to time and watch the pieces pile up. Sometimes this is for revenge against the company that "treats us like machines," "uses us like tools." More often it's just for a break, a chance to talk, kid around, take a drink of water. But the most common motive is one that I hadn't expected.

Young workers like to let the work pile up just so they can race to catch up with the line. This creates a few minutes of seemingly purposeful exertion. It makes hills and troughs, minor goals and fulfillments while you're waiting for the day to end or the line to break down.

I have spent the last two years examining the way people cope with routine and monotonous work. I expected to find resentment, and I found it. I expected to find boredom, and I found it. I expected to find sabotage, and I found it in clever forms that I could never have imagined.

But the most dramatic thing I found was quite the opposite of nonco-operation. *People passionately want to work.*

Whatever creativity goes into sabotage, a more amazing ingenuity goes into manufacturing goals and satisfactions on jobs where measurable achievement has been all but rationalized out. Somehow in an unending flow of parts or papers, with operations subdivided beyond any recognizable unit of accomplishment, people still find ways to define certain stacks of work as "theirs," certain piles as "today's" and "tomorrow's."

Almost everyone wants to feel she is getting something accomplished —to see that stack of paddles, the growing pile of dark meat, or to master the job blindfolded since there's not much to master the other way.

Which is not to say that workers don't also resent and resist the subdivision and trivialization of their jobs.

At the Fair Plan Insurance Company a young clerk named Ellen told me about a not quite so co-operative game.

"The other day when I was proofreading endorsements I noticed some guy had insured his store for $165,000 against vandalism and $5,000 against fire. Now that's bound to be a mistake. They probably got it backwards.

"I was just about to show it to Gloria [the supervisor] when I figured, 'Wait a minute! I'm not supposed to read these forms. I'm just supposed to check one column against another. And they do check. So it couldn't be counted as my error.'

"Then I thought about this poor guy when his store burns down and they tell him he's only covered for $5,000. But I figured the hell with it. It'll get straightened out one way or another."

I must have looked disapproving at that moment.

"Listen," she apologized, "for all I know he took out the insurance just to burn down the store himself." Then growing angry: "Goddamn it! They don't explain this stuff to me. I'm not supposed to understand it. I'm supposed to check one column against the other.

"If they're gonna give me a robot's job to do, I'm gonna do it like a robot."

I met a few more people who played that passive resistance game— "gonna be as dumb as they think I am." But not too many. And as a matter of fact, when I questioned further it turned out that Ellen had reported the error after all. For most people it is hard and uncomfortable to do a bad job.

At Lordstown, Ohio, General Motors runs the fastest assembly line in the world, manned by a work force whose average age is twenty-four. At 101 cars an hour, each young worker has thirty-six seconds to perform his assigned snaps, knocks, twists, or squirts on each passing vehicle.

I visited Lordstown the week before a strike amid union charges of speed-up, company charges of sabotage, and a great deal of national publicity about "the new worker," "the changing work ethic."

While a young Vega worker and his friends argued in the living room about the strike and disciplinary layoffs, I talked to his mother in the kitchen. Someone in the supermarket where she works had said that those young kids were "just lazy."

"One thing, Tony is not lazy. He'll take your car apart and put it together any day. . . . the slightest knock and he takes care of it. And he never will leave it half done. He even cleans up after himself.

"And I'm not lazy either. I love to cook. But supposing they gave me a job just cracking eggs with bowls moving past on a line. Pretty soon I'd get to a point where I'd wish the next egg was rotten just to spoil their whole cake."

Occasionally Lordstown workers toss in a rotten egg of their own by dropping an ignition key down the gas tank, lighting a work glove, locking it in the trunk, and waiting to see how far down the line it will be stopped, or just scratching a car as it goes past because you can't keep up with the pace.

But sabotage, though much publicized, is really quite limited. Much of the ingenuity at Lordstown goes into creating escape devices and games that can be squeezed into the thirty-six-second cycle.

No ingenuity at all goes into building cars.

I wasn't particularly surprised by the negative things I saw in factories: speed, heat, humiliation, monotony. I'm sure the reader will have guessed that I began this research prepared to expose and denounce "the system."

It was the positive things I saw that touched me the most. Not that people are beaten down (which they are) but that they almost always pop up. Not that people are bored (which they are) but the ways they find to make it interesting. Not that people hate their work (which they do) but that even so, they try to make something out of it.

In factories and offices around this country work is systematically reduced to the most minute and repetitious tasks. Supervision ranges from counting bones, raising hands to use the bathroom, issuing "report cards" with number and letter grades for quantity, quality, co-operation, dependability, attendance, etc.

Through all this workers make a constant effort, sometimes creative, sometimes pathetic, sometimes violent, to put meaning and dignity back into their daily acitivity.

I realize now, much more deeply than ever, that work is a human need following right after the need for food and the need for love.

The crime of modern industry is not forcing us to work, but denying us real work. For no matter what tricks people play on themselves to make the day's work meaningful, management seems determined to remind them, "You are just tools for our use."

* * *

1975

Desmond Morris

TERRITORIAL BEHAVIOR

A territory is a defended space. In the broadest sense, there are three kinds of human territory: tribal, family and personal.

It is rare for people to be driven to physical fighting in defense of these "owned" spaces, but fight they will, if pushed to the limit. The invading army encroaching on national territory, the gang moving into a rival district, the trespasser climbing into an orchard, the burglar breaking into a house, the bully pushing to the front of a queue, the driver trying to steal a parking space, all of these intruders are liable to be met with resistance varying from the vigorous to the savagely violent. Even if the law is on the side of the intruder, the urge to protect a territory may be so strong that otherwise peaceful citizens abandon all their usual controls and inhibitions. Attempts to evict families from their homes, no matter how socially valid the reasons, can lead to siege conditions reminiscent of the defense of a medieval fortress.

The fact that these upheavals are so rare is a measure of the success of Territorial Signals as a sytem of dispute prevention. It is sometimes cynically stated that "all property is theft," but in reality it is the opposite. Property, as owned space which is *displayed* as owned space, is a special kind of sharing system which reduces fighting much more than it causes it. Man is a co-operative species, but he is also competitive, and his struggle for dominance has to be structured in some way if chaos is to be avoided. The establishment of territorial rights is one such structure. It limits dominance geographically. I am dominant in my territory and you are dominant in yours. In other words, dominance is shared out spatially, and we all have some. Even if I am weak and unintelligent and you can dominate me when we meet on neutral ground, I can still enjoy a thoroughly dominant role as soon as I retreat to my private base. Be it ever so humble, there is no place like a home territory.

Of course, I can still be intimidated by a particularly dominant individual who enters my home base, but his encroachment will be dangerous for him and he will think twice about it, because he will know that here my urge to resist will be dramatically magnified and my usual subservience banished. Insulted at the heart of my own territory, I may easily explode into battle—either symbolic or real—with a result that may be damaging to both of us.

In order for this to work, each territory has to be plainly advertised as such. Just as a dog cocks its leg to deposit its personal scent on the trees in its locality, so the human animal cocks its leg symbolically all over his home base. But because we are predominantly visual animals we employ mostly visual signals, and it is worth asking how we do this at the three levels: tribal, family, and personal.

First: the Tribal Territory. We evolved as tribal animals, living in comparatively small groups, probably of less than a hundred, and we existed like that for millions of years. It is our basic social unit, a group in which everyone knows everyone else. Essentially, the tribal territory consisted of a home base surrounded by extended hunting grounds. Any neighboring tribe intruding on our social space would be repelled and driven away. As these early tribes swelled into agricultural supertribes, and eventually into industrial nations, their territorial defense systems became increasingly elaborate. The tiny, ancient home base of the hunting tribe became the great capital city, the primitive warpaint became the flags, emblems, uniforms, and regalia of the specialized military, and the war-chants became national anthems, marching songs, and bugle calls. Territorial boundary-lines hardened into fixed borders, often conspicuously patrolled and punctuated with defensive structures—forts and lookout posts, checkpoints and great walls, and, today, customs barriers.

Today each nation flies its own flag, a symbolic embodiment of its territorial status. But patriotism is not enough. The ancient tribal hunter lurking inside each citizen finds himself unsatisfied by membership in such a vast conglomeration of individuals, most of whom are totally unknown to him personally. He does his best to feel that he shares a common territorial defense with them all, but the scale of the operation has become inhuman. It is hard to feel a sense of belonging with a tribe of fifty million or more. His answer is to form sub-groups, nearer to his ancient pattern, smaller, and more personally known to him—the local club, the teenage gang, the union, the specialist society, the sports association, the political party, the college fraternity, the social clique, the protest group, ahd the rest. Rare indeed is the individual who does not belong to at least one of these splinter groups, and take from it a sense of tribal allegiance and brotherhood. Typical of all these groups is the development of Territorial Signals—badges, costumes, headquarters, banners, slogans, and all the other displays of group identity. This is where the action is, in terms of tribal territorialism, and only when a major war breaks out does the emphasis shift upwards to the higher group level of the nations.

Each of these modern pseudo-tribes sets up its own special kind of home base. In extreme cases non-members are totally excluded, in others they are allowed in as visitors with limited rights and under a control system of special rules. In many ways they are like miniature nations, with their own flags and emblems and their own border guards. The exclusive club has its own "customs barrier": the doorman who checks your "passport" (your membership card) and prevents strangers from passing in unchallenged. There is a government: the club committee; and often special displays of the tribal elders: the photographs or portraits of previous officials on the walls. At the heart of the specialized territories there is a powerful feeling of security and importance, a sense of shared defense against the outside world. Much of the club chatter, both serious and joking, directs itself against the rottenness of everything outside the club boundaries—in that "other world" beyond the protected portals.

In social organizations which embody a strong class system, such as military units and large business concerns, there are many territorial rules, often unspoken, which interfere with the official hierarchy. High-status individuals, such as officers or managers, could in theory enter any of the regions occupied by the lower levels in the peck order, but they limit this power in a striking way. An officer seldom enters a sergeant's mess or a barrack room unless it is for a formal inspection. He respects those regions as alien territories even though he has the power to go there by virtue of his dominant role. And in businesses, part of the appeal of unions, over and above their obvious functions, is that with their officials, headquarters, and meetings they add a sense of territorial power for the staff workers. It is almost as if each military organization and business concern consists of two warring tribes: the officers versus the other ranks, and the management versus the workers. Each has its special home base within the system, and the territorial defense pattern thrusts itself into what, on the surface, is a pure social hierarchy. Negotiations between managements and unions are tribal battles fought out over the neutral ground of a boardroom table, and are as much concerned with territorial display as they are with resolving problems of wages and conditions. Indeed, if one side gives in too quickly and accepts the other's demands, the victors feel strangely cheated and deeply suspicious that it may be a trick. What they are missing is the protracted sequence of ritual and counter-ritual that keeps alive their group territorial identity.

Likewise, many of the hostile displays of sports fans and teenage gangs are primarily concerned with displaying their group image to rival fan-clubs and gangs. Except in rare cases, they do not attack one another's headquarters, drive out the occupants, and reduce them to a submissive, subordinate condition. It is enough to have scuffles on the borderlands between the two rival territories. This is particularly clear at football matches, where the fan-club headquarters becomes temporarily shifted from the club-house to a section of the stands, and where minor fighting breaks out at the unofficial boundary line between the massed groups of rival supporters. Newspaper reports play up the few accidents and injuries which do occur on such occasions, but when these are studied in relation to the total numbers of displaying fans involved it is clear that the serious incidents represent only a tiny fraction of the overall group behavior. For every actual punch or kick there are a thousand war-cries, war dances, chants, and gestures.

Second: the Family Territory. Essentially, the family is a breeding unit and the family territory is a breeding ground. At the center of this space, there is the nest—the bedroom—where, tucked up in bed, we feel at our most territorially secure. In a typical house the bedroom is upstairs, where a safe nest should be. This puts it farther away from the entrance hall, the area where contact is made, intermittently, with the outside world. The less private reception rooms, where intruders are allowed access, are the next line of defense. Beyond them, outside the walls of the building, there is often a symbolic remnant of the ancient feeding grounds—a garden. Its symbolism often extends to the plants and animals it contains, which cease to be nutritional and become merely decorative—flowers and pets. But like a true territorial space it has a conspicuously displayed boundary-line, the garden fence, wall, or railings. Often no more than a token barrier, this is the outer territorial demarcation, separating the private world for the family from the public world beyond. To cross it puts any visitor or intruder at an immediate disadvantage. As he crosses the threshold, his dominance wanes, slightly but unmistakably. He is entering an area where he senses that he must ask permission to do simple things that he would consider a right elsewhere. Without lifting a finger, the territorial owners exert their dominance. This is done by all the hundreds of small ownership "markers" they have deposited on their family territory: the ornaments, the "possessed" objects positioned in the rooms and on the walls; the furnishings, the furniture, the colors, the patterns, all owner-chosen and all making this particular home base unique to them.

It is one of the tragedies of modern architecture that there has been a standardization of these vital territorial living units. One of the most important aspects of a home is that it should be similar to other homes only in a general way, and that in detail it should have many differences, making it a particular home. Unfortunately, it is cheaper to build a row of houses, or a block of flats, so that all the family living-units are identical, but the territorial urge rebels against this trend and house-owners struggle as best they can to make their mark on their mass-produced properties. They do this with garden-design, with front-door colors, with curtain patterns, with wallpaper and all the other decorative elements that together create a unique and different family environment. Only when they have completed this nest-building do they feel truly "at home" and secure.

When they venture forth as a family unit they repeat the process in a minor way. On a day-trip to the seaside, they load the car with personal belongings and it becomes their temporary, portable territory. Arriving at the beach they stake out a small territorial claim, marking it with rugs, towels, baskets, and other belongings to which they can return from their seaboard wanderings. Even if they all leave it at once to bathe, it retains a characteristic territorial quality and other family groups arriving will recognize this by setting up their own "home" bases at a respectful distance. Only when the whole beach has filled up with these marked spaces will newcomers start to position themselves in such a way that the inter-base distance becomes reduced. Forced to pitch between several existing beach territories they will feel a momentary sensation of intrusion, and the established "owners" will feel a similar sensation of invasion, even though they are not being directly inconvenienced.

The same territorial scene is being played out in parks and fields and on riverbanks, wherever family groups gather in their clustered units. But if rivalry for spaces creates mild feelings of hostility, it is true to say that, without the territorial system of sharing and space-limited dominance, there would be chaotic disorder.

Third: the Personal Space. If a man enters a waiting-room and sits at one end of a long row of empty chairs, it is possible to predict where the next man to enter will seat himself. He will not sit next to the first man, nor will he sit at the far end, right away from him. He will choose a position about halfway between these two points. The next man to enter will take the largest gap left, and sit roughly in the middle of that, and so on, until eventually the latest newcomer will be forced to select a seat that places him right next to one of the already seated men. Similar patterns can be observed in cinemas, public urinals, airplanes, trains, and buses. This is a reflection of the fact that we all carry with us, everywhere we go, a portable territory called a Personal Space. If people move inside this space, we feel threatened. If they keep too far outside it, we feel rejected. The result is a subtle series of spatial adjustments, usually operating quite unconsciously and producing ideal compromises as far as this is possible. If a situation becomes too crowded, then we adjust our reactions accordingly and allow our personal space to shrink. Jammed into an elevator, a rush-hour compartment, or a packed room, we give up altogether and allow body-to-body contact, but when we relinquish our Personal Space in this way, we adopt certain special techniques. In essence, what we do is to convert these other bodies into "nonpersons." We studiously ignore them, and they us. We try not to face them if we can possibly avoid it. We wipe all expressiveness from our faces, letting them go blank. We may look up at the ceiling or down at the floor, and we reduce body movements to a minimum. Packed together like sardines in a tin, we stand dumbly still, sending out as few social signals as possible.

Even if the crowding is less severe, we still tend to cut down our social interactions in the presence of large numbers. Careful observations of children in play groups revealed that if they are high-density groupings there is less social interaction between the individual children, even though there is theoretically more opportunity for such contacts. At the same time, the high-density groups show a higher frequency of aggressive and destructive behavior patterns in their play. Personal Space—"elbow room"—is a vital commodity for the human animal, and one that cannot be ignored without risking serious trouble.

Of course, we all enjoy the excitement of being in a crowd, and this reaction cannot be ignored. But there are crowds and crowds. It is pleasant enough to be in a "spectator crowd," but not so appealing to find yourself in the middle of a rush-hour crush. The difference between the two is that the spectator crowd is all facing in the same direction and concentrating on a distant point of interest. Attending a theater, there are twinges of rising hostility toward the stranger who sits down immediately in front of you or the one who squeezes into the seat next to you. The shared armrest can become a polite, but distinct, territorial boundary-dispute region. However, as soon as the show begins, these invasions of Personal Space are forgotten and the attention is focused beyond the small space where the crowding is taking place. Now, each member of the audience feels himself spatially related, not to his cramped neighbors, but to the actor on the stage, and this distance is, if anything, too great. In the rush-hour crowd, by contrast, each member of the pushing throng is competing with his neighbors all the time. There is no escape to a spatial relation with a distant actor, only the pushing, shoving bodies all around.

Those of us who have to spend a great deal of time in crowded conditions become gradually better able to adjust, but no one can ever become completely immune to invasions of Personal Space. This is because they remain forever associated with either powerful hostile or equally powerful loving feelings. All through our childhood we will have been held to be loved and held to be hurt, and anyone who invades our Personal Space when we are adults is, in effect, threatening to extend his behavior into one of these two highly charged areas of human interaction. Even if his motives are clearly neither hostile nor sexual, we still find it hard to suppress our reactions to his close approach. Unfortunately, different countries have different ideas about exactly how close is close. It is easy enough to test your own "space reaction": when you are talking to someone in the street or in any open space, reach out with your arm and see where the nearest point on his body comes. If you hail from western Europe, you will find that he is at roughly fingertip distance from you. In other words, as you reach out, your fingertips will just about make contact with his shoulder. If you come from eastern Europe you will find you are standing at "wrist distance." If you come from the Mediterranean region you will find that you are much closer to your companion, at little more than "elbow distance."

Trouble begins when a member of one of these cultures meets and talks to one from another. Say a British diplomat meets an Italian or an Arab diplomat at an embassy function. They start talking in a friendly way, but soon the fingertips man begins to feel uneasy. Without knowing quite why, he starts to back away gently from his companion. The companion edges forward again. Each tries in his way to set up a Personal Space relationship that suits his own background. But it is impossible to do. Every time the Mediterranean diplomat advances to a distance that feels comfortable for him, the British diplomat feels threatened. Every time the Briton moves back, the other feels rejected. Attempts to adjust this situation often lead to a talking pair shifting slowly across a room, and many an embassy reception is dotted with western-European fingertip-distance men pinned against the walls by eager elbow-distance men. Until such differences are fully understood and allowances made, these minor differences in "body territories" will continue to act as an alienation factor which may interfere in a subtle way with diplomatic harmony and other forms of international transaction.

If there are distance problems when engaged in conversation, then there are clearly going to be even bigger difficulties where people must work privately in a shared space. Close proximity of others, pressing against the invisible boundaries of our personal body-territory, makes it difficult to concentrate on nonsocial matters. Flat-mates, students sharing a study, sailors in the cramped quarters of a ship, and office staff in crowded work-places, all have to face this problem. They solve it by "cocooning." They use a variety of devices to shut themselves off from the others present. The best possible cocoon, of course, is a small private room—a den, a private office, a study, or a studio—which physically obscures the presence of other nearby territory-owners. This is the ideal situation for non-social work, but the space-sharers cannot enjoy this luxury. Their cocooning must be symbolic. They may, in certain cases, be able to erect small physical barriers, such as screens and partitions, which give substance to their invisible Personal Space boundaries, but when this cannot be done, other means must be sought. One of these is the "favored object." Each space-sharer develops a preference, repeatedly expressed until it becomes a fixed pattern, for a particular chair, or table, or alcove. Others come to respect this, and friction is reduced. This sytem is often formally arranged (this is my desk, that is yours), but even where it is not, favored places soon develop. Professor Smith has a favorite chair in the library. It is not formally his, but he always uses it and others avoid it. Seats around a mess-room table, or a boardroom table, become almost personal property for specific individuals. Even in the home, father has his favorite chair for reading the newspaper or watching television. Another device is the blinkers-posture. Just as a horse that over-reacts to other horses and the distractions of the noisy race-course is given a pair of blinkers to shield its eyes, so people studying privately in a public place put on pseudo-blinkers in the form of shielding hands. Resting their elbows on the table, they sit with their hands screening their eyes from the scene on either side.

A third method of reinforcing the body-territory is to use personal markers. Books, papers, and other personal belongings are scattered around the favored site to render it more privately owned in the eyes of companions. Spreading out one's belongings is a well-known trick in public-transport situations, where a traveler tries to give the impression that seats next to him are taken. In many contexts carefully arranged personal markers can act as an effective territorial display, even in the absence of the territory owner. Experiments in a library revealed that placing a pile of magazines on the table in one seating position successfully reserved that place for an average of 77 minutes. If a sports-jacket was added, draped over the chair, then the "reservation effect" lasted for over two hours.

In these ways, we strengthen the defenses of our Personal Spaces, keeping out intruders with the minimum of open hostility. As with all territorial behavior, the object is to defend space with signals rather than with fists and at all three levels—the tribal, the family, and the personal —it is a remarkably efficient system of space-sharing. It does not always seem so, because newspapers and newscasts inevitably magnify the exceptions and dwell on those cases where the signals have failed and wars have broken out, gangs have fought, neighboring families have feuded, or colleagues have clashed, but for every territorial signal that has failed, there are millions of others that have not. They do not rate a mention in the news, but they nevertheless constitute a dominant feature of human society—the society of a remarkably territorial animal.

1977

THE READER

1. *Morris predicts people's behavior when they are selecting seats (p. 335). Does observation confirm his prediction? Does the balancing of threat and rejection seem like a good explanation?*
2. *Is racism territorial?*
3. *Although he clearly recognizes that territorial behavior can lead to trouble, Morris speaks approvingly of it as "a remarkably efficient system of space-sharing." If you wanted to challenge his argument, where would you start—his definitions, his evidence, his conclusions?*

THE WRITER

1. *The essay is obviously organized to discuss territorial behavior on three levels. Does it progress from level to level? Is there any repetition? To what degree is each level an independent subessay?*
2. *Describe tribal subdivision in a large social unit like a high school or college. What are the Territorial Signals?*

Judith Viorst

GOOD AS GUILT

Without guilt
What is man? An animal, isn't he?
A wolf forgiven at his meat,
A beetle innocent in his copulation.

—Archibald MacLeish

Anything *isn't* possible, the realities of love and our bodies persuade us. We aren't unbounded, and never will be free of the limits imposed upon us by the forbidden and the impossible—including the limits imposed upon us by guilt.

For whether or not we humans are the only creatures capable of guilt, we undoubtedly do it better than beetles or wolves. And although our guilty feelings haven't put an end to the Seven Deadly Sins or persuaded us to obey all Ten Commandments, they have without question slowed us down considerably.

Nevertheless we must recognize that while guilt deprives us of numerous gratifications, we and our world would be monstrous minus guilt. For the freedoms we lose, our constraints and taboos, are necessary losses—part of the price we pay for civilization.

Our guilt becomes our own when, at around the age of five, we begin to develop a superego, a conscience, when the "No, you can'ts" and the "Shame on you's" which used to be outside us regroup as our internal critical voice. Our guilt becomes our own when instead of feeling, "Better not do it; they will not like it," that "they" is no longer our mother and father but—us.

For we do not arrive in this world with a commitment to certain admirable moral precepts. We are not born intending to be good. We want, we want, we want, and only slowly relinquish reaching out and grabbing. But control cannot be called conscience until we are able to take it inside us and make it out own, until—in spite of the fact that the wrongs we have done or imagined will never be punished or known—we nonetheless feel that clutch in the stomach, that chill upon the soul, that self-inflicted misery called guilt.

True guilt, it can be argued, is not the fear of our parents' wrath or the loss of their love. True guilt, it can be argued, is the fear of our conscience's wrath, the loss of *its* love.

We resolve our oedipal conflicts by acquiring a conscience which—like our parents—limits and restrains. Our conscience is our parents installed in our mind. Later identifications, with teachers and preachers, with friends, with superstars and heroes, will modify what we value and what we forbid. And the emergence, over the years, of increasingly complex cognitive skills, will ready the ground for more complex moral ideas. Indeed, it is now believed that the stages of our moral reasoning (psychologist Lawrence Kohlberg says there are six) parallel the development of our thinking processes. But although our conscience is based on emotion and thought, and although it evolves and changes over time, and although it is built upon feelings from earlier stages, and although it expands beyond oedipal issues to take in all kinds of conflicts and concerns, this superego, this part of our self that contains our moral restraints and our ideals, is born of our primal struggles with lawless passions, is born of our *inner* submission to human law.

And if we breach those moral restraints or abandon those ideals, our conscience will observe, reproach, condemn.

And if we breach those moral restraints or abandon those ideals, our conscience will arrange to make us feel guilty.

There is, however, good and bad, appropriate and inappropriate guilt. There is deficient guilt and also excessive guilt. A few of us may know people who lack the capacity to have feelings of guilt about anything. But most of us know people (and a number of us *are* people) who are able to muster up guilt about virtually everything.

I am one of those people.

I feel guilty whenever my children are unhappy.

I feel guilty whenever one of my houseplants dies.

I feel guilty whenever I fail to floss after eating.

I feel guilty whenever I tell the whitest of lies.

I feel guilty whenever I step on a bug deliberately—all cockroaches excepted.

I feel guilty whenever I cook with a pat of butter that I have dropped on the kitchen floor.

And because, if there were room, I could easily list several hundred more of such genuinely guilt-provoking items, I would say that I am suffering from an excessive, indiscriminate sense of guilt.

Indiscriminate guilt is also the failure to distinguish between forbidden thoughts and forbidden deeds. Thus wicked wishes equal wicked acts. And although we adults believe that we have long ago learned to tell the two apart, our conscience may cruelly condemn us not just for the murder we carry out but for the murder that we harbor in our heart. And although we very well know that wishing does not make it so, it nevertheless may make us feel very guilty.

This lack of discrimination is one of the ways that we display excessive guilt. Disproportionate punitiveness is another. For guilty acts which require no more than a gentle "I'm sorry," a mental slap on the wrist, may inspire astonishing acts of self-flagellation: "I did it, how could I do it, only a low-down no-good moral monster could do it, and I hereby sentence this criminal—me—to death." This excessive punishing guilt is somewhat like pouring a whole cup of salt on an egg-salad sandwich. No one is disputing that perhaps the sandwich needs salt but—*not that much.*

Another form of excess might be called omnipotent guilt, which rests on the illusion of control—the illusion, for example, that we have absolute power over our loved ones' well-being. And so, if they suffer or fail or fall ill in body or in mind, we have no doubt that we alone are to blame, that had we done it differently, or had we done it better, we surely would have been able to prevent it.

A rabbi, for instance, tells of paying condolence calls—one winter afternoon—on two different families where elderly women had died.

At the first house, the bereaved son told the rabbi: "If only I had sent my mother to Florida and gotten her out of this cold and snow, she would be alive today. It's my fault that she died."

At the second house, the other bereaved son told the rabbi: "If only I hadn't insisted on my mother's going to Florida, she would be alive today. That long airplane ride, the abrupt change of climate, was more than she could take. It's my fault that she's dead."

The point here is this: By blaming ourself, we can believe in our life-controlling powers. By blaming ourself, we are saying that we would rather feel guilty than helpless, than not in control.

Others may have a need to believe that Someone Up There has control, that terrible things do not happen without a cause, that if they are struck by tragedy and devastating loss, they are struck because in some way they deserve it. There are those who cannot accept the thought that suffering is random or that evil men prosper and sorrows befall the good. And so they add to their suffering the conviction that they suffer because they should, that their pain is sufficient proof that they are guilty.

A woman whose child had been desperately ill once described to me an astonishing conversation she'd had with God, a God in whom, by the way, she had most earnestly proclaimed she did not believe. "You ought to be ashamed of yourself. You really should," she reproached Him. "What a bully you turned out to be. If you want to punish a disbeliever, punish the disbeliever—not her child. Stop picking on my daughter! Pick on me!"

Analyst Selma Fraiberg writes that a healthy conscience produces guilt feelings commensurate with the act and that guilt feelings serve to prevent our repeating such acts. "But the neurotic conscience," she writes, "behaves like a gestapo[1] headquarters within the personality, mercilessly tracking down dangerous or potentially dangerous ideas and every remote relative of these ideas, accusing, threatening, tormenting in an interminable inquisition to establish guilt for trivial offenses or crimes committed in dreams. Such guilt feelings have the effect of putting the whole personality under arrest. . . . "

Such feelings are excessive, neurotic guilt.

Neurotic guilt may be fed by the events of pre-oedipal years—by the anxiety and anger evoked by early separations or struggles with parents. Thus, for instance, our conscience may exercise an I-was-left-because-I-was-bad-and-therefore-I-deserve-to-be-punished punitiveness. Or it may harshly condemn the parts of ourself that our parents—whose love we so deeply feared losing—condemned. Or it may carry a great load of anger once directed against our mother and our father and now vigorously redirected against ourself. As one psychoanalyst told me, "I think, in general, that anything that leaves the child on his own to grapple with anxiety and rage will predispose him to play it all out on a repetitive inner stage—to get stuck with inappropriate levels and kinds of guilt as an adult."

Such guilt may make us feel that if we ever kiss a fellow, we'll grow hair on our teeth. And if we ever talk back to our mother, we'll give her a heart attack. And if we decide to do what we are desperately longing to do—and it is wonderful—we shouldn't be doing it.

And sometimes, alas, like Dr. Spielvogel's frantic, fictional patient Alexander Portnoy[2]—we *cannot* do it:

> Can't smoke, hardly drink, no drugs, don't borrow money or play cards, can't tell a lie without beginning to sweat as though I'm passing over the equator. Sure, I say *fuck* a lot, but I assure you, that's about the sum of my success with transgressing. . . . Why is a little turbulence so beyond my means? Why must the least deviation from respectable conventions cause me such inner hell? When I *hate* those fucking conventions? When I know *better* than the taboos! Doctor, my doctor, what do you say, LET'S PUT THE ID BACK IN YID! Liberate this nice Jewish boy's libido, will you please? Raise the prices if you have to—I'll pay anything! Only enough cowering in the face of the deep, dark pleasures!

Not everyone is as acutely aware as Portnoy, or his creator, Philip Roth, of the moral inhibitions with which we live. We may consciously feel we are freer than we are. For an important aspect of guilt is that it frequently works upon us without our knowing about it, that we can suffer the consequences of unconscious guilt.

Now we know what our conscious guilt feels like—we know the

1. Secret state police from 1933 of the Nazi regime in Germany. 2. Protagonist of Philip Roth's novel *Portnoy's Complaint*.

tension and the distress—but our unconscious guilt can only be known indirectly. And among the signs that may attest to the presence of unconscious guilt is a powerful need to injure ourself, a persistent need to get or to give ourself punishment.

Criminals leaving self-damaging clues (including Nixon, perhaps, and his Watergate tapes) are very often impelled by unconscious guilt. And so is the husband who, having spent the afternoon with a friend, comes home with her watch in the pocket of his shirt. And so is Dick who, having had a bitter fight with his father, smashes up his Chevy and gets himself hurt. And so is Rita who, watching her boss raise hell with his secretary, fleetingly thinks, "I'm glad it's her, not me"—and then promptly pays for her thought by accidentally spilling hot tea all over her lap.

And so are these erstwhile lovers, Ellie and Marvin.

> Ellie and Marvin
> Have been having secret meetings twice a week
> For the past six months
> But have thus far failed to consummate
> Their passion
> Because
> While both of them agree
> That marital fidelity
> Is not only unrealistic but also
> Irrelevant,
> She has developed migraines, and
> He has developed these sharp shooting pains
> In his chest, and
> She's got impetigo, and
> He's got pinkeye.

> Ellie and Marvin
> Drive forty miles to sneaky luncheonettes
> In separate cars
> But have thus far done no more than
> Heavy necking
> Because
> While both of them agree
> That sexual exclusivity
> Is not only adolescent but also
> Retrograde,
> She has developed colitis, and
> He has developed these dull throbbing pains
> In his back, and
> She's started biting her nails, and
> He's smoking again.

Ellie and Marvin
Yearn to have some love in the afternoon
At a motor hotel
But have thus far only had a lot of
Coffee
Because
He is convinced that his phone is being tapped, and
She is convinced that a man in a trench coat is following her, and
He says what if the motor hotel catches fire, and
She says what if she talks some night in her sleep, and
She thinks her husband is acting suspiciously hostile, and
He thinks his wife is acting suspiciously nice, and
He keeps cutting his face with his double-edge razor, and
She keeps closing her hand in the door of her car, so
While both of them agree
That guilt is not only neurotic but also
Obsolete,
They've also agreed
To give up
Secret meetings.

Unconscious guilt, however, may extract much higher prices than colitis, migraines, backaches or mild paranoia. It may insist on a lifetime of penance and pain. And this guilt may derive from any act or omission, from any thought, that our conscience in its infinite wisdom deems wicked. Thus our mother's ill health, our parents' divorce, our secret envies and hates, our solitary sexual gratifications—any and all can become our blame and our shame. And if the new brother or sister we didn't want and wish wish wish would disappear does in fact—by illness or accident—die, we may hold ourself responsible, we—not knowing we think it—might think: "Why did I kill him? Why didn't I save him? Why?"

And our lives may crash on the rocks of our unconscious guilt.

It was Freud who first observed that analysts sometimes work with patients who ferociously resist relief from their symptoms, who seem to hold on for dear life to emotional pain, and who cling to this pain because it gives them the punishment that they don't even know they want for crimes they don't even know that they have committed. He notes ruefully, however, that a neurosis which has defied an analyst's best efforts may suddenly vanish if the patient gets into an unhappy marriage, loses all his money or becomes dangerously ill. "In such instances," writes Freud, "one form of suffering has been replaced by another; and we see that all that mattered was that it should be possible to maintain a certain amount of suffering."

But sometimes people are guilty and people should suffer, including people like you and people like me. Sometimes guilt is appropriate and good. Not all guilt is neurotic—to be cured, to be analyzed away. We would be moral monsters if it could. But some of us exhibit certain deficiencies in our capacity for guilt.

I have a friend named Elizabeth who cannot acknowledge guilt because, in her mind, the guilty are shot at dawn. She has to be perfect, sinless, error-free. And so she will say, "The car was smacked up," because she would choke on the words "I smacked up the car." And she also will say, "His feelings got hurt," because she cannot accept that she hurt his feelings. At best she can say, "We forgot to buy tickets and now they're all sold out," when she was the only "we" in charge of tickets. And as for certain more drastic acts—she once had a love affair with her husband's best friend—she managed to persuade both herself and her husband that she was guiltless because he had driven her to it!

Elizabeth is quite capable of telling right from wrong. She is, however, incapable of believing that she could experience guilt—and survive.

Another kind of deficient guilt is displayed by people who punish themselves after they have committed some dreadful act, but who then go on to commit these dreadful acts again and again, again and again. For although their conscience acknowledges that what they did was wrong, and exacts quite brutal payments for their sins, their guilt never functions for them as a warning signal. It serves them only to punish, not to prevent.

It is known that certain criminals are actually seeking punishment in order to expiate unconscious guilt. It is known that certain criminals are suffering from distorted, not absent, guilt feelings. There are, however, the so-called psychopathic personalities who seem to display a genuine lack of guilt, whose antisocial and criminal acts, whose repetitive acts of destructiveness and depravity, occur with no restraint and no remorse. These psychopaths cheat and rob and lie and damage and destroy with remarkable emotional impunity. These psychopaths spell out for us, in letters ten feet high, what kind of world this world would be without guilt.

But we don't have to be a psychopath to allow some person or group to stand in the place of our individual conscience. And yet this too can lead to deficient guilt. For when we relinquish to others our sense of moral responsibility, we may become free of central moral constraints. This giving over of conscience can turn ordinary people into lynch mobs and operators of crematoria. And it may enable any of us to act in certain ways which on our own we would surely regard as unthinkable.

In a famous experiment testing conscience versus obedience to authority, experimental psychologist Stanley Milgram brought people into a Yale University psychology laboratory to engage—or so they were told—in a study of memory and learning. The experimenter explained that the issue to be explored was the impact of punishment on learning, and to that end the subject designated "teacher" was asked to administer a learning test to a "learner" strapped in a chair in another room—and to give him an electric shock whenever his answer was wrong. The shocks were executed by a series of thirty switches which ranged from slight (15 volts) to severe (450 volts), and the teacher was told that, with each wrong answer, he was to give the learner the next higher shock. Conflict began when the learner went from grunts to vehement protests to agonized screams, and the teacher became increasingly uneasy and wished to stop. But each time he hesitated, the person in authority urged him to continue, insisting that he must complete the experiment. And despite the concern for the level of shocking pain that was being inflicted, a large number of teachers continued to push the switches all the way up to the highest voltage.

The teachers did not know that the learners were actors, and that they were only simulating distress. The teachers believed that the shocks were painfully real. But some of them persuaded themselves that what they were doing was for a noble cause—the pursuit of truth. And some of them persuaded themselves that "He was so stupid and stubborn he deserved to get shocked." And some of them were simply unable, despite their conviction that what they were doing was wrong, to make an open break with the person running the experiment—to challenge authority.

Milgram notes that a "commonly offered explanation is that those who shocked the victim at the most severe level were monsters, the sadistic fringe of society. But if one considers that almost two-thirds of the participants fall into the category of 'obedient' subjects and that they represented ordinary people drawn from working, managerial and professional classes, the argument becomes very shaky."

It is tempting to read about that experiment and imagine ourselves walking out the door, able to know right from wrong and to act on that knowledge. It is tempting to think that our conscience would prevail. It is tempting to think that put to the test, we would be counted among the morally pure. And some of us would be. And some of us would fail. But all of us, in the course of our life, will engage in acts we know to be morally wrong. And when we do, the healthy response is guilt.

Healthy guilt is appropriate—in quantity and quality—to the deed. Healthy guilt leads to remorse but not self-hate. Healthy guilt discourages us from repeating our guilty act without shutting down a wide range of our passions and pleasures.

We need to be able to know when what we are doing is morally wrong.

We need to be able to know and acknowledge our guilt.

The philosopher Martin Buber, respectful of this need, tells us that "there exists real guilt," that there is value in the "paining and admonishing heart" and that reparation, reconciliation, renewal require a conscience "that does not shy away from the glance into the depths and that already in admonishing envisages the way that leads across it. . . .

"Man," says Buber, "is the being who is capable of becoming guilty and is capable of illuminating his guilt."

We seem to be more familiar with the prohibiting parts of our conscience, the parts that limit our pleasures and water our joys, the parts that are always watching us to judge, condemn and mobilize our guilt. But our conscience also contains our ego ideal—our values and higher aspirations, the parts that speak to our "oughts" instead of our "don'ts." And another task of our conscience is to say in effect, "Good for you" and "You did well," to encourage us and approve of us and praise and reward and love us for meeting, or striving to meet, this ego ideal.

Our ego ideal is composed of our most wishful, hopeful visions of our self. Our ego ideal is composed of our noblest goals. And while it is an impossible dream that can never be fulfilled, our reachings toward it provide a deep sense of well-being. Our ego ideal is precious to us because it repairs a loss of our earlier childhood, the loss of our image of self as perfect and whole, the loss of a major portion of our infantile, limitless, ain't-I-wonderful narcissism which we had to give up in the face of compelling reality. Modified and reshaped into ethical goals and moral standards and a vision of what at our finest we might be, our dream of perfection lives on—our lost narcissism lives on—in our ego ideal.

It is true that we will feel guilt when we fall short of our ego ideal or when we override our moral restraints. It is true that guilt will make us less happy, less free. If we could believe in "anything goes," we could go merrily—guiltlessly—on our way. But without ideals and restraints, what would we be? A wolf forgiven at his meat. A beetle innocent in his copulation. Something beyond the bounds of humanity.

We cannot be full human beings without the loss of some of our anything-goes moral freedom.

We cannot be full human beings without acquiring a capacity for guilt.

1986

THE READER

1. Viorst describes what she calls a tempting way to react to accounts of the Milgram experiment (p. 345). Do you react that way? She follows that with a "But . . ." sentence. What were the signals that such a sentence was coming? Is it logically satisfying?

2. Are there any signs in Viorst's essay that she is a psychoanalyst?

THE WRITER

1. What is Viorst's basic point? How is it served by her initial stress on guilt that is excessive?

2. Write a paragraph on guilt from another professional or personal point of view—for example, a coach, a policeman, a student.

Lewis Thomas

THE LONG HABIT

We continue to share with our remotest ancestors the most tangled and evasive attitudes about death, despite the great distance we have come to understanding some of the profound aspects of biology. We have as much distaste for talking about personal death as for thinking about it; it is an indelicacy, like talking in mixed company about venereal disease or abortion in the old days. Death on a grand scale does not bother us in the same special way: we can sit around a dinner table and discuss war, involving 60 million volatilized human deaths, as though we were talking about bad weather; we can watch abrupt bloody death every day, in color, on films and television, without blinking back a tear. It is when the numbers of dead are very small, and very close, that we begin to think in scurrying circles. At the very center of the problem is the naked cold deadness of one's own self, the only reality in nature of which we can have absolute certainty, and it is unmentionable, unthinkable. We may be even less willing to face the issue at first hand than our predecessors because of a secret new hope that maybe it will go away. We like to think, hiding the thought, that with all the marvelous ways in which we seem now to lead nature around by the nose, perhaps we can avoid the central problem if we just become, next year, say, a bit smarter.

"The long habit of living," said Thomas Browne, "indisposeth us to dying." These days, the habit has become an addiction: we are hooked on living, the tenacity of its grip on us, and ours on it, grows in intensity. We cannot think of giving it up, even when living loses its zest—even when we have lost the zest for zest.

We have come a long way in our technologic capacity to put death off, and it is imaginable that we might learn to stall it for even longer periods, perhaps matching the life-spans of the Abkhasian Russians, who are said to go on, springily, for a century and a half. If we can rid ourselves of some of our chronic, degenerative diseases, and cancer, strokes and coronaries, we might go on and on. It sounds attractive and reasonable, but it is no certainty. If we became free of disease, we would make a much better run of it for the last decade or so, but might still terminate on about the same schedule as now. We may be like the genetically different lines of mice, or like Hayflick's different tissue-culture lines, programmed to die after a predetermined number of days clocked by their genomes. If this is the way it is, some of us will continue to wear out and come unhinged in the sixth decade, and some much later, depending on genetic timetables.

If we ever do achieve freedom from most of today's diseases, or even complete freedom from disease, we will perhaps terminate by drying out and blowing away on a light breeze, but we will still die.

Most of my friends do not like this way of looking at it. They prefer to take it for granted that we only die because we get sick, with one lethal ailment or another, and if we did not have our diseases we might go on indefinitely. Even biologists choose to think this about themselves, despite the evidences of the absolute inevitability of death that surround their professional lives. Everything dies, all around, trees, plankton, lichens, mice, whales, flies, mitochondria. In the simplest creatures it is sometimes difficult to see it as death, since the strands of replicating DNA they leave behind are more conspicuously the living parts of themselves than with us (not that it is fundamentally any different, but it seems so). Flies do not develop a ward round[1] of diseases that carry them off, one by one. They simply age, and die, like flies.

We hanker to go on, even in the face of plain evidence that long, long lives are not necessarily pleasurable in the kind of society we have arranged thus far. We will be lucky if we can postpone the search for new technologies for a while, until we have discovered some satisfactory things to do with the extra time. Something will surely have to be found to take the place of sitting on the porch reexamining one's watch.

Perhaps we would not be so anxious to prolong life if we did not detest so much the sickness of withdrawal. It is astonishing how little information we have about this universal process, with all the other dazzling advances in biology. It is almost as though we wanted not to know about it. Even if we could imagine the act of death in isolation, without any preliminary stage of being struck down by disease, we would be fearful of it.

There are signs that medicine may be taking a new interest in the process, partly from interest, partly from an embarrassed realization that we have not been handling this aspect of disease with as much skill as physicians once displayed, back in the days before they became convinced that disease was their solitary and sometimes defeatable enemy. It used to be the hardest and most important of all the services of a good doctor to be on hand at the time of death, and to provide comfort, usually in the home. Now it is done in hospitals, in secrecy (one of the reasons for the increased fear of death these days may be that so many people are totally unfamiliar with it; they never actually see it happen in real life). Some of our technology permits us to deny its existence, and we maintain

1. That is, the variety of ailments a doctor sees during his circuit among the patients in a hospital ward.

flickers of life for long stretches in one community of cells or another, as though we were keeping a flag flying. Death is not a sudden all-at-once affair; cells go down in sequence, one by one. You can, if you like, recover great numbers of them many hours after the lights have gone out, and grow them out in cultures. It takes hours, even days, before the irreversible word finally gets around to all the provinces.

We may be about to rediscover that dying is not such a bad thing to do after all. Sir William Osler took this view; he disapproved of people who spoke of the agony of death, maintaining that there was no such thing.

In a 19th-century memoir about an expedition in Africa, there is a story about an explorer who was caught by a lion, crushed across the chest in the animal's great jaws, and saved in the instant by a lucky shot from a friend. Later, he remembered the episode in clear detail. He was so amazed by the extraordinary sense of peace and calm, and total painlessness, associated with his partial experience of being killed, that he constructed a theory that all creatures are provided with a protective physiologic mechanism, switched on at the verge of death, carrying them through in a haze of tranquility.

I have seen agony in death only once, in a patient with rabies, who remained acutely aware of every stage in the process of his own disintegration over a 24-hour period, right up to his final moment. It was as though, in the special neuropathology of rabies, the switch had been prevented from turning.

We will be having new opportunities to learn more about the physiology of death at first hand, from the increasing numbers of cardiac patients who have been through the whole process and then back again. Judging from what has been found out thus far, from the first generation of people resuscitated from cardiac standstill (already termed the Lazarus syndrome), Osler seems to have been right. Those who remember parts or all of their episodes do not recall any fear, or anguish. Several people who remained conscious throughout, while appearing to have been quite dead, could only describe a remarkable sensation of detachment. One man underwent coronary occlusion with cessation of the heart and dropped for all practical purposes dead in front of a hospital, and within a few minutes his heart had been restarted by electrodes and he breathed his way back into life. According to his account, the strangest thing was that there were so many people around him, moving so urgently, handling his body with such excitement, while all his awareness was of quietude.

In a recent study of the reaction to dying in patients with obstructive disease of the lungs, it was concluded that the process was considerably more shattering for the professional observers than the observed. Most of the patients appeared to be preparing themselves with equanimity for death, as though intuitively familiar with the business. One elderly woman reported that the only painful and distressing part of the process was in being interrupted; on several occasions she was provided with conventional therapeutic measures to maintain oxygenation or restore fluids and electrolytes, and each time she found the experience of coming back harrowing, she deeply resented the interference with her dying.

I find myself surprised by the thought that dying is an all-right thing to do, but perhaps it should not surprise. It is, after all, the most ancient and fundamental of biologic functions, with its mechanisms worked out with the same attention to detail, the same provision for the advantage of the organism, the same abundance of genetic information for guidance through the stages, that we have long since become accustomed to finding in all the crucial acts of living.

Very well. But even so, if the transformation is a co-ordinated, integrated physiologic process in its initial, local stages, there is still that permanent vanishing of consciousness to be accounted for. Are we to be stuck forever with this problem? Where on earth does it go? Is it simply stopped dead in its tracks, lost in humus, wasted? Considering the tendency of nature to find uses for complex and intricate mechanisms, this seems to me unnatural. I prefer to think of it as somehow separated off at the filaments of its attachment, and then drawn like an easy breath back into the membrane of its origin, a fresh memory for a biospherical nervous system, but I have no data on the matter.

This is for another science, another day. It may turn out, as some scientists suggest, that we are forever precluded from investigating consciousness, by a sort of indeterminacy principle that stipulates that the very act of looking will make it twitch and blur out of sight. It this is true, we will never learn. I envy some of my friends who are convinced about telepathy; oddly enough, it is my European scientist acquaintances who believe it most freely and take it most lightly. All their aunts have received Communications, and there they sit, with proof of the motility of consciousness at their fingertips, and the making of a new science. It is discouraging to have had the wrong aunts, and never the ghost of a message.

1973

THE READER

1. "They simply age, and die, like flies" (p. 349). What makes this sentence, which concludes the opening section of this brief essay, effective? What does Thomas establish in this opening section? What does he consider in the next section, which constitutes the bulk of his essay? What is the logic that connects the two, and what is the basic assumption underlying the second section?
2. What does this essay have in common with Thomas's "On Magic in Medicine" (p. 370)? Is Thomas ever "unscientific"? Can you infer

from these two essays his estimate of science—what it can do and what it can't do?

Elisabeth Kübler-Ross

ON THE FEAR OF DEATH

Let me not pray to be sheltered from
dangers but to be fearless in facing
them.
  Let me not beg for the stilling of
my pain but for the heart to conquer it.
  Let me not look for allies in life's
battlefield but to my own strength.
  Let me not crave in anxious fear to
be saved but hope for the patience to
win my freedom.
  Grant me that I may not be a
coward, feeling your mercy in my
success alone; but let me find the grasp
of your hand in my failure.

RABINDRANATH TAGORE,
Fruit-Gathering

Epidemics have taken a great toll of lives in past generations. Death in infancy and early childhood was frequent and there were few families who didn't lose a member of the family at an early age. Medicine has changed greatly in the last decades. Widespread vaccinations have practically eradicated many illnesses, at least in western Europe and the United States. The use of chemotherapy, especially the antibiotics, has contributed to an ever decreasing number of fatalities in infectious diseases. Better child care and education has effected a low morbidity and mortality among children. The many diseases that have taken an impressive toll among the young and middle-aged have been conquered. The number of old people is on the rise, and with this fact come the number of people with malignancies and chronic diseases associated more with old age.

Pediatricians have less work with acute and life-threatening situations as they have an ever increasing number of patients with psychosomatic disturbances and adjustment and behavior problems. Physicians have more people in their waiting rooms with emotional problems than they have ever had before, but they also have more elderly patients who not only try to live with their decreased physical abilities and limitations but who also face loneliness and isolation with all its pains and anguish. The majority of these people are not seen by a psychiatrist. Their needs have to be elicited and gratified by other professional people, for instance, chaplains and social workers. It is for them that I am trying to outline the changes that have taken place in the last few decades, changes that are ultimately responsible for the increased fear of death, the rising number of emotional problems, and the greater need for understanding of and coping with the problems of death and dying.

When we look back in time and study old cultures and people, we are impressed that death has always been distasteful to man and will probably always be. From a psychiatrist's point of view this is very understandable and can perhaps best be explained by our basic knowledge that, in our unconscious, death is never possible in regard to ourselves. It is inconceivable for our unconscious to imagine an actual ending of our own life here on earth, and if this life of ours has to end, the ending is always attributed to a malicious intervention from the outside by someone else. In simple terms, in our unconscious mind we can only be killed; it is inconceivable to die of a natural cause or of old age. Therefore death in itself is associated with a bad act, a frightening happening, something that in itself calls for retribution and punishment.

One is wise to remember these fundamental facts as they are essential in understanding some of the most important, otherwise unintelligible communications of our patients.

The second fact that we have to comprehend is that in our unconscious mind we cannot distinguish between a wish and a deed. We are all aware of some of our illogical dreams in which two completely opposite statements can exist side by side—very acceptable in our dreams but unthinkable and illogical in our wakening state. Just as our unconscious mind cannot differentiate betwee the wish to kill somebody in anger and the act of having done so, the young child is unable to make this distinction. The child who angrily wishes his mother to drop dead for not having gratified his needs will be traumatized greatly by the actual death of his mother—even if this event is not linked closely in time with his destructive wishes. He will always take part or the whole blame for the loss of his mother. He will always say to himself—rarely to others—"I did it, I am responsible, I was bad, therefore Mommy left me." It is well to remember that the child will react in the same manner if he loses a parent by divorce, separation, or desertion. Death is often seen by a child as an impermanent thing and has therefore little distinction from a divorce in which he may have an opportunity to see a parent again.

Many a parent will remember remarks of their children such as, "I will bury my doggy now and next spring when the flowers come up again, he will get up." Maybe it was the same wish that motivated the ancient Egyptians to supply their dead with food and goods to keep them happy and the old American Indians to bury their relatives with their belongings.

When we grow older and begin to realize that our omnipotence is really not so omnipotent, that our strongest wishes are not powerful enough to make the impossible possible, the fear that we have contributed to the death of a loved one diminishes—and with it the guilt. The fear remains diminished, however, only so long as it is not challenged too strongly. Its vestiges can be seen daily in hospital corridors and in people associated with the bereaved.

A husband and wife may have been fighting for years, but when the partner dies, the survivor will pull his hair, whine and cry louder and beat his chest in regret, fear and anguish, and will hence fear his own death more than before, still believing in the law of talion—an eye for an eye, a tooth for a tooth—"I am responsible for her death, I will have to die a pitiful death in retribution."

Maybe this knowledge will help us understand many of the old customs and rituals which have lasted over the centuries and whose purpose is to diminish the anger of the gods or the people as the case may be, thus decreasing the anticipated punishment. I am thinking of the ashes, the torn clothes, the veil, the *Klage Weiber*[1] of the old days—they are all means to ask you to take pity on them, the mourners, and are expressions of sorrow, grief, and shame. If someone grieves, beats his chest, tears his hair, or refuses to eat, it is an attempt at self-punishment to avoid or reduce the anticipated punishment for the blame that he takes on the death of a loved one.

This grief, shame, and guilt are not very far removed from feelings of anger and rage. The process of grief always includes some qualities of anger. Since none of us likes to admit anger at a deceased person, these emotions are often disguised or repressed and prolong the period of grief or show up in other ways. It is well to remember that it is not up to us to judge such feelings as bad or shameful but to understand their true meaning and origin as something very human. In order to illustrate this I will again use the example of the child—and the child in us. The five-year-old who loses his mother is both blaming himself for her disappear-

1. Wailing wives.

ance and being angry at her for having deserted him and for no longer gratifying his needs. The dead person then turns into something the child loves and wants very much but also hates with equal intensity for this severe deprivation.

The ancient Hebrews regarded the body of a dead person as something unclean and not to be touched. The early American Indians talked about the evil spirits and shot arrows in the air to drive the spirits away. Many other cultures have rituals to take care of the "bad" dead person, and they all originate in this feeling of anger which still exists in all of us, though we dislike admitting it. The tradition of the tombstone may originate in this wish to keep the bad spirits deep down in the ground, and the pebbles that many mourners put on the grave are left-over symbols of the same wish. Though we call the firing of guns at military funerals a last salute, it is the same symbolic ritual as the Indian used when he shot his spears and arrows into the skies.

I give these examples to emphasize that man has not basically changed. Death is still a fearful, frightening happening, and the fear of death is a universal fear even if we think we have mastered it on many levels.

What has changed is our way of coping and dealing with death and dying and our dying patients.

Having been raised in a country in Europe where science is not so advanced, where modern techniques have just started to find their way into medicine, and where people still live as they did in this country half a century ago, I may have had an opportunity to study a part of the evolution of mankind in a shorter period.

I remember as a child the death of a farmer. He fell from a tree and was not expected to live. He asked simply to die at home, a wish that was granted without questioning. He called his daughters into the bedroom and spoke with each one of them alone for a few moments. He arranged his affairs quietly, though he was in great pain, and distributed his belongings and his land, none of which was to be split until his wife should follow him in death. He also asked each of his children to share in the work, duties, and tasks that he had carried on until the time of the accident. He asked his friends to visit him once more, to bid good-bye to them. Although I was a small child at the time, he did not exclude me or my siblings. We were allowed to share in the preparations of the family just as we were permitted to grieve with them until he died. When he did die, he was left at home, in his own beloved home which he had built, and among his friends and neighbors who went to take a last look at him where he lay in the midst of flowers in the place he had lived in and loved so much. In that country today there is still no make-believe slumber room, no embalming, no false makeup to pretend sleep. Only the signs of very disfiguring illnesses are covered up with bandages and only infectious cases are removed from the home prior to the burial.

Why do I describe such "old-fashioned" customs? I think they are an indication of our acceptance of a fatal outcome, and they help the dying patient as well as his family to accept the loss of a loved one. If a patient is allowed to terminate his life in the familiar and beloved environment, it requires less adjustment for him. His own family knows him well enough to replace a sedative with a glass of his favorite wine; or the smell of a home-cooked soup may give him the appetite to sip a few spoons of fluid which, I think is still more enjoyable than an infusion. I will not minimize the need for sedatives and infusions and realize full well from my own experience as a country doctor that they are sometimes life-saving and often unavoidable. But I also know that patience and familiar people and foods could replace many a bottle of intravenous fluids given for the simple reason that it fulfills the physiological need without involving too many people and/or individual nursing care.

The fact that children are allowed to stay at home where a fatality has stricken and are included in the talk, discussions, and fears gives them the feeling that they are not alone in the grief and gives them the comfort of shared responsibility and shared mourning. It prepares them gradually and helps them view death as part of life, an experience which may help them grow and mature.

This is in great contrast to a society in which death is viewed as taboo, discussion of it is regarded as morbid, and children are excluded with the presumption and pretext that it would be "too much" for them. They are then sent off to relatives, often accompanied with some unconvincing lies of "Mother has gone on a long trip" or other unbelievable stories. The child senses that something is wrong, and his distrust in adults will only multiply if other relatives add new variations of the story, avoid his questions or suspicions, shower him with gifts as a meager substitute for a loss he is not permitted to deal with. Sooner or later the child will become aware of the changed family situation and, depending on the age and personality of the child, will have an unresolved grief and regard this incident as a frightening, mysterious, in any case very traumatic experience with untrustworthy grownups, which he has no way to cope with.

It is equally unwise to tell a little child who lost her brother that God loved little boys so much that he took little Johnny to heaven. When this little girl grew up to be a woman she never solved her anger at God, which resulted in a psychotic depression when she lost her own little son three decades later.

We would think that our great emancipation, our knowledge of science and of man, has given us better ways and means to prepare ourselves and our families for this inevitable happening. Instead the days are gone when a man was allowed to die in peace and dignity in his own home.

The more we are making advancements in science, the more we seem to fear and deny the reality of death. How is this possible?

We use euphemisms, we make the dead look as if they were asleep, we ship the children off to protect them from the anxiety and turmoil around the house if the patient is fortunate enough to die at home, we don't allow children to visit their dying parents in the hospitals, we have long and controversial discussions about whether patients should be told the truth —a question that rarely arises when the dying person is tended by the family physician who has known him from delivery to death and who knows the weaknesses and strengths of each member of the family.

I think there are many reasons for this flight away from facing death calmly. One of the most important facts is that dying nowadays is more gruesome in many ways, namely, more lonely, mechanical, and dehumanized; at times it is even difficult to determine technically when the time of death has occurred.

Dying becomes lonely and impersonal because the patient is often taken out of his familiar environment and rushed to an emergency room. Whoever has been very sick and has required rest and comfort especially may recall his experience of being put on a stretcher and enduring the noise of the ambulance siren and hectic rush until the hospital gates open. Only those who have lived through this may appreciate the discomfort and cold necessity of such transportation which is only the beginning of a long order—hard to endure when you are well, difficult to express in words when noise, light, pumps, and voices are all too much to put up with. It may well be that we might consider more the patient under the sheets and blankets and perhaps stop our well-meant efficiency and rush in order to hold the patient's hand, to smile, or to listen to a question. I include the trip to the hospital as the first episode in dying, as it is for many. I am putting it exaggeratedly in contrast to the sick man who is left at home—not to say that lives should not be saved if they can be saved by a hospitalization but to keep the focus on the patient's experience, his needs and his reactions.

When a patient is severely ill, he is often treated like a person with no right to an opinion. It is often someone else who makes the decision if and when and where a patient should be hospitalized. It would take so little to remember that the sick person too has feelings, has wishes and opinions, and has—most important of all—the right to be heard.

Well, our presumed patient has now reached the emergency room. He will be surrounded by busy nurses, orderlies, interns, residents, a lab technician perhaps who will take some blood, an electrocardiogram technician who takes the cardiogram. He may be moved to X-ray and he will overhear opinions of his condition and discussions and questions to members of the family. He slowly but surely is beginning to be treated like a thing. He is no longer a person. Decisions are made often without his opinion. If he tries to rebel he will be sedated and after hours of waiting and wondering whether he has the strength, he will be wheeled into the operating room or intensive treatment unit and become an object of great concern and great financial investment.

He may cry for rest, peace, and dignity, but he will get infusions, transfusions, a heart machine, or tracheotomy[2] if necessary. He may want one single person to stop for one single minute so that he can ask one single question—but he will get a dozen people around the clock, all busily preoccupied with his heart rate, pulse, electrocardiogram or pulmonary functions, his secretions or excretions but not with him as a human being. He may wish to fight it all but it is going to be a useless fight since all this is done in the fight for his life, and if they can save his life they can consider the person afterwards. Those who consider the person first may lose precious time to save his life! At least this seems to be the rationale or justification behind all this—or is it? Is the reason for this increasingly mechanical, depersonalized approach our own defensiveness? Is this approach our own way to cope with and repress the anxieties that a terminally or critically ill patient evokes in us? Is our concentration on equipment, on blood pressure our desperate attempt to deny the impending death which is so frightening and discomforting to us that we displace all our knowledge onto machines, since they are less close to us than the suffering face of another human being which would remind us once more of our lack of omnipotence, our own limits and failures, and last but not least perhaps our own mortality?

Maybe the question has to be raised: Are we becoming less human or more human? * * * [I]t is clear that whatever the answer may be, the patient is suffering more—not physically, perhaps, but emotionally. And his needs have not changed over the centuries, only our ability to gratify them.

1969

2. The surgical opening of a passage through the neck into the trachea.

THE READER

1. Thomas, in "The Long Habit" (p. 348), also speaks of dying. To what extent is he in harmony with Kübler-Ross? What differences do you find? What is the special contribution of each author?
2. To speak of rights, as Kübler-Ross does in the last pages of her essay, is to raise the question of where they come from. For example, the Declaration of Independence (p. 510) implies that the rights it asserts come from God. From what source would you expect Kübler-Ross to derive the rights she speaks of?
3. Kübler-Ross doubts the rationale for efficiency in medical care but, at the same time, recognizes the life-saving results of this efficiency. There is obviously a dilemma here. What are the extreme opposite positions that define the dilemma? What is the best intermediate or compromise position?

THE WRITER

1. *How is Kübler-Ross's essay organized? What difference does it make that she postpones presenting generalizations about her subject until late in her discussion?*
2. *Kübler-Ross opens her discussion with a quotation. Read Shakespeare's Sonnet 73 and Hopkins's "Sping and Fall: To a Young Child" (below). Would these poems be appropriate for introducing her essay? Why, or why not?*

73

That time of year thou mayst in me behold
When yellow leaves, or none, or few, do hang
Upon those boughs which shake against the cold,
Bare ruined choirs, where late the sweet birds sang.
In me thou see'st the twilight of such day
As after sunset fadeth in the west;
Which by and by black night doth take away,
Death's second self, that seals up all in rest.
In me thou see'st the glowing of such fire,
That on the ashes of his youth doth lie,
As the deathbed whereon it must expire,
Consumed with that which it was nourished by.
This thou perceiv'st, which makes thy love more strong,
To love that well which thou must leave ere long.

—William Shakespeare

SPRING AND FALL

TO A YOUNG CHILD

Margaret, are you grieving
Over Goldengrove unleaving?
Leaves, like the things of man, you
With your fresh thoughts care for, can you?
Ah! as the heart grows older
It will come to such sights colder
By and by, nor spare a sigh
Though worlds of wanwood leafmeal lie;
And yet you *will* weep and know why.
Now no matter, child, the name:
Sorrow's springs are the same.
Nor mouth had, no nor mind, expressed
What heart heard of, ghost [soul] guessed:
It is the blight man was born for,
It is Margaret you mourn for.

—Gerard Manley Hopkins

3. Write a brief comparison between Thomas and Kübler-Ross along the lines suggested above ("The Reader," question 1).

Ethics

Samuel L. Clemens

ADVICE TO YOUTH

Being told I would be expected to talk here, I inquired what sort of a talk I ought to make. They said it should be something suitable to youth —something didactic, instructive, or something in the nature of good advice. Very well. I have a few things in my mind which I have often longed to say for the instruction of the young; for it is in one's tender early years that such things will best take root and be most enduring and most valuable. First, then, I will say to you, my young friends—and I say it beseechingly, urgingly—

Always obey your parents, when they are present. This is the best policy in the long run, because if you don't they will make you. Most parents think they know better than you do, and you can generally make more by humoring that superstition than you can by acting on your own better judgment.

Be respectful to your superiors, if you have any, also to strangers, and sometimes to others. If a person offend you, and you are in doubt as to whether it was intentional or not, do not resort to extreme measures; simply watch your chance and hit him with a brick. That will be sufficient. If you shall find that he had not intended any offense, come out frankly and confess yourself in the wrong when you struck him; acknowledge it like a man and say you didn't mean to. Yes, always avoid violence; in this age of charity and kindliness, the time has gone by for such things. Leave dynamite to the low and unrefined.

Go to bed early, get up early—this is wise. Some authorities say get up with the sun; some others say get up with one thing, some with another. But a lark is really the best thing to get up with. It gives you a splendid reputation with everybody to know that you get up with the lark; and if you get the right kind of a lark, and work at him right, you can easily train him to get up at half past nine, every time—it is no trick at all.

Now as to the matter of lying. You want to be very careful about lying; otherwise you are nearly sure to get caught. Once caught, you can never again be, in the eyes of the good and the pure, what you were before. Many a young person has injured himself permanently through a single clumsy and illfinished lie, the result of carelessness born of incomplete training. Some authorities hold that the young ought not to lie at all. That, of course, is putting it rather stronger than necessary; still, while I cannot go quite so far as that, I do maintain, and I believe I am right, that the young ought to be temperate in the use of this great art until practice and experience shall give them that confidence, elegance, and precision which alone can make the accomplishment graceful and profitable. Patience, diligence, painstaking attention to detail—these are the requirements; these, in time, will make the student perfect; upon these, and upon these only, may he rely as the sure foundation for future eminence. Think what tedious years of study, thought, practice, experience, went to the equipment of that peerless old master who was able to impose upon the whole world the lofty and sounding maxim that "truth is mighty and will prevail"—the most majestic compound fracture of fact which any of woman born has yet achieved. For the history of our race, and each individual's experience, are sown thick with evidence that a truth is not hard to kill and that a lie told well is immortal. There is in Boston a monument of the man who discovered anaesthesia; many people are aware, in these latter days, that that man didn't discover it at all, but stole the discovery from another man. Is this truth mighty, and will it prevail? Ah no, my hearers, the monument is made of hardy material, but the lie it tells will outlast it a million years. An awkward, feeble, leaky lie is a thing which you ought to make it your unceasing study to avoid; such a lie as that has no more real permanence than an average truth. Why, you might as well tell the truth at once and be done with it. A feeble, stupid, preposterous lie will not live two years—except it be a slander upon somebody. It is indestructible, then, of course, but that is no merit of yours. A final word: begin your practice of this gracious and beautiful art early—begin now. If I had begun earlier, I could have learned how.

Never handle firearms carelessly. The sorrow and suffering that have been caused through the innocent but heedless handling of firearms by the young! Only four days ago, right in the next farmhouse to the one where I am spending the summer, a grandmother, old and gray and sweet, one of the loveliest spirits in the land, was sitting at her work, when her young grandson crept in and got down an old, battered, rusty gun which had not been touched for many years and was supposed not to be loaded, and pointed it at her, laughing and threatening to shoot. In her fright she ran screaming and pleading toward the door on the other side of the room; but as she passed him he placed the gun almost against her very breast and pulled the trigger! He had supposed it was not loaded. And he was right—it wasn't. So there wasn't any harm done. It is the only case of that kind I ever heard of. Therefore, just the same, don't you meddle with old unloaded firearms; they are the most deadly and unerring things that have ever been created by man. You don't have to take any pains at all with them; you don't have to have a rest, you don't have to have any sights on the gun, you don't have to take aim, even. No, you just pick out a relative and bang away, and you are sure to get him. A youth who can't hit a cathedral at thirty yards with a Gatling gun in three-quarters of an hour, can take up an old empty musket and bag his grandmother every time, at a hundred. Think what Waterloo[1] would have been if one of the armies had been boys armed with old muskets supposed not to be loaded, and the other army had been composed of their female relations. The very thought of it makes one shudder.

There are many sorts of books; but good ones are the sort for the young to read. Remember that. They are a great, an inestimable, an unspeakable means of improvement. Therefore be careful in your selection, my young friends; be very careful; confine yourselves exclusively to Robertson's Sermons, Baxter's *Saint's Rest, The Innocents Abroad,* and works of that kind.[2]

But I have said enough. I hope you will treasure up the instructions which I have given you, and make them a guide to your feet and a light to your understanding. Build your character thoughtfully and painstakingly upon these precepts, and by and by, when you have got it built, you will be surprised and gratified to see how nicely and sharply it resembles everybody else's.

1882   1923

1. The bloody battle (1815) in which Napoleon suffered his final defeat at the hands of English and German troops under the Duke of Wellington.
2. The five volumes of sermons by Frederick William Robertson (1816–1853), an English clergyman, and Richard Baxter's *Saints' Everlasting Rest* (1650) were once well-known religious works. *The Innocents Abroad* is Clemens's own collection of humorous travel sketches.

THE READER

1. How much of Clemens's advice applies only to the young? How much of it is to be taken seriously?
2. What does Clemens assume about his audience? How many of these assumptions would hold true today?

THE WRITER

1. Is this piece unified? Does it have a thesis sentence? If you think it is unified, in what does the unity consist? If you think it is not unified, where are the breaks? Would it have seemed more unified when it was given as a speech?
2. What "image" or "personality" does Clemens project or assume?

What does he do that creates his image or personality?
3. *Write a brief essay comparing what Clemens says about lying with what Didion says about it in "On Keeping a Notebook" (p. 414).*

Michael Levin

THE CASE FOR TORTURE

It is generally assumed that torture is impermissible, a throwback to a more brutal age. Enlightened societies reject it outright, and regimes suspected of using it risk the wrath of the United States.

I believe this attitude is unwise. There are situations in which torture is not merely permissible but morally mandatory. Moreover, these situations are moving from the realm of imagination to fact.

Death: Suppose a terrorist has hidden an atomic bomb on Manhattan Island which will detonate at noon on July 4 unless ... (here follow the usual demands for money and release of his friends from jail). Suppose, further, that he is caught at 10 a.m. of the fateful day, but—preferring death to failure—won't disclose where the bomb is. What do we do? If we follow due process—wait for his lawyer, arraign him—millions of people will die. If the only way to save those lives is to subject the terrorist to the most excruciating possible pain, what grounds can there be for not doing so? I suggest there are none. In any case, I ask you to face the question with an open mind.

Torturing the terrorist is unconstitutional? Probably. But millions of lives surely outweigh constitutionality. Torture is barbaric? Mass murder is far more barbaric. Indeed, letting millions of innocents die in deference to one who flaunts his guilt is moral cowardice, an unwillingness to dirty one's hands. If you caught the terrorist, could you sleep nights knowing that millions died because you couldn't bring yourself to apply the electrodes?

Once you concede that torture is justified in extreme cases, you have admitted that the decision to use torture is a matter of balancing innocent lives against the means needed to save them. You must now face more realistic cases involving more modest numbers. Someone plants a bomb on a jumbo jet. He alone can disarm it, and his demands cannot be met (or if they can, we refuse to set a precedent by yielding to his threats). Surely we can, we must, do anything to the extortionist to save the passengers. How can we tell 300, or 100, or 10 people who never asked to be put in danger, "I'm sorry, you'll have to die in agony, we just couldn't bring ourselves to ..."

Here are the results of an informal poll about a third, hypothetical, case. Suppose a terrorist group kidnapped a newborn baby from a hospital. I asked four mothers if they would approve of torturing kidnappers if that were necessary to get their own newborns back. All said yes, the most "liberal" adding that she would like to administer it herself.

I am not advocating torture as punishment. Punishment is addressed to deeds irrevocably past. Rather, I am advocating torture as an acceptable measure for preventing future evils. So understood, it is far less objectionable than many extant punishments. Opponents of the death penalty, for example, are forever insisting that executing a murderer will not bring back his victim (as if the purpose of capital punishment were supposed to be resurrection, not deterrence or retribution). But torture, in the cases described, is intended not to bring anyone back but to keep innocents from being dispatched. The most powerful argument against using torture as a punishment or to secure confessions is that such practices disregard the rights of the individual. Well, if the individual is all that important—and he is—it is correspondingly important to protect the rights of individuals threatened by terrorists. If life is so valuable that it must never be taken, the lives of the innocents must be saved even at the price of hurting the one who endangers them.

Better precedents for torture are assassination and pre-emptive attack. No Allied leader would have flinched at assassinating Hitler, had that been possible. (The Allies did assassinate Heydrich.) Americans would be angered to learn that Roosevelt could have had Hitler killed in 1943—thereby shortening the war and saving millions of lives—but refused on moral grounds. Similarly, if nation A learns that nation B is about to launch an unprovoked attack, A has a right to save itself by destroying B's military capability first. In the same way, if the police can by torture save those who would otherwise die at the hands of kidnappers or terrorists, they must.

Idealism: There is an important difference between terrorists and their victims that should mute talk of the terrorists' "rights." The terrorist's victims are at risk unintentionally, not having asked to be endangered. But the terrorist knowingly initiated his actions. Unlike his victims, he volunteered for the risks of his deed. By threatening to kill for profit or idealism, he renounces civilized standards, and he can have no complaint if civilization tries to thwart him by whatever means necessary.

Just as torture is justified only to save lives (not extort confessions or recantations), it is justifiably administered only to those *known* to hold innocent lives in their hands. Ah, but how can the authorities ever be sure they have the right malefactor? Isn't there a danger of error and abuse? Won't We turn into Them?

Questions like these are disingenuous in a world in which terrorists proclaim themselves and perform for television. The name of their game is public recognition. After all, you can't very well intimidate a government into releasing your freedom fighters unless you announce that it is your group that has seized its embassy. "Clear guilt" is difficult to define, but when 40 million people see a group of masked gunmen seize an airplane on the evening news, there is not much question about who the perpetrators are. There will be hard cases where the situation is murkier. Nonetheless, a line demarcating the legitimate use of torture can be drawn. Torture only the obviously guilty, and only for the sake of saving innocents, and the line between Us and Them will remain clear.

There is little danger that the Western democracies will lose their way if they choose to inflict pain as one way of preserving order. Paralysis in the face of evil is the greater danger. Some day soon a terrorist will threaten tens of thousands of lives, and torture will be the only way to save them. We had better start thinking about this.

1982

THE READER

1. When, in the author's view, is torture permissible? When is it not permissible? What distinguishes the two situations?
2. Why is torture justified to save lives? That is, what assumption is made in this case?
3. Why is torture not justified as punishment or to extort confessions? That is, what assumption is being made in these cases?
4. Who will judge as to when torture is permissible and, indeed, "morally mandatory"? What ensures that that judgment will be correct?

THE WRITER

1. Why does Levin need to ask the reader to face the question posed in his third paragraph "with an open mind"?
2. In the first part of his essay, Levin gives three hypothetical examples. Why does he arrange them in the order he does?
3. Write a brief essay in which you discuss what effect the use of torture has upon the persons applying torture.

Barbara Grizzuti Harrison

ABORTION

If there is one issue on which sane and reasonable people cannot agree to disagree, it is abortion. And even to say that is to make an inflammatory statement: People on both sides of the issue—pro-choice (or pro-abortion) and anti-abortion (or pro-life)—refuse, for the most part, to acknowledge that honor and decency can attach to anyone in the other camp.

You see what I mean: pro-choice/pro-abortion; anti-abortion/pro-life —even the semantics of abortion defeat dialogue. And to occupy a middle ground, to admit to being pushed in one direction, pulled in another, by the claims of conscience, compassion, and reality, is intolerable (others would say unconscionable): People call you names.

Smugness or stridency overwhelms rational discourse; and the voices we hear from most frequently—the loudest voices—are often both smug *and* strident, which is to say arrogant. The arrogance of (some) anti-abortionists is flagrant: to burn a clinic is not an act conceived in humility. There is another kind of arrogance that expresses itself in the unwarranted assumption that anyone who takes a position against abortion is punitive, anti-sexual, lacking in compassion, or mindlessly following an imperative imposed upon her by a "patriarchal" religion.

Partly in an effort to resolve my own psychic tug of war, I sought to hear the quiet voices of conviction from whom we do not often hear.

I thought, while I was at it, that I might as well start at home. I have a 17-year-old son, a 16-year-old daughter. My daughter said: "Abortion is murder." My son said, "The woman should decide for herself." My daughter, however, added: "It's different from other murders, though, because nobody means to do evil; there isn't any desire to kill."

She was expressing—without knowing it—a sophisticated theological concept: that of subjective, as opposed to objective, sin.

Catholics who do not oppose abortion take refuge in this theological loophole: Miriam Walcott, a lay leader, formerly Catholic chaplain at Brown University, says that while she is "personally repelled by abortion, it is specifically inaccurate to ascribe sin, such as murder, where none is intended within the conscience of the individual choosing to have an abortion."

Catholics for a Free Choice, a national organization with state and local chapters, quotes the Second Vatican Council Declaration on Religious Liberty, saying that people who possess "civil rights are not to be

367

hindered in leading their lives in accordance with their conscience." Joan Harriman, of Catholics for Alternatives, whose activities include "nonjudgmental pregnancy counseling," says that "abortion is often the lesser evil in service of the greater good. I am concerned with when 'ensoulment' takes place; and second-trimester abortions are awful to contemplate. But I can't contemplate making a choice for another woman, either."

A friend I value for her generosity as much as for her integrity says adamantly that if my daughter were to have an abortion, she would refuse to drive her to a clinic: "I couldn't aid and abet you. I'm beginning to feel immoral because I don't try to dissuade friends who are choosing to have abortions. I allow the vehemence of my feelings to embarrass me, so my protest comes out sounding like a little romantic squeak."

My friend is Jewish, and secular; and she "couldn't care less when 'ensoulment' takes place. That's splitting hairs and focusing attention away from the kind of society we're creating. I see abortion as the worst kind of denial of our bodies. We are our bodies. If we deny the limits inherent in being a physical creature, society approaches an ideal of mechanical perfection. Mongoloid children or thalidomide babies can live happy and good lives. The trouble is that they are intimations of our mortality."

Another friend of mine, an active member of a mainline Protestant church, says, "I know how terribly destructive it is for a mother to give up a child for adoption; and how much adopted children suffer from a sense of identity loss. On one side guilt, on the other side longing. When my extended family gets together, I see three faces that probably would not be here if abortion had been legal 20 years ago—three adopted children. I love those children, and I'm glad they're alive. But I think of their mothers. How terrible it must have been—how terrible it is—for them."

Elizabeth Moore is a welfare mother of six who works for Feminists for Life. When anti-abortionists brought a fetus to a National Organization for Women conference on abortion, she publicly denounced their action on the ground that it was "hurtful to dialogue." Active in the civil rights movement and in the peace movement, she is opposed to "all forms of violence—handguns, nukes, capital punishment."

Clearly not an ultraconservative, she takes issue with what has unfortunately become known as the "pro-family" line: she supports the proposed equal rights amendment, day-care centers, shelters for battered wives and sex education in the public schools. "Abortion," she says, "is not an alternative to sharing jobs and wealth. Abortion does not cure poverty."

Pam Cira, also of Feminists for Life, says, "Feminism grew out of the anger of women who did not want their value to be determined by men. How can we turn around and arbitrarily devalue the fetus? How can I support a Nestlé boycott and turn around and support the destruction of life *in utero*?"

"I wish we could talk to one another," she said. "This is a heartbreaking issue, and if we shout, the Women's Movement will be destroyed."

Some women are reluctant to speak. One very prominent religious reproaches herself for her silence: "A significant amount of blame must go to women like me who delivered the pro-life movement into the hands of people who care nothing about the hungry of the world, nothing about social justice, and who are not pro-life but merely anti-abortion.

"In talking about abortion," she continued, "we are talking about relationships: the relationship between the woman and the father, the relationship between the woman and the fetus, and our relationship to God, whose essence is creation and who calls us to be co-creators in the search for social justice. We say that a woman's body is her own, but we can't forget that moral decisions always come out of the perspective of being related. A human being is never *not* related."

"I was driving once with a group of poor Mexican-American women," she said, "and we passed a car with a bumper that said 'Abortion Is Murder.' By the time we reached our destination, every single woman in that car had admitted to having an abortion. They were scared to tell their husbands they were pregnant, and scared to tell them they were aborting. They had no options. Socially and economically, they saw no way out."

Like my daughter, I believe that abortion is murder. But I would drive my daughter to a clinic. I don't know how to fit this reality into a tidy moral or logical equation. But I do know that the arrogance one hears from the loud voices on both sides of this issue stems from the implicit assumption that the function of morality is to make one comfortable; whereas in fact the function of morality is to make one profoundly uncomfortable—it is only out of that discomfort, that spiritual or psychic itch, vexation and turmoil—that authentic ethical decisions can be made.

1980

Lewis Thomas

ON MAGIC IN MEDICINE

Medicine has always been under pressure to provide public explanations for the diseases with which it deals, and the formulation of comprehensive, unifying theories has been the most ancient and willing preoccupation of the profession. In the earliest days, hostile spirits needing exorcism were the principal pathogens, and the shaman's duty was simply the development of improved techniques for incantation. Later on, especially in the Western world, the idea that the distribution of body fluids among various organs determined the course of all illnesses took hold, and we were in for centuries of bleeding, cupping, sweating, and purging in efforts to intervene. Early in this century the theory of autointoxication evolved, and a large part of therapy was directed at emptying the large intestine and keeping it empty. Then the global concept of focal infection became popular, accompanied by the linked notion of allergy to the presumed microbial pathogens, and no one knows the resulting toll of extracted teeth, tonsils, gallbladders, and appendixes: the idea of psychosomatic influences on disease emerged in the 1930s and, for a while, seemed to sweep the field.

Gradually, one by one, some of our worst diseases have been edited out of such systems by having their causes indisputably identified and dealt with. Tuberculosis was the paradigm. This was the most chronic and inexorably progressive of common human maladies, capable of affecting virtually every organ in the body and obviously influenced by crowding, nutrition, housing, and poverty; theories involving the climate in general, and night air and insufficient sunlight in particular, gave rise to the spa as a therapeutic institution. It was not until the development of today's effective chemotherapy that it became clear to everyone that the disease had a single, dominant, central cause. If you got rid of the tubercle bacillus you were rid of the disease.

But that was some time ago, and today the idea that complicated diseases can have single causes is again out of fashion. The microbial infections that can be neatly coped with by antibiotics are regarded as lucky anomalies. The new theory is that most of today's human illnesses, the infections aside, are multifactorial in nature, caused by two great arrays of causative mechanisms: 1) the influence of things in the environment and 2) one's personal life-style. For medicine to become effective in dealing with such diseases, it has become common belief that the environment will have to be changed, and personal ways of living will also have to be transformed, and radically.

These things may turn out to be true, for all I know, but it will take a long time to get the necessary proofs. Meanwhile, the field is wide open for magic.

One great difficulty in getting straightforward answers is that so many of the diseases in question have unpredictable courses, and some of them have a substantial tendency toward spontaneous remission. In rheumatoid arthritis, for instance, when such widely disparate therapeutic measures as copper bracelets, a move to Arizona, diets low in sugar or salt or meat or whatever, and even an inspirational book have been accepted by patients as useful, the trouble in evaluation is that approximately 35 percent of patients with this diagnosis are bound to recover no matter what they do. But if you actually have rheumatoid arthritis or, for that matter, schizophrenia, and then get over it, or if you are a doctor and observe this to happen, it is hard to be persuaded that it wasn't *something* you did that was responsible. Hence you need very large numbers of patients and lots of time, and a cool head.

Magic is back again, and in full force. Laetrile cures cancer, acupuncture is useful for deafness and low-back pain, vitamins are good for anything, and meditation, yoga, dancing, biofeedback, and shouting one another down in crowded rooms over weekends are specifics for the human condition. Running, a good thing to be doing for its own sake, has acquired the medicinal value formerly attributed to rare herbs from Indonesia.

There is a recurring advertisement, placed by Blue Cross on the op-ed page of *The New York Times*, which urges you to take advantage of science by changing your life habits, with the suggestion that if you do so, by adopting seven easy-to-follow items of life-style, you can achieve eleven added years beyond what you'll get if you don't. Since today's average figure is around seventy-two for all parties in both sexes, this might mean going on until at least the age of eighty-three. You can do this formidable thing, it is claimed, by simply eating breakfast, exercising regularly, maintaining normal weight, not smoking cigarettes, not drinking excessively, sleeping eight hours each night, and not eating between meals.

The science which produced this illumination was a careful study by California epidemiologists, based on a questionnaire given to about seven thousand people. Five years after the questionnaire, a body count was made by sorting through the county death certificates, and the 371 people who had died were matched up with their answers to the questions. To be sure, there were more deaths among the heavy smokers and drinkers, as you might expect from the known incidence of lung cancer in smokers and cirrhosis and auto accidents among drinkers. But there was also a higher mortality among those who said they didn't eat breakfast, and even higher in those who took no exercise, no exercise at all, not even going off in the family car for weekend picnics. Being up to 20 percent overweight was not so bad, surprisingly, but being *underweight* was clearly associated with a higher death rate.

The paper describing these observations has been widely quoted, and not just by Blue Cross. References to the Seven Healthy Life Habits keep turning up in popular magazines and in the health columns of newspapers, always with that promise of eleven more years.

The findings fit nicely with what is becoming folk doctrine about disease. You become ill because of not living right. If you get cancer it is, somehow or other, your own fault. If you didn't cause it by smoking or drinking or eating the wrong things, it came from allowing yourself to persist with the wrong kind of personality, in the wrong environment. If you have a coronary occlusion, you didn't run enough. Or you were too tense, or you *wished* too much, and didn't get a good enough sleep. Or you got fat. Your fault.

But eating breakfast? It is a kind of enchantment, pure magic.

You have to read the report carefully to discover that there is another, more banal way of explaining the findings. Leave aside the higher deaths in heavy smokers and drinkers, for there is no puzzle in either case; these are dangerous things to do. But it is hard to imagine any good reason for dying within five years from not eating a good breakfast, or any sort of breakfast.

The other explanation turns cause and effect around. Among the people in that group of seven thousand who answered that they don't eat breakfast, don't go off on picnics, are underweight, and can't sleep properly, there were surely some who were already ill when the questionnaire arrived. They didn't eat breakfast because they couldn't stand the sight of food. They had lost their appetites, were losing weight, didn't feel up to moving around much, and had trouble sleeping. They didn't play tennis or go off on family picnics because they didn't *feel* good. Some of these people probably had an undetected cancer, perhaps of the pancreas; others may have had hypertension or early kidney failure or some other organic disease which the questionnaire had no way of picking up. The study did not ascertain the causes of death in the 371, but just a few deaths from such undiscerned disorders would have made a significant statistical impact. The author of the paper was careful to note these possible interpretations, although the point was not made strongly, and the general sense you have in reading it is that you can live on and on if only you will eat breakfast and play tennis.

The popular acceptance of the notion of Seven Healthy Life Habits, as a way of staying alive, says something important about today's public attitudes, or at least the attitudes in the public mind, about disease and dying. People have always wanted causes that are simple and easy to comprehend, and about which the individual can *do* something. If you believe that you can ward off the common causes of premature death—cancer, heart disease, and stroke, diseases whose pathogenesis we really do not understand—by jogging, hoping, and eating and sleeping regularly, these are good things to believe even if not necessarily true. Medicine has survived other periods of unifying theory, constructed to explain all of human disease, not always as benign in their effects as this one is likely to be. After all, if people can be induced to give up smoking, stop overdrinking and overeating, and take some sort of regular exercise, most of them are bound to feel the better for leading more orderly, regular lives, and many of them are surely going to look better.

Nobody can say an unfriendly word against the sheer goodness of keeping fit, but we should go carefully with the promises.

There is also a bifurcated ideological appeal contained in the seven-life-habits doctrine, quite apart from the subliminal notion of good luck in the numbers involved (7 come 11). Both ends of the political spectrum can find congenial items. At the further right, it is attractive to hear that the individual, the good old freestanding, free-enterprising American citizen, is responsible for his own health and when things go wrong it is his own damn fault for smoking and drinking and living wrong (and he can jolly well pay for it). On the other hand, at the left, it is nice to be told that all our health problems, including dying, are caused by failure of the community to bring up its members to live properly, and if you really want to improve the health of the people, research is not the answer; you should upheave the present society and invent a better one. At either end, you can't lose.

In between, the skeptics in medicine have a hard time of it. It is much more difficult to be convincing about ignorance concerning disease mechanisms than it is to make claims for full comprehension, especially when the comprehension leads, logically or not, to some sort of action. When it comes to serious illness, the public tends, understandably, to be more skeptical about the skeptics, more willing to believe the true believers. It is medicine's oldest dilemma, not to be settled by candor or by any kind of rhetoric; what it needs is a lot of time and patience, waiting for science to come in, as it has in the past, with the solid facts.

1979

THE READER

1. *What would be a sensible response to a recommendation of the Seven Healthy Life Habits?*
2. *Thomas speaks of "folk doctrine about disease" (p. 372). Are there folk doctrines about other things? How are they similar or different?*
3. *In this essay, Thomas calls himself a skeptic. What evidence does he give of a similar skepticism in "The Long Habit" (p. 348)? What other features of his presumed personality are common to both essays?*

THE WRITER

1. *In the second paragraph, Thomas uses the word* paradigm. *First define the term from the way Thomas uses it in that paragraph, and then compare that definition with what you find in the dictionary. Explain how Thomas might say that the study by the California epidemiologists that defined the Seven Healthy Life Habits (p. 371) was also a paradigm—for successful research, in their case. Does such an explanation require that you define a place for magic in the paradigm for successful research?*

2. *On p. 372, Thomas argues for turning cause and effect (in the California study) around so that, for example, what was the effect (sickness) becomes a cause and what was a cause (failure to exercise) becomes an effect. This is obviously a potent argumentative tactic. Suggest some other applications in politics or international affairs. Explain one of your examples in a paragraph or two.*

Stephen Jay Gould

THE TERRIFYING NORMALCY OF AIDS

Disney's Epcot Center in Orlando, Fla., is a technological tour de force and a conceptual desert. In this permanent World's Fair, American industrial giants have built their versions of an unblemished future. These masterful entertainments convey but one message, brilliantly packaged and relentlessly expressed: progress through technology is the solution to all human problems. G.E. proclaims from Horizons: "If we can dream it, we can do it." A.T.&T. speaks from on high within its giant golf ball: We are now "unbounded by space and time." United Technologies bubbles from the depths of Living Seas: "With the help of modern technology, we feel there's really no limit to what can be accomplished."

Yet several of these exhibits at the Experimental Prototype Community of Tomorrow, all predating last year's space disaster, belie their stated message from within by using the launch of the shuttle as a visual metaphor for technological triumph. The Challenger disaster may represent a general malaise, but it remains an incident. The AIDS pandemic, an issue that may rank with nuclear weaponry as the greatest danger of our era, provides a more striking proof that mind and technology are not omnipotent and that we have not canceled our bond to nature.

In 1984, John Platt, a biophysicist who taught at the University of Chicago for many years, wrote a short paper for private circulation. At a time when most of us were either ignoring AIDS, or viewing it as a contained and peculiar affliction of homosexual men, Platt recognized that the limited data on the origin of AIDS and its spread in America suggested a more frightening prospect: we are all susceptible to AIDS, and the disease has been spreading in a simple exponential manner.

Exponential growth is a geometric increase. Remember the old kiddy problem: if you place a penny on square one of a checkerboard and double the number of coins on each subsequent square—2, 4, 8, 16, 32 . . . —how big is the stack by the 64th square? The answer: about as high as the universe is wide. Nothing in the external environment inhibits this increase, thus giving to exponential processes their relentless character. In the real, noninfinite world, of course, some limit will eventually arise, and the process slows down, reaches a steady state, or destroys the entire system: the stack of pennies falls over, the bacterial cells exhaust their supply of nutrients.

Platt noticed that data for the initial spread of AIDS fell right on an exponential curve. He then followed the simplest possible procedure of extrapolating the curve unabated into the 1990's. Most of us were incredulous, accusing Platt of the mathematical gamesmanship that scientists call "curve fitting." After all, aren't exponential models unrealistic? Surely we are not all susceptible to AIDS. Is it not spread only by odd practices to odd people? Will it not, therefore, quickly run its short course within a confined group?

Well, hello 1987—worldwide data still match Platt's extrapolated curve. This will not, of course, go on forever. AIDS has probably already saturated the African areas where it probably originated, and where the sex ratio of afflicted people is 1-to-1, male-female. But AIDS still has far to spread, and may be moving exponentially, through the rest of the world. We have learned enough about the cause of AIDS to slow its spread, if we can make rapid and fundamental changes in our handling of that most powerful part of human biology—our own sexuality. But medicine, as yet, has nothing to offer as a cure and precious little even for palliation.

This exponential spread of AIDS not only illuminates its, and our, biology, but also underscores the tragedy of our moralistic misperception. Exponential processes have a definite time and place of origin, an initial point of "inoculation"—in this case, Africa. We didn't notice the spread at first. In a population of billions, we pay little attention when 1 increases to 2, or 8 to 16, but when 1 million becomes 2 million, we panic, even though the rate of doubling has not increased.

The infection has to start somewhere, and its initial locus may be little more than an accident of circumstance. For a while, it remains confined to those in close contact with the primary source, but only by accident of proximity, not by intrinsic susceptibility. Eventually, given the power and lability of human sexuality, it spreads outside the initial group and into the general population. And now AIDS has begun its march through our own heterosexual community.

What a tragedy that our moral stupidity caused us to lose precious time, the greatest enemy in fighting an exponential spread, by downplaying the danger because we thought that AIDS was a disease of three irregular groups of minorities: minorities of life style (needle users), of sexual preference (homosexuals) and of color (Haitians). If AIDS had first been imported from Africa into a Park Avenue apartment, we would not have dithered as the exponential march began.

The message of Orlando—the inevitability of technological solutions —is wrong, and we need to understand why.

Our species has not won its independence from nature, and we cannot do all that we can dream. Or at least we cannot do it at the rate required to avoid tragedy, for we are not unbounded from time. Viral diseases are preventable in principle, and I suspect that an AIDS vaccine will one day be produced. But how will this discovery avail us if it takes until the millenium, and by then AIDS has fully run its exponential course and saturated our population, killing a substantial percentage of the human race? A fight against an exponential enemy is primarily a race against time.

We must also grasp the perspective of ecology and evolutionary biology and recognize, once we reinsert ourselves properly into nature, that AIDS represents the ordinary workings of biology, not an irrational or diabolical plague with a moral meaning. Disease, including epidemic spread, is a natural phenomenon, part of human history from the beginning. An entire subdiscipline of my profession, paleopathology, studies the evidence of ancient diseases preserved in the fossil remains of organisms. Human history has been marked by episodic plagues. More native peoples died of imported disease than ever fell before the gun during the era of colonial expansion. Our memories are short, and we have had a respite, really, only since the influenza pandemic at the end of World War I, but AIDS must be viewed as a virulent expression of an ordinary natural phenomenon.

I do not say this to foster either comfort or complacency. The evolutionary perspective is correct, but utterly inappropriate for our human scale. Yes, AIDS is a natural phenomenon, one of a recurring class of pandemic diseases. Yes, AIDS may run through the entire population, and may carry off a quarter or more of us. Yes, it may make no *biological* difference to Homo sapiens in the long run: there will still be plenty of us left and we can start again. Evolution cares as little for its agents— organisms struggling for reproductive success—as physics cares for individual atoms of hydrogen in the sun. But we care. These atoms are our neighbors, our lovers, our children and ourselves. AIDS is both a natural phenomenon and, potentially, the greatest natural tragedy in human history.

The cardboard message of Epcot fosters the wrong attitudes; we must both reinsert ourselves into nature and view AIDS as a natural phenomenon in order to fight properly. If we stand above nature and if technology is all-powerful, then AIDS is a horrifying anomaly that must be trying to tell us something. If so, we can adopt one of two attitudes, each potentially fatal. We can either become complacent, because we believe the message of Epcot and assume that medicine will soon generate a cure, or we can panic in confusion and seek a scapegoat for something so irregular that it must have been visited upon us to teach us a moral lesson.

But AIDS is not irregular. It is part of nature. So are we. This should galvanize us and give us hope, not prompt the worst of all responses: a kind of "new-age" negativism that equates natural with what we must accept and cannot, or even should not, change. When we view AIDS as natural, and when we recognize both the exponential property of its spread and the accidental character of its point of entry into America, we can break through our destructive tendencies to blame others and to free ourselves of concern.

If AIDS is natural, then there is no *message* in its spread. But by all that science has learned and all that rationality proclaims, AIDS works by a *mechanism*—and we can discover it. Victory is not ordained by any principle of progress, or any slogan of technology, so we shall have to fight like hell, and be watchful. There is no message, but there is a mechanism.

1987

Michael Stone

SHOULD TESTING FOR THE AIDS VIRUS BE MANDATORY?

Testing has become the most controversial issue surrounding AIDS. Should marriage applicants, hospital patients, and visitors to sexually-transmitted-disease (STD) clinics be required to undergo tests for AIDS antibodies? Short of that, should such tests be routinely made available? A recent conference run by the CDC[1] and attended by about 800 health officials focused on these questions. The overwhelming consensus was

1. Centers for Disease Control.

that tests should not be required—but that's not likely to end the dispute.

Many AIDS experts seem to be influenced in their opinions on testing by their approach to the disease. Health officials and epidemiologists deal with whole populations. While they are often concerned with the legal and ethical implications of testing, their overriding objection is pragmatic. Most of them simply don't believe that such measures will stem the spread of the virus, and some worry about the psychological effects of a positive result. "Mandatory testing needs effective treatment," says Health Commissioner Joseph. "But right now, I can't offer that treatment."

Clinical doctors, on the other hand, approach AIDS on case-by-case terms. They view testing as a requisite to treatment and responsible social behavior; many can't understand why health authorities around the country won't undertake the same measures long used to fight gonorrhea, syphilis, and other sexually transmitted diseases. In a recent survey conducted by *MD* magazine, more than half of the 1,500 doctors in private practice who were queried supported mandatory testing for marriage applicants.

"This is the first time in history that we have the means of diagnosing a disease and we're not using it," says Dr. Redfield of Walter Reed. "In just three years, we figured out the etiology of this disease and developed a test for it, and now, three years later, we're still not fully using that knowledge. We did screen blood when we found out that blood was less than one percent of AIDS transmission. But in New York, where one out of every 50 male Army applicants is seropositive, they are still not testing in the VD clinics. If you don't look for the virus, you're not going to find it." (In fact, the City Health Department has been running tests at an STD clinic as part of an epidemiological study. So far, after about 200 tests, the study has found no positives who are not members or sex partners of members of high-risk groups.)

The testing issue is complicated by civil-liberties concerns. Most health officials distinguish between AIDS and other sexually transmitted diseases on the basis of AIDS's association with homosexuality and drug use—and its extreme virulence. Many authorities say they cannot guarantee the confidentiality of test results; as a result, carriers of the virus could be exposed to discrimination by employers, landlords, and insurers, among other groups.

But Dr. Redfield, for one, thinks the health risks far outweigh the threat to civil liberties. What's more, he argues that even without a cure, an accurate diagnosis can be immensely helpful. "There are a number of things that can be done," he says. "If I know you're positive, I can monitor the progress of the virus. If you're in the first four stages—okay. If you're in the fifth or sixth stage, we're aggressive. We practice medicine appropriately. We don't misdiagnose.

"Second, you don't have to become a cardiac cripple. I can give you drugs that stop opportunistic infections. We don't see a lot of *Pneumocystis carinii* pneumonia [at Walter Reed]. That's the No. 1 cause of death among AIDS patients. We can give them a prophylactic drug—Fansidar—that can stop recurrence. But the timing is very important.

"Third, we let you prognosticate. I tell you how this virus is. I give you the opportunity to know and to plan where you are in your life.

"Fourth, I allow you the opportunity to make a decision whether you want to infect others. A positive result is not a death sentence. It's not unhelpable, and testing does make the difference. Clinically, as a doctor, it makes an amazing difference to me to know the immunological status of my patient. It allows me to intervene at the greatest risk-benefit ratio to him."

There's disagreement, too, over the effects a diagnosis—one way or the other—would have. If it takes a positive test to make people modify their behavior, as some proponents of mandatory testing claim, does that mean they won't change if they know they're negative? Shouldn't everyone practice "safer sex" regardless of his or her status?

Homosexual men in New York and San Francisco began to change their behavior even before widespread testing became available. Studies show that knowing someone who suffers or died from AIDS is more likely to prompt change than knowing one's sero-status. But waiting for that kind of personal understanding of the disease may take too long. Even though homosexuals changed their sexual behavior dramatically, their communities are now 50 to 60 percent seropositive.

So far, no states require testing and almost all testing services are anonymous. Of the people who do come in for a test, 22 percent nationally test positive, indicating that the system is attracting at-risk groups; even Redfield advocates setting up more anonymous-test sites to encourage more people to come in. But Dr. Redfield also thinks that authorities should strongly encourage testing in which the subject is identified and his or her sex partners are traced. "I think most people are not threatened by name-linked testing," he says. "We asked 29 seropositive women we saw at Walter Reed for their sexual contacts. Of the 23 contacts they gave us, we found 17 were infected. We should be using the same classic public-health approach to AIDS that we use for other sexually transmitted diseases."

Last month, New York State ordered about 250 STD, family-planning, and prenatal-care clinics to provide free, voluntary testing for the AIDS virus. Five of these clinics are in New York City. In addition, the City Health Department operates two anonymous-testing clinics and encourages people who fear they are at risk to get tested. But Health Commissioner Joseph feels that tracing partners is impractical in the high-risk groups. With an estimated 500,000 seropositives in New York, the time and money needed to track even a small fraction of their contacts would be better spent on education or research. "Some of the people we deal with can't remember who they slept with last night, much less five years ago," says one community worker. The Health Department does encourage a carrier to notify his or her partners, however, and offers to help.

Colorado has taken a somewhat more aggressive approach than New York and most other states. Testing in Colorado is required to be name-linked—that is, whoever gets tested has to give a name (at the anonymous-test sites, the subjects are usually given just a number). However, since no identification is asked for, many test subjects simply give a pseudonym. That ensures confidentiality, says Colorado health chief Dr. Thomas Vernon, but allows counselors to develop closer relationships with their subjects than they would if the system were anonymous.

Still, Dr. Vernon thinks the system should become far more aggressive in tracing contacts in groups and communities that have a low incidence of infection. "If I had known who the 150 positives were in Colorado in 1981," he says, "I could have prevented the 20,000 infected today."

In certain special situations, health officials generally support mandatory testing. Blood and organ donors, of course, must be screened for infectiousness. Military recruits are tested in part because of the financial burden AIDS cases could create and because in some cases soldiers are expected to serve as a transfusion source for their colleagues.

Many of these issues may be radically altered by advances in diagnostic research. The technology is already in place for a highly accurate test that could be performed during the course of a routine doctor's visit. If approved by the FDA, a quick test could dramatically affect the costs, logistics, and epidemiology of current testing.

Some experts worry that as testing becomes more common, it will polarize the population into antibody positives and negatives. Already, clubs are being formed that issue negative-status-confirmation cards to members. If the antibody-positive group overwhelmingly includes the anticipated categories—homosexuals, IV-drug users, and people from communities with high drug use—then AIDS may again become the "other guy's disease." Indeed, if heterosexual, white, middle-class Americans no longer regard AIDS as an imminent threat to them, the growing effort to contain it may falter.

1987

Thomas Murray

THE GROWING DANGER

My son Peter is twelve, and lately the cuffs of his pants have been racing up his ankles—a sure sign that growth hormone is coursing through his body. He's on about the same growth schedule that I was. By my fourteenth birthday I was already just shy of six feet, and hopeful of four or five inches more. I thought that would be enough to give me a shot at playing basketball in college. Alas, I'd reached my limit. Lacking any notable physical talents, I had to rely on guile; if you can't shoot over the guy, get him looking one way and then scurry past on the other side. (As we used to say, "Fake left, go right.") Recent happenings in genetic engineering make me wonder if something similar, albeit unintentional, is going on there: Is our attention being directed one way while what's important is slipping by on the other side?

At least since 1980, worries about using recombinant DNA technology to alter "human nature" have focused on gene therapy—the direct and intentional alteration of genetic material to treat disease. On June 20 of that year the general secretaries of three national organizations, for Protestants, Jews, and Catholics, wrote the President to warn: "History has shown us that there will always be those who believe it appropriate to 'correct' our mental and social structures by genetic means, so as to fit their vision of humanity. This becomes more dangerous when the basic tools to do so are finally at hand. Those who would play God will be tempted as never before."

Nothing garners attention as quickly as a nice little scandal; within a month of the letter, Dr. Martin Cline of UCLA provided one by experimenting on two patients with beta-zero thalassemia, a genetic condition that causes severe anemia. Cline removed some of their bone marrow, treated it with recombinant DNA containing normal hemoglobin genes, then reinserted it into the bone (after making room by killing some of the remaining marrow cells with radiation). The hope was that the treated cells would multiply and produce normal hemoglobin.

They didn't. Worse, Cline didn't have the approval of the UCLA committee that oversees research with human subjects. When the affair became public, the National Institutes of Health (NIH) stripped Cline of $162,000 in grant money and demanded strict supervision of his research. For those suspicious of human gene therapy, the case was proof that scientists couldn't be trusted to regulate themselves.

Since then, such work has proceeded very cautiously. A presidential commission gave its tentative blessing to gene therapy with somatic cells

381

—those that don't pass the altered genes on to future generations. The NIH's watchdog recombinant DNA advisory committee set up a "human gene therapy subcommittee," which has suggested "points to consider" for doctors who propose to tinker with genes. Among them: whether the benefits of the treatment outweigh the risks, how to choose patients fairly, and how to publicize the results of the research. Thanks to the brouhaha over gene therapy, no great threats to humanity are likely to slip by in the near future—at least not on that side.

But there's another side to genetic engineering that has the power to alter us physically and socially. Rather than directly altering our genes, it can modify our bodies by supplementing the natural supply of important regulatory hormones with genetically engineered ones. A prime example is biosynthetically manufactured human growth hormone—hGH. Except for one additional amino acid—methionine (which appears to have no effect on its action)—biosynthetic hGH is identical to the hormone that promotes natural growth.

Produced in the pituitary gland, hGH plays a key role in determining how tall we'll become. So-called pituitary dwarfs usually lack an adequate supply of bioactive hGH. To treat them, for more than twenty years we've been harvesting pituitaries from human cadavers, each of which yields a minute quantity of hGH. Until recently the supply was barely adequate. In 1979 genetic engineers cloned the gene carrying instructions for making hGH, inserted it into a microorganism, and coaxed the bug to produce the human hormone. Just in time, it appears, because some hGH recovered from human pituitaries seems to have been contaminated with the slow virus that causes Creutzfeldt-Jakob disease (CJD), a degenerative infection of the brain. In April 1985 the Food and Drug Administration (FDA) halted the sale of natural growth hormone, and shortly thereafter approved Genentech's[1] biosynthetic version. Since no human tissue is used in producing it, there's no danger of contamination with the CJD virus. Also, we're no longer limited by the scarcity of cadaver pituitaries, and other uses for hGH can be explored.

Biotechnology came to the rescue of kids deficient in growth hormone. But if hGH injections can make extremely short children a bit taller, what can it do for those who aren't dwarfs, but just shorter than average? What about the youngster who would have been only of average height? And what about the basketball player for whom a couple of inches more might mean the difference between the schoolyard and the NBA? In short (no pun intended), why not use hGH to give your child the advantages that come with being tall?

Years ago, at an FDA hearing, I speculated that once biosynthetic hGH was approved, people would want to use it for all sorts of non-

---

1. A major American biotechnology company.

therapeutic purposes. One member of the FDA committee told me that several parents had already asked her if they could get the drug for their kids, who weren't hGH-deficient. All, she recalled, were physicians. Rebecca Kirkland, who does clinical trials of biosynthetic hGH at the Baylor College of Medicine, recently said she's had inquiries from five parents wanting to get hGH for their normal children.

Why would parents want to go to such expense (treatment with biosynthetic hGH costs roughly $10,000 a year), cause their children pain (the shots hurt a bit), and risk unknown long-term side effects? Quite simply, because it's advantageous to be tall—within limits. A modest body of scientific evidence supports the commonsense observation that taller people often get the nod over their shorter counterparts, because they're perceived as more intelligent, good-looking, likable, extroverted, and attractive. Being very much taller than the average is a mixed blessing, to be sure. But being a few inches above average seems to help.

A survey at the University of Pittsburgh in 1968 found that starting salaries for graduates varied with height: roughly $300 an inch up to six feet two inches. In a study of men whose heights had been recorded twenty-five years earlier, a graduate student at Washington University in St. Louis demonstrated a "height bonus" of approximately $400 per inch.

When a researcher at Eastern Michigan University presented two hypothetical job candidates to recruiters, one eight inches taller than the other, 72 percent preferred the taller one, 27 percent said there was no difference, and only one chose the shorter applicant, And much has been made of the fact that the taller candidate for President usually wins. Only two presidents—Madison and Benjamin Harrison—were shorter than the average American male of their eras.

If some parents want to give their child the edge that height seems to confer, what's wrong with that? If it's O.K. to spend $2,500 on orthodontics, to buy your kid private tennis and music lessons, or to spend $10,000 a year and up for prep school and private college, what's a few thousand bucks more to buy a couple of inches? The kid could turn out to be a klutz at tennis, have a tin ear, and major in Michelob, but taller is taller.

In this century, we make a strong presumption in favor of liberty. Before we interfere with the right of parents to bring up their children as they judge best, we demand strong reasons for doing so. Can we find them in the case of hGH?

Let me ask a skeptical question: What's the disease for which human growth hormone is the cure? Philosophers have a difficult time agreeing on the definition of disease, but most would recognize a physiological deficiency in hGH as a genuine disease, and hGH injections as a reasonable treatment. There are some kids, though, who aren't measurably deficient in hGH but who are very short. Their shortness can be the consequence of any one of numerous medical problems, or they may fall into the category of "familial short stature"—that is, short like mom or pop. Either way, can their shortness ever be a disability? A disability is a condition that interferes with the tasks of everyday living. If people are so short that they qualify for the elevator riddle,[2] their shortness may well be a disability. Disabilities usually justify medical intervention. But what if a person isn't suffering from a disease, and isn't so short that the lack of height becomes a disability? What if it's merely a disadvantage?

Even if hGH turns out to be physiologically harmless—some experts have warned of possible effects on glucose regulation, as well as an increased risk of atherosclerosis and high blood pressure—there may be psychological consequences to treating children with the hormone. The unmistakable message given to a child is that shortness is a grave enough problem to justify the considerable expense, inconvenience, and discomfort of hGH treatment. It's likely to increase the child's self-consciousness about height. And since children rarely grow as much with the hormone as they or their parents hope, disappointment is likely.

A study of hGH-deficient children and their families found that the most psychologically mature kids weren't those who grew the most but those whom parents and other adults had treated appropriately for their age rather than their size. Kids who were encouraged to pursue interests where their height wasn't a disadvantage were much happier with themselves.

People differ in so many ways: in intelligence, charm, quickness of hand and foot, facility with words, wit, etc. But when we put children through hGH treatments, we focus almost entirely on their height (where they don't "measure up") and ignore their other talents and abilities. Understandably, short kids receiving hGH may come to feel that they're inadequate and inferior.

All other things being equal, taller basketball players are more effective than shorter ones. Height is an advantage in basketball and some other sports. In almost all other realms of human endeavor, though, height bears no relationship to the ability to do a job well. But in a culture that regularly imputes desirable characteristics to tall people and undesirable ones to short ones, shortness is surely a disadvantage. (Even our language is laden with "heightisms": we look up to people we admire, look down on those we don't.)

Like other "isms," such as racism and sexism, heightism involves making unwarranted judgments about people based on irrelevant criteria. Does anyone believe the solution to racism is to find a drug that lightens black skin? The mind boggles at the possible biotechnological

---

2. Why did the man always take the elevator to the sixth floor, then walk up four more flights to his apartment? Because he could only reach the button for the sixth floor [author's note].

remedies for sexism. And yet those who want to give their kids hGH are proposing just this sort of technological end-run around heightism.

If we choose to allow hGH to be used for non-disease, non-disabling shortness, then we must make a choice. Either we let those who can afford it buy it for their children, or we make it available at public expense to all children whose parents want it.

Suppose we let it be sold. The children of rich parents will have one more leg up, so to speak, on their peers. You could ask, what's one more advantage in the light of all the others available to people with means? But the prospect of two classes—one tall and monied, the other short and poor—is ugly and disquieting. It would allow injustice to be piled upon injustice.

Suppose we take the other route and provide hGH to anyone who wants it. If all parents (short and tall alike) rushed out to get hGH shots for their kids, the average height of the entire population might increase. But in all likelihood the distribution of height in the population wouldn't change much, if at all. There would still be the taller and the shorter, and since we're doing nothing to diminish heightism, discrimination against the shorter would continue. Some people would benefit, of course—for example, the stockholders in Genentech (which holds the patent for making biosynthetic hGH) and those who produce fabrics (since everyone will be wearing bigger sizes). Meanwhile, at considerable social expense, kids would get their three shots a week with a little pain and, we hope, minimal side effects.

Inevitably, a few eager parents would want to regain the edge for their kids and try to get bigger doses of hGH, like those athletes who take increasing amounts of anabolic steroids in the hope of obtaining an advantage over their rivals. In both cases, individuals pursue their own interests, only to make everyone worse off.

Whether hGH is available just to those who can pay for it or to everyone, the results would be unfortunate. In one instance, we use biotechnology to reinforce the advantages of wealth; in the other, we incur enormous expense and unknown risks without making anyone better off. The wisest course is to restrict hGH to cases of disease and disability.

Although hGH may be the first biosynthetic hormone to tempt us to improve on human nature, it won't be the last. Imagine what we might do with a hormone that prompted damaged nerves to regenerate. Someone would wonder whether it would also stimulate growth in the brain. And soon we'd be trying to enlarge our brains, however misguided that might be, scientifically or morally.

It also occurs to me that simply by writing this article I may spur some parents to seek out growth hormone for their child of normal height. I fervently hope not. But the temptation posed by hGH, and by other fruits of biotechnology as yet unripened, will be great. And it will require all our collective common sense to use them wisely.

1987

THE READER

1. How does Murray's "Fake left, go right" apply to his discussion of genetic engineering?
2. Considering the possibility that hGH could be sold, Murray raises "the prospect of two classes—one tall and monied, the other short and poor." Judging by his data, assess the likelihood of this outcome. How important is it to his argument?
3. Murray would restrict availability of hGH to cases of disease and disability, but earlier he has acknowledged the difficulty of defining disease. How seriously does he take that difficulty? How seriously do you take it?

THE WRITER

1. The author is perfectly clear about the wisest course to follow with hGH. Why doesn't he just stop there, without adding the two final paragraphs? What is the tone of these two paragraphs? How does he feel about what he is saying?
2. Murray teaches in a medical school. How well suited is this essay to an audience of prospective doctors?
3. Without worrying about scientific plausibility in your examples, try to draw a line between responsible and irresponsible use of biosynthetic hormones.

Willard Gaylin

WHAT YOU SEE IS THE REAL YOU

It was, I believe, the distinguished Nebraska financier Father Edward J. Flanagan[1] who professed to having "never met a bad boy." Having, myself, met a remarkable number of bad boys, it might seem that either our experiences were drastically different or we were using the word "bad" differently. I suspect neither is true, but rather that the Father was appraising the "inner man," while I, in fact, do not acknowledge the existence of inner people.

Since we psychoanalysts have unwittingly contributed to this confusion, let one, at least, attempt a small rectifying effort. Psychoanalytic data—which should be viewed as supplementary information—is, unfortunately, often viewed as alternative (and superior) explanation. This has

1. Founder (1917) of Boys Town, a self-governing community for homeless and abandoned boys, for which he was also an energetic fund raiser.

led to the prevalent tendency to think of the "inner" man as the real man and the outer man as an illusion or pretender.

While psychoanalysis supplies us with an incredibly useful tool for explaining the motives and purposes underlying human behavior, most of this has little bearing on the moral nature of that behavior.

Like roentgenology, psychoanalysis is a fascinating, but relatively new, means of illuminating the person. But few of us are prepared to substitute an X-ray of Grandfather's head for the portrait that hangs in the parlor. The inside of the man represents another view, not a truer one. A man may not always be what he appears to be, but what he appears to be is always a significant part of what he is. A man is the sum total of all his behavior. To probe for unconscious determinants of behavior and then define him in their terms exclusively, ignoring his overt behavior altogether, is a greater distortion than ignoring the unconscious completely.

Kurt Vonnegut has said, "You are what you pretend to be," which is simply another way of saying, you are what we (all of us) perceive you to be, not what you think you are.

Consider for a moment the case of the ninety-year-old man on his deathbed (surely the Talmud must deal with this?) joyous and relieved over the success of his deception. For ninety years he has shielded his evil nature from public observation. For ninety years he has affected courtesy, kindness, and generosity—suppressing all the malice he knew was within him while he calculatedly and artificially substituted grace and charity. All his life he had been fooling the world into believing he was a good man. This "evil" man will, I predict, be welcomed into the Kingdom of Heaven.

Similarly, I will not be told that the young man who earns his pocket money by mugging old ladies is "really" a good boy. Even my generous and expansive definition of goodness will not accommodate that particular form of self-advancement.

It does not count that beneath the rough exterior he has a heart—or, for that matter, an entire innards—of purest gold, locked away from human perception. You are for the most part what you seem to be, not what you would wish to be, nor, indeed, what you believe yourself to be.

Spare me, therefore, your good intentions, your inner sensitivities, your unarticulated and unexpressed love. And spare me also those tedious psychohistories which—by exposing the goodness inside the bad man, and the evil in the good—invariably establish a vulgar and perverse egalitarianism, as if the arrangement of what is outside and what inside makes no moral difference.

Saint Francis[2] may, in his unconscious, indeed have been compensat-

2. Saint Francis of Assisi, who early in the thirteenth century renounced parental wealth, entered on a life of poverty, and founded the Franciscan order of begging friars.

ing for, and denying, destructive, unconscious Oedipal impulses identical to those which Atilla projected and acted on. But the similarity of the unconscious constellations in the two men matters precious little, if it does not distinguish between them.

I do not care to learn that Hitler's heart was in the right place. A knowledge of the unconscious life of the man may be an adjunct to understanding his behavior. It is *not* a substitute for his behavior in describing him.

The inner man is a fantasy. If it helps you to identify with one, by all means, do so; preserve it, cherish it, embrace it, but do not present it to others for evaluation or consideration, for excuse or exculpation, or, for that matter, for punishment or disapproval.

Like any fantasy, it serves your purposes alone. It has no standing in the real world which we share with each other. Those character traits, those attitudes, that behavior—that strange and alien stuff sticking out all over you—*that's the real you!*

1977

THE READER

1. Gaylin makes a key distinction between the inner and the outer man. Why is it necessary for him to start with this distinction?
2. Gaylin says in his first paragraph that he does "not acknowledge the existence of inner people," while in his fourth paragraph he says that "the inside of the man represents another view, not a truer one." How can you account for this seeming contradiction?
3. Compare the approach to human personality taken by Gaylin with that of Goldberg, also a psychotherapist, in "In Harness: The Male Condition" (p. 280). Do they seem to agree on the nature of human personality? Explain.

THE WRITER

1. Gaylin finds in the relation between an X-ray and a portrait an analogy for the relation between the inner man and the outer man. How accurate is this analogy?
2. Discuss the effectiveness of the examples in the essay, and suggest others that Gaylin might have used.
3. Write a paragraph commenting on the appropriateness of Gaylin's title.

History

Walt Whitman

DEATH OF ABRAHAM LINCOLN

I shall not easily forget the first time I ever saw Abraham Lincoln. It must have been about the 18th or 19th of February, 1861. It was rather a pleasant afternoon, in New York city, as he arrived there from the West, to remain a few hours, and then pass on to Washington, to prepare for his inauguration. I saw him in Broadway, near the site of the present Post-office. He came down, I think from Canal street, to stop at the Astor House. The broad spaces, sidewalks, and streets in the neighborhood, and for some distance, were crowded with solid masses of people, many thousands. The omnibuses and other vehicles had all been turn'd off, leaving an unusual hush in that busy part of the city. Presently two or three shabby hack barouches made their way with some difficulty through the crowd, and drew up at the Astor House entrance. A tall figure stepp'd out of the centre of these barouches, paus'd leisurely on the sidewalk, look'd up at the granite walls and looming architecture of the grand old hotel—then, after a relieving stretch of arms and legs, turn'd round for over a minute to slowly and good-humoredly scan the appearance of the vast and silent crowds. There were no speeches—no compliments—no welcome—as far as I could hear, not a word said. Still much anxiety was conceal'd in the quiet. Cautious persons had fear'd some mark'd insult or indignity to the President-elect—for he possess'd no personal popularity at all in New York City, and very little political. But it was evidently tacitly agreed that if the few political supporters of Mr. Lincoln present would entirely abstain from any demonstration on their side, the immense majority, who were anything but supporters, would abstain on their sides also. The result was a sulky, unbroken silence, such as certainly never before characterized so great a New York crowd.

Almost in the same neighborhood I distinctly remember'd seeing

Lafayette on his visit to America in 1825. I had also personally seen and heard, various years afterward, how Andrew Jackson, Clay, Webster, Hungarian Kossuth, Filibuster Walker, the Prince of Wales on his visit, and other *célèbres*, native and foreign, had been welcom'd there—all that indescribable human roar and magnetism, unlike any other sound in the universe—the glad exulting thunder-shouts of countless unloos'd throats of men! But on this occasion, not a voice—not a sound. From the top of an omnibus, (driven up one side, close by, and block'd by the curbstone and the crowds), I had, I say, a capital view of it all, and especially of Mr. Lincoln, his look and gait—his perfect composure and coolness—his unusual and uncouth height, his dress of complete black, stovepipe hat push'd back on the head, dark-brown complexion, seam'd and wrinkled yet canny-looking face, black, bushy head of hair, disproportionately long neck, and his hands held behind as he stood observing the people. He look'd with curiosity upon that immense sea of faces, and the sea of faces return'd the look with similar curiosity. In both there was a dash of comedy, almost farce, such as Shakspere puts in his blackest tragedies. The crowd that hemm'd around consisted I should think of thirty to forty thousand men, not a single one his personal friend—while I have no doubt, (so frenzied were the ferments of the time,) many an assassin's knife and pistol lurk'd in hip or breast-pocket there, ready, soon as break and riot came.

But no break or riot came. The tall figure gave another relieving stretch or two of arms and legs; then with moderate pace, and accompanied by a few unknown-looking persons, ascended the portico-steps of the Astor House, disappear'd through its broad entrance—and the dumb-show ended.

I saw Abraham Lincoln often the four years following that date. He changed rapidly and much during his Presidency—but this scene, and him in it, are indelibly stamp'd upon my recollection. As I sat on the top of my omnibus, and had a good view of him, the thought, dim and inchoate then, has since come out clear enough, that four sorts of genius, four mighty and primal hands, will be needed to the complete limning of this man's future portrait—the eyes and brains and finger-touch of Plutarch and Eschylus and Michel Angelo, assisted now by Rabelais.

And now—(Mr. Lincoln passing on from this scene to Washington, where he was inaugurated, amid armed cavalry, and sharpshooters at every point—the first instance of the kind in our history—and I hope it will be the last)—now the rapid succession of well-known events, (too well-known—I believe, these days, we almost hate to hear them mention'd)—the national flag fired on at Sumter—the uprising of the North, in paroxysms of astonishment and rage—the chaos of divided councils—the call for troops—the first Bull Run—the stunning cast-down, shock, and dismay of the North—and so in full flood the Secession war. Four years of lurid, bleeding, murky, murderous war. Who paint those years, with all their scenes?—the hard-fought engagements—the defeats, plans, failures—the gloomy hours, days, when our Nationality seem'd hung in pall of doubt, perhaps death—the Mephistophelean sneers of foreign lands and attachés—the dreaded Scylla of European interference, and the Charybdis of the tremendously dangerous latent strata of seccession sympathizers throughout the free States, (far more numerous than is supposed)—the long marches in summer—the hot sweat, and many a sunstroke, as on the rush to Gettysburg in '63—the night battles in the woods, as under Hooker at Chancellorsville—the camps in winter—the military prisons—the hospitals—(alas! alas! the hospitals.)

The Secession war? Nay, let me call it the Union war. Though whatever call'd, it is even yet too near us—too vast and too closely overshadowing—its branches unform'd yet, (but certain,) shooting too far into the future—and the most indicative and mightiest of them yet ungrown. A great literature will yet arise out of the era of those four years, those scenes—era compressing centuries of native passion, first-class pictures, tempests of life and death—an inexhaustible mine for the histories, drama, romance, and even philosophy, of peoples to come—indeed the verteber[1] of poetry and art, (of personal character too,) for all future America—far more grand, in my opinion, to the hands capable of it, than Homer's siege of Troy, or the French wars to Shakspere.

But I must leave these speculations, and come to the theme I have assign'd and limited myself to. Of the actual murder of President Lincoln, though so much has been written, probably the facts are yet very indefinite in most persons' minds. I read from my memoranda, written at the time, and revised frequently and finally since.

The day, April 14, 1865, seems to have been a pleasant one throughout the whole land—the moral atmosphere pleasant too—the long storm, so dark, so fratricidal, full of blood and doubt and gloom, over and ended at last by the sunrise of such an absolute National victory, and utter breakdown of Secessionism—we almost doubted our own senses! Lee had capitulated beneath the apple-tree of Appomattox. The other armies, the flanges of the revolt, swiftly follow'd. And could it really be, then? Out of all the affairs of this world of woe and failure and disorder, was there really come the confirm'd, unerring sign of plan, like a shaft of pure light —of rightful rule—of God? So the day, as I say, was propitious. Early herbage, early flowers, were out. (I remember where I was stopping at the time, the season being advanced, there were many lilacs in full bloom. By one of those caprices that enter and give tinge to events without being at all a part of them, I find myself always reminded of the great tragedy of that day by the sight and odor of these blossoms.[2] It never fails.)

1. Vertebra.
2. Cf. Whitman's elegy on Lincoln, "When

Lilacs Last in the Dooryard Bloom'd" (1865–66).

But I must not dwell on accessories. The deed hastens. The popular afternoon paper of Washington, the little *Evening Star*, has spatter'd all over its third page, divided among the advertisements in a sensational manner, in a hundred different places, "*The President and his Lady will be at the Theatre this evening. . . .*" (Lincoln was fond of the theatre. I have myself seen him there several times. I remember thinking how funny it was that he, in some respects the leading actor in the stormiest drama known to real history's stage through centuries, should sit there and be so completely interested and absorb'd in those human jackstraws, moving about with their silly little gestures, foreign spirit, and flatulent text.)

On this occasion the theatre was crowded, many ladies in rich and gay costumes, officers in their uniforms, many well-known citizens, young folks, the usual clusters of gas-lights, the usual magnetism of so many people, cheerful, with perfumes, music of violins and flutes—(and over all, and saturating all, that vast, vague wonder, *Victory*, the nation's victory, the triumph of the Union, filling the air, the thought, the sense, with exhilaration more than all music and perfumes.)

The President came betimes, and, with his wife, witness'd the play from the large stage-boxes of the second tier, two thrown into one, and profusely drap'd with the national flag. The acts and scenes of the piece —one of those singularly written compositions which have at least the merit of giving entire relief to an audience engaged in mental action or business excitements and cares during the day, as it makes not the slightest call on either the moral, emotional, esthetic, or spiritual nature —a piece, (*Our American Cousin,*) in which, among other characters so call'd, a Yankee, certainly such a one as was never seen, or the least like it ever seen, in North America, is introduced in England, with a varied fol-de-rol of talk, plot, scenery, and such phantasmagoria as goes to make up a modern popular drama—had progress'd through perhaps a couple of its acts, when in the midst of this comedy, or non-such, or whatever it is to be call'd, and to offset it, or finish it out, as if in Nature's and the great Muse's mockery of those poor mimes, came interpolated that scene, not really or exactly to be described at all, (for on the many hundreds who were there it seems to this hour to have left a passing blur, a dream, a blotch)—and yet partially to be described as I now proceed to give it. There is a scene in the play representing a modern parlor, in which two unprecedented English ladies are inform'd by the impossible Yankee that he is not a man of fortune, and therefore undesirable for marriage-catching purposes; after which, the comments being finish'd, the dramatic trio make exit, leaving the stage clear for a moment. At this period came the murder of Abraham Lincoln. Great as all its manifold train, circling round it, and stretching into the future for many a century, in the politics, history, art &c., of the New World, in point of fact the main thing, the actual murder, transpired with the quiet and simplicity of any commonest occurrence—the bursting of a bud or pod in the growth of vegetation, for instance. Through the general hum following the stage pause, with the change of positions, came the muffled sound of a pistol-shot, which not one-hundredth part of the audience heard at the time—and yet a moment's hush—somehow, surely, a vague startled thrill—and then, through the ornamented, draperied, starr'd and striped space-way of the President's box, a sudden figure, a man, raises himself with hands and feet, stands a moment on the railing, leaps below to the stage, (a distance of perhaps fourteen or fifteen feet), falls out of position, catching his boot-heel in the copious drapery, (the American flag,) falls on one knee, quickly recovers himself, rises as if nothing had happen'd, (he really sprains his ankle, but unfelt then)—and so the figure, Booth, the murderer, dress'd in plain black broadcloth, bare-headed, with full, glossy, raven hair, and his eyes like some mad animal's flashing with light and resolution, yet with a certain strange calmness, holds aloft in one hand a large knife—walks along not much back from the footlights—turns fully toward the audience his face of statuesque beauty, lit by those basilisk eyes, flashing with desperation, perhaps insanity—launches out in a firm and steady voice the words *Sic semper tyrannis*[3]—and then walks with neither slow nor very rapid pace diagonally across to the back of the stage, and disappears. (Had not all this terrible scene—making the mimic ones preposterous—had it not all been rehears'd, in blank, by Booth, beforehand?)

A moment's hush—a scream—the cry of *"murder"*—Mrs. Lincoln leaning out of the box, with ashy cheeks and lips, with involuntary cry, pointing to the retreating figure, *"He has kill'd the President."* And still a moment's strange, incredulous suspense—and then the deluge! then that mixture of horror, noises, uncertainty—(the sound, somewhere back, of a horse's hoofs clattering with speed)—the people burst through chairs and railings, and break them up—there is inextricable confusion and terror—women faint—quite feeble persons fall, and are trampl'd on—many cries of agony are heard—the broad stage suddenly fills to suffocation with a dense and motley crowd, like some horrible carnival—the audience rush generally upon it, at least the strong men do—the actors and actresses are all there in their play-costumes and painted faces, with mortal fright showing through the rouge—the screams and calls, confused talk—redoubled, trebled—two or three manage to pass up water from the stage to the President's box—others try to clamber up—&c., &c.

In the midst of all this, the soldiers of the President's guard, with others, suddenly drawn to the scene, burst in—(some two hundred altogether)—they storm the house, through all the tiers, especially the upper

---

3. "Thus always to tyrants."

ones, inflam'd with fury, literally charging the audience with fix'd bayonets, muskets, and pistols, shouting "*Clear out! clear out! you sons of — —
—*".... Such a wild scene, or a suggestion of it rather, inside the playhouse that night.

Outside, too, in the atmosphere of shock and craze, crowds of people,
fill'd with frenzy, ready to seize any outlet for it, come near committing
murder several times on innocent individuals. One such case was especially exciting. The infuriated crowd, through some chance, got started
against one man, either for words he utter'd, or perhaps without any
cause at all, and were proceeding at once to actually hang him on a
neighboring lamp-post, when he was rescued by a few heroic policemen,
who placed him in their midst, and fought their way slowly and amid
great peril toward the station-house. It was a fitting episode of the whole
affair. The crowd rushing and eddying to and fro—the night, the yells,
the pale faces, many frighten'd people trying in vain to extricate themselves—the attack'd man, not yet freed from the jaws of death, looking
like a corpse—the silent, resolute, half-dozen policemen, with no weapons but their little clubs, yet stern and steady through all those eddying
swarms—made a fitting side-scene to the grand tragedy of the murder.
They gain'd the station house with the protected man, whom they placed
in security for the night, and discharged him in the morning.

And in the midst of that pandemonium, infuriated soldiers, the audience and the crowd, the stage, and all its actors and actresses, its paint-
pots, spangles, and gas-lights—the life blood from those veins, the best
and sweetest of the land, drips slowly down, and death's ooze already
begins its little bubbles on the lips.

Thus the visible incidents and surroundings of Abraham Lincoln's
murder, as they really occur'd. Thus ended the attempted secession of
these States: thus the four years' war. But the main things come subtly
and invisibly afterward, perhaps long afterward—neither military, political, nor (great as those are,) historical. I say, certain secondary and
indirect results, out of the tragedy of this death, are, in my opinion,
greatest. Not the event of the murder itself. Not that Mr. Lincoln strings
the principal points and personages of the period, like beads, upon the
single string of his career. Not that his idiosyncrasy, in its sudden appearance and disappearance, stamps this Republic with a stamp more mark'd
and enduring than any yet given by any one man—(more even than
Washington's;)—but, join'd with these, the immeasurable value and
meaning of that whole tragedy lies, to me, in senses finally dearest to a
nation, (and here all our own)—the imaginative and artistic senses—the
literary and dramatic ones. Not in any common or low meaning of those
terms, but a meaning precious to the race, and to every age. A long and
varied series of contradictory events arrives at last at its highest poetic,
single, central, pictorial *dénouement*. The whole involved, baffling, mul-

tiform whirl of the secession period comes to a head, and is gather'd in one brief flash of lightning-illumination—one simple, fierce deed. Its sharp culmination, and as it were solution, of so many bloody and angry problems, illustrates those climax-moments on the stage of universal Time, where the historic Muse at one entrance, and the tragic Muse at the other, suddenly ringing down the curtain, close an immense act in the long drama of creative thought, and give it radiation, tableau, stranger than fiction. Fit radiation—fit close! How the imagination—how the student loves these things! America, too, is to have them. For not in all great deaths, not far or near—not Caesar in the Roman senate-house, or Napoleon passing away in the wild night-storm at St. Helena—not Paleologus,[4] falling, desperately fighting, piled over dozens deep with Grecian corpses—not calm old Socrates, drinking the hemlock—outvies that terminus of the secession war, in one man's life, here in our midst, in our time—that seal of the emancipation of three million slaves—that parturition and delivery of our at last really free Republic, born again, henceforth to commence its career of genuine homogeneous Union, compact, consistent with itself.

Nor will ever future American Patriots and Unionists, indifferently over the whole land, or North or South, find a better moral to their lesson. The final use of the greatest men of a Nation is, after all, not with reference to their deeds in themselves, or their direct bearing on their times or lands. The final use of a heroic-eminent life—especially of a heroic-eminent death—is its indirect filtering into the nation and the race, and to give, often at many removes, but unerringly, age after age, color and fibre to the personalism of the youth and maturity of that age, and of mankind. Then, there is a cement to the whole people, subtler, more underlying, than any thing in written constitution, or courts or armies—namely, the cement of a death identified thoroughly with that people, at its head, and for its sake. Strange, (is it not?) that battles, martyrs, agonies, blood, even assassination, should so condense—perhaps only really, lastingly condense—a Nationality.

I repeat it—the grand deaths of the race—the dramatic deaths of every nationality—are its most important inheritance-value—in some respects beyond its literature and art—(as the hero is beyond his finest portrait, and the battle itself beyond its choicest song or epic.) Is not here indeed the point underlying all tragedy? the famous pieces of the Grecian masters—and all masters? Why, if the old Greeks had had this man, what trilogies of plays—what epics—would have been made out of him! How the rhapsodes would have recited him! How quickly that quaint tall form would have enter'd into the region where men vitalize gods, and gods divinify men! But Lincoln, his times, his death—great as any, any age—

4. Emperor Constantine XI, who yielded Constantinople to the Turks in 1453.

belong altogether to our own, and are autochthonic.[5] (Sometimes indeed
I think our American days, our own stage—the actors we know and have
shaken hands, or talk'd with—more fateful than any thing in Eschylus[6]—
more heroic than the fighters around Troy—afford kings of men for our
Democracy prouder than Agamemnon—models of character cute and
hardy as Ulysses—deaths more pitiful than Priam's.)

When centuries hence, (as it must, in my opinion, be centuries hence
before the life of these States, or of Democracy, can be really written and
illustrated,) the leading historians and dramatists seek for some personage, some special event, incisive enough to mark with deepest cut, and
mnemonize, this turbulent nineteenth century of ours, (not only these
States, but all over the political and social world)—something, perhaps,
to close that gorgeous procession of European feudalism, with all its
pomp and caste-prejudices, (of whose long train we in America are yet so
inextricably the heirs)—something to identify with terrible identification, by far the greatest revolutionary step in the history of the United
States, (perhaps the greatest of the world, our century)—the absolute
extirpation and erasure of slavery from the States—those historians will
seek in vain for any point to serve more thoroughly their purpose, than
Abraham Lincoln's death.

Dear to the Muse—thrice dear to Nationality—to the whole human
race—precious to this Union—precious to Democracy—unspeakably
and forever precious—their first great Martyr Chief.

1882

5. Aboriginal, indigenous.
6. Eschylus (i.e., Aeschylus): Greek tragic
dramatist (525-456 B.C.) whose plays, like
Homer's epics, dealt with such figures of the
Trojan War as Agamemnon, leader of the
Greek forces; Ulysses, whose return to Ith-
aca after the war took ten years; and Priam,
slaughtered king of Troy.

THE READER

1. Whitman says that "four sorts of genius" would be needed to give a
complete portrait of Lincoln. What does he mean by this? Look up
more about each of the four people he mentions, and determine what
each might contribute to a complete picture of Lincoln.
2. Whitman says that the murder of Lincoln "transpired with the quiet
and simplicity of any commonest occurrence—the bursting of a bud or
pod in the growth of vegetation, for instance." What meaning and
effect does this metaphor convey?
3. At the end, Whitman speaks grandly of Lincoln's significance for far
more than the citizens of the still United States. As he sees it, what do
all these people have in common that would allow for this more-than-
national significance?
4. Compare Whitman's practice as a biographer with the theory set forth
by Woolf in "The New Biography" (p. 420).

THE WRITER

1. Whitman delivered this piece as a lecture. How might it have differed if he had composed it as an essay to be read rather than a lecture to be heard?
2. The events of the assassination lead Whitman to mention his perception of Lincoln's fondness for the theater. What does he do to make this particular observation serve a larger purpose?
3. How does Whitman convey the sense of horror and confusion in the scene when Lincoln is shot? Using some of Whitman's techniques, write an account of a similar scene which produces a strong emotional effect.
4. Using a dictionary if you like, explain the different meanings of the different names for the war. Be sure to consider our own name, which Whitman does not use—the Civil War. Does this difference about names imply a difference about attitudes toward the war? Toward Lincoln?
5. Using the details Whitman provides, write a movie or TV script for one of the scenes he describes. What things will the camera "see" and focus on?

Hannah Arendt

DENMARK AND THE JEWS

At the Wannsee Conference,[1] Martin Luther, of the Foreign Office, warned of great difficulties in the Scandinavian countries, notably in Norway and Denmark. (Sweden was never occupied, and Finland, though in the war on the side of the Axis, was one country the Nazis never even approached on the Jewish question. This surprising exception of Finland, with some two thousand Jews, may have been due to Hitler's great esteem for the Finns, whom perhaps he did not want to subject to threats and humiliating blackmail.) Luther proposed postponing evacuations from Scandinavia for the time being, and as far as Denmark was concerned, this really went without saying, since the country retained its independent government, and was respected as a neutral state, until the fall of 1943, although it, along with Norway, had been invaded by the German Army in April, 1940. There existed no Fascist or Nazi movement in Denmark worth mentioning, and therefore no collaborators. In Norway, however, the Germans had been able to find enthusiastic supporters; indeed, Vidkun Quisling, leader of the pro-Nazi and anti-Semitic Norwegian party, gave his name to what later became

1. A meeting of German officials on "the Jewish question."

known as a "quisling government." The bulk of Norway's seventeen
hundred Jews were stateless, refugees from Germany; they were seized
and interned in a few lightning operations in October and November,
1942. When Eichmann's office ordered their deportation to Auschwitz,
some of Quisling's own men resigned their government posts. This may
not have come as a surprise to Mr. Luther and the Foreign Office, but
what was much more serious, and certainly totally unexpected, was that
Sweden immediately offered asylum, and even Swedish nationality, to all
who were persecuted. Dr. Ernst von Weizsäcker, Undersecretary of
State of the Foreign Office, who received the proposal, refused to discuss
it, but the offer helped nevertheless. It is always relatively easy to get out
of a country illegally, whereas it is nearly impossible to enter the place of
refuge without permission and to dodge the immigration authorities.
Hence, about nine hundred people, slightly more than half of the small
Norwegian community, could be smuggled into Sweden.

It was in Denmark, however, that the Germans found out how fully
justified the Foreign Office's apprehensions had been. The story of the
Danish Jews is *sui generis*, and the behavior of the Danish people and
their government was unique among all the countries in Europe—
whether occupied, or a partner of the Axis, or neutral and truly independent. One is tempted to recommend the story as required reading in
political science for all students who wish to learn something about the
enormous power potential inherent in non-violent action and in resistance to an opponent possessing vastly superior means of violence. To be
sure, a few other countries in Europe lacked proper "understanding of
the Jewish question," and actually a majority of them were opposed to
"radical" and "final" solutions. Like Denmark, Sweden, Italy, and Bulgaria proved to be nearly immune to anti-Semitism, but of the three that
were in the German sphere of influence, only the Danes dared speak out
on the subject to their German masters. Italy and Bulgaria sabotaged
German orders and indulged in a complicated game of double-dealing
and double-crossing, saving their Jews by a tour de force of sheer ingenuity, but they never contested the policy as such. That was totally different
from what the Danes did. When the Germans approached them rather
cautiously about introducing the yellow badge, they were simply told
that the King would be the first to wear it, and the Danish government
officials were careful to point out that anti-Jewish measures of any sort
would cause their own immediate resignation. It was decisive in this
whole matter that the Germans did not even succeed in introducing the
vitally important distinction between native Danes of Jewish origin, of
whom there were about sixty-four hundred, and the fourteen hundred
German Jewish refugees who had found asylum in the country prior to
the war and who now had been declared stateless by the German government. This refusal must have surprised the Germans no end, since it

appeared so "illogical" for a government to protect people to whom it had categorically denied naturalization and even permission to work. (Legally, the prewar situation of refugees in Denmark was not unlike that in France, except that the general corruption in the Third Republic's civil services enabled a few of them to obtain naturalization papers, through bribes or "connections," and most refugees in France could work illegally, without a permit. But Denmark, like Switzerland, was no country *pour se débrouiller*[2].) The Danes, however, explained to the German officials that because the stateless refugees were no longer German citizens, the Nazis could not claim them without Danish assent. This was one of the few cases in which statelessness turned out to be an asset, although it was of course not statelessness per se that saved the Jews but, on the contrary, the fact that the Danish government had decided to protect them. Thus, none of the preparatory moves, so important for the bureaucracy of murder, could be carried out, and operations were postponed until the fall of 1943.

What happened then was truly amazing; compared with what took place in other European countries, everything went topsy-turvey. In August, 1943—after the German offensive in Russia had failed, the Afrika Korps had surrendered in Tunisia, and the Allies had invaded Italy—the Swedish government canceled its 1940 agreement with Germany which had permitted German troops the right to pass through the country. Thereupon, the Danish workers decided that they could help a bit in hurrying things up; riots broke out in Danish shipyards, where the dock workers refused to repair German ships and then went on strike. The German military commander proclaimed a state of emergency and imposed martial law, and Himmler thought this was the right moment to tackle the Jewish question, whose "solution" was long overdue. What he did not reckon with was that—quite apart from Danish resistance—the German officials who had been living in the country for years were no longer the same. Not only did General von Hannecken, the military commander, refuse to put troops at the disposal of the Reich plenipotentiary, Dr. Werner Best; the special S.S. units (*Einsatz-kommandos*) employed in Denmark very frequently objected to "the measures they were ordered to carry out by the central agencies"—according to Best's testimony of Nuremberg. And Best himself, an old Gestapo man and former legal adviser to Heydrich, author of a then famous book on the police, who had worked for the military government in Paris to the entire satisfaction of his superiors, could not longer be trusted, although it is doubtful that Berlin ever learned the extent of his unreliability. Still, it was clear from the beginning that things were not going well, and Eichmann's office sent one of its best men to Denmark—Rolf Günther,

2. For wangling—using bribery to circumvent bureaucratic regulations.

whom no one had ever accused of not possessing the required "ruthless toughness." Günther made no impression on his colleagues in Copenhagen, and now von Hannecken refused even to issue a decree requiring all Jews to report for work.

Best went to Berlin and obtained a promise that all Jews from Denmark would be sent to Theresienstadt[3] regardless of their category—a very important concession, from the Nazis' point of view. The night of October 1 was set for their seizure and immediate departure—ships were ready in the harbor—and since neither the Danes nor the Jews nor the German troops stationed in Denmark could be relied on to help, police units arrived from Germany for a door-to-door search. At the last moment, Best told them that they were not permitted to break into apartments, because the Danish police might then interfere, and they were not supposed to fight it out with the Danes. Hence they could seize only those Jews who voluntarily opened their doors. They found exactly 477 people, out of a total of more then 7,800, at home and willing to let them in. A few days before the date of doom, a German shipping agent, Georg F. Duckwitz, having probably been tipped off by Best himself, had revealed the whole plan to Danish government officials, who, in turn, had hurriedly informed the heads of the Jewish community. They, in marked contrast to Jewish leaders in other countries, had then communicated the news openly in the synagogues on the occasion of the New Year services. The Jews had just time enough to leave their apartments and go into hiding, which was very easy in Denmark, because, in the words of the judgment, "all sections of the Danish people, from the King down to simple citizens," stood ready to receive them.

They might have remained in hiding until the end of the war if the Danes had not been blessed with Sweden as a neighbor. It seemed reasonable to ship the Jews to Sweden, and this was done with the help of the Danish fishing fleet. The cost of transportation for people without means—about a hundred dollars per person—was paid largely by wealthy Danish citizens, and that was perhaps the most astounding feat of all, since this was a time when Jews were paying for their own deportation, when the rich among them were paying fortunes for exit permits (in Holland, Slovakia, and, later, in Hungary) either by bribing the local authorities or by negotiating "legally" with the S.S., who accepted only hard currency and sold exit permits, in Holland, to the tune of five or ten thousand dollars per person. Even in places where Jews met with genuine sympathy and a sincere willingness to help, they had to pay for it, and the chances poor people had of escaping were nil.

It took the better part of October to ferry all the Jews across the five to fifteen miles of water that separates Denmark from Sweden. The Swedes

---

3. A camp for certain classes of prisoners who were to receive special treatment.

received 5,919 refugees, of whom at least 1,000 were of German origin, 1,310 were half-Jews, and 686 were non-Jews married to Jews. (Almost half the Danish Jews seem to have remained in the country and survived the war in hiding.) The non-Danish Jews were better off than ever before, they all received permission to work. The few hundred Jews whom the German police had been able to arrest were shipped to Theresienstadt. They were old or poor people, who either had not received the news in time or had not been able to comprehend its meaning. In the ghetto, they enjoyed greater privileges than any other group because of the never-ending "fuss" made about them by Danish institutions and private persons. Forty-eight persons died, a figure that was not particularly high, in view of the average age of the group. When everything was over, it was the considered opinion of Eichmann that "for various reasons the action against the Jews in Denmark has been a failure," whereas the curious Dr. Best declared that "the objective of the operation was not to seize a great number of Jews but to clean Denmark of Jews, and this objective has now been achieved."

Politically and psychologically, the most interesting aspect of this incident is perhaps the role played by the German authorities in Denmark, their obvious sabotage of orders from Berlin. It is the only case we know of in which the Nazis met with open native resistance, and the result seems to have been that those exposed to it changed their minds. They themselves apparently no longer looked upon the extermination of a whole people as a matter of course. They had met resistance based on principle, and their "toughness" had melted like butter in the sun, they had even been able to show a few timid beginnings of genuine courage. That the ideal of "toughness," except, perhaps, for a few half-demented brutes, was nothing but a myth of self-deception, concealing a ruthless desire for conformity at any price, was clearly revealed at the Nuremberg Trials, where the defendants accused and betrayed each other and assured the world that they "had always been against it" or claimed, as Eichmann was to do, that their best qualities had been "abused" by their superiors. (In Jerusalem, he accused "those in power" of having abused his "obedience." "The subject of a good government is lucky, the subject of a bad government is unlucky. I had no luck.") The atmosphere had changed, and although most of them must have known that they were doomed, not a single one of them had the guts to defend the Nazi ideology. Werner Best claimed at Nuremberg that he had played a complicated double role and that it was thanks to him that the Danish officials had been warned of the impending catastrophe; documentary evidence showed, on the contrary, that he himself had proposed the Danish operation in Berlin, but he explained that this was all part of the game. He was extradited to Denmark and there condemned to death, but he appealed the sentence, with surprising results; because of "new evidence," his sentence was commuted to five years in prison, from which he was released soon afterward. He must have been able to prove to the satisfaction of the Danish court that he really had done his best.

1963

Michael Arlen

GRIEFSPEAK

When Robert Kennedy was shot, the reporters were already there—the cameras, the lights, the heralds of the people standing upon chairs and tabletops, trailing wire and tape recorders, the black tubelike microphones stretched out arclike into the room (that kitchen). He was shot, and it was real—a life, a death, the *event*, confusion, motion, people running, the man on the floor, young girls in straw hats crying, policemen, people pushing, yelling, the man on the floor, dying, dead, dying. It was all there for a moment, for a short while (it is perhaps this moment, stretching out forward and backward in our imaginations, that now remains), this event, this God knows what it was, and then the hands of people began to touch it. Inevitably, one will say. Inevitably. *Je suis touriste ici moi-même.*[1] Soft hands, tired hands, sincere hands, oh those sincere hands touching it (and him), poking it, rubbing it, plumping it, patting it. The men in rumpled shirts, hastily buttoned coats, were on the tabletops (our witness-technicians), on sidewalks, in corridors, holding aloft their microphones and cameras. The other men, in better-fitting suits and serious expressions, were inside some room—it all seemed like the same room (some underground chamber), but it could not have been. They talked—to each other, out to us. "I suppose," said Charles Kuralt, "we ought to be giving some comfort to the country in times like this. . . ." Griefspeak. "I don't know about the rest of you," John Chancellor said, "but in the last few hours I seem to have lost part of my self-respect." Somebody handed a piece of paper to Edwin Newman. "I have some new information here," said Edwin Newman. "Sirhan has ordered two books." He looked at the piece of paper. "One is by Madame Blavatsky. The other is by C. W. Ledbetter. We don't know the meaning of this as yet. Or whether it has anything to do with the alleged, the—we want to remind you that all this is tentative, because in this country no man is guilty until judged by a court of law." They talked of irony awhile. It was a time for discovering ironies. It was ironic about "the

1. "I'm a tourist here myself."

family." It was ironic that he was shot at the time of his "greatest triumph." It was ironic that "he had spoken out so often against violence." It was ironic that only yesterday he had rescued one of his children from the surf at Malibu. "Excuse me, John," said Edwin Newman. "We just got this on Madame Blavatsky. She lived from 1830 to 1891 and was a Theosophist—although I want to say that we're not yet sure what relationship, if any, this has to the . . ." "I just thought of another irony," said Sander Vanocur. "In a speech just a few days ago Senator Kennedy said, 'We were killed in Oregon. I hope to be resurrected in Los Angeles.'" A psychiatrist appeared at some point to say he thought the violence in our country derived from showing films like Bonnie and Clyde. There were discussions across the nation about brain surgery. "I think each one of us is guilty," Mike Wallace said. Telephone calls from prominent people to the family were duly logged and reported. CBS announced telephone calls from President Johnson, Vice-President Humphrey, Governor Reagan, and Senator Mansfield. NBC announced telephone calls from President Johnson, Governor Reagan, Robert McNamara, and Mayor Daley. The police chief of Los Angeles appeared before the press and spoke calmly and effectively. "I'll give you boys a moment to get your machines adjusted," he said before beginning. Prime Minister Harold Wilson was interviewed via satellite. The BBC announced "prayers for America." There were scenes of the coffin being placed into the plane in Los Angeles and being taken out of the plane in New York. There was an interview with Cardinal Cushing. Lord Harlech said that violence in America had become "an international scandal." There were interviews by satellite with former Prime Minister Macmillan and Romain Gary. There was an interview with an old gentleman seated in a chair upon a lawn, who had once been Robert Kennedy's grade-school principal. "I remember him very well," he said. "One day he brought one of these animals to school with him. A little pig, I think it was." They showed us the inside of the cathedral. Norman Mailer was standing at vigil around the coffin. "I think Nick Katzenbach is there," said an announcer. "There is George Plimpton. Ed, is that George Plimpton?" "No," said Edwin Newman. "But I think Mayor Lindsay is now coming down the aisle." They showed us Ethel Kennedy. Mrs. Robert Kennedy was seated in church beside a child, her head bent low over the child. The camera zoomed in. "How does one comfort a child at a time like that?" asked Edwin Newman. There was a Chevrolet ad. A man and a girl were seated on top of a convertible singing about "the big new savings on all regular Chevrolets." The song ended. "And on Chevelles too," the girl said with a wink. CBS was running off a Western. A man and a very blond girl with frizzy hair were hiding behind some curtains. There were advance shots of the route to be taken by the funeral procession. There were shots of tree-lined streets in

Washington. "He often enjoyed a brisk walk down streets such as these," a voice informed us. There were pictures of the White House. Leonard Bernstein, it was announced, would handle the musical arrangements. There were more scenes of Ethel Kennedy in church. There were scenes at Union Station. There were distant views of Hickory Hill. "He liked fresh air," said another voice. Jerome Wilson of WCBS had a number of people seated around him. "I realize it is hard for you to talk at a time like this," he said to a young man who had been a Citizen for Kennedy, "but what did you young people *especially* like about him?" The young man thought for a moment. "We especially liked him because he had leverage," he said. "I think I can say that business would have been happy with Robert Kennedy," said Roswell Gilpatric. They showed us the crowds lined up outside Saint Patrick's. "Young and old alike are joined in grief," an announcer said. They showed us the flags flying on the office buildings on Park Avenue. Some were flying at half-mast, some were not. "The flags fly at half-mast all across this mourning city," an announcer said. They showed us people filing by the coffin. They showed us the train on the way to Washington. They showed us the railroad stations. They showed us the train tracks. "What was it . . . what was the *mystique* that the Kennedy family had?" asked Johnny Carson. "Ethel Kennedy must now begin to build anew," Gabe Pressman said. The Red Cross, one learned, had already distributed four thousand cups of cold drink. They showed us the Lincoln Memorial. They showed us the Joint Chiefs of Staff. "As time goes on," said Louis Nizer, "the pain from his passing will diminish." They showed us John Kennedy's widow in church. I watched the television on and off those days, and the strangely disconnected people on the streets, in crowds, in the lines that rolled around Saint Patrick's down to Forty-fourth Street. "The people have come by to pay their last respects," the voices said. "The people file by . . . the people wait . . . the people touch . . . the people grieve. . . ." They showed us that throng of men and women waiting outside the station at Trenton—kids with American flags, parents in their shirtsleeves, the long train tracks, the crowded platform. "The question," the announcer said, "is how much the train has been slowed down en route from Newark." No. The question all along (we had known three days ago who had been killed) was who was dead.

1969

THE READER

1. What is the significance of the title?
2. Isolate a sample of Arlen's sentences. How many of them are cast in the form of straight observation—"It is . . ." There are . . ." "Mike Wallace said . . ."? What effect does this distribution have on the essay?
3. Whitman (p. 389) writes about Lincoln. The differences between his

memorial and Arlen's essay are many and great. List a few. To what
degree do they seem to be caused by differences between the two
events? To what degree do they seem to be caused by differences
between the two writers? Is it possible to distinguish the causes in that
way? If not, what causes can you distinguish?
4. Is this essay an indictment of television?

THE WRITER

1. Arlen's essay is one long paragraph. Is there any organizational
scheme? Is there a topic sentence, either explicit or implicit? Where
might Arlen have made paragraph divisions? What would he have
gained and what would he have lost by making more divisions?
2. Mostly Arlen describes and quotes. What are the signs of his distress
about the treatment of Robert Kennedy's assassination?
3. Write a paragraph answering the question at the end.
4. Read Whitman's account of the death of Lincoln (p. 389). Then,
imagining that TV had already been invented in Lincoln's time, write
an account, similar to Arlen's, of how TV might have covered Lincoln's death.
5. Imitating Arlen's style, write an account as it might be presented on
TV of some event you have witnessed.

Michael Herr

"HOW BAD DO YOU WANT TO GET TO DANANG?"

You could be in the most protected space in Vietnam and still know
that your safety was provisional, that early death, blindness, loss of legs,
arms or balls, major and lasting disfigurement—the whole rotten deal—
could come in on the freaky-fluky as easily as in the so-called expected
ways, you heard so many of those stories it was a wonder anyone was left
alive to die in firefights and mortar-rocket attacks. After a few weeks,
when the nickel had jarred loose and dropped and I saw that everyone
around me was carrying a gun, I also saw that any one of them could go off
at any time, putting you where it wouldn't matter whether it had been an
accident or not. The roads were mined, the trails booby-trapped, satchel
charges and grenades blew up jeeps and movie theaters, the VC[1] got
work inside all the camps as shoeshine boys and laundresses and honey-
dippers,[2] they'd starch your fatigues and burn your shit and then go home
and mortar your area. Saigon and Cholon and Danang held such hostile

1. Vietcong.   2. Latrine cleaners.

vibes that you felt you were being dry-sniped every time someone looked at you, and choppers fell out of the sky like fat poisoned birds a hundred times a day. After a while I couldn't get on one without thinking that I must be out of my fucking mind.

Fear and motion, fear and standstill, no preferred cut there, no way even to be clear about which was really worse, the wait or the delivery. Combat spared far more men than it wasted, but everyone suffered the time between contact, especially when they were going out every day looking for it; bad going on foot, terrible in trucks and APC's,[3] awful in helicopters, the worst, traveling so fast toward something so frightening. I can remember times when I went half dead with my fear of the motion, the speed and direction already fixed and pointed one way. It was painful enough just flying "safe" hops between firebases and lz's;[4] if you were ever on a helicopter that had been hit by ground fire your deep, perpetual chopper anxiety was guaranteed. At least actual contact when it was happening would draw long ragged strands of energy out of you, it was juicy, fast and refining, and traveling toward it was hollow, dry, cold and steady, it never let you alone. All you could do was look around at the other people on board and see if they were as scared and numbed out as you were. If it looked like they weren't you thought they were insane, if it looked like they were it made you feel a lot worse.

I went through that thing a number of times and only got a fast return on my fear once, a too classic hot landing with the heat coming from the trees about 300 yards away, sweeping machine-gun fire that sent men head down into swampy water, running on their hands and knees toward the grass where it wasn't blown flat by the rotor blades, not much to be running for but better than nothing. The helicopter pulled up before we'd all gotten out, leaving the last few men to jump twenty feet down between the guns across the paddy and the gun on the chopper door. When we'd all reached the cover of the wall and the captain had made a check, we were amazed to see that no one had even been hurt, except for one man who'd sprained both his ankles jumping. Afterwards, I remembered that I'd been down in the muck worrying about leeches. I guess you could say that I was refusing to accept the situation.

"Boy, you sure get offered some shitty choices," a Marine once said to me, and I couldn't help but feel that what he really meant was that you didn't get offered any at all. Specifically, he was just talking about a couple of C-ration cans, "dinner," but considering his young life you couldn't blame him for thinking that if he knew one thing for sure, it was that there was no one anywhere who cared less about what *he* wanted. There wsn't anybody he wanted to thank for his food, but he was grateful that he was still alive to eat it, that the motherfucker hadn't scarfed him up first. He hadn't been anything but tired and scared for six months and he'd lost a lot, mostly people, and seen far too much, but he was breathing in and breathing out, some kind of choice all by itself.

He had one of those faces, I saw that face at least a thousand times at a hundred bases and camps, all the youth sucked out of the eyes, the color drawn from the skin, cold white lips, you knew he wouldn't wait for any of it to come back. Life had made him old, he'd live it out old. All those faces, sometimes it was like looking into faces at a rock concert, locked in, the event had them; or like students who were very heavily advanced, serious beyond what you'd call their years if you didn't know for yourself what the minutes and hours of those years were made up of. Not just like all the ones you saw who looked like they couldn't drag their asses through another day of it. (How do you feel when a nineteen-year-old kid tells you from the bottom of his heart that he's gotten too old for this kind of shit?) Not like the faces of the dead or wounded either, they could look more released than overtaken. These were the faces of boys whose whole lives seemed to have backed up on them, they'd be a few feet away but they'd be looking back at you over a distance you knew you'd never really cross. We'd talk, sometimes fly together, guys going out on R&R,[5] guys escorting bodies, guys who'd flipped over into extremes of peace or violence. Once I flew with a kid who was going home, he looked back down once at the ground where he'd spent the year and spilled his whole load of tears. Sometimes you even flew with the dead.

Once I jumped on a chopper that was full of them. The kid in the Op[6] shack had said that there would be a body on board, but he'd been given some wrong information. "How bad do you want to get to Danang?" he'd asked me, and I'd said, "Bad."

When I saw what was happening I didn't want to get on, but they'd made a divert and a special landing for me, I had to go with the chopper I'd drawn, I was afraid of looking squeamish. (I remember, too, thinking that a chopper full of dead men was far less likely to get shot down than one full of living.) They weren't even in bags. They'd been on a truck near one of the firebases in the DMZ[7] that was firing support for Khe Sanh, and the truck had hit a Command-detonated mine, then they'd been rocketed. The Marines were always running out of things, even food, ammo and medicine, it wsn't so strange that they'd run out of bags too. The men had been wrapped around in ponchos, some of them carelessly fastened with plastic straps, and loaded on board. There was a small space cleared for me between one of them and the door gunner, who looked pale and so tremendously furious that I thought he was angry with me and I couldn't look at him for a while. When we went up the wind blew through the ship and made the ponchos shake and tremble until the one next to me blew back in a fast brutal flap, uncovering the face. They hadn't even closed his eyes for him.

The gunner started hollering as loud as he could, "Fix it! Fix it!," maybe he thought the eyes were looking at him, but there wasn't anything I could do. My hand went there a couple of times and I couldn't, and then I did. I pulled the poncho tight, lifted his head carefully and tucked the poncho under it, and then I couldn't believe that I'd done it. All during the ride the gunner kept trying to smile, and when we landed at Dong Ha he thanked me and ran off to get a detail. The pilots jumped down and walked away without looking back once, like they'd never seen that chopper before in their lives. I flew the rest of the way to Danang in a general's plane.

1977

Kildare Dobbs

THE SHATTERER OF WORLDS

Before that morning in 1945 only a few conventional bombs, none of which did any great damage, had fallen on the city. Fleets of U.S. bombers had, however, devastated many cities round about, and Hiroshima had begun a program of evacuation which had reduced its population from 380,000 to some 245,000. Among the evacuees were Emiko and her family.

"We were moved out to Otake, a town about an hour's train-ride out of the city," Emiko told me. She had been a fifteen-year-old student in 1945. Fragile and vivacious, versed in the gentle traditions of the tea ceremony and flower arrangement, Emiko still had an air of the frail school-child when I talked with her. Every day, she and her sister Hideko used to commute into Hiroshima to school. Hideko was thirteen. Their father was an antique-dealer and he owned a house in the city, although it was empty now. Tetsuro, Emiko's thirteen-year-old brother, was at the Manchurian front with the Imperial Army. Her mother was kept busy looking after the children, for her youngest daughter Eiko was sick with heart trouble, and rations were scarce. All of them were undernourished.

The night of August 5, 1945, little Eiko was dangerously ill. She was not expected to live. Everybody took turns watching by her bed, soothing her by massaging her arms and legs. Emiko retired at 8:30 (most Japanese people go to bed early) and at midnight was roused to take her turn with the sick girl. At 2 A.M. she went back to sleep.

While Emiko slept, the *Enola Gay*, a U.S. B-29 carrying the world's first operational atom bomb, was already in the air. She had taken off from the Pacific island of Iwo Jima at 1:45 A.M., and now Captain William Parsons, U.S.N. ordnance expert, was busy in her bomb-hold with the final assembly of Little Boy. Little Boy looked much like an outsize T.N.T. block-buster but the crew knew there was something different about him. Only Parsons and the pilot, Colonel Paul Tibbets, knew exactly in what manner Little Boy was different. Course was set for Hiroshima.

Emiko slept.

On board the *Enola Gay* co-pilot Captain Robert Lewis was writing up his personal log. "After leaving Iwo," he recorded, "we began to pick up some low stratus and before very long we were flying on top of an undercast. Outside of a thin, high cirrus and the low stuff, it's a very beautiful day."

Emiko and Hideko were up at six in the morning. They dressed in the uniform of their women's college—white blouse, quilted hat, and black skirt—breakfasted and packed their aluminum lunch-boxes with white rice and eggs. These they stuffed into their shoulder bags as they hurried for the seven-o'clock train to Hiroshima. Today there would be no classes. Along with many women's groups, high school students, and others, the sisters were going to work on demolition. The city had begun a project of clearance to make fire-breaks in its downtown huddle of wood and paper buildings.

It was a lovely morning.

While the two young girls were at breakfast, Captain Lewis, over the Pacific, had made an entry in his log. "We are loaded. The bomb is now alive, and it's a funny feeling knowing it's right in back of you. Knock wood!"

In the train Hideko suddenly said she was hungry. She wanted to eat her lunch. Emiko dissuaded her: she'd be much hungrier later on. The two sisters argued, but Hideko at last agreed to keep her lunch till later. They decided to meet at the main station that afternoon and catch the five-o'clock train home. By now they had arrived at the first of Hiroshima's three stations. This was where Hideko got off, for she was to work in a different area from her sister. "Sayonara!" she called. "Goodbye." Emiko never saw her again.

There had been an air-raid at 7 A.M., but before Emiko arrived at Hiroshima's main station, two stops farther on, the sirens had sounded the all-clear. Just after eight, Emiko stepped off the train, walked through the station, and waited in the morning sunshine for her streetcar.

At about the same moment Lewis was writing in his log. "There'll be a short intermission while we bomb our target."

It was hot in the sun, Emiko saw a class-mate and greeted her. Together they moved back into the shade of a high concrete wall to chat.

Emiko looked up at the sky and saw, far up in the cloudless blue, a single
B-29.

It was exactly 8:10 A.M. The other people waiting for the streetcar saw
it too and began to discuss it anxiously. Emiko felt scared. She felt that at
all costs she must go on talking to her friend. Just as she was thinking this,
there was a tremendous greenish-white flash in the sky. It was far brighter
than the sun. Emiko afterwards remembered vaguely that there was a
roaring or a rushing sound as well, but she was not sure, for just at that
moment she lost consciousness.

"About 15 seconds after the flash," noted Lewis, 30,000 feet high and
several miles away, "there were two very distinct slaps on the ship from
the blast and the shock wave. That was all the physical effect we felt. We
turned the ship so that we could observe the results."

When Emiko came to, she was lying on her face about forty feet away
from where she had been standing. She was not aware of any pain. Her
first thought was: "I'm alive!" She lifted her head slowly and looked about
her. It was growing dark. The air was seething with dust and black
smoke. There was a smell of burning. Emiko felt something trickle into
her eyes, tested it in her mouth. Gingerly she put a hand to her head, then
looked at it. She saw with a shock that it was covered with blood.

She did not give a thought to Hideko. It did not occur to her that her
sister who was in another part of the city could possibly have been in
danger. Like most of the survivors, Emiko assumed she had been close to
a direct hit by a conventional bomb. She thought it had fallen on the post-
office next to the station. With a hurt child's panic, Emiko, streaming
with blood from gashes in her scalp, ran blindly in search of her mother
and father.

The people standing in front of the station had been burned to death
instantly (a shadow had saved Emiko from the flash). The people inside
the station had been crushed by falling masonry. Emiko heard their faint
cries, saw hands scrabbling weakly from under the collapsed platform.
All around her the maimed survivors were running and stumbling away
from the roaring furnace that had been a city. She ran with them toward
the mountains that ring the landward side of Hiroshima.

From the *Enola Gay*, the strangers from North America looked down
at their handiwork. "There, in front of our eyes," wrote Lewis, "was
without a doubt the greatest explosion man had ever witnessed. The city
was nine-tenths covered with smoke of a boiling nature, which seemed to
indicate buildings blowing up, and a large white cloud which in less than
three minutes reached 30,000 feet, then went to at least 50,000 feet."

Far below, on the edge of this cauldron of smoke, at a distance of some
2,500 yards from the blast's epicenter, Emiko ran with the rest of the
living. Some who could not run limped or dragged themselves along.
Others were carried. Many, hideously burned, were screaming with pain;

when they tripped they lay where they had fallen. There was a man whose face had been ripped open from mouth to ear, another whose forehead was a gaping wound. A young soldier was running with a foot-long splinter of bamboo protruding from one eye. But these, like Emiko, were the lightly wounded.

Some of the burned people had been literally roasted. Skin hung from their flesh like sodden tissue paper. They did not bleed but plasma dripped from their seared limbs.

The *Enola Gay*, mission completed, was returning to base. Lewis sought words to express his feelings, the feelings of all the crew. "I might say," he wrote, "I might say 'My God! What have we done?'"

Emiko ran. When she had reached the safety of the mountain she remembered that she still had her shoulder bag. There was a small first-aid kit in it and she applied ointment to her wounds and to a small cut in her left hand. She bandaged her head.

Emiko looked back at the city. It was a lake of fire. All around her the burned fugitives cried out in pain. Some were scorched on one side only. Others, naked and flayed, were burned all over. They were too many to help and most of them were dying. Emiko followed the walking wounded along a back road, still delirious, expecting suddenly to meet her father and mother.

The thousands dying by the roadside called feebly for help or water. Some of the more lightly injured were already walking in the other direction, back towards the flames. Others, with hardly any visible wounds, stopped, turned ashy pale, and died within minutes. No one knew then that they were victims of radiation.

Emiko reached the suburb of Nakayama.

Far off in the *Enola Gay*, Lewis, who had seen none of this, had been writing, "If I live a hundred years, I'll never get those few minutes out of my mind. Looking at Captain Parsons, why he is as confounded as the rest, and he is supposed to have known everything and expected this to happen...."

At Nakayama, Emiko stood in line at a depot where rice-balls were being distributed. Though it distressed her that the badly maimed could hardly feed themselves, the child found she was hungry. It was about 6 P.M. now. A little farther on, at Gion, a farmer called her by name. She did not recognize him, but it seemed he came monthly to her home to collect manure. The farmer took Emiko by the hand, led her to his own house, where his wife bathed her and fed her a meal of white rice. Then the child continued on her way. She passed another town where there were hundreds of injured. The dead were being hauled away in trucks. Among the injured a woman of about forty-five was waving frantically and muttering to herself. Emiko brought this woman a little water in a pumpkin leaf. She felt guilty about it; the schoolgirls had been warned not to give water to the seriously wounded. Emiko comforted herself with the thought that the woman would die soon anyway.

At Koi, she found standing-room in a train. It was heading for Otake with a full load of wounded. Many were put off at Ono, where there was a hospital; and two hours later the train rolled into Otake station. It was around 10 P.M.

A great crowd had gathered to look for their relations. It was a nightmare, Emiko remembered years afterwards; people were calling their dear kinfolk by name, searching frantically. It was necessary to call them by name, since most were so disfigured as to be unrecognizable. Doctors in the town council offices stitched Emiko's head-wounds. The place was crowded with casualties lying on the floor. Many died as Emiko watched.

The town council authorities made a strange announcement. They said a new and mysterious kind of bomb had fallen in Hiroshima. People were advised to stay away from the ruins.

Home at midnight, Emiko found her parents so happy to see her that they could not even cry. They could only give thanks that she was safe. Then they asked, "Where is your sister?"

For ten long days, while Emiko walked daily one and a half miles to have her wounds dressed with fresh gauze, her father searched the rubble of Hiroshima for his lost child. He could not have hoped to find her alive. All, as far as the eye could see, was a desolation of charred ashes and wreckage, relieved only by a few jagged ruins and by the seven estuarial rivers that flowed through the waste delta. The banks of these rivers were covered with the dead and in the rising tidal waters floated thousands of corpses. On one broad street in the Hakushima district the crowds who had been thronging there were all naked and scorched cadavers. Of thousands of others there was no trace at all. A fire several times hotter than the surface of the sun had turned them instantly to vapor.

On August 11 came the news that Nagasaki had suffered the same fate as Hiroshima; it was whispered that Japan had attacked the United States mainland with similar mysterious weapons. With the lavish circumstantiality of rumor, it was said that two out of a fleet of six-engined trans-Pacific bombers had failed to return. But on August 15, speaking for the first time over the radio to his people, the Emperor Hirohito announced his country's surrender. Emiko heard him. No more bombs! she thought. No more fear! The family did not learn till June the following year that this very day young Tetsuro had been killed in action in Manchuria.

Emiko's wounds healed slowly. In mid-September they had closed with a thin layer of pinkish skin. There had been a shortage of antiseptics and Emiko was happy to be getting well. Her satisfaction was short-lived. Mysteriously she came down with diarrhea and high fever. The fever continued for a month. Then one day she started to bleed from the gums, her mouth and throat became acutely inflamed, and her hair started to fall out. Through her delirium the child heard the doctors whisper by her pillow that she could not live. By now the doctors must have known that ionizing radiation caused such destruction of the blood's white cells that victims were left with little or no resistance against infection.

Yet Emiko recovered.

The wound on her hand, however, was particularly troublesome and did not heal for a long time.

As she got better, Emiko began to acquire some notion of the fearful scale of the disaster. Few of her friends and acquaintances were still alive. But no one knew precisely how many had died in Hiroshima. To this day the claims of various agencies conflict.

According to General Douglas MacArthur's headquarters, there were 78,150 dead and 13,083 missing.[1] The United States Atomic Bomb Casualty Commission claims there were 79,000 dead. Both sets of figures are probably far too low. There's reason to believe that at the time of the surrender Japanese authorities lied about the number of survivors, exaggerating it to get extra medical supplies. The Japanese welfare ministry's figures of 260,000 dead and 163,263 missing may well be too high. But the very order of such discrepancies speaks volumes about the scale of the catastrophe. The dead were literally uncountable.

This appalling toll of human life had been exacted from a city that had been prepared for air attack in a state of full wartime readiness. All civil-defense services had been overwhelmed from the first moment and it was many hours before any sort of organized rescue and relief could be put into effect.

It's true that single raids using so-called conventional weapons on other cities such as Tokyo and Dresden inflicted far greater casualties. And that it could not matter much to a victim whether he was burnt alive by a fire-storm caused by phosphorus, or by napalm or by nuclear fission. Yet in the whole of human history so savage a massacre had never before been inflicted with a single blow. And modern thermonuclear weapons are upwards of 1,000 times more powerful and deadly than the Hiroshima bomb.

The white scar I saw on Emiko's small, fine-boned hand was a tiny metaphor, a faint but eloquent reminder of the scar on humanity's conscience.

1968

---

1. Douglas MacArthur (1880–1964): American army officer, Allied Supreme Commander in the Southwest Pacific (1942) and of occupied Japan following World War II (1945–51).

Joan Didion

ON KEEPING A NOTEBOOK

"'That woman Estelle,'" the note reads, "'is partly the reason why George Sharp and I are separated today.' *Dirty crepe-de-Chine wrapper, hotel bar, Wilmington RR, 9:45 a.m. August Monday morning.*"

Since the note is in my notebook, it presumably has some meaning to me. I study it for a long while. At first I have only the most general notion of what I was doing on an August Monday morning in the bar of the hotel across from the Pennsylvania Railroad station in Wilmington, Delaware (waiting for a train? missing one? 1960? 1961? why Wilmington?), but I do remember being there. The woman in the dirty crepe-de-Chine wrapper had come down from her room for a beer, and the bartender had heard before the reason why George Sharp and she were separated today. "Sure," he said, and went on mopping the floor. "You told me." At the other end of the bar is a girl. She is talking, pointedly, not to the man beside her but to a cat lying in the triangle of sunlight cast through the open door. She is wearing a plaid silk dress from Peck & Peck, and the hem is coming down.

Here is what it is: the girl has been on the Eastern Shore, and now she is going back to the city, leaving the man beside her, and all she can see ahead are the viscous summer sidewalks and the 3 a.m. long-distance calls that will make her lie awake and then sleep drugged through all the steaming mornings left in August (1960? 1961?). Because she must go directly from the train to lunch in New York, she wishes that she had a safety pin for the hem of the plaid silk dress, and she also wishes that she could forget about the hem and the lunch and stay in the cool bar that smells of disinfectant and malt and make friends with the woman in the crepe-de-Chine wrapper. She is afflicted by a little self-pity, and she wants to compare Estelles. That is what that was all about.

Why did I write it down? In order to remember, of course, but exactly what was it I wanted to remember? How much of it actually happened? Did any of it? Why do I keep a notebook at all? It is easy to deceive oneself on all those scores. The impulse to write things down is a peculiarly compulsive one, inexplicable to those who do not share it, useful only accidentally, only secondarily, in the way that any compulsion tries to justify itself. I suppose that it begins or does not begin in the cradle. Although I have felt compelled to write things down since I was five years old, I doubt that my daughter ever will, for she is a singularly blessed and accepting child, delighted with life exactly as life presents

414

itself to her, unafraid to go to sleep and unafraid to wake up. Keepers of private notebooks are a different breed altogether, lonely and resistant rearrangers of things, anxious malcontents, children afflicted apparently at birth with some presentiment of loss.

My first notebook was a Big Five tablet, given to me by my mother with the sensible suggestion that I stop whining and learn to amuse myself by writing down my thoughts. She returned the tablet to me a few years ago; the first entry is an account of a woman who believed herself to be freezing to death in the Arctic night, only to find, when day broke, that she had stumbled onto the Sahara Desert, where she would die of the heat before lunch. I have no idea what turn of a five-year-old's mind could have prompted so insistently "ironic" and exotic a story, but it does reveal a certain predilection for the extreme which has dogged me into adult life; perhaps if I were analytically inclined I would find it a truer story than any I might have told about Donald Johnson's birthday party or the day my cousin Brenda put Kitty Litter in the aquarium.

So the point of my keeping a notebook has never been, nor is it now, to have an accurate factual record of what I have been doing or thinking. That would be a different impulse entirely, an instinct for reality which I sometimes envy but do not possess. At no point have I ever been able successfully to keep a diary; my approach to daily life ranges from the grossly negligent to the merely absent, and on those few occasions when I have tried dutifully to record a day's events, boredom has so overcome me that the results are mysterious at best. What is this business about "shopping, typing piece, dinner with E, depressed"? Shopping for what? Typing what piece? Who is E? Was this "E" depressed, or was I depressed? Who cares?

In fact I have abandoned altogether that kind of pointless entry; instead I tell what some would call lies. "That's simply not true," the members of my family frequently tell me when they come up against my memory of a shared event. "The party was *not* for you, the spider was *not* a black widow, *it wasn't that way at all.*" Very likely they are right, for not only have I always had trouble distinguishing between what happened and what merely might have happened, but I remain unconvinced that the distinction, for my purposes, matters. The cracked crab that I recall having for lunch the day my father came home from Detroit in 1945 must certainly be embroidery, worked into the day's pattern to lend verisimilitude; I was ten years old and would not now remember the cracked crab. The day's events did not turn on cracked crab. And yet it is precisely that fictitious crab that makes me see the afternoon all over again, a home movie run all too often, the father bearing gifts, the child weeping, an exercise in family love and guilt. Or that is what it was to me. Similarly, perhaps it never did snow that August in Vermont; perhaps there never were flurries in the night wind, and maybe no one else felt the ground hardening and summer already dead even as we pretended to bask in it, but that was how it felt to me, and it might as well have snowed, could have snowed, did snow.

How it felt to me: that is getting closer to the truth about a notebook. I sometimes delude myself about why I keep a notebook, imagine that some thrifty virtue derives from preserving everything observed. See enough and write it down, I tell myself, and then some morning when the world seems drained of wonder, some day when I am only going through the motions of doing what I am supposed to do, which is write—on that bankrupt morning I will simply open my notebook and there it will all be, a forgotten account with accumulated interest, paid passage back to the world out there: dialogue overheard in hotels and elevators and at the hatcheck counter in Pavillon (one middle-aged man shows his hat check to another and says, "That's my old football number"); impressions of Bettina Aptheker and Benjamin Sonnenberg and Teddy ("Mr. Acapulco") Stauffer; careful *aperçus* about tennis bums and failed fashion models and Greek shipping heiresses, one of whom taught me a significant lesson (a lesson I could have learned from F. Scott Fitzgerald, but perhaps we all must meet the very rich for ourselves) by asking, when I arrived to interview her in her orchid-filled sitting room on the second day of a paralyzing New York blizzard, whether it was snowing outside.

I imagine, in other words, that the notebook is about other people. But of course it is not. I have no real business with what one stranger said to another at the hat-check counter in Pavillon; in fact I suspect that the line "That's my old football number" touched not my own imagination at all, but merely some memory of something once read, probably "The Eighty-Yard Run." Nor is my concern with a woman in a dirty crepe-de-Chine wrapper in a Wilmington bar. My stake is always, of course, in the unmentioned girl in the plaid silk dress. *Remember what it was to be me:* that is always the point.

It is a difficult point to admit. We are brought up in the ethic that others, any others, all others, are by definition more interesting than ourselves; taught to be diffident, just this side of self-effacing. ("You're the least important person in the room and don't forget it," Jessica Mitford's governess would hiss in her ear on the advent of any social occasion; I copied that into my notebook because it is only recently that I have been able to enter a room without hearing some such phrase in my inner ear.) Only the very young and the very old may recount their dreams at breakfast, dwell upon self, interrupt with memories of beach picnics and favorite Liberty lawn dresses and the rainbow trout in a creek near Colorado Springs. The rest of us are expected, rightly, to affect absorption in other people's favorite dresses, other people's trout.

And so we do. But our notebooks give us away, for however dutifully we record what we see around us, the common denominator of all we see is always, transparently, shamelessly, the implacable "I." We are not talking here about the kind of notebook that is patently for public consumption, a structural conceit for binding together a series of graceful *pensées*;[1] we are talking about something private, about bits of the mind's string too short to use, an indiscriminate and erratic assemblage with meaning only for its maker.

And sometimes even the maker has difficulty with the meaning. There does not seem to be, for example, any point in my knowing for the rest of my life that, during 1964, 720 tons of soot fell on every square mile of New York City, yet there it is in my notebook, labeled "FACT." Nor do I really need to remember that Ambrose Bierce liked to spell Leland Stanford's[2] name "£eland $tanford" or that "smart women almost always wear black in Cuba," a fashion hint without much potential for practical application. And does not the relevance of these notes seem marginal at best?:

> In the basement museum of the Inyo County Courthouse in Independence, California, sign pinned to a mandarin coat: "This MANDARIN COAT was often worn by Mrs. Minnie S. Brooks when giving lectures on her TEAPOT COLLECTION."
> Redhead getting out of car in front of Beverly Wilshire Hotel, chinchilla stole, Vuitton bags with tags reading:
> > MRS LOU FOX
> > HOTEL SAHARA
> > VEGAS

Well, perhaps not entirely marginal. As a matter of fact, Mrs. Minnie S. Brooks and her MANDARIN COAT pull me back into my own childhood, for although I never knew Mrs. Brooks and did not visit Inyo County until I was thirty, I grew up in just such a world, in houses cluttered with Indian relics and bits of gold ore and ambergris and the souvenirs my Aunt Mercy Farnsworth brought back from the Orient. It is a long way from that world to Mrs. Lou Fox's world, where we all live now, and is it not just as well to remember that? Might not Mrs. Minnie S. Brooks help me to remember what I am? Might not Mrs. Lou Fox help me to remember what I am not?

But sometimes the point is harder to discern. What exactly did I have in mind when I noted down that it cost the father of someone I know $650 a month to light the place on the Hudson in which he lived before the Crash?[3] What use was I planning to make of this line by Jimmy Hoffa: "I

1. Thoughts, reflections.
2. A nineteenth-century American million-

aire.
3. The stock market crash of 1929.

may have my faults, but being wrong ain't one of them"? And although I
think it interesting to know where the girls who travel with the Syndicate
have their hair done when they find themselves on the West Coast, will I
ever make suitable use of it? Might I not be better off just passing it on to
John O'Hara? What is a recipe for sauerkraut doing in my notebook?
What kind of magpie keeps this notebook? "He was born the night the
Titanic went down." That seems a nice enough line, and I even recall who
said it, but is it not really a better line in life than it could ever be in
fiction?

But of course that is exactly it: not that I should ever use the line, but
that I should remember the woman who said it and the afternoon I heard
it. We were on her terrace by the sea, and we were finishing the wine left
from lunch, trying to get what sun there was, a California winter sun.
The woman whose husband was born the night the Titanic went down
wanted to rent her house, wanted to go back to her children in Paris. I
remember wishing that I could afford the house, which cost $1,000 a
month. "Someday you will," she said lazily. "Someday it all comes."
There in the sun on her terrace it seemed easy to believe in someday, but
later I had a low-grade afternoon hangover and ran over a black snake on
the way to the supermarket and was flooded with inexplicable fear when I
heard the checkout clerk explaining to the man ahead of me why she was
finally divorcing her husband. "He left me no choice," she said over and
over as she punched the register. "He has a little seven-month-old baby
by her, he left me no choice." I would like to believe that my dread then
was for the human condition, but of course it was for me, because I
wanted a baby and did not then have one and because I wanted to own
the house that cost $1,000 a month to rent and because I had a hangover.

It all comes back. Perhaps it is difficult to see the value in having one's
self back in that kind of mood, but I do see it; I think we are well advised
to keep on nodding terms with the people we used to be whether we find
them attractive company or not. Otherwise they turn up unannounced
and surprise us, come hammering on the mind's door at 4 a.m. of a bad
night and demand to know who deserted them, who betrayed them, who
is going to make amends. We forget all too soon the things we thought
we could never forget. We forget the loves and the betrayals alike, forget
what we whispered and what we screamed, forget who we were. I have
already lost touch with a couple of people I used to be; one of them, a
seventeen-year-old, presents little threat, although it would be of some
interest to me to know again what it feels like to sit on a river levee
drinking vodka-and-orange-juice and listening to Les Paul and Mary
Ford and their echoes sing "How High the Moon" on the car radio. (You
see I still have the scenes, but I no longer perceive myself among those
present, no longer could even improvise the dialogue.) The other one, a
twenty-three-year-old, bothers me more. She was always a good deal of

trouble, and I suspect she will reappear when I least want to see her, skirts too long, shy to the point of aggravation, always the injured party, full of recriminations and little hurts and stories I do not want to hear again, at once saddening me and angering me with her vulnerability and ignorance, an apparition all the more insistent for being so long banished.

It is a good idea, then, to keep in touch, and I suppose that keeping in touch is what notebooks are all about. And we are all on our own when it comes to keeping those lines open to ourselves: your notebook will never help me, nor mine you. *"So what's new in the whiskey business?"* What could that possibly mean to you? To me it means a blonde in a Pucci bathing suit sitting with a couple of fat men by the pool at the Beverly Hills Hotel. Another man approaches, and they all regard one another in silence for a while. "So what's new in the whiskey business?" one of the fat men finally says by way of welcome, and the blonde stands up, arches one foot and dips it in the pool, looking all the while at the cabaña where Baby Pignatari is talking on the telephone. That is all there is to that, except that several years later I saw the blonde coming out of Saks Fifth Avenue in New York with her California complexion and a voluminous mink coat. In the harsh wind that day she looked old and irrevocably tired to me, and even the skins in the mink coat were not worked the way they were doing them that year, not the way she would have wanted them done, and there is the point of the story. For a while after that I did not like to look in the mirror, and my eyes would skim the newspapers and pick out only the deaths, the cancer victims, the premature coronaries, the suicides, and I stopped riding the Lexington Avenue IRT[4] because I noticed for the first time that all the strangers I had seen for years—the man with the seeing-eye dog, the spinster who read the classified pages every day, the fat girl who always got off with me at Grand Central—looked older than they once had.

It all comes back. Even that recipe for sauerkraut: even that brings it back. I was on Fire Island when I first made that sauerkraut, and it was raining, and we drank a lot of bourbon and ate the sauerkraut and went to bed at ten, and I listened to the rain and the Atlantic and felt safe. I made the sauerkraut again last night and it did not make me feel any safer, but that is, as they say, another story.

1968

4. A New York City subway line; one of its stops is the Grand Central railway terminal.

THE READER

1. *What distinction does Didion make between a diary and a notebook?*
2. *What uses does a notebook have for Didion?*
3. *Didion says she uses her notebook to "tell what some would call lies." Why does she do this? Would some people call these things truths? Why?*

4. What does Didion imply is the difference between a notebook and a diary?

5. Is the visit Didion describes in "On Going Home" (p. 40) an effort to keep in touch with the people we used to be (p. 418)? One test would be to check "On Going Home" for phrases and observations like those she quotes from her notebooks. Are there any?

THE WRITER

1. Didion says that "we are brought up in the ethic that others . . . are by definition more interesting than ourselves." Explain whether she believes this can be harmful to one's development as a writer.

2. Didion says: "How it felt to me: that is getting closer to the truth about a notebook." What writing strategies does she use to convey "how it felt"?

3. Try keeping a notebook for a week, jotting down the sort of things that Didion does. At the end of the week, take one or two of your entries and expand on them, as Didion does with the entries on Mrs. Minnie S. Brooks and Mrs. Lou Fox.

4. Read Woolf's "The New Biography" (p. 420), and write a brief comparison of Woolf's metaphors of granite and rainbow with Didion's distinction between the facts of "what happened and what merely might have happened." Are the two writers talking about the same basic distinction or not?

5. References to her notebooks give you a lot of biographical detail about Didion's life, as do her essays "On Going Home" (p. 40) and "Georgia O'Keeffe" (p. 673). Restricting yourself to that information, sketch out as much of her biography as you can, and then write a paragraph of that biography. For advice about writing a biography, you might consult Woolf's "The New Biography" (below).

Virginia Woolf

THE NEW BIOGRAPHY

"The aim of biography," said Sir Sidney Lee, who had perhaps read and written more lives than any man of his time, "is the truthful transmission of personality," and no single sentence could more neatly split up into two parts the whole problem of biography as it presents itself to us today. On the one hand there is truth; on the other there is personality. And if we think of truth as something of granite-like solidity and of personality as something of rainbow-like intangibility and reflect that the aim of biography is to weld these two into one seamless whole, we shall admit that the problem is a stiff one and that we need not wonder if biographers have for the most part failed to solve it.

For the truth of which Sir Sidney speaks, the truth which biography demands, is truth in its hardest, most obdurate form; it is truth as truth is to be found in the British Museum; it is truth out of which all vapor of falsehood has been pressed by the weight of research. Only when truth had been thus established did Sir Sidney Lee use it in the building of his monument; and no one can be so foolish as to deny that the piles he raised of such hard facts, whether one is called Shakespeare or King Edward the Seventh, are worthy of all our respect. For there is a virtue in truth; it has an almost mystic power. Like radium, it seems able to give off forever and ever grains of energy, atoms of light. It stimulates the mind, which is endowed with a curious susceptibility in this direction as no fiction, however artful or highly colored, can stimulate it. Truth being thus efficacious and supreme, we can only explain the fact that Sir Sidney's life of Shakespeare is dull, and that his life of Edward the Seventh is unreadable, by supposing that though both are stuffed with truth, he failed to choose those truths which transmit personality. For in order that the light of personality may shine through, facts must be manipulated; some must be brightened; others shaded; yet, in the process, they must never lose their integrity. And it is obvious that it is easier to obey these precepts by considering that the true life of your subject shows itself in action which is evident rather than in that inner life of thought and emotion which meanders darkly and obscurely through the hidden channels of the soul. Hence, in the old days, the biographer chose the easier path. A life, even when it was lived by a divine, was a series of exploits. The biographer, whether he was Izaak Walton or Mrs. Hutchinson or that unknown writer who is often so suprisingly eloquent on tombstones and memorial tablets, told a tale of battle and victory. With their stately phrasing and their deliberate artistic purpose, such records transmit personality with a formal sincerity which is perfectly satisfactory of its kind. And so, perhaps, biography might have pursued its way, draping the robes decorously over the recumbent figures of the dead, had there not arisen toward the end of the eighteenth century one of those curious men of genius who seem able to break up the stiffness into which the company has fallen by speaking in his natural voice. So Boswell spoke. So we hear booming out from Boswell's page the voice of Samuel Johnson. "No, sir; stark insensibility," we hear him say. Once we have heard those words we are aware that there is an incalculable presence among us which will go on ringing and reverberating in widening circles however times may change and ourselves. All the draperies and decencies of biography fall to the ground. We can no longer maintain that life consists in actions only or in works. It consists in personality. Something has been liberated beside which all else seems cold and colorless. We are freed from a servitude which is now seen to be intolerable. No longer need we pass solemnly and stiffly from camp to council chamber. We may sit, even with the great and good, over the table and talk.

Through the influence of Boswell, presumably, biography all through the nineteenth century concerned itself as much with the lives of the sedentary as with the lives of the active. It sought painstakingly and devotedly to express not only the outer life of work and activity but the inner life of emotion and thought. The uneventful lives of poets and painters were written out as lengthily as the lives of soldiers and statesmen. But the Victorian biography was a parti-colored, hybrid, monstrous birth. For though truth of fact was observed as scrupulously as Boswell observed it, the personality which Boswell's genius set free was hampered and distorted. The convention which Boswell had destroyed settled again, only in a different form, upon biographers who lacked his art. Where the Mrs. Hutchinsons and the Izaak Waltons had wished to prove that their heroes were prodigies of courage and learning the Victorian biographer was dominated by the idea of goodness. Noble, upright, chaste, severe; it is thus that the Victorian worthies are presented to us. The figure is almost always above life size in top hat and frock coat, and the manner of presentation becomes increasingly clumsy and laborious. For lives which no longer express themselves in action take shape in innumerable words. The conscientious biographer may not tell a fine tale with a flourish, but must toil through endless labyrinths and embarrass himself with countless documents. In the end he produces an amorphous mass, a life of Tennyson, or of Gladstone, in which we go seeking disconsolately for voice or laughter, for curse or anger, for any trace that this fossil was once a living man. Often, indeed, we bring back some invaluable trophy, for Victorian biographies are laden with truth; but always we rummage among them with a sense of the prodigious waste, of the artistic wrongheadedness of such a method.

With the twentieth century, however, a change came over biography, as it came over fiction and poetry. The first and most visible sign of it was the difference in size. In the first twenty years of the new century biographies must have lost half their weight. Mr. Strachey compressed four stout Victorians into one slim volume; M. Maurois boiled the usual two volumes of a Shelley life into one little book the size of a novel. But the diminution of size was only the outward token of an inward change. The point of view had completely altered. If we open one of the new school of biographies its bareness, its emptiness makes us at once aware that the author's relation to his subject is different. He is no longer the serious and sympathetic companion, toiling even slavishly in the footsteps of his hero. Whether friend or enemy, admiring or critical, he is an equal. In any case, he preserves his freedom and his right to independent judgment. Moreover, he does not think himself constrained to follow every step of the way. Raised upon a little eminence which his independence has made for him, he sees his subject spread about him. He chooses; he synthesizes; in short, he has ceased to be the chronicler; he has become an artist.

Few books illustrate the new attitude to biography better than *Some People*,[1] by Harold Nicolson. In his biographies of Tennyson and of Byron Mr. Nicolson followed the path which had been already trodden by Mr. Strachey and others. Here he has taken a step on his own initiative. For here he has devised a method of writing about people and about himself as though they were at once real and imaginary. He has succeeded remarkably, if not entirely, in making the best of both worlds. *Some People* is not fiction because it has the substance, the reality of truth. It is not biography because it has the freedom, the artistry of fiction. And if we try to discover how he has won the liberty which enables him to present us with these extremely amusing pages we must in the first place credit him with having had the courage to rid himself of a mountain of illusion. An English diplomat is offered all the bribes which usually induce people to swallow humbug in large doses with composure. If Mr. Nicolson wrote about Lord Curzon it should have been solemnly. If he mentioned the Foreign Office it should have been respectfully. His tone toward the world of Bognors[2] and Whitehall should have been friendly but devout. But thanks to a number of influences and people, among whom one might mention Max Beerbohm and Voltaire, the attitude of the bribed and docile official has been blown to atoms. Mr. Nicolson laughs. He laughs at Lord Curzon; he laughs at the Foreign Office; he laughs at himself. And since his laughter is the laughter of the intelligence it has the effect of making us take the people he laughs at seriously. The figure of Lord Curzon concealed behind the figure of a drunken valet is touched off with merriment and irreverence; yet of all the studies of Lord Curzon which have been written since his death none makes us think more kindly of that preposterous but, it appears, extremely human man.

So it would seem as if one of the great advantages of the new school to which Mr. Nicolson belongs is the lack of pose, humbug, solemnity. They approach their bigwigs fearlessly. They have no fixed scheme of the universe, no standard of courage or morality to which they insist that he shall conform. The man himself is the supreme object of their curiosity. Further, and it is this chiefly which has so reduced the bulk of biography, they maintain that the man himself, the pith and essence of his character, shows itself to the observant eye in the tone of a voice, the

---

1. "Nine semi-biographical sketches concerning which the author says, 'Many are purely imaginary. Such truths as they may contain are only half-truths'" (*Book Review Digest*, 1927).

2. Bognors: a seaside resort in Sussex featuring many convalescent homes; Whitehall: the British civil-service administration, much of it housed on the street of this name.

turn of a head, some little phrase or anecdote picked up in passing. Thus in two subtle phrases, in one passage of brilliant description, whole chapters of the Victorian volume are synthesized and summed up. *Some People* is full of examples of this new phase of the biographer's art. Mr. Nicolson wants to describe a governess and he tells us that she had a drop at the end of her nose and made him salute the quarter-deck. He wants to describe Lord Curzon, and he makes him lose his trousers and recite "Tears, Idle Tears." He does not cumber himself with a single fact about them. He waits till they have said or done something characteristic, and then he pounces on it with glee. But, though he waits with an intention of pouncing which might well make his victims uneasy if they guessed it, he lays suspicion by appearing himself in his own proper person in no flattering light. He has a scrubby dinner jacket, he tells us; a pink bumptious face, curly hair, and a curly nose. He is as much the subject of his own ironies and observation as they are. He lies in wait for his own absurdities as artfully as for theirs. Indeed, by the end of the book we realize that the figure which has been most completely and most subtly displayed is that of the author. Each of the supposed subjects holds up in his or her small bright diminishing mirror a different reflection of Harold Nicolson. And though the figure thus revealed is not noble or impressive or shown in a very heroic attitude, it is for these very reasons extremely like a real human being. It is thus, he would seem to say, in the mirrors of our friends, that we chiefly live.

To have contrived this effect is a triumph not of skill only, but of those positive qualities which we are likely to treat as if they were negative— freedom from pose, from sentimentality, from illusion. And the victory is definite enough to leave us asking what territory it has won for the art of biography. Mr. Nicolson has proved that one can use many of the devices of fiction in dealing with real life. He has shown that a little fiction mixed with fact can be made to transmit personality very effectively. But some objections or qualifications suggest themselves. Undoubtedly the figures in *Some People* are all rather below life size. The irony with which they are treated, though it has its tenderness, stunts their growth. It dreads nothing more than that one of these little beings should grow up and become serious or perhaps tragic. And, again, they never occupy the stage for more than a few brief moments. They do not want to be looked at very closely. They have not a great deal to show us. Mr. Nicolson makes us feel, in short, that he is playing with very dangerous elements. An incautious movement and the book will be blown sky high. He is trying to mix the truth of real life and the truth of fiction. He can only do it by using no more than a pinch of either. For though both truths are genuine, they are antagonistic; let them meet and they destroy each other. Even here, where the imagination is not deeply engaged, when we find people whom we know to be real like Lord Oxford or Lady Colefax, mingling with Miss Plimsoll and Marstock, whose reality we doubt, the one casts suspicion upon the other. Let it be fact, one feels, or let it be fiction; the imagination will not serve under two masters simultaneously.

And here we again approach the difficulty which, for all his ingenuity, the biographer still has to face. Truth of fact and truth of fiction are incompatible; yet he is now more than ever urged to combine them. For it would seem that the life which is increasingly real to us is the fictitious life; it dwells in the personality rather than in the act. Each of us is more Hamlet, Prince of Denmark, than he is John Smith of the Corn Exchange. Thus, the biographer's imagination is always being stimulated to use the novelists's art of arrangement, suggestion, dramatic effect to expound the private life. Yet if he carries the use of fiction too far, so that he disregards the truth, or can only introduce it with incongruity, he loses both worlds; he has neither the freedom of fiction nor the substance of fact. Boswell's astonishing power over us is based largely upon his obstinate veracity, so that we have implicit belief in what he tells us. When Johnson says "No, sir; stark insensibility," the voice has a ring in it because we have been told, soberly and prosaically, a few pages earlier, that Johnson "was entered a Commoner of Pembroke, on the 31st of October, 1728, being then in his nineteenth year." We are in the world of brick and pavement; of birth, marriage, and death; of Acts of Parliament; of Pitt and Burke and Sir Joshua Reynolds. Whether this is a more real world than the world of Bohemia and Hamlet and Macbeth we doubt; but the mixture of the two is abhorrent.

Be that as it may we can assure ourselves by a very simple experiment that the days of Victorian biography are over. Consider one's own life; pass under review a few years that one has actually lived. Conceive how Lord Morley would have expounded them; how Sir Sidney Lee would have documented them; how strangely all that has been most real in them would have slipped through their fingers. Nor can we name the biographer whose art is subtle and bold enough to present that queer amalgamation of dream and reality, that perpetual marriage of granite and rainbow. His method still remains to be discovered. But Mr. Nicolson with his mixture of biography and autobiography, of fact and fiction, of Lord Curzon's trousers and Miss Plimsoll's nose, waves his hand airily in a possible direction.

1958

THE READER

1. Explain the significance of the metaphors of "granite" and "rainbow" in Woolf's first paragraph.
2. Woolf says that for some biographers a life was "a series of exploits." What more does she think a good biography should be? Why?
3. Why does Woolf object to the presentation of figures "above life size"

in biography?
4. What are the differences between a biographer who is a "chronicler" and one who is an "artist"?
5. Explain why Woolf thinks that "truth of fact and truth of fiction are incompatible."

THE WRITER

1. What does Woolf mean when she says that in the new school of biography "the figure which has been most completely and most subtly displayed is that of the author"? How "truthful" can such a biography be?
2. Why does Woolf call the new biography an "art"? How does it differ from the biography of "facts" displaying "the weight of research"?
3. Make a list of facts and actions that would be important in writing a brief autobiography or a biography of someone you know well. Make a list of personality traits for yourself or the other person selected. Then, using Woolf's essay as a guide, write a brief autobiographical or biographical sketch.
4. How far does Woolf follow her theory of what a good biography should be in her sketch of her father, Leslie Stephen (p. 83)?

Frances FitzGerald

REWRITING AMERICAN HISTORY

Those of us who grew up in the fifties believed in the permanence of our American-history textbooks. To us as children, those texts were the truth of things: they were American history. It was not just that we read them before we understood that not everything that is printed is the truth, or the whole truth. It was that they, much more than other books, had the demeanor and trappings of authority. They were weighty volumes. They spoke in measured cadences: imperturbable, humorless, and as distant as Chinese emperors. Our teachers treated them with respect, and we paid them abject homage by memorizing a chapter a week. But now the textbook histories have changed, some of them to such an extent that an adult would find them unrecognizable.

One current junior-high-school American history begins with a story about a Negro cowboy called George McJunkin. It appears that when McJunkin was riding down a lonely trail in New Mexico one cold spring morning in 1925 he discovered a mound containing bones and stone implements, which scientists later proved belonged to an Indian civilization ten thousand years old. The book goes on to say that scientists now believe there were people in the Americas at least twenty thousand years ago. It discusses the Aztec, Mayan, and Incan civilizations and the meaning of the word "culture" before introducing the European explorers.

Another history text—this one for the fifth grade—begins with the story of how Henry B. Gonzalez, who is a member of Congress from Texas, learned about his own nationality. When he was ten years old, his teacher told him he was an American because he was born in the United States. His grandmother, however, said, "The cat was born in the oven. Does that make him bread?" After reporting that Mr. Gonzalez eventually went to college and law school, the book explains that "the melting pot idea hasn't worked out as some thought it would," and that now "some people say that the people of the United States are more like a salad bowl than a melting pot."

Poor Columbus! He is a minor character now, a walk-on in the middle of American history. Even those books that have not replaced his picture with a Mayan temple or an Iroquois mask do not credit him with discovering America—even for the Europeans. The Vikings, they say, preceded him to the New World, and after that the Europeans, having lost or forgotten their maps, simply neglected to cross the ocean again for five hundred years. Columbus is far from being the only personage to have suffered from time and revision. Captain John Smith, Daniel Boone, and Wild Bill Hickok—the great self-promoters of American history—have all but disappeared, taking with them a good deal of the romance of the American frontier. General Custer has given way to Chief Crazy Horse; General Eisenhower no longer liberates Europe single-handed; and, indeed, most generals, even to Washington and Lee, have faded away, as old soldiers do, giving place to social reformers such as William Lloyd Garrison and Jacob Riis. A number of black Americans have risen to prominence: not only George Washington Carver but Frederick Douglass and Martin Luther King, Jr. W. E. B. Du Bois now invariably accompanies Booker T. Washington. In addition, there is a mystery man called Crispus Attucks, a fugitive slave about whom nothing seems to be known for certain except that he was a victim of the Boston Massacre and thus became one of the first casualties of the American Revolution. Thaddeus Stevens has been reconstructed—his character changed, as it were, from black to white, from cruel and vindictive to persistent and sincere. As for Teddy Roosevelt, he now champions the issue of conservation instead of charging up San Juan Hill. No single President really stands out as a hero, but all Presidents—except certain unmentionables in the second half of the nineteenth century—seem to have done as well as could be expected, given difficult circumstances.

Of course, when one thinks about it, it is hardly surprising that modern scholarship and modern perspectives have found their way into children's books. Yet the changes remain shocking. Those who in the sixties complained of the bland optimism, the chauvinism, and the materialism of their old civics text did so in the belief that, for all their protests, the texts would never change. The thought must have had something reassuring about it, for that generation never noticed when its complaints began to take effect and the songs about radioactive rainfall and houses made of ticky-tacky began to appear in the textbooks. But this is what happened.

The history texts now hint at a certain level of unpleasantness in American history. Several books, for instance, tell the story of Ishi, the last "wild" Indian in the continental United States, who, captured in 1911 after the massacre of his tribe, spent the final four and a half years of his life in the University of California's museum of anthropology, in San Francisco. At least three books show the same stunning picture of the breaker boys, the child coal miners of Pennsylvania—ancient children with deformed bodies and blackened faces who stare stupidly out from the entrance to a mine. One book quotes a soldier on the use of torture in the American campaign to pacify the Philippines at the beginning of the century. A number of books say that during the American Revolution the patriots tarred and feathered those who did not support them, and drove many of the loyalists from the country. Almost all the present-day history books note that the United States interned Japanese-Americans in detention camps during the Second World War.

Ideologically speaking, the histories of the fifties were implacable, seamless. Inside their covers, America was perfect: the greatest nation in the world, and the embodiment of democracy, freedom, and technological progress. For them, the country never changed in any important way: its values and its political institutions remained constant from the time of the American Revolution. To my generation—the children of the fifties —these texts appeared permanent just because they were so self-contained. Their orthodoxy, it seemed, left no handholds for attack, no lodging for decay. Who, after all, would dispute the wonders of technology or the superiority of the English colonists over the Spanish? Who would find fault with the pastorale of the West or the Old South? Who would question the anti-Communist crusade? There was, it seemed, no point in comparing these visions with reality, since they were the public truth and were thus quite irrelevant to what existed and to what anyone privately believed. They were—or so it seemed—the permanent expression of mass culture in America.

But now the texts have changed, and with them the country that American children are growing up into. The society that was once uniform is now a patchwork of rich and poor, old and young, men and women, blacks, whites, Hispanics, and Indians. The system that ran so smoothly by means of the Constitution under the guidance of benevolent conductor Presidents is now a rattletrap affair. The past is no highway to the present; it is a collection of issues and events that do not fit together and that lead in no single direction. The word "progress" has been replaced by the word "change": children, the modern texts insist, should learn history so that they can adapt to the rapid changes taking place around them. History is proceeding in spite of us. The present, which was once portrayed in the concluding chapters as a peaceful haven of scientific advances and Presidential inaugurations, is now a tangle of problems: race problems, urban problems, foreign-policy problems, problems of pollution, poverty, energy depletion, youthful rebellion, assassination, and drugs. Some books illustrate these problems dramatically. One, for instance, contains a picture of a doll half buried in a mass of untreated sewage; the caption reads, "Are we in danger of being overwhelmed by the products of our society and wastage created by their production? Would you agree with this photographer's interpretation?" Two books show the same picture of an old black woman sitting in a straight chair in a dingy room, her hands folded in graceful resignation; the surrounding text discusses the problems faced by the urban poor and by the aged who depend on Social Security. Other books present current problems less starkly. One of the texts concludes sagely:

> Problems are part of life. Nations face them, just as people face them, and try to solve them. And today's Americans have one great advantage over past generations. Never before have Americans been so well equipped to solve their problems. They have today the means to conquer poverty, disease, and ignorance. The technetronic age has put that power into their hands.

Such passages have a familiar ring. Amid all the problems, the deus ex machina[1] of science still dodders around in the gloaming of pious hope.

Even more surprising than the emergence of problems is the discovery that the great unity of the texts has broken. Whereas in the fifties all texts represented the same political view, current texts follow no pattern of orthodoxy. Some books, for instance, portray civil-rights legislation as a series of actions taken by a wise, paternal government; others convey some suggestion of the social upheaval involved and make mention of such people as Stokely Carmichael and Malcolm X.[2] In some books, the Cold War has ended; in others, it continues, with Communism threatening the free nations of the earth.

The political diversity in the books is matched by a diversity of pedagogical approach. In addition to the traditional narrative histories, with their endless streams of facts, there are so-called "discovery," or "inquiry," texts, which deal with a limited number of specific issues in

1. God from a machine. A reference to early plays in which a god, lowered to the stage by mechanical means, solved the drama's problems; thus, an artificial solution to a difficulty.
2. Radical black leaders of the 1960s.

American history. These tests do not pretend to cover the past; they focus on particular topics, such as "stratification in Colonial society" or "slavery and the American Revolution," and illustrate them with documents from primary and secondary sources. The chapters in these books amount to something like case studies, in that they include testimony from people with different perspectives or conflicting views on a single subject. In addition, the chapters provide background information, explanatory notes, and a series of questions for the student. The questions are the heart of the matter, for when they are carefully selected they force students to think much as historians think: to define the point of view of the speaker, analyze the ideas presented, question the relationship between events, and so on. One text, for example, quotes Washington, Jefferson, and John Adams on the question of foreign alliances and then asks, "What did John Adams assume that the international situation would be after the American Revolution? What did Washington's attitude toward the French alliance seem to be? How do you account for his attitude?" Finally, it asks, "Should a nation adopt a policy toward alliances and cling to it consistently, or should it vary its policies toward other countries as circumstances change?" In these books, history is clearly not a list of agreed-upon facts or a sermon on politics but a babble of voices and a welter of events which must be ordered by the historian.

In matters of pedagogy, as in matters of politics, there are not two sharply differentiated categories of books; rather, there is a spectrum. Politically, the books run from moderate left to moderate right; pedagogically, they run from the traditional history sermons, through a middle ground of narrative texts with inquiry-style questions and of inquiry texts with long stretches of narrative, to the most rigorous of case-study books. What is common to the current texts—and makes all of them different from those of the fifties—is their engagement with the social sciences. In eighth-grade histories, the "concepts" of social sciences make fleeting appearances. But these "concepts" are the very foundation stones of various elementary-school social-studies series. The 1970 Harcourt Brace Jovanovich[3] series, for example, boasts in its preface of "a horizontal base or ordering of conceptual schemes" to match its "vertical arm of behavioral themes." What this means is not entirely clear, but the books do proceed from easy questions to hard ones, such as—in the sixth-grade book—"How was interaction between merchants and citizens different in the Athenian and Spartan social systems?" Virtually all the American-history texts for older children include discussions of "role," "status," and "culture." Some of them stage debates between eminent social scientists in roped-off sections of the text; some include essays on economics or sociology; some contain pictures and short biographies of

---

3. Major textbook publisher.

social scientists of both sexes and of diverse races. Many books seem to accord social scientists a higher status than American Presidents.

Quite as striking as these political and pedagogical alterations is the change in the physical appearance of the texts. The schoolbooks of the fifties showed some effort in the matter of design: they had maps, charts, cartoons, photographs, and an occasional four-color picture to break up the columns of print. But beside the current texts they look as naïve as Soviet fashion magazines. The print in the fifties books is heavy and far too black, the colors muddy. The photographs are conventional news shots—portraits of Presidents in three-quarters profile, posed "action" shots of soldiers. The other illustrations tend to be Socialist-realist-style[4] drawings (there are a lot of hefty farmers with hoes in the Colonial-period chapters) or incredibly vulgar made-for-children paintings of patriotic events. One painting shows Columbus standing in full court dress on a beach in the New World from a perspective that could have belonged only to the Arawaks.[5] By contrast, the current texts are paragons of sophisticated modern design. They look not like People or Family Circle but, rather, like Architectural Digest or Vogue. * * * The amount of space given to illustrations is far greater than it was in the fifties; in fact, in certain "slow-learner" books the pictures far outweigh the text in importance. However, the illustrations have a much greater historical value. Instead of made-up paintings or anachronistic sketches, there are cartoons, photographs, and paintings drawn from the periods being treated. The chapters on the Colonial period will show, for instance, a ship's carved prow, a Revere bowl, a Copley[6] painting—a whole gallery of Early Americana. The nineteenth century is illustrated with nineteenth-century cartoons and photographs—and the photographs are all of high artistic quality. As for the twentieth-century chapters, they are adorned with the contents of a modern-art museum.

The use of all this art and high-quality design contains some irony. The nineteenth-century photographs of child laborers or urban slum apartments are so beautiful that they transcend their subjects. To look at them, or at the Victor Gatto painting of the Triangle shirtwaist-factory fire, is to see not misery or ugliness but an art object. In the modern chapters, the contrast between style and content is just as great: the color photographs of junk yards or polluted rivers look as enticing as Gourmet's photographs of food. The book that is perhaps the most stark in its description of modern problems illustrates the horrors of nuclear testing with a pretty Ben Shahn picture of the Bikini explosion,[7] and the poten-

4. Socialist realism, which originated in the Soviet Union, is a style of art in which the communal labor of farmers and industrial workers is glorified in works of poster-like crudity.
5. American Indians, then inhabiting the Caribbean area.
6. The reference is to John Singleton Copley (1738–1815), greatest of the American old masters; he specialized in portraits and historical paintings.
7. The Bikini atoll, part of the Marshall Is-

tial for global ecological disaster with a color photograph of the planet swirling its mantle of white clouds. Whereas in the nineteen-fifties the texts were childish in the sense that they were naïve and clumsy, they are now childish in the sense that they are polymorphous-perverse. American history is not dull any longer; it is a sensuous experience.

The surprise that adults feel in seeing the changes in history texts must come from the lingering hope that there is, somewhere out there, an objective truth. The hope is, of course, foolish. All of us children of the twentieth century know, or should know, that there are no absolutes in human affairs, and thus there can be no such thing as perfect objectivity. We know that each historian in some degree creates the world anew and that all history is in some degree contemporary history. But beyond this knowledge there is still a hope for some reliable authority, for some fixed stars in the universe. We may know that journalists cannot be wholly unbiased and that "balance" is an imaginary point between two extremes, and yet we hope that Walter Cronkite will tell us the truth of things. In the same way, we hope that our history will not change—that we learned the truth of things as children. The texts, with their impersonal voices, encourage this hope, and therefore it is particularly disturbing to see how they change, and how fast.

Slippery history! Not every generation but every few years the content of American-history books for children changes appreciably. Schoolbooks are not, like trade books,[8] written and left to their fate. To stay in step with the cycles of "adoption"[9] in school districts across the country, the publishers revise most of their old texts or substitute new ones every three or four years. In the process of revision, they not only bring history up to date but make changes—often substantial changes—in the body of the work. History books for children are thus more contemporary than any other form of history. How should it be otherwise? Should students read histories written ten, fifteen, thirty years ago? In theory, the system is reasonable—except that each generation of children reads only one generation of schoolbooks. The transient history is those children's history forever—their particular version of America.

1979

---

lands in the Pacific, was the site of American nuclear-bomb testing from 1946 to 1958. Ben Shahn (1898–1969) was an American painter and graphic artist with strong social and po-

litical concerns.
8. Books written for a general audience, as opposed to textbooks.
9. Choice of required textbooks.

THE READER

1. What sorts of difference does FitzGerald find between the history textbooks of the fifties and those of today? In what ways—according to what she states or implies—have the texts been improved? Does she see any changes for the worse?
2. On p. 429, FitzGerald says that in the new texts, "the word 'progress'

has been replaced by the word 'change.'" What is the difference between these two words? What does the replacement imply?

3. Is FitzGerald showing that the new textbooks give a truer account of American history?

THE WRITER

1. By "rewriting," does FitzGerald mean changing the facts of history? What is the relationship between the facts of history and history textbooks?

2. Why does FitzGerald give the story about George McJunkin (p. 426)? Was his discovery important?

3. Compare the process of "rewriting" or "revision" of history described by FitzGerald with Sommers's discussion of revision strategies (p. 232).

4. Write a brief account of the revisions you would like to see in some textbook you have used.

Edward Hallett Carr

THE HISTORIAN AND HIS FACTS

What is history? Lest anyone think the question meaningless or superfluous, I will take as my text two passages relating respectively to the first and second incarnations of *The Cambridge Modern History*. Here is Acton in his report of October 1896 to the Syndics of the Cambridge University Press on the work which he had undertaken to edit:

> It is a unique opportunity of recording, in the way most useful to the greatest number, the fullness of the knowledge which the nineteenth century is about to bequeath. . . . By the judicious division of labor we should be able to do it, and to bring home to every man the last document, and the ripest conclusions of international research.
>
> Ultimate history we cannot have in this generation; but we can dispose of conventional history, and show the point we have reached on the road from one to the other, now that all information is within reach, and every problem has become capable of solution.

And almost exactly sixty years later Professor Sir George Clark, in his general introduction to the second *Cambridge Modern History*, commented on this belief of Acton and his collaborators that it would one day be possible to produce "ultimate history," and went on:

> Historians of a later generation do not look forward to any such prospect. They expect their work to be superseded again and again. They consider that knowledge of the past has come down through one or more human minds, has been "processed" by them, and therefore cannot consist of elemental and

> impersonal atoms which nothing can alter. . . . The exploration seems to be
> endless, and some impatient scholars take refuge in scepticism, or at least in
> the doctrine that, since all historical judgments involve persons and points of
> view, one is as good as another and there is no "objective" historical truth.

Where the pundits contradict each other so flagrantly the field is open to
enquiry. I hope that I am sufficiently up-to-date to recognize that anything written in the 1890's must be nonsense. But I am not yet advanced
enough to be committed to the view that anything written in the 1950's
necessarily makes sense. Indeed, it may already have occurred to you that
this enquiry is liable to stray into something even broader than the
nature of history. The clash between Acton and Sir George Clark is a
reflection of the change in our total outlook on society over the interval
between these two pronouncements. Acton speaks out of the positive
belief, the clear-eyed self-confidence of the later Victorian age; Sir
George Clark echoes the bewilderment and distracted scepticism of the
beat generation. When we attempt to answer the question, What is
history?, our answer, consciously or unconsciously, reflects our own
position in time, and forms part of our answer to the broader question,
what view we take of the society in which we live. I have no fear that my
subject may, on closer inspection, seem trivial. I am afraid only that I may
seem presumptuous to have broached a question so vast and so important.

The nineteenth century was a great age for facts. "What I want," said
Mr. Gradgrind in *Hard Times*, "is Facts. . . . Facts alone are wanted in
life." Nineteenth-century historians on the whole agreed with him.
When Ranke in the 1830's, in legitimate protest against moralizing
history, remarked that the task of the historian was "simply to show how
it really was [*wie es eigentlich gewesen*]" this not very profound aphorism
had an astonishing success. Three generations of German, British, and
even French historians marched into battle intoning the magic words,
"*Wie es eigentlich gewesen*" like an incantation—designed, like most
incantations, to save them from the tiresome obligation to think for
themselves. The Positivists, anxious to stake out their claim for history as
a science, contributed the weight of their influence to this cult of facts.
First ascertain the facts, said the positivists, then draw your conclusions
from them. In Great Britain, this view of history fitted in perfectly with
the empiricist tradition which was the dominant strain in British philosophy from Locke to Bertrand Russell. The empirical theory of knowledge
presupposes a complete separation between subject and object. Facts,
like sense-impressions, impinge on the observer from outside, and are
independent of his consciousness. The process of reception is passive:
having received the data, he then acts on them. *The Shorter Oxford
English Dictionary*, a useful but tendentious work of the empirical school,

clearly marks the separateness of the two processes by defining a fact as "a datum of experience as distinct from conclusions." This is what may be called the common-sense view of history. History consists of a corpus of ascertained facts. The facts are available to the historian in documents, inscriptions, and so on, like fish on the fishmonger's slab. The historian collects them, takes them home, and cooks and serves them in whatever style appeals to him. Acton, whose culinary tastes were austere, wanted them served plain. In his letter of instructions to contributors to the first *Cambridge Modern History* he announced the requirement "that our Waterloo must be one that satisfies French and English, German and Dutch alike; that nobody can tell, without examining the list of authors where the Bishop of Oxford laid down the pen, and whether Fairbairn or Gasquet, Liebermann or Harrison took it up." Even Sir George Clark, critical as he was of Acton's attitude, himself contrasted the "hard core of facts" in history with the "surrounding pulp of disputable interpretation"—forgetting perhaps that the pulpy part of the fruit is more rewarding than the hard core. First get your facts straight, then plunge at your peril into the shifting sands of interpretation—that is the ultimate wisdom of the empirical, common-sense school of history. It recalls the favorite dictum of the great liberal journalist C. P. Scott: "Facts are sacred, opinion is free."

Now this clearly will not do. I shall not embark on a philosophical discussion of the nature of our knowledge of the past. Let us assume for present purposes that the fact that Caesar crossed the Rubicon and the fact that there is a table in the middle of the room are facts of the same or of a comparable order, that both these facts enter our consciousness in the same or in a comparable manner, and that both have the same objective character in relation to the person who knows them. But, even on this bold and not very plausible assumption, our argument at once runs into the difficulty that not all facts about the past are historical facts, or are treated as such by the historian. What is the criterion which distinguishes the facts of history from other facts about the past?

What is a historical fact? This is a crucial question into which we must look a little more closely. According to the common-sense view, there are certain basic facts which are the same for all historians and which form, so to speak, the backbone of history—the fact, for example, that the Battle of Hastings was fought in 1066. But this view calls for two observations. In the first place, it is not with facts like these that the historian is primarily concerned. It is no doubt important to know that the great battle was fought in 1066 and not in 1065 or 1067, and that it was fought at Hastings and not at Eastbourne or Brighton. The historian must not get these things wrong. But when points of this kind are raised, I am reminded of Housman's remark[1] that "accuracy is a duty, not a virtue." To praise a historian for his accuracy is like praising an architect for using well-seasoned timber or properly mixed concrete in his building. It is a necessary condition of his work, but not his essential function. It is precisely for matters of this kind that the historian is entitled to rely on what have been called the "auxiliary sciences" of history—archaeology, epigraphy, numismatics, chronology, and so forth. The historian is not required to have the special skills which enable the expert to determine the origin and period of a fragment of pottery or marble, or decipher an obscure inscription, or to make the elaborate astronomical calculations necessary to establish a precise date. These so-called basic facts which are the same for all historians commonly belong to the category of the raw materials of the historian rather than of history itself. The second observation is that the necessity to establish these basic facts rests not on any quality in the facts themselves, but on an *a priori* decision of the historian. In spite of C. P. Scott's motto, every journalist knows today that the most effective way to influence opinion is by the selection and arrangement of the appropriate facts. It used to be said that facts speak for themselves. This is, of course, untrue. The facts speak only when the historian calls on them: It is he who decides to which facts to give the floor, and in what order or context. It was, I think, one of Pirandello's characters who said that a fact is like a sack—it won't stand up till you've put something in it. The only reason why we are interested to know that the battle was fought at Hastings in 1066 is that historians regard it as a major historical event. It is the historian who has decided for his own reasons that Caesar's crossing of that petty stream, the Rubicon, is a fact of history, whereas the crossing of the Rubicon by millions of other people before or since interests nobody at all. The fact that you arrived in this building half an hour ago on foot, or on a bicycle, or in a car, is just as much a fact about the past as the fact that Caesar crossed the Rubicon. But it will probably be ignored by historians. Professor Talcott Parsons once called science "a selective system of cognitive orientations to reality." It might perhaps have been put more simply. But history is, among other things, that. The historian is necessarily selective. The belief in a hard core of historical facts existing objectively and independently of the interpretation of the historian is a preposterous fallacy, but one which it is very hard to eradicate.

Let us take a look at the process by which a mere fact about the past is transformed into a fact of history. At Stalybridge Wakes in 1850, a vendor of gingerbread, as the result of some petty dispute, was deliberately kicked to death by an angry mob. Is this a fact of history? A year ago I should unhesitatingly have said "no." It was recorded by an eyewitness

1. In the preface to his critical edition of Manilius, *Astronomicon*, an obscure Latin work.

in some little-known memoirs;[2] but I had never seen it judged worthy of mention by any historian. A year ago Dr. Kitson Clark cited it in his Ford lectures in Oxford. Does this make it into a historical fact? Not, I think, yet. Its present status, I suggest, is that it has been proposed for membership of the select club of historical facts. It now awaits a seconder and sponsors. It may be that in the course of the next few years we shall see this fact appearing first in footnotes, then in the text, of articles and books about nineteenth-century England, and that in twenty or thirty years' time it may be a well established historical fact. Alternatively, nobody may take it up, in which case it will relapse into the limbo of unhistorical facts about the past from which Dr. Kitson Clark has gallantly attempted to rescue it. What will decide which of these two things will happen? It will depend, I think, on whether the thesis or interpretation in support of which Dr. Kitson Clark cited this incident is accepted by other historians as valid and significant. Its status as a historical fact will turn on a question of interpretation. This element of interpretation enters into every fact of history.

May I be allowed a personal reminiscence? When I studied ancient history in this university many years ago, I had as a special subject "Greece in the period of the Persian Wars." I collected fifteen or twenty volumes on my shelves and took it for granted that there, recorded in these volumes, I had all the facts relating to my subject. Let us assume—it was very nearly true—that those volumes contained all the facts about it that were then known, or could be known. It never occurred to me to enquire by what accident or process of attrition that minute selection of facts, out of all the myriad facts that must have once been known to somebody, had survived to become *the* facts of history. I suspect that even today one of the fascinations of ancient and mediaeval history is that it gives us the illusion of having all the facts at our disposal within a manageable compass: the nagging distinction between the facts of history and other facts about the past vanishes because the few known facts are all facts of history. As Bury, who had worked in both periods, said, "the records of ancient and mediaeval history are starred with lacunae." History has been called an enormous jig-saw with a lot of missing parts. But the main trouble does not consist of the lacunae. Our picture of Greece in the fifth century b.c. is defective not primarily because so many of the bits have been accidentally lost, but because it is, by and large, the picture formed by a tiny group of people in the city of Athens. We know a lot about what fifth-century Greece looked like to an Athenian citizen; but hardly anything about what it looked like to a Spartan, a Corinthian, or a Theban—not to mention a Persian, or a slave or other non-citizen resident in Athens. Our picture has been preselected and

2. Lord George Sanger: *Seventy Years a Showman* (London: J. M. Dent & Sons, 1926), pp. 188–9 [Carr's note].

predetermined for us, not so much by accident as by people who were consciously or unconsciously imbued with a particular view and thought the facts which supported that view worth preserving. In the same way, when I read in a modern history of the Middle Ages that the people of the Middle Ages were deeply concerned with religion, I wonder how we know this, and whether it is true. What we know as the facts of mediaeval history have almost all been selected for us by generations of chroniclers who were professionally occupied in the theory and practice of religion, and who therefore thought it supremely important, and recorded everything relating to it, and not much else. The picture of the Russian peasant as devoutly religious was destroyed by the revolution of 1917. The picture of mediaeval man as devoutly religious, whether true or not, is indestructible, because nearly all the known facts about him were preselected for us by people who believed it, and wanted others to believe it, and a mass of other facts, in which we might possibly have found evidence to the contrary, has been lost beyond recall. The dead hand of vanished generations of historians, scribes, and chroniclers has determined beyond the possibility of appeal the pattern of the past. "The history we read," writes Professor Barraclough, himself trained as a mediaevalist, "though based on facts, is, strictly speaking, not factual at all, but a series of accepted judgments."

But let us turn to the different, but equally grave, plight of the modern historian. The ancient or mediaeval historian may be grateful for the vast winnowing process which, over the years, has put at his disposal a manageable corpus of historical facts. As Lytton Strachey said in his mischievous way, "ignorance is the first requisite of the historian, ignorance which simplifies and clarifies, which selects and omits." When I am tempted, as I sometimes am, to envy the extreme competence of colleagues engaged in writing ancient or mediaeval history, I find consolation in the reflection that they are so competent mainly because they are so ignorant of their subject. The modern historian enjoys none of the advantages of this built-in ignorance. He must cultivate this necessary ignorance for himself—the more so the nearer he comes to his own times. He has the dual task of discovering the few significant facts and turning them into facts of history, and of discarding the many insignificant facts as unhistorical. But this is the very converse of the nineteenth-century heresy that history consists of the compilation of a maximum number of irrefutable and objective facts. Anyone who succumbs to this heresy will either have to give up history as a bad job, and take to stamp-collecting or some other form of antiquarianism, or end in a madhouse. It is this heresy, which during the past hundred years has had such devastating effects on the modern historian, producing in Germany, in Great Britain, and in the United States a vast and growing mass of dry-as-dust factual histories, of minutely specialized monographs, of would-be historians knowing more and more about less and less, sunk without trace in an ocean of facts. It was, I suspect, this heresy—rather than the alleged conflict between liberal and Catholic loyalties—which frustrated Acton as a historian. In an early essay he said of his teacher Döllinger: "He would not write with imperfect materials, and to him the materials were always imperfect."[3] Acton was surely here pronouncing an anticipatory verdict on himself, on that strange phenomenon of a historian whom many would regard as the most distinguished occupant the Regius Chair of Modern History in this university has ever had—but who wrote no history. And Acton wrote his own epitaph in the introductory note to the first volume of the *Cambridge Modern History*, published just after his death, when he lamented that the requirements pressing on the historian "threaten to turn him from a man of letters into the compiler of an encyclopedia." Something had gone wrong. What had gone wrong was the belief in this untiring and unending accumulation of hard facts as the foundation of history, the belief that facts speak for themselves and that we cannot have too many facts, a belief at that time so unquestioning that few historians then thought it necessary—and some still think it unneces-sary today—to ask themselves the question: What is history?

The nineteenth-century fetishism of facts was completed and justified by a fetishism of documents. The documents were the Ark of the Cove-nant in the temple of facts. The reverent historian approached them with bowed head and spoke of them in awed tones. If you find it in the documents, it is so. But what, when we get down to it, do these docu-ments—the decrees, the treaties, the rent-rolls, the blue books, the official correspondence, the private letters and diaries—tell us? No docu-ment can tell us more than what the author of the document thought—what he thought had happened, what he thought ought to happen or would happen, or perhaps only what he wanted others to think he thought, or even only what he himself thought he thought. None of this means anything until the historian has got to work on it and deciphered it. The facts, whether found in documents or not, have still to be processed by the historian before he can make any use of them: the use he makes of them is, if I may put it that way, the processing process.

Let me illustrate what I am trying to say by an example which I happen to know well. When Gustav Stresemann, the Foreign Minister of the Weimar Republic, died in 1929, he left behind him an enormous mass—300 boxes full—of papers, official, semiofficial, and private, nearly all relating to the six years of his tenure of office as Foreign Minister. His friends and relatives naturally thought that a monument should be raised to the memory of so great a man. His faithful secretary Bernhardt got to work; and within three years there appeared three massive volumes, of

3. Later Acton said of Döllinger that "it was given him to form his philosophy of history on the largest induction ever available to man" [Carr's note].

some 600 pages each, of selected documents from the 300 boxes, with the impressive title *Stresemanns Vermächtnis*.[4] In the ordinary way the documents themselves would have moldered away in some cellar or attic and disappeared for ever; or perhaps in a hundred years or so some curious scholar would have come upon them and set out to compare them with Bernhardt's text. What happened was far more dramatic. In 1945 the documents fell into the hands of the British and the American governments, who photographed the lot and put the photostats at the disposal of scholars in the Public Record Office in London and in the National Archives in Washington, so that, if we have sufficient patience and curiosity, we can discover exactly what Bernhardt did. What he did was neither very unusual nor very shocking. When Stresemann died, his Western policy seemed to have been crowned with a series of brilliant successes—Locarno, the admission of Germany to the League of Nations, the Dawes and Young plans and the American loans, the withdrawal of allied occupation armies from the Rhineland. This seemed the important and rewarding part of Stresemann's foreign policy; and it was not unnatural that it should have been over-represented in Bernhardt's selection of documents. Stresemann's Eastern policy, on the other hand, his relations with the Soviet Union, seemed to have led nowhere in particular; and, since masses of documents about negotiations which yielded only trivial results were not very interesting and added nothing to Stresemann's reputation, the process of selection could be more rigorous. Stresemann in fact devoted a far more constant and anxious attention to relations with the Soviet Union, and they played a far larger part in his foreign policy as a whole, than the reader of the Bernhardt selection would surmise. But the Bernhardt volumes compare favorably, I suspect, with many published collections of documents on which the ordinary historian implicitly relies.

This is not the end of my story. Shortly after the publication of Bernhardt's volumes, Hitler came into power. Stresemann's name was consigned to oblivion in Germany, and the volumes disappeared from circulation: many, perhaps most, of the copies must have been destroyed. Today *Stresemanns Vermächtnis* is a rather rare book. But in the West Stresemann's reputation stood high. In 1935 an English publisher brought out an abbreviated translation of Bernhardt's work—a selection from Bernhardt's selection; perhaps one third of the original was omitted. Sutton, a well-known translator from the German, did his job competently and well. The English version, he explained in the preface, was "slightly condensed, but only by the omission of a certain amount of what, it was felt, was more ephemeral matter ... of little interest to English readers or students." This again is natural enough. But the result

4. *Stresemann's Legacy.*

is that Stresemann's Eastern policy, already under-represented in Bernhardt, recedes still further from view, and the Soviet Union appears in Sutton's volumes merely as an occasional and rather unwelcome intruder in Stresemann's predominantly Western foreign policy. Yet it is safe to say that, for all except a few specialists, Sutton and not Bernhardt—and still less the documents themselves—represents for the Western world the authentic voice of Stresemann. Had the documents perished in 1945 in the bombing, and had the remaining Bernhardt volumes disappeared, the authenticity and authority of Sutton would never have been questioned. Many printed collections of documents gratefully accepted by historians in default of the originals rest on no securer basis than this.

But I want to carry the story one step further. Let us forget about Bernhardt and Sutton, and be thankful that we can, if we choose, consult the authentic papers of a leading participant in some important events in recent European history. What do the papers tell us? Among other things they contain records of some hundreds of Stresemann's conversations with the Soviet ambassador in Berlin and of a score or so with Chicherin.[5] These records have one feature in common. They depict Stresemann as having the lion's share of the conversations and reveal his arguments as invariably well put and cogent, while those of his partner are for the most part scanty, confused, and unconvincing. This is a familiar characteristic of all records of diplomatic conversations. The documents do not tell us what happened, but only what Stresemann thought had happened. It was not Sutton or Bernhardt, but Stresemann himself, who started the process of selection. And, if we had, say Chicherin's records of these same conversations, we should still learn from them only what Chicherin thought, and what really happened would still have to be reconstructed in the mind of the historian. Of course, facts and documents are essential to the historian. But do not make a fetish of them. They do not by themselves constitute history; they provide in themselves no ready-made answer to this tiresome question: What is history?

At this point I should like to say a few words on the question of why nineteenth-century historians were generally indifferent to the philosophy of history. The term was invented by Voltaire, and has since been used in different senses; but I shall take it to mean, if I use it at all, our answer to the question: What is history? The nineteenth century was, for the intellectuals of Western Europe, a comfortable period exuding confidence and optimism. The facts were on the whole satisfactory; and the inclination to ask and answer awkward questions about them was correspondingly weak. Ranke piously believed that divine providence would take care of the meaning of history if he took care of the facts; and

5. Soviet foreign minister from 1918 to 1928.

Burckhardt with a more modern touch of cynicism observed that "we are not initiated into the purposes of the eternal wisdom." Professor Butterfield as late as 1931 noted with apparent satisfaction that "historians have reflected little upon the nature of things and even the nature of their own subject." But my predecessor in these lectures, Dr. A. L. Rowse, more justly critical, wrote of Sir Winston Churchill's *The World Crisis*—his book about the First World War—that, while it matched Trotsky's *History of the Russian Revolution* in personality, vividness, and vitality, it was inferior in one respect: it had "no philosophy of history behind it." British historians refused to be drawn, not because they believed that history had no meaning, but because they believed that its meaning was implicit and self-evident. The liberal nineteenth-century view of history had a close affinity with the economic doctrine of *laissez-faire*—also the product of a serene and self-confident outlook on the world. Let everyone get on with his particular job, and the hidden hand would take care of the universal harmony. The facts of history were themselves a demonstration of the supreme fact of a beneficent and apparently infinite progress towards higher things. This was the age of innocence, and historians walked in the Garden of Eden, without a scrap of philosophy to cover them, naked and unashamed before the god of history. Since then, we have known Sin and experienced a Fall; and those historians who today pretend to dispense with a philosophy of history are merely trying, vainly and self-consciously, like members of a nudist colony, to recreate the Garden of Eden in their garden suburb. Today the awkward question can no longer be evaded. * * *

During the past fifty years a good deal of serious work has been done on the question: What is history? It was from Germany, the country which was to do so much to upset the comfortable reign of nineteenth-century liberalism, that the first challenge came in the 1880's and 1890's to the doctrine of the primacy and autonomy of facts in history. The philosophers who made the challenge are now little more than names: Dilthey is the only one of them who has recently received some belated recognition in Great Britain. Before the turn of the century, prosperity and confidence were still too great in this country for any attention to be paid to heretics who attacked the cult of facts. But early in the new century, the torch passed to Italy, where Croce began to propound a philosophy of history which obviously owed much to German masters. All history is "contemporary history," declared Croce,[6] meaning that history consists

6. The context of this celebrated aphorism is as follows: "The practical requirements which underlie every historical judgment give to all history the character of 'contemporary history,' because, however remote in time events thus recounted may seem to be, the history in reality refers to present needs and present situations wherein those events vibrate" [Carr's note].

essentially in seeing the past through the eyes of the present and in the light of its problems, and that the main work of the historian is not to record, but to evaluate; for, if he does not evaluate, how can he know what is worth recording? In 1910 the American philosopher, Carl Becker, argued in deliberately provocative language that "the facts of history do not exist for any historian till he creates them." These challenges were for the moment little noticed. It was only after 1920 that Croce began to have a considerable vogue in France and Great Britain. This was not perhaps because Croce was a subtler thinker or a better stylist than his German predecessors, but because, after the First World War, the facts seemed to smile on us less propitiously than in the years before 1914, and we were therefore more accessible to a philosophy which sought to diminish their prestige. Croce was an important influence on the Oxford philosopher and historian Collingwood, the only British thinker in the present century who has made a serious contribution to the philosophy of history. He did not live to write the systematic treatise he had planned; but his published and unpublished papers on the subject were collected after his death in a volume entitled *The Idea of History*, which appeared in 1945.

The views of Collingwood can be summarized as follows. The philosophy of history is concerned neither with "the past by itself" nor with "the historian's thought about it by itself," but with "the two things in their mutual relations." (This dictum reflects the two current meanings of the word "history"—the enquiry conducted by the historian and the series of past events into which he enquires.) "The past which a historian studies is not a dead past, but a past which in some sense is still living in the present." But a past act is dead, *i.e.* meaningless to the historian, unless he can understand the thought that lay behind it. Hence "all history is the history of thought," and "history is the re-enactment in the historian's mind of the thought whose history he is studying." The reconstitution of the past in the historian's mind is dependent on empirical evidence. But it is not in itself an empirical process, and cannot consist in a mere recital of facts. On the contrary, the process of reconstitution governs the selection and interpretation of the facts: this, indeed, is what makes them historical facts. "History," says Professor Oakeshott, who on this point stands near to Collingwood, "is the historian's experience. It is 'made' by nobody save the historian: to write history is the only way of making it."

This searching critique, though it may call for some serious reservations, brings to light certain neglected truths.

In the first place, the facts of history never come to us "pure," since they do not and cannot exist in a pure form: they are always refracted through the mind of the recorder. It follows that when we take up a work of history, our first concern should be not with the facts which it contains but with the historian who wrote it. Let me take as an example the great historian in whose honor and in whose name these lectures were founded. Trevelyan, as he tells us in his autobiography, was "brought up at home on a somewhat exuberantly Whig tradition"; and he would not, I hope, disclaim the title if I described him as the last and not the least of the great English liberal historians of the Whig tradition. It is not for nothing that he traces back his family tree, through the great Whig historian George Otto Trevelyan, to Macaulay, incomparably the greatest of the Whig historians. Dr. Trevelyan's finest and maturest work *England under Queen Anne* was written against that background, and will yield its full meaning and significance to the reader only when read against that background. The author, indeed, leaves the reader with no excuse for failing to do so. For if, following the technique of connoisseurs of detective novels, you read the end first, you will find on the last few pages of the third volume the best summary known to me of what is nowadays called the Whig interpretation of history; and you will see that what Trevelyan is trying to do is to investigate the origin and development of the Whig tradition, and to root it fairly and squarely in the years after the death of its founder, William III. Though this is not, perhaps, the only conceivable interpretation of the events of Queen Anne's reign, it is a valid and, in Trevelyan's hands, a fruitful interpretation. But, in order to appreciate it at its full value, you have to understand what the historian is doing. For if, as Collingwood says, the historian must re-enact in thought what has gone on in the mind of his *dramatis personae*, so the reader in his turn must re-enact what goes on in the mind of the historian. Study the historian before you begin to study the facts. This is, after all, not very abstruse. It is what is already done by the intelligent undergraduate who, when recommended to read a work by that great scholar Jones of St. Jude's, goes round to a friend at St. Jude's to ask what sort of chap Jones is, and what bees he has in his bonnet. When you read a work of history, always listen out for the buzzing. If you can detect none, either you are tone deaf or your historian is a dull dog. The facts are really not at all like fish on the fishmonger's slab. They are like fish swimming about in a vast and sometimes inaccessible ocean; and what the historian catches will depend partly on chance, but mainly on what part of the ocean he chooses to fish in and what tackle he chooses to use—these two factors being, of course, determined by the kind of fish he wants to catch. By and large, the historian will get the kind of facts he wants. History means interpretation. Indeed, if, standing Sir George Clark on his head, I were to call history "a hard core of interpretation surrounded by a pulp of disputable facts," my statement would, no doubt, be one-sided and misleading, but no more so, I venture to think, than the original dictum.

The second point is the more familiar one of the historian's need of imaginative understanding for the minds of the people with whom he is dealing, for the thought behind their acts: I say "imaginative understanding," not "sympathy," lest sympathy should be supposed to imply agreement. The nineteenth century was weak in mediaeval history, because it was too much repelled by the superstitious beliefs of the Middle Ages and by the barbarities which they inspired, to have any imaginative understanding of mediaeval people. Or take Burckhardt's censorious remark about the Thirty Years' War: "It is scandalous for a creed, no matter whether it is Catholic or Protestant, to place its salvation above the integrity of the nation." It was extremely difficult for a nineteenth-century liberal historian, brought up to believe that it is right and praiseworthy to kill in defense of one's country, but wicked and wrong-headed to kill in defense of one's religion, to enter into the state of mind of those who fought the Thirty Years' War. This difficulty is particularly acute in the field in which I am now working. Much of what has been written in English-speaking countries in the last ten years about the Soviet Union, and in the Soviet Union about the English-speaking countries, has been vitiated by this inability to achieve even the most elementary measure of imaginative understanding of what goes on in the mind of the other party, so that the words and actions of the other are always made to appear malign, senseless, or hypocritical. History cannot be written unless the historian can achieve some kind of contact with the mind of those about whom he is writing.

The third point is that we can view the past, and achieve our understanding of the past, only through the eyes of the present. The historian is of his own age, and is bound to it by the conditions of human existence. The very words which he uses—words like democracy, empire, war, revolution—have current connotations from which he cannot divorce them. Ancient historians have taken to using words like *polis* and *plebs* in the original, just in order to show that they have not fallen into this trap. This does not help them. They, too, live in the present, and cannot cheat themselves into the past by using unfamiliar or obsolete words, any more than they would become better Greek or Roman historians if they delivered their lectures in a *chlamys* or a *toga*. The names by which successive French historians have described the Parisian crowds which played so prominent a role in the French revolution—*les sansculottes, le peuple, la canaille, les bras-nus*—are all, for those who know the rules of the game, manifestos of a political affiliation and of a particular interpretation. Yet the historian is obliged to choose: the use of language forbids him to be neutral. Nor is it a matter of words alone. Over the past hundred years the changed balance of power in Europe has reversed the attitude of British historians to Frederick the Great. The changed balance of power within the Christian churches between Catholicism and Protestantism has profoundly altered their attitude to such figures as Loyola, Luther, and Cromwell. It requires only a superficial knowledge of the work of French historians of the last forty years on the French revolution to recognize how deeply it has been affected by the Russian revolution of 1917. The historian belongs not to the past but to the present. Professor Trevor-Roper tells us that the historian "ought to love the past." This is a dubious injunction. To love the past may easily be an expression of the nostalgic romanticism of old men and old societies, a symptom of loss of faith and interest in the present or future.[7] Cliché for cliché, I should prefer the one about freeing oneself from "the dead hand of the past." The function of the historian is neither to love the past nor to emancipate himself from the past, but to master and understand it as the key to the understanding of the present.

If, however, these are some of the sights of what I may call the Collingwood view of history, it is time to consider some of the dangers. The emphasis on the role of the historian in the making of history tends, if pressed to its logical conclusion, to rule out any objective history at all: history is what the historian makes. Collingwood seems indeed, at one moment, in an unpublished note quoted by his editor, to have reached this conclusion:

> St. Augustine looked at history from the point of view of the early Christian; Tillemont, from that of a seventeenth-century Frenchman; Gibbon, from that of an eighteenth-century Englishman; Mommsen, from that of a nineteenth-century German. There is no point in asking which was the right point of view. Each was the only one possible for the man who adopted it.

This amounts to total scepticism, like Froude's remark that history is "a child's box of letters with which we can spell any word we please." Collingwood, in his reaction against "scissors-and-paste history," against the view of history as a mere compilation of facts, comes perilously near to treating history as something spun out of the human brain, and leads back to the conclusion referred to by Sir George Clark in the passage which I quoted earlier, that "there is no 'objective' historical truth." In place of the theory that history has no meaning, we are offered here the theory of an infinity of meanings, none any more right than any other— which comes to much the same thing. The second theory is surely as untenable as the first. It does not follow that, because a mountain appears to take on different shapes from different angles of vision, it has objectively either no shape at all or an infinity of shapes. It does not follow that, because interpretation plays a necessary part in establishing the facts of history, and because no existing interpretation is wholly objective, one interpretation is as good as another, and the facts of history are in principle not amenable to objective interpretation. I shall have to consider at a later stage what exactly is meant by objectivity in history.

7. Compare Nietzsche's view of history: "To old age belongs the old man's business of looking back and casting up his accounts, of seeking consolation in the memories of the past, in historical culture" [Carr's note].

But a still greater danger lurks in the Collingwood hypothesis. If the historian necessarily looks at his period of history through the eyes of his own time, and studies the problems of the past as a key to those of the present, will he not fall into a purely pragmatic view of the facts, and maintain that the criterion of a right interpretation is its suitability to some present purpose? On this hypothesis, the facts of history are nothing, interpretation is everything. Nietzsche had already enunciated the principle: "The falseness of an opinion is not for us any objection to it. . . . The question is how far it is life-furthering, life-preserving, species-preserving, perhaps species-creating." The American pragmatists moved, less explicitly and less wholeheartedly, along the same line. Knowledge is knowledge for some purpose. The validity of the knowledge depends on the validity of the purpose. But, even where no such theory has been professed, the practice has often been no less disquieting. In my own field of study, I have seen too many examples of extravagant interpretation riding roughshod over facts, not to be impressed with the reality of this danger. It is not surprising that perusal of some of the more extreme products of Soviet and anti-Soviet schools of historiography should sometimes breed a certain nostalgia for that illusory nineteenth-century heaven of purely factual history.

How then, in the middle of the twentieth century, are we to define the obligation of the historian to his facts? I trust that I have spent a sufficient number of hours in recent years chasing and perusing documents, and stuffing my historical narrative with properly footnoted facts, to escape the imputation of treating facts and documents too cavalierly. The duty of the historian to respect his facts is not exhausted by the obligation to see that his facts are accurate. He must seek to bring into the picture all known or knowable facts relevant, in one sense or another, to the theme on which he is engaged and to the interpretation proposed. If he seeks to depict the Victorian Englishman as a moral and rational being, he must not forget what happened at Stalybridge Wakes in 1850. But this, in turn, does not mean that he can eliminate interpretation, which is the lifeblood of history. Laymen—that is to say, non-academic friends or friends from other academic disciplines—sometimes ask me how the historian goes to work when he writes history. The commonest assumption appears to be that the historian divides his work into two sharply distinguishable phases or periods. First, he spends a long preliminary period reading his source and filling his notebooks with facts: then, when this is over, he puts away his sources, takes out his notebooks, and writes his book from beginning to end. This is to me an unconvincing and unplausible picture. For myself, as soon as I have got going on a few of what I take to be the capital sources, the itch becomes too strong and I begin to write—not necessarily at the beginning, but somewhere, anywhere. Thereafter, reading and writing go on simultaneously. The writing is added to, subtracted from, re-shaped, cancelled, as I go on reading. The reading is guided and directed and made fruitful by the writing: the more I write, the more I know what I am looking for, the better I understand the significance and relevance of what I find. Some historians probably do all this preliminary writing in their head without using pen, paper, or typewriter, just as some people play chess in their heads without recourse to board and chess-men: this is a talent which I envy, but cannot emulate. But I am convinced that, for any historian worth the name, the two processes of what economists call "input" and "output" go on simultaneously and are, in practice, parts of a single process. If you try to separate them, or to give one priority over the other, you fall into one of two heresies. Either you write scissors-and-paste history without meaning or significance; or you write propaganda or historical fiction, and merely use facts of the past to embroider a kind of writing which has nothing to do with history.

Our examination of the relation of the historian to the facts of history finds us, therefore, in an apparently precarious situation, navigating delicately between the Scylla of an untenable theory of history as an objective compilation of facts, of the unqualified primacy of fact over interpretation, and the Charybdis of an equally untenable theory of history as the subjective product of the mind of the historian who establishes the facts of history and masters them through the process of interpretation, between a view of history having the center of gravity in the past and the view having the center of gravity in the present. But our situation is less precarious than it seems. We shall encounter the same dichotomy of fact and interpretation again in these lectures in other guises—the particular and the general, the empirical and the theoretical, the objective and the subjective. The predicament of the historian is a reflection of the nature of man. Man, except perhaps in earliest infancy and in extreme old age, is not totally involved in his environment and unconditionally subject to it. On the other hand, he is never totally independent of it and its unconditional master. The relation of man to his environment is the relation of the historian to his theme. The historian is neither the humble slave, nor the tyrannical master, of his facts. The relation between the historian and his facts is one of equality, of give-and-take. As any working historian knows, if he stops to reflect what he is doing as he thinks and writes, the historian is engaged on a continuous process of molding his facts to his interpretation and his interpretation to his facts. It is impossible to assign primacy to one over the other.

The historian starts with the provisional selection of facts and a provisional interpretation in the light of which that selection has been made— by others as well as by himself. As he works, both the interpretation and the selection and ordering of facts undergo subtle and perhaps partly unconscious changes through the reciprocal action of one or the other.

And this reciprocal action also involves reciprocity between present and past, since the historian is part of the present and the facts belong to the past. The historian and the facts of history are necessary to one another. The historian without his facts is rootless and futile; the facts without their historian are dead and meaningless. My first answer therefore to the question, What is history?, is that it is a continuous process of interaction between the historian and his facts, an unending dialogue between the present and the past.

1961

THE READER

1. In his discussion of the facts of history, Carr distinguishes between "a mere fact about the past" and "a fact of history." Into which category should Bettelheim's encounter with the infirmary guard go (p. 40)?
2. If you were commissioned to write a history of the semester or of a particular group during the semester, what would be your most important "facts of history"?

THE WRITER

1. Carr begins with a question but does not answer it until the last sentence. What are the main steps of the discussion leading to his answer? The answer takes the form of a definition. Which is the most important of the defining words?
2. Carr says that the historian's "facts are really not at all like fish on the fishmonger's slab. They are like fish swimming about in a vast and sometimes inaccessible ocean; and what the historian catches will depend partly on chance, but mainly on what part of the ocean he chooses to fish in and what tackle he chooses to use—these two factors being, of course, determined by the kind of fish he wants to catch." How appropriate a description is this of the way other kinds of writers use facts—for example, the scientist, the psychologist, the novelist, the familiar essayist?
3. Write a brief "history" of an event, keeping in mind what Carr says about what the historian does.

Politics and Government

George Orwell

SHOOTING AN ELEPHANT

In Moulmein, in Lower Burma, I was hated by large numbers of people —the only time in my life that I have been important enough for this to happen to me. I was sub-divisional police officer of the town, and in an aimless, petty kind of way anti-European feeling was very bitter. No one had the guts to raise a riot, but if a European woman went through the bazaars alone somebody would probably spit betel juice over her dress. As a police officer I was an obvious target and was baited whenever it seemed safe to do so. When a nimble Burman tripped me up on the football field and the referee (another Burman) looked the other way, the crowd yelled with hideous laughter. This happened more than once. In the end the sneering yellow faces of young men that met me everywhere, the insults hooted after me when I was at a safe distance, got badly on my nerves. The young Buddhist priests were the worst of all. There were several thousands of them in the town and none of them seemed to have anything to do except stand on street corners and jeer at Europeans.

All this was perplexing and upsetting. For at that time I had already made up my mind that imperialism was an evil thing and the sooner I chucked up my job and got out of it the better. Theoretically—and secretly, of course—I was all for the Burmese and all against their oppressors, the British. As for the job I was doing, I hated it more bitterly than I can perhaps make clear. In a job like that you see the dirty work of Empire at close quarters. The wretched prisoners huddling in the stinking cages of the lock-ups, the grey, cowed faces of the long-term convicts, the scarred buttocks of the men who had been flogged with bamboos—all these oppressed me with an intolerable sense of guilt. But I could get nothing into perspective. I was young and ill-educated and I had had to think out my problems in the utter silence that is imposed on every

Englishman in the East. I did not even know that the British Empire is dying, still less did I know that it is a great deal better than the younger empires that are going to supplant it. All I knew was that I was stuck between my hatred of the empire I served and my rage against the evil-spirited little beasts who tried to make my job impossible. With one part of my mind I thought of the British Raj[1] as an unbreakable tyranny, as something clamped down, in *saecula saeculorum*,[2] upon the will of prostrate peoples; with another part I thought that the greatest joy in the world would be to drive a bayonet into a Buddhist priest's guts. Feelings like these are the normal by-products of imperialism; ask any Anglo-Indian official, if you can catch him off duty.

One day something happened which in a roundabout way was enlightening. It was a tiny incident in itself, but it gave me a better glimpse than I had had before of the real nature of imperialism—the real motives for which despotic governments act. Early one morning the sub-inspector at a police station the other end of town rang me up on the 'phone and said that an elephant was ravaging the bazaar. Would I please come and do something about it? I did not know what I could do, but I wanted to see what was happening and I got on to a pony and started out. I took my rifle, an old .44 Winchester and much too small to kill an elephant, but I thought the noise might be useful *in terrorem*. Various Burmans stopped me on the way and told me about the elephant's doings. It was not, of course, a wild elephant, but a tame one which had gone "must."[3] It had been chained up, as tame elephants always are when their attack of "must" is due, but on the previous night it had broken its chain and escaped. Its mahout, the only person who could manage it when it was in that state, had set out in pursuit, but had taken the wrong direction and was now twelve hours' journey away, and in the morning the elephant had suddenly reappeared in the town. The Burmese population had no weapons and were quite helpless against it. It had already destroyed somebody's bamboo hut, killed a cow and raided some fruit-stalls and devoured the stock; also it had met the municipal rubbish van and, when the driver jumped out and took to his heels, had turned the van over and inflicted violences upon it.

The Burmese sub-inspector and some Indian constables were waiting for me in the quarter where the elephant had been seen. It was a very poor quarter, a labyrinth of squalid bamboo huts, thatched with palm-leaf, winding all over a steep hillside. I remember that it was a cloudy, stuffy morning at the beginning of the rains. We began questioning the people as to where the elephant had gone and, as usual, failed to get any definite information. That is invariably the case in the East; a story always sounds clear enough at a distance, but the nearer you get to the

1. The imperial government of British India and Burma. 2. Forever and ever.
3. Gone into sexual heat.

scene of events the vaguer it becomes. Some of the people said that the
elephant had gone in one direction, some said that he had gone in
another, some professed not even to have heard of any elephant. I had
almost made up my mind that the whole story was a pack of lies, when we
heard yells a little distance away. There was a loud, scandalized cry of
"Go away, child! Go away this instant!" and an old woman with a switch
in her hand came round the corner of a hut, violently shooing away a
crowd of naked children. Some more women followed, clicking their
tongues and exclaiming; evidently there was something that the children
ought not to have seen. I rounded the hut and saw a man's dead body
sprawling in the mud. He was an Indian, a black Dravidian coolie, almost
naked, and he could not have been dead many minutes. The people said
that the elephant had come suddenly upon him round the corner of the
hut, caught him with its trunk, put its foot on his back and ground him
into the earth. This was the rainy season and the ground was soft, and his
face had scored a trench a foot deep and a couple of yards long. He was
lying on his belly with arms crucified and head sharply twisted to one
side. His face was coated with mud, the eyes wide open, the teeth bared
and grinning with an expression of unendurable agony. (Never tell me,
by the way, that the dead look peaceful. Most of the corpses I have seen
looked devilish.) The friction of the great beast's foot had stripped the
skin from his back as neatly as one skins a rabbit. As soon as I saw the dead
man I sent an orderly to a friend's house nearby to borrow an elephant
rifle. I had already sent back the pony, not wanting it to go mad with
fright and throw me if it smelt the elephant.

The orderly came back in a few minutes with a rifle and five cartridges,
and meanwhile some Burmans had arrived and told us that the elephant
was in the paddy fields below, only a few hundred yards away. As I started
forward practically the whole population of the quarter flocked out of the
houses and followed me. They had seen the rifle and were all shouting
excitedly that I was going to shoot the elephant. They had not shown
much interest in the elephant when he was merely ravaging their homes,
but it was different now that he was going to be shot. It was a bit of fun to
them, as it would be to an English crowd; besides they wanted the meat.
It made me vaguely uneasy. I had no intention of shooting the elephant—
I had merely sent for the rifle to defend myself if necessary—and it is
always unnerving to have a crowd following you. I marched down the
hill, looking and feeling a fool, with the rifle over my shoulder and an
ever-growing army of people jostling at my heels. At the bottom, when
you got away from the huts, there was a metalled road and beyond that a
miry waste of paddy fields a thousand yards across, not yet ploughed but
soggy from the first rains and dotted with coarse grass. The elephant was
standing eight yards from the road, his left side towards us. He took not
the slightest notice of the crowd's approach. He was tearing up bunches

of grass, beating them against his knees to clean them and stuffing them into his mouth.

I had halted on the road. As soon as I saw the elephant I knew with perfect certainty that I ought not to shoot him. It is a serious matter to shoot a working elephant—it is comparable to destroying a huge and costly piece of machinery—and obviously one ought not to do it if it can possibly be avoided. And at that distance, peacefully eating, the elephant looked no more dangerous than a cow. I thought then and I think now that his attack of "must" was already passing off; in which case he would merely wander harmlessly about until the mahout came back and caught him. Moreover, I did not in the least want to shoot him. I decided that I would watch him for a little while to make sure that he did not turn savage again, and then go home.

But at that moment I glanced round at the crowd that had followed me. It was an immense crowd, two thousand at the least and growing every minute. It blocked the road for a long distance on either side. I looked at the sea of yellow faces above the garish clothes—faces all happy and excited over this bit of fun, all certain that the elephant was going to be shot. They were watching me as they would watch a conjurer about to perform a trick. They did not like me, but with the magical rifle in my hands I was momentarily worth watching. And suddenly I realized that I should have to shoot the elephant after all. The people expected it of me and I had got to do it; I could feel their two thousand wills pressing me forward, irresistibly. And it was at this moment, as I stood there with the rifle in my hands, that I first grasped the hollowness, the futility of the white man's dominion in the East. Here was I, the white man with his gun, standing in front of the unarmed native crowd—seemingly the leading actor of the piece; but in reality I was only an absurd puppet pushed to and fro by the will of those yellow faces behind. I perceived in this moment that when the white man turns tyrant it is his own freedom that he destroys. He becomes a sort of hollow, posing dummy, the conventionalized figure of a sahib. For it is the condition of his rule that he shall spend his life in trying to impress the "natives," and so in every crisis he has got to do what the "natives" expect of him. He wears a mask, and his face grows to fit it. I had got to shoot the elephant. I had committed myself to doing it when I sent for the rifle. A sahib has got to act like a sahib; he has got to appear resolute, to know his own mind and do definite things. To come all that way, rifle in hand, with two thousand people marching at my heels, and then to trail feebly away, having done nothing—no, that was impossible. The crowd would laugh at me. And my whole life, every white man's life in the East, was one long struggle not to be laughed at.

But I did not want to shoot the elephant. I watched him beating his bunch of grass against his knees, with that preoccupied grandmotherly air that elephants have. It seemed to me that it would be murder to shoot him. At that age I was not squeamish about killing animals, but I had never shot an elephant and never wanted to. (Somehow it always seems worse to kill a *large* animal.) Besides, there was the beast's owner to be considered. Alive, the elephant was worth at least a hundred pounds; dead, he would only be worth the value of his tusks, five pounds, possibly. But I had got to act quickly. I turned to some experienced-looking Burmans who had been there when we arrived, and asked them how the elephant had been behaving. They all said the same thing: he took no notice of you if you left him alone, but he might charge if you went too close to him.

It was perfectly clear to me what I ought to do. I ought to walk up to within, say, twenty-five yards of the elephant and test his behavior. If he charged, I could shoot; if he took no notice of me, it would be safe to leave him until the mahout came back. But also I knew that I was going to do no such thing. I was a poor shot with a rifle and the ground was soft mud into which one would sink at every step. If the elephant charged and I missed him, I should have about as much chance as a toad under a steam-roller. But even then I was not thinking particularly of my own skin, only of the watchful yellow faces behind. For at that moment, with the crowd watching me, I was not afraid in the ordinary sense, as I would have been if I had been alone. A white man mustn't be frightened in front of "natives"; and so, in general, he isn't frightened. The sole thought in my mind was that if anything went wrong those two thousand Burmans would see me pursued, caught, trampled on and reduced to a grinning corpse like that Indian up the hill. And if that happened it was quite probable that some of them would laugh. That would never do. There was only one alternative. I shoved the cartridges into the magazine and lay down on the road to get a better aim.

The crowd grew very still, and a deep, low, happy sigh, as of people who see the theatre curtain go up at last, breathed from innumerable throats. They were going to have their bit of fun after all. The rifle was a beautiful German thing with cross-hair sights. I did not then know that in shooting an elephant one would shoot to cut an imaginary bar running from ear-hole to ear-hole. I ought, therefore, as the elephant was sideways on, to have aimed straight at his ear-hole; actually I aimed several inches in front of this, thinking the brain would be further forward.

When I pulled the trigger I did not hear the bang or feel the kick—one never does when a shot goes home—but I heard the devilish roar of glee that went up from the crowd. In that instant, in too short a time, one would have thought, even for the bullet to get there, a mysterious, terrible change had come over the elephant. He neither stirred nor fell, but every line of his body had altered. He looked suddenly stricken, shrunken, immensely old, as though the frightful impact of the bullet had paralysed him without knocking him down. At last, after what seemed a long time—it might have been five seconds, I dare say—he sagged flabbily to his knees. His mouth slobbered. An enormous senility seemed to have settled upon him. One could have imagined him thousands of years old. I fired again into the same spot. At the second shot he did not collapse but climbed with desperate slowness to his feet and stood weakly upright, with legs sagging and head drooping. I fired a third time. That was the shot that did for him. You could see the agony of it jolt his whole body and knock the last remnant of strength from his legs. But in falling he seemed for a moment to rise, for as his hind legs collapsed beneath him he seemed to tower upward like a huge rock toppling, his trunk reaching skywards like a tree. He trumpeted, for the first and only time. And then down he came, his belly towards me, with a crash that seemed to shake the ground even where I lay.

I got up. The Burmans were already racing past me across the mud. It was obvious that the elephant would never rise again, but he was not dead. He was breathing very rhythmically with long rattling gasps, his great mound of a side painfully rising and falling. His mouth was wide open—I could see far down into caverns of pale pink throat. I waited a long time for him to die, but his breathing did not weaken. Finally I fired my two remaining shots into the spot where I thought his heart must be. The thick blood welled out of him like red velvet, but still he did not die. His body did not even jerk when the shots hit him, the tortured breathing continued without a pause. He was dying, very slowly and in great agony, but in some world remote from me where not even a bullet could damage him further. I felt that I had got to put an end to that dreadful noise. It seemed dreadful to see the great beast lying there, powerless to move and yet powerless to die, and not even to be able to finish him. I sent back for my small rifle and poured shot after shot into his heart and down his throat. They seemed to make no impression. The tortured gasps continued as steadily as the ticking of a clock.

In the end I could not stand it any longer and went away. I heard later that it took him half an hour to die. Burmans were bringing dahs[3] and baskets even before I felt, and I was told they had stripped his body almost to the bones by the afternoon.

Afterwards, of course, there were endless discussions about the shooting of the elephant. The owner was furious, but he was only an Indian and could do nothing. Besides, legally I had done the right thing, for a mad elephant has to be killed, like a mad dog, if its owner fails to control it. Among the Europeans opinion was divided. The older men said I was right, the younger men said it was a damn shame to shoot an elephant for killing a coolie, because an elephant was worth more than any damn

___
3. Butcher knives.

Coringhee coolie. And afterwards I was very glad that the coolie had been killed; it put me legally in the right and it gave me a sufficient pretext for shooting the elephant. I often wondered whether any of the others grasped that I had done it solely to avoid looking a fool.

1936

THE READER

1. *What issue does Orwell address, and what kind of evidence is proper to it? Does he actually prove anything?*
2. *Does Robley (see question 2 under "The Writer," below) show any sign that he recognizes what Orwell calls "the futility of the white man's dominion in the East" (p. 453)? Could it be that this dominion was not futile for Robley, or in his day?*

THE WRITER

1. *The proportion of this essay devoted to narrative is relatively high. What effect(s) does Orwell aim at? How does he organize his essay? Where does he state his thesis? Would he have done better to argue his thesis directly rather than mainly by example? Why, or why not?*
2. *The following is a sketch from* The Graphic *(London) of January 21, 1888, written by a Major-General H. G. Robley:*

SHOOTING A MAN-EATING CROCODILE

It is tedious work waiting for the man-eater to come out of the water, but a fat native child as a lure will make the monster speedily walk out of his aqueous lair. Contracting the loan of a chubby infant, however, is a matter of some negotiation, and it is perhaps not to be wondered at that mammas occasionally object to their offspring being pegged down as food for a great crocodile; but there are always some parents to be found whose confidence in the skill of the British sportsman is unlimited. My sketch [omitted here] gives a view of the collapse of the man-eater, who, after viewing the tempting morsel tethered carefully to a bamboo near the water's edge, makes a rush through the sedges. The sportsman, hidden behind a bed of reeds, then fires, the bullet penetrates the heart, and the monster is dead in a moment. The little bait, whose only alarm has been caused by the report of the rifle, is now taken home by its doting mother for its matutinal banana. The natives wait to get the musky flesh of the animal, and the sportsman secures the scaly skin and the massive head of porous bone as a trophy.

There are probably educational and social similarities between Robley and Orwell, and, of course, both were imperial Englishmen in a colonial setting. However, the differences between the two men are far more striking. Briefly and basically, what are they? How are these similarities and differences reflected in the essays' styles?
3. *Compare Robley's sketch with Swift's "A Modest Proposal" (p. 489). How can you tell that Robley is not ironic and that Swift is? If you can't*

tell, what does your uncertainty suggest about the nature of irony?
4. Adapt Robley's sketch to meet an ironic purpose like Swift's.

Ngũgĩ wa Thiong'o

DECOLONIZING THE MIND

I was born into a large peasant family: father, four wives and about twenty-eight children. I also belonged, as we all did in those days, to a wider extended family and to the community as a whole.

We spoke Gĩkũyũ as we worked in the fields. We spoke Gĩkũyũ in and outside the home. I can vividly recall those evenings of story-telling around the fireside. It was mostly the grown-ups telling the children but everybody was interested and involved. We children would re-tell the stories the following day to other children who worked in the fields picking the pyrethrum flowers, tea-leaves or coffee beans of our European and African landlords.

The stories, with mostly animals as the main characters, were all told in Gĩkũyũ. Hare, being small, weak but full of innovative wit and cunning, was our hero. We identified with him as he struggled against the brutes of prey like lion, leopard, hyena. His victories were our victories and we learned that the apparently weak can outwit the strong. We followed the animals in their struggle against hostile nature—drought, rain, sun, wind—a confrontation often forcing them to search for forms of co-operation. But we were also interested in their struggles amongst themselves, and particularly between the beasts and the victims of prey. These twin struggles, against nature and other animals, reflected real-life struggles in the human world.

Not that we neglected stories with human beings as the main characters. There were two types of characters in such human-centered narratives: the species of truly human beings with qualities of courage, kindness, mercy, hatred of evil, concern for others; and a man-eat-man two-mouthed species with qualities of greed, selfishness, individualism and hatred of what was good for the larger co-operative community. Co-operation as the ultimate good in a community was a constant theme. It could unite human beings with animals against ogres and beasts of prey, as in the story of how dove, after being fed with castor-oil seeds, was sent to fetch a smith working far away from home and whose pregnant wife was being threatened by these man-eating two-mouthed ogres.

There were good and bad story-tellers. A good one could tell the same story over and over again, and it would always be fresh to us, the listeners.

He or she could tell a story told by someone else and make it more alive and dramatic. The differences really were in the use of words and images and the inflection of voices to effect different tones.

We therefore learned to value words for their meaning and nuances. Language was not a mere string of words. It had a suggestive power well beyond the immediate and lexical meaning. Our appreciation of the suggestive magical power of language was reinforced by the games we played with words through riddles, proverbs, transpositions of syllables, or through nonsensical but musically arranged words.[1] So we learned the music of our language on top of the content. The language, through images and symbols, gave us a view of the world, but it had a beauty of its own. The home and the field were then our pre-primary school but what is important, for this discussion, is that the language of our evening teachins, and the language of our immediate and wider community, and the language of our work in the fields were one.

And then I went to school, a colonial school, and this harmony was broken. The language of my education was no longer the language of my culture. I first went to Kamaandura, missionary run, and then to another called Maanguuũ run by nationalists grouped around the Gĩkũyũ Independent and Karinga Schools Association. Our language of education was still Gĩkũyũ. The very first time I was ever given an ovation for my writing was over a composition in Gĩkũyũ. So for my first four years there was still harmony between the language of my formal education and that of the Limuru peasant community.

It was after the declaration of a state of emergency over Kenya in 1952 that all the schools run by patriotic nationalists were taken over by the colonial regime and were placed under District Education Boards chaired by Englishmen. English became the language of my formal education. In Kenya, English became more than a language: it was *the* language, and all the others had to bow before it in deference.

Thus one of the most humiliating experiences was to be caught speaking Gĩkũyũ in the vicinity of the school. The culprit was given corporal punishment—three to five strokes of the cane on bare buttocks—or was made to carry a metal plate around the neck with inscriptions such as I AM STUPID or I AM A DONKEY. Sometimes the culprits were fined money they could hardly afford. And how did the teachers catch the culprits? A button was initially given to one pupil who was supposed to hand it over to whoever was caught speaking his mother tongue. Whoever had the button at the end of the day would sing who had given it to him and the

1. Example from a tongue twister: "Kaana ka Nikoora koona koora koora: na ko koora koona kaana ka Nikoora koora koora." I'm indebted to Wangui wa Goro for this example. "Nichola's child saw a baby frog and ran away: and when the baby frog saw Nichola's child it also ran away." A Gĩkũyũ speaking child has to get the correct tone and length of vowel and pauses to get it right. Otherwise it becomes a jumble of *k*'s and *r*'s and *na*'s [author's note].

ensuing process would bring out all the culprits of the day. Thus children were turned into witchhunters and in the process were being taught the lucrative value of being a traitor to one's immediate community.

The attitude to English was the exact opposite: any achievement in spoken or written English was highly rewarded; prizes, prestige, applause; the ticket to higher realms. English became the measure of intelligence and ability in the arts, the sciences, and all the other branches of learning. English became *the* main determinant of a child's progress up the ladder of formal education.

As you may know, the colonial system of education in addition to its apartheid racial demarcation had the structure of a pyramid: a broad primary base, a narrowing secondary middle, and an even narrower university apex. Selections from primary into secondary were through an examination, in my time called Kenya African Preliminary Examination, in which one had to pass six subjects ranging from Maths to Nature Study and Kiswahili. All the papers were written in English. Nobody could pass the exam who failed the English language paper no matter how brilliantly he had done in the other subjects. I remember one boy in my class of 1954 who had distinctions in all subjects except English, which he had failed. He was made to fail the entire exam. He went on to become a turn boy in a bus company. I who had only passes but a credit in English got a place at the Alliance High School, one of the most elitist institutions for Africans in colonial Kenya. The requirements for a place at the University, Makerere University College, were broadly the same: nobody could go on to wear the undergraduate red gown, no matter how brilliantly they had performed in all the other subjects unless they had a credit—not even a simple pass!—in English. Thus the most coveted place in the pyramid and in the system was only available to the holder of an English language credit card. English was the official vehicle and the magic formula to colonial elitedom.

Literary education was now determined by the dominant language while also reinforcing that dominance. Orature (oral literature) in Kenyan languages stopped. In primary school I now read simplified Dickens and Stevenson alongside Rider Haggard. Jim Hawkins, Oliver Twist, Tom Brown—not Hare, Leopard and Lion—were now my daily companions in the world of imagination. In secondary school, Scott and G. B. Shaw vied with more Rider Haggard, John Buchan, Alan Paton, Captain W. E. Johns. At Makerere I read English: from Chaucer to T. S. Eliot with a touch of Graham Greene.

Thus language and literature were taking us further and further from ourselves to other selves, from our world to other worlds.

What was the colonial system doing to us Kenyan children? What were the consequences of, on the one hand, this systematic suppression of our languages and the literature they carried, and on the other the elevation of English and the literature it carried? To answer those questions, let me first examine the relationship of language to human experience, human culture, and the human perception of reality.

Language, any language, has a dual character: it is both a means of communication and a carrier of culture. Take English. It is spoken in Britain and in Sweden and Denmark. But for Swedish and Danish people English is only a means of communication with non-Scandinavians. It is not a carrier of their culture. For the British, and particularly the English, it is additionally, and inseparably from its use as a tool of communication, a carrier of their culture and history. Or take Swahili in East and Central Africa. It is widely used as a means of communication across many nationalities. But it is not the carrier of a culture and history of many of those nationalities. However in parts of Kenya and Tanzania, and particularly in Zanzibar, Swahili is inseparably both a means of communication and a carrier of the culture of those people to whom it is a mother-tongue.

Language as communication has three aspects or elements. There is first what Karl Marx once called the language of real life,[2] the element basic to the whole notion of language, its origins and development: that is, the relations people enter into with one another in the labor process, the links they necessarily establish among themselves in the act of a people, a community of human beings, producing wealth or means of life like food, clothing, houses. A human community really starts its historical being as a community of co-operation in production through the division of labor; the simplest is between man, woman and child within a household; the more complex divisions are between branches of production such as those who are sole hunters, sole gatherers of fruits or sole workers in metal. Then there are the most complex divisions such as those in modern factories where a single product, say a shirt or a shoe, is the result of many hands and minds. Production is co-operation, is communication, is language, is expression of a relation between human beings and it is specifically human.

The second aspect of language as communication is speech and it imitates the language of real life, that is communication in production. The verbal signposts both reflect and aid communication or the relations

2. "The production of ideas, of conceptions, of consciousness, is at first directly interwoven with the material activity and the material intercourse of men, the languge of real life. Conceiving, thinking, the mental intercourse of men, appear at this stage as the direct efflux of their material behaviour. The same applies to mental production as expressed in the language of politics, laws, morality, religion, metaphysics, etc., of a people. Men are the producers of their conceptions, ideas etc.—real active men, as they are conditioned by a definite development of their productive forces and of the intercourse corresponding to these, up to its furthest form." Marx and Engels, German Ideology, the first part published under the title *Feuerbach: Opposition of the Materialist and Idealist Outlooks*, London: 1973, p. 8 [author's note].

established between human beings in the production of their means of life. Language as a system of verbal signposts makes that production possible. The spoken word is to relations between human beings what the hand is to the relations between human beings and nature. The hand through tools mediates between human beings and nature and forms the language of real life: spoken words mediate between human beings and form the language of speech.

The third aspect is the written signs. The written word imitates the spoken. Where the first two aspects of language as communication through the hand and the spoken word historically evolved more or less simultaneously, the written aspect is a much later historical development. Writing is representation of sounds with visual symbols, from the simplest knot among shepherds to tell the number in a herd or the hieroglyphics among the Agĩkũyũ gicaandi singers and poets of Kenya, to the most complicated and different letter and picture writing systems of the world today.

In most societies the written and the spoken languages are the same, in that they represent each other: what is on paper can be read to another person and be received as that language which the recipient has grown up speaking. In such a society there is broad harmony for a child between the three aspects of language as communication. His interaction with nature and with other men is expressed in written and spoken symbols or signs which are both a result of that double interaction and a reflection of it. The association of the child's sensibility is with the language of his experience of life.

But there is more to it: communication between human beings is also the basis and process of evolving culture. In doing similar kinds of things and actions over and over again under similar circumstances, similar even in their mutability, certain patterns, moves, rhythms, habits, attitudes, experiences and knowledge emerge. Those experiences are handed over to the next generation and become the inherited basis for their further actions on nature and on themselves. There is a gradual accumulation of values which in time become almost self-evident truths governing their conception of what is right and wrong, good and bad, beautiful and ugly, courageous and cowardly, generous and mean in their internal and external relations. Over a time this becomes a way of life distinguishable from other ways of life. They develop a distinctive culture and history. Culture embodies those moral, ethical and aesthetic values, the set of spiritual eyeglasses, through which they come to view themselves and their place in the universe. Values are the basis of a people's identity, their sense of particularity as members of the human race. All this is carried by language. Language as culture is the collective memory bank of a people's experience in history. Culture is almost indistinguishable from the language that makes possible its genesis, growth, banking, articulation and indeed its transmission from one generation to the next.

Language as culture also has three important aspects. Culture is a product of the history which it in turn reflects. Culture in other words is a product and a reflection of human beings communicating with one another in the very struggle to create wealth and to control it. But culture does not merely reflect that history, or rather it does so by actually forming images or pictures of the world of nature and nurture. Thus the second aspect of language as culture is as an image-forming agent in the mind of a child. Our whole conception of ourselves as a people, individually and collectively, is based on those pictures and images which may or may not correctly correspond to the actual reality of the struggles with nature and nurture which produced them in the first place. But our capacity to confront the world creatively is dependent on how these images correspond or not to that reality, how they distort or clarify the reality of our struggles. Language as culture is thus mediating between me and my own self; between my own self and other selves; between me and nature. Language is mediating in my very being. And this brings us to the third aspect of language as culture. Culture transmits or imparts those images of the world and reality through the spoken and the written language, that is through a specific language. In other words, the capacity to speak, the capacity to order sounds in a manner that makes for mutual comprehension between human beings is universal. This is the universality of language, a quality specific to human beings. It corresponds to the universality of the struggle against nature and that between human beings. But the particularity of the sounds, the words, the word order into phrases and sentences, and the specific manner, or laws, of their ordering is what distinguishes one language from another. Thus a specific culture is not transmitted through language in its universality but in its particularity as the language of a specific community with a specific history. Written literature and orature are the main means by which a particular language transmits the images of the world contained in the culture it carries.

Language as communication and as culture are then products of each other. Communication creates culture: culture is a means of communication. Language carries culture, and culture carries, particularly through orature and literature, the entire body of values by which we come to perceive ourselves and our place in the world. How people perceive themselves affects how they look at their culture, at their politics and at the social production of wealth, at their entire relationship to nature and to other beings. Language is thus inseparable from ourselves as a community of human beings with a specific form and character, a specific history, a specific relationship to the world.

So what was the colonialist imposition of a foreign language doing to us children?

The real aim of colonialism was to control the people's wealth: what they produced, how they produced it, and how it was distributed; to control, in other words, the entire realm of the language of real life. Colonialism imposed its control of the social production of wealth through military conquest and subsequent political dictatorship. But its most important area of domination was the mental universe of the colonized, the control, through culture, of how people perceived themselves and their relationship to the world. Economic and political control can never be complete or effective without mental control. To control a people's culture is to control their tools of self-definition in relationship to others.

For colonialism this involved two aspects of the same process: the destruction or the deliberate undervaluing of a people's culture, their art, dances, religions, history, geography, education, orature and literature, and the conscious elevation of the language of the colonizer. The domination of a people's language by the languages of the colonizing nations was crucial to the domination of the mental universe of the colonized.

Take language as communication. Imposing a foreign language, and suppressing the native languages as spoken and written, were already breaking the harmony previously existing between the African child and the three aspects of language. Since the new language as a means of communication was a product of and was reflecting the "real language of life" elsewhere, it could never as spoken or written properly reflect or imitate the real life of that community. This may in part explain why technology always appears to us as slightly external, *their* product and not *ours*. The word "missile" used to hold an alien far-away sound until I recently learned its equivalent in Gĩkũyũ, *ngurukuhĩ*, and it made me apprehend it differently. Learning, for a colonial child, became a cerebral activity and not an emotionally felt experience.

But since the new, imposed languages could never completely break the native languages as spoken, their most effective area of domination was the third aspect of language as communication, the written. The language of an African child's formal education was foreign. The language of the books he read was foreign. The language of his conceptualization was foreign. Thought, in him, took the visible form of a foreign language. So the written language of a child's upbringing in the school (even his spoken language within the school compound) became divorced from his spoken language at home. There was often not the slightest relationship between the child's written world, which was also the language of his schooling, and the world of his immediate environment in the family and the community. For a colonial child, the harmony existing between the three aspects of language as communication was irrevocably broken. This resulted in the disassociation of the sensibility of that child from his natural and social environment, what we might call colonial alienation. The alienation became reinforced in the teaching of history, geography, music, where bourgeois Europe was always the center of the universe.

This disassociation, divorce, or alienation from the immediate environment becomes clearer when you look at colonial language as a carrier of culture.

Since culture is a product of the history of a people which it in turn reflects, the child was now being exposed exclusively to a culture that was a product of a world external to himself. He was being made to stand outside himself to look at himself. *Catching Them Young* is the title of a book on racism, class, sex, and politics in children's literature by Bob Dixon. "Catching them young" as an aim was even more true of a colonial child. The images of this world and his place in it implanted in a child take years to eradicate, if they ever can be.

Since culture does not just reflect the world in images but actually, through those very images, conditions a child to see that world in a certain way, the colonial child was made to see the world and where he stands in it as seen and defined by or reflected in the culture of the language of imposition.

And since those images are mostly passed on through orature and literature it meant the child would now only see the world as seen in the literature of his language of adoption. From the point of view of alienation, that is of seeing oneself from outside oneself as if one was another self, it does not matter that the imported literature carried the great humanist tradition of the best in Shakespeare, Goethe, Balzac, Tolstoy, Gorky, Brecht, Sholokhov, Dickens. The location of this great mirror of imagination was necessarily Europe and its history and culture and the rest of the universe was seen from that center.

But obviously it was worse when the colonial child was exposed to images of his world as mirrored in the written languages of his colonizer. Where his own native languages were associated in his impressionable mind with low status, humiliation, corporal punishment, slow-footed intelligence and ability or downright stupidity, non-intelligibility and barbarism, this was reinforced by the world he met in the works of such geniuses of racism as a Rider Haggard or a Nicholas Monserrat; not to mention the pronouncement of some of the giants of western intellectual and political establishment, such as Hume (". . . the negro is naturally inferior to the whites . . ."), Thomas Jefferson (". . . the blacks . . . are inferior to the whites on the endowments of both body and mind . . ."), or Hegel with his Africa comparable to a land of childhood still enveloped in the dark mantle of the night as far as the development of self-conscious history was concerned. Hegel's statement that there was nothing harmo-

nious with humanity to be found in the African character is representative of the racist images of Africans and Africa such a colonial child was
bound to encounter in the literature of the colonial languages. The
results could be disastrous.

In her paper read to the conference on the teaching of African literature in schools held in Nairobi in 1973, entitled "Written Literature and
Black Images," the Kenyan writer and scholar Professor Mĩcere Mũgo
related how a reading of the description of Gagool as an old African
woman in Rider Haggard's *King Solomon's Mines* had for a long time
made her feel mortal terror whenever she encountered old African women. In his autobiography *This Life* Sydney Poitier describes how, as a
result of the literature he had read, he had come to associate Africa with
snakes. So on arrival in Africa and being put up in a modern hotel in a
modern city, he could not sleep because he kept on looking for snakes
everywhere, even under the bed. These two have been able to pinpoint
the origins of their fears. But for most others the negative image becomes
internalized and it affects their cultural and even political choices in
ordinary living.

Thus Léopold Sédar Senghor[3] has said very clearly that although the
colonial language had been forced upon him, if he had been given the
choice he would still have opted for French. He becomes lyrical in his
subservience to French:

> We express ourselves in French since French has a universal vocation and
> since our message is also addressed to French people and others. In our
> languages [i.e. African languages] the halo that surrounds the words is by
> nature merely that of sap and blood; French words send out thousands of rays
> like diamonds.

Senghor has now been rewarded by being anointed to an honored place
in the French Academy—that institution for safe-guarding the purity of
the French language.

In Malawi, Banda[4] has erected his own monument by way of an
institution, The Kamuzu Academy, designed to aid the brightest pupils
of Malawi in their mastery of English.

> It is a grammar school designed to produce boys and girls who will be sent to
> universities like Harvard, Chicago, Oxford, Cambridge and Edinburgh and
> be able to compete on equal terms with others elsewhere.
>
> The President has instructed that Latin should occupy a central place in
> the curriculum. All teachers must have had at least some Latin in their
> academic background. Dr Banda has often said that no one can fully master
> English without knowledge of languages such as Latin and French . . .

3. Léopold Sédar Senghor: African statesman
and poet, born in 1906, became president of
the republic of Senegal in 1960.

4. Hastings Kamuzu Banda: born in 1902 (?),
became president of Malawi in 1966.

For good measure no Malawian is allowed to teach at the academy—none is good enough—and all the teaching staff has been recruited from Britain. A Malawian might lower the standards, or rather, the purity of the English language. Can you get a more telling example of hatred of what is national, and a servile worship of what is foreign even though dead?

In history books and popular commentaries on Africa, too much has been made of the supposed differences in the policies of the various colonial powers, the British indirect rule (or the pragmatism of the British in their lack of a cultural program!) and the French and Portuguese conscious program of cultural assimilation. These are a matter of detail and emphasis. The final effect was the same: Senghor's embrace of French as this language with a universal vocation is not so different from Chinua Achebe's[5] gratitude in 1964 to English—"those of us who have inherited our English language may not be in a position to appreciate the value of the inheritance." The assumptions behind the practice of those of us who have abandoned our mother-tongues and adopted European ones as the creative vehicles of our imagination, are not different either.

Thus the 1962 conference of "African Writers of English expression" was only recognizing, with approval and pride of course, what through all the years of selective education and rigorous tutelage, we had already been led to accept: the "fatalistic logic of the unassailable position of English in our literature." The logic was embodied deep in imperialism; and it was imperialism and its effects that we did not examine at Makerere. It is the final triumph of a system of domination when the dominated start singing its virtues.

1986

5. Chinua Achebe: Nigerian novelist, poet, and essayist, born in 1930.

THE READER

1. "Culture is . . . an image-forming agent in the mind of a child" (p. 462). Is the author right? How do you know? How can this statement be tested?
2. What distinctions does Ngũgĩ make between language as communication and language as culture? What connections between the two does he see?
3. What connections does Ngũgĩ draw between language and colonialism?
4. Ngũgĩ uses different verbs to describe the relation between language and reality. List some. If you grant his idea about that relation, is his conclusion inevitable?
5. On p. 457, Ngũgĩ speaks movingly of the power of language and literature to define the selves of the speakers and then of the division between English and Gĩkũyũ in his experience. His context is colonial, but the idea is plausible in other contexts—popular culture, for in-

stance. To what degree do rock music and cult movies provide analogies to his experience of his native Gĩkũyũ?

THE WRITER

1. On p. 462, Ngũgĩ makes an important distinction between images and reality. How does he use this distinction in his essay?

2. On p. 465, Ngũgĩ speaks of other Africans who have adopted French or English. What does he think of them? Can he share a culture with them?

3. When Ngũgĩ wrote the book from which this piece is taken, he said it would be the last time he would write in English. Address a letter to Ngũgĩ either applauding his decision or attempting to change his mind.

4. Write a brief essay comparing Ngũgĩ's view of the political effects of language with Orwell's (p. 241).

Charles R. Morris

CIVIL DISOBEDIENCE

The assignment of primacy to the moral over the political resonates comfortably within the American tradition, however revolutionary its implications. The radical Black Panthers, with a wry sense of nuance, adopted the Declaration of Independence as their official platform. ("It is the Right of the People ... it is their duty, to throw off such Government.") The higher claim of the civil rights movement over legal authority was formally stated by Martin Luther King in his famous "Letter from a Birmingham Jail" of 1963. The letter was a response to a group of Southern white clergymen who had criticized King for breaking local laws during a series of demonstrations. It is notable not only for its claim that civil disobedience is a legitimate technique to advance the cause of equal rights, but for its attempt to lay down a formal set of rules for its application and practice.

King argued that his violation of the law in Birmingham qualified as "legitimate" civil disobedience, as the concept was developed in the teachings and writings of Gandhi. In King's view, the pressing reality of social injustice in the South made action imperative. The lawbreaking was not casual, for King had carefully ascertained the facts of the law beforehand. He had negotiated fruitlessly and at great length with local officials. He had "purified" himself with prayer and meditation before his action. He had taken care that he would break the law nonviolently. The laws violated were either unjust laws—they applied only to a minority or they were undemocratically passed—or proper laws being applied unjustly. Finally, the violation was "open and loving," and King was willing to accept whatever penalty was imposed.

Civil disobedience became something of an intellectual industry in the mid-1960s. It was not a new idea, of course. Aside from Gandhi and Sam Adams, there was Henry David Thoreau, who had refused to pay taxes in 1848 to protest against the Mexican War; there were the Boston abolitionists who had forcibly prevented the return of fugitive slaves, and, if one cared to stretch the gospels a bit, there was even Jesus. The underlying assumption was that there was a higher law that took precedence over political codes. The problem for philosophers and moralists was to define that higher law and to establish the circumstances that made civil disobedience permissible. Some of the attempts were ingenious; in my view, none of them was wholly successful. One fairly typical formulation, that of John Rawls,[1] defined civil disobedience as a "public, nonviolent, conscientious yet political act contrary to law usually done with the aim of bringing about a change in the law or policies of the government." The public character of the act was necessary if it was to result in the desired changes. The "conscientious" requirement meant that the lawbreaking was reasoned and principled—that the lawbreakers, in effect, could point to the higher law they were obeying, could demonstrate why it imposed a superior obligation, and could show that there was no available recourse within the current legal framework.

It was more difficult to demonstrate why civil disobedience had to be nonviolent. Most theorists, in company with King's Birmingham letter, argued that nonviolence advertised the lawbreakers' continued respect for the law and increased the effectiveness of the protest. But that rings more of tactical advice than of moral canon. By 1963, in fact, an important element in SNCC[2]—oxymoronically but understandably—had rejected nonviolence and were carrying guns. Howard Zinn, who had become a sort of quasi-official SNCC theorist, insisted that change may *require* violence, citing sources as diverse as Albert Camus, Frederick Douglass, Ralph Waldo Emerson, and Reinhold Niebuhr. While scholars like Rawls, Ronald Dworkin, and Morris Cohen were constructing high-minded hypotheses drawn from civil rights or anti-Vietnam protests, Zinn was calling for takeovers of university buildings, "smashing a hospital gate" to keep the hospital from closing, "occupying a skyscraper and living in it," "running up bills and sending them to the federal government," forcibly keeping the police out of the ghettos, and other fevered products of a rich academic imagination. Violence, as H. Rap Brown, a later SNCC chairman, jeered, was "as American as cherry pie."

1. John Rawls: Harvard philosophy professor.
2. The Student Nonviolent Coordinating Committee, an organization formed in the 1960s to further the civil-rights movement and to oppose the Vietnam War.

It may not be possible to construct a truly consistent theory of "legitimate" or "permissible" civil disobedience. Locke and Hume argued that selective disobedience entails rejection of the entire government. If individuals are the final arbiters of the law, the entire structure of authority must eventually collapse. Rawls and Zinn struggle to avoid that logic, but the arguments of both, if they have little else in common, are circular —each selects specific incidents of civil disobedience he approves of and then searches for principles to fit them. Nor is historical precedent of much help. Thoreau was more quirky than principled, and admitted that he enjoyed picking and choosing which laws to obey. Emerson made a hero and martyr of John Brown,[3] who was probably a psychopath. Gandhi, at least in his Indian phase, and Sam Adams were forthright revolutionaries, not reformists; their civil disobedience was merely a tactic in the larger treason.

It is easy to conceive of instances where the law should be disobeyed. The logic of Nuremberg,[4] after all, rested on the principle of a higher duty. But when the most extreme cases have been allowed for, the argument quickly collapses into mere subjectivity. Rawls maintains that "each person must decide for himself whether the circumstances justify civil disobedience," although he hastens to add that "it does not follow that one is to decide as one pleases." The distinction may be sufficient guide for a Harvard philosophy professor but is rather harder to employ as the platform of a mass movement. The early proclivity of the Kennedy administration to prefer tranquillity and ordered change over strict justice sprang from an instinctive Burkean[5] reliance on settled institutions. As pragmatic liberals they were prepared to accept, even embrace, change. But their insistence that it proceed incrementally and at a pace that could be readily absorbed by the existing political structure seemed arid and unfeeling in the face of the pressing issues that were churning to the surface first in the South and later in Vietnam. And, to an extent, their position was arid and unfeeling, and in the case of Vietnam, casually arrogant as well. But if pragmatism proved an inadequate guide as the country careened toward the confrontations of the late 1960s, it remained to be shown whether deduction from principles of individual morality could provide a more reliable compass.

1984

3. John Brown: American abolitionist (1800–59), hanged for leading a raid on the federal arsenal at Harpers Ferry, Virginia.
4. Site of the war-crimes trials of Nazi leaders after World War II.

5. A reference to Edmund Burke (1729–97), British political writer and statesman, influential spokesman for European conservatives.

THE READER

1. This is a historical account of civil disobedience. What are Morris's data? What are the phenomena he is observing in order to write his history? Arrange them on a scale from the most factual and objective to the most abstract and general. Where does his emphasis fall?

2. *Morris permits himself some indirect judgments of people involved in civil disobedience. Cite some examples. Are they coherent enough to show Morris's own attitude toward civil disobedience? If so, what is it?*

THE WRITER

1. *On p. 468, Morris says that theorists "argued that nonviolence advertised the lawbreakers' continued respect for the law and increased the effectiveness of the protest." He then goes on to say, "That rings more of tactical advice than of moral canon." Write a paragraph to amplify his judgment or to refute it by explaining the moral grounds for the theorists' argument.*

2. *Choose a sentence expressing one of Morris's indirect judgments ("The Reader," question 2). Rewrite it, first, so that no judgment is expressed and, then, so as to express a different judgment.*

Ralph W. Conant

THE JUSTIFICATION OF CIVIL PROTEST, NONVIOLENT AND VIOLENT

There is substantial agreement among legal and political thinkers that nonviolent challenges to the policies and laws of civil authority are an indispensable mechanism of corrective change in a democratic society. Insofar as possible, procedures for challenge which may involve open and deliberate disobedience should be built into the laws and policies of the system, for such procedures give the system a quality of resilience and flexibility, the capacity to absorb constructive attack from within.

As George Lakay has pointed out, one great strength of democratic institutions is that they build a degree of conflict into the decision-making structure just so that conflicts can be resolved publicly and without violence. Adequately designed democratic institutions deliberately reflect shifting views and power relations of interest groups and the normal workings of compromise and settlement, and equilibrium is usually maintained. Civil disobedience, and other forms of civil protest, are resorted to when political adversaries exhaust means of compromise in the political arena. Then the less powerful of the adversaries is forced to carry his challenge into a legal procedure or to the public in a show of protest.

Agreement on a policy of deliberate tolerance of peaceful challenge does not imply automatic agreement on what conditions *justify* challenges that involve disobedience. Moreover, agreement on a policy of tolerance toward nonviolent civil disobedience bears no necessary relationship at all to the question of the justification of civil protest involving violence, as riots and insurrection always do.

Nonviolent civil disobedience is justified under the following circumstances:

1. When an oppressed group is deprived of lawful channels for remedying its condition; conversely, a resort to civil disobedience is never politically legitimate where methods of due process in both the legal and political systems are available as remedies.

2. As a means of resisting or refusing to participate in an obvious and intolerable evil perpetrated by civil authorities (for example, a policy of genocide or enslavement).

3. When government takes or condones actions that are inconsistent with values on which the society and the political system are built, and thus violates the basic assumptions on which the regime's legitimacy rests.

4. When it is certain that the law or policy in question violates the constitution of the regime and, therefore, would be ruled unconstitutional by proper authority if challenged.

5. When a change in law or policy is demanded by social or economic need in the community and the normal procedures of law and politics are inadequate, obstructed or held captive by antilegal forces.

6. When the actions of government have become so obnoxious to one's own personal ethics (value system) that one would feel hypocritical in submitting to a law that enforces these actions: for example, the Fugitive Slave Law.

It seems to me that a citizen is justified in originating or participating in an act of civil disobedience under any of these circumstances, and, as Herbert Kelman[1] has argued, that an act of civil disobedience in such circumstances should be generally regarded as *obligatory* in terms of the highest principles of citizenship. This does not mean that acts of civil disobedience should be ignored by civil authorities; on the contrary, aside from the damage such a policy would do to effectiveness of the act of civil disobedience, it must be considered the obligation of the regime to punish a law breaker *so long as the violated law is in force.* As William Buckley[2] has argued, it is the individual's right to refuse to go along with

1. Herbert Kelman (b. 1927, Austria): psychologist and educator noted for his work on

the ethics of social intervention.
2. William Buckley, Jr. (b. 1925): magazine

his community, but the community, not the individual, must specify the consequences. For the regime to act otherwise would be to concede the right of personal veto over every act of government. At the same time, a conscientious challenge to civil authority (with full expectation of punishment) aimed at repairing a serious flaw in the system of justice is a step every citizen should know how to *decide* to take.

When Is Civil Protest Involving Violence Justified?

Americans like to think of themselves as a peace-loving people, yet violence is and always has been an important and sometimes indispensable instrument of social, economic and political change in our national history. We do not need to be reminded of the role it has played in United States foreign policy and in domestic relations.

The fact is that Americans are *both* peace-loving and willing to resort to violence when other avenues of goal achievement seem closed or ineffective. In our national history violence was the ultimate instrument in our conquest of the lands on the North American continent that now comprise the nation. Violence freed the American colonists from British rule and later insured freedom of the seas (1812–1815). Violence abolished slavery, established the bargaining rights of labor, twice put down threatening tyrannies in Europe and once in the Asian Pacific. In the present day, violence is the unintended instrument of black citizens to break through oppressive discrimination in housing, employment, education and political rights.

Americans have always taken the position that violence could be justified *as an instrument of last resort* in the achievement of critical national goals or in the face of external threat.

While it is true that we have always felt most comfortable about government-sponsored violence and especially violence in response to an external threat, we have often rationalized *post factum* the use of violence by aggrieved segments of the population *when the cause was regarded as a just one in terms of our deeply held egalitarian values.* The anti-draft riots during the Civil War are one example; labor strife that finally led to legitimizing workers' bargaining rights is another. Two or three generations from now, the ghetto riots (and even the spasmodic insurrection that is bound to follow) will be seen as having contributed to the perfection of our system of egalitarian values. Thus, I conclude that violence in the cause of hewing to our most cherished goals of freedom, justice and equal opportunity for all our citizens is and will remain as indispensable a corrective ingredient in our system as peaceful acts of civil disobedience. The sole qualification is that all other avenues of legitimate and peaceful

---

editor, author, influential advocate of conservatism in America.

change first be substantially closed, exhausted or ineffective.

When an aggrieved segment of the population finds it necessary to resist, riot or commit deliberate acts of insurrection, the government must respond firmly to enforce the law, to protect people and property from the consequences of violence, but it must, with equal energy and dedication, seek out the causes of the outbursts and move speedily to rectify any injustices that are found at the root of the trouble.

1968

THE READER

1. *Conant lists six circumstances in which he believes nonviolent civil disobedience is justified. Which of these six have similar bases for justification? Are some bases stronger than others?*
2. *Under what circumstances does Conant believe violence is justified?*
3. *What does Conant believe the obligations of government are? Is this view consistent with his other views?*

THE WRITER

1. *What assumptions does Conant seem to be making about his audience?*
2. *Conant asserts that violence is sometimes justified, and that nonviolent civil disobedience is sometimes justified. Does he offer the same or different kinds of support for these two assertions? Is the case for one stronger than the case for the other?*
3. *Conant asserts that a citizen not only is justified in engaging in an act of civil disobedience under some circumstances, but also has an obligation to do so. Write a brief essay supporting or opposing his view.*
4. *Write a brief essay comparing Conant's views with those of Morris (p. 467) or King (below).*

Martin Luther King, Jr.

LETTER FROM BIRMINGHAM JAIL[1]

My Dear Fellow Clergymen:

While confined here in the Birmingham city jail, I came across your recent statement calling my present activities "unwise and untimely."

1. This response to a published statement by eight fellow clergymen from Alabama (Bishop C. C. J. Carpenter, Bishop Joseph A. Durick, Rabbi Milton L. Grafman, Bishop Paul Hardin, Bishop Holan B. Harmon, the Reverend George M. Murray, the Reverend Edward V. Ramage and the Reverend Earl Stallings) was composed under somewhat constricting circumstances. Begun on the margins of the newspaper in which the statement appeared while I was in jail, the letter was continued on scraps of writing paper supplied by a friendly Negro trusty, and concluded on a pad my attorneys were eventually permitted to leave me. Although the text remains in substance unaltered, I have indulged in the author's prerogative of polishing it for publication [King's note].

Seldom do I pause to answer criticism of my work and ideas. If I sought to answer all the criticisms that cross my desk, my secretaries would have little time for anything other than such correspondence in the course of the day, and I would have no time for constructive work. But since I feel that you are men of genuine good will and that your criticisms are sincerely set forth, I want to try to answer your statement in what I hope will be patient and reasonable terms.

I think I should indicate why I am here in Birmingham, since you have been influenced by the view which argues against "outsiders coming in." I have the honor of serving as president of the Southern Christian Leadership Conference, an organization operating in every southern state, with headquarters in Atlanta, Georgia. We have some eighty-five affiliated organizations across the South, and one of them is the Alabama Christian Movement for Human Rights. Frequently we share staff, educational, and financial resources with our affiliates. Several months ago the affiliate here in Birmingham asked us to be on call to engage in a nonviolent direct-action program if such were deemed necessary. We readily consented, and when the hour came we lived up to our promise. So I, along with several members of my staff, am here because I was invited here. I am here because I have organizational ties here.

But more basically, I am in Birmingham because injustice is here. Just as the prophets of the eighth century B.C. left their villages and carried their "thus saith the Lord" far beyond the boundaries of their home towns, and just as the Apostle Paul left his village of Tarsus and carried the gospel of Jesus Christ to the far corners of the Greco-Roman world, so am I compelled to carry the gospel of freedom beyond my own home town. Like Paul, I must constantly respond to the Macedonian call for aid.

Moreover, I am cognizant of the interrelatedness of all communities and states. I cannot sit idly by in Atlanta and not be concerned about what happens in Birmingham. Injustice anywhere is a threat to justice everywhere. We are caught in an inescapable network of mutuality, tied in a single garment of destiny. Whatever affects one directly, affects all indirectly. Never again can we afford to live with the narrow, provincial "outside agitator" idea. Anyone who lives inside the United States can never be considered an outsider anywhere within its bounds.

You deplore the demonstrations taking place in Birmingham. But your statement, I am sorry to say, fails to express a similar concern for the conditions that brought about the demonstrations. I am sure that none of you would want to rest content with the superficial kind of social analysis that deals merely with effects and does not grapple with underlying causes. It is unfortunate that demonstrations are taking place in Birmingham, but it is even more unfortunate that the city's white power structure left the Negro community with no alternative.

In any nonviolent campaign there are four basic steps: collection of the facts to determine whether injustices exist; negotiation; self-purification; and direct action. We have gone through all these steps in Birmingham. There can be no gainsaying the fact that racial injustice engulfs this community. Birmingham is probably the most thoroughly segregated city in the United States. Its ugly record of brutality is widely known. Negroes have experienced grossly unjust treatment in the courts. There have been more unsolved bombings of Negro homes and churches in Birmingham than in any other city in the nation. These are the hard, brutal facts of the case. On the basis of these conditions, Negro leaders sought to negotiate with the city fathers. But the latter consistently refused to engage in good-faith negotiation.

Then, last September, came the opportunity to talk with leaders of Birmingham's economic community. In the course of the negotiations, certain promises were made by the merchants—for example, to remove the stores' humiliating racial signs. On the basis of these promises, the Reverend Fred Shuttlesworth and the leaders of the Alabama Christian Movement for Human Rights agreed to a moratorium on all demonstrations. As the weeks and months went by, we realized that we were the victims of a broken promise. A few signs, briefly removed, returned; the others remained.

As in so many past experiences, our hopes had been blasted, and the shadow of deep disappointment settled upon us. We had no alternative except to prepare for direct action, whereby we would present our very bodies as a means of laying our case before the conscience of the local and the national community. Mindful of the difficulties involved, we decided to undertake a process of self-purification. We began a series of workshops on nonviolence, and we repeatedly asked ourselves: "Are you able to accept blows without retaliating?" "Are you able to endure the ordeal of jail?" We decided to schedule our direct-action program for the Easter season, realizing that except for Christmas, this is the main shopping period of the year. Knowing that a strong economic-withdrawal program would be the by-product of direct action, we felt that this would be the best time to bring pressure to bear on the merchants for the needed change.

Then it occurred to us that Birmingham's mayoral election was coming up in March, and we speedily decided to postpone action until after election day. When we discovered that the Commissioner of Public Safety, Eugene "Bull" Connor, had piled up enough votes to be in the run-off, we decided again to postpone action until the day after the run-off so that the demonstrations could not be used to cloud the issues. Like many others, we wanted to see Mr. Connor defeated, and to this end we endured postponement after postponement. Having aided in this community need, we felt that our direct-action program could be delayed no longer.

You may well ask, "Why direct action? Why sit-ins, marches, and so forth? Isn't negotiation a better path?" You are quite right in calling for negotiation. Indeed, this is the very purpose of direct action. Nonviolent direct action seeks to create such a crisis and foster such a tension that a community which has constantly refused to negotiate is forced to confront the issue. It seeks so to dramatize the issue that it can no longer be ignored. My citing the creation of tension as part of the work of the nonviolent-resister may sound rather shocking. But I must confess that I am not afraid of the word "tension." I have earnestly opposed violent tension, but there is a type of constructive, nonviolent tension which is necessary for growth. Just as Socrates felt that it was necessary to create a tension in the mind so that individuals could rise from the bondage of myths and half-truths to the unfettered realm of creative analysis and objective appraisal, so must we see the need for nonviolent gadflies to create the kind of tension in society that will help men rise from the dark depths of prejudice and racism to the majestic heights of understanding and brotherhood.

The purpose of our direct-action program is to create a situation so crisis-packed that it will inevitably open the door to negotiation. I therefore concur with you in your call for negotiation. Too long has our beloved Southland been bogged down in a tragic effort to live in monologue rather than dialogue.

One of the basic points in your statement is that the action that I and my associates have taken in Birmingham is untimely. Some have asked: "Why didn't you give the new city administration time to act?" The only answer that I can give to this query is that the new Birmingham administration must be prodded about as much as the outgoing one, before it will act. We are sadly mistaken if we feel that the election of Albert Boutwell as mayor will bring the millennium to Birmingham. While Mr. Boutwell is a much more gentle person than Mr. Connor, they are both segregationists, dedicated to maintenance of the status quo. I have hoped that Mr. Boutwell will be reasonable enough to see the futility of massive resistance to desegregation. But he will not see this without pressure from devotees of civil rights. My friends, I must say to you that we have not made a single gain in civil rights without determined legal and nonviolent pressure. Lamentably, it is an historical fact that privileged groups seldom give up their privileges voluntarily. Individuals may see the moral light and voluntarily give up their unjust posture; but, as Reinhold Niebuhr has reminded us, groups tend to be more immoral than individuals.

We know through painful experience that freedom is never voluntarily given by the oppressor; it must be demanded by the oppressed. Frankly, I have yet to engage in a direct-action campaign that was "well timed" in the view of those who have not suffered unduly from the disease of segregation. For years now I have heard the word "Wait!" It rings in the ear of every Negro with piercing familiarity. This "Wait" has almost always meant "Never." We must come to see, with one of our distinguished jurists, that "justice too long delayed is justice denied."

We have waited for more than 340 years for our constitutional and God-given rights. The nations of Asia and Africa are moving with jetlike speed toward gaining political independence, but we still creep at horse-and-buggy pace toward gaining a cup of coffee at a lunch counter. Perhaps it is easy for those who have never felt the stinging darts of segregation to say, "Wait." But when you have seen vicious mobs lynch your mothers and fathers at will and drown your sisters and brothers at whim; when you have seen hate-filled policemen curse, kick, and even kill your black brothers and sisters; when you see the vast majority of your twenty million Negro brothers smothering in an airtight cage of poverty in the midst of an affluent society; when you suddenly find your tongue twisted and your speech stammering as you seek to explain to your six-year-old daughter why she can't go to the public amusement park that has just been advertised on television, and see tears welling up in her eyes when she is told that Funtown is closed to colored children, and see ominous clouds of inferiority beginning to form in her little mental sky, and see her beginning to distort her personality by develop-ing an unconscious bitterness toward white people; when you have to concoct an answer for a five-year-old son who is asking, "Daddy, why do white people treat colored people so mean?"; when you take a cross-country drive and find it necessary to sleep night after night in the uncomfortable corners of your automobile because no motel will accept you; when you are humiliated day in and day out by nagging signs reading "white" and "colored"; when your first name becomes "nigger," your middle name becomes "boy" (however old you are) and your last name becomes "John," and your wife and mother are never given the respected title "Mrs."; when you are harried by day and haunted by night by the fact that you are a Negro, living constantly at tiptoe stance, never quite knowing what to expect next, and are plagued with inner fears and outer resentments; when you are forever fighting a degenerating sense of "nobodiness"—then you will understand why we find it difficult to wait. There comes a time when the cup of endurance runs over, and men are no longer willing to be plunged into the abyss of despair. I hope, sirs, you can understand our legitimate and unavoidable impatience.

You express a great deal of anxiety over our willingness to break laws. This is certainly a legitimate concern. Since we so diligently urge people to obey the Supreme Court's decision of 1954 outlawing segregation in the public schools, at first glance it may seem rather paradoxical for us consciously to break laws. One may well ask: "How can you advocate breaking some laws and obeying others?" The answer lies in the fact that there are two types of laws: just and unjust. I would be the first to advocate obeying just laws. One has not only a legal but a moral responsibility to obey just laws. Conversely, one has a moral responsibility to disobey unjust laws. I would agree with St. Augustine that "an unjust law is no law at all."

Now, what is the difference between the two? How does one determine whether a law is just or unjust? A just law is a man-made code that squares with the moral law or the law of God. An unjust law is a code that is out of harmony with the moral law. To put it in the terms of St. Thomas Aquinas: An unjust law is a human law that is not rooted in eternal law and natural law. Any law that uplifts human personality is just. Any law that degrades human personality is unjust. All segregation statutes are unjust because segregation distorts the soul and damages the personality. It gives the segregator a false sense of superiority and the segregated a false sense of inferiority. Segregation, to use the terminology of the Jewish philosopher Martin Buber, substitutes an "I-it" relationship for an "I-thou" relationship and ends up relegating persons to the status of things. Hence segregation is not only politically, economically, and sociologically unsound, it is morally wrong and sinful. Paul Tillich has said that sin is separation. Is not segregation an existential expression of man's tragic separation, his awful estrangement, his terrible sinfulness? Thus it is that I can urge men to obey the 1954 decision of the Supreme Court, for it is morally right; and I can urge them to disobey segregation ordinances, for they are morally wrong.

Let us consider a more concrete example of just and unjust laws. An unjust law is a code that a numerical or power majority group compels a minority group to obey but does not make binding on itself. This is difference made legal. By the same token, a just law is a code that a majority compels a minority to follow and that it is willing to follow itself. This is sameness made legal.

Let me give another explanation. A law is unjust if it is inflicted on a minority that, as a result of being denied the right to vote, had no part in enacting or devising the law. Who can say that the legislature of Alabama which set up that state's segregation laws was democratically elected? Throughout Alabama all sorts of devious methods are used to prevent Negroes from becoming registered voters, and there are some counties in which, even though Negroes constitute a majority of the population, not a single Negro is registered. Can any law enacted under such circumstances be considered democratically structured?

Sometimes a law is just on its face and unjust in its application. For instance, I have been arrested on a charge of parading without a permit.

Now, there is nothing wrong in having an ordinance which requires a permit for a parade. But such an ordinance becomes unjust when it is used to maintain segregation and to deny citizens the First-Amendment privilege of peaceful assembly and protest.

I hope you are able to see the distinction I am trying to point out. In no sense do I advocate evading or defying the law, as would the rabid segregationist. That would lead to anarchy. One who breaks an unjust law must do so openly, lovingly, and with a willingness to accept the penalty. I submit that an individual who breaks a law that conscience tells him is unjust, and who willingly accepts the penalty of imprisonment in order to arouse the conscience of the community over its injustice, is in reality expressing the highest respect for law.

Of course, there is nothing new about this kind of civil disobedience. It was evidenced sublimely in the refusal of Shadrach, Meshach, and Abednego to obey the laws of Nebuchadnezzar, on the ground that a higher moral law was at stake. It was practiced superbly by the early Christians, who were willing to face hungry lions and the excruciating pain of chopping blocks rather than submit to certain unjust laws of the Roman Empire. To a degree, academic freedom is a reality today because Socrates practiced civil disobedience.[2] In our own nation, the Boston Tea Party represented a massive act of civil disobedience.

We should never forget that everything Adolf Hitler did in Germany was "legal" and everything the Hungarian freedom fighters[3] did in Hungary was "illegal." It was "illegal" to aid and comfort a Jew in Hitler's Germany. Even so, I am sure that, had I lived in Germany at the time, I would have aided and comforted my Jewish brothers. If today I lived in a Communist country where certain principles dear to the Christian faith are suppressed, I would openly advocate disobeying that country's antireligious laws.

I must make two honest confessions to you, my Christian and Jewish brothers. First, I must confess that over the past few years I have been gravely disappointed with the white moderate. I have almost reached the regrettable conclusion that the Negro's great stumbling block in his stride toward freedom is not the White Citizen's Counciler or the Ku Klux Klanner, but the white moderate, who is more devoted to "order" than to justice; who prefers a negative peace which is the absence of tension to a positive peace which is the presence of justice; who constantly says, "I agree with you in the goal you seek, but I cannot agree with your methods of direct action"; who paternalistically believes he

2. The ancient Greek philosopher Socrates was tried by the Athenians for corrupting their youth through his skeptical, questioning manner of teaching. He refused to change his ways, and was condemned to death.

3. In the anti-Communist revolution of 1956, which was quickly put down by the Russian army.

can set the timetable for another man's freedom; who lives by a mythical concept of time and who constantly advises the Negro to wait for a "more convenient season." Shallow understanding from people of good will is more frustrating than absolute misunderstanding from people of ill will. Lukewarm acceptance is much more bewildering than outright rejection.

I had hoped that the white moderate would understand that law and order exist for the purpose of establishing justice and that when they fail in this purpose they become the dangerously structured dams that block the flow of social progress. I had hoped that the white moderate would understand that the present tension in the South is a necessary phase of the transition from an obnoxious negative peace, in which the Negro passively accepted his unjust plight, to a substantive and positive peace, in which all men will respect the dignity and worth of human personality. Actually, we who engage in nonviolent direct action are not the creators of tension. We merely bring to the surface the hidden tension that is already alive. We bring it out in the open, where it can be seen and dealt with. Like a boil that can never be cured so long as it is covered up but must be opened with all its ugliness to the natural medicines of air and light, injustice must be exposed, with all the tension its exposure creates, to the light of human conscience and the air of national opinion, before it can be cured.

In your statement you assert that our actions, even though peaceful, must be condemned because they precipitate violence. But is this a logical assertion? Isn't this like condemning a robbed man because his possession of money precipitated the evil act of robbery? Isn't this like condemning Socrates because his unswerving commitment to truth and his philosophical inquiries precipitated the act by the misguided populace in which they made him drink hemlock? Isn't this like condemning Jesus because his unique God-consciousness and never-ceasing devotion to God's will precipitated the evil act of crucifixion? We must come to see that, as the federal courts have consistently affirmed, it is wrong to urge an individual to cease his efforts to gain his basic constitutional rights because the quest may precipitate violence. Society must protect the robbed and punish the robber.

I had also hoped that the white moderate would reject the myth concerning time in relation to the struggle for freedom. I have just received a letter from a white brother in Texas. He writes: "All Christians know that the colored people will receive equal rights eventually, but it is possible that you are in too great a religious hurry. It has taken Christianity almost two thousand years to accomplish what it has. The teachings of Christ take time to come to earth." Such an attitude stems from a tragic misconception of time, from the strangely irrational notion that there is something in the very flow of time that will inevitably cure all ills. Actually, time itself is neutral; it can be used either destructively or constructively. More and more I feel that the people of ill will have used time much more effectively than have the people of good will. We will have to repent in this generation not merely for the hateful words and actions of the bad people, but for the appalling silence of the good people. Human progress never rolls in on wheels of inevitability; it comes through the tireless efforts of men willing to be co-workers with God, and without this hard work, time itself becomes an ally of the forces of social stagnation. We must use time creatively, in the knowledge that the time is always ripe to do right. Now is the time to make real the promise of democracy and transform our pending national elegy into a creative psalm of brotherhood. Now is the time to lift our national policy from the quicksand of racial injustice to the solid rock of human dignity.

You speak of our activity in Birmingham as extreme. At first I was rather disappointed that fellow clergymen would see my nonviolent efforts as those of an extremist. I began thinking about the fact that I stand in the middle of two opposing forces in the Negro community. One is a force of complacency, made up in part of Negroes who, as a result of long years of oppression, are so drained of self-respect and a sense of "somebodiness" that they have adjusted to segregation; and in part of a few middle-class Negroes who, because of a degree of academic and economic security and because in some ways they profit by segregation, have become insensitive to the problems of the masses. The other force is one of bitterness and hatred, and it comes perilously close to advocating violence. It is expressed in the various black nationalist groups that are springing up across the nation, the largest and best-known being Elijah Muhammad's Muslim movement. Nourished by the Negro's frustration over the continued existence of racial discrimination, this movement is made up of people who have lost faith in America, who have absolutely repudiated Christianity, and who have concluded that the white man is an incorrigible "devil."

I have tried to stand between these two forces, saying that we need emulate neither the "do-nothingism" of the complacent nor the hatred and despair of the black nationalist. For there is the more excellent way of love and nonviolent protest. I am grateful to God that, through the influence of the Negro church, the way of nonviolence became an integral part of our struggle.

If this philosophy had not emerged, by now many streets of the South would, I am convinced, be flowing with blood. And I am further convinced that if our white brothers dismiss as "rabblerousers" and "outside agitators" those of use who employ nonviolent direct action, and if they refuse to support our nonviolent efforts, millions of Negroes will, out of frustration and despair, seek solace and security in black-nationalist ideologies—a development that would inevitably lead to a frightening racial nightmare.

Oppressed people cannot remain oppressed forever. The yearning for freedom eventually manifests itself, and that is what has happened to the American Negro. Something within has reminded him of his birthright of freedom, and something without has reminded him that it can be gained. Consciously or unconsciously, he has been caught up by the Zeitgeist,[4] and with his black brothers of Africa and his brown and yellow brothers of Asia, South America, and the Caribbean, the United States Negro is moving with a sense of great urgency toward the promised land of racial justice. If one recognizes this vital urge that has engulfed the Negro community, one should readily understand why public demonstrations are taking place. The Negro has many pent-up resentments and latent frustrations, and he must release them. So let him march; let him make prayer pilgrimages to the city hall; let him go on freedom rides—and try to understand why he must do so. If his repressed emotions are not released in nonviolent ways, they will seek expression through violence; this is not a threat but a fact of history. So I have not said to my people, "Get rid of your discontent." Rather, I have tried to say that this normal and healthy discontent can be channeled into the creative outlet of nonviolent direct action. And now this approach is being termed extremist.

But though I was initially disappointed at being categorized as an extremist, as I continued to think about the matter I gradually gained a measure of satisfaction from the label. Was not Jesus an extremist for love: "Love your enemies, bless them that curse you, do good to them that hate you, and pray for them which despitefully use you, and persecute you." Was not Amos an extremist for justice: "Let justice roll down like waters and righteousness like an ever-flowing stream." Was not Paul an extremist for the Christian gospel: "I bear in my body the marks of the Lord Jesus." Was not Martin Luther an extremist: "Here I stand; I cannot do otherwise, so help me God." And John Bunyan: "I will stay in jail to the end of my days before I make a butchery of my conscience." And Abraham Lincoln: "This nation cannot survive half slave and half free." And Thomas Jefferson: "We hold these truths to be self-evident, that all men are created equal. . . ." So the question is not whether we will be extremists, but what kind of extremists we will be. Will we be extremists for hate or for love? Will we be extremists for the preservation of injustice or for the extension of justice? In that dramatic scene on Calvary's hill three men were crucified. We must never forget that all three were crucified for the same crime—the crime of extremism. Two were extremists for immorality, and thus fell below their environment. The other, Jesus Christ, was an extremist for love, truth, and goodness, and thereby rose above his environment. Perhaps the South, the nation,

4. The spirit of the times.

and the world are in dire need of creative extremists.

I had hoped that the white moderate would see this need. Perhaps I was too optimistic; perhaps I expected too much. I suppose I should have realized that few members of the oppressor race can understand the deep groans and passionate yearnings of the oppressed race, and still fewer have the vision to see that injustice must be rooted out by strong, persistent, and determined action. I am thankful, however, that some of our white brothers in the South have grasped the meaning of this social revolution and committed themselves to it. They are still all too few in quantity, but they are big in quality. Some—such as Ralph McGill, Lillian Smith, Harry Golden, James McBridge Dabbs, Ann Braden, and Sarah Patton Boyle—have written about our struggle in eloquent and prophetic terms. Others have marched with us down nameless streets of the South. They have languished in filthy, roach-infested jails, suffering the abuse and brutality of policemen who view them as "dirty nigger-lovers." Unlike so many of their moderate brothers and sisters, they have recognized the urgency of the moment and sensed the need for powerful "action" antidotes to combat the disease of segregation.

Let me take note of my other major disappointment. I have been so greatly disappointed with the white church and its leadership. Of course, there are some notable exceptions. I am not unmindful of the fact that each of you has taken some significant stands on this issue. I commend you, Reverend Stallings, for your Christian stand on this past Sunday, in welcoming Negroes to your worship service on a nonsegregated basis. I commend the Catholic leaders of this state for integrating Spring Hill College several years ago.

But despite these notable exceptions, I must honestly reiterate that I have been disappointed with the church. I do not say this as one of those negative critics who can always find something wrong with the church. I say this as a minister of the gospel, who loves the church; who was nurtured in its bosom; who has been sustained by its spiritual blessings and who will remain true to it as long as the cord of life shall lengthen.

When I was suddenly catapulted into the leadership of the bus protest in Montgomery, Alabama, a few years ago, I felt we would be supported by the white church. I felt that the white ministers, priests, and rabbis of the South would be among our strongest allies. Instead, some have been outright opponents, refusing to understand the freedom movement and misrepresenting its leaders; all too many others have been more cautious than courageous and have remained silent behind the anesthetizing security of stainedglass windows.

In spite of my shattered dreams, I came to Birmingham with the hope that the white religious leadership of this community would see the justice of our cause and, with deep moral concern, would serve as the channel through which our just grievances could reach the power structure. I had hoped that each of you would understand. But again I have been disappointed.

I have heard numerous southern religious leaders admonish their worshipers to comply with a desegregation decision because it is the law, but I have longed to hear white ministers declare: "Follow this decree because integration is morally right and because the Negro is your brother." In the midst of blatant injustices inflicted upon the Negro, I have watched white churchmen stand on the sideline and mouth pious irrelevancies and sanctimonious trivialities. In the midst of a mighty struggle to rid our nation of racial and economic injustice, I have heard many ministers say: "Those are social issues, with which the gospel has no real concern." And I have watched many churches commit themselves to a completely otherworldly religion which makes a strange, un-Biblical distinction between body and soul, between the sacred and the secular.

I have traveled the length and breadth of Alabama, Mississippi, and all the other southern states. On sweltering summer days and crisp autumn mornings I have looked at the South's beautiful churches with their lofty spires pointing heavenward. I have beheld the impressive outlines of her massive religious-education buildings. Over and over I have found myself asking: "What kind of people worship here? Who is their God? Where were their voices when the lips of Governor Barnett dripped with words of interposition and nullification? Where were they when Governor Wallace gave a clarion call for defiance and hatred? Where were their voices of support when bruised and weary Negro men and women decided to rise from the dark dungeons of complacency to the bright hills of creative protest?"

Yes, these questions are still in my mind. In deep disappointment I have wept over the laxity of the church. But be assured that my tears have been tears of love. There can be no deep disappointment where there is not deep love. Yes, I love the church. How could I do otherwise? I am in the rather unique position of being the son, the grandson, and the great-grandson of preachers. Yes, I see the church as the body of Christ. But, oh! How we have blemished and scarred that body through social neglect and through fear of being nonconformists.

There was a time when the church was very powerful—in the time when the early Christians rejoiced at being deemed worthy to suffer for what they believed. In those days the church was not merely a thermometer that recorded the ideas and principles of popular opinion; it was a thermostat that transformed the mores of society. Whenever the early Christians entered a town, the people in power became disturbed and immediately sought to convict the Christians for being "disturbers of the peace" and "outside agitators." But the Christians pressed on, in the conviction that they were "a colony of heaven," called to obey God rather than man. Small in number, they were big in commitment. They were too God-intoxicated to be "astronomically intimidated." By their effort and example they brought an end to such ancient evils as infanticide and gladiatorial contests.

Things are different now. So often the contemporary church is a weak, ineffectual voice with an uncertain sound. So often it is an archdefender of the status quo. Far from being disturbed by the presence of the church, the power structure of the average community is consoled by the church's silent—and often even vocal—sanction of things as they are.

But the judgment of God is upon the church as never before. If today's church does not recapture the sacrificial spirit of the early church, it will lose its authenticity, forfeit the loyalty of millions, and be dismissed as an irrelevant social club with no meaning for the twentieth century. Every day I meet young people whose disappointment with the church has turned into outright disgust.

Perhaps I have once again been too optimistic. Is organized religion too inextricably bound to the status quo to save our nation and the world? Perhaps I must turn my faith to the inner spiritual church, the church within the church, as the true *ekklesia*[5] and the hope of the world. But again I am thankful to God that some noble souls from the ranks of organized religion have broken loose from the paralyzing chains of conformity and joined us as active partners in the struggle for freedom. They have left their secure congregations and walked the streets of Albany, Georgia, with us. They have gone down the highways of the South on tortuous rides for freedom. Yes, they have gone to jail with us. Some have been dismissed from their churches, have lost the support of their bishops and fellow ministers. But they have acted in the faith that right defeated is stronger than evil triumphant. Their witness has been the spiritual salt that has preserved the true meaning of the gospel in these troubled times. They have carved a tunnel of hope through the dark mountain of disappointment.

I hope the church as a whole will meet the challenge of this decisive hour. But even if the church does not come to the aid of justice, I have no despair about the future. I have no fear about the outcome of our struggle in Birmingham, even if our motives are at present misunderstood. We will reach the goal of freedom in Birmingham and all over the nation, because the goal of America is freedom. Abused and scorned though we may be, our destiny is tied up with America's destiny. Before the pilgrims landed at Plymouth, we were here. Before the pen of Jefferson etched the majestic words of the Declaration of Independence across the pages of history, we were here. For more than two centuries our forebears labored in this country without wages; they made cotton king; they built the

5. The Greek New Testament word for the early Christian church.

homes of their masters while suffering gross injustice and shameful humiliation—and yet out of a bottomless vitality they continued to thrive and develop. If the inexpressible cruelties of slavery could not stop us, the opposition we now face will surely fail. We will win our freedom because the sacred heritage of our nation and the eternal will of God are embodied in our echoing demands.

Before closing I feel impelled to mention one other point in your statement that has troubled me profoundly. You warmly commended the Birmingham police force for keeping "order" and "preventing violence." I doubt that you would have so warmly commended the police force if you had seen its dogs sinking their teeth into unarmed, nonviolent Negroes. I doubt that you would so quickly commend the policemen if you were to observe their ugly and inhumane treatment of Negroes here in the city jail; if you were to watch them push and curse old Negro women and young Negro girls; if you were to see them slap and kick old Negro men and young boys; if you were to observe them, as they did on two occasions, refuse to give us food because we wanted to sing our grace together. I cannot join you in your praise of the Birmingham police department.

It is true that the police have exercised a degree of discipline in handling the demonstrators. In this sense they have conducted themselves rather "nonviolently" in public. But for what purpose? To preserve the evil system of segregation. Over the past few years I have consistently preached that nonviolence demands that the means we use must be as pure as the ends we seek. I have tried to make clear that it is wrong to use immoral means to attain moral ends. But now I must affirm that it is just as wrong, or perhaps even more so, to use moral means to preserve immoral ends. Perhaps Mr. Connor and his policemen have been rather nonviolent in public, as was Chief Pritchett in Albany, Georgia, but they have used the moral means of nonviolence to maintain the immoral end of racial injustice. As T. S. Eliot has said, "The last temptation is the greatest treason: To do the right deed for the wrong reason."

I wish you had commended the Negro sit-inners and demonstrators of Birmingham for their sublime courage, their willingness to suffer, and their amazing discipline in the midst of great provocation. One day the South will recognize its real heroes. They will be the James Merediths,[6] with the noble sense of purpose that enables them to face jeering and hostile mobs, and with the agonizing loneliness that characterizes the life of the pioneer. They will be old, oppressed, battered Negro women, symbolized in a seventy-two-year-old woman in Montgomery, Alabama, who rose up with a sense of dignity and with her people decided not to

6. Meredith was the first black to enroll at the University of Mississippi.

ride segregated buses, and who responded with ungrammatical profundity to one who inquired about her weariness: "My feets is tired, but my soul is at rest." They will be the young high school and college students, the young ministers of the gospel and a host of their elders, courageously and nonviolently sitting in at lunch counters and willingly going to jail for conscience' sake. One day the South will know that when these disinherited children of God sat down at lunch counters, they were in reality standing up for what is best in the American dream and for the most sacred values in our Judaeo-Christian heritage, thereby bringing our nation back to those great wells of democracy which were dug deep by the founding fathers in their formulation of the Constitution and the Declaration of Independence.

Never before have I written so long a letter. I'm afraid it is much too long to take your precious time. I can assure you that it would have been much shorter if I had been writing from a comfortable desk, but what else can one do when he is alone in a narrow jail cell, other than write long letters, think long thoughts, and pray long prayers?

If I have said anything in this letter that overstates the truth and indicates an unreasonable impatience, I beg you to forgive me. If I have said anything that understates the truth and indicates my having a patience that allows me to settle for anything less than brotherhood, I beg God to forgive me.

I hope this letter finds you strong in the faith. I also hope that circumstances will soon make it possible for me to meet each of you, not as an integrationist or a civil-rights leader but as a fellow clergyman and a Christian brother. Let us all hope that the dark clouds of racial prejudice will soon pass away and the deep fog of misunderstanding will be lifted from our fear-drenched communities, and in some not too distant tomorrow the radiant stars of love and brotherhood will shine over our great nation with all their scintillating beauty.

Yours for the cause of Peace and Brotherhood,
MARTIN LUTHER KING, JR.

1963

James Thurber

THE RABBITS WHO CAUSED ALL THE TROUBLE

Within the memory of the youngest child there was a family of rabbits who lived near a pack of wolves. The wolves announced that they did not like the way the rabbits were living. (The wolves were crazy about the way they themselves were living, because it was the only way to live.) One night several wolves were killed in an earthquake and this was blamed on the rabbits, for it is well known that rabbits pound on the ground with their hind legs and cause earthquakes. On another night one of the wolves was killed by a bolt of lightning and this was also blamed on the rabbits, for it is well known that lettuce-eaters cause lightning. The wolves threatened to civilize the rabbits if they didn't behave, and the rabbits decided to run away to a desert island. But the other animals, who lived at a great distance, shamed them, saying, "You must stay where you are and be brave. This is no world for escapists. If the wolves attack you, we will come to your aid, in all probability." So the rabbits continued to live near the wolves and one day there was a terrible flood which drowned a great many wolves. This was blamed on the rabbits, for it is well known that carrot-nibblers with long ears cause floods. The wolves descended on the rabbits, for their own good, and imprisoned them in a dark cave, for their own protection.

When nothing was heard about the rabbits for some weeks, the other animals demanded to know what had happened to them. The wolves replied that the rabbits had been eaten and since they had been eaten the affair was a purely internal matter. But the other animals warned that they might possibly unite against the wolves unless some reason was given for the destruction of the rabbits. So the wolves gave them one. "They were trying to escape," said the wolves, "and, as you know, this is no world for escapists."

Moral: Run, don't walk, to the nearest desert island.

1955

Jonathan Swift

A MODEST PROPOSAL

For Preventing the Children of Poor People in Ireland from Being a Burden to Their Parents or Country, and for Making Them Beneficial to the Public

It is a melancholy object to those who walk through this great town[1] or travel in the country, when they see the streets, the roads, and cabin doors, crowded with beggars of the female-sex, followed by three, four, or six children, all in rags and importuning every passenger for an alms. These mothers, instead of being able to work for their honest livelihood, are forced to employ all their time in strolling to beg sustenance for their helpless infants, who, as they grow up, either turn thieves for want of work, or leave their dear native country to fight for the Pretender in Spain, or sell themselves to the Barbadoes.[2]

I think it is agreed by all parties that this prodigious number of children in the arms, or on the backs, or at the heels of their mothers, and frequently of their fathers, is in the present deplorable state of the kingdom a very great additional grievance; and therefore whoever could find out a fair, cheap, and easy method of making these children sound, useful members of the commonwealth would deserve so well of the public as to have his statue set up for a preserver of the nation.

But my intention is very far from being confined to provide only for the children of professed beggars; it is of a much greater extent, and shall take in the whole number of infants at a certain age who are born of parents in effect as little able to support them as those who demand our charity in the streets.

As to my own part, having turned my thoughts for many years upon this important subject, and maturely weighed the several schemes of other projectors,[3] I have always found them grossly mistaken in their computation. It is true, a child just dropped from its dam may be supported by her milk for a solar year, with little other nourishment; at most

1. Dublin.
2. Many poor Irish sought to escape poverty by emigrating to the Barbadoes and other western English colonies, paying for transport by binding themselves to work for a landowner there for a period of years. The Pretender, claimant to the English throne, was barred from succession after his father, King James II, was deposed in a Protestant revolution; thereafter, many Irish Catholics joined the Pretender in his exile in France and Spain, and in his unsuccessful attempts at counterrevolution.
3. People with projects; schemers.

not above the value of two shillings,[4] which the mother may certainly get, or the value in scraps, by her lawful occupation of begging; and it is exactly at one year old that I propose to provide for them in such a manner as instead of being a charge upon their parents or the parish, or wanting food and raiment for the rest of their lives, they shall on the contrary contribute to the feeding, and partly to the clothing, of many thousands.

There is likewise another great advantage in my scheme, that it will prevent those voluntary abortions, and that horrid practice of women murdering their bastard children, alas, too frequent among us, sacrificing the poor innocent babes, I doubt, more to avoid the expense than the shame, which would move tears and pity in the most savage and inhuman breast.

The number of souls in this kingdom being usually reckoned one million and a half, of these I calculate there may be about two hundred thousand couple whose wives are breeders; from which number I subtract thirty thousand couples who are able to maintain their own children, although I apprehend there cannot be so many under the present distresses of the kingdom; but this being granted, there will remain an hundred and seventy thousand breeders. I again subtract fifty thousand for those women who miscarry, or whose children die by accident or disease within the year. There only remain an hundred and twenty thousand children of poor parents annually born. The question therefore is, how this number shall be reared and provided for, which, as I have already said, under the present situation of affairs, is utterly impossible by all the methods hitherto proposed. For we can neither employ them in handicraft or agriculture; we neither build houses (I mean in the country) nor cultivate land. They can very seldom pick up a livelihood by stealing till they arrive at six years old, except where they are of towardly parts;[5] although I confess they learn the rudiments much earlier, during which time they can however be looked upon only as probationers, as I have been informed by a principal gentleman in the county of Cavan, who protested to me that he never knew above one or two instances under the age of six, even in a part of the kingdom so renowned for the quickest proficiency in that art.

I am assured by our merchants that a boy or a girl before twelve years old is no salable commodity; and even when they come to this age they will not yield above three pounds, or three pounds and half a crown[6] at most on the Exchange; which cannot turn to account either to the parents or the kingdom, the charge of nutriment and rags having been at least four times that value.

4. A shilling used to be worth about twenty-five cents.
5. Promising abilities.
6. A pound was twenty shillings; a crown, five shillings.

I shall now therefore humbly propose my own thoughts, which I hope will not be liable to the least objection.

I have been assured by a very knowing American of my acquaintance in London, that a young healthy child well nursed is at a year old a most delicious, nourishing, and wholesome food, whether stewed, roasted, baked, or boiled; and I make no doubt that it will equally serve in a fricassee or a ragout.

I do therefore humbly offer it to public consideration that of the hundred and twenty thousand children, already computed, twenty thousand may be reserved for breed, whereof only one fourth part to be males, which is more than we allow to sheep, black cattle, or swine; and my reason is that these children are seldom the fruits of marriage, a circumstance not much regarded by our savages, therefore one male will be sufficient to serve four females. That the remaining hundred thousand may at a year old be offered in sale to the persons of quality and fortune through the kingdom, always advising the mother to let them suck plentifully in the last month, so as to render them plump and fat for a good table. A child will make two dishes at an entertainment for friends; and when the family dines alone, the fore or hind quarter will make a reasonable dish, and seasoned with a little pepper or salt will be very good boiled on the fourth day, especially in winter.

I have reckoned upon a medium that a child just born will weigh twelve pounds, and in a solar year if tolerably nursed increaseth to twenty-eight pounds.

I grant this food will be somewhat dear, and therefore very proper for landlords, who, as they have already devoured most of the parents, seem to have the best title to the children.

Infant's flesh will be in season throughout the year, but more plentiful in March, and a little before and after. For we are told by a grave author, an eminent French physician,[7] that fish being a prolific diet, there are more children born in Roman Catholic countries about nine months after Lent than at any other season; therefore, reckoning a year after Lent, the markets will be more glutted than usual, because the number of popish infants is at least three to one in this kingdom; and therefore it will have one other collateral advantage, by lessening the number of Papists among us.[8]

I have already computed the charge of nursing a beggar's child (in which list I reckon all cottagers, laborers, and four fifths of the farmers) to be about two shillings per annum, rags included; and I believe no gentleman would repine to give ten shillings for the carcass of a good fat child, which, as I have said, will make four dishes of excellent nutritive

7. The sixteenth-century comic writer François Rabelais.
8. The speaker is addressing Protestant Anglo-Irish, who were the chief landowners and administrators, and his views of Catholicism in Ireland and abroad echo theirs.

meat, when he hath only some particular friend or his own family to dine with him. Thus the squire will learn to be a good landlord, and grow popular among the tenants; the mother will have eight shillings net profit, and be fit for work till she produces another child.

Those who are more thrifty (as I must confess the times require) may flay the carcass; the skin of which artificially[9] dressed will make admirable gloves for ladies, and summer boots for fine gentlemen.

As to our city of Dublin, shambles[1] may be appointed for this purpose in the most convenient parts of it, and butchers we may be assured will not be wanting; although I rather recommend buying the children alive, and dressing them hot from the knife as we do roasting pigs.

A very worthy person, a true lover of his country, and whose virtues I highly esteem, was lately pleased in discoursing on this matter to offer a refinement upon my scheme. He said that many gentlemen of this kingdom, having of late destroyed their deer, he conceived that the want of venison might be well supplied by the bodies of young lads and maidens, not exceeding fourteen years of age nor under twelve, so great a number of both sexes in every county being now ready to starve for want of work and service; and these to be disposed of by their parents, if alive, or otherwise by their nearest relations. But with due deference to so excellent a friend and so deserving a patriot, I cannot be altogether in his sentiments; for as to the males, my American acquaintance assured me from frequent experience that their flesh was generally tough and lean, like that of our schoolboys, by continual exercise, and their taste disagreeable; and to fatten them would not answer the charge. Then as to the females, it would, I think with humble submission, be a loss to the public, because they soon would become breeders themselves: and besides, it is not improbable that some scrupulous people might be apt to censure such a practice (although indeed very unjustly) as a little bordering upon cruelty; which, I confess, hath always been with me the strongest objection against any project, how well soever intended.

But in order to justify my friend, he confessed that this expedient was put into his head by the famous Psalmanazar, a native of the island Formosa,[2] who came from thence to London above twenty years ago, and in conversation told my friend that in his country when any young person happened to be put to death, the executioner sold the carcass to persons of quality as a prime dainty; and that in his time the body of a plump girl of fifteen, who was crucified for an attempt to poison the emperor, was sold to his Imperial Majesty's prime minister of state, and other great mandarins of the court, in joints from the gibbet, at four hundred crowns.

9. Skillfully.
1. Slaughterhouses.
2. Actually a Frenchman, George Psalmanazar had passed himself off as from Formosa (now Taiwan) and had written a fictitious book about his "homeland," with descriptions of human sacrifice and cannibalism.

Neither indeed can I deny that if the same use were made of several plump young girls in this town, who without one single groat[3] to their fortunes cannot stir abroad without a chair,[4] and appear at the playhouse and assemblies in foreign fineries which they never will pay for, the kingdom would not be the worse.

Some persons of a desponding spirit are in great concern about that vast number of poor people who are aged, diseased, or maimed, and I have been desired to employ my thoughts what course may be taken to ease the nation of so grievous an encumbrance. But I am not in the least pain upon that matter, because it is very well known that they are every day dying and rotting by cold and famine, and filth and vermin, as fast as can be reasonably expected. And as to the younger laborers, they are now in almost as hopeful a condition. They cannot get work, and consequently pine away for want of nourishment to a degree that if at any time they are accidentally hired to common labor, they have not strength to perform it; and thus the country and themselves are happily delivered from the evils to come.

I have too long digressed, and therefore shall return to my subject. I think the advantages by the proposal which I have made are obvious and many, as well as of the highest importance.

For first, as I have already observed, it would greatly lessen the number of Papists, with whom we are yearly overrun, being the principal breeders of the nation as well as our most dangerous enemies; and who stay at home on purpose to deliver the kingdom to the Pretender, hoping to take their advantage by the absence of so many good Protestants, who have chosen rather to leave their country than to stay at home and pay tithes against their conscience to an Episcopal curate.

Secondly, the poorer tenants will have something valuable of their own, which by law may be made liable to distress,[5] and help to pay their landlord's rent, their corn and cattle being already seized and money a thing unknown.

Thirdly, whereas the maintenance of an hundred thousand children, from two years old and upwards, cannot be computed at less than ten shillings a piece per annum, the nation's stock will be thereby increased fifty thousand pounds per annum, besides the profit of a new dish introduced to the tables of all gentlemen of fortune in the kingdom who have any refinement in taste. And the money will circulate among ourselves, the goods being entirely of our own growth and manufacture.

Fourthly, the constant breeders, besides the gain of eight shillings sterling per annum by the sale of their children, will be rid of the charge of maintaining them after the first year.

Fifthly, this food would likewise bring great custom to taverns, where

3. An English coin worth about four pennies.   5. Seizure for the payment of debts.
4. A sedan chair.

the vintners will certainly be so prudent as to procure the best receipts for dressing it to perfection, and consequently have their houses frequented by all the fine gentlemen, who justly value themselves upon their knowledge in good eating; and a skillful cook, who understands how to oblige his guests, will contrive to make it as expensive as they please.

Sixthly, this would be a great inducement to marriage, which all wise nations have either encouraged by rewards or enforced by laws and penalties. It would increase the care and tenderness of mothers toward their children, when they were sure of a settlement for life to the poor babes, provided in some sort by the public, to their annual profit instead of expense. We should see an honest emulation among the married women, which of them could bring the fattest child to the market. Men would become as fond of their wives during the time of their pregnancy as they are now of their mares in foal, their cows in calf, or sows when they are ready to farrow; nor offer to beat or kick them (as is too frequent a practice) for fear of a miscarriage.

Many other advantages might be enumerated. For instance, the addition of some thousand carcasses in our exportation of barreled beef, the propagation of swine's flesh, and improvement in the art of making good bacon, so much wanted among us by the great destruction of pigs, too frequent at our tables, which are no way comparable in taste or magnificence to a well-grown, fat, yearling child, which roasted whole will make a considerable figure at a lord mayor's feast or any other public entertainment. But this and many others I omit, being studious of brevity.

Supposing that one thousand families in this city would be constant customers for infants' flesh, besides others who might have it at merry meetings, particularly weddings and christenings, I compute that Dublin would take off annually about twenty thousand carcasses, and the rest of the kingdom (where probably they will be sold somewhat cheaper) the remaining eighty thousand.

I can think of no one objection that will possibly be raised against this proposal, unless it should be urged that the number of people will be thereby much lessened in the kingdom. This I freely own, and it was indeed one principal design in offering it to the world. I desire the reader will observe, that I calculate my remedy for this one individual kingdom of Ireland and for no other that ever was, is, or I think ever can be upon earth. Therefore let no man talk to me of other expedients: of taxing our absentees at five shillings a pound: of using neither clothes nor household furniture except what is of our own growth and manufacture: of utterly rejecting the materials and instruments that promote foreign luxury: of curing the expensiveness of pride, vanity, idleness, and gaming in our women: of introducing a vein of parsimony, prudence, and temperance: of learning to love our country, in the want of which we differ even from

Laplanders and the inhabitants of Topinamboo[6]: of quitting our animosi-
ties and factions, nor acting any longer like the Jews, who were murdering one another at the very moment their city was taken: of being a little
cautious not to sell our country and conscience for nothing: of teaching
landlords to have at least one degree of mercy toward their tenants: lastly,
of putting a spirit of honesty, industry, and skill into our shopkeepers;
who, if a resolution could now be taken to buy only our native goods,
would immediately unite to cheat and exact upon us in the price, the
measure, and the goodness, nor could ever yet be brought to make one
fair proposal of just dealing, though often and earnestly invited to it.[7]

Therefore I repeat, let no man talk to me of these and the like expedients, till he hath at least some glimpse of hope that there will ever be
some hearty and sincere attempt to put them in practice.

But as to myself, having been wearied out for many years with offering
vain, idle, visionary thoughts, and at length utterly despairing of success,
I fortunately fell upon this proposal, which, as it is wholly new, so it hath
something solid and real, of no expense and little trouble, full in our own
power, and whereby we can incur no danger in disobliging England. For
this kind of commodity will not bear exportation, the flesh being of too
tender a consistence to admit a long continuance in salt, although perhaps I could name a country[8] which would be glad to eat up our whole
nation without it.

After all, I am not so violently bent upon my own opinion as to reject
any offer proposed by wise men, which shall be found equally innocent,
cheap, easy, and effectual. But before something of that kind shall be
advanced in contradiction to my scheme, and offering a better, I desire
the author or authors will be pleased maturely to consider two points.
First, as things now stand, how they will be able to find food and raiment
for an hundred thousand useless mouths and backs. And secondly, there
being a round million of creatures in human figure throughout this
kingdom, whose sole subsistence put into a common stock would leave
them in debt two millions of pounds sterling, adding those who are
beggars by profession to the bulk of farmers, cottagers, and laborers, with
their wives and children who are beggars in effect; I desire those politicians who dislike my overture, and may perhaps be so bold to attempt an
answer, that they will first ask the parents of these mortals whether they
would not at this day think it a great happiness to have been sold for food
at a year old in the manner I prescribe, and thereby have avoided such a
perpetual scene of misfortunes as they have since gone through by the
oppression of landlords, the impossibility of paying rent without money
or trade, the want of common sustenance, with neither house nor clothes
to cover them from the inclemencies of the weather, and the most

6. A district in Brazil.   seriously in various previous works.
7. Swift himself had made these proposals   8. England.

inevitable prospect of entailing the like or greater miseries upon their breed forever.

I profess, in the sincerity of my heart, that I have not the least personal interest in endeavoring to promote this necessary work, having no other motive than the public good of my country, by advancing our trade, providing for infants, relieving the poor, and giving some pleasure to the rich. I have no children by which I can propose to get a single penny; the youngest being nine years old, and my wife past childbearing.

1729

THE READER

1. At what point do you begin to suspect that Swift is using irony? What further evidence accumulates to make you certain that Swift is being ironic?
2. Does the essay shock you? Was it Swift's purpose to shock you?
3. What is the main target of Swift's attack? What subsidiary targets are there? Does Swift offer any serious solutions for the problems and conditions he is describing?

THE WRITER

1. This essay has been called one of the best examples of sustained irony in the English language. Irony is difficult to handle because there is always the danger that the reader will miss the irony and take what is said literally. What does Swift do to try to prevent this?
2. Why does Swift use such phrases as "just dropped from its dam," "whose wives are breeders," "one fourth part to be males"?
3. What devices of argument, apart from the use of irony, does Swift use that could be successfully applied to other subjects?
4. In the study questions for Orwell's "Shooting an Elephant" (p. 450), there is a brief sketch from The Graphic of 1888, "Shooting a Man-eating Crocodile." How can you tell that this sketch is not ironic and that "A Modest Proposal" is? If you can't tell, what does your uncertainty suggest about the nature of irony?
5. Write your own modest proposal for something, keeping in mind Swift's technique.

Niccolò Machiavelli

THE MORALS OF THE PRINCE[1]

On the Reasons Why Men Are Praised or Blamed—Especially Princes

It remains now to be seen what style and principles a prince ought to adopt in dealing with his subjects and friends. I know the subject has been treated frequently before, and I'm afraid people will think me rash for trying to do so again, especially since I intend to differ in this discussion from what others have said. But since I intend to write something useful to an understanding reader, it seemed better to go after the real truth of the matter than to repeat what people have imagined. A great many men have imagined states and princedoms such as nobody ever saw or knew in the real world, for there's such a difference between the way we really live and the way we ought to live that the man who neglects the real to study the ideal will learn how to accomplish his ruin, not his salvation. Any man who tries to be good all the time is bound to come to ruin among the great number who are not good. Hence a prince who wants to keep his post must learn how not to be good, and use that knowledge, or refrain from using it, as necessity requires.

Putting aside, then, all the imaginary things that are said about princes, and getting down to the truth, let me say that whenever men are discussed (and especially princes because they are prominent), there are certain qualities that bring them either praise or blame. Thus some are considered generous, others stingy (I use a Tuscan term, since "greedy" in our speech means a man who wants to take other people's goods. we call a man "stingy" who clings to his own); some are givers, others grabbers; some cruel, others merciful; one man is treacherous, another faithful; one is feeble and effeminate, another fierce and spirited; one humane, another proud; one lustful, another chaste; one straightforward, another sly; one harsh, another gentle; one serious, another playful; one religious, another skeptical, and so on. I know everyone will agree that among these many qualities a prince certainly ought to have all those that are considered good. But since it is impossible to have and exercise them all, because the conditions of human life simply do not allow it, a prince must be shrewd enough to avoid the public disgrace of those vices that would lose him his state. If he possibly can, he should also guard against vices that will not lose him his state; but if he cannot prevent them, he should not be too worried about indulging them. And furthermore, he

1. From *The Prince*, a book on statecraft written for Giuliano de' Medici (1479-1516), a member of one of the most famous and powerful families of Renaissance Italy.

497

should not be too worried about incurring blame for any vice without which he would find it hard to save his state. For if you look at matters carefully, you will see that something resembling virtue, if you follow it, may be your ruin, while something else resembling vice will lead, if you follow it, to your security and well-being.

On Liberality and Stinginess

Let me begin, then, with the first of the qualities mentioned above, by saying that a reputation for liberality is doubtless very fine; but the generosity that earns you that reputation can do you great harm. For if you exercise your generosity in a really virtuous way, as you should, nobody will know of it, and you cannot escape the odium of the opposite vice. Hence if you wish to be widely known as a generous man, you must seize every opportunity to make a big display of your giving. A prince of this character is bound to use up his entire revenue in works of ostentation. Thus, in the end, if he wants to keep a name for generosity, he will have to load his people with exorbitant taxes and squeeze money out of them in every way he can. This is the first step in making him odious to his subjects; for when he is poor, nobody will respect him. Then, when his generosity has angered many and brought rewards to a few, the slightest difficulty will trouble him, and at the first approach of danger, down he goes. If by chance he foresees this, and tries to change his ways, he will immediately be labeled a miser.

Since a prince cannot use this virtue of liberality in such a way as to become known for it unless he harms his own security, he won't mind, if he judges prudently of things, being known as a miser. In due course he will be thought the more liberal man, when people see that his parsimony enables him to live on his income, to defend himself against his enemies, and to undertake major projects without burdening his people with taxes. Thus he will be acting liberally toward all those people from whom he takes nothing (and there are an immense number of them), and in a stingy way toward those people on whom he bestows nothing (and they are very few). In our times, we have seen great things being accomplished only by men who have had the name of misers; all the others have gone under. Pope Julius II, though he used his reputation as a generous man to gain the papacy, sacrificed it in order to be able to make war; the present king of France has waged many wars without levying a single extra tax on his people, simply because he could take care of the extra expenses out of the savings from his long parsimony. If the present king of Spain had a reputation for generosity, he would never have been able to undertake so many campaigns, or win so many of them.

Hence a prince who prefers not to rob his subjects, who wants to be able to defend himself, who wants to avoid poverty and contempt, and who doesn't want to become a plunderer, should not mind in the least if people consider him a miser; this is simply one of the vices that enable him to reign. Someone may object that Caesar used a reputation for generosity to become emperor, and many other people have also risen in the world, because they were generous or were supposed to be so. Well, I answer, either you are a prince already, or you are in the process of becoming one; in the first case, this reputation for generosity is harmful to you, in the second case it is very necessary. Caesar was one of those who wanted to become ruler in Rome; but after he had reached his goal, if he had lived, and had not cut down on his expenses, he would have ruined the empire itself. Someone may say: there have been plenty of princes, very successful in warfare, who have had a reputation for generosity. But I answer: either the prince is spending his own money and that of his subjects, or he is spending someone else's. In the first case, he ought to be sparing; in the second case, he ought to spend money like water. Any prince at the head of his army, which lives on loot, extortion, and plunder, disposes of other people's property, and is bound to be very generous; otherwise, his soldiers would desert him. You can always be a more generous giver when what you give is not yours or your subjects'; Cyrus, Caesar, and Alexander[2] were generous in this way. Spending what belongs to other people does no harm to your reputation, rather it enhances it; only spending your own substance harms you. And there is nothing that wears out faster than generosity; even as you practice it, you lose the means of practicing it, and you become either poor and contemptible or (in the course of escaping poverty) rapacious and hateful. The thing above all against which a prince must protect himself is being contemptible and hateful; generosity leads to both. Thus, it's much wiser to put up with the reputation of being a miser, which brings you shame without hate, than to be forced—just because you want to appear generous—into a reputation for rapacity, which brings shame on you and hate along with it.

On Cruelty and Clemency: Whether It Is Better to Be Loved or Feared

Continuing now with our list of qualities, let me say that every prince should prefer to be considered merciful rather than cruel, yet he should be careful not to mismanage this clemency of his. People thought Cesare Borgia[3] was cruel, but that cruelty of his reorganized the Romagna, united it, and established it in peace and loyalty. Anyone who views the matter realistically will see that this prince was much more merciful than the people of Florence, who, to avoid the reputation of cruelty, allowed

2. Persian, Roman, and Macedonian con-   later) and duke of Romagna, which he subju-
querors and rulers in ancient times.   gated in 1499–1502.
3. The son of Pope Alexander VI (referred to

Pistoia to be destroyed.[4] Thus, no prince should mind being called cruel
for what he does to keep his subjects united and loyal; he may make
examples of a very few, but he will be more merciful in reality than those
who, in their tenderheartedness, allow disorders to occur, with their
attendant murders and lootings. Such turbulence brings harm to an
entire community, while the executions ordered by a prince affect only
one individual at a time. A new prince, above all others, cannot possibly
avoid a name for cruelty, since new states are always in danger. And
Virgil, speaking through the mouth of Dido,[5] says:

> My cruel fate
> And doubts attending an unsettled state
> Force me to guard my coast from foreign foes.

Yet a prince should be slow to believe rumors and to commit himself to
action on the basis of them. He should not be afraid of his own thoughts;
he ought to proceed cautiously, moderating his conduct with prudence
and humanity, allowing neither overconfidence to make him careless, nor
overtimidity to make him intolerable.

Here the question arises: is it better to be loved than feared, or vice
versa? I don't doubt that every prince would like to be both; but since it is
hard to accommodate these qualities, if you have to make a choice, to be
feared is much safer than to be loved. For it is a good general rule about
men, that they are ungrateful, fickle, liars and deceivers, fearful of danger
and greedy for gain. While you serve their welfare, they are all yours,
offering their blood, their belongings, their lives, and their children's
lives, as we noted above—so long as the danger is remote. But when the
danger is close at hand, they turn against you. Then, any prince who has
relied on their words and has made no other preparations will come to
grief; because friendships that are bought at a price, and not with greatness and nobility of soul, may be paid for but they are not acquired, and
they cannot be used in time of need. People are less concerned with
offending a man who makes himself loved than one who makes himself
feared: the reason is that love is a link of obligation which men, because
they are rotten, will break any time they think doing so serves their
advantage; but fear involves dread of punishment, from which they can
never escape.

Still, a prince should make himself feared in such a way that, even if he
gets no love, he gets no hate either; because it is perfectly possible to be
feared and not hated, and this will be the result if only the prince will
keep his hands off the property of his subjects or citizens, and off their
women. When he does have to shed blood, he should be sure to have a
strong justification and manifest cause; but above all, he should not

4. By unchecked rioting between opposing
factions (1502).

5. Queen of Carthage and tragic heroine of
Virgil's epic, The Aeneid.

confiscate people's property, because men are quicker to forget the death of a father than the loss of a patrimony. Besides, pretexts for confiscation are always plentiful, it never fails that a prince who starts living by plunder can find reasons to rob someone else. Excuses for proceeding against someone's life are much rarer and more quickly exhausted.

But a prince at the head of his armies and commanding a multitude of soldiers should not care a bit if he is considered cruel; without such a reputation, he could never hold his army together and ready for action. Among the marvelous deeds of Hannibal,[6] this was prime: that, having an immense army, which included men of many different races and nations, and which he led to battle in distant countries, he never allowed them to fight among themselves or to rise against him, whether his fortune was good or bad. The reason for this could only be his inhuman cruelty, which, along with his countless other talents, made him an object of awe and terror to his soldiers; and without the cruelty, his other qualities would never have sufficed. The historians who pass snap judgments on these matters admire his accomplishments and at the same time condemn the cruelty which was their main cause.

When I say, "His other qualities would never have sufficed," we can see that this is true from the example of Scipio,[7] an outstanding man not only among those of his own time, but in all recorded history; yet his armies revolted in Spain, for no other reason than his excessive leniency in allowing his soldiers more freedom than military discipline permits. Fabius Maximus rebuked him in the senate for this failing, calling him the corrupter of the Roman armies. When a lieutenant of Scipio's plundered the Locrians,[8] he took no action in behalf of the people, and did nothing to discipline that insolent lieutenant; again, this was the result of his easygoing nature. Indeed, when someone in the senate wanted to excuse him on this occasion, he said there are many men who knew better how to avoid error themselves than how to correct error in others. Such a soft temper would in time have tarnished the fame and glory of Scipio, had he brought it to the office of emperor; but as he lived under the control of the senate, this harmful quality of his not only remained hidden but was considered creditable.

Returning to the question of being feared or loved, I conclude that since men love at their own inclination but can be made to fear at the inclination of the prince, a shrewd prince will lay his foundations on what is under his own control, not on what is controlled by others. He should simply take pains not to be hated, as I said.

6. Carthaginian general who led a massive but unsuccessful invasion of Rome in 218–203 B.C.
7. The Roman general whose successful invasion of Carthage in 203 B.C. caused Hannibal's army to be recalled from Rome. The episode described here occurred in 206 B.C.
8. A people of Sicily, defeated by Scipio in 205 B.C. and placed under Q. Pleminius; *Fabius Maximus:* not only a senator but a high public official and general who had fought against Hannibal in Italy.

The Way Princes Should Keep Their Word

How praiseworthy it is for a prince to keep his word and live with integrity rather than by craftiness, everyone understands; yet we see from recent experience that those princes have accomplished most who paid little heed to keeping their promises, but who knew how craftily to manipulate the minds of men. In the end, they won out over those who tried to act honestly.

You should consider then, that there are two ways of fighting, one with laws and the other with force. The first is properly a human method, the second belongs to beasts. But as the first method does not always suffice, you sometimes have to turn to the second. Thus a prince must know how to make good use of both the beast and the man. Ancient writers made subtle note of this fact when they wrote that Achilles and many other princes of antiquity were sent to be reared by Chiron the centaur,[9] who trained them in his discipline. Having a teacher who is half man and half beast can only mean that a prince must know how to use both these two natures, and that one without the other has no lasting effect.

Since a prince must know how to use the character of beasts, he should pick for imitation the fox and the lion. As the lion cannot protect himself from traps, and the fox cannot defend himself from wolves, you have to be a fox in order to be wary of traps, and a lion to overawe the wolves. Those who try to live by the lion alone are badly mistaken. Thus a prudent prince cannot and should not keep his word when to do so would go against his interest, or when the reasons that made him pledge it no longer apply. Doubtless if all men were good, this rule would be bad; but since they are a sad lot, and keep no faith with you, you in your turn are under no obligation to keep it with them.

Besides, a prince will never lack for legitimate excuses to explain away his breaches of faith. Modern history will furnish innumerable examples of this behavior, showing how many treaties and promises have been made null and void by the faithlessness of princes, and how the man succeeded best who knew best how to play the fox. But it is a necessary part of this nature that you must conceal it carefully; you must be a great liar and hypocrite. Men are so simple of mind, and so much dominated by their immediate needs, that a deceitful man will always find plenty who are ready to be deceived. One of many recent examples calls for mention. Alexander VI[1] never did anything else, never had another thought, except to deceive men, and he always found fresh material to work on. Never was there a man more convincing in his assertions, who sealed his

9. Half man and half horse, the mythical Chiron was said to have taught the arts of war and peace, including hunting, medicine, music, and prophecy; Achilles: foremost among the Greek heroes in the Trojan War. 1. Pope from 1492 to 1503.

promises with more solemn oaths, and who observed them less. Yet his deceptions were always successful, because he knew exactly how to manage this sort of business.

In actual fact, a prince may not have all the admirable qualities we listed, but it is very necessary that he should seem to have them. Indeed, I will venture to say that when you have them and exercise them all the time, they are harmful to you; when you just seem to have them, they are useful. It is good to appear merciful, truthful, humane, sincere, and religious; it is good to be so in reality. But you must keep your mind so disposed that, in case of need, you can turn to the exact contrary. This has to be understood: a prince, and especially a new prince, cannot possibly exercise all those virtues for which men are called "good." To preserve the state, he often has to do things against his word, against charity, against humanity, against religion. Thus he has to have a mind ready to shift as the winds of fortune and the varying circumstances of life may dictate. And as I said above, he should not depart from the good if he can hold to it, but he should be ready to enter on evil if he has to.

Hence a prince should take great care never to drop a word that does not seem imbued with the five good qualities noted above; to anyone who sees or hears him, he should appear all compassion, all honor, all human-ity, all integrity, all religion. Nothing is more necessary than to seem to have this last virtue. Men in general judge more by the sense of sight than by the sense of touch, because everyone can see but only a few can test by feeling. Everyone sees what you seem to be, few know what you really are; and those few do not dare take a stand against the general opinion, supported by the majesty of the government. In the actions of all men, and especially of princes who are not subject to a court of appeal, we must always look to the end. Let a prince, therefore, win victories and uphold his state; his methods will always be considered worthy, and everyone will praise them, because the masses are always impressed by the superfi-cial appearance of things, and by the outcome of an enterprise. And the world consists of nothing but the masses; the few who have no influence when the many feel secure. A certain prince of our own time, whom it's just as well not to name,[2] preaches nothing but peace and mutual trust, yet he is the determined enemy of both; and if on several different occasions he had observed either, he would have lost both his reputation and his throne.

1513

2. Probably Ferdinand of Spain, then allied with the house of Medici.

THE READER

1. *Toward the end of the first paragraph, Machiavelli says, "The man who neglects the real to study the ideal will learn how to accomplish his ruin." Explain the logical relation between that statement and the*

statements of the last two sentences of that paragraph.
2. *Speaking of a prince, Machiavelli uses a moral, personal vocabulary: "liberality"/"stinginess," "cruelty"/"clemency," "loved"/"feared," etc. Other vocabularies are possible. For example, the stinginess of a miser (p. 498) might be fiscal responsibility. Provide alternatives for some of the other terms in his moral, personal vocabulary.*
3. *Machiavelli speaks about government by a prince. To what degree do his observations and advice apply to a democracy?*

THE WRITER

1. *On p. 503, the author speaks of five admirable qualities: compassion, honor, humanity, integrity, and religion. How admirable do you think he believes those qualities to be? Base your answer on your sense of what matters to him in this essay. What would you say he admires most?*
2. *Machiavelli clearly says a prince should seem to be virtuous. Write a one-page strategy paper for Machiavelli as if you were the media consultant to a prince, or for yourself as if you were the media consultant to a candidate.*
3. *Machiavelli sees men as "a sad lot" and has a generally bleak view of human behavior. What would be the best logical strategy for an argument in refutation? Can you get any help from King (p. 473) or Lincoln (below) or the Declaration of Independence (p. 510)?*

Abraham Lincoln

SECOND INAUGURAL ADDRESS

At this second appearing to take the oath of the presidential office, there is less occasion for an extended address than there was at the first. Then a statement, somewhat in detail, of a course to be pursued, seemed fitting and proper. Now, at the expiration of four years, during which public declarations have been constantly called forth on every point and phase of the great contest which still absorbs the attention, and engrosses the energies of the nation, little that is new could be presented. The progress of our arms, upon which all else chiefly depends, is as well known to the public as to myself; and it is, I trust, reasonably satisfactory and encouraging to all. With high hope for the future, no prediction in regard to it is ventured.

On the occasion corresponding to this four years ago, all thoughts were anxiously directed to an impending civil war. All dreaded it—all sought to avert it. While the inaugural address was being delivered from this place, devoted altogether to saving the Union without war, insurgent agents were in the city seeking to destroy it without war—seeking to dissolve the Union, and divide effects, by negotiation. Both parties deprecated war; but one of them would make war rather than let the nation survive; and the other would accept war rather than let it perish. And the war came.

One-eighth of the whole population were colored slaves, not distributed generally over the Union, but localized in the Southern part of it. These slaves constituted a peculiar and powerful interest. All knew that this interest was, somehow, the cause of the war. To strengthen, perpetuate, and extend this interest was the object for which the insurgents would rend the Union, even by war; while the government claimed no right to do more than to restrict the territorial enlargement of it. Neither party expected for the war, the magnitude, or the duration, which it has already attained. Neither anticipated that the cause of the conflict might cease with, or even before, the conflict itself should cease. Each looked for an easier triumph, and a result less fundamental and astounding. Both read the same Bible, and pray to the same God; and each invokes His aid against the other. It may seem strange that any men should dare to ask a just God's assistance in wringing their bread from the sweat of other men's faces; but let us judge not that we be not judged.[1] The prayers of both could not be answered; that of neither has been answered fully. The Almighty has His own purposes. "Woe unto the world because of offenses! for it must needs be that offenses come; but woe to that man by whom the offense cometh!"[2] If we shall suppose that American slavery is one of those offenses which, in the providence of God, must needs come, but which, having continued through His appointed time, He now wills to remove, and that He gives to both North and South, this terrible war, as the woe due to those by whom the offense came, shall we discern therein any departure from those divine attributes which the believers in a Living God always ascribe to Him? Fondly do we hope—fervently do we pray—that this mightly scourge of war may speedily pass away. Yet, if God wills that it continue, until all the wealth piled by the bondman's two hundred and fifty years of unrequited toil shall be sunk, and until every drop of blood drawn with the lash, shall be paid by another drawn with the sword, as was said three thousand years ago, so still it must be said "the judgments of the Lord are true and righteous altogether."[3]

With malice toward none; with charity for all; with firmness in the right, as God gives us to see the right, let us strive on to finish the work we are in; to bind up the nation's wounds; to care for him who shall have

1. Lincoln alludes to Jesus' statement in the Sermon on the Mount—"Judge not, that ye be not judged" (Matthew vii.1)—and to God's curse on Adam—"In the sweat of thy face shalt thou eat bread, till thou return unto the ground" (Genesis iii.19).
2. From Jesus' speech to his disciples (Matthew xviii.7).
3. Psalms xix.9.

borne the battle, and for his widow, and his orphan—to do all which may achieve and cherish a just, and a lasting peace, among ourselves, and with all nations.

1865

Thomas Jefferson

ORIGINAL DRAFT OF THE DECLARATION OF INDEPENDENCE

A DECLARATION OF THE REPRESENTATIVES OF THE UNITED STATES OF AMERICA, IN GENERAL CONGRESS ASSEMBLED.

When in the course of human events it becomes necessary for a people to advance from that subordination in which they have hitherto remained, & to assume among the powers of the earth the equal & independant station to which the laws of nature & of nature's god entitle them, a decent respect to the opinions of mankind requires that they should declare the causes which impel them to the change.

We hold these truths to be sacred & undeniable; that all men are created equal & independant, that from that equal creation they derive rights inherent & inalienable, among which are the preservation of life, & liberty, & the spirit of happiness; that to secure these ends, governments are instituted among men, deriving their just powers from the consent of the governed; that whenever any form of government shall become destructive of these ends, it is the right of the people to alter or to abolish it, & to institute new government, laying it's foundation on such principles & organising it's powers in such form, as to them shall seem most likely to effect their safety & happiness. prudence indeed will dictate that governments long established should not be changed for light & transient causes: and accordingly all experience hath shewn that mankind are more disposed to suffer while evils are sufferable, than to right themselves by abolishing the forms to which they are accustomed. but when a long train of abuses & usurpations, begun at a distinguished period, & pursuing invariably the same object, evinces a design to subject them to arbitrary power, it is their right, it is their duty, to throw off such government & to provide new guards for their future security. such has been the patient sufferance of these colonies; & such is now the necessity which constrains them to expunge their former systems of government. The history of his present majesty, is a history of unremitting injuries and usurpations, among which no one fact stands single or solitary to contradict the uniform tenor of the rest, all of which have in direct object the establishment of an absolute tyranny over these states. to prove this, let facts be submitted to a candid world, for the truth of which we pledge a faith yet unsullied by falsehood.

he has refused his assent to laws the most wholesome and necessary for the public good:

he has forbidden his governors to pass laws of immediate & pressing importance, unless suspended in their operation till his assent should be obtained; and when so suspended, he has neglected utterly to attend to them.

he has refused to pass other laws for the accommodation of large districts of people unless those people would relinquish the right of representation, a right inestimable to them, & formidable to tyrants alone:[1]

he has dissolved Representative houses repeatedly & continually, for opposing with manly firmness his invasions on the rights of the people:

he has refused for a long space of time to cause others to be elected, whereby the legislative powers, incapable of annihilation, have returned to the people at large for their exercise, the state remaining in the mean time exposed to all the dangers of invasion from without, &, convulsions within:

he has suffered the administration of justice totally to cease in some of these colonies, refusing his assent to laws for establishing judiciary powers:

he has made our judges dependant on his will alone, for the tenure of their offices, and amount of their salaries:

he has erected a multitude of new offices by a self-assumed power, & sent hither swarms of officers to harrass our people & eat out their substance:

he has kept among us in times of peace standing armies & ships of war:

he has affected[2] to render the military, independent of & superior to the civil power:

he has combined with others to subject us to a jurisdiction foreign to our constitutions and unacknowledged by our laws; giving his assent to their pretended acts of legislation, for quartering large bodies of

1. At this point in the manuscript a strip containing the following clause is inserted: "He called together legislative bodies at places unusual, unco[mfortable, & distant from] the depository of their public records for the sole purpose of fatiguing [them into compliance] with his measures:" Missing parts in the Library of Congress text are supplied from the copy made by Jefferson for George Wythe. This copy is in the New York Public Library. The fact that this passage was omitted from John Adams's transcript suggests that it was not a part of Jefferson's original rough draft.
2. Tried.

armed troops among us;

for protecting them by a mock-trial from punishment for any murders they should commit on the inhabitants of these states;

for cutting off our trade with all parts of the world;

for imposing taxes on us without our consent;

for depriving us of the benefits of trial by jury

he has endeavored to prevent the population of these states; for that purpose obstructing the laws for naturalization of foreigners; refusing to pass others to encourage their migrations hither; & raising the conditions of new appropriations of lands;

for transporting us beyond seas to be tried for pretended offences:

for taking away our charters & altering fundamentally the forms of our governments;

for suspending our own legislatures & declaring themselves invested with power to legislate for us in all cases whatsoever:

he has abdicated government here, withdrawing his governors, & declaring us out of his allegiance & protection:

he has plundered our seas, ravaged our coasts, burnt our towns & destroyed the lives of our people:

he is at this time transporting large armies of foreign mercenaries to compleat the works of death, desolation & tyranny, already begun with circumstances of cruelty & perfidy unworthy the head of a civilized nation:

he has endeavored to bring on the inhabitants of our frontiers the merciless Indian savages, whose known rule of warfare is an undistinguished destruction of all ages, sexes, & conditions of existence:

he has incited treasonable insurrections of our fellow-citizens, with the allurements of forfeiture & confiscation of our property:

he has waged cruel war against human nature itself, violating it's most sacred rights of life & liberty in the persons of a distant people who never offended him, captivating & carrying them into slavery in another hemisphere, or to incur miserable death in their transportation thither. this piratical warfare, the opprobrium of *infidel* powers, is the warfare of the CHRISTIAN king of Great Britain. determined to keep open a market where MEN should be bought & sold; he has prostituted his negative for suppressing every legislative attempt to prohibit or to restrain this execrable commerce: and that this assemblage of horrors might want no fact of distinguished die, he is now exciting those very people to rise in arms among us, and to purchase that liberty of which *he* has deprived them, by murdering the people upon whom *he* also obtruded them; thus paying off former crimes committed against the *liberties* of one people, with crimes which he urges them to commit against the *lives* of another.

in every stage of these oppressions we have petitioned for redress in the most humble terms; our repeated petitions have been answered by repeated injury. a prince whose character is thus marked by every act which may define a tyrant, is unfit to be the ruler of a people who mean to be free. future ages will scarce believe that the hardiness of one man, adventured within the short compass of twelve years only, on so many acts of tyranny without a mask, over a people fostered & fixed in principles of liberty.

Nor have we been wanting in attentions to our British brethren. we have warned them from time to time of attempts by their legislature to extend a jurisdiction over these our states. we have reminded them of the circumstances of our emigration & settlement here, no one of which could warrant so strange a pretension: that these were effected at the expence of our own blood & treasure, unassisted by the wealth or the strength of Great Britain: that in constituting indeed our several forms of government, we had adopted one common king, thereby laying a foundation for perpetual league & amity with them; but that submission to their [Parliament, was no Part of our Constitution, nor ever in Idea, if History may be]³ credited: and we appealed to their native justice & magnanimity, as to the ties of our common kindred to disavow these usurpations which were likely to interrupt our correspondence & connection. they too have been deaf to the voice of justice & of consanguinity, & when occasions have been given them, by the regular course of their laws, of removing from their councils the disturbers of our harmony, they have by their free election re-established them in power. at this very time too they are permitting their chief magistrate to send over not only soldiers of our common blood, but Scotch & foreign mercenaries to invade & deluge us in blood. these facts have given the last stab to agonizing affection, and manly spirit bids us to renounce for ever these unfeeling brethren. we must endeavor to forget our former love for them, and to hold them as we hold the rest of mankind, enemies in war, in peace friends. we might have been a free & a great people together; but a communication of grandeur & of freedom it seems is below their dignity. be it so, since they will have it: the road to glory & happiness is open to us too; we will climb it in a separate state, and acquiesce in the necessity which pronounces our everlasting Adieu!

We therefore the representatives of the United States of America in General Congress assembled do, in the name & by authority of the good people of these states, reject and renounce all allegiance & subjection to the kings of Great Britain & all others who may hereafter claim by, through, or under them; we utterly dissolve & break off all political connection which may have heretofore subsisted between us & the

3. An illegible passage is supplied from John Adams's transcription.

people or parliament of Great Britain; and finally we do assert and declare these colonies to be free and independant states, and that as free & independant states they shall hereafter have power to levy war, conclude peace, contract alliances, establish commerce, & to do all other acts and things which independant states may of right do. And for the support of this declaration we mutually pledge to each other our lives, our fortunes, & our sacred honour.
1776

Thomas Jefferson and Others

THE DECLARATION OF INDEPENDENCE

IN CONGRESS, JULY 4, 1776
THE UNANIMOUS DECLARATION OF THE
THIRTEEN UNITED STATES OF AMERICA

When in the Course of human events it becomes necessary for one people to dissolve the political bands which have connected them with another, and to assume among the powers of the earth, the separate and equal station to which the Laws of Nature and of Nature's God entitle them, a decent respect to the opinions of mankind requires that they should declare the causes which impel them to the separation.

We hold these truths to be self-evident, that all men are created equal, that they are endowed by their Creator with certain unalienable Rights, that among these are Life, Liberty and the pursuit of Happiness. That to secure these rights, Governments are instituted among Men, deriving their just powers from the consent of the governed. That whenever any Form of Government becomes destructive of these ends, it is the Right of the People to alter or to abolish it, and to institute new Government, laying its foundation on such principles and organizing its powers in such form, as to them shall seem most likely to affect their Safety and Happiness. Prudence, indeed, will dictate that Governments long established should not be changed for light and transient causes; and accordingly all experience hath shewn that mankind are more disposed to suffer, while evils are sufferable, than to right themselves by abolishing the forms to which they are accustomed. But when a long train of abuses and usurpations, pursuing invariably the same Object evinces a design to reduce them under absolute Despotism, it is their right, it is their duty, to throw off such Government, and to provide new Guards for their future security. Such has been the patient sufferance of these Colonies; and such is now the necessity which constrains them to alter their former Systems of Government. The history of the present King of Great Britain is a history of repeated injuries and usurpations, all having in direct object the establishment of an absolute Tyranny over these States. To prove this, let Facts be submitted to a candid world.

He has refused his Assent to Laws, the most wholesome and necessary for the public good.

He has forbidden his Government to pass laws of immediate and pressing importance, unless suspended in their operation till his Assent should be obtained; and when so suspended, he has utterly neglected to attend to them.

He has refused to pass other Laws for the accommodation of large districts of people, unless those people would relinquish the right of Representation in the Legislature, a right inestimable to them and formidable to tyrants only.

He has called together legislative bodies at places unusual, uncomfortable, and distant from the depository of their Public Records, for the sole purpose of fatiguing them into compliance with his measures.

He has dissolved Representative Houses repeatedly, for opposing with manly firmness his invasions on the rights of the people.

He has refused for a long time, after such dissolutions, to cause others to be elected; whereby the Legislative Powers, incapable of Annihilation, have returned to the People at large for their exercise; the State remaining in the mean time exposed to all the dangers of invasion from without, and convulsions within.

He has endeavored to prevent the population of these States; for that purpose obstructing the Laws for Naturalization of Foreigners; refusing to pass others to encourage their migration hither, and raising the conditions of new Appropriations of Lands.

He has obstructed the Administration of Justice, by refusing his Assent to Laws for establishing Judiciary Powers.

He has made Judges dependent on his Will alone, for the tenure of their offices, and the amount and payment of their salaries.

He has erected a multitude of New Offices, and sent hither swarms of Officers to harass our people, and eat out their substance.

He has kept among us, in times of peace, Standing Armies without the Consent of our legislatures.

He has affected to render the Military independent of and superior to the Civil Power.

He has combined with others to subject us to a jurisdiction foreign to our constitution, and unacknowledged by our laws; giving his Assent to their Acts of pretended Legislation: For quartering large bodies of armed troops among us: For protecting them, by a mock Trial, from punishment for any Murders which they should commit on the Inhabitants of these States: For cutting off our Trade with all parts of the world: For imposing Taxes on us without our Consent: For depriving us in many cases, of the benefits of Trial by Jury; For transporting us beyond Seas to be tried for pretended offenses: for abolishing the free System of English Laws in a neighboring Province, establishing therein an Arbitrary government, and enlarging its Boundaries so as to render it at once an example and fit instrument for introducing the same absolute rule into these Colonies: For taking away our Charters, abolishing our most valuable Laws and altering fundamentally the Forms of our Governments: For suspending our own Legislatures, and declaring themselves invested with power to legislate for us in all cases whatsoever.

He has abdicated Government here, by declaring us out of his Protection and waging War against us.

He has plundered our seas, ravaged our Coasts, burnt our towns, and destroyed the lives of our people.

He is at this time transporting large Armies of foreign Mercenaries to complete the works of death, desolation and tyranny, already begun with circumstances of Cruelty & Perfidy scarcely paralleled in the most barbarous ages, and totally unworthy the Head of a civilized nation.

He has constrained our fellow Citizens taken Captive on the high Seas to bear Arms against their Country, to become the executioners of their friends and Brethren, or to fall themselves by their Hands.

He has excited domestic insurrections amongst us, and has endeavored to bring on the inhabitants of our frontiers, the merciless Indian Savages, whose known rule of warfare, is an undistinguished destruction of all ages, sexes, and conditions.

In every stage of these Oppressions We have Petitioned for Redress in the most humble terms: Our repeated Petitions have been answered only by repeated injury. A Prince, whose character is thus marked by every act which may define a Tyrant, is unfit to be the ruler of a free people.

Nor have We been wanting in attention to our British brethren. We have warned them from time to time of attempts by their legislature to extend an unwarrantable jurisdiction over us. We have reminded them of the circumstances of our emigration and settlement here. We have appealed to their native justice and magnanimity, and we have conjured them by the ties of our common kindred to disavow these usurpations, which would inevitably interrupt our connections and correspondence. They too have been deaf to the voice of justice and of consanguinity. We must, therefore, acquiesce in the necessity, which denounces our Separation, and hold them, as we hold the rest of mankind, Enemies in War, in Peace Friends.

We, THEREFORE the Representatives of the UNITED STATES OF AMERICA, in General Congress, Assembled, appealing to the Supreme

Judge of the world for the rectitude of our intentions, do, in the Name, and by Authority of the good People of these Colonies, solemnly publish and declare, That these United Colonies are, and of Right ought to be FREE AND INDEPENDENT STATES; that they are Absolved from all Allegiance to the British Crown, and that all political connection between them and the State of Great Britain, is and ought to be totally dissolved; and that as Free and Independent States, they have full Power to levy War, conclude Peace, contract Alliances, establish Commerce, and to do all other Acts and Things which Independent States may of right do. And for the support of this Declaration, with a firm reliance on the protection of Divine Providence, we mutually pledge to each other our Lives, our Fortunes, and our sacred Honor.

1776

THE READER

1. Find the key terms and phrases of the Declaration (such as "these truths . . . self-evident," "created equal," "unalienable Rights," and so on), and determine how fully they are defined by the contexts in which they occur. Why are no formal definitions given for them?
2. The signers of the Declaration appeal both to general principles and to factual evidence in presenting their case. Which of the appeals to principle could still legitimately be made today by a nation eager to achieve independence? In other words, how far does the Declaration reflect unique events of history, and how far does it reflect universal aspirations and ideals?

THE WRITER

1. The Declaration of Independence was addressed to several audiences: the king of Great Britain, the people of Great Britain, the people of America, and the world at large. Show ways in which the final draft was adapted for its several audiences.
2. Closely examine the second paragraph of both the original draft and the final version of the Declaration. How have the revisions of the final version increased its effectiveness over the first draft?
3. The Declaration has often been called a classic example of deductive argument: setting up general statements, relating particular cases to them, and drawing conclusions. Trace this pattern through the document, noting the way each part is developed. Would the document have been as effective if the long middle part had either come first or been left out entirely? Explain.
4. Using only what is implied in the Declaration, write a brief definition for one of the key terms referred to in question 1 under "The Reader."
5. Burgess refers to the "dangerous naiveté" of the Declaration (p. 265). Read Burgess's remark in its context, and then write a paragraph or two supporting or opposing his view.

E. B. White

DEMOCRACY

We received a letter from the Writers' War Board the other day asking for a statement on "The Meaning of Democracy." It presumably is our duty to comply with such a request, and it is certainly our pleasure.

Surely the Board knows what democracy is. It is the line that forms on the right. It is the don't in don't shove. It is the hole in the stuffed shirt through which the sawdust slowly trickles; it is the dent in the high hat. Democracy is the recurrent suspicion that more than half of the people are right more than half of the time. It is the feeling of privacy in the voting booths, the feeling of communion in the libraries, the feeling of vitality everywhere. Democracy is a letter to the editor. Democracy is the score at the beginning of the ninth. It is an idea which hasn't been disproved yet, a song the words of which have not gone bad. It's the mustard on the hot dog and the cream in the rationed coffee. Democracy is a request from a War Board, in the middle of a morning in the middle of a war, wanting to know what democracy is.

1943

THE READER

1. Look up democracy in a standard desk dictionary. Of the several meanings given, which one best applies to White's definition? Does more than one apply?
2. If White were writing this piece today, which of his examples might he change and which would he probably retain?

THE WRITER

1. White's piece is dated July 3, 1943, the middle of World War II. How did the occasion shape what White says about democracy?
2. Translate White's definition into nonmetaphorical language. (For example, "It is the line that forms on the right" might be translated by "It has no special privileges.") Determine what is lost in the translation or, in other words, what White has gained by using figurative language.
3. If you didn't know that White was the author of "Some Remarks on Humor" (p. 663), what specific features of his use of metaphor in that piece might enable you to guess that he was?
4. Using White's technique for definition, write a definition of an abstraction such as love, justice, or beauty.

Science

James C. Rettie

"BUT A WATCH IN THE NIGHT": A SCIENTIFIC FABLE

Out beyond our solar system there is a planet called Copernicus. It came into existence some four or five billion years before the birth of our Earth. In due course of time it became inhabited by a race of intelligent men.

About 750 million years ago the Copernicans had developed the motion picture machine to a point well in advance of the stage that we have reached. Most of the cameras that we now use in motion picture work are geared to take twenty-four pictures per second on a continuous strip of film. When such film is run through a projector, it throws a series of images on the screen and these change with a rapidity that gives the visual impression of normal movement. If a motion is too swift for the human eye to see it in detail, it can be captured and artificially slowed down by means of the slow-motion camera. This one is geared to take many more shots per second—ninety-six or even more than that. When the slow motion film is projected at the normal speed of twenty-four pictures per second, we can see just how the jumping horse goes over a hurdle.

What about motion that is too slow to be seen by the human eye? That problem has been solved by the use of the time-lapse camera. In this one, the shutter is geared to take only one shot per second, or one per minute, or even one per hour—depending upon the kind of movement that is being photographed. When the time-lapse film is projected at the normal speed of twenty-four pictures per second, it is possible to see a bean sprout growing up out of the ground. Time-lapse films are useful in the study of many types of motion too slow to be observed by the unaided, human eye.

The Copernicans, it seems, had time-lapse cameras some 757 million years ago and they also had superpowered telescopes that gave them a clear view of what was happening upon this Earth. They decided to make a film record of the life history of Earth and to make it on the scale of one picture per year. The photography has been in progress during the last 757 million years.

In the near future, a Copernican interstellar expedition will arrive upon our Earth and bring with it a copy of the time-lapse film. Arrangements will be made for showing the entire film in one continuous run. This will begin at midnight of New Year's eve and continue day and night without a single stop until midnight of December 31. The rate of projection will be twenty-four pictures per second. Time on the screen will thus seem to move at the rate of twenty-four years per second; 1440 years per minute; 86,400 years per hour; approximately two million years per day; and sixty-two million years per month. The normal lifespan of individual man will occupy about three seconds. The full period of Earth history that will be unfolded on the screen (some 757 million years) will extend from what the geologists call Pre-Cambrian times[1] up to the present. This will, by no means, cover the full time-span of the Earth's geological history but it will embrace the period since the advent of living organisms.

During the months of January, February, and March the picture will be desolate and dreary. The shape of the land masses and the oceans will bear little or no resemblance to those that we know. The violence of geological erosion will be much in evidence. Rains will pour down on the land and promptly go booming down to the seas. There will be no clear streams anywhere except where the rains fall upon hard rock. Everywhere on the steeper ground the stream channels will be filled with boulders hurled down by rushing waters. Raging torrents and dry stream beds will keep alternating in quick succession. High mountains will seem to melt like so much butter in the sun. The shifting of land into the seas, later to be thrust up as new mountains, will be going on at a grand scale.

Early in April there will be some indication of the presence of single-celled living organisms in some of the warmer and sheltered coastal waters. By the end of the month it will be noticed that some of these organisms have become multicellular. A few of them, including the Trilobites, will be encased in hard shells.

Toward the end of May, the first vertebrates will appear, but they will still be aquatic creatures. In June about 60 per cent of the land area that we know as North America will be under water. One broad channel will occupy the space where the Rocky Mountains now stand. Great deposits

1. 500,000,000 years or more before the present.

of limestone will be forming under some of the shallower seas. Oil and gas deposits will be in process of formation—also under shallow seas. On land there will still be no sign of vegetation. Erosion will be rampant, tearing loose particles and chunks of rock and grinding them into sand and silt to be spewed out by the streams into bays and estuaries.

About the middle of July the first land plants will appear and take up the tremendous job of soil building. Slowly, very slowly, the mat of vegetation will spread, always battling for its life against the power of erosion. Almost foot by foot, the plant life will advance, lacing down with its root structures whatever pulverized rock material it can find. Leaves and stems will be giving added protection against the loss of the soil foothold. The increasing vegetation will pave the way for the land animals that will live upon it.

Early in August the seas will be teeming with fish. This will be what geologists call the Devonian period.[2] Some of the races of these fish will be breathing by means of lung tissue instead of through gill tissues. Before the month is over, some of the lung fish will go ashore and take on a crude lizard-like appearance. Here are the first amphibians.

In early September the insects will put in their appearance. Some will look like huge dragonflies and will have a wing spread of 24 inches. Large portions of the land masses will now be covered with heavy vegetation that will include the primitive spore-propagating trees. Layer upon layer of this plant growth will build up, later to appear as the coal deposits. About the middle of this month, there will be evidence of the first seed-bearing plants and the first reptiles. Heretofore, the land animals will have been amphibians that could reproduce their kind only by depositing a soft egg mass in quiet waters. The reptiles will be shown to be freed from the aquatic bond because they can reproduce by means of a shelled egg in which the embryo and its nurturing liquids are sealed and thus protected from destructive evaporation. Before September is over, the first dinosaurs will be seen—creatures destined to dominate the animal realm for about 140 million years and then to disappear.

In October there will be series of mountain uplifts along what is now the eastern coast of the United States. A creature with feathered limbs— half bird and half reptile in appearance—will take itself into the air. Some small and rather unpretentious animals will be seen to bring forth their young in a form that is a miniature replica of the parents and to feed these young on milk secreted by mammary glands in the female parent. The emergence of this mammalian form of animal life will be recognized as one of the great events in geologic time. October will also witness the high water mark of the dinosaurs—creatures ranging in size from that of the modern goat to monsters like Brontosaurus that weighed some 40

2. 405,000,000–345,000,000 years ago.

tons. Most of them will be placid vegetarians, but a few will be hideous-looking carnivores, like Allosaurus and Tyrannosaurus. Some of the herbivorous dinosaurs will be clad in bony armor for protection against their flesh-eating comrades.

November will bring pictures of a sea extending from the Gulf of Mexico to the Arctic in space now occupied by the Rocky Mountains. A few of the reptiles will take to the air on bat-like wings. One of these, called Pteranodon, will have a wingspread of 15 feet. There will be a rapid development of the modern flowering plants, modern trees, and modern insects. The dinosaurs will disappear. Toward the end of the month there will be a tremendous land disturbance in which the Rocky Mountains will rise out of the sea to assume a dominating place in the North American landscape.

As the picture runs on into December it will show the mammals in command of the animal life. Seed-bearing trees and grasses will have covered most of the land with a heavy mantle of vegetation. Only the areas newly thrust up from the sea will be barren. Most of the streams will be crystal clear. The turmoil of geologic erosion will be confined to localized areas. About December 25 will begin the cutting of the Grand Canyon of the Colorado River. Grinding down through layer after layer of sedimentary strata, this stream will finally expose deposits laid down in Pre-Cambrian times. Thus in the walls of that canyon will appear geological formations dating from recent times to the period when the Earth had no living organisms upon it.

The picture will run on through the latter days of December and even up to its final day with still no sign of mankind. The spectators will become alarmed in the fear that man has somehow been left out. But not so; sometime about noon on December 31 (one million years ago) will appear a stooped, massive creature of man-like proportions. This will be Pithecanthropus, the Java ape man. For tools and weapons he will have nothing but crude stone and wooden clubs. His children will live a precarious existence threatened on the one side by hostile animals and on the other by tremendous climatic changes. Ice sheets—in places 4000 feet deep—will form in the northern parts of North America and Eurasia. Four times this glacial ice will push southward to cover half the continents. With each advance the plant and animal life will be swept under or pushed southward. With each recession of the ice, life will struggle to reestablish itself in the wake of the retreating glaciers. The woolly mammoth, the musk ox, and the caribou all will fight to maintain themselves near the ice line. Sometimes they will be caught and put into cold storage—skin, flesh, blood, bones and all.

The picture will run on through supper time with still very little evidence of man's presence on the Earth. It will be about 11 o'clock when Neanderthal man appears. Another half hour will go by before the appearance of Cro-Magnon man living in caves and painting crude animal pictures on the walls of his dwelling. Fifteen minutes more will bring Neolithic man, knowing how to chip stone and thus produce sharp cutting edges for spears and tools. In a few minutes more it will appear that man has domesticated the dog, the sheep and, possibly, other animals. He will then begin the use of milk. He will also learn the arts of basket weaving and the making of pottery and dugout canoes.

The dawn of civilization will not come until about five or six minutes before the end of the picture. The story of the Egyptians, the Babylonians, the Greeks, and the Romans will unroll during the fourth, the third and the second minute before the end. At 58 minutes and 43 seconds past 11:00 P.M. (just 1 minute and 17 seconds before the end) will come the beginning of the Christian era. Columbus will discover the new world 20 seconds before the end. The Declaration of Independence will be signed just 7 seconds before the final curtain comes down.

In those few moments of geologic time will be the story of all that has happened since we became a nation. And what a story it will be! A human swarm will sweep across the face of the continent and take it away from the . . . red men. They will change it far more radically than it has ever been changed before in a comparable time. The great virgin forests will be seen going down before ax and fire. The soil, covered for eons by its protective mantle of trees and grasses, will be laid bare to the ravages of water and wind erosion. Streams that had been flowing clear will, once again, take up a load of silt and push it toward the seas. Humus and mineral salts, both vital elements of productive soil, will be seen to vanish at a terrifying rate. The railroads and highways and cities that will spring up may divert attention, but they cannot cover up the blight of man's recent activities. In great sections of Asia, it will be seen that man must utilize cow dung and every scrap of available straw or grass for fuel to cook his food. The forests that once provided wood for this purpose will be gone without a trace. The use of these agricultural wastes for fuel, in place of returning them to the land, will be leading to increasing soil impoverishment. Here and there will be seen a dust storm darkening the landscape over an area a thousand miles across. Man-creatures will be shown counting their wealth in terms of bits of printed paper representing other bits of a scarce but comparatively useless yellow metal that is kept buried in strong vaults. Meanwhile, the soil, the only real wealth that can keep mankind alive on the face of this Earth is savagely being cut loose from its ancient moorings and washed into the seven seas.

We have just arrived upon this Earth. How long will we stay?

1948

Edward O. Wilson

THE SUPERORGANISM

In March 1983 I returned to South America to begin a new program of study on tropical ants. I was interested in the way the communication systems and division of labor of these insects adapt them to their environment. My first stop was the field site of the Minimum Critical Size Project of the World Wildlife Fund, located in Amazonian forest sixty miles north of Manaus,[1] Brazil. I was accompanied by Thomas Lovejoy, the young and vigorous vice-president for science of WWF-US, who had conceived the project in the late 1970s. We joined an assortment of researchers, students, and assistants who were working back and forth between Manaus and the site on weekly tours. Camaraderie came easily and was genuine; our shared values were implicit, forming a bond too strong to allow much discussion of why we had come together in this unlikely place. We talked only about organisms, in endless technical detail.

My hosts were not ordinary field biologists. They did not affect the verbal delicacy and critical reserve of typical academics encountered on leave from comfortable bases in Berkeley, Ann Arbor, and Cambridge. Their manner was self-confident and achievement-oriented, tough in a pleasant way, and they reminded me a bit of settlers I had met in Australia and New Guinea (and the Israeli biologist who pointed out the house where he had commanded a company during the 1967 war, as we returned from a field trip to the Dead Sea). Even though the World Wildlife Fund is operating on a slender budget, its Amazon Project is truly pioneering on a large scale. Planned to run into the next century, it is designed to answer one of the key questions of ecology and conservation practice: how extensive does a wildlife preserve have to be to sustain permanently most or all of the kinds of plants and animals protected within its boundaries?

We know that when a species loses part of its range,[2] it is in greater danger of extinction. Expressed in loosely mathematical terms, the chance that a population of organisms will go extinct in a given year increases as its living space is cut back and its numbers are held at correspondingly lower numbers. All populations fluctuate in size to some extent, but those kept at a low maximum are more likely to zigzag all the way down to zero than those permitted to fluctuate at higher levels. For example, a population of ten grizzly bears living on one hundred square

1. Capital of the state of West Brazil, located on the left bank of the Río Negro.   2. Native habitat.

miles of land will probably disappear much earlier than a population of a thousand grizzly bears living on ten thousand square miles of similar land; the thousand could persist for centuries or, so far as ordinary human awareness is concerned, forever.

This simple fact of nature bears heavily on the design of nature reserves. When a piece of primeval forest is set aside and the surrounding forest cleared, it becomes an island in an agricultural sea. Like wave-lapped Puerto Rico or Bali, it has lost most of its connections with other natural land habitats from which new immigrations can occur. Over a period of years the number of plant and animal species will fall to a new and predictable level. Some impoverishment of diversity is inevitable even if men never put an ax to a single tree in the reserve. This natural decline presents biologists with a problem that is technically difficult and soluble only through the chancing of risky compromises. The reserve they recommend must be small enough to be economically reasonable. They cannot ask that an entire country be set aside. But they have the obligation to insist that the patch be made large enough to sustain the fauna and flora. It is their job to prove that a certain minimum area is required, to list as completely as possible which species will be saved in the reserve, and for approximately how long.

The tropical rain forest north of Manaus, like that in many other parts of the Amazon basin, is being clear-cut from the edge inward. It is being lifted up from the ground entire like a carpet rolled off a bare floor, leaving behind vast stretches of cattle range and cropland that need artificial fertilization to sustain even marginal productivity for more than two or three years. A rain forest in Brazil differs fundamentally from a deciduous woodland in Pennsylvania or Germany in the way its key resources are distributed. A much greater fraction of organic matter is bound up in the tissues of the standing trees, so that the leaf litter and humus are only a few inches deep. When the forest is felled and burned, the hard equatorial downpours quickly wash away the thin blanket of top soil.

Although I had this general information in advance, I was still shaken by the sight of newly cleared land around Manaus. The pans and hillocks of lateritic[3] clay, littered with blackened tree stumps, bore the look of a freshly deserted battlefield. Spherical termite mounds sprouted from the fallen wood in an ill-fated population explosion, while vultures and swifts wheeled overhead in representation of the mostly vanished bird fauna. Bony white cattle, forlorn replacements of a magnificent heritage, clustered in small groups around the scattered watersheds. Near midday the heat of the sun bounced up from the bare patches of soil to hit with an almost tactile force. It was another world altogether from the shadowed

---

3. From decayed rock, a residue red in color.

tunnels of the nearby forest, and a constant reminder of what had happened: tens of thousands of species had been scraped away as by a giant hand and will not be seen in that place for generations, if ever. The action can be defended (with difficulty) on economic grounds, but it is like burning a Renaissance painting to cook dinner.

The Brazilian authorities have sanctioned the opening of the wilderness on the basis of a logical formula: the impoverished Northeast has people and no land, the Amazon has land and no people; join them together and build a nation. But they are also well aware of the problems of environmental degradation. More recently, influenced by biologists such as Warwick Kerr, Paulo Nogueira Neto, and Paulo Vanzolini, they have begun to forge a policy of preservation. Now by law, honored at least in principle, half of the forest must be left standing. Of equal importance, more than twenty Amazonian reserves and parks have been set aside in key areas where the greatest number of species of plants and animals are thought to exist. Most are over a thousand square miles in extent, the minimum area that, according to Princeton University's John Terborgh and other experts on the subject, is needed to hold the number of disappearing species to less than 1 percent of the initial complement over the next century. In other words, the formula is meant to ensure that 99 out of every 100 kinds of organisms will still be present in the year 2100. With reserves of this size there is hope even for the harpy eagle and the jaguar, of which single individuals need three square miles or more to survive, as well as the flourish of rare orchids, monkeys, river fish, and brilliant toucans and macaws that symbolize the admirable élan[4] of Brazil itself.

But this leaves the smaller reserves elsewhere in Brazil and in the more densely populated countries of South and Central America. The American and Brazilian scientists at the Manaus project are addressing the problem in the following way. At the edge of the cutting, where the rain forest begins and continues virtually unbroken north to Venezuela, they have marked off a series of twenty plots ranging in size from one to a thousand hectares (a hectare is 100 meters on the side and equals 2.47 acres). In each plot they survey the most easily classified and monitored of the big organisms, including the trees, butterflies, birds, monkeys, and other large mammals. Then, with the cooperation of the landowners, they supervise the clearing of the surrounding land, leaving the plots behind as forest islands in a newly created agricultural sea. The surveys were begun in 1980 and will be continued for many years. Eventually the data should reveal how much faster the smaller island-reserves lose their species than larger ones, which kinds of animals and plants decline the most rapidly, why they become extinct, and, most crucially, the mini-

4. Ardor, spirit.

mum area needed to hold on to the greater part of the diversity of life. No process being addressed by modern science is more complicated or, in my opinion, more important.

We rode in a World Wildlife Fund truck to a camp just inside the forest border at Fazenda Esteio, where the biologists were conducting one of the initial surveys. True to the philosophy of the sponsoring organization, the camp was a tiny clearing with a temporary shelter just large enough to hold a few hammocks, plus a cook's shed and fireplace, and nothing more. To my delight I found that I could roll out of my hammock in the morning, take twenty steps, and be in virgin rain forest. For five days I stayed in the woods except for meals and as little sleep as I needed to keep going.

I savored the cathedral feeling expressed by Darwin in 1832 when he first encountered tropical forest near Rio de Janeiro ("wonder, astonishment & sublime devotion, fill & elevate the mind"). And once again I could hold still for long intervals to study a few centimeters of tree trunk or ground, finding some new organism at each shift of focus. The intervals of total silence, often prolonged, became evidence of the intensity of the enveloping life. Several times a day I heard what may be the most distinctive sound of the primary tropical forest: a sharp crack like a rifle shot, followed by a whoosh and a solid thump. Somewhere a large tree, weakened by age and rot and top heavy from layers of vines, has chosen that moment to fall and end decades or centuries of life. The process is random and continuous, a sprinkling of events through the undisturbed portion of the forest. The broad trunk snaps or keels over to lever up the massive root system, the branches plow down through the canopies of neighboring trees at terrifying speed, and the whole thunders to the ground in a cloud of leaves, trailing lianas,[5] and fluttering insects. There may be a hundred thousand trees within earshot of any place the hiker stands in the forest, so that the odds of hearing one coming down on a given day are high. But the chance of being close enough to be struck by any part of the tree is remote, comparable to that of stepping on a poisonous snake or coming round the bend of a trail one day to meet a mother jaguar with cubs. Still, the lifetime risk builds up cumulatively, like that in daily flights aboard single-engined airplanes, so that those who spend years in the forest count falling trees as an important source of danger.

Most of the time I worked with a restless energy to get ahead on several research projects I had in mind. I opened logs and twigs like presents on Christmas morning, entranced by the endless variety of insects and other small creatures that scuttled away to safety. None of these organisms was repulsive to me; each was beautiful, with a name and special meaning. It

5. Climbing tropical vine.

is the naturalist's privilege to choose almost any kind of plant or animal for examination and be able to commence productive work within a relatively short time. In the tropical forest, with thousands of mostly unknown species all around, the number of discoveries per investigator per day is probably greater than anywhere else in the world.

As if to dramatize the point, an insect I most wanted to find made its appearance soon after my arrival at Fazenda Esteio, with no effort of my own and literally at my feet. It was the leafcutter ant (*Atta cephalotes*), one of the most abundant and visually striking animals of the New World tropics. The *saúva*, as it is called locally, is a prime consumer of fresh vegetation, rivaled only by man, and a leading agricultural pest in Brazil. I had devoted years of research to the species in the laboratory but never studied it in the field. At dusk on the first day in camp, as the light failed to the point where we found it difficult to make out small objects on the ground, the first worker ants came scurrying purposefully out of the surrounding forest. They were brick red in color, about a quarter inch in length, and bristling with short, sharp spines. Within minutes, several hundred had arrived and formed two irregular files that passed on either side of the hammock shelter. They ran in a nearly straight line across the clearing, their paired antennae scanning right and left, as though drawn by some directional beam from the other side. Within an hour, the trickle expanded to twin rivers of tens of thousands of ants running ten or more abreast. The columns could be traced easily with the aid of a flashlight. They came up from a huge earthen nest a hundred yards from the camp on a descending slope, crossed the clearing, and disappeared again into the forest. By climbing through tangled undergrowth we were able to locate one of their main targets, a tall tree bearing white flowers high in its crown. The ants streamed up the trunk, scissored out pieces of leaves and petals with their sharp-toothed mandibles, and headed home carrying the fragments over their heads like little parasols. Some floated the pieces to the ground, where most were picked up and carried away by newly arriving nestmates. At maximum activity, shortly before midnight, the trails were a tumult of ants bobbing and weaving past each other like miniature mechanical toys.

For many visitors to the forest, even experienced naturalists, the foraging expeditions are the whole of the matter, and individual leafcutter ants seem to be inconsequential ruddy specks on a pointless mission. But a closer look transforms them into beings of another order. If we magnify the scene to human scale, so that an ant's quarter-inch length grows into six feet, the forager runs along the trail for a distance of about ten miles at a velocity of 16 miles an hour. Each successive mile is covered in three minutes and forty-five seconds, about the current (human) world record. The forager picks up a burden of 750 pounds and speeds back toward the nest at 15 miles an hour—hence, four-minute miles. This marathon is repeated many times during the night and in many localities on through the day as well.

From research conducted jointly by biologists and chemists, it is known that the ants are guided by a secretion paid onto the soil through the sting, in the manner of ink being drawn out of a pen. The crucial molecule is methyl-4-methylpyrrole-2-carboxylate, which is composed of a tight ring of carbon and nitrogen atoms with short side chains made of carbon and oxygen. The pure substance has an innocuous odor, judged by various people to be faintly grassy, sulphurous, or fruitlike with a hint of naphtha[6] (I'm not sure I can smell it at all). But whatever the impact on human beings, it is an ichor[7] of extraordinary power for the ants. One milligram, a quantity that would just about cover the printed letters in this sentence, if dispensed with theoretical maximum efficiency, is enough to excite billions of workers into activity or to lead a short column of them three times around the world. The vast difference between us and them has nothing to do with the trail substance itself, which is a biochemical material of unexceptional structure. It lies entirely in the unique sensitivity of the sensory organs and brains of the insects.

One millimeter above the ground, where ants exist, things are radically different from what they seem to the gigantic creatures who peer down from a thousand times that distance. The ants do not follow the trail substance as a liquid trace on the soil, as we are prone to think. It comes up to them as a cloud of molecules diffusing through still air at the ground surface. The foragers move inside a long ellipsoidal space in which the gaseous material is dense enough to be detected. They sweep their paired antennae back and forth in advance of the head to catch the odorant molecules. The antennae are the primary sensory centers of the ant. Their surfaces are furred with thousands of nearly invisible hairs and pegs, among which are scattered diminutive plates and bottle-necked pits. Each of these sense organs is serviced by cells that carry electrical impulses into the central nerve of the antenna. Then relay cells take over and transmit the messages to the integrating regions of the brain. Some of the antennal organs react to touch, while others are sensitive to slight movements of air, so that the ant responds instantaneously whenever the nest is breached by intruders. But most of the sensors monitor the chemicals that swirl around the ant in combinations that change through each second of its life. Human beings live in a world of sight and sound, but social insects exist primarily by smell and taste. In a word, we are audiovisual where they are chemical.

The oddness of the insect sensory world is illustrated by the swift sequence of events that occurs along the odor trail. When a forager takes a wrong turn to the left and starts to run away from the track, its left

6. Low-grade petroleum.
7. From Greek mythology, an ethereal fluid that flowed in the veins of ancient gods.

antenna breaks out of the odor space first and is no longer stimulated by the guiding substance. In a few thousandths of a second, the ant perceives the change and pulls back to the right. Twisting right and left in response to the vanishing molecules, it follows a tightly undulating course between the nest and the tree. During the navigation it must also dodge moment by moment through a tumult of other runners. If you watch a foraging worker from a few inches away with the unaided eye, it seems to touch each passerby with its antennae, a kind of tactile probe. Slow-motion photography reveals that it is actually sweeping the tips of the antennae over parts of the other ant's body to smell it. If the surface does not present exactly the right combination of chemicals—the colony's unique odor signature—the ant attacks at once. It may simultaneously spray an alarm chemical from special glands located in the head capsule, causing others in the vicinity to rush to the site with their mandibles gaping.

An ant colony is organized by no more than ten or twenty such signals, most of which are chemical secretions leaked or sprayed from glands. The workers move with swiftness and precision through a life that human beings have come to understand only with the aid of mathematical diagrams and molecular formulas. We can also simulate the behavior. Computer technology has made it theoretically possible to create a mechanical ant that duplicates the observed activity. But the machine, if for some reason we chose to build one, would be the size of a small automobile, and even then I doubt if it would tell us anything new about the ant's inner nature.

At the end of the trail the burdened foragers rush down the nest hole, into throngs of nestmates and along tortuous channels that end near the water table fifteen feet or more below. The ants drop the leaf sections onto the floor of a chamber, to be picked up by workers of a slightly smaller size who clip them into fragments about a millimeter across. Within minutes still smaller ants take over, crush and mold the fragments into moist pellets, and carefully insert them into a mass of similar material. This mass ranges in size between a clenched fist and a human head, is riddled with channels, and resembles a gray cleaning sponge. It is the garden of the ants: on its surface a symbiotic fungus grows which, along with the leaf sap, forms the ants' sole nourishment. The fungus spreads like a white frost, sinking its hyphae into the leaf paste to digest the abundant cellulose and proteins held there in partial solution.

The gardening cycle proceeds. Worker ants even smaller than those just described pluck loose strands of the fungus from places of dense growth and plant them onto the newly constructed surfaces. Finally, the very smallest—and most abundant—workers patrol the beds of fungal strands, delicately probing them with their antennae, licking their surfaces clean, and plucking out the spores and hyphae of alien species of mold. These colony dwarfs are able to travel through the narrowest channels deep within the garden masses. From time to time they pull tufts of fungus loose and carry them out to feed their larger nestmates.

The leafcutter economy is organized around this division of labor based on size. The foraging workers, about as big as houseflies, can slice leaves but are too bulky to cultivate the almost microscopic fungal strands. The tiny gardener workers, somewhat smaller than this printed letter I, can grow the fungus but are too weak to cut the leaves. So the ants form an assembly line, each successive step being performed by correspondingly smaller workers, from the collection of pieces of leaves out of doors to the manufacture of leaf paste to the cultivation of dietary fungi deep within the nest.

The defense of the colony is also organized according to size. Among the scurrying workers can be seen a few soldier ants, three hundred times heavier than the gardener workers. Their sharp mandibles are powered by massive adductor muscles that fill the swollen, quarter-inch wide head capsules. Working like miniature wire clippers, they chop enemy insects into pieces and easily slice through human skin. These behemoths are especially adept at repelling large invaders. When entomologists digging into a nest grow careless, their hands become nicked all over as if pulled through a thorn bush. I have occasionally had to pause to staunch the flow of blood from a single bite, impressed by the fact that a creature one-millionth my size could stop me with nothing but its jaws.

No other animals have evolved the ability to turn fresh vegetation into mushrooms. The evolutionary event occurred only once, millions of years ago, somewhere in South America. It gave the ants an enormous advantage: they could now send out specialized workers to collect the vegetation while keeping the bulk of their populations safe in subterranean retreats. As a result, all of the different kinds of leafcutters together, comprising fourteen species in the genus *Atta* and twenty-three in *Acromyrmex*, dominate a large part of the American tropics. They consume more vegetation than any other group of animals, including the more abundant forms of caterpillars, grasshoppers, birds, and mammals. A single colony can strip an orange tree or bean patch overnight, and the combined populations inflict over a billion dollars' worth of damage yearly. It was with good reason that the early Portuguese settlers called Brazil the Kingdom of the Ants.

At full size, a colony contains three to four million workers and occupies three thousand or more underground chambers. The earth it excavates forms a pile twenty feet across and three to four feet high. Deep inside the nest sits the mother queen, a giant insect the size of a newborn mouse. She can live at least ten years and perhaps as long as twenty. No one has had the persistence to determine the true longevity.

In my laboratory I have an individual collected in Guyana[8] fourteen years ago. When she reaches eighteen, and breaks the proved longevity record of the seventeen-year locusts, my students and I will open a bottle of champagne to celebrate. In her lifetime an individual can produce over twenty million offspring, which translates into the following: a mere three hundred ants, a small fraction of the number emerging from a single colony in a year, can give birth to more ants than there are human beings on Earth.

The queen is born as a tiny egg, among thousands laid daily by the old mother queen. The egg hatches as a grublike larva, which is fed and laved incessantly throughout its month-long existence by the adult worker nurses. Through some unknown treatment, perhaps a special diet controlled by the workers, the larva grows to a relatively huge size. She then transforms into a pupa, whose waxy casement is shaped like an adult queen in fetal position, with legs, wings, and antennae folded tightly against the body. After several weeks the full complement of adult organs develops within this cuticle, and the new queen emerges. From the beginning she is fully adult and grows no more in size. She also possesses the same genes as her sisters, the colony workers. Their smaller size and pedestrian behavior is not due to heredity but rather to the different treatment they received as larvae.

In bright sunshine following a heavy rain, the virgin queen comes to the surface of the nest and flies up into the air to join other queens and the darkly pigmented, big-eyed males. Four or five males seize and inseminate her in quick succession, while she is still flying through the air. Their sole function now completed, they die within hours without returning to the home nest. The queen stores their sperm in her spermatheca, a tough muscular bag located just above and behind her ovaries. These reproductive cells live like independent microorganisms for years, passively waiting until they are released into the oviduct to meet an egg and create a new female ant. If the egg passes through the oviduct and to the outside without receiving a sperm, it produces a male. The queen can control the sex of her offspring, as well as the number of new workers and queens she produces, by opening or shutting the passage leading from her sperm-storage organ to the oviduct.

The newly inseminated queen descends to the ground. Raking her legs forward, she breaks off her wings, painlessly because they are composed of dead, membranous tissue. She wanders in a random pattern until she finds a patch of soft, bare soil, then commences to excavate a narrow tunnel straight down. Several hours later, when the shaft has been sunk to a depth of about ten inches, the queen widens its bottom into a small room. She is now set to start a garden and a colony of her own. But there is

8. Coastal nation in northeast South America, formerly British Guiana.

a problem in this life-cycle strategy. The queen has completely separated herself from the mother colony. Where can she obtain a culture of the vital symbiotic fungus to start the garden? Answer: she has been carrying it all along in her mouth. Just before leaving home, the young queen gathered a wad of fungal strands and inserted it into a pocket in the floor of her oral cavity, just back of the tongue. Now she passes the pellet out onto the floor of the nest and fertilizes it with droplets of feces.

As the fungus proliferates in the form of a whitish mat, the queen lays eggs on and around its surface. When the young larvae hatch, they are fed with other eggs given to them by the queen. At the end of their development, six weeks later, they transform into small workers. These new adults quickly take over the ordinary tasks of the colony. When still only a few days old, they proceed to enlarge the nest, work the garden, and feed the queen and larvae with tufts of the increasingly abundant fungus. In a year the little band has expanded into a force of a thousand workers, and the queen has ceased almost all activity to become a passive eating and egg-laying machine. She retains that exclusive role for the rest of her life. The measure of her Darwinian success is whether some of her daughters born five or ten years down the line grow into queens, leave on nuptial flights, and—rarest of all achievements—found new colonies of their own. In the world of the social insects, by the canons of biological organization, colonies beget colonies; individuals do not directly beget individuals.

People often ask me whether I see any human qualities in an ant colony, any form of behavior that even remotely mimics human thought and feeling. Insects and human beings are separated by more than 600 million years of evolution, but a common ancestor did exist in the form of one of the earliest multicellular organisms. Does some remnant of psychological continuity exist across that immense phylogenetic gulf? The answer is that I open an ant colony as I would the back of a Swiss watch. I am enchanted by the intricacy of its parts and the clean, thrumming precision. But I never see the colony as anything more than an organic machine.

Let me qualify that metaphor. The leafcutter colony is a superorganism. The queen sits deep in the central chambers, the vibrant growing tip from which all the workers and new queens originate. But she is not in any sense the leader or the repository of an organizational blueprint. No command center directs the colony. The social master plan is partitioned into the brains of the all-female workers, whose separate programs fit together to form a balanced whole. Each ant automatically performs certain tasks and avoids others according to its size and age. The superorganism's brain is the entire society; the workers are the crude analogue of its nerve cells. Seen from above and at a distance, the leafcutter colony resembles a gigantic amoeba. Its foraging columns snake out like pseudopods to engulf and shred plants, while their stems pull the green pieces down holes into the fungus gardens. Through a unique step in evolution taken millions of years ago, the ants captured a fungus, incorporated it into the superorganism, and so gained the power to digest leaves. Or perhaps the relation is the other way around: perhaps the fungus captured the ants and employed them as a mobile extension to take leaves into the moist underground chambers.

In either case, the two now own each other and will never pull apart. The ant-fungus combination is one of evolution's master clockworks, tireless, repetitive, and precise, more complicated than any human invention and unimaginably old. To find a colony in the South American forest is like coming upon some device left in place ages ago by an extraterrestrial visitor for a still undisclosed purpose. Biologists have only begun to puzzle out its many parts.

Because of modern science the frontier is no longer located along the retreating wall of the great rain forest. It is in the bodies and lives of the leafcutters and thousands of other species found for the most part on the other side of that tragic line.

1984

Michael J. Katz

ON THE WINGS OF AN ANGEL: AN EXPLORATION OF THE LIMITS OF BIOLOGICAL ENTERPRISE

When you have eliminated the impossible, whatever remains, however improbable, must be the truth.
—SHERLOCK HOLMES in *The Sign of the Four*

Biologists rarely use the word "impossible." To a biologist, the range of the possible is so large, the potential biological entities so overwhelmingly numerous, that the impossible is only a tiny issue.

To a biologist, impossibilities are the wall at the edge of the physical universe—real and formidable constraints, but constraints lying somewhere far away, somewhere in the realm of the physicist.

The biologist sees these physical constraints as if through the wrong end of a telescope. Demagnified and miniaturized, the limits of the physical universe form toy fences in someone else's province. With more than 1,500 species of daisies in Europe alone and more than 2,000 species of crickets world-wide, with 30,000 different proteins specific to the brain of the rat, biologists have little room on their desks for perpetual motion machines or for rockets that travel faster than the speed of light.

The mainstream of biological tradition is natural history, the record of Nature's accomplishments, the careful charting of the possible. Moreover, biologists are artisans at heart; they want to do things and make things, and they actively seek out the possible. Beyond this, however, I suspect that there is a more fundamental reason that biologists rarely speak in terms of the impossible. Perhaps there are no biological impossibilities. Perhaps, deep within the true province of biology, everything is possible.

The Province of Biology

The wide range of the possible in biology depends on the unique and peculiar province of the living. Living beings form a special realm of science, filled with eye-popping collages of butterflies, sheets of grasses, mildewing molds, people, bears, whales, and bats, eggs and embryos, grandmothers and grandfathers. Biology is about life, and life is organisms.

We know them well, these organisms. We pass them every day as we walk on the grass, under the trees, past the birds and squirrels. Gardening, we run our hands through the cool earth, crumbles of plant detritus, worms, larvae, hundreds of thousands of microorganisms. We know them by touch, smell, and sight; and those organisms that never come within our grasps, such as the gulls at the shore, we know by sight and sound.

But most of all, we know the human organisms. We know our parents and our friends; we know strangers on the bus, on the street, and in the stores; and, of course, we know ourselves. How many times a day do we look at our hands? A hundred? A thousand? We feel our toes from outside and from inside. We hear our heartbeats at night. We smell our sweat, we taste our blood. We are not all physicists or economists or mathematicians, but we are all biologists. We know organisms, and most of us know them quite well.

Biological organisms fall into a few general types but into innumerable specific varieties. In fact, each organism is essentially unique. Human "identical" twins differ in many ways; for example, their fingerprints are different. Even a pair of cloned organisms are sufficiently complex so that, during their creation, the stochasticism of the world can insinuate itself and change a molecule here or an organelle there and in this way produce two slightly different individuals. The complexity and the individuality of its particular items of study—that is, organisms—are certainly characteristic of the biological realm, but these features do not distinguish biology from physics or metallurgy or economics. Each of these disciplines faces items of study that have many interactive parts, with those parts forming unique wholes. What is it, then, that distinguishes biology from other sciences?

Ontogeny. Organisms are patterns of matter that are at once complex and individual, and the features that distinguish these patterns from other complex and individual patterns of the natural world are the two sequential processes that produce organisms; ontogeny and phylogeny.

Ontogeny is the history of a living entity from conception through birth to maturity and death, the laying out of all the stages in its transformation from an unspecialized embryonic form to a particular and idiomatic machine. Ontogenies come in all shapes and sizes. At one extreme, bacteria go through an ontogeny that is entirely internal: the transformations from a single parent cell to two daughter cells are a series of changes of molecules *inside* the cell. On the other hand, multicellular organisms, such as squid, butterflies, and people, begin as single fertile cells—zygotes—and transform into unified collections of millions of cells. The ontogeny of a multicellular organism is a cascade of intracellular, cellular, and extracellular changes that establish whole cities of specialized cells. During the ontogeny of a multicellular organism, interactive pockets of cells are geographically segregated into organs and tissues connected by highways of nerves and vessels. The construction of these cities is continuously dynamic, and it proceeds inexorably in a particular sequence, the characteristic ontogeny of that organism.

An ontogeny is stereotyped and highly reproducible. It is like a phonograph record; when conception sets the needle in the first groove (and given that the basic machinery has an appropriate supply of energy), it plays out the full music of a life. Random dust will always change the notes a bit along the way. Sometimes the environment intervenes to turn the volume up or down. Occasionally, the needle gets caught by a scratch and falls into the endless loops of a cancer. Usually, however, a scratch or even a jarring of the turntable causes only a skip in the sequence as the needle falls into a different groove and proceeds once again resolutely on its inevitable path.

Ontogenies are dogged things, and organisms are those highly complex patterns produced by ontogenies. It is ontogeny—the repeated generation of stereotyped yet complex patterns—that first sets the biological realm apart from the other spheres of natural science.

Phylogeny

This is the book of the generations of Adam. . . . And Adam lived an hundred and thirty years, and begat a son in his own likeness, after his image; and

called his name Seth. . . . And Seth lived an hundred and five years and begat
Enos. . . . And Enos lived ninety years and begat Cainan. . . . And Cainan
lived seventy years and begat Mahalaleel. . . . And Lamech lived an hundred
eighty and two years and begat a son: and he called his name Noah . . . and
Noah was five hundred years old: and Noah begat Shem, Ham, and Japheth.
—GENESIS, Chapter 5

Generation after generation, organisms beget like organisms. This is
phylogeny, the ancestral lineages of organisms. Ontogenies are the life
histories of individual organisms, and phylogenies are the repeated un-
foldings of ontogenies. Our ancestors are our phylogeny.

Biological time is different from physical time, and the biological clock
of phylogenies ticks in generations. In one hundred years, a human
phylogeny contains five generations, a buttercup phylogeny one hundred
generations, a fruit fly phylogeny 2,500 generations, and a bacterial
phylogeny can contain 2.5 million generations.

A human phylogeny of five generations is, on the whole, a very short
time, and it represents an almost unchanging set of transformations. The
striking similarities between ancestors and descendants transcend a
handful of generations—how often have we heard: "He certainly reminds me of his grandfather." Those differences that do show up during a
few generations are really rather subtle, and each child is inordinately
more like his parents than he is different from them. A few generations of
phylogeny is a biologically stable time interval, but a million or ten
million generations is quite another story.

In the course of millions of generations, the difference between members of a phylogeny can become so marked that we say the original
organism has evolved into a new organism. "Evolution" means
"change," and long phylogenies tend to change. If traced back into the
dim reaches of time, the human phylogeny contains all manner of different creatures: apes, small bright-eyed mammals, dog-sized sharp-toothed
reptiles, flat snub-nosed amphibians, and even fish. If we take a patient
astronomical view, we can see clearly that we have evolved from our
ancestors. Phylogenies slowly evolve, and evolving phylogenies characterize the biological realm.

One distinguishing characteristic of the province of biology is ontogeny, the recurrent stereotyped re-creation of a very complex pattern.
The other distinguishing characteristic of the biological realm is phylogeny, the ancestral lineage of these ontogenies. While an ontogeny is a
relatively stable sequence, a phylogeny is a slowly evolving sequence of
ontogenies. When we ask what is impossible in biology—in biology
specifically, above and beyond physics and chemistry, besides psychology and economics, separate from mathematics and the arts—we are
asking what is impossible in ontogeny and in phylogeny.

The Richness of Natural Ontogenies and Phylogenies

If there is a constant in biology, it is its exuberant variety. A major contributor to this rich unpredictability of living things is unnecessary complexity: biological systems often contain more machinery than is necessary to make them work properly. Excess complexities permeate life. At the molecular level, there is the DNA that does not code for any proteins—noncoding DNA can outnumber coding DNA a hundredfold in some cells. Then, there are the "futile metabolic cycles" in cells, circular chemical reactions that go back and forth producing and unproducing the same molecules and depleting energy stores to no apparent purpose.

Another example of unnecessary complexity is the blood-clotting cascade. When you cut your finger, blood proteins immediately begin to clump together, the wound is soon dammed up, and the cut stops bleeding within five to ten minutes. To staunch the blood flow, the initial injury sets off a waterfall of from eight to thirteen separate chemical reactions in two chains, with each chemical transformation giving rise to the next in an orderly sequence. At least thirteen different proteins— coagulation factors—form the normal clotting cascades in humans, and if one of these factors is missing the person can have a bleeding disorder such as hemophilia.

The complete blood-clotting cascade is quite complex, and a theoretical biologist would be hard-pressed to predict its actual details from a priori considerations, from first principles, or from the requirements of blood-clotting systems. One of the factors—Hageman Factor or Factor XII—even appears to be unnecessary. Those people who, through genetic disorders, develop without any Factor XII do not have bleeding problems; and whales, dolphins, and porpoises, all of which survive injuries quite normally, do not have any Factor XII.

Complex and elusive intricacies also characterize the tissue level of biological organization. Consider the corpus callosum, one of the largest bundles of axons in the human brain. Although it interconnects most areas of the cerebral hemispheres, its function is so subtle that for years no one understood exactly what it does. The five out of a thousand individuals born without a corpus callosum cannot normally be distinguished from those with one. The corpus callosum is found only in placental mammals: other mammals (such as opossums and kangaroos) and all nonmammals live quite happily without it. Only through an ingenious series of psychological experiments did Roger Sperry finally show how the two halves of the brain normally use the corpus callosum as their most intimate route of self-communication.

From his desk, the theoretical biologist could not determine the role of the corpus callosum with certainty, and he could not predict its appearance or its use in those animals that have acquired one during the last 200 million years. Who could have imagined that the human brain contains two separate minds, a right mind and a left mind, each localized in one of the major cerebral hemispheres? Normally, the two minds are in such close touch that they think alike, they trade thoughts instantaneously, they share the same sensations and emotions, and they act as one. All this intimacy flows through the corpus callosum, and the intercommunication is smooth and efficient. At the same time, each separate brain is a powerful and complete mind. Amazingly, without a corpus callosum, the nervous system still functions as a smooth and efficient unit—one brain, to almost all outward appearance. Normally two brains make each human, and two brains are a wonderful but unnecessary complexity.

The corpus callosum is not a necessity, but is it just a frill? Two minds are not a necessity, but is the second one a frill? Such questions, with words like "frill" or even "necessity," are slightly askew. They are difficult to answer because they are built from peculiarly human judgments. As Richard Bentley[1] wrote (in the late seventeenth century):

> All pulchritude is relative. . . . We ought not . . . to believe that the banks of the ocean are really deformed, because they have not the form of a regular bulwark; nor that the mountains are out of shape, because they are not exact pyramids or cones; nor that the stars are unskillfully placed, because they are not situated at uniform distance. These are not natural irregularities, but with respect to our fancies only; nor are they incommodious to the true uses of life and the designs of man's being on earth.

Nature need not adhere to human standards, and she need not follow human principles. Nature does as she does, and we can only be secure in our science when we act as natural historians, conscientiously describing the natural record retrospectively. We walk a precipitous course when we attempt a priori evaluations based on anthropocentric standards.

Ontogenies and phylogenies are not limited to the simplest or the most efficient paths. In the natural realm, organisms are not built by engineers who, with an overall plan in mind, use only the most appropriate materials, the most effective design, and the most reliable construction techniques. Instead, organisms are patchworks containing appendixes, uvulas, earlobes, dewclaws, adenoids, warts, eyebrows, underarm hair, wisdom teeth, and toenails. They are a meld of ancestral parts integrated step by step during their development through a set of tried and true ontogenetic mechanisms. These mechanisms ensure matching between disparate elements such as nerves and muscles, but they have no overall vision. Natural ontogenies and natural phylogenies are not limited by

1. Richard Bentley: English clergyman, classical scholar, and critic (1662–1742).

principles of parsimony,[2] and they have no teleology.[3] Possible organisms can be overdetermined, unnecessarily complex, or inefficiently designed.

Many Roads

Two roads diverged in a yellow wood,
And sorry I could not travel both
And be one traveler, long I stood
And looked down one as far as I could
To where it bent in the undergrowth;

Then took the other, as just as fair,
And having perhaps the better claim,
Because it was grassy and wanted wear;
Though as for that the passing there
Had worn them really about the same. . . .

—ROBERT FROST

The constraints in building organisms are usually insufficient to limit Nature to only one blueprint, and a wide range of alternate constructions have evolved. There is no one "right" way to build an eye. The octopus and the human both have eyes that appear quite similar, but the human eye is built exactly inside out when compared to the [eye of the] octopus. In an octopus, light passing through the lens falls directly on the photoreceptors, while in a person, light must travel through many layers of cells and axons before reaching the photoreceptors, which are themselves pointing the wrong way—that is, toward the back of the eye. Likewise, Nature has used a number of radically different designs for building wings: bat wings, for instance, are modified hands, while insect wings are entirely separate appendages.

Even molecules themselves can have architectural latitude. Although certain parts of a biological molecule are fairly immutable, there is often no one right overall molecule. For instance, insulin is an essential protein hormone that is built of about fifty subunits (amino acids). Three to five of these subunits differ between the insulin molecules of pigs, cows, and humans. Nonetheless, the insulins from pigs and cows are perfectly acceptable substitutes for human insulin, and both pig and cow insulin are commonly used to treat human diabetes.

In terms of many roads, the capricious courses of phylogenies are most

2. Occam's razor, a principle formulated by the English philosopher William of Occam or Ockham (?1300–?49) maintaining that entities should not be multiplied unnecessarily —i.e., that the simplest of competing theories should be preferred to more complex ones and that explanations of unknown phenomena should be sought in the known.
3. Explanation of nature or natural processes that can be attributed to design or purpose.

telling. Evolution has followed the exigencies of the times under the whims of chance and the accidents of history. Had the continents not drifted apart, Australian fauna and flora would undoubtedly be less peculiar—Australia would probably have had indigenous hoofed animals and indigenous apes, animal groups that never developed on that island. Had Alexander Fleming not discovered penicillin, penicillin-resistant bacteria would be a freakish oddity rather than ubiquitous inhabitants of our planet. Extant organisms are legacies of habits acquired by their ancestors, but these habits coalesced from a plethora of possibilities.

What Nature Cannot Do in Ontogeny and Phylogeny

I am Rose my eyes are blue
I am Rose and who are you
I am Rose and when I sing
I am Rose like anything

—GERTRUDE STEIN

Science fiction comes in two varieties. On one hand are the tales that explore worlds harboring phenomena that scientists think are impossible. These stories ask the questions of dreams: How would people spend their evenings if everyone had a perpetual motion machine in the basement? How soon would you get bored if you lived forever?

Then there are those tales that explore worlds that just might exist. They ask the questions of science: In what language could we talk to an extraterrestrial creature? What could we do with self-reproducing automata? What will people do when the sun goes out?

The standard science fiction of biology certainly falls into both of these categories, but which biological tall tales are the stories of dreams and which the stories of science?

Consider, for a moment, the mushroom—"the elf of plants," Emily Dickinson called it. Actually mushrooms are only distantly related to plants. They are many-celled fungi, relatively advanced organisms with cell walls but with no ability to manufacture their own food (e.g., no photosynthetic machinery), no ability to move, and no nervous system. We are all aware that many animals are fungivorous, but it took science fiction to popularize the idea that mushrooms could be carnivorous. In *The Wonderful Flight to the Mushroom Planet*, for instance, Eleanor Cameron invented the mushroom people of the mysterious planet Basidium-X, who must eat chicken eggs to remain healthy. The stories of dreams? Surprisingly not. Carnivorous mushrooms actually exist here on earth: certain species of woodland toadstools trap and eat worms—and from worms it may be only a small step to chickens. Carnivorous mushrooms, once in the realm of science fiction, are now unequivocally science fact.

Or, consider the square organism, once a creature confined to E. A. Abbott's *Flatland*, where all "Professional Men and Gentlemen are Squares." Today, the square organism has found a home on our well-worn earth, swimming in the brine pools of the Middle East. There tiny, flat, transparent bacteria in the form of thin square sheets float like ghostly salt crystals, mimicking the perfect planar polygons and belying the notion that—to reduce their surface-to-volume ratios—cells must be spheres.

Carnivorous mushrooms and square bacteria bring a smile to the biologist, but they do not stretch the bounds of biology because they can be explained by mechanisms that sit somewhere on Nature's cluttered shelf of standard organismic machinery. True, the biologist may have to hunt around a bit among the everyday mitochondria,[4] the familiar Krebs cycles, and the mundane cyclic AMPs to retrieve all of the appropriate mechanisms. He will certainly have to spend some time in serious study to find how these mechanisms have been stuck together in each of their peculiar combinations. Nonetheless, somewhere in a corner of her cupboard Nature is sure to have just the right bits and pieces to construct these natural oddities.

Nature regularly builds baby carnivorous mushrooms from spores of parent carnivorous mushrooms and replicates daughter square bacteria from parent square bacteria, and Nature derived the parent carnivorous mushrooms from other preexisting mushrooms and the parent square bacteria from other preexisting bacteria. Strange as they are, carnivorous mushrooms and square bacteria—the incarnations of biological tall tales —are neither ontogenetically nor phylogenetically impossible.

Angels, on the other hand, are somewhat different. Although they adorn the spiritual world, our natural world has no angels. Why is this? While it is not absolutely impossible, it is nonetheless difficult for Nature to construct an angel from an extant phylogeny. Besides the arms and legs of a human, an angel has a set of wings along its back. Wings are complex structures sculpted of muscles, bones, and nerves; and angels' wings are covered with feathers. To introduce wings or any other complex appendage into an existing organismal lineage, Nature needs the appropriate raw materials and organizational blueprint—preexisting structures that can be transformed—because complex biological forms

---

4. "Mitochondria": various round or long cellular organelles found outside the nucleus that produce energy for the cell through cellular respiration; "Krebs cycles": sequences of reactions in the living organism in which oxidation of acetic acid or an acetyl equivalent provides energy for storage in phosphate bonds; "AMPs": mononucleotides of adenine originally isolated from mammalian muscle that are reversibly convertible to ADP and ATP in metabolic reactions.

cannot be created ex *nihilo*.[5]

For angels' wings, the preexisting structures are simply not available. The wings of the natural extant flying vertebrates—the birds and bats—are direct modifications of preexisting front limbs. The muscles, bones, and nerves were already there in ancestral organisms, and Nature proceeded to evolve wings by stretching, shrinking, folding, and bending those elements. Furthermore, through all of the transmogrifications, the overall organization of the front limb has remained the same during evolution. For example, the upper limb always has a single long bone, the humerus, and the lower limb always has a pair of parallel long bones, the radius and the ulna.

The back of a mammal has no structures that can be stretched or shrunk, folded or bent into a wing. To make an angel, the ground plan of the existing elements must be tampered with and new structures must be generated without precedent. This Nature cannot easily do.

Angels are probably destined to remain spiritual, and winged horses like Pegasus are likely to be forever myths; but biologists do not consider them impossible. Instead, they are put into another realm: they are highly improbable biological phenomena. Improbable biological phenomena cannot easily be pieced together by Nature from any of the mechanisms in her crowded cupboard of organismic machinery. Without the coincidence of a number of highly improbable events, Nature cannot generate a winged horse or an angel in an existing phylogeny.

What a Biologist Cannot Do

He said "I look for butterflies
That sleep among the wheat;
I make them into mutton pies,
And sell them in the street.
I sell them unto men," he said
"Who sail on stormy seas;
And that's the way I get my bread—
A trifle, if you please."

—LEWIS CARROLL

With the development of his complex and specialized brain, man has taken a place beside Nature as a biological creator. Nature creates through ontogenies and phylogenies, but man is an engineer and can construct biological forms from other beginnings and through other ad hoc processes. Man is not limited to the natural routes of creation, and in the laboratory he can generate biological phenomena that would be

5. Out of nothing.

highly improbable in nature.

A protein, an organelle, a cell, a tissue, an organism—each is made of a great many different parts, and in each case these parts are organized in a particular and characteristic design. The many parts and unique designs are found at every level—we see them whether we look at an elephant from a distance or we examine its gall bladder under a microscope. These biological items are truly complex in all ways. Not only are they composed of many different parts interrelated in unique designs, their fabrication is complex. In most cases, the parts of a biological item will not fully self-assemble. You cannot shake a beaker of salts and amino acids and make insulin, and you cannot stir a soup of cells and make a mouse. To build a protein or an animal, one must carefully put all of the parts together in their single proper order. One must impose detailed external information—templets—on the raw materials.

Biological items form only a small subset of all the possible items that one might construct from the same raw materials. This means that, as an architect, the biologist cannot merely choose the right bricks and mortar, but he must also draw up the right plan and then contrive to interweave the building blocks into just the right design. This is a difficult set of tasks. Often the parts are tiny and cannot be easily moved about or stored by themselves, isolated from their natural settings. Moreover, gluing these tiny parts together in such a way as to create the proper order at all levels, from macroscopic to microscopic to molecular, takes extreme patience, steady hands, X-ray vision, and highly specialized, Rube Goldberg contraptions.[6]

In the face of these problems, biologists have been undauntedly optimistic, twiddling and fiddling, tinkering with bones and nerves, gingerly reconstructing hormones, and rearranging genes. The job of building a biological item entirely from scratch is usually too overwhelming to be practical. The fabrication of a biological item from extant biological scraps, however, and the sculpting of new biological items from preexisting ones, these have become everyday operations in the laboratory. In baby newts, embryonic eyes are transplanted to tail buds, where they eventually mature and send out nerves. The adult newts, three-eyed oddities [such as Nature has never seen,] swim in laboratory aquaria with two eyes fore and one aft. In embryonic chicks, extra limb buds are grafted alongside the normal ones; later, the adult chickens run through the laboratory flailing supernumerary appendages. Mouse and human cells are fused to form hybrid mammalian cells, biological items never found in nature but powerful tools for mapping human chromosomes. Copies of human insulin genes are inserted into yeast or bacterial cells, and these tiny and primitive creatures, as different from us as any orga-

6. Devices invented by the American cartoonist Reuben L. Goldberg that accomplish simple tasks by complex means.

nisms on earth, will now manufacture human proteins. In the lab, the biologist is busily creating highly improbable biological phenomena.

Building Ontogenies and Phylogenies

Given the range, the power, and the detailed precision of modern technologies, is there anything that the biologist cannot do within the bounds of the physical constraints of the universe? Today's biologists have the faith that it is possible to construct almost any biological item from precursor materials.

A gene, a protein, a cell, a tissue, an organism—these all seem to be in the realm of possibility. It may not always be practical to create these items from the most elemental materials. Nonetheless, new genes can be manufactured by mutating and rearranging existing genes, and short proteins can be made to order from their constituent amino acids. Primal protocells can be formed in appropriate man-made molecular soups, and new and complex cell types can be pieced together by fusing whole cells or combining parts of cells. New tissues can be designed by growing cells on artificial templets. New organisms can be constructed by mutations, by genetic engineering, and by embryonic reconstructions such as grafts and transplants.

Biologists can build improbable biological items in the laboratory, but the hallmarks of the biological realm are more than individual biological items. Life is not a DNA molecule or a nerve cell or a kumquat or a wolf spider. Life is a special set of sequences; it is the autonomous and recurrent stereotyped re-creation of certain very complex patterns. Life is a child growing and becoming a mother and eventually a grandmother. Can the biologist create new grandmothers, that is, can he generate ontogenies and phylogenies never before seen in nature?

The answer is yes, although the new ontogenies and phylogenies take advantage of natural cascades of developmental events that are normally found in preexisting ontogenies. To begin, the biologist makes an improbable change in some developmental event; for example, he grafts a frog eye primordium into the side of a newt embryo. In nature, the two sets of tissues would never interact, but in the laboratory the hybrid organism undergoes an ontogeny. The frog cells form an eye and send an optic nerve into the newt nervous system; concurrently, the newt skin cells form a lens and the newt nervous system accommodates the aberrant nerves. Frog cells integrate with newt cells, newt cells mesh with frog cells, and the strange three-eyed chimera that develops unfolds through a truly new ontogeny.

Similarly, new phylogenies—ancestral lineages never before seen in nature—take advantage of natural cascades of ontogenies that are normally found in preexisting phylogenies. Here, the biologist makes an improbable change in the stuff of inheritance; for example, he grafts a sequence of human DNA into the DNA of a bacterium. In nature, the two sets of genes would never interact, but in the laboratory the hybrid bacterium divides and quickly becomes a grandmother. All of her children and grandchildren will manufacture certain human proteins, and a truly new phylogeny has been founded.

Such ontogenies and phylogenies are new, but they are not unnatural. Once triggered, they unfold spontaneously and thereby enter the natural realm, producing surprising wonders like three-eyed frog-newts and insulin-secreting germs or carnivorous mushrooms and square bacteria. Man-made ontogenies and phylogenies are autonomous and recurrent stereotyped re-creations of certain very complex patterns, just as are naturally initiated ontogenies and phylogenies. In the laboratory, it is only the initiating event that may have been "unnatural."

When the biologist founds a new ontogeny or phylogeny, he can, of course, understand the initial improbable event. Many times, he can also understand the initial event when Nature founds a new ontogeny or phylogeny. But in nature initial events can sometimes remain arcane. As Dr. Seuss wrote in *The 500 Hats of Bartholomew Cubbins*:

> But neither Bartholomew Cubbins, nor King Derwin himself, nor anyone else in the Kingdom of Didd could ever explain how the strange thing had happened. They could only say it just "happened to happen" and was not very likely to happen again.

In the province of biology, buttermilk-thick with life and under the patience of millions of generations, Nature sometimes stumbles on the extremely improbable, and arcane initial events can indeed be quite natural. They just "happen to happen" and are "not very likely to happen again." Moreover, when they happen in a natural ontogeny or phylogeny, arcane events can trigger sequences that are as natural as apples. It is the initiating event in the generation of an angel that would undoubtedly be arcane, but the autonomous development of an angel from a tiny wisp of an angelic embryo or the spontaneous unfolding of a lineage of angels, once set on their way, become natural phenomena no more impossible than the development of an oak from an acorn or the spontaneous unfolding of the ancestral lineage of the great Bach family.[7]

Biological Possibilities

What is an impossibility? I think that for the biological realm, the requirements are rather special. Not only must we be able to write science fiction about it, we must also be able to imagine it as a part of a

---

7. A German family of musicians and composers, the most famous of whom was Johann Sebastian Bach (1685–1750).

natural ontogeny and phylogeny. Truly biological entities are always enmeshed in a developmental and an evolutionary sequence: they are dynamic, they have a lifespan, they have ancestors, and they beget progeny. In this way, a biological impossibility would be something—be it an organelle, a cell, or a creature—that we could imagine in an ontogeny or in a phylogeny but that cannot ever exist in the real world.

Physically impossible organisms, such as hedgehogs that can run faster than the speed of light and perpetual motion bees, can be dreamt by the physicist, but I cannot easily imagine a biologically impossible organism. When we have eliminated the physically impossible, when we remain within the constraints set by the physical limits of the universe, whatever remains—no matter how improbable—must be considered biologically possible. With the biologist as creator, the improbable has ofttimes become probable. But, Nature herself is wild and rich and her splendor is unconstrained. Afternoons poking about the Woods Hole seashore among the horseshoe crabs, the seaweed, and the tunicates or munching blue-eyed scallops and beach peas on a rocky island in Penobscot Bay or chipping ornate brachiopods from the shale of the Chagrin River make me hesitate to think that I could ever dream of a creature that might not creep out from among the cattails one windy spring morning.

1985

Konrad Z. Lorenz

THE TAMING OF THE SHREW

Though Nature, red in tooth and claw,
With ravine, shrieked against his creed.
TENNYSON, *In Memoriam*

All shrews are particularly difficult to keep; this is not because, as we are led proverbially to believe, they are hard to tame, but because the metabolism of these smallest of mammals is so very fast that they will die of hunger within two or three hours if the food supply fails. Since they feed exclusively on small, living animals, mostly insects, and demand, of these, considerably more than their own weight every day, they are most exacting charges. At the time of which I am writing, I had never succeeded in keeping any of the terrestrial shrews alive for any length of time; most of those that I happened to obtain had probably only been caught because they were already ill and they died almost at once. I had never succeeded in procuring a healthy specimen. Now the order Insectivora is very low in the genealogical hierarchy of mammals and is, therefore, of particular interest to the comparative ethologist. Of the whole group, there was only one representative with whose behavior I was tolerably familiar, namely the hedgehog, an extremely interesting animal of whose ethology Professor Herter of Berlin has made a very thorough study. Of the behavior of all other members of the family practically nothing is known. Since they are nocturnal and partly subterranean animals, it is nearly impossible to approach them in field observation, and the difficulty of keeping them in captivity had hitherto precluded their study in the laboratory. So the Insectivores were officially placed on my program.

First I tried to keep the common mole. It was easy to procure a healthy specimen, caught to order in the nursery gardens of my father-in-law, and I found no difficulty in keeping it alive. Immediately on its arrival, it devoured an almost incredible quantity of earthworms which, from the very first moment, it took from my hand. But, as an object of behavior study, it proved most disappointing. Certainly, it was interesting to watch its method of disappearing in the space of a few seconds under the surface of the ground, to study its astoundingly efficient use of its strong, spadeshaped fore-paws, and to feel their amazing strength when one held the little beast in one's hand. And again, it was remarkable with what surprising exactitude it located, by smell, from underground, the earthworms which I put on the surface of the soil in its terrarium. But these observations were the only benefits I derived from it. It never became any tamer and it never remained above ground any longer than it took to devour its prey; after this, it sank into the earth as a submarine sinks into the water. I soon grew tired of procuring the immense quantities of living food it required and, after a few weeks, I set it free in the garden.

It was years afterwards, on an excursion to that extraordinary lake, the Neusiedlersee, which lies on the Hungarian border of Austria, that I again thought of keeping an insectivore. This large stretch of water, though not thirty miles from Vienna, is an example of the peculiar type of lake found in the open steppes of Eastern Europe and Asia. More than thirty miles long and half as broad, its deepest parts are only about five feet deep and it is much shallower on the average. Nearly half its surface is overgrown with reeds which form an ideal habitat for all kinds of water birds. Great colonies of white, purple, and grey heron and spoonbills live among the reeds and, until a short while ago, glossy ibis were still to be found here. Greylag geese breed here in great numbers and, on the eastern, reedless shore, avocets and many other rare waders can regularly be found. On the occasion of which I am speaking, we, a dozen tired zoologists, under the experienced guidance of my friend Otto Koenig, were wending our way, slowly and painfully, through the forest of reeds. We were walking in single file, Koenig first, I second, with a few students in our wake. We literally left a wake, an inky-black one in pale grey water. In the reed forests of Lake Neusiedel, you walk knee deep in slimy, black ooze, wonderfully perfumed by sulphureted-hydrogen-producing bacteria. This mud clings tenaciously and only releases its hold on your foot with a loud, protesting plop at every step.

After a few hours of this kind of wading you discover aching muscles whose very existence you had never suspected. From the knees to the hips you are immersed in the milky, clay-colored water characteristic of the lake, which, among the reeds, is populated by myriads of extremely hungry leeches conforming to the old pharmaceutical recipe, *"Hirudines medicinales maxime affamati."*[1] The rest of your person inhabits the upper air, which here consists of clouds of tiny mosquitoes whose blood-thirsty attacks are all the more exasperating because you require both your hands to part the dense reeds in front of you and can only slap your face at intervals. The British ornithologist who may perhaps have envied us some of our rare specimens will perceive that bird watching on Lake Neusiedel is not, after all, an entirely enviable occupation.

We were thus wending our painful way through the rushes when suddenly Koenig stopped and pointed mutely towards a pond, free from reeds, that stretched in front of us. At first, I could only see whitish water, dark blue sky and green reeds, the standard colors of Lake Neusiedel. Then, suddenly, like a cork popping up on to the surface, there appeared, in the middle of the pool, a tiny black animal, hardly bigger than a man's thumb. And for a moment I was in the rare position of a zoologist who sees a specimen and is not able to classify it, in the literal sense of the word: I did not know to which class of vertebrates the object of my gaze belonged. For the first fraction of a second I took it for the young of some diving bird of a species unknown to me. It appeared to have a beak and it swam on the water like a bird, not in it as a mammal. It swam about in narrow curves and circles, very much like a whirligig beetle, creating an extensive wedge-shaped wake, quite out of proportion to the tiny animal's size. Then a second little beast popped up from below, chased the first one with a shrill, bat-like twitter, then both dived and were gone. The whole episode had not lasted five seconds.

I stood open-mouthed, my mind racing. Koenig turned round with a broad grin, calmly detached a leech that was sticking like a leech to his wrist, wiped away the trickle of blood from the wound, slapped his cheek, thereby killing thirty-five mosquitoes, and asked, in the tone of an examiner, "What was that?" I answered as calmly as I could, "water shrews," thanking, in my heart, the leech and the mosquitoes for the respite they had given me to collect my thoughts. But my mind was racing on: water shrews ate fishes and frogs which were easy to procure in any quantity;

1. "In medicine, the hungriest leech is best." Until modern times, patients were bled as a remedy for various ills, and doctors kept live leeches for the purpose.

water shrews were less subterranean than most other insectivores; they were the very insectivore to keep in captivity. "That's an animal I must catch and keep," I said to my friend. "That is easy," he responded. "There is a nest with young under the floor mat of my tent." I had slept that night in his tent and Koenig had not thought it worth-while to tell me of the shrews; such things are, to him, as much a matter of course as wild little spotted crakes feeding out of his hand, or as any other wonders of his queer kingdom in the reeds.

On our return to the tent that evening, he showed me the nest. It contained eight young which, compared with their mother, who rushed away as we lifted the mat, were of enormous size. They were considerably more than half her length and must each have weighed well between a fourth and a third of their dam: that is to say, the whole litter weighed, at a very modest estimate, twice as much as the old shrew. Yet they were still quite blind and the tips of their teeth were only just visible in their rosy mouths. And two days later when I took them under my care, they were still quite unable to eat even the soft abdomens of grasshoppers, and in spite of evident greed, they chewed interminably on a soft piece of frog's meat without succeeding in detaching a morsel from it. On our journey home, I fed them on the squeezed-out insides of grasshoppers and finely minced frog's meat, a diet on which they obviously throve. Arrived home in Altenberg, I improved on this diet by preparing a food from the squeezed-out insides of mealworm larvae, with some finely chopped small, fresh fishes, worked into a sort of gravy with a little milk. They consumed large quantities of this food, and their little nest-box looked quite small in comparison with the big china bowl whose contents they emptied three times a day. All these observations raise the problem of how the female water shrew succeeds in feeding her gigantic litter. It is absolutely impossible that she should do so on milk alone. Even on a more concentrated diet my young shrews devoured the equivalent of their own weight daily and this meant nearly twice the weight of a grown shrew. Yet, at that time of their lives, young shrews could not possibly engulf a frog or a fish brought whole to them by their mother, as my charges indisputably proved. I can only think that the mother feeds her young by regurgitation of chewed food. Even thus, it is little short of miraculous that the adult female should be able to obtain enough meat to sustain herself and her voracious progeny.

When I brought them home, my young watershrews were still blind. They had not suffered from the journey and were as sleek and fat as one could wish. Their black, glossy coats were reminiscent of moles, but the white color of their underside, as well as the round, streamlined contours of their bodies, reminded me distinctly of penguins, and not, indeed, without justification: both the streamlined form and the light underside are adaptations to a life in the water. Many free-swimming animals, mammals, birds, amphibians and fishes, are silvery-white below in order to be invisible to enemies swimming in the depths. Seen from below, the shining white belly blends perfectly with the reflecting surface film of the water. It is very characteristic of these water animals that the dark dorsal and the white ventral colors do not merge gradually into each other as is the case in "counter-shaded" land animals whose coloring is calculated to make them invisible by eliminating the contrasting shade on their undersides. As in the killer whale, in dolphins, and in penguins, the white underside of the watershrew is divided from the dark upper side by a sharp line which runs, often in very decorative curves, along the animal's flank. Curiously enough, this borderline between black and white showed considerable variations in individuals and even on both sides of one animal's body. I welcomed this, since it enabled me to recognize my shrews personally.

Three days after their arrival in Altenberg my eight shrew babies opened their eyes and began, very cautiously, to explore the precincts of their nest-box. It was now time to remove them to an appropriate container, and on this question I expended much hard thinking. The enormous quantity of food they consumed and, consequently, of excrement they produced, made it impossible to keep them in an ordinary aquarium whose water, within a day, would have become a stinking brew. Adequate sanitation was imperative for particular reasons; in ducks, grebes, and all waterfowl, the plumage must be kept perfectly dry if the animal is to remain in a state of health, and the same premise may reasonably be expected to hold good of the shrew's fur. Now water which has been polluted soon turns strongly alkaline and this I knew to be very bad for the plumage of waterbirds. It causes saponification of the fat to which the feathers owe their waterproof quality, and the bird becomes thoroughly wet and is unable to stay on the water. I hold the record, as far as I know hitherto unbroken by any other birdlover, for having kept dabchicks alive and healthy in captivity for nearly two years, and even then they did not die but escaped, and may still be living. My experience with these birds proved the absolute necessity of keeping the water perfectly clean: whenever it became a little dirty I noticed their feathers beginning to get wet, a danger which they anxiously tried to counteract by constantly preening themselves. I had, therefore, to keep these little grebes in crystal clear water which was changed every day, and I rightly assumed that the same would be necessary for my water shrews.

I took a large aquarium tank, rather over a yard in length and about two feet wide. At each end of this, I placed two little tables, and weighed them down with heavy stones so that they would not float. Then I filled up the tank until the water was level with the tops of the tables. I did not at first push the tables close against the panes of the tank, which was rather narrow, for fear that the shrews might become trapped underwater in the blind alley beneath a table and drown there; this precaution, however, subsequently proved unnecessary. The water shrew which, in its natural state, swims great distances under the ice, is quite able to find its way to the open surface in much more difficult situations. The nest-box, which was placed on one of the tables, was equipped with a sliding shutter, so that I could imprison the shrews whenever the container had to be cleaned. In the morning, at the hour of general cage-cleaning, the shrews were usually at home and asleep, so that the procedure caused them no appreciable disturbance. I will admit that I take great pride in devising, by creative imagination, suitable containers for animals of which nobody, myself included, has had any previous experience, and it was particularly gratifying that the contraption described above proved so satisfactory that I never had to alter even the minutest detail.

When first my baby shrews were liberated in this container they took a very long time to explore the top of the table on which their nest-box was standing. The water's edge seemed to exert a strong attraction; they approached it ever and again, smelled the surface and seemed to feel along it with the long, fine whiskers which surround their pointed snouts like a halo and represent not only their most important organ of touch but the most important of all their sensory organs. Like other aquatic mammals, the water shrew differs from the terrestrial members of its class in that its nose, the guiding organ of the average mammal, is of no use whatsoever in its underwater hunting. The water shrew's whiskers are actively mobile like the antennae of an insect or the fingers of a blind man.

Exactly as mice and many other small rodents would do under similar conditions, the shrews interrupted their careful exploration of their new surroundings every few minutes to dash wildly back into the safe cover of their nest-box. The survival value of this peculiar behavior is evident: the animal makes sure, from time to time that it has not lost its way and that it can, at a moment's notice, retreat to the one place it knows to be safe. It was a queer spectacle to see those podgy black figures slowly and carefully whiskering their way forward and, in the next second, with lightning speed, dash back to the nest-box. Queerly enough, they did not run straight through the little door, as one would have expected, but in their wild dash for safety they jumped, one and all, first onto the roof of the box and only then, whiskering along its edge, found the opening and slipped in with a half somersault, their back turned nearly vertically downward. After many repetitions of this maneuver, they were able to find the opening without feeling for it; they "knew" perfectly its whereabouts yet still persisted in the leap onto the roof. They jumped onto it and immediately vaulted in through the door, but they never, as long as they lived, found out that the leap and vault which had become their habit was really quite unnecessary and that they could have run in directly without this extraordinary detour. We shall hear more about this dominance of path habits in the water shrew presently.

It was only on the third day, when the shrews had become thoroughly acquainted with the geography of their little rectangular island, that the largest and most enterprising of them ventured into the water. As is so often the case with mammals, birds, reptiles, and fishes, it was the largest and most handsomely colored male which played the role of leader. First he sat on the edge of the water and thrust in the fore part of his body, at the same time frantically paddling with his forelegs but still clinging with his hind ones to the board. Then he slid in, but in the next moment took fright, scampered madly across the surface very much after the manner of a frightened duckling, and jumped out onto the board at the opposite end of the tank. There he sat, excitedly grooming his belly with one hind paw, exactly as coypus and beavers do. Soon he quieted down and sat still for a moment. Then he went to the water's edge a second time, hesitated for a moment, and plunged in; diving immediately, he swam ecstatically about underwater, swerving upward and downward again, running quickly along the bottom, and finally jumping out of the water at the same place as he had first entered it.

When I first saw a water shrew swimming I was most struck by a thing which I ought to have expected but did not: at the moment of diving, the little black and white beast appears to be made of silver. Like the plumage of ducks and grebes, but quite unlike the fur of most water mammals, such as seals, otters, beavers or coypus, the fur of the water shrew remains absolutely dry under water, that is to say, it retains a thick layer of air while the animal is below the surface. In the other mammals mentioned above, it is only the short, woolly undercoat that remains dry, the superficial hair tips becoming wet, wherefore the animal looks its natural color when underwater and is superficially wet when it emerges. I was already aware of the peculiar qualities of the waterpfoof fur of the shrew, and, had I given it a thought, I should have known that it would look, under water, exactly like the air-retaining fur on the underside of a water beetle or on the abdomen of a water spider. Nevertheless the wonderful, transparent silver coat of the shrew was, to me, one of those delicious surprises that nature has in store for her admirers.

Another surprising detail which I only noticed when I saw my shrews in the water was that they have a fringe of stiff, erectile hairs on the outer side of their fifth toes and on the underside of their tails. These form collapsible oars and a collapsible rudder. Folded and inconspicuous as long as the animal is on dry land, they unfold the moment it enters the water and broaden the effective surface of the propelling feet and of the steering tail by a considerable area.

Like penguins, the water shrews looked rather awkward and ungainly on dry land but were transformed into objects of elegance and grace on entering the water. As long as they walked, their strongly convex underside made them look pot-bellied and reminiscent of an old, overfed dachshund. But under water, the very same protruding belly balanced harmoniously the curve of their back and gave a beautifully symmetrical streamline which, together with their silver coating and the elegance of their movements, made them a sight of entrancing beauty.

When they had all become familiar with the water, their container was one of the chief attractions that our research station had to offer to any visiting naturalists or animal lovers. Unlike all other mammals of their size, the water shrews were largely diurnal and, except in the early hours of the morning, three or four of them were constantly on the scene. It was exceedingly interesting to watch their movements upon and under the water. Like the whirligig beetle, Gyrinus, they could turn in an extremely small radius without diminishing their speed, a faculty for which the large rudder surface of the tail with its fringe of erectile hairs is evidently essential. They had two different ways of diving, either by taking a little jump as grebes or coots do and working their way down at a steep angle, or by simply lowering their snout under the surface and paddling very fast till they reached "planing speed," thus working their way downward on the principle of the inclined plane—in other words, performing the converse movement of an ascending airplane. The water shrew must expend a large amount of energy in staying down since the air contained in its fur exerts a strong pull upwards. Unless it is paddling straight downwards, a thing it rarely does, it is forced to maintain a constant minimum speed, keeping its body at a slightly downward angle in order not to float to the surface. While swimming under water the shrew seems to flatten, broadening its body in a peculiar fashion, in order to present a better planing surface to the water. I never saw my shrews try to cling by their claws to any underwater objects, as the dipper is alleged to do. When they seemed to be running along the bottom, they were really swimming close above it, but perhaps the smooth gravel on the bottom of the tank was unsuitable for holding on to and it did not occur to me then to offer them a rougher surface. They were very playful when in the water and chased one another loudly twittering on the surface, or silently in the depths. Unlike any other mammal, but just like water birds, they could rest on the surface; this they used to do, rolling partly over and grooming themselves. Once out again, they instantly proceeded to clean their fur—one is almost tempted to say "preen" it, so similar was their behavior to that of ducks which have just left the water after a long swim.

Most interesting of all was their method of hunting under water. They came swimming along with an erratic course, darting a foot or so forward very swiftly in a straight line, then starting to gyrate in looped turns at reduced speed. While swimming straight and swiftly their whiskers were, as far as I could see, laid flat against their head, but while circling they were erect and bristled out in all directions, as they sought contact with some prey. I have no reason to believe that vision plays any part in the water shrew's hunting, except perhaps in the activation of its tactile search. My shrews may have noticed visually the presence of the live tadpoles or little fishes which I put in the tank, but in the actual hunting of its prey the animal is exclusively guided by its sense of touch, located in the wide-spreading whiskers on its snout. Certain small free-swimming species of catfish find their prey by exactly the same method. When these fishes swim fast and straight, the long feelers on their snout are depressed but, like the shrew's whiskers, are stiffly spread out when the fish becomes conscious of the proximity of potential prey; like the shrew, the fish then begins to gyrate blindly in order to establish contact with its prey. It may not even be necessary for the water shrew actually to touch its prey with one of its whiskers. Perhaps, at very close range, the water vibration caused by the movements of a small fish, a tadpole or a water insect is perceptible by those sensitive tactile organs. It is quite impossible to determine this question by mere observation, for the action is much too quick for the human eye. There is a quick turn and a snap and the shrew is already paddling shorewards with a wriggling creature in its maw.

In relation to its size, the water shrew is perhaps the most terrible predator of all vertebrate animals, and it can even vie with the invertebrates, including the murderous Dytiscus larva. It has been reported by A. E. Brehm that water shrews have killed fish more than sixty times heavier than themselves by biting out their eyes and brain. This happened only when the fish were confined in containers with no room for escape. The same story has been told to me by fishermen on Lake Neusiedel, who could not possibly have heard Brehm's report. I once offered to my shrews a large edible frog. I never did it again, nor could I bear to see out to its end the cruel scene that ensued. One of the shrews encountered the frog in the basin and instantly gave chase, repeatedly seizing hold of the creature's legs; although it was kicked off again it did not cease in its attack and finally, the frog, in desperation, jumped out of the water and onto one of the tables, where several shrews raced to the pursuer's assistance and buried their teeth in the legs and hindquarters of the wretched frog. And now, horribly, they began to eat the frog alive, beginning just where each one of them happened to have hold of it; the poor frog croaked heartrendingly, as the jaws of the shrews munched audibly in chorus. I need hardly be blamed for bringing this experiment to an abrupt and agitated end and putting the lacerated frog out of its misery. I never offered the shrews large prey again but only such as would be killed at the first bite or two. Nature can be very cruel indeed; it is not out of pity that most of the larger predatory animals kill their prey quickly. The lion has to finish off a big antelope or a buffalo very quickly indeed in order not to get hurt itself, for a beast of prey which has to hunt daily cannot afford to receive even a harmless scratch in effecting a kill; such scratches would soon add up to such an extent as to put the killer out of action. The same reason has forced the python and other large snakes to evolve a quick and really humane method of killing the well-armed mammals that are their natural prey. But where there is no danger of the victim doing damage to the killer, the latter shows no pity whatsoever. The hedgehog which, by virtue of its armor, is quite immune to the bite of a snake, regularly proceeds to eat it, beginning at the tail or in the middle of its body, and in the same way the water shrew treats its innocuous prey. But man should abstain from judging his innocently-cruel fellow creatures, for even if nature sometimes "shrieks against his creed," what pain does he himself not inflict upon the living creatures that he hunts for pleasure and not for food?

The mental qualities of the water shrew cannot be rated very high. They were quite tame and fearless of me and never tried to bite when I took them in my hand, nor did they ever try to evade it, but, like little tame rodents, they tried to dig their way out if I held them for too long in the hollow of my closed fist. Even when I took them out of their container and put them on a table or on the floor, they were by no means thrown into a panic but were quite ready to take food out of my hand and even tried actively to creep into it if they felt a longing for cover. When, in such an unwonted environment, they were shown their nest-box, they plainly showed that they knew it by sight and instantly made for it, and even pursued it with upraised heads if I moved the box along above them, just out of their reach. All in all, I really may pride myself that I have tamed the shrew, or at least one member of that family.

In their accustomed surroundings, my shrews proved to be very strict creatures of habit. I have already mentioned the remarkable conservatism with which they persevered in their unpractical way of entering their nest-box by climbing onto its roof and then vaulting, with a half turn, in through the door. Something more must be said about the unchanging tenacity with which these animals cling to their habits once they have formed them. In the water shrew, the path habits, in particular, are of a really amazing immutability; I hardly know another instance to which the saying, "As the twig is bent, so the tree is inclined," applies so literally.

In a territory unknown to it, the water shrew will never run fast except under pressure of extreme fear, and than it will run blindly along, bumping into objects and usually getting caught in a blind alley. But, unless the little animal is severely frightened, it moves in strange surroundings, only step by step, whiskering right and left all the time and following a path that is anything but straight. Its course is determined by a hundred fortuitous factors when it walks that way for the first time. But, after a few repetitions, it is evident that the shrew recognizes the locality in which it finds itself and that it repeats, with the utmost exactitude, the movements which it performed the previous time. At the same time, it is noticeable that the animal moves along much faster whenever it is repeating what it has already learned. When placed on a path which it has already traversed a few times, the shrew starts on its way slowly, carefully whiskering. Suddenly it finds known bearings, and now rushes forward a short distance, repeating exactly every step and turn which it executed on the last occasion. Then, when it comes to a spot where it ceases to know the way by heart, it is reduced to whiskering again and to feeling its way step by step. Soon, another burst of speed follows and the same thing is repeated, bursts of speed alternating with very show progress. In the beginning of this process of learning their way, the shrews move along at an extremely slow average rate and the little bursts of speed are few and far between. But gradually the little laps of the course which have been "learned by heart" and which can be covered quickly begin to increase in length as well as in number until they fuse and the whole course can be completed in a fast, unbroken rush.

Often, when such a path habit is almost completely formed, there still remains one particularly difficult place where the shrew always loses its bearings and has to resort to its senses of smell and touch, sniffing and whiskering vigorously to find out where the next reach of its path "joins on." Once the shrew is well settled in its path habits it is as strictly bound to them as a railway engine to its tracks and as unable to deviate from them by even a few centimeters. If it diverges from its path by so much as an inch, it is forced to stop abruptly, and laboriously regain its bearings. The same behavior can be caused experimentally by changing some small detail in the customary path of the animal. Any major alteration in the habitual path threw the shrews into complete confusion. One of their paths ran along the wall adjoining the wooden table opposite to that on which the nest box was situated. This table was weighted with two stones lying close to the panes of the tank, and the shrews, running along the wall, were accustomed to jump on and off the stones which lay right in their path. If I moved the stones out of the runway, placing both together in the middle of the table, the shrews would jump right up into the air in the place where the stone should have been; they came down with a jarring bump, were obviously disconcerted and started whiskering cautiously right and left, just as they behaved in an unknown environment. And then they did a most interesting thing: they went back the way they had come, carefully feeling their way until they had again got their bearings. Then, facing round again, they tried a second time with a rush and jumped and crashed down exactly as they had done a few seconds before. Only then did they seem to realize that the first fall had not been their own fault but was due to a change in the wonted pathway, and now they proceeded to explore the alteration, cautiously sniffing and bewhiskering the place where the stone ought to have been. This method of going back to the start, and trying again always reminded me of a small boy who, in reciting a poem, gets stuck and begins again at an earlier verse.

In rats, as in many small mammals, the process of forming a path habit, for instance in learning a maze, is very similar to that just described; but a rat is far more adaptable in its behavior and would not dream of trying to jump over a stone which was not there. The preponderance of motor habit over present perception is a most remarkable peculiarity of the water shrew. One might say that the animal actually disbelieves its senses if they report a change of environment which necessitates a sudden alteration in its motor habits. In a new environment a water shrew would be perfectly able to see a stone of that size and consequently to avoid it or to run over it in a manner well adapted to the spatial conditions; but once a habit is formed and has become ingrained, it supersedes all better knowledge. I know of no animal that is a slave to its habits in so literal a sense as the water shrew. For this animal the geometric axiom that a straight line is the shortest distance between two points simply does not hold good. To them, the shortest line is always the accustomed path and, to a certain extent, they are justified in adhering to this principle: they run with amazing speed along their pathways and arrive at their destination much sooner than they would if, by whiskering and nosing, they tried to go straight. They will keep to the wonted path, even though it winds in such a way that it crosses and recrosses itself. A rat or mouse would be quick to discover that it was making an unnecessary detour, but the water shrew is no more able to do so than is a toy train to turn off at right angles at a level crossing. In order to change its route, the water shrew must change its whole path habit, and this cannot be done at a moment's notice but gradually, over a long period of time. An unnecessary, loop-shaped detour takes weeks and weeks to become a little shorter, and after months it is not even approximately straight. The biological advantage of such a path habit is obvious: it compensates the shrew for being nearly blind and enables it to run exceedingly fast without wasting a minute on orientation. On the other hand it may, under unusual circumstances, lead the shrew to destruction. It has been reported, quite plausibly, that water shrews have broken their necks by jumping into a pond which had been recently drained. In spite of the possibility of such mishaps, it would be shortsighted if one were simply to stigmatize the water shrew as stupid because it solves the spatial problems of its daily life in quite a different way from man. On the contrary, if one thinks a little more deeply, it is very wonderful that the same result, namely a perfect orientation in space, can be brought about in two so widely divergent ways: by true observation, as we achieve it, or, as the water shrew does, by learning by heart every possible spatial contingency that may arise in a given territory.

Among themselves, my water shrews were surprisingly good-natured. Although, in their play, they would often chase each other, twittering with a great show of excitement, I never saw a serious fight between them until an unfortunate accident occurred: one morning, I forgot to reopen the little door of the nest-box after cleaning out their tank. When at last I remembered, three hours had elapsed—a very long time for the swift metabolism of such small insectivores. Upon the opening of the door, all the shrews rushed out and made a dash for the food tray. In their haste to get out, not only did they soil themselves all over but they apparently discharged, in their excitement, some sort of glandular secretion, for a strong, musk-like odor accompanied their exit from the box. Since they appeared to have incurred no damage by their three hours' fasting, I turned away from the box to occupy myself with other things. However, on nearing the container soon afterwards, I heard an unusually loud, sharp twittering and, on my hurried approach, found my eight shrews locked in deadly battle. Two were even then dying and, though I consigned them at once to separate cages, two more died in the course of the day. The real cause of this sudden and terrible battle is hard to ascertain but I cannot help suspecting that the shrews, owing to the sudden change in the usual odor, had failed to recognize each other and had fallen upon each other as they would have done upon strangers. The four survivors quieted down after a certain time and I was able to reunite them in the original container without fear of further mishap.

I kept those four remaining shrews in good health for nearly seven months and would probably have had them much longer if the assistant whom I had engaged to feed them had not forgotten to do so. I had been obliged to go to Vienna and, on my return in the late afternoon, was met by that usually reliable fellow who turned pale when he saw me, thereupon remembering that he had forgotten to feed the shrews. All four of them were alive but very weak; they ate greedily when we fed them but died nonetheless within a few hours. In other words, they showed exactly the same symptoms as the shrews which I had formerly tried to keep; this confirmed my opinion that the latter were already dying of hunger when they came into my possession.

To any advanced animal keeper who is able to set up a large tank, preferably with running water, and who can obtain a sufficient supply of small fish, tadpoles, and the like, I can recommend the water shrew as one of the most gratifying, charming, and interesting objects of care. Of course it is a somewhat exacting charge. It will eat raw chopped heart (the customary substitute for small live prey) only in the absence of something better and it cannot be fed exclusively on this diet for long periods.

Moreover, really clean water is indispensable. But if these clear-cut requirements be fulfilled, the water shrew will not merely remain alive but will really thrive, nor do I exclude the possibility that it might even breed in captivity.

1952

THE READER

1. What features of the shrew's behavior does Lorenz select for special emphasis? What conclusions does he draw about these features?
2. Lorenz employs a narrative framework in which to describe the shrews. Make a list of narrative events and a list of major characteristics of the shrew. Do you as a reader react differently to the facts about shrew behavior because they are embedded in narrative?

THE WRITER

1. Lorenz discusses a field trip and some other matters before he reports his laboratory observations. What is the effect of this organization?
2. Though this is mainly a report of his observations, Lorenz includes matters that are not necessary to the report of strictly controlled observation of the shrew's habits. Indicate some of the places where his discussion moves beyond strict reporting. Characterize the roles he assumes in these passages. Do these other roles or revelations of personality compromise or support his claim to being a scientist?
3. Write an account of the characteristics of some animal, either domesticated or wild, embedding them in a brief narrative.

Stephen Jay Gould

OUR ALLOTTED LIFETIMES

Meeting with Henry Ford in E. L. Doctorow's *Ragtime*, J. P. Morgan praises the assembly line as a faithful translation of nature's wisdom:

> Has it occurred to you that your assembly line is not merely a stroke of industrial genius but a projection of organic truth? After all, the interchangeability of parts is a rule of nature. . . . All mammals reproduce in the same way and share the same designs of self-nourishment, with digestive and circulatory systems that are recognizably the same, and they enjoy the same senses. . . . Shared design is what allows taxonomists to classify mammals as mammals.

An imperious tycoon should not be met with equivocation; nonetheless, I can only reply "yes, and no" to Morgan's pronouncement. Morgan was wrong if he thought that large mammals are geometric replicas of small ones. Elephants have relatively smaller brains and thicker legs than mice, and these differences record a general rule of mammalian design, not the idiosyncracies of particular animals.

Morgan was right in arguing that large animals are essentially similar to small members of their group. The similarity, however, does not lie in a constant shape. The basic laws of geometry dictate that animals must change their shape in order to perform the same function at different sizes. I remind readers of the classical example, first discussed by Galileo in 1638: the strength of an animal's leg is a function of its cross-sectional area (length × length); the weight that the leg must support varies as the animal's volume (length × length × length). If a mammal did not alter the relative thickness of its legs as it got larger, it would soon collapse since body weight would increase much faster than the supporting strength of limbs. Instead, large mammals have relatively thicker leg bones than small mammals. To remain the same in function, animals must change their form.

The study of these changes in form is called "scaling theory." Scaling theory has uncovered a remarkable regularity of changing shape over the 25-millionfold range of mammalian weight from shrew to blue whale. If we plot brain weight versus body weight for all mammals on the so-called mouse-to-elephant (or shrew-to-whale) curve, very few species deviate far from a single line expressing the general rule: brain weight increases only two-thirds as fast as body weight as we move from small to large mammals. (We share with bottle-nosed dolphins the honor of greatest deviance from the curve.)

We can often predict these regularities from the physical behavior of objects. The heart, for example, is a pump. Since all mammalian hearts are similar in function, small hearts will pump considerably faster than large ones (imagine how much faster you could work a finger-sized toy bellows than the giant model that fuels a blacksmith's large forge). On the mouse-to-elephant curve for mammals, the length of a heartbeat increases between one-fourth and one-third as fast as body weight as we move from small to large mammals. The generality of this conclusion has just been affirmed in an interesting study by J. E. Carrel and R. D. Heathcote on the scaling of heart rate in spiders. They used a cool laser beam to illuminate the hearts of resting spiders and drew a crab spider-to-tarantula curve for eighteen species spanning nearly a thousandfold range of body weight. Again, scaling is very regular with heart rate increasing four-tenths as fast as body weight (or .409 times as fast, to be exact).

We may extend this conclusion for hearts to a very general statement about the pace of life in small versus large animals. Small animals tick through life far more rapidly than large ones—their hearts work more quickly, they breathe more frequently, their pulse beats much faster.

Most importantly, metabolic rate, the so-called fire of life, scales only three-fourths as fast as body weight in mammals. Large mammals generate much less heat per unit of body weight to keep themselves going. Tiny shrews move frentically, eating nearly all their waking lives to keep their metabolic fire burning at its maximal rate among mammals; blue whales glide majestically, their hearts beating the slowest rhythm among active, warmblooded creatures.

If we consider the scaling of lifetime among mammals, an intriguing synthesis of these disparate data seems to suggest itself. We have all had enough experience with mammalian pets of various sizes to understand that small mammals tend to live for a shorter time than large ones. In fact, the scaling of mammalian lifetime follows a regular curve at about the same rate as heartbeat and breath time—between one-fourth and one-third as fast as body weight as we move from small to large animals. (Again, Homo sapiens emerges as a very peculiar animal. We live far longer than a mammal of our body size should. I have argued elsewhere that humans evolved by a process called "neoteny"—the retention of shapes and growth rates that characterize juvenile stages of our primate ancestors. I also believe that neoteny is responsible for our elevated longevity. Compared with other mammals, all stages of human life— from juvenile features to adulthood—arise "too late." We are born as helpless embryos after a long gestation; we mature late after an extended childhood; we die, if fortune be kind, at ages otherwise reached only by the very largest warmblooded creatures.)

Usually, we pity the pet mouse or gerbil that lived its full span of a year or two at most. How brief its life, while we endure for the better part of a century. As the main theme of this column, I want to argue that such pity is misplaced (our personal grief, of course, is quite another matter; with this, science does not deal). J. P. Morgan of Ragtime was right—small and large mammals are essentially similar. Their lifetimes are scaled to their life's pace, and all endure for approximately the same amount of biological time. Small mammals tick fast, burn rapidly, and live for a short time; large ones live long at a stately pace. Measured by their own internal clocks, mammals of different sizes tend to live for the same amount of time.

Yet we are prevented from grasping this important and comforting concept by a deeply ingrained habit of Western thought. We are trained from earliest memory to regard absolute Newtonian time as the single valid measuring stick in a rational and objective world. We impose our kitchen clock, ticking equably, upon all things. We marvel at the quickness of a mouse, express boredom at the torpor of a hippopotamus. Yet each is living at the appropriate pace of its own biological clock.

I do not wish to deny the importance of absolute, astronomical time to organisms. Animals must measure it to lead successful lives. Deer must know when to regrow their antlers, birds when to migrate. Animals track the day–night cycle with their circadian rhythms; jet lag is the price we pay for moving much faster than nature intended. Bamboos can somehow count 120 years before flowering again.

But absolute time is not the appropriate measuring stick for all biological phenomena. Consider the song of the humpback whale. These magnificent animals sing with such volume that their sounds travel through water for thousands of miles, perhaps even around the world, as their leading student Roger S. Payne has suggested. E. O. Wilson has described the awesome effect of these vocalizations: "The notes are eerie yet beautiful to the human ear. Deep basso groans and almost inaudibly high soprano squeaks alternate with repetitive squeals that suddenly rise or fall in pitch." We do not know the function of these songs. Perhaps they enable whales to find each other and to stay together during their annual transoceanic migrations.

Each whale has its own characteristic song; the highly complex patterns are repeated over and over again with great faithfulness. No scientific fact that I have learned in the last decade struck me with more force than Payne's report that the length of some songs may extend for more than half an hour. I have never been able to memorize the five-minute first Kyrie of the B-minor Mass[1] (and not for want of trying); how could a whale sing for thirty minutes and then repeat itself accurately? Of what possible use is a thirty-minute repeat cycle—far too long for a human to recognize: we would never grasp it as a single song (without Payne's recording machinery and much study after the fact). But then I remembered the whale's metabolic rate, the enormously slow pace of its life compared with ours. What do we know about a whale's perception of thirty minutes? A humpback may scale the world to its own metabolic rate: its half-hour song may be our minute waltz.[2] From any point of view, the song is spectacular; it is the most elaborate single display so far discovered in any animal. I merely urge the whale's point of view as an appropriate perspective.

We can provide some numerical precision to support the claim that all mammals, on average, live for the same amount of biological time. In a method developed by W. R. Stahl, B. Gunther, and E. Guerra in the late 1950s and early 1960s, we search the mouse-to-elephant equations for biological properties that scale at the same rate against body weight. For example, Gunther and Guerra give the following equations for mammalian breath time and heartbeat time versus body weight.

---

1. By Johann Sebastian Bach; the movement is woven together from many independent musical lines.

2. The reference is to the "Minute Waltz," by Frédéric Chopin, which is not only brief but fast-moving.

$$\text{breath time} = .0000470 \, \text{body}^{0.28}$$
$$\text{heartbeat time} = .0000119 \, \text{body}^{0.28}$$

(Nonmathematical readers need not be overwhelmed by the formalism. The equations simply mean that both breath time and heartbeat time increase about .28 times as fast as body weight as we move from small to large mammals.) If we divide the two equations, body weight cancels out because it is raised to the same power.

$$\frac{\text{breath time}}{\text{heartbeat time}} = \frac{.0000470 \, \text{body}^{0.28}}{.0000119 \, \text{body}^{0.28}} = 4.0$$

This says that the ratio of breath time to heartbeat time is 4.0 in mammals of any body size. In other words, all mammals, whatever their size, breathe once for each four heartbeats. Small animals breathe and beat their hearts faster than large animals, but both breath and heart slow up at the same relative rate as mammals get larger.

Lifetime also scales at the same rate to body weight (.28 times as fast as we move from small to large mammals). This means that the ratio of both breath time and heartbeat time to lifetime is also constant over the whole range of mammalian size. When we perform an exercise similar to that above, we find that all mammals, regardless of their size, tend to breathe about 200 million times during their lives (their hearts, therefore, beat about 800 million times). Small mammals breathe fast, but live for a short time. Measured by the sensible internal clocks of their own hearts or the rhythm of their own breathing, all mammals live about the same time. (Astute readers, having counted their breaths, may have calculated that they should have died long ago. But *Homo sapiens* is a markedly deviant mammal in more ways than braininess alone. We live about three times as long as mammals of our body size "should," but we breathe at the "right" rate and thus live to breathe about three times as much as an average mammal of our body size.)

The mayfly lives but a day as an adult. It may, for all I know, experience that day as we live a lifetime. Yet all is not relative in our world, and such a short glimpse of it must invite distortion in interpreting events ticking on longer scales. In a brilliant metaphor, the pre-Darwinian evolutionist Robert Chambers spoke of a mayfly watching the metamorphosis of a tadpole into a frog (from *Vestiges of the Natural History of Creation*, 1844):

> Suppose that an ephemeron [a mayfly], hovering over a pool for its one April day of life, were capable of observing the fry of the frog in the waters below. In its aged afternoon, having seen no change upon them for such a long time, it would be little qualified to conceive that the external branchiae [gills] of these creatures were to decay, and be replaced by internal lungs, that feet were to be developed, the tail erased, and the animal then to become a denizen of the land.

Human consciousness arose but a minute before midnight on the geologic clock. Yet we mayflies, ignorant perhaps of the messages buried in earth's long history, try to bend an ancient world to our purposes. Let us hope that we are still in the morning of our April day.

1977

Nigel Calder

HEADS AND TAILS

During the comet *Halley's* * * * visit to the sun in 1910, reputable observers said that it broke up. At the time this was widely believed to be true but, after the comet departed, calmer opinions prevailed and the reports were seen as the products of imagination working on certain jets and streamers visible in the comet's head. Like the planet Vulcan, it was an example of people seeing what they expected to see: there would have been no such suggestion a hundred years earlier.

An amiable mathematician told me how he once thought Saturday was Sunday. All the evidence of Saturday bustle around him failed to shake his conviction and he rebuked an astonished newspaper-seller for fobbing people off with yesterday's papers. Only in the evening, when he went to deliver a society lecture and found no one there, did the truth begin to dawn. Again, the annals of war are full of instances of troops, ships and aircraft being misidentified and efficiently destroyed by "friendly" forces. Christopher Columbus's belief was that he had sailed west to Asia and we all connive in it to this day by calling the American natives "Indians." And there is no reason to doubt the sincerity of those who spot flying saucers.

A rich vein of experimental psychology was opened in the late 1940s when Jerome Bruner of Harvard began researching into influences on human perception. In a series of classic experiments with Cecile Goodman and Leo Postman, he showed (1) that valuable coins look larger than they really are, (2) that emotionally loaded words like "crime" and "bitch" are harder to read than bland words, and (3) that when people are shown a false playing card, say a red six of clubs, they are likely to report it as a six of hearts. In this playing-card experiment a person may hesitate uneasily for quite a while before he sees the deception and typically exclaims, "My God!" The historian of science Thomas Kuhn has drawn the parallel between this experiment and the reluctant shifts of ideas in science.

Expect strange sights in the sky and you are liable to see them. A medical student, Ambroise Paré, wins pride of place in the chronicles of wishful seeing for his observations of the comet of 1528. He was an able young man who went on to be a surgeon to four kings of France and invented, among other practical novelties, ligatures for stopping arterial bleeding. Yet in all honesty he described the comet as being bloody in color, which is plausible, but also stocked with weapons and arrayed with hideous human heads, which seems unlikely.

A malodorous comet demonstrates even better how ideas influence perceptions. Medieval scholars in Europe, who deferred to ancient wisdom and considered that comets inhabited the upper atmosphere of the Earth, also suspected them of being Devil's work. So it is not altogether surprising to learn that certain medieval monks swore they smelled a comet, or that the odor was of suitably devilish sulphurous gas. This report of halleytosis won approval in a book already mentioned, *Cometomantia* of 1684, which used it as evidence against those over-zealous astronomers who wanted to displace all comets into deep space, far beyond the orbit of the Moon.

In the matter of the break-up of comets, the first psychological effect to manifest itself was blindness of the kind that prevented the Europeans seeing "new" stars: it was followed by the eager supersight which affords a grand view of invisible objects and processes. An historian of ancient Greece, Ephorus by name, reported that in 371 B.C. a comet broke into pieces; and he was reviled by Nero's tutor, Lucius Seneca, as an irresponsible gossip. Even though Johann Kepler had also said that comets could break up, by the nineteenth century the possibility was either forgotten or regarded as a grotesque fiction. Multiple tails of comets were seen often enough but multiple heads were unthinkable.

When, in the winter of 1845–6, a comet called *Biela* became oddly pear-shaped and then divided into two distinct comets, one of the astronomers who observed them, James Challis of Cambridge, averted his gaze. A week later he took another peep and *Biela* was still flaunting its rude duality. He had never heard of such a thing and for several more days the cautious Challis hesitated before he announced it to his astronomical colleagues. Meanwhile American astronomers in Washington D.C. and New Haven, equally surprised but possibly more confident in their own sobriety, had already staked their claim to the discovery. Challis excused his slowness in reporting the event by saying that he was busy looking for the new planet beyond Uranus. When later in the same year he was needlessly beaten to the discovery of that planet (Neptune) by German astronomers, Challis explained that he had been preoccupied with his work on comets.

After *Biela*'s fission similar sights became commonplace, not because nature embarked on a frenzy of comet smashing but because astronomers' visual neurones were at last prepared to register such events. In fact, splitting comets became the popular thing to see, whether or not they really happened. For example, the great comet *Donati* (1858) was reported as coming to pieces but it almost certainly did not do so. And inevitably the most famous comet, *Halley*, was supposed to conform with the latest fashion in 1910, and to fall apart. A considered, and one might say considerate, view of those reports is that *Halley* was on the verge of disruption in 1910, but survived intact.

On the other hand, several other comets certainly have split since *Biela*, some of them being well documented in photographs. Zdenek Sekanina, a Czechoslovak-born astronomer in Cometsville, has put the stamp of certified break-up on *Sawerthal* (1888), *Campbell* (1914), *Whipple-Fedtke-Tevzadze* (1943), *Honda* (1955) and *Tago-Sato-Kosaka* (1969). The ones with cumbersome names deserve to split up, but that cannot be said for *West* (1976). This was the great comet that the public did not see, because news editors, feeling foolish after they promoted *Kohoutek* of 1973 as the spectacle of the century, virtually banned any mention of comets from their papers and television screens. The head of *West* divided itself into four pieces and in the process threw out streamers of dust every two or three days, which gave the comet a fanned, peacock-like tail. Paolo Toscanelli described *Halley* in those terms, in 1456, but any inference would be rash.

In the twelfth century, by Brian Marsden's retrospective calculations, a comet passed extremely close to the Sun and broke up into at least two pieces. (It may have been a conspicuous comet of A.D. 1106.) One of the pieces came back in 1882 as the "Great September Comet" and again grazed the Sun; another, on an almost indistinguishable orbit, appeared in 1965 as the comet *Ikeya-Seki*. There is in fact a group of "sungrazers," sharing very similar orbits, and they have been spawned over many centuries by successive break-ups, from a single parent comet. The "Great March Comet" of 1843 was one of them, and so were at least seven since then. *Pereyra* of 1963 passed within a mere 60,000 kilometers of the bright solar surface, while the "Great Southern Comet" of 1887 may have collided with the Sun.

The visual system is adept at filling in details in a cartoon, seeing the Man in the Moon and generally perceiving unreal patterns. The ink-blot tests with which psychologists used to plague people are a case in point; another is the interpretation of comet haloes and streamers as bleeding heads or splitting heads. The most celebrated discovery in the history of astronomy was the Canals of Mars. In 1877 Giovanni Schiaparelli of Milan reported that he could see channels crossing the face of that planet and by the end of the century Percival Lowell, founder of a famous observatory at Flagstaff, Arizona, had mapped an intricate network of dozens of canals.

The martians' planet-wide irrigation system was, for Lowell, the dismaying sign of an advanced civilization fighting the growing aridity of the planet. The American comet hunter, Edward Barnard, wittily disposed of the fiction: he operated what was, at the time, the most advanced telescope in the world, and he said that it was too powerful to show the Canals of Mars. Yet (there is always a "yet" in science) the ghosts of Schiaparelli and Lowell can have one last snigger. In 1971 a spacecraft sent back pictures of Mars showing huge valleys, including a natural rift eighty kilometers wide and five thousand kilometers long—one of the features mapped by the "canal" enthusiasts. Of the martian civilization there was of course no sign, but the channels were not all imaginary. And there were also immense volcanoes on Mars: the jesting Barnard had seen them himself, but did not dare mention them for fear of ridicule.

Some illusions are deep-seated in the machinery of our brains, which compel us, for instance, to interpret the sky as a flattened dome so that the Moon and the comets always look much bigger on the horizon than when they are overhead. Telescopes, too, can deceive and many an eager amateur mistakes a stray reflection in his instrument for a new-found comet. An observatory in tsarist Russia had a telescope that was well adapted to the discovery of companions of the stars, because a flaw in the glass made it see everything double. But when misperceptions and misconceptions ferment together the results can be more vivid than that.

The discoveries of Isaac Newton and Edmond Halley did not at once dispose of devilish connotations of comets. On the contrary, the realization that comets move in great ellipses around the Sun helped to modernize the notions of Hell. What better punishment for sinners than to be condemned to ride on a comet for ever and experience a fearful alternation of freezing in the outer darkness and roasting when the comet brushed past the Sun? The cheerful idea that the comet of 44 B.C. was Caesar on his way to Heaven was thus revised to stock comets with the souls of the damned, not on their way but there already, in a brand-new, eighteenth-century, whirly version of Hell.

Astronomers had more sense than that. They knew that comets were free-ranging lumps of light that were necessary to sustain all living folk, like those who made their home on the Sun. Nowadays the bad habit of attending to only those past ideas that pointed more or less directly towards modern scientific theories is being corrected by historians of science, and from these professional investigators of theories long since dead we learn what creative errors surrounded the attempts to explain the illuminations of the sky, two to three centuries ago. By then the misunderstandings about light were no longer quite as bizarre as the ancient proposition that eyes acted like lasers and looked around by sending out beams, as in the "darting glances" favored by some novelists. But there was a persistent confusion between light and its sources. Most of us nowadays can distinguish a lamp from the dust of photons that it throws in our eyes. Our predecessors, though, were infected with the old concept of "fire" as an element in its own right, and in any case, not knowing about plasmas heated by nuclear reactions, they found the light of the Sun and the stars mysterious.

Even Newton, who founded the modern science of light in his spare time and certainly knew the difference between rays and sources, was at a loss to say how the Sun could burn undiminished for thousands of years (billions of years, as we now know). The comets came like cosmic cavalry to the rescue: Newton said that God arranged for the Sun to be reinforced by comets that fell into it as a result of fatal changes in their orbits. Here too, he thought, was an explanation for the new star seen by Tycho Brahe in 1572. Astrophysicists today would say it was a natural H-bomb going off, in the destructive explosion of a giant star; for Newton it was a star that suddenly acquired new splendor thanks to a goodly stoking of comet-fuel.

Newton was no Newtonian, in the austere nineteenth-century sense of one content to contemplate the celestial clockwork. The taming of imagination by algebra dates not from the *Principia* of 1687 but from Karl Friedrich Gauss's *Theoria Motus Corporum* of 1809. In the intervening century astronomers, clergymen and laymen continued to regard comets as manifestations of divine purpose. Taking their cue from Newton, they wondered about the light of comets and about their life-giving properties, whether in watering the Earth or conveying some vital principle that might breathe life into all the orbs of the sky. Such ideas foreshadowed a twentieth-century proposition that the Earth might have been seeded with the first bacteria by a comet's tail * * *.

The cheekiest of all ideas about the cosmos was William Herschel's belief that the nearest star was peopled: " . . . we need not hesitate to admit that the Sun is richly stored with inhabitants." Herschel flourished a hundred years after Newton and his name is one of the most celebrated in the history of astronomy. He was a Hanoverian musician living at Bath in England, and was catapulted to fame when his telescope revealed the large planet Uranus, the first major piece of the Solar System to be noticed since prehistoric times. Many astronomers had already seen the planet but mistook it for a star. In the post-Halley era Herschel naturally announced his discovery as a new comet, and it fell to others to infer that it was a planet lying far beyond Saturn and a hundred times larger than the Earth.

Concerning comet light and its contribution to the habitability of the Sun, Herschel pictured alien creatures going about their business on the solid surface of the Sun which underlay an atmosphere of light that was replenished, as Newton had said, by an influx of comets. Cosmic light was thus a special kind of life-giving stuff that nature could manipulate, in this case into a shell around the sun that illuminated the solar surface as well as the Solar System. Even in Herschel's day, to say that the Sun was cool could earn you a certificate of insanity, but he supposed that the solar rays generated heat only when absorbed in a suitable medium, such as the Earth's atmosphere. And he offered visible evidence in support of the proposition: what were the familiar dark sunspots but chinks in the light offering glimpses of a cooler surface below? Present-day reckonings of the internal temperature of the Sun guarantee that any inhabitants of that world must be, to say the least, jumping like fleas on a hotplate, and sunspots are known to be magnetic storms.

Yet the adherents of these ideas about light are entitled to more than a posthumous chuckle, because their line of reasoning led them to conclusions that the latest astrophysics regards as sensationally correct. The marshaling of the supposed light-stuff around the heavy Sun indicated to eighteenth-century astronomers that light was subject to the action of gravity. The luminiferous comets, moving in obedience to Newton's law, provided equally graphic proof. But the ability of gravity to bend light and slow it down was to be the basis of General Relativity. Albert Einstein arrived at it armed with less devious notions about the nature of light, and the anticipation might be dismissed as a chance intersection of two very different lines of thought, had it not also led to General Relativity's most breathtaking deduction. The eighteenth-century theory of light predicted black holes.

The man to say so first was a clergyman at Thornhill near Leeds: John Michell. At Cambridge he had initiated the modern study of magnetism and of earthquakes; he also identified the double stars and gave Herschel a correspondence course in telescope-making. Michell set down the idea of an invisible star in a paper that was published in 1784 and resurrected in 1979 by Simon Schaffer, an historian at Cambridge. The original black hole arose in Michell's mind from the thought that a large and massive star would, by its powerful gravity, slow down the light that it emitted. In the extreme case a star could choke off its light entirely, and Michell calculated that a star with five hundred times the Sun's diameter, and the same density, would be invisible. The French theorist Pierre-Simon de Laplace arrived at the same idea in 1796 (and has often been credited with originating it) but he reckoned the size of the black-hole star at half the diameter given by Michell. General Relativity agrees with Michell: the Rector of Thornhill turns out to have been more accurate as well as earlier than the great Laplace.

Astronomy is thus a four-legged animal standing on sound and false ideas at the front and false observations at the rear. Amazingly the beast can limp forward, sometimes even gallop, from one discovery to the next. And lurching on its way to valuable information about the nature and history of the universe it has in passing exposed the character of those ephemera, the tails of comets.

1980

Arthur Koestler

GRAVITY AND THE HOLY GHOST

"If I have been able to see farther than others," said Newton, "it was because I stood on the shoulders of giants." One of the giants was Johannes Kepler (1571–1630) whose three laws of planetary motion provided the foundation on which the Newtonian universe was built. They were the first "natural laws" in the modern sense: precise, verifiable statements expressed in mathematical terms; at the same time, they represent the first attempt at a synthesis of astronomy and physics which, during the preceding two thousand years, had developed on separate lines.

Astronomy before Kepler had been a purely descriptive geometry of the skies. The motion of stars and planets had been represented by the device of epicycles and eccentrics—an imaginary clockwork of circles turning on circles turning on circles. Copernicus, for instance, had used forty-eight wheels to represent the motion of the five known planets around the sun. These wheels were purely fictitious, and meant as such—they enabled astronomers to make more or less precise predictions, but, above all, they satisfied the dogma that all heavenly motion must be uniform and in perfect circles. Though the planets moved neither uniformly nor in perfect circles, the imaginary cogwheels did, and thereby "saved the appearances."

Kepler's discoveries put an end to this state of affairs. He reconciled astronomy with physics, and substituted for the fictitious clockwork a universe of material bodies not unlike the earth, freely floating and turning in space, moved by forces acting on them. His most important book bears the provocative title: *A New Astronomy Based on Causation, or Physics of the Sky* (1609). It contains the first and second of Kepler's three laws. The first says that the planets move around the sun not in circles but in elliptic orbits; the second says that a planet moves in its orbit not at uniform speed but at a speed that varies according to its position, and is defined by a simple and beautiful law: the line connecting planet and sun sweeps over equal areas in equal times. The third law establishes an equally elegant mathematical correlation between the length of a planet's year and its mean distance from the sun.

Kepler did not start his career as an astronomer, but as a student of theology (at the Lutheran University of Thuebingen); yet already as a student he was attracted by the Copernican idea of a sun-centered universe. Now Canon Copernicus's book, *On the Revolutions of the Heavenly Spheres*, had been published in the year of his death, 1543; that is, fifty years before Kepler first heard of him; and during that half century it had attracted very little attention. One of the reasons was its supreme unreadability, which made it into an all-time worst-seller: its first edition of a thousand copies was never sold out. Kepler was the first Continental astronomer to embrace the Copernican theory. His *Mysterium Cosmographicum*, published in 1597 (fifty-four years after Copernicus's death) started the great controversy—Galileo entered the scene fifteen years later.

The reason why the idea of a sun-centered universe appealed to Kepler was repeatedly stated by himself: "I often defended the opinions of Copernicus in the disputations of the candidates and I composed a careful disputation on the first motion which consists in the rotation of the earth; then I was adding to this the motion of the earth around the sun *for physical or, if you prefer, metaphysical reasons.*" I have emphasized the last words because they contain the leitmotif of Kepler's quest, and because he used the same expression in various passages in his works. Now what were those "physical or, if you prefer, metaphysical reasons" which made Kepler prefer to put the sun into the center of the universe instead of the earth?

> My ceaseless search concerned primarily three problems, namely, the number, size, and motion of the planets—why they are just as they are and not otherwise arranged. I was encouraged in my daring inquiry by that beautiful analogy between the stationary objects, namely, the sun, the fixed stars, and the space between them, with God the Father, the Son, and the Holy Ghost. I shall pursue this analogy in my future cosmographical work.

Twenty-five years later, when he was over fifty, Kepler repeated his credo: "It is by no means permissible to treat this analogy as an empty comparison; it must be considered by its Platonic form and archetypal quality as one of the primary causes."

He believed in this to the end of his life. Yet gradually the analogy underwent a significant change:

> The sun in the middle of the moving stars, himself at rest and yet the source of motion, carries the image of God the Father and Creator. He distributes his motive force through a medium which contains the moving bodies, even as the Father creates through the Holy Ghost.

Thus the "moving bodies"—that is, the planets—are now brought into the analogy. The Holy Ghost no longer merely fills the space between the motionless sun and the motionless fixed stars. It has become an active force, a *vis motrix*, which *drives* the planets. Nobody before Kepler had postulated, or even suspected, the existence of a physical force acting between the sun and the planets. Astronomy was not concerned with physical forces, nor with the causes of the heavenly motions, merely with their description. The passages which I have just quoted are the first intimation of the forthcoming marriage between physics and astronomy—the act of betrothal, as it were. By looking at the sky, not through the eyes of the geometrician only, but of the physicist concerned with natural causes, he hit upon a question which nobody had asked before. The question was: "Why do the planets closer to the sun move faster than those which are far away? What is the mathematical relation between a planet's distance from the sun and the length of its year?"

These questions could only occur to one who had conceived the revolutionary hypothesis that the motion of the planet—and therefore its velocity and the duration of its year—was governed by a physical force emanating from the sun. Every astronomer knew, of course, that the greater their distance from the sun the slower the planets moved. But this phenomenon was taken for granted, just as it was taken for granted that boys will be boys and girls will be girls, as an irreducible fact of creation. Nobody asked the cause of it because physical causes were not assumed to enter into the motion of heavenly bodies. The greatness of the philosophers of the scientific revolution consisted not so much in finding the right answers but in asking the right questions; in seeing a problem where nobody saw one before; in substituting a "why" for a "how."

Kepler's answer to the question why the outer planets move slower than the inner ones, and how the speed of their motion is related to their distance from the sun, was as follows:

> There exists only one moving soul in the center of all the orbits that is the sun which drives the planets the more vigorously the closer the planet is, but whose force is quasi-exhausted when acting on the outer planets because of the long distance and the weakening of the force which it entails.

Later on he commented: "If we substitute for the word 'soul' the word 'force,' then we get just the principle which underlies my 'Physics of the Skies.' As I reflected that this cause of motion *diminishes in proportion to distance* just as the light of the sun diminishes in proportion to distance from the sun, I came to the conclusion that this force must be substantial —'substantial' not in the literal sense but . . . in the same manner as we say that light is something substantial, meaning by this an unsubstantial entity emanating from a substantial body."

We notice that Kepler's answer came *before* the question—that it was the answer that begot the question. The answer, the starting point, was the analogy between God the Father and the sun—the former acting through the Holy Ghost, the latter through a physical force. The planets must obey the law of the sun—the law of God—the mathematical law of nature; and the Holy Ghost's action through empty space diminishes, as the light emanating from the sun does, with distance. The degenerate, purely descriptive astronomy which originated in the period of the Greek decline, and continued through the Dark and Middle Ages until Kepler, did not ask for meaning and causes. But Kepler was convinced that physical causes operate between heavenly, just as between earthly, bodies, and more specifically that the sun exerts a physical force on the planets. It was this conviction which enabled him to formulate his laws. Physics became the auxiliary matrix which secured his escape from the blocked situation into which astronomy had maneuvered itself.

The blockage—to cut a very long story short—was due to the fact that Tycho de Brahe[1] had improved the instruments and methods of star-gazing, and produced observational data of a hitherto unequaled abundance and precision; and the new data did not fit into the traditional schemes. Kepler, who served his apprenticeship under Tycho, was given the task of working out the orbit of Mars. He spent six years on the task and covered nine thousand foliosheets with calculations in his small handwriting without getting anywhere. When at last he believed he had succeeded he found to his dismay that certain observed positions of Mars differed from those which his theory demanded by magnitudes up to eight minutes arc. Eight minutes arc is approximately one-quarter of the apparent diameter of the moon.

This was a catastrophe. Ptolemy, and even Copernicus, could afford to neglect a difference of eight minutes, because their observations were accurate only within a margin of ten minutes, anyway. "But," Kepler wrote in the New Astronomy, "but for us, who by divine kindness were given an accurate observer such as Tycho Brahe, for us it is fitting that we should acknowledge this divine gift and put it to use. . . . Henceforth I shall lead the way toward that goal according to my ideas. For if I had believed that we could ignore these eight minutes, I would have patched up by hypothesis accordingly. But since it was not permissible to ignore them, those eight minutes point the road to a complete reformation of astronomy. . . ."

Thus a theory, built on years of labor and torment, was instantly thrown away because of a discord of eight miserable minutes arc. Instead of cursing those eight minutes as a stumbling block, he transformed them into the cornerstone of a new science. For those eight minutes arc had at last made him realize that the field of astronomy in its traditional framework was well and truly blocked.

One of the recurrent frustrations and tragedies in the history of thought is caused by the uncertainty whether it is possible to solve a

1. Danish astronomer (1546–1601).

given problem by traditional methods previously applied to problems which seem to be of the same nature. Who can say how many lives were wasted and good minds destroyed in futile attempts to square the circle, or to construct a *perpetuum mobile?*[2] The proof that these problems are *insoluble* was in each case an original discovery in itself (such as Maxwell's second law of thermodynamics);[3] and such proofs could only be found by looking at the problem from a point of view outside its traditional matrix. On the other hand, the mere knowledge that a problem is soluble means that half the game is already won.

The episode of the eight minutes arc had convinced Kepler that his problem—the orbit of Mars—was insoluble so long as he felt bound by the traditional rules of sky-geometry. Implied in those rules was the dogma of "uniform motion in perfect circles." *Uniform* motion he had already discarded before the crisis; now he felt that the even more sacred one of *circular* motion must also go. The impossibility of constructing a circular orbit which would satisfy all existing observations suggested to him that the circle must be replaced by some other curve.

> The conclusion is quite simply that the planet's path is not a circle—it curves inward on both sides and outward again at opposite ends. Such a curve is called an oval. The orbit is not a circle but an oval figure.

This oval orbit was a wild, frightening new departure for him. To be fed up with cycles and epicycles, to mock the slavish imitators of Aristotle was one thing; to assign an entirely new, lopsided, implausible path for the heavenly bodies was quite another. Why indeed an oval? There is something in the perfect symmetry of spheres and circles which has a deep, reassuring appeal to the unconscious mind—otherwise it could not have survived two millennia. The oval lacks that archetypal appeal. It has an arbitrary, distorted form. It destroyed the dream of the "harmony of the spheres," which lay at the origin of the whole quest. At times he felt like a criminal, or worse: a fool. All he had to say in his own defense was: "I have cleared the Augean stables of astronomy of cycles and spirals, and left behind me only a single cartful of dung."

That cartful of dung—nonuniform motion in noncircular orbits—could only be justified and explained by arguments derived not from geometry, but from physics. A phrase kept humming in his ear like a catchy tune, and crops up in his writings over and again: there is a force in the sun which moves the planets, there is a force in the sun. . . . And since there is a force in the sun, there must exist some simple relationship between the planet's distance from the sun, and its speed. A light shines

2. A hypothetical machine which, once set in motion, would continue in motion forever unless stopped by some external force or by its own the wearing out.

3. The second law of thermodynamics, put

forward not by James Clerk Maxwell, but by Rudolf Julius Emmanuel Clausius (1822-1888), provides an explanation of why a perpetual-motion machine cannot exist.

the brighter the nearer one is to its source, and the same must apply to the force of the sun: the closer the planet to it, the quicker it will move. This had been his instinctive conviction; but now he thought that he had found the proof of it. "Ye physicists, prick your ears, for now we are going to invade your territory." The next six chapters in the *Astronomia Nova* are a report on that invasion into celestial physics, which had been out of bounds for astronomy since Plato. He had found the second matrix which would unblock his problem.

That excursion was something of a comedy of errors—which nevertheless ended with finding the truth. Since he had no notion of the principle of inertia, which makes a planet persist in its tangential motion under its own momentum, and had only a vague intuition of gravity, he had to invent a force which, emanating from the sun, sweeps the planet round its path like a broom. In the second place, to account for the eccentricity of the orbits he had to postulate that the planets were "huge round magnets" whose poles pointed always in the same direction so that they would alternately be drawn closer to and be repelled by the sun. But although today the whole thing seems cockeyed, his intuition that there are *two antagonistic forces* acting on the planets, guided him in the right direction. A single force, as previously assumed—the divine Prime Mover and its allied hierarchy of angels—would never produce elliptic orbits and periodic changes of speed. These could only be the result of some dynamic tug of war going on in the sky—as indeed there is. The concept of two antagonistic forces provided rules for a new game in which elliptic orbits and velocities depending on solar distance have their legitimate place.

He made many mistakes during that wild flight of thought; but "as if by miracle"—as he himself remarked—the mistakes canceled out. It looks as if at times his conscious critical faculties had been anesthetized by the creative impulse, by the impatience to get to grips with the physical forces in the solar system. The problem of the planetary orbits had been hopelessly bogged down in its purely geometrical frame of reference, and when he realized that he could not get it unstuck he tore it out of that frame and removed it into the field of physics. That there were inconsistencies and impurities in his method did not matter to him in the heat of the moment, hoping that somehow they would right themselves later on —as they did. This inspired cheating—or, rather, borrowing on credit— is a characteristic and recurrent feature in the history of science. The latest example is subatomic physics, which may be said to live on credit —in the pious hope that one day its inner contradictions and paradoxes will somehow resolve themselves.

Kepler's determination of the orbit of Mars became the unifying link between the two formerly separate realms of physics and astronomy. His was the first serious attempt at explaining the mechanism of the solar system in terms of physical forces; and once the example was set, physics and cosmology could never again be divorced.

1964

THE READER

1. *Why, according to Koestler, was it so difficult for Kepler to discard the notion of circular movement for the heavenly bodies, and why was it difficult to conceive of physical forces acting between the heavenly bodies? Are there any ideas in your own way of thinking that might be similarly difficult to discard or to accept? Perhaps Bronowski's "The Reach of Imagination" (p. 133) and "The Nature of Scientific Reasoning" (p. 574) may help you in thinking or writing about these questions.*

2. *What was the role of Tycho Brahe's observations, fact finding, and data gathering in the formulation of Kepler's thought? Did the facts speak for themselves and make a true conception of the solar system evident at once? Explain the reasons for your answer.*

3. *On p. 570, Koestler says of Kepler, "Instead of cursing those eight minutes as a stumbling block, he transformed them into the cornerstone of a new science." What does this statement mean? Is a difference of such small scale between theory and observation necessarily significant in itself? If so, of what? Do you know of similar differences between expectation and actual behavior in your own personal relationships? How have you handled such discrepancies?*

THE WRITER

1. *What effect is produced by the essay's title, "Gravity and the Holy Ghost"? What relationship between the two terms in the title does the essay explore? Which of the two terms is more familiar to you? Which do you think you know more about? Write an account of your understanding of them.*

2. *Koestler says that "the greatness of the philosophers of the scientific revolution consisted not so much in finding the right answers but in asking the right questions." On the basis of your reading of "Humanities and Science" (p. 188), do you think Thomas would agree or disagree? Put your answer in the form of a brief essay.*

Jacob Bronowski

THE NATURE OF SCIENTIFIC REASONING

What is the insight in which the scientist tries to see into nature? Can it indeed be called either imaginative or creative? To the literary man the question may seem merely silly. He has been taught that science is a large collection of facts; and if this is true, then the only seeing which scientists need to do is, he supposes, seeing the facts. He pictures them, the colorless professionals of science, going off to work in the morning into the universe in a neutral, unexposed state. They then expose themselves like a photographic plate. And then in the darkroom or laboratory they develop the image, so that suddenly and startlingly it appears, printed in capital letters, as a new formula for atomic energy.

Men who have read Balzac and Zola[1] are not deceived by the claims of these writers that they do no more than record the facts. The readers of Christopher Isherwood[2] do not take him literally when he writes "I am a camera." Yet the same readers solemnly carry with them from their schooldays this foolish picture of the scientist fixing by some mechanical process the facts of nature. I have had of all people a historian tell me that science is a collection of facts, and his voice had not even the ironic rasp of one filing cabinet reproving another.

It seems impossible that this historian had ever studied the beginnings of a scientific discovery. The Scientific Revolution can be held to begin in the year 1543 when there was brought to Copernicus, perhaps on his deathbed, the first printed copy of the book he had finished about a dozen years earlier. The thesis of this book is that the earth moves around the sun. When did Copernicus go out and record this fact with his camera? What appearance in nature prompted his outrageous guess? And in what odd sense is this guess to be called a neutral record of fact?

Less than a hundred years after Copernicus, Kepler published (between 1609 and 1619) the three laws which describe the paths of the planets. The work of Newton and with it most of our mechanics spring from these laws. They have a solid, matter-of-fact sound. For example, Kepler says that if one squares the year of a planet, one gets a number which is proportional to the cube of its average distance from the sun. Does anyone think that such a law is found by taking enough readings and then squaring and cubing everything in sight? If he does, then, as a scientist, he is doomed to a wasted life; he has as little prospect of making a scientific discovery as an electronic brain has.

1. Honoré de Balzac and Émile Zola, nine-   2. Modern English novelist and playwright.
teenth-century French novelists.

It was not this way that Copernicus and Kepler thought, or that scientists think today. Copernicus found that the orbits of the planets would look simpler if they were looked at from the sun and not from the earth. But he did not in the first place find this by routine calculation. His first step was a leap of imagination—to lift himself from the earth, and put himself wildly, speculatively into the sun. "The earth conceives from the sun," he wrote; and "the sun rules the family of stars." We catch in his mind an image, the gesture of the virile man standing in the sun, with arms outstretched, overlooking the planets. Perhaps Copernicus took the picture from the drawings of the youth with outstretched arms which the Renaissance teachers put into their books on the proportions of the body. Perhaps he had seen Leonardo's drawings of his loved pupil Salai. I do not know. To me, the gesture of Copernicus, the shining youth looking outward from the sun, is still vivid in a drawing which William Blake in 1780 based on all these: the drawing which is usually called *Glad Day*.

Kepler's mind, we know, was filled with just such fanciful analogies; and we know what they were. Kepler wanted to relate the speeds of the planets to the musical intervals. He tried to fit the five regular solids into their orbits. None of these likenesses worked, and they have been forgotten; yet they have been and they remain the stepping stones of every creative mind. Kepler felt for his laws by way of metaphors, he searched mystically for likenesses with what he knew in every strange corner of nature. And when among these guesses he hit upon his laws, he did not think of their numbers as the balancing of a cosmic bank account, but as a revelation of the unity in all nature. To us, the analogies by which Kepler listened for the movement of the planets in the music of the spheres are farfetched. Yet are they more so than the wild leap by which Rutherford and Bohr in our own century found a model for the atom in, of all places, the planetary system?

No scientific theory is a collection of facts. It will not even do to call a theory true or false in the simple sense in which every fact is either so or not so. The Epicureans held that matter is made of atoms two thousand years ago and we are now tempted to say that their theory was true. But if we do so we confuse their notion of matter with our own. John Dalton in 1808 first saw the structure of matter as we do today, and what he took from the ancients was not their theory but something richer, their image: the atom. Much of what was in Dalton's mind was as vague as the Greek notion, and quite as mistaken. But he suddenly gave life to the new facts of chemistry and the ancient theory together, by fusing them to give what neither had: a coherent picture of how matter is linked and built up from different kinds of atoms. The act of fusion is the creative act.

All science is the search for unity in hidden likenesses. The search may be on a grand scale, as in the modern theories which try to link the fields of gravitation and electromagnetism. But we do not need to be browbeaten by the scale of science. There are discoveries to be made by snatching a small likeness from the air too, if it is bold enough. In 1935 the Japanese physicist Hideki Yukawa wrote a paper which can still give heart to a young scientist. He took as his starting point the known fact that waves of light can sometimes behave as if they were separate pellets. From this he reasoned that the forces which hold the nucleus of an atom together might sometimes also be observed as if they were solid pellets. A schoolboy can see how thin Yukawa's analogy is, and his teacher would be severe with it. Yet Yukawa without a blush calculated the mass of the pellet he expected to see, and waited. He was right; his meson was found, and a range of other mesons, neither the existence nor the nature of which had been suspected before. The likeness had borne fruit.

The scientist looks for order in the appearances of nature by exploring such likenesses. For order does not display itself of itself; if it can be said to be there at all, it is not there for the mere looking. There is no way of pointing a finger or camera at it; order must be discovered and, in a deep sense, it must be created. What we see, as we see it, is mere disorder.

This point has been put trenchantly in a fable by Karl Popper. Suppose that someone wished to give his whole life to science. Suppose that he therefore sat down, pencil in hand, and for the next twenty, thirty, forty years recorded in notebook after notebook everything that he could observe. He may be supposed to leave out nothing: today's humidity, the racing results, the level of cosmic radiation and the stockmarket prices and the look of Mars, all would be there. He would have compiled the most careful record of nature that has ever been made; and, dying in the calm certainty of a life well spent, he would of course leave his notebooks to the Royal Society. Would the Royal Society thank him for the treasure of a lifetime of observation? It would not. The Royal Society would treat his notebooks exactly as the English bishops have treated Joanna Southcott's box.[3] It would refuse to open them at all, because it would know without looking that the notebooks contain only a jumble of disorderly and meaningless items.

Science finds order and meaning in our experience, and sets about this in quite a different way. It sets about it as Newton did in the story which he himself told in his old age, and of which the schoolbooks give only a caricature. In the year 1665, when Newton was twenty-two, the plague broke out in southern England, and the University of Cambridge was closed. Newton therefore spent the next eighteen months at home,

3. Joanna Southcott was a nineteenth-century English farm servant who claimed to be a prophetess. She left behind a box which was to be opened in a time of national emergency in the presence of all the English bishops. In 1927, a bishop agreed to officiate; when the box was opened, it was found to contain only some odds and ends.

removed from traditional learning, at a time when he was impatient for knowledge and, in his own phrase, "I was in the prime of my age for invention." In this eager, boyish mood, sitting one day in the garden of his widowed mother, he saw an apple fall. So far the books have the story right; we think we even know the kind of apple; tradition has it that it was a Flower of Kent. But now they miss the crux of the story. For what struck the young Newton at the sight was not the thought that the apple must be drawn to the earth by gravity; that conception was older than Newton. What struck him was the conjecture that the same force of gravity, which reaches to the top of the tree, might go on reaching out beyond the earth and its air, endlessly into space. Gravity might reach the moon: this was Newton's new thought; and it might be gravity which holds the moon in her orbit. There and then he calculated what force from the earth (falling off as the square of the distance) would hold the moon, and compared it with the known force of gravity at tree height. The forces agreed; Newton says laconically, "I found them answer pretty nearly." Yet they agreed only nearly: the likeness and the approximation go together, for no likeness is exact. In Newton's science modern science is full grown.

It grows from a comparison. It has seized a likeness between two unlike appearances; for the apple in the summer garden and the grave moon overhead are surely as unlike in their movements as two things can be. Newton traced in them two expressions of a single concept, gravitation: and the concept (and the unity) are in that sense his free creation. The progress of science is the discovery at each step of a new order which gives unity to what had long seemed unlike.

* * *

1953, 1965

THE READER

1. In his opening paragraph, Bronowski pictures what the "literary man," or perhaps the ordinary nonscientist, thinks of as the nature of science. Is this a fair representation of the layman's view? What features of science or of the presentation of science might contribute to the development of that view? How does the process depicted in that paragraph compare with the actual activity of a scientist, as described in the account of his own work given by Lorenz in "The Taming of the Shrew" (p. 543) or in the account of Kepler given by Koestler in "Gravity and the Holy Ghost" (p. 567)?

2. Bronowski recounts the famous story of Newton and the apple. What general principle about science is the author exemplifying in this story?

3. In "The Reach of Imagination" (p. 133), Bronowski shows the work of imagination in Newton's thinking of the moon as a huge ball, thrown hard, and in Galileo's imaginary experiment with unequal weights. In

what particular ways do these examples relate to and supplement Bronowski's remarks on science in "The Nature of Scientific Reasoning"?

THE WRITER

1. *On p. 574, Bronowski says: "I have had of all people a historian tell me that science is a collection of facts, and his voice had not even the ironic rasp of one filing cabinet reproving another." Is that image appropriate to the point he wants to make? Can you find other such uses of language in the selection?*
2. *In his fourth paragraph, Bronowski indicates that an electronic brain has little or no chance of making a scientific discovery. Do you agree? Why, or why not? Develop your answer in a brief essay.*

Stephen Jay Gould

DARWIN'S MIDDLE ROAD

"We began to sail up the narrow strait lamenting," narrates Odysseus. "For on the one hand lay Scylla, with twelve feet all dangling down; and six necks exceeding long, and on each a hideous head, and therein three rows of teeth set thick and close, full of black death. And on the other mighty Charybdis sucked down the salt sea water. As often as she belched it forth, like a cauldron on a great fire she would seethe up through all her troubled deeps." Odysseus managed to swerve around Charybdis, but Scylla grabbed six of his finest men and devoured them in his sight—"the most pitiful thing mine eyes have seen of all my travail in searching out the paths of the sea."

False lures and dangers often come in pairs in our legends and metaphors—consider the frying pan and the fire, or the devil and the deep blue sea. Prescriptions for avoidance either emphasize a dogged steadiness—the straight and narrow of Christian evangelists—or an averaging between unpleasant alternatives—the golden mean of Aristotle. The idea of steering a course between undesirable extremes emerges as a central prescription for a sensible life.

The nature of scientific creativity is both a perennial topic of discussion and a prime candidate for seeking a golden mean. The two extreme positions have not been directly competing for allegiance of the unwary. They have, rather, replaced each other sequentially, with one now in the ascendency, the other eclipsed.

The first—inductivism—held that great scientists are primarily great observers and patient accumulators of information. For new and significant theory, the inductivists claimed, can only arise from a firm foundation of facts. In this architectural view, each fact is a brick in a structure built without blueprints. Any talk or thought about theory (the completed building) is fatuous and premature before the bricks are set. Inductivism once commanded great prestige within science, and even represented an "official" position of sorts, for it touted, however falsely, the utter honesty, complete objectivity, and almost automatic nature of scientific progress towards final and incontrovertible truth.

Yet, as its critics so rightly claimed, inductivism also depicted science as a heartless, almost inhuman discipline offering no legitimate place to quirkiness, intuition, and all the other subjective attributes adhering to our vernacular notion of genius. Great scientists, the critics claimed, are distinguished more by their powers of hunch and synthesis, than their skill in experiment or observation. The criticisms of inductivism are certainly valid and I welcome its dethroning during the past thirty years as a necessary preclude to better understanding. Yet, in attacking it so strongly, some critics have tried to substitute an alternative equally extreme and unproductive in its emphasis on the essential subjectivity of creative thought. In this "eureka" view, creativity is an ineffable something, accessible only to persons of genius. It arises like a bolt of lightning, unanticipated, unpredictable and unanalyzable—but the bolts strike only a few special people. We ordinary mortals must stand in awe and thanks. (The name refers, of course, to the legendary story of Archimedes running naked through the streets of Syracuse shouting eureka [I have discovered it] when water displaced by his bathing body washed the scales abruptly from his eyes and suggested a method for measuring volumes.)

I am equally disenchanted by both these opposing extremes. Inductivism reduces genius to dull, rote operations; eurekaism grants it an inaccessible status more in the domain of intrinsic mystery than in a realm where we might understand and learn from it. Might we not marry the good features of each view, and abandon both the elitism of eurekaism and the pedestrian qualities of inductivism? May we not acknowledge the personal and subjective character of creativity, but still comprehend it as a mode of thinking that emphasizes or exaggerates capacities sufficiently common to all of us that we may at least understand if not hope to imitate?

In the hagiography of science, a few men hold such high positions that all arguments must apply to them if they are to have any validity. Charles Darwin, as the principal saint of evolutionary biology, has therefore been presented both as an inductivist and as a primary example of eurekaism. I will attempt to show that these interpretations are equally inadequate, and that recent scholarship on Darwin's own odyssey towards the theory of natural selection supports an intermediate position.

So great was the prestige of inductivism in his own day, that Darwin himself fell under its sway and, as an old man, falsely depicted his youthful accomplishments in its light. In an autobiography, written as a lesson in morality for his children and not intended for publication, he penned some famous lines that misled historians for nearly a hundred years. Describing his path to the theory of natural selection, he claimed: "I worked on true Baconian principles, and without any theory collected facts on a wholesale scale."[1]

The inductivist interpretation focuses on Darwin's five years aboard the *Beagle* and explains his transition from a student for the ministry to the nemesis of preachers as the result of his keen powers of observation applied to the whole world. Thus, the traditional story goes, Darwin's eyes opened wider and wider as he saw, in sequence, the bones of giant South American fossil mammals, the turtles and finches of the Galapagos, and the marsupial fauna of Australia. The truth of evolution and its mechanism of natural selection crept up gradually upon him as he sifted facts in a sieve of utter objectivity.

The inadequacies of this tale are best illustrated by the falsity of its conventional premier example—the so-called Darwin's finches of the Galapagos. We now know that although these birds share a recent and common ancestry on the South American mainland, they have radiated into an impressive array of species on the outlying Galapagos. Few terrestrial species manage to cross the wide oceanic barrier between South America and the Galapagos. But the fortunate migrants often find a sparsely inhabited world devoid of the competitors that limit their opportunities on the crowded mainland. Hence, the finches evolved into roles normally occupied by other birds and developed their famous set of adaptations for feeding—seed crushing, insect eating, even grasping and manipulating a cactus needle to dislodge insects from plants. Isolation—both of the islands from the mainland and among the islands themselves—provided an opportunity for separation, independent adaptation, and speciation.

According to the traditional view, Darwin discovered these finches, correctly inferred their history, and wrote the famous lines in his notebook: "If there is the slightest foundation for these remarks the zoology of Archipelagoes will be worth examining; for such facts would undermine the stability of Species." But, as with so many heroic tales from Washington's cherry tree to the piety of Crusaders, hope rather than truth motivates the common reading. Darwin found the finches to be sure. But he didn't recognize them as variants of a common stock. In fact, he didn't even record the island of discovery for many of them—some of his labels just read "Galapagos Islands." So much for his immedi-

<hr>

1. Francis Bacon (1561–1626): English philosopher, statesman, and essayist, and the first apostle of inductivism.

ate recognition of the role of isolation in the formation of new species. He reconstructed the evolutionary tale only after his return to London, when a British Museum ornithologist correctly identified all the birds as finches.

The famous quotation from his notebook refers to Galapagos tortoises and to the claim of native inhabitants that they can "at once pronounce from which Island any Tortoise may have been brought" from subtle differences in size and shape of body and scales. This is a statement of different, and much reduced, order from the traditional tale of finches. For the finches are true and separate species—a living example of evolution. The subtle differences among tortoises represent minor geographic variation within a species. It is a jump in reasoning, albeit a valid one as we now know, to argue that such small differences can be amplified to produce a new species. All creationists, after all, acknowledged geographic variation (consider human races), but argued that it could not proceed beyond the rigid limits of a created archetype.

I don't wish to downplay the pivotal influence of the *Beagle* voyage on Darwin's career. It gave him space, freedom and endless time to think in his favored mode of independent self-stimulation. (His ambivalence towards university life, and his middling performance there by conventional standards, reflected his unhappiness with a curriculum of received wisdom.) He writes from South America in 1834: "I have not one clear idea about cleavage, stratification, lines of upheaval. I have no books, which tell me much and what they do I cannot apply to what I see. In consequence I draw my own conclusions, and most gloriously ridiculous ones they are." The rocks and plants and animals that he saw did provoke him to the crucial attitude of doubt—midwife of all creativity. Sydney, Australia—1836. Darwin wonders why a rational God would create so many marsupials on Australia since nothing about its climate or geography suggests any superiority for pouches: "I had been lying on a sunny bank and was reflecting on the strange character of the animals of this country as compared to the rest of the World. An unbeliever in everything beyond his own reason might exclaim, 'Surely two distinct Creators must have been at work.'"

Nonetheless, Darwin returned to London without an evolutionary theory. He suspected the truth of evolution, but had no mechanism to explain it. Natural selection did not arise from any direct reading of the *Beagle's* facts, but from two subsequent years of thought and struggle as reflected in a series of remarkable notebooks that have been unearthed and published during the past twenty years. In these notebooks, we see Darwin testing and abandoning a number of theories and pursuing a multitude of false leads—so much for his later claim about recording facts with an empty mind. He read philosophers, poets, and economists, always searching for meaning and insight—so much for the notion that

582   STEPHEN JAY GOULD

natural selection arose inductively from the *Beagle's* facts. Later, he labelled one notebook as "full of metaphysics on morals."

Yet if this tortuous path belies the Scylla of inductivism, it has engendered an equally simplistic myth—the Charybdis of eurekaism. In his maddeningly misleading autobiography, Darwin does record a eureka and suggests that natural selection struck him as a sudden, serendipitous flash after more than a year of groping frustration:

> In October 1838, that is, fifteen months after I had begun my systematic inquiry, I happened to read for amusement Malthus on Population,[2] and being well prepared to appreciate the struggle for existence which everywhere goes on from long-continued observation of the habits of animals and plants, it at once struck me that under these circumstances favorable variations would tend to be preserved, and unfavorable ones to be destroyed. The result of this would be the formation of new species. Here, then, I had at last got a theory by which to work.

Yet, again, the notebooks belie Darwin's later recollections—in this case by their utter failure to record, at the time it happened, any special exultation over his Malthusian insight. He inscribes it as a fairly short and sober entry without a single exclamation point, though he habitually used two or three in moments of excitement. He did not drop everything and reinterpret a confusing world in its light. On the very next day, he wrote an even longer passage on the sexual curiosity of primates.

The theory of natural selection arose neither as a workmanlike induction from nature's facts, nor as a mysterious bolt from Darwin's subconscious, triggered by an accidental reading of Malthus. It emerged instead as the result of a conscious and productive search, proceeding in a ramifying but ordered manner, and utilizing both the facts of natural history and an astonishingly broad range of insights from disparate disciplines far from his own. Darwin trod the middle path between inductivism and eurekaism. His genius is neither pedestrian nor inaccessible.

Darwinian scholarship has exploded since the centennial of the *Origin*[3] in 1959. The publication of Darwin's notebooks and the attention devoted by several scholars to the two crucial years between the *Beagle's* docking and the demoted Malthusian insight has clinched the argument for a "middle path" theory of Darwin's creativity. Two particularly important works focus on the broadest and narrowest scales. Howard E. Gruber's masterful intellectual and psychological biography of this phase in Darwin's life, *Darwin on Man*, traces all the false leads and turning points in Darwin's search. Gruber shows that Darwin was continually proposing, testing, and abandoning hypotheses, and that he never simply collected facts in a blind way. He began with a fanciful theory involving

2. Thomas Malthus, whose work on population was published under several titles be-   tween 1798 and 1817.
3. *The Origin of Species* (1859).

the idea that new species arise with a prefixed life span, and worked his way gradually, if fitfully, towards an idea of extinction by competition in a world of struggle. He recorded no exultation upon reading Malthus, because the jigsaw puzzle was only missing a piece or two at the time.

Silvan S. Schweber has reconstructed, in detail as minute as the record will allow, Darwin's activities during the few weeks before Malthus (The Origin of the Origin Revisited, *Journal of the History of Biology*, 1977). He argues that the final pieces arose not from new facts in natural history, but from Darwin's intellectual wanderings in distant fields. In particular, he read a long review of social scientist and philosopher Auguste Comte's most famous work, the *Cours de philosophie positive*.[4] He was particularly struck by Comte's insistence that a proper theory be predictive and at least potentially quantitative. He then turned to Dugald Stewart's *On the Life and Writing of Adam Smith*, and imbibed the basic belief of the Scottish economists that theories of overall social structure must begin by analyzing the unconstrained actions of individuals. (Natural selection is, above all, a theory about the struggle of individual organisms for success in reproduction.) Then, searching for quantification, he read a lengthy analysis of work by the most famous statistician of his time—the Belgian Adolphe Quetelet. In the review of Quetelet, he found, among other things, a forceful statement of Malthus's quantitative claim—that population would grow geometrically and food supplies only arithmetically, thus guaranteeing an intense struggle for existence. In fact, Darwin had read the Malthusian statement several times before; but only now was he prepared to appreciate its significance. Thus, he did not turn to Malthus by accident, and he already knew what it contained. His "amusement," we must assume, consisted only in a desire to read in its original formulation the familiar statement that had so impressed him in Quetelet's secondary account.

In reading Schweber's detailed account of the moments preceding Darwin's formulation of natural selection, I was particularly struck by the absence of deciding influence from his own field of biology. The immediate precipitators were a social scientist, an economist, and a statistician. If genius has any common denominator, I would propose breadth of interest and the ability to construct fruitful analogies between fields.

In fact, I believe that the theory of natural selection should be viewed as an extended analogy—whether conscious or unconscious on Darwin's part I do not know—to the laissez faire economics of Adam Smith. The essence of Smith's argument is a paradox of sorts: if you want an ordered economy providing maximal benefits to all, then let individuals compete and struggle for their own advantages. The result, after appropriate sorting and elimination of the inefficient, will be a stable and harmonious

4. *Course in Positivist Philosophy* (1830–42).

polity. Apparent order arises naturally from the struggle among individuals, not from predestined principles or higher control. Dugald Stewart epitomized Smith's system in the book Darwin read:

> The most effective plan for advancing a people . . . is by allowing every man, as long as he observes the rules of justice, to pursue his own interest in his own way, and to bring both his industry and his capital into the freest competition with those of his fellow citizens. Every system of policy which endeavors . . . to draw towards a particular species of industry a greater share of the capital of the society than would naturally go to it . . . is, in reality, subversive of the great purpose which it means to promote.

As Schweber states: "The Scottish analysis of society contends that the combined effect of individual actions results in the institutions upon which society is based, and that such a society is a stable and evolving one and functions without a designing and directing mind."

We know that Darwin's uniqueness does not reside in his support for the idea of evolution—scores of scientists had preceded him in this. His special contribution rests upon his documentation and upon the novel character of his theory about how evolution operates. Previous evolutionists had proposed unworkable schemes based on internal perfecting tendencies and inherent directions. Darwin advocated a natural and testable theory based on immediate interaction among individuals (his opponents considered it heartlessly mechanistic). The theory of natural selection is a creative transfer to biology of Adam Smith's basic argument for a rational economy: the balance and order of nature does not arise from a higher, external (divine) control, or from the existence of laws operating directly upon the whole, but from struggle among individuals for their own benefits (in modern terms, for the transmission of their genes to future generations through differential success in reproduction).

Many people are distressed to hear such an argument. Does it not compromise the integrity of science if some of its primary conclusions originate by analogy from contemporary politics and culture rather than from data of the discipline itself? In a famous letter to Engels, Karl Marx identified the similarities between natural selection and the English social scene:

> It is remarkable how Darwin recognizes among beasts and plants his English society with its division of labor, competition, opening up of new markets, 'invention,' and the Malthusian 'struggle for existence.' It is Hobbes' *bellum omnium contra omnes* (the war of all against all).[5]

Yet Marx was a great admirer of Darwin—and in this apparent paradox lies resolution. For reasons involving all the themes I have emphasized here—that inductivism is inadequate, that creativity demands breadth,

5. From the English philosopher Thomas Hobbes's *Leviathan* (1651).

and that analogy is a profound source of insight—great thinkers cannot be divorced from their social background. But the source of an idea is one thing; its truth or fruitfulness is another. The psychology and utility of discovery are very different subjects indeed. Darwin may have cribbed the idea of natural selection from economics, but it may still be right. As the German socialist Karl Kautsky wrote in 1902: "The fact that an idea emanates from a particular class, or accords with their interests, of course proves nothing as to its truth or falsity." In this case, it is ironic that Adam Smith's system of laissez faire does not work in his own domain of economics, for it leads to oligopoly and revolution, rather than to order and harmony. Struggle among individuals does, however, seem to be the law of nature.

Many people use such arguments about social context to ascribe great insights primarily to the indefinable phenomenon of good luck. Thus, Darwin was lucky to be born rich, lucky to be on the *Beagle*, lucky to live amidst the ideas of his age, lucky to trip over Parson Malthus—essentially little more than a man in the right place at the right time. Yet, when we read of his personal struggle to understand, the breadth of his concerns and study, and the directedness of his search for a mechanism of evolution, we understand why Pasteur made his famous quip that fortune favors the prepared mind.[6]

1980

6. Louis Pasteur (1822–95): French chemist.

Tom Bethell

AGNOSTIC EVOLUTIONISTS

The first time I saw Colin Patterson was at the American Museum of Natural History in New York City in the spring of 1983. He was in the office of Donn Rosen, a curator in the museum's department of ichthyology, which is the branch of zoology that deals with fishes. Patterson, a paleontologist specializing in fossil fishes, was staring through a binocular microscope at a slice of codfish. In his mid-fifties and balding, he was wearing black corduroys and a smoking-jacket affair of the kind that I associate with the Sloane Square poets of the "angry young man" generation—the generation to which Patterson belongs by age, and perhaps by temperament. I would later spend time with him in London, at the British Museum of Natural History, where he is a senior paleontologist, and at Cambridge University, where we attended a lecture by the famous

Harvard paleontologist Stephen Jay Gould. He often conveyed an impression of moody rebelliousness: he is authoritative, the kind of person others defer to in a discussion; he is habitually pessimistic; and he seemed not at all sanguine about his brushes with other scientists—encounters that by the late 1970s had become quite frequent. Those with whom Patterson has been arguing are mostly paleontologists and evolutionary biologists—researchers and academics who have devoted their careers, their lives, to upholding and fine-tuning the ideas about the origins and the development of species introduced by Charles Darwin in the second half of the nineteenth century. Patterson, it seemed, was no longer sure he believed in evolutionary theory, and he was saying so. Or, perhaps more accurately, he was saying that evolutionists—like the creationists they periodically do battle with—are nothing more than believers themselves.

In 1978, Patterson wrote an introductory book called *Evolution*, which was published by the British Museum. A year later, he received a letter from Luther Sunderland, an electrical engineer in upstate New York and a creationist-activist, asking why *Evolution* did not include any "direct illustrations of evolutionary transitions." Patterson's reply included the following:

> You say I should at least "show a photo of the fossil from which each type of organism was derived." I will lay it on the line—there is not one such fossil for which one could make a watertight argument. The reason is that statements about ancestry and descent are not applicable in the fossil record. Is *Archaeopteryx* the ancestor of all birds? Perhaps yes, perhaps no: there is no way of answering the question. It is easy enough to make up stories of how one form gave rise to another, and to find reasons why the stages should be favoured by natural selection. But such stories are not part of science, for there is no way of putting them to the test.

By 1981, Patterson's doubts about evolutionary theory were finding their way to the public. A sentence in a brochure he wrote that year for the British Museum began: "If the theory of evolution is true . . . " In the fall of 1981, Patterson addressed the Systematics Discussion Group at the American Museum of Natural History. Once a month, the group meets in an upstairs classroom at the museum, opposite the dinosaur exhibit hall. The audience in any given month is likely to be made up of museum staff, graduate students from nearby universities, and the occasional amateur like Norman Macbeth, the author of *Darwin Retried*. (Systematics is a science of classification; taxonomists working in systematics study the way taxonomic groups relate to one another in nature.) There may be no more than fifteen people on hand when the discussion focuses on, say, fossil rodent teeth; or there may be 150 or more when Richard C. Lewontin, the renowned geneticist and author, gives a talk on the meaning (if any) of adaptation in biology.

Patterson 's address was titled "Evolutionism and Creationism." Patterson is not a creationist, but he had been trying to think like one as a sort of experiment. "It's true," he told his audience, "that for the last eighteen months or so I've been kicking around non-evolutionary or even anti-evolutionary ideas." He went on:

> I think always before in my life when I've got up to speak on a subject I've been confident of one thing—that I know more about it than anybody in the room, because I've worked on it. Well, this time it isn't true. I'm speaking on two subjects, evolutionism and creationism, and I believe it's true to say that I know nothing whatever about either of them.
>
> One of the reasons I started taking this anti-evolutionary view, or let's call it a non-evolutionary view, was that last year I had a sudden realization. For over twenty years I had thought I was working on evolution in some way. One morning I woke up and something had happened in the night, and it struck me that I had been working on this stuff for more than twenty years, and there was not one thing I knew about it. It's quite a shock to learn that one can be so misled for so long. Either there was something wrong with me or there was something wrong with evolutionary theory. Naturally I know there is nothing wrong with me, so for the last few weeks I've tried putting a simple question to various people and groups.
>
> Question is: Can you tell me anything you know about evolution? Any one thing, any one thing that is true?

In the public mind, challenges to Darwin's theory of evolution are associated with biblical creationists who periodically remove their children from schoolrooms where they are being taught that man evolved from monkeys. Most Americans know about the Scopes trial of 1925, in which a Tennessee high school teacher was fined $100 for teaching evolutionary theory. Four years ago there was the trial in San Diego in which Kelly Seagraves, director of the Creation Science Research Center, unsuccessfully sued the state of California over regulations governing the teaching of evolution in California public schools. (Seagraves wanted science teachers to be required to mention pertinent passages from the Book of Genesis.) What most people do not know is that for much of this century, and especially in recent years, scientists have been fighting among themselves about Darwin and his ideas.

Scientists are largely responsible for keeping the public in the dark about these in-house arguments. When they see themselves as beleaguered by opponents outside the citadel of science, they tend to put their differences aside and unite to defeat the heathen. The layman sees only the closed ranks. At the moment, with creationism apparently quiescent, we can, if we listen hard enough, hear fresh murmurs of dissent within the scientific walls. These debates are more complicated, perhaps, than the old contest, Science vs. Religion, but they are at least as interesting, and sometimes as heated.

One of the least publicized and least understood challenges to Darwin and the theory of evolution—and surely one of the more fascinating, in its sweep and rigor—involves a school of taxonomists called cladists. (A "clade" is a branch, from the Greek *klados*; "cladist" is pronounced with a long *a*.) Particularly interesting—vexing, evolutionary biologists would say (and do)—are those who toil in what is called transformed cladistics, and who might be thought of as agnostic evolutionists. Like many who have broken with a faith and challenged an orthodoxy, the transformed cladists are perhaps best defined by an opponent—in this case, the British biologist Beverly Halstead. Asked not long ago in a BBC interview what he thought of transformed cladistics, Halstead replied: "Well, I object to it! I mean, this is going back to Aristotle. It is not pre-Darwinian, it is Aristotelian. From Darwin's day to the present we've understood there's a time element; we've begun to understand evolution. What they are doing in transformed cladistics is to say, Let's forget about evolution, let's forget about process, let's simply consider pattern."

Since Darwin's time, biologists have been absorbed in process: Where did we come from? How did everything in nature get to be what it now is? How will things continue to alter? The transformed cladists—they are sometimes called pattern cladists—are not concerned primarily with time or process. To understand why, it helps to know that they are trained in taxonomy: they are rigorous, scrupulous labelers. Their job as taxonomists is to discover and name the various groups found in nature— a task first assigned to Adam by God, according to Genesis—and put them into one category or another. Taxonomists try to determine not how groups came into existence but what groups exist, among both present-day and fossil organisms. To understand that cladists believe this knowledge must be acquired before ideas about process can be tested is to understand the natural tension that exists between taxonomists and evolutionary biologists.

The transformed cladists have escalated the battle. In the 1940s and 1950s, years which witnessed the growth of evolutionary biology, taxonomists allowed themselves what might be called a bit of artistic license. (They called it the new systematics.) This occurred in part, no doubt, because taxonomy had come to be thought of as dull and stuffy—particularly by evolutionists like Sir Julian Huxley (the grandson of Darwin's contemporary champion Thomas Henry Huxley), who believed it was high time to cease being "bogged down in semantics and definitions." (Sir Julian said this in 1959 at the University of Chicago during a centennial celebration for Darwin's *On the Origin of Species*.) Taxonomists, in other words, were regarded as bookkeepers and accountants in need of a little loosening up. In his 1959 book *Nature & Man's Fate*, Garrett Hardin, a professor of human ecology at the University of California at

Santa Barbara, quoted a zoologist as giving this advice: "Whoever wants to hold to firm rules should give up taxonomic work. Nature is much too disorderly for such a man."

The transformed cladists think otherwise, and have sought to re-establish taxonomic rigor. In doing so, they have come to think that it is the evolutionists who have the problem—the problem being slipshod methodology. Colin Patterson, perhaps the leading transformed cladist, has enunciated what might be regarded as the cladists' battle cry: "The concept of ancestry is not accessible by the tools we have." Patterson and his fellow cladists argue that a common ancestor can only be hypothe-sized, not identified in the fossil record. A group of people can be brought together for a family reunion on the basis of birth documents, tombstone inscriptions, and parish records—evidence of process, one might say. But in nature there are no parish records; there are only fossils. And a fossil, Patterson told me once, is a "mess on a rock." Time, change, process, evolution—none of this, the cladists argue, can be read from rocks.

What can be discerned in nature, according to the cladists, are pat-terns—relationships between things, not between eras. There can be no absolute tracing back. There can be no certainty about parent-offspring links. There are only inferences drawn from fossils. To the cladists, the science of evolution is in large part a matter of faith—faith different, but not all *that* different, from that of the creationists.

"I really put my foot in it," Patterson told me that day I first met him nearly two years ago. We were in a restaurant on Columbus Avenue near the Museum of Natural History, and he was recalling the talk he had given eighteen months earlier to the systematics discussion group. "I compared evolution and creation and made a case that the two were equivalent. I was all fired up, and I said what I thought. I went through merry hell for about a year. Almost everybody except the people at the museum objected. Lots of academics wrote. Deluges of mail. 'Here we are trying to combat a political argument,' they said, 'and you give them ammunition!'"

He ordered something from the menu and said:"One has to live with one's colleagues. They hold the theory very dear. I found out that what you say will be taken in 'political' rather than rational terms."

Patterson told me that he regarded the theory of evolution as "often unnecessary" in biology. "In fact," he said, "they could do perfectly well without it." Nevertheless, he said, it was presented in textbooks as though it were "the unified field theory of biology," holding the whole subject together—and binding the profession to it. "Once something has that status," he said, "it becomes like religion."

The founding father of cladistics was an entomologist named Willi Hennig. Hennig was born in what is now East Germany and spent the bulk of his career there, studying and classifying flies. At some point in the mid-1960s (there is very little biographical information available about him) he turned up in West Germany; he died there, at the age of 63, in 1976. His principal work is *Phylogenetic Systematics*, an updated version of which was translated into English and published in the United States in 1966 by the University of Illinois Press. It is a difficult book, and an enormously influential one. By the 1970s, as the prominent evolutionary biologist Ernst Mayr wrote in *The Growth of Biological Thought*, a virtual Hennig cult had developed. A Willi Hennig Society was formed in 1980, and its fourth annual meeting, held last summer in London, was attended by some 250 scientists from around the world. Last month, the society published the first issue of its new quarterly journal, *Cladistics*. According to David Hull, the philosopher of science (he was at the meeting too), "among evolutionary biologists, cladistics is what everyone is arguing about."

At the heart of cladistics are the concepts of "plesiomorphy" and "paraphyly." A characteristic, or trait, is said to be plesiomorphic if it is found in a group of organisms of more general scope than the specific group under consideration. Thus, while all primates have hair, hair is also a characteristic of a more general class of creatures—mammals. What Hennig called the fallacy of plesiomorphy is the belief that a characteristic (like hair) identifies and helps to define a particular species or order of animal life when in fact it can be found among a broader group.

Hennig also objected to the still common practice in biology of identifying a grouping of animal life only by the absence of certain characteristics. (His reasoning was Aristotelian; in *On the Parts of Animals*, Aristotle wrote that "there can be no specific forms of a negation, of Featherless, for instance or of Footless, as there are of Feathered or Footed.") It was the lack of precision that bothered Hennig: a feathered animal is one thing (a bird); a non-feathered animal is anything (except a bird). Groups in nature defined by an absence of characteristics Hennig called paraphyletic.

By calling attention to the paraphyletic traits, Hennig helped revive the rigor taxonomy once prided itself on. Colin Patterson and other transformed cladists have moved on to examine—and call into question —the crucial role that paraphyletic groups and species play in evolutionary theory. In his 1981 talk at the Museum of Natural History, for example, Patterson touched on the subject of invertebrates. Invertebrates make up one of the two general categories of animals. The grouping comprises a huge and often bewildering diversity of animals, from the simplest single-cell protozoan to insects, clams, worms, and crabs. Every schoolchild learns that what brings this wide array of creatures under one heading is their shared lack of a backbone. Cladists like Patterson have asked: Why group them this way? What function does it serve? The problem they have is this: the term *invertebrate* does not serve a scientific function; it is too nebulous, too inexact for that. (It also accurately describes strawberries and chairs.) What the term *invertebrate* does serve, the cladists maintain, is a rhetorical function: it makes possible the claim, found in many textbooks, that "vertebrates evolved from invertebrates." According to the cladistic reading, the last two words of the four-word statement do not contain any information that is not asserted as factual by the first two words; "vertebrates evolved" simply means that the first vertebrate had parents without backbones. The transformed cladists claim that "vertebrates evolved from invertebrates" is a disguised tautology.

In his museum talk, Patterson said that groups defined only by negative traits have "no existence in nature, and they cannot possibly convey knowledge, though they appear to when you first hear them." Evolutionary biologists maintain that negatively defined groups make sense and serve a purpose; they tend to accuse the cladists, as one writer recently did in the magazine *Science*, of engaging in "verbal legerdemain." But Patterson and his colleagues point their fingers back at the evolutionists. Patterson for one has called the paraphyletic groups "voids."

What evolutionary theory does, the cladists say, is make claims about something that cannot be determined by studying fossils. They say that the "tree of life," with its paraphyletic branches, is nothing more than a hypothesis, a reasonable guess.

Nor do they believe it will ever be anything more than that. When asked about this in an interview, Patterson said: "I don't think we shall ever have any access to any form of tree which we can call factual." He was then asked: "Do you believe it to be, then, no reality?" He replied: "Well, isn't it strange that this is what it comes to, that you have to ask me whether I believe it, as if it mattered whether I believe it or not. Yes, I do believe it. But in saying that, it is obvious it is faith."

Cladists do not spend their time on the lecture circuit drumming up sentiment against Darwin. Some of them would like it if all the talk about evolution just quietly went away. Evolution is not important to the work they do. That work involves finding the positive and verifiable characteristics of the various species and determining how all these species fit together in the animal kingdom—what patterns exist in nature. Their interest is the here and now, not how it all came to be.

I recently spent some time with two cladists on the staff of the Museum of Natural History. I first met with Gareth Nelson, who in 1982 was named chairman of the department of ichthyology. Nelson graduated from the University of Hawaii in 1966 and he joined the museum staff a year later. The walls of Nelson's office were lined with boxes of articles from scientific journals, and a large table was covered with papers and jars stuffed with small, silvery fish preserved in alcohol: anchovies. Nelson is just about the world's expert on anchovies, although he told me that the number of people studying them (three or four) is much smaller than the number of anchovy species (there are 150 known species, and Nelson believes there are many more). This disparity between the magnitude of the scientific "problem" and the number of people working on it is a commonplace in biology. Most laymen think that the experts have pretty exhaustively studied the earth's biota, when they have barely scratched the surface.

Nelson put the issue of evolution this way: in order to understand what we actually know, we must first look at what it is that the evolutionists claim to know for certain. He said that if you turn to a widely used college text like Alfred Romer's *Vertebrate Paleontology*, published by the University of Chicago Press in 1966 and now in its third edition, you will find such statements as "mammals evolved from reptiles," and "birds are descended from reptiles." (Very rarely, at least in the current literature, will you find the claim that a given species evolved from another given species.) The trouble with general statements like "mammals evolved from reptiles," Nelson said, is that the "ancestral groups are taxonomic artifacts." These groups "do not have any characters that are unique," he said. "They do not have defining characters, and therefore they are not real groups." I asked Nelson to name some of these allegedly "unreal" groups. He replied: invertebrates, fishes, reptiles, apes. According to Nelson, this does not by any means exhaust the list of negatively defined groups. Statements imputing ancestry to such groups have no real meaning, he said.

I asked Nelson about the fossil record. Don't we know that evolutionary theory is true from the fossils? Like most people, I thought the natural history museums had pretty well worked out the fossil sequences, much as in an automobile museum you can find the "ancestors" of contemporary cars lined up in sequence: Thunderbird back to Model T.

"Usually with fossils all you find are a few nuts and bolts," Nelson said. "An odd piston ring, maybe, or different pieces of a carburetor that are spread out or piled on top of one another, but not in their correct arrangement."

He maintained that too much importance has been attached to fossils. "And it's easy to understand why," he said. "You put in all this effort studying them, and you get out a little bit. Therefore you are persuaded that that little bit must be very important. I can get ten times more information per unit with recent fishes. So if you put in all that effort on fossils, you are inclined to say that the information you get is worth ten times as much."

Nelson said it was quite common for paleontologists to go to all the trouble of digging up fossils without realizing that the animals in question were still walking about. (Think of spending months hunting for a book in used-book stores without realizing it was still in print.) "Say you dig up a 50-million-year-old beetle," he said. "It looks like it belongs to a certain family, but there may be 30,000 species in the family. What do you do? Go through all 30,000? No, you just give it an appropriate-sounding name, *Eocoleoptera*, say. If it is a species that has been in existence for 50 million years, somebody else will have to find that out, because you don't have enough time. You're out digging in the rocks, not poking through beetle collections in museums."

I asked him about anchovy fossils. How far back do they go? "Well," he said, "Lance Grande, who was a student here recently, studied that, and it turns out that all the fossils previously described as anchovies are not anchovies at all." (Grande is now an assistant curator in the department of geology at the Field Museum of Natural History in Chicago.) "In other words," Nelson said, "the people who described them did not do a very good job. So the fossil record of anchovies was reduced to zero. However, there was something in the British Museum that I think Colin Patterson told Grande about, something from the Miocene in Cyprus; maybe 10 million years old. And it turned out to be an anchovy—the only known fossil. It has not yet been described in detail, but there is information suggesting it is the same kind of animal we find inhabiting the Mediterranean today."

A week or two after I met with Nelson I spoke to Norman Platnick, a curator in the museum's entomology department and an expert on spiders. On my way to see him on the fifth floor, I was joined in the elevator by a couple of lab assistants who were wheeling on a cart what looked like a dinosaur head. (I was reminded that for a long time the museum had the wrong head on its brontosaurus. One of the few bits of conventional wisdom about paleontology is that entire animals can be reconstructed from scraps of bone. Paleontologists now repudiate the idea, first enunciated by the French anatomist Baron Cuvier in the early 1800s. Steve Farris, a professor in the department of ecology and evolution at the State University of New York at Stony Brook and the president of the Hennig Society, told me that Cuvier erected a monument to his own error in the form of a cement statue of an iguanodon, now at the Crystal Palace outside London. "The animal that Cuvier imagined was four-footed and resembled a rhinoceros," Farris said. "The complete skeleton of the iguanodon is now known—the animal was bipedal, with a long tail." As for the idea that the relationship of early animals to present-day ones is well established, Farris said: "When they are writing for a general audience, a lot of paleontologists do try to give that impression.")

Not far from the elevator I found Platnick's orderly office: spiders (dead) inside little labeled bottles; book-filled shelves; journal articles neatly stacked. It would seem that professional biologists spend at least as much time studying each other's work as they do the world around them.

Platnick, who is rather square-shaped and bearded, told me that when he was an undergraduate at a small Appalachian college, he would go along with his wife when she collected millipedes. "But I was a wretched millipede collector," he said. "When we arrived home, all I would have in my jars would be spiders." So he started to study them. Today he has a Ph.D. from Harvard, and he and Nelson are co-authors of a book recently published by Columbia University Press entitled *Systematics and Biogeography: Cladistics and Vicariance.*

Spiders, which go back to the Devonian period, 400 million years ago, belong to the class Arachnida and the phylum Arthropoda. They are among the "invertebrates," in other words, and are not well preserved in the fossil record. About 35,000 species of spiders have been identified, Platnick said, "but there may be three times that many in the world." He thought there were perhaps four full-time systematists examining spiders in the United States, "and perhaps another dozen who teach at small colleges and do some research." There is an American Arachnological Society, with 475 members worldwide, some of them amateurs. They meet once a year and discuss scorpions and daddy-long-legs, as well as spiders.

"Most of the spiders I look at may have been looked at by two or three people in history," Platnick said, adding that he would most likely be dead before anyone looked at them again.

I asked Platnick what was known about spider phylogeny, or ancestry.

"Very little," he said. "We still don't know a hill of beans about that." We certainly don't know, he said, what species the animal belonged to that was the ancestor of the very first spider. All we know of such an animal is that it was *not* a spider. We don't even know of any links in the (presumed) 400-million-year chain of spider ancestry.

"I do not ever say that this spider is ancestral to that one," Platnick said firmly.

"Does anyone?"

"I don't know of a single case in the modern literature where it's claimed that one spider is the ancestor of another."

Some spiders have been well preserved in amber. Even so, Platnick said, "very few spider fossils have been so well preserved that you can put a species name on them." After a pause he added: "You don't learn much from fossils."

In view of Platnick's comments about our knowledge of spider ancestry, I was curious to know what he thought of the following passage from a well-known high school biology text, *Life: An Introduction to Biology,* by George Simpson and William S. Beck, first published in 1957 by Harcourt Brace Jovanovich and still in print.

> An animal is not classified as an arachnid because it has four or five pairs of
> legs rather than three. It is classified in the Arachnida because it has the same
> ancestry as other arachnids, and a different ancestry from insects over some
> hundreds of millions of years, as attested by all the varying characteristics of
> the two groups and by large numbers of fossil representatives of both.

At that he threw himself back in his chair, and burst out laughing.

In this passage, Simpson and Beck were practicing the verbal sleight of
hand that has been common in evolutionary biology since the 1940s. All
we know for sure is that there is a group of organisms (in this case spiders)
that are identifiable as a group because they have certain unique characteristics. They have spinnerets for spinning silk, for instance, and thus we
can say that all organisms with spinnerets are spiders. (They share other
unique features, too.)

If we want to explain why thousands of members of a group have
features uniquely in common, that is another matter entirely. We can, if
we like, posit a theoretical common ancestor in the ur-spider, which
transmitted spider traits to all its descendants. That is precisely what
Darwin did in On the Origin of Species. But Simpson and Beck do
something very different. They say that the composition of the class
Arachnida was determined by examining not the features of spiders but
their ancestral lines. But no such pedigrees are known to science—not just
with respect to spiders but with respect to all groups of organisms.

The point stressed by the cladists is this: unless we know the taxonomic relationships of organisms—what makes each unique and different from the other—we cannot possibly guess at the ancestral
relationships. Things in nature here and now must be ranked according
to their taxonomic relationship before they can be placed in a family tree.
Thus the speculations of evolutionists ("Do X and Y have a common
ancestor?") must be subordinate to the findings of taxonomists ("X and Y
have features not shared by anything else"). If fossils came with pedigrees
attached, this laborious method of comparison would not be necessary;
but of course they don't.

"Stephen Jay Gould does his work without bothering about cladistics, I
assure you," Platnick said, citing a recent paper by Niels Bonde, a
paleontologist at the University of Copenhagen. Platnick went on to say
that "the literature is replete with such statements as 'fossil X is the
ancestor of some other taxon,' when it has not even been shown that
fossil X is the closest relative of that taxon." (By "closest relative" he
means that the two taxa form a group having unique characteristics.)
"This is seen most commonly in accounts of human paleontology, but it
is by no means restricted to it," Platnick said.

One reason why many laymen readily accept evolution as fact is that
they have seen the famous "horse sequence" reproduced in textbooks.

The sequence, which shows a gradual increase in the size of the horse with time, is dear to the hearts of textbook writers, in large part because it is on display at the American Museum of Natural History. For obvious reasons, the museum staff are uncomfortable going on record about the horse sequence, but when Niles Eldridge, a curator in the department of invertebrates at the museum and co-author, with Stephen Jay Gould, of the "punctuated equilibria" theory of evolution (organisms stay the same for millions of years, then change quickly rather than gradually, as Darwin believed), was asked about it once, he said:

> There have been an awful lot of stories, some more imaginative than others, about what the nature of that history [of life] really is. The most famous example, still on exhibit downstairs, is the exhibit on horse evolution prepared perhaps fifty years ago. That has been presented as the literal truth in textbook after textbook. Now I think that that is lamentable, particularly when the people who propose these kinds of stories may themselves be aware of the speculative nature of some of that stuff.

When I brought the subject up with Platnick, he said that he thought horse fossils had not yet been properly classified, or even exhaustively studied. I wanted to know whether Platnick believed that evolution has occurred. He said he did, and that the evidence was to be found in the existing hierarchical structure of nature. All organisms can, as it were, be placed within an internested set of "boxes." The box labeled "gazelles" fits in the larger box labeled "ungulates" (animals with hoofs), which fits inside the "mammals" box, which fits inside "tetrapods" (four-footed animals), which fits inside "vertebrates." The grand task of taxonomy, Platnick said, is to describe this hierarchical pattern precisely, and in particular to define the traits that delineate the boundaries of each "box."

Whether taxonomy will ever fill in all the blanks in the pattern is a question Platnick cannot answer. One problem, he said, is the shortage of taxonomists. "Systematics," he said, "doesn't have the glamour to attract research funds." Research grants have increasingly gone to molecular and biochemical studies; the result is that support for taxonomy at many institutions has, he said, "withered away." This bothered Platnick. "I am fully prepared to stand up to any biologist who says evolutionary theory is more important, or more basic. Without the results of systematics there is nothing to be explained."

I wanted to find out what those on the other side—the evolutionary biologists and paleontologists—had to say about what the cladists are saying. First I went to the bookshelf. In his 1969 book *The Triumph of the Darwinian Method* (recently reprinted by the University of Chicago Press), Michael T. Ghiselin, one of Darwin's greatest admirers, seems to be taking on the cladists (or trying to) when he writes:

Instead of finding patterns in nature and deciding that because of their conspicuousness they seem important, we discover the underlying mechanisms that impose order on natural phenomena, whether we see that order or not, and then derive the structure of our classification system from this understanding.

I next looked in *Hen's Teeth and Horse's Toes*, Stephen Jay Gould's volume of essays on natural history. "No debate in evolutionary biology has been more intense during the past decade than the challenges raised by cladistics against traditional schemes of classification," Gould writes. He is not sympathetic to cladistics ("its leading exponents in America are among the most contentious scientists I have ever encountered"), but in his essay "What, If Anything, Is a Zebra?" he admits that "behind the names and the nastiness lies an important set of principles." These he enunciates, only to repudiate. He acknowledges that a strict taxonomy would eliminate groups like apes and fishes. But when cladists go this far, "many biologists rebel, and rightly, I think." Like his Harvard colleague Edward O. Wilson, the Frank B. Baird Professor of Science, Gould opts for the "admittedly vague and qualitative, but not therefore unimportant notion of overall similarity" of form.

I decided it would be a good idea to talk with a scientist who believes strongly in evolutionary theory. Last May, I traveled to Boston to meet with Richard C. Lewontin, a geneticist, a one-time president of the Society for the Study of Evolution, a well-known writer on science, and currently Agassiz Professor of Zoology at Harvard. I had seen a quote from Lewontin used as a chapter head in a book titled *Science on Trial*, by Douglas Futuyma. The quote, as edited, read: "Evolution is fact, not theory.... Birds evolve from nonbirds, humans evolve from nonhumans."

Lewontin was uncharacteristically attired in a scientist's regulation white lab coat when I first saw him (instead of his usual blue work shirt). We talked a bit about his stand against biological determinism. Finally it was time to get around to the point of my visit. What about these claims: evolution is fact; birds evolve from nonbirds, humans from nonhumans? The cladists disapproved, I said.

He paused for a split second and said: "Those are very weak statements, I agree." Then he made one of the clearest statements about evolution I have heard. He said; "Those statements flow simply from the assertion that all organisms have parents. It is an empirical claim, I think, that all living organisms have living organisms as parents. The second empirical claim is that there was a time on earth when there were no mammals. Now, if you allow me those two claims as empirical, then the claim that mammals arose from non-mammals is simply a conclusion. It's the deduction from two empirical claims. But that's all I want to claim for it. You can't make the direct empirical statement that mammals arose from non-mammals."

Lewontin had made what seemed to me to be a deduction—a materialist's deduction. "The only problem is that it appears to be based on evidence derived from fossils," I said. "But the cladists say they don't really have that kind of information."

"Of course they don't," Lewontin said. "In fact, the stuff I've written on creationism, which isn't much, has always made that point. There is a vast weight of empirical evidence about the universe which says that unless you invoke supernatural causes, the birds could not have arisen from muck by any natural processes. Well, if the birds couldn't have arisen from muck by any natural processes, then they had to arise from non-birds. The only alternative is to say that they did arise from muck— because God's finger went out and touched that muck. That is to say, there was a non-natural process. And that's really where the action is. Either you think that complex organisms arose by non-natural phenomena, or you think that they arose by natural phenomena. If they arose by natural phenomena, they had to evolve. And that's all there is to it. And that's the only claim I'm making."

He reached for a copy of his 1982 book *Human Diversity*, and said: "Look, I'm a person who says in this book that we don't know anything about the ancestors of the human species." (He writes on page 163: "Despite the excited and optimistic claims that have been made by some paleontologists, no fossil hominid species can be established as our direct ancestor. . . .") "All the fossils which have been dug up and are claimed to be ancestors—we haven't the faintest idea whether they are ancestors. Because all you've got, and the cladists are right . . . " He got up and began to do his famous rat-a-tat-tat with a piece of chalk on the blackboard. "All you've got is Homo Sapiens there, you've got *that* fossil there, you've got another fossil *there* . . . this is time here . . . and it's up to you to draw the lines. Because there *are* no lines. I don't think any one of them is likely to be the direct ancestor of the human species. But how would you know it's *that* [pat] one?

"The only way you can know that some fossil is the direct ancestor is that it's so human that it *is* human. There is a contradiction there. If it is different enough from humans to be interesting, then you don't know whether it's an ancestor or not. And if it's similar enough to be human, then it's not interesting."

He returned to his chair and looked out at the slanting rain. "So," he said. "Look, we're not ever going to know what the direct ancestor is."

What struck me about Lewontin's argument was how much it depended on his premise that all organisms have parents. In a sense, his argument includes the assertion that evolutionary theory is true. Lewontin maintains that his premise is "empirical," but this is so only in the (admittedly important) sense that it has never to our knowledge been falsified. No one has ever found an organism that is known not to have parents, or a parent. This is the strongest evidence on behalf of evolution.

Our belief, or "faith," that, as Patterson says, "all organisms have parents" ultimately derives from our acceptance of the philosophy of materialism. It is hard for us to understand (so long has materialism been the natural habitat of Western thought) that this philosophy was not always accepted. In one of his essays on natural history reprinted in *Ever Since Darwin*, Stephen Jay Gould suggests that Darwin delayed publishing his theory of evolution by natural selection because he was, perhaps unconsciously, waiting for the climate of materialism to become more firmly established. In his 1838 *M Notebook* Darwin wrote: "To avoid stating how far, I believe, in Materialism, say only that emotions, instincts, degrees of talent, which are hereditary are so because brain of child resembles parent stock." Darwin realized that the climate *had* changed—that evolution was "in the air"—in 1858 when he was jolted by Alfred Russel Wallace's paper outlining a theory of the mechanism of evolution very similar to his own.

The theory of evolution has never been falsified. On the other hand, it is also surely true that the positive evidence for evolution is very much weaker than most laymen imagine, and than many scientists want us to imagine. Perhaps, as Patterson says, that positive evidence is missing entirely. The human mind, alas, seems on the whole to find such uncertainty intolerable. Most people want certainty in one form (Darwin) or another (the Bible). Only evolutionary agnostics like Patterson and Nelson and the other cladists seem willing to live with doubt. And that, surely, is the only truly scientific outlook.

1986

THE READER

1. What, according to Bethell, is "the only true scientific outlook"? Do you agree? Is this view generally supported by other essays on science in this section, or are there exceptions?
2. What is the difference between the kind of work done by taxonomists and by evolutionary biologists?
3. What is meant by "the philosophy of materialism"?
4. What question, specifically, is at issue in the discussion of evolution presented here?

THE WRITER

1. Does Bethell have a thesis? If so, by what means does he demonstrate or develop it?
2. Write a brief explanation of the relationship between Bethell's title and the body of the article.

Literature and the Arts

Eudora Welty

ONE WRITER'S BEGINNINGS

I learned from the age of two or three that any room in our house, at any time of day, was there to read in, or to be read to. My mother read to me. She'd read to me in the big bedroom in the mornings, when we were in her rocker together, which ticked in rhythm as we rocked, as though we had a cricket accompanying the story. She'd read to me in the diningroom on winter afternoons in front of the coal fire, with our cuckoo clock ending the story with "Cuckoo," and at night when I'd got in my own bed. I must have given her no peace. Sometimes she read to me in the kitchen while she sat churning, and the churning sobbed along with any story. It was my ambition to have her read to me while I churned; once she granted my wish, but she read off my story before I brought her butter. She was an expressive reader. When she was reading "Puss in Boots,"[1] for instance, it was impossible not to know that she distrusted all cats.

It had been startling and disappointing to me to find out that story books had been written by *people*, that books were not natural wonders, coming up of themselves like grass. Yet regardless of where they came from, I cannot remember a time when I was not in love with them—with the books themselves, cover and binding and the paper they were printed on, with their smell and their weight and with their possession in my arms, captured and carried off to myself. Still illiterate, I was ready for them, committed to all the reading I could give them.

Neither of my parents had come from homes that could afford to buy many books, but though it must have been something of a strain on his salary, as the youngest officer in a young insurance company, my father

---

1. A fairy tale.

was all the while carefully selecting and ordering away for what he and Mother thought we children should grow up with. They bought first for the future.

Besides the bookcase in the livingroom, which was always called "the library," there were the encyclopedia tables and dictionary stand under windows in our diningroom. Here to help us grow up arguing around the diningroom table were the Unabridged Webster, the Columbia Encyclopedia, Compton's Pictured Encyclopedia, the Lincoln Library of Information, and later the Book of Knowledge. And the year we moved into our new house, there was room to celebrate it with the new 1925 edition of the Britannica, which my father, his face always deliberately turned toward the future, was of course disposed to think better than any previous edition.

In "the library," inside the mission-style bookcase with its three diamond-latticed glass doors, with my father's Morris chair and the glass-shaded lamp on its table beside it, were books I could soon begin on—and I did, reading them all alike and as they came, straight down their rows, top shelf to bottom. There was the set of Stoddard's Lectures, in all its late nineteenth-century vocabulary and vignettes of peasant life and quaint beliefs and customs, with matching halftone illustrations: Vesuvius erupting, Venice by moonlight, gypsies glimpsed by their campfires. I didn't know then the clue they were to my father's longing to see the rest of the world. I read straight through his other love-from-afar: the Victrola Book of the Opera, with opera after opera in synopsis, with portraits in costume of Melba, Caruso, Galli-Curci, and Geraldine Farrar,[2] some of whose voices we could listen to on our Red Seal records.

My mother read secondarily for information; she sank as a hedonist into novels. She read Dickens in the spirit in which she would have eloped with him. The novels of her girlhood that had stayed on in her imagination, besides those of Dickens and Scott and Robert Louis Stevenson,[3] were *Jane Eyre, Trilby, The Woman in White, Green Mansions, King Solomon's Mines.*[4]Marie Corelli's[5] name would crop up but I understood she had gone out of favor with my mother, who had only kept *Ardath* out of loyalty. In time she absorbed herself in Galsworthy, Edith Wharton, above all in Thomas Mann of the *Joseph* volumes.[6]

St. Elmo was not in our house; I saw it often in other houses. This wildly

2. Nellie Melba (1861–1931); Enrico Caruso (1837–1921); Amelita Galli-Curci (1889–1964); Geraldine Farrar (1882–1967).
3. Charles Dickens (1812–70); Sir Walter Scott (1771–1832); Robert Louis Stevenson (1850–94). The first was English, the others Scottish.
4. Respectively by Charlotte Brontë (1816–55), George Du Maurier (1834–96), Wilkie Collins (1824–89), William Henry Hudson (1841–1922), Sir H. Rider Haggard (1856–1925). All were English.
5. The pen name of Mary Mackay (1855–1924), a popular and prolific English novelist.
6. John Galsworthy (1867–1933), English; Edith Wharton (1862–1937), American; Thomas Mann (1875–1955), German, whose *Joseph* novels appeared in four parts, from 1933 to 1943.

popular Southern novel is where all the Edna Earles in our population started coming from. They're all named for the heroine, who succeded in bringing a dissolute, sinning roué and atheist of a lover (St. Elmo) to his knees. My mother was able to forgo it. But she remembered the classic advice given to rose growers on how to water their bushes long enough: "Take a chair and St. *Elmo*."[7]

To both my parents I owe my early acquaintance with a beloved Mark Twain. There was a full set of Mark Twain and a short set of Ring Lardner in our bookcase,[8] and those were the volumes that in time united us all, parents and children.

Reading everything that stood before me was how I came upon a worn old book without a back that had belonged to my father as a child. It was called *Sanford and Merton.* Is there anyone left who recognizes it, I wonder? It is the famous moral tale written by Thomas Day in the 1780s, but of him no mention is made on the title page of *this* book; here it is *Sanford and Merton in Words of One Syllable* by Mary Godolphin. Here are the rich boy and the poor boy and Mr. Barlow, their teacher and interlocutor, in long discourses alternating with dramatic scenes—danger and rescue allotted to the rich and the poor respectively. It may have only words of one syllable, but one of them is "quoth." It ends with not one but two morals, both engraved on rings: "Do what you ought, come what may," and "If we would be great, we must first learn to be good."

This book was lacking its front cover, the back held on by strips of pasted paper, now turned golden, in several layers, and the pages stained, flecked, and tattered around the edges; its garish illustrations had come unattached but were preserved, laid in. I had the feeling even in my heedless childhood that this was the only book my father as a little boy had had of his own. He had held onto it, and might have gone to sleep on its coverless face: he had lost his mother when he was seven. My father had never made any mention to his own children of the book, but he had brought it along with him from Ohio to our house and shelved it in our bookcase.

My mother had brought from West Virginia that set of Dickens; those books looked sad, too—they had been through fire and water before I was born, she told me, and there they were, lined up—as I later realized, waiting for *me.*

I was presented, from as early as I can remember, with books of my own, which appeared on my birthday and Christmas morning. Indeed, my parents could not give me books enough. They must have sacrificed to give me on my sixth or seventh birthday—it was after I became a reader for myself—the ten-volume set of Our Wonder World. These

7. By Augusta Jane Evans (1835–1909).
8. Mark Twain: the pen name of Samuel Langhorne Clemens (1835–1910); Ring
(Ringgold Wilmer) Lardner (1885–1933). Both were American.

were beautifully made, heavy books I would lie down with on the floor in front of the diningroom hearth, and more often than the rest volume 5, *Every Child's Story Book*, was under my eyes. There were the fairy tales —Grimm, Andersen, the English, the French, "Ali Baba and the Forty Thieves"; and there was Aesop and Reynard the Fox; there were the myths and legends, Robin Hood, King Arthur, and St. George and the Dragon, even the history of Joan of Arc; a whack of *Pilgrim's Progress* and a long piece of *Gulliver*.[9] They all carried their classic illustrations. I located myself in these pages and could go straight to the stories and pictures I loved; very often "The Yellow Dwarf" was first choice, with Walter Crane's Yellow Dwarf in full color making his terrifying appearance flanked by turkeys.[1] Now that volume is as worn and backless and hanging apart as my father's poor *Sanford and Merton*. The precious page with Edward Lear's "Jumblies"[2] on it has been in danger of slipping out for all these years. One measure of my love for Our Wonder World was that for a long time I wondered if I would go through fire and water for it as my mother had done for Charles Dickens; and the only comfort was to think I could ask my mother to do it for me.

I believe I'm the only child I know of who grew up with this treasure in the house. I used to ask others, "Did you have Our Wonder World?" I'd have to tell them The Book of Knowledge could not hold a candle to it.

I live in gratitude to my parents for initiating me—and as early as I begged for it, without keeping me waiting—into knowledge of the word, into reading and spelling, by way of the alphabet. They taught it to me at home in time for me to begin to read before starting to school. I believe the alphabet is no longer considered an essential piece of equipment for traveling through life. In my day it was the keystone to knowledge. You learned the alphabet as you learned to count to ten, as you learned "Now I lay me" and the Lord's Prayer and your father's and mother's name and address and telephone number, all in case you were lost.

My love for the alphabet, which endures, grew out of reciting it but, before that, out of seeing the letters on the page. In my own story books, before I could read them for myself, I fell in love with various winding, enchanting-looking initials drawn by Walter Crane at the heads of fairy tales. In "Once upon a time," an "O" had a rabbit running it as a treadmill, his feet upon flowers. When the day came, years later, for me to see the Book of Kells,[3] all the wizardry of letter, initial, and word swept over me a thousand times over, and the illumination, the gold, seemed a part of the word's beauty and holiness that had been there from the start.

9. Respectively by John Bunyan (1628–88) and Jonathan Swift (1667–1745). Both were English.
1. A fairy tale illustrated by Walter Crane (1845–1915), popular illustrator of children's books.

2. A narrative poem about creatures called Jumblies who went to sea in a sieve. Edward Lear (1812–88), English, wrote nonsense poems for children.
3. An illustrated Irish manuscript of the four Gospels from the eighth or ninth century.

Learning stamps you with its moments. Childhood's learning is made up of moments. It isn't steady. It's a pulse.

In a children's art class, we sat in a ring on kindergarten chairs and drew three daffodils that has just been picked out of the yard; and while I was drawing, my sharpened pencil and the cup of the yellow daffodil gave off whiffs just alike. That the pencil doing the drawing should give off the same smell as the flower it drew seemed a part of the art lesson—as shouldn't it be? Children, like animals, use all their senses to discover the world. Then artists come along and discover it the same way, all over again. Here and there, it's the same world. Or now and then we'll hear from an artist who's never lost it.

In my sensory education I include my physical awareness of the *word*. Of a certain word, that is; the connection it has with what it stands for. At around age six, perhaps, I was standing by myself in our front yard waiting for supper, just at that hour in a late summer day when the sun is already below the horizon and the risen full moon in the visible sky stops being chalky and begins to take on light. There comes the moment, and I saw it then, when the moon goes from flat to round. For the first time it met my eyes as a globe. The word "moon" came into my mouth as though fed to me out of a silver spoon. Held in my mouth the moon became a word. It had the roundness of a Concord grape Grandpa took off his vine and gave me to suck out of its skin and swallow whole, in Ohio.

This love did not prevent me from living for years in foolish error about the moon. The new moon just appearing in the west was the rising moon to me. The new should be rising. And in early childhood the sun and moon, those opposite reigning powers, I just as easily assumed rose in east and west respectively in their opposite sides of the sky, and like partners in a reel they advanced, sun from the east, moon from the west, crossed over (when I wasn't looking) and went down on the other side. My father couldn't have known I believed that when, bending behind me and guiding my shoulder, he positioned me at our telescope in the front yard and, with careful adjustment of the focus, brought the moon close to me.

The night sky over my childhood Jackson[4] was velvety black. I could see the full constellations in it and call their names; when I could read, I knew their myths. Though I was always waked for eclipses, and indeed carried to the window as an infant in arms and shown Halley's Comet[5] in my sleep, and though I'd been taught at our diningroom table about the solar system and knew the earth revolved around the sun, and our moon around us, I never found out the moon didn't come up in the west until I was a writer and Herschel Brickell, the literary critic, told me after I

4. Jackson, Mississippi, where Welty grew up.

5. A comet named after Edmund Halley (1656–1742), English astronomer.

misplaced it in a story. He said valuable words to me about my new profession: "Always be sure you get your moon in the right part of the sky."

My mother always sang to her children. Her voice came out just a little bit in the minor key. "Wee Willie Winkie's" song was wonderfully sad when she sang the lullabies.

"Oh, but now there's a record. She could have her own record to listen to," my father would have said. For there came a Victrola record of "Bobby Shafftoe" and "Rock-a-Bye Baby,"[6] all of Mothers's lullabies, which could be played to take her place. Soon I was able to play her my own lullabies all day long.

Our Victrola stood in the diningroom. I was allowed to climb onto the seat of a diningroom chair to wind it, start the record turning, and set the needle playing. In a second I'd jumped to the floor, to spin or march around the table as the music called for—now there were all the other records I could play too. I skinned back onto the chair just in time to lift the needle at the end, stop the record and turn it over, then change the needle. That brass receptable with a hole in the lid gave off a metallic smell like human sweat, from all the hot needles that were fed it. Winding up, dancing, being cocked to start and stop the record, was of course all in one the act of listening—to "Overture to Daughter of the Regiment," "Selections from The Fortune Teller," "Kiss Me Again," "Gypsy Dance from Carmen," "Stars and Stripes Forever," "When the Midnight Choo-Choo Leaves for Alabam," or whatever. came next.[7] Movement must be at the very heart of listening.

Ever since I was first read to, then started reading to myself, there has never been a line read that I didn't hear. As my eyes followed the sentence, a voice was saying it silently to me. It isn't my mother's voice, or the voice of any person I can identify, certainly not my own. It is human, but inward, and it is inwardly that I listen to it. It is to me the voice of the story or the poem itself. The cadence, whatever it is that asks you to believe, the feeling that resides in the printed word, reaches me through the reader-voice. I have supposed, but never found out, that this is the case with all readers—to read as listeners—and with all writers, to write as listeners. It may be part of the desire to write. The sound of what

6. "Wee Willie Winkie": a nursery rhyme of 1841 in which sleep is personified; "Bobby Shafftoe": a traditional sea chantey dating from about 1750; "Rock-a-Bye Baby": words from Mother Goose's Melodies (1765) set to music in 1884.

7. Daughter of the Regiment: an opera (1840) by the Italian composer Gaetano Donizetti; The Fortune Teller: an operetta (1898) by the American Victor Herbert; "Kiss Me Again": a song from Herbert's Mlle. Modiste (1905); Carmen: an opera (1875) by the French composer Georges Bizet; "Stars and Stripes Forever": a march (1897) by the American John Philip Sousa (the "March King"); "When the Midnight Choo-Choo Leaves for Alabam": a popular song (1912) by the American Irving Berlin.

falls on the page begins the process of testing it for truth, for me. Whether I am right to trust so far I don't know. By now I don't know whether I could do either one, reading or writing, without the other.

My own words, when I am at work on a story, I hear too as they go, in the same voice that I hear when I read in books. When I write and the sound of it comes back to my ears, then I act to make my changes. I have always trusted this voice.

1985

THE READER

1. *On p. 604, Welty devotes a paragraph to drawing a daffodil in children's art class. What is the relation of that paragraph to the one about the initial "O" just before and to the one about the full moon just after?*
2. *Welty concludes by talking of "trust" and "truth." What meaning does she give to these words?*
3. *When she speaks of her father's belief about the 1925 edition of the* Britannica *or puts quotation marks around "the library," Welty suggests that her mature judgment differs from her parents' judgment. How significant is her mature judgment on these matters? How does the answer to this question relate to the meaning she gives to "trust" and "truth" (see question 2, above)?*

THE WRITER

1. *Welty speaks of her "sensory education." What does she mean?*
2. *Welty got her sensory education before television. Suppose she had watched children's television as a child. Write a couple of sentences in her voice explaining its function in her sensory education. Write a paragraph in your own voice explaining its function in your sensory education.*

John Gardner

WHAT WRITERS DO

Everyone knows at least in a general way what writers—that is, writers of fiction—do. They write fiction. But even for writers themselves it's not easy to say just what that means. We listen to the sentence "They write fiction" and nod impatiently, as if the thing were too obvious to need saying, which in a way it is, because we all agree, as speakers of English, on what "they" means, and "write" and "fiction." But maybe we nodded too hastily. What *do* we mean, to start with the easiest question, by "they"—that is, "writers"?

Most of us are snobs and would be inclined to say at once that we need not concern ourselves with the obvious fact that writers are of various sorts ranging from, say, John Jakes (of the Bicentennial series) to Kurt Vonnegut, to Herman Melville. As warthogs, IRS agents, and zebras are all animals, these dissimilar beings—Jakes, Vonnegut, and Melville—are all writers; but though the problem here might amuse a chimpanzee or a positivist, it does not seem, to us snobs, worth attention. The word *writers*, and the pronoun we substitute for it, has various meanings, but the only one we really care about is the one which refers to the class represented by Melville. The trouble with this hasty, respectable judgment lies of course in the fact that every individual writer, even a stern-minded person like Melville, is different people at different times. In one mood, or in one crowd, the serious writer writes fairy tales; in another he writes ponderous novels; in still another, dirty limericks. A great writer is not great because he never writes dirty limericks but because, if he does write one, he tries to write a very good one.

Any writer who's worked in various forms can tell you from experience that it all feels like writing. Some people may feel that they're "really" writing when they work on their novels and just fooling around when they write bedtime stories for their children; but that can mean only one of two things, I think: either that the writer has a talent for writing novels and not much talent for writing children's stories, or else that the writer is a self-important donzel who writes both miserable novels and miserable children's stories. I would say that even in a given work a writer is many different people. Just at the moment when his novel is most serious —most strenuously laboring to capture some profound idea through meticulous analysis of characters in action—the Melvillian heavyweight suddenly notices (as John Jakes would do) that the serving-girl in the corner has lowered her bodice a little, trying to catch the central character's eye. I don't mean that our serious writer's mind has wandered; I mean that another side of him, after vigorous signaling, has gotten his attention. Or to put it another way, wanting to write like Tolstoi at his solemnest, he has suddenly discovered in himself an urge to write like, say, Henry Fielding. If he gives in to the impulse, as he may or may not, and pursues the romance the lowered bodice has invited, he may suddenly, at the height of idealistic love, or the depth of debauchery, find himself feeling a little cynical somehow, or puritanically pious; or he may find himself distracted by the ferns outside the window, which lure him to delicate appositions and fluttering rhythms, lyricism for its own sake.

What's happening here, of course, is not that several writers inside the one writer's head are clubbing each other for control of the typewriter keys. The true writer's mind is not a jungle but a noble democracy, in which all parties have their say, even the crazy ones, even the most violently passionate, because otherwise justice, balance, sanity are impossible. Wanting to write like Tolstoi at his solemnest, the writer finds a part of himself rising to object to a hint of pompous braying, agrarian bigotry, righteousness unredeemed by humor. Swinging toward Fielding, the writer finds a part of himself complaining about the absence of high-mindedness. Scanning possibilities like a chess-playing computer, weighing the votes of his innumerable selves, following now this leading voice, now that, the writer-multitude finds out, page by page and draft by draft, the sane and passionate whole which is his novel.

Every fine writer has within him a John Jakes, a Marquis de Sade, a James Michener, a William Gass, a Melville. If his multitude of selves is rich but anarchic, uncontrollable, so that his work bulges here with pornography, here with dry philosophy, he is likely to be a "serious" writer but not a very good one. If for one reason or another his selection of selves is limited, he is likely to be a lesser writer. Some writers are limited because they are, simply, not very rich personalities: they contain in them no Melville, no Marquis de Sade. Other writers are limited because, though rich in selves, they voluntarily disenfranchise large segments of their inner population to satisfy the whim of some market: they avoid ideas, or sex, or—as in the stock "*New Yorker* story"—unfashionable emotion.

Writers whose stock of selves is limited by simplicity of personality we dismiss—uncharitably but not unjustly—as stupid. Writers limited by concern about market we dismiss as commercial. How do we distinguish these lesser kinds of writers from the serious, even sublime writer who limits himself by the choice of some relatively simple form—Shakespeare in the sonnets, Hawthorne in his stories for children? And how, we may as well ask in the same breath, does the simplicity of a sonnet or children's story differ from the simplicity of a porno or mystery thriller?

If you accept my metaphor of the writer as democracy, the answer to both questions seems obvious. The whole community cannot get together on a porno or the usual emotionally simpleminded thriller, at least so long as the porno or thriller remain recognizable themselves, conscious and intentional distortions of human experience. (Ross Macdonald is the superior mystery writer he is precisely because he refuses to abide by the usual rules of his form, consistently writing, so to speak, better than necessary.) On the other hand, the sonnet and children's story—or the parable, tale, yarn, sketch, and so on—do not of necessity oversimplify or distort. When the whole community argues about war, pollution, or energy, it argues in one way; when it argues about building swing-sets on playgrounds, it argues in another. I think no part of a writer need be suppressed to write *Charlotte's Web* or the juveniles of Joan Aiken. It is true, of course, that the children's story, like the traditional gothic tale, tends to use a very special language; but it is not a language into which large parts of our common experience cannot be translated.

One might put it this way: important thought is important only insofar as it communicates with those at whom it is aimed; no sensible human being goes on talking when all of his audience has walked away. Great children's literature talks about the complexity of human experience in a way interesting and meaningful to children; bad children's literature talks about what some mistaken person imagines children care about. The bad children's writer writes as he does either because, being of limited personality, he thinks children care about no more than he does, or because, being commercial, he wants to satisfy formulas made up by fools and statisticians.

Great children's writers, like great writers of any other kind, are complex, multitudinous of self. To speak only of living American writers, think of the children's fiction of Nancy Willard, Hilma Wolitzer, or Susan Shreve. All of these writers, as it happens—not by chance—are also respectable writers of adult fiction or poetry. For contrast think of Maxine Kumin or Raoul Dahl, occasionally unsatisfying writers both for children and for adults because, in each case, one side of the writer's personality—the angrily righteous—overwhelms the democratic balance with pious despotism.

So much for the "they" in the truism about writers, "They write fiction." Let me turn to "write."

Writing is an action, a different action from talking. The only conceivable reason for engaging in writing is to make something relatively permanent which one might otherwise forget. That would seem to imply that one thinks there is some value in the thing not to be forgotten—either some value already achieved, as in the case of a good recipe for scalloped potatoes, or some potential value, as in the case of a love poem which stinks at the moment but has the right spirit and might get better under revision. Writers of the Melvillian class, that is, "serious" writers, write only in the second sense: they write works that with luck and devotion may be improved by revision—or, in the end, works that have been so improved, so that we may class them with other human treasures, such as good recipes for scalloped potatoes. If one looks at the first drafts of even the greatest writers, like Tolstoi and Dostoevski, one sees that literary art does not come flying like Athena, fully formed, from Zeus' head. Indeed, the first-draft stupidity of great writers is a shocking and comforting thing to see. What one learns from studying successive drafts is that the writer did not know what he meant to say until he said it. A typo of "murder" for "mirror" can change the whole plot of a novel.

To put all this another way, what oral storytellers seem to do is figure out certain parts of the world by telling stories about those parts. The Greeks, as you know, made much of this. Whereas most civilizations feared and hated blindness, the Greeks elevated it, at least as a symbol: the blind man was the man who had to see with his tongue, understanding the world by telling of it. What writers do is somewhat different. They figure out the world by talking about it, then looking at what they've said and changing it. I don't mean, of course, that oral storytellers don't polish and repolish; I only mean to say that there's a great difference between the power and precision of the two instruments—a difference as great as that between, say, a reading glass and a microscope. Think again of Homer. A fair pile of prehomeric poetry survives, all of it fairly good, most of it battle poetry, all the battle pieces relatively short, at least in comparison with the *Iliad*. The standard heroic poem before Homer's time probably ran to about the length of one or two books of the *Iliad*. It may be true, as tradition says, that Homer was a blind oral poet, like Demodokos, his character in the *Odyssey*; but it does not seem likely. Homer appeared at the very moment when writing was reintroduced in ancient Greece, and the complexity of his poems—repeated, cunningly varied references to bows, looms, Odysseus' bed and the great phallic pillar which supports it—images we're forced to describe, finally, as richly and ingeniously symbolic—can only be accounted for in one of two ways: either by a theory that Homer was vastly more intelligent than any other human being who ever lived, or by a theory that Homer wrote things down, studied them patiently and stubbornly, like Beethoven, and, like Beethoven, endlessly, brilliantly revised.

Or think of the sudden, astonishing rise of serious "popular" literature in the late Middle Ages and early Renaissance; I mean the use, in writers like Boccaccio, Chaucer, and Shakespeare, of salacious stories and folktales as the base of psychologically and philosophically serious literature. Before Boccaccio's time, as has recently been pointed out, writers used parchment. To make a Bible you had to kill three hundred cows. Books cost a lot, in money and cattle-blood. One used parchment only for things of the greatest importance—religious writings, cathedral plans, the shopping lists of kings. Then in Boccaccio's time paper was introduced, so that suddenly it was possible for Boccaccio to write down a dirty joke he'd heard, fool around with it a little—change the farmer's daughter to a nun, for instance, or introduce comically disparate high-class symbolism—and produce the *Decameron*. Chaucer did the same only better. We have two drafts—by no means all that once existed—of Chaucer's story borrowed from Boccaccio, *Troilus and Criseyde*. For artists, writing has always meant, in effect, the art of endless revising.

Now let me turn to the third term in the formula "They write fiction." What oral storytellers tell and retell we call legends, a tricky word that, if we derive it from the Latin, means "that which is read," and if we take it (by false etymology, a once common one) from Anglo-Saxon, means—as a result of the softening of g to y—*lying*. Even in the beginning no one knew what to do with that. The primary meaning of *legend* in the Middle Ages was "a saint's life." In any case, *fiction* was from the beginning something else: it can only come from the Latin and means "something shaped, molded, or devised." As everyone knows, the origins of words don't prove much; but it seems true that we still use fiction in the original sense, not to describe some noble old lie which can be told, with no great loss, in a variety of ways, but to describe a specific kind of made-up story, a story we think valuable precisely because of the way it's been shaped. You can tell the legend or fairy tale of *Jack and the Beanstalk* pretty much any way you please, as long as you don't throw out Jack, the giant, the colored beans, or the beanstalk. Jack can make three trips, or two, or one; he can trade in the cow (or something) for the colored beans either on the way in to town or at the fair; and so on. To tell Faulkner's *As I Lay Dying,* Joyce's "The Dead," or William Gass' "In the Heart of the Heart of the Country," one has to use the writer's exact words or all is lost. The essential difference between what we think of as "fiction" and what we think of as "legend" is that, relatively at least, the shaping in fiction counts more heavily.

In the broadest and perhaps most important sense, fiction can go wrong in two ways: it fails as basic legend or it fails in its artifice. Most of the fiction one reads—I mean contemporary fiction, but the same may be said of fiction done in Dickens' day, most of it by now ground to dust by time's selectivity—is trash. It makes no real attempt at original and interesting style, and the story it tells is boring. This is simply to say, of course, that if fiction moves too far from its model, legend, and abandons story, it fails to satisfy our age-old expectations; if it does not move far enough, telling its story without concern for style, it fails to satisfy other, newer expectations. What writers do, if they haven't been misled by false canons of taste or some character defect, is try to make up an interesting story and tell it in an authentically interesting way—that is, some way that, however often we may read it, does not turn out to be boring.

The odds against a writer's achieving a real work of art are astronomical. Most obviously the "they" of our "They write fiction" formula—in other words, the writer's personality—may go wrong. Every good writer is many things—a symbolist, a careful student of character, a person of strong opinions, a lover of pure tale or adventure. In a bad or just ordinary novel, the writer's various selves war with one another. We feel, as we read, not one commanding voice but a series of jarringly different voices, even voices in sharp and confusing disagreement.

The war of the writer's selves can result in great fiction only in the case of an extraordinarily great writer, which is to say, an almost supernaturally wise man—one who has the rare gift of being able to see through his own soul's trickery. Very few people of the kind who make good writers —rather childlike people, as psychologists have often pointed out—are wise in life. They become wise, if they do, by revision—by looking over what they've written down again and again, a hundred times, two hundred, each time in a slightly different mood, with a different model ringing in their ears: one day the writer looks over what he's written just after spending a few hours reading Tolstoi; another day he rereads his own work just after seeing a play by Samuel Beckett, or some simple-minded but good-hearted movie like *The Sound of Music*, or just after returning from his mother's funeral. That process, endless revision and rereading—in different moods, with different models in mind—is the writer's chief hope.

Or anyway it is his chief hope if he has known all along what fiction is and has been trying to write real fiction. I have said that true fiction is, in effect, oral-storytelling written down and fixed, perfected by revision. Let me refine that a little now. What is it that the writer is trying to achieve—or ought to be—as he endlessly fiddles with rough drafts?

A true work of fiction is a wonderfully simple thing—so simple that most so-called serious writers avoid trying it, feeling they ought to do something more important and ingenious, never guessing how incredibly difficult it is. A true work of fiction does all of the following things, and does them elegantly, efficiently: It creates a vivid and continuous dream in the reader's mind; it is implicitly philosophical; it fulfills or at least deals with all of the expectations it sets up; and it strikes us, in the end, not simply as a thing done but as a shining performance.

I will not elaborate that description in much detail. Some of it I've mentioned before, here and there; some of it seems to me to need no elaboration. I've said, first, that fiction creates a vivid and continuous dream in the reader's mind. Any reader knows at a glance that that is true, and that if a given work does not bring a vivid and continuous dream to the reader—almost instantly, after five or six words—the fiction is either bad or, what may be the same thing, a so-called metafiction. One can derive all the principles of effective fiction from the idea that the writer must make his dream vivid and continuous. The dream is not vivid, of course, if too many words are abstract, not concrete, if too many verbs are passive, too many metaphors familiar or dull, and so on; and the dream is not continuous if some element in the writing distracts the reader from the story to thoughts about the stupidity of the writer—his inability to use proper grammar, his excessive loquacity, his deviation into sentimentality, mannerism, or frigidity, and so on. If the student writer can get rid of every one of those common errors which regularly undermine vividness and continuousness, a finite list not difficult to spell out, then that student can consistently avoid writing bad fiction. Whether or not he can write *great* fiction is of course another matter, one of genius or the lack of it. When the writer is finally writing true fiction, the best he is capable of, he may well discover that he'd better start making some carefully calculated mistakes, disguise his insipidity.

It's the law of the vivid and continuous dream—for it is, I think, something close to an aesthetic law for fiction—that makes writing fiction what I've described as a "wonderfully simple thing." All the writer has to do is see with absolute clarity and vividness, and describe without mistake exactly what he's seen. That was Faulkner's genius—to see very clearly. No one forgets his image of the falling lantern and the fire starting in "Shingles for the Lord," or his image of a Negro shanty's dirt yard, "smooth as an old, worn nickle." What offends in Faulkner, as has often been remarked, is his failure to value that clarity of vision, again and again mucking it up—especially toward the end—with outrageously mannered prose, that is, prose calculated to obscure the vision and call attention to the writer. Joyce did the same. At the end of his life, clear-headedly looking back, he thought "The Dead" the finest thing he'd ever done, and Tolstoi's "How Much Land Does a Man Need?" the finest work of fiction ever written. It had been Joyce himself, of course, who made the claim that the writer should be inconspicuous in his work, like God off in the corner of the universe paring his nails. In Dubliners and Portrait he'd been true to that ideal; from that point on—however great the books in certain ways—Joyce went for mannerism, and the sad truth is he carried most of twentieth-century fiction with him.

To do the wonderfully simple thing real writers do at their best, one needs only to look clearly and levelly at one's character and his situation. If the writer sees his character clearly, and if the character is, as all human beings in fact are, unique in certain respects, that character will inevitably behave in ways no one else would behave in that precise situation. It will prove impossible to write a story which could be equally well played in a film version by Robert Redford, Dustin Hoffman, Alan Arkin, Richard Dreyfus, or Frank Sinatra. If the writer sees each and every one of his characters clearly—even the most minor walk-ons—he can never for a moment slip into cliché. Following actions and reactions second by second through a significant chain of events, keeping a sharp eye out to catch every wince or grin or twitch, always checking his imagination against experience (how do misers really behave in the world), the writer almost cannot help coming up with a dream worth following—not a passive dream, of course, but one the reader struggles with, judges, tries to second-guess, a dream of reality more vivid and powerful than all but the rarest, keenest moments of reality itself.

Of course part of what makes this dream so vivid and powerful is that, like our best nightmares, the dream is thematic, or, as I put it earlier, it is implicitly philosophical. I would say that, at their best, both fiction and philosophy do the same thing, only fiction does it better—though slower. Philosophy is by essence abstract, a sequence of general argument controlled in its profluence by either logic (in old-fashioned systematic philosophy) or emotional coherence (in the intuitive philosophies of, say, Nietzsche and Kierkegaard). We read the argument and it seems to flow along okay, make sense, but what we ask is, "Is this true of my mailman?" or, "Do I really follow the Golden Rule because, unlike Prussian officers, I am a coward? Do I *know* any good Prussian officers?" Fiction comes at questions from the other end. It traces or explores some general argument by examining a particular case in which the universal case seems implied; and in place of logic or emotional coherence—the philosopher's stepping stones—fictional argument is controlled by mimesis: we are persuaded that the characters would indeed do and say exactly what we are told they do and say, whether the characters are lifelike human beings or a congress of insects given human traits. If the mimesis convinces us, then the question we ask is opposite to that we ask of philosophical argument; that is, we ask, "Is this true *in general?*" Convinced by Captain Ahab, we want to know if in some way his story, the story of a madman, applies to all human beings, mad or sane. In great fiction the writer, inching along from particular to particular, builds into his work arrows or vectors pointing us toward the general. He does this, we know, in numerous ways—by relating his particulars to some symbolic system recalling a familiar set of questions of values, by playing his plot off against some old and familiar plot, as Joyce does in *Ulysses*, by old-fashioned allegory, by explicit authorial comment, by arranging that his characters discuss the important issues within the story (the method of Tolstoi and Dostoevski), or by some other means.

What happens in great fiction is that, while we are occupied with the vividness and convincingness of detail—admiring, for instance, the fact that Captain Ahab's personal crew is made up of Chinese never before seen on the ship until now, with the first lowering of the longboats—we are also occupied with the neatness and power of the philosophical argument. When reading great fiction, one never feels that the writer has wandered from the subject. The true writer sets up for us some important question, in dramatic form, and explores it clear-mindedly, relentlessly. We read of Raskolnikov's initial indecision about whether or not he has the right to commit murder, and we instantly recognize the universal significance of the question and lean forward tensely, waiting to see what will happen. We delight in the particulars—the fact that he is very nearly caught on the stairs—and we delight simultaneously in seeing the implied universals. It's in this sense that true fiction is implicitly philosophical.

I need say nothing about the next standard I've mentioned, that fiction at its best satisfies our expectations. At the end of a mystery, we want all the questions answered, red herrings explained away, false clues justified, and so on. In a more serious kind of novel, we want all important issues dealt with, no character left hiding forever behind the tree where the author put him and forgot him. It may be that, finishing the novel, we at first imagine that some thread was left untied—for instance, some symbolic idea. Two different characters may have been subtly identified as Eden serpents, and as we finish the novel we at first can't see how the double identification was resolved. Carefully rereading, we discover that the seeming contradiction was indeed resolved, and the belated satisfaction of our expectation gives pleasure. But whether the satisfaction is immediate or purposely delayed, it must sooner or later come.

Finally, I've said that in the best fiction we get not just a piece of work —efficient energy which moves something—but a "shining performance." We say not just "What a true and good book!" but "What magnificent writing!" To win our applause, it cannot have the fake magnificence of mannerism—flights of purple prose, advance-guard trickery, artifice aimed solely at calling attention to the artificer. It must have the true magnificence of beautiful (some would prefer to say "interesting") technique: adequate and "inspired"—that is, revised, rerevised, polished to near perfection. We recognize this at once, I think, in acting. Some actors do a perfectly good job—we are never distracted to the actor behind the character played—while other actors do a brilliant job: we do think of the actor, not as a human being at war with the part being played, but as an artist whose skills come singing through the part, making the character more interesting and "real" than we could have hoped or dreamed from a reading of the script.

What the writers I care most about do is take fiction as the single most important thing in life after life itself—life itself being both their raw material and the object of their celebration. They do it not for ego but simply to make something singularly beautiful. Fiction is their religion and comfort: when they are depressed, they go not to church or psychoanalysis but to Salinger or Joyce, early Malamud, parts of Faulkner, Tolstoi, or the Bible as book. They write, themselves, to make things equally worthy of trust, not stories of creeps and cynics but stories of people capable of a measure of heroism, capable of strong and honest feeling at least some of the time, capable of love and sacrifice—capable of all this, and available as models for imitation. Everything true writers do, I think, from laborious plotting on butcher paper or three-by-five cards to laborious revision, draft after draft, they do to create characters—the center and heart of all true fiction—characters who will serve till Messiah comes, characters whose powerful existence in our minds make a real-life messiah unnecessary. Imperfect, even childish human beings, writers raise themselves up by the techniques of fiction to something much better than even the best of writers are in everyday life: ordinary mortals transmuted for the moment into apostles.

1981

Northrop Frye

THE MOTIVE FOR METAPHOR

For the past twenty-five years I have been teaching and studying English literature in a university. As in any other job, certain questions stick in one's mind, not because people keep asking them, but because they're the questions inspired by the very fact of being in such a place. What good is the study of literature? Does it help us to think more clearly, or feel more sensitively, or live a better life than we could without it? What is the function of the teacher and scholar, or of the person who calls himself, as I do, a literary critic? What difference does the study of literature make in our social or political or religious attitude? In my early days I thought very little about such questions, not because I had any of the answers, but because I assumed that anybody who asked them was naïve. I think now that the simplest questions are not only the hardest to answer, but the most important to ask, so I'm going to raise them and try to suggest what my present answers are. I say try to suggest, because there are only more or less inadequate answers to such questions—there aren't any right answers. The kind of problem that literature raises is not the kind that you ever "solve." Whether my answers are any good or not, they represent a fair amount of thinking about the questions. As I can't see my audience, I have to choose my rhetorical style in the dark, and I'm taking the classroom style, because an audience of students is the one I feel easiest with.

There are two things in particular that I want to discuss with you. In school, and in university, there's a subject called "English" in English-speaking countries. English means, in the first place, the mother tongue. As that, it's the most practical subject in the world: you can't understand anything or take any part in your society without it. Wherever illiteracy is a problem, it's as fundamental a problem as getting enough to eat or a place to sleep. The native language takes precedence over every other subject of study: nothing else can compare with it in its usefulness. But then you find that every mother tongue, in any developed or civilized society, turns into something called literature. If you keep on studying "English," you find yourself trying to read Shakespeare and Milton. Literature, we're told, is one of the arts, along with painting and music, and, after you've looked up all the hard words and the Classical allusions and learned what words like imagery and diction are supposed to mean, what you use in understanding it, or so you're told, is your imagination. Here you don't seem to be in quite the same practical and useful area: Shakespeare and Milton, whatever their merits, are not the kind of thing you must know to hold any place in society at all. A person who knows nothing about literature may be an ignoramus, but many people don't mind being that. Every child realizes that literature is taking him in a different direction from the immediately useful, and a good many children complain loudly about this. Two questions I want to deal with, then, are, first: what is the relation of English as the mother tongue to English as a literature? Second: What is the social value of the study of literature, and what is the place of the imagination that literature addresses itself to, in the learning process?

Let's start with the different ways there are of dealing with the world we're living in. Suppose you're shipwrecked on an uninhabited island in the South Seas. The first thing you do is to take a long look at the world around you, a world of sky and sea and earth and stars and trees and hills. You see this world as objective, as something set over against you and not yourself or related to you in any way. And you notice two things about this objective world. In the first place, it doesn't have any conversation. It's full of animals and plants and insects going on with their own business, but there's nothing that responds to you: it has no morals and no intelligence, or at least none that you can grasp. It may have a shape and a meaning, but it doesn't seem to be a human shape or a human meaning. Even if there's enough to eat and no dangerous animals, you feel lonely and frightened and unwanted in such a world.

In the second place, you find that looking at the world, as something set over against you, splits your mind in two. You have an intellect that feels curious about it and wants to study it, and you have feelings or emotions that see it as beautiful or austere or terrible. You know that both these attitudes have some reality, at least for you. If the ship you were wrecked in was a Western ship, you'd probably feel that your intellect tells you more about what's really there in the outer world, and that your emotions tell you more about what's going on inside you. If your background were Oriental, you'd be more likely to reverse this and say that the beauty or terror was what was really there, and that your instinct to count and classify and measure and pull to pieces was what was inside your mind. But whether your point of view is Western or Eastern, intellect and emotion never get together in your mind as long as you're simply looking at the world. They alternate, and keep you divided between them.

The language you use on this level of the mind is the language of consciousness or awareness. It's largely a language of nouns and adjectives. You have to have names for things, and you need qualities like "wet" or "green" or "beautiful" to describe how things seem to you. This is the speculative or contemplative position of the mind, the position in which the arts and sciences begin, although they don't stay there very long. The sciences begin by accepting the facts and the evidence about an outside world without trying to alter them. Science proceeds by accurate measurement and description, and follows the demands of the reason rather than the emotions. What it deals with is there, whether we like it or not. The emotions are unreasonable: for them it's what they like and don't like that comes first. We'd be naturally inclined to think that the arts follow the path of emotion, in contrast to the sciences. Up to a point they do, but there's a complicating factor.

That complicating factor is the contrast between "I like this" and "I don't like this." In this Robinson Crusoe life I've assigned you, you may have moods of complete peacefulness and joy, moods when you accept your island and everything around you. You wouldn't have such moods very often, and when you had them, they'd be moods of identification, when you felt that the island was a part of you and you a part of it. That is not the feeling of consciousness or awareness, where you feel split off from everything that's not your perceiving self. Your habitual state of mind is the feeling of separation which goes with being conscious, and the feeling "this is not a part of me" soon becomes "this is not what I want." Notice the word "want": we'll be coming back to it.

So you soon realize that there's a difference between the world you're living in and the world you want to live in. The world you want to live in is a human world, not an objective one: it's not an environment but a home; it's not the world you see but the world you build out of what you see. You go to work to build a shelter or plant a garden, and as soon as you start to work you've moved into a different level of human life. You're not separating only yourself from nature now, but constructing a human world and separating it from the rest of the world. Your intellect and emotions are now both engaged in the same activity, so there's no longer any real distinction between them. As soon as you plant a garden or a crop, you develop the conception of a "weed," the plant you don't want in there. But you can't say that "weed" is either an intellectual or an emotional conception, because it's both at once. Further, you go to work because you feel you have to, and because you want something at the end of the work. That means that the important categories of your life are no longer the subject and the object, the watcher and the things being watched: the important categories are what you have to do and what you want to do—in other words, necessity and freedom.

One person by himself is not a complete human being, so I'll provide you with another shipwrecked refugee of the opposite sex and an eventual family. Now you're a member of a human society. This human society after a while will transform the island into something with a human shape. What that human shape is, is revealed in the shape of the work you do: the buildings, such as they are, the paths through the woods, the planted crops fenced off against whatever animals want to eat them. These things, these rudiments of city, highway, garden, and farm, are the human form of nature, or the form of human nature, whichever you like. This is the area of the applied arts and sciences, and it appears in our society as engineering and agriculture and medicine and architecture. In this area we can never say clearly where the art stops and the science begins, or vice versa.

The language you use on this level is the language of practical sense, a language of verbs or words of action and movement. The practical world, however, is a world where actions speak louder than words. In some way it's a higher level of existence than the speculative level, because it's doing something about the world instead of just looking at it, but in itself it's a much more primitive level. It's the process of adapting to the environment, or rather of transforming the environment in the interests of one species, that goes on among animals and plants as well as human beings. The animals have a good many of our practical skills: some insects make pretty fair architects, and beavers know quite a lot about engineering. In this island, probably, and certainly if you were alone, you'd have about the ranking of a second-rate animal. What makes our practical life really human is a third level of the mind, a level where consciousness and practical skill come together.

This third level is a vision or model in your mind of what you want to construct. There's that word "want" again. The actions of man are prompted by desire, and some of these desires are needs, like food and warmth and shelter. One of these needs is sexual, the desire to reproduce and bring more human beings into existence. But there's also a desire to bring a social human form into existence: the form of cities and gardens and farms that we call civilization. Many animals and insects have this social form too, but man knows that he has it: he can compare what he does with what he can imagine being done. So we begin to see where the imagination belongs in the scheme of human affairs. It's the power of constructing possible models of human experience. In the world of the imagination, anything goes that's imaginatively possible, but nothing really happens. If it did happen, it would move out of the world of imagination into the world of action.

We have three levels of the mind now, and a language for each of them, which in English-speaking societies means an English for each of them. There's the level of consciousness and awareness, where the most important thing is the difference between me and everything else. The English of this level is the English of ordinary conversation, which is mostly monologue, as you'll soon realize if you do a bit of eavesdropping, or listening to yourself. We can call it the language of self-expression. Then there's the level of social participation, the working or technological language of teachers and preachers and politicians and advertisers and lawyers and journalists and scientists. We've already called this the language of practical sense. Then there's the level of imagination, which produces the literary language of poems and plays and novels. They're not really different languages, of course, but three different reasons for using words.

On this basis, perhaps, we can distinguish the arts from the sciences. Science begins with the world we have to live in, accepting its data and trying to explain its laws. From there, it moves towards the imagination: it becomes a mental construct, a model of a possible way of interpreting experience. The further it goes in this direction, the more it tends to speak the language of mathematics, which is really one of the languages of the imagination, along with literature and music. Art, on the other hand, begins with the world we construct, not with the world we see. It starts with the imagination, and then works towards ordinary experience: that is, it tries to make itself as convincing and recognizable as it can. You can see why we tend to think of the sciences as intellectual and the arts as emotional: one starts with the world as it is, the other with the world we want to have. Up to a point it is true that science gives an intellectual view of reality, and that the arts try to make the emotions as precise and disciplined as sciences do the intellect. But of course it's nonsense to think of the scientist as a cold unemotional reasoner and the artist as somebody who's in a perpetual emotional tizzy. You can't distinguish the arts from the sciences by the mental processes the people in them use: they both operate on a mixture of hunch and common sense. A highly developed science and and a highly developed art are very close together, psychologically and otherwise.

Still, the fact that they start from opposite ends, even if they do meet in the middle, makes for one important difference between them. Science learns more and more about the world as it goes on: it evolves and improves. A physicist today knows more physics than Newton did, even if he's not as great a scientist. But literature begins with the possible model of experience, and what it produces is the literary model we call the classic. Literature doesn't evolve or improve or progress. We may have dramatists in the future who will write plays as good as *King Lear*, though they'll be very different ones, but drama as a whole will never get better than *King Lear*. *King Lear* is it, as far as drama is concerned; so is *Oedipus Rex*, written two thousand years earlier than that, and both will be models of dramatic writing as long as the human race endures. Social conditions may improve: most of us would rather live in nineteenth-century United States than in thirteenth-century Italy, and for most of us Whitman's celebration of democracy makes a lot more sense than Dante's Inferno. But it doesn't follow that Whitman is a better poet than Dante: literature won't line up with that kind of improvement.

So we find that everything that does improve, including science, leaves the literary artist out in the cold. Writers don't seem to benefit much by the advance of science, although they thrive on superstitions of all kinds. And you certainly wouldn't turn to contemporary poets for guidance or leadership in the twentieth-century world. You'd hardly go to Ezra Pound, with his fascism and social credit and Confucianism and anti-semitism. Or to Yeats, with his spiritualism and fairies and astrology. Or to D. H. Lawrence, who'll tell you that it's a good thing for servants to be flogged because that restores the precious current of blood-reciprocity between servant and master. Or to T. S. Eliot, who'll tell you that to have a flourishing culture we should educate an élite, keep most people living in the same spot, and never disestablish the Church of England. The novelists seem to be a little closer to the world they're living in, but not much. When Communists talk about the decadence of bourgeois culture, this is the kind of thing they always bring up. Their own writers don't seem to be any better, though; just duller. So the real question is a bigger one. Is it possible that literature, especially poetry, is something that a scientific civilization like ours will eventually outgrow? Man has always wanted to fly, and thousands of years ago he was making sculptures of winged bulls and telling stories about people who flew so high on artificial wings that the sun melted them off. In an Indian play fifteen hundred years old, *Sakuntala*, there's a god who flies around in a chariot that to a modern reader sounds very much like a private aeroplane. Interesting that the writer had so much imagination, but do we need such stories now that we have private aeroplanes?

This is not a new question: it was raised a hundred and fifty years ago by Thomas Love Peacock, who was a poet and novelist himself, and a very brilliant one. He wrote an essay called *Four Ages of Poetry*, with his tongue of course in his cheek, in which he said that poetry was the mental rattle that awakened the imagination of mankind in its infancy, but that now, in an age of science and technology, the poet has outlived his social function. "A poet in our times," said Peacock, "is a semi-barbarian in a civilized community. He lives in the days that are past. His ideas, thoughts, feelings, associations, are all with barbarous manners, obsolete customs, and exploded superstitions. The march of his intellect is like that of a crab, backwards." Peacock's essay annoyed his friend Shelley, who wrote another essay called *A Defence of Poetry* to refute it. Shelley's essay is a wonderful piece of writing, but it's not likely to convince anyone who needs convincing. I shall be spending a good deal of my time on this question of the relevance of literature in the world of today, and I can only indicate the general lines my answer will take. There are two points I can make now, one simple, the other more difficult.

The simple point is that literature belongs to the world man constructs, not to the world he sees; to his home, not his environment. Literature's world is a concrete human world of immediate experience. The poet uses images and objects and sensations much more than he uses abstract ideas; the novelist is concerned with telling stories, not with working out arguments. The world of literature is human in shape, a world where the sun rises in the east and sets in the west over the edge of a flat earth in three dimensions, where the primary realities are not atoms or electrons but bodies, and the primary forces not energy or gravitation but love and death and passion and joy. It's not surprising if writers are often rather simple people, not always what we think of as intellectuals, and certainly not always any freer of silliness or perversity than anyone else. What concerns us is what they produce, not what they are, and poetry, according to Milton, who ought to have known, is "more simple, sensuous and passionate" than philosophy or science.

The more difficult point takes us back to what we said when we were on that South Sea island. Our emotional reaction to the world varies from "I like this" to "I don't like this." The first, we said, was a state of identity, a feeling that everything around us was part of us, and the second is the ordinary state of consciousness, or separation, where art and science begin. Art begins as soon as "I don't like this" turns into "this is not the way I could imagine it." We notice in passing that the creative and the neurotic minds have a lot in common. They're both dissatisfied with what they see; they both believe that something else ought to be there, and they try to pretend it is there or to make it be there. The differences are more important, but we're not ready for them yet.

At the level of ordinary consciousness the individual man is the centre of everything, surrounded on all sides by what he isn't. At the level of practical sense, or civilization, there's a human circumference, a little cultivated world with a human shape, fenced off from the jungle and inside the sea and the sky. But in the imagination anything goes that can be imagined, and the limit of the imagination is a totally human world. Here we recapture, in full consciousness, that original lost sense of identity with our surroundings, where there is nothing outside the mind of man, or something identical with the mind of man. Religions present us with visions of eternal and infinite heavens or paradises which have the form of the cities and gardens of human civilization, like the Jerusalem and Eden of the Bible, completely separated from the state of frustration and misery that bulks so large in ordinary life. We're not concerned with these visions as religion, but they indicate what the limits of the imagination are. They indicate too that in the human world the imagination has no limits, if you follow me. We said that the desire to fly produced the aeroplane. But people don't get into planes because they want to fly; they get into planes because they want to get somewhere else faster. What's produced the aeroplane is not so much a desire to fly as a rebellion against the tyranny of time and space. And that's a process that can never stop, no matter how high our Titovs[1] and Glenns[2] may go.

---

1. Gherman S. Titov, Russian astronaut and first man to make a multi-orbital flight (August 1961).

2. John H. Glenn, astronaut and first American to make an orbital flight (February 1962).

For each of these six talks I've taken a title from some work of literature, and my title for this one is "The Motive for Metaphor," from a
poem of Wallace Stevens. Here's the poem:

> You like it under the trees in autumn,
> Because everything is half dead.
> The wind moves like a cripple among the leaves
> And repeats words without meaning.
>
> In the same way, you were happy in spring,
> With the half colors of quarter-things,
> The slightly brighter sky, the melting clouds,
> The single bird, the obscure moon—
>
> The obscure moon lighting an obscure world
> Of things that would never be quite expressed,
> Where you yourself were never quite yourself
> And did not want nor have to be,
>
> Desiring the exhilarations of changes:
> The motive for metaphor, shrinking from
> The weight of primary noon,
> The A B C of being,
>
> The ruddy temper, the hammer
> Of red and blue, the hard sound—
> Steel against intimation—the sharp flash,
> The vital, arrogant, fatal, dominant X.

What Stevens calls the weight of primary noon, the A B C of being, and
the dominant X is the objective world, the world set over against us.
Outside literature, the main motive for writing is to describe this world.
But literature itself uses language in a way which associates our minds
with it. As soon as you use associative language, you begin using figures
of speech. If you say this talk is dry and dull, you're using figures associat-
ing it with bread and breadknives. There are two main kinds of association, analogy and identity, two things that are like each other and two
things that are each other. You can say with Burns, "My love's like a red,
red rose," or you can say with Shakespeare:

> Thou that art now the world's fresh ornament
> And only herald to the gaudy spring.

One produces the figure of speech called the simile; the other produces
the figure called metaphor.

In descriptive writing you have to be careful of associative language.
You'll find that analogy, or likeness to something else, is very tricky to
handle in description, because the differences are as important as the
resemblances. As for metaphor, where you're really saying "this *is* that,"
you're turning your back on logic and reason completely, because logi-

cally two things can never be the same thing and still remain two things. The poet, however, uses these two crude, primitive, archaic forms of thought in the most uninhibited way, because his job is not to describe nature, but to show you a world completely absorbed and possessed by the human mind. So he produces what Baudelaire called a "suggestive magic including at the same time object and subject, the world outside the artist and the artist himself." The motive for metaphor, according to Wallace Stevens, is a desire to associate, and finally to identify, the human mind with what goes on outside it, because the only genuine joy you can have is in those rare moments when you feel that although we may know in part, as Paul says, we are also a part of what we know.

1964

THE READER

1. At what point in his essay does Frye come to the meaning of his title? What does this essay say the motive for metaphor is? Does it seem to you to be a satisfactory motive?
2. How far does Frye go in this essay toward responding to the simple, big questions he starts out with? Has he clarified for you or answered any of these questions? Is there indication in the essay that this is a beginning of the discussion, with more to follow?
3. What are the three kinds of English Frye talks about in his essay? Do we really need three kinds—isn't one enough?
4. Why do you have to take so much English in school when you already know how to use English even before you start school?

THE WRITER

1. Why does Frye ask his reader to imagine him- or herself a castaway on a South Sea island? Are you ever likely to be in that position, or is it a bit far-fetched? Is it just a colorful way to get his point across? If so, what is his point?
2. Does Frye anticipate a possible objection that metaphor distorts the truth and misleads us as to the way things really are? Why, or why not?
3. Why doesn't literature get any better, the way science does? Can literature be any good, seeing that it doesn't improve? Given the fact that it doesn't improve, shouldn't much of it be outdated? Cast your answer to these questions in the form of two brief essays, one addressed to an English teacher, one addressed to a fellow student majoring in science. How do your two essays differ?

Carl Gustav Jung

THE POET

Creativeness, like the freedom of the will, contains a secret. The psychologist can describe both these manifestations as processes, but he can find no solution of the philosophical problems they offer. Creative man is a riddle that we may try to answer in various ways, but always in vain, a truth that has not prevented modern psychology from turning now and again to the question of the artist and his art. Freud thought that he had found a key in his procedure of deriving the work of art from the personal experiences of the artist. It is true that certain possibilities lay in this direction, for it was conceivable that a work of art, no less than a neurosis, might be traced back to those knots in psychic life that we call the complexes. It was Freud's great discovery that neuroses have a causal origin in the psychic realm—that they take their rise from emotional states and from real or imagined childhood experiences. Certain of his followers, like Rank and Stekel, have taken up related lines of enquiry and have achieved important results. It is undeniable that the poet's psychic disposition permeates his work root and branch. Nor is there anything new in the statement that personal factors largely influence the poet's choice and use of his materials. Credit, however, must certainly be given to the Freudian school for showing how far-reaching this influence is and in what curious ways it comes to expression.

Freud takes the neurosis as a substitute for a direct means of gratification. He therefore regards it as something inappropriate—a mistake, a dodge, an excuse, a voluntary blindness. To him it is essentially a shortcoming that should never have been. Since a neurosis, to all appearances, is nothing but a disturbance that is all the more irritating because it is without sense or meaning, few people will venture to say a good word for it. And a work of art is brought into questionable proximity with the neurosis when it is taken as something which can be analysed in terms of the poet's repressions. In a sense it finds itself in good company, for religion and philosophy are regarded in the same light by Freudian psychology. No objection can be raised if it is admitted that this approach amounts to nothing more than the elucidation of those personal determinants without which a work of art is unthinkable. But should the claim be made that such an anlaysis accounts for the work of art itself, then a categorical denial is called for. The personal idiosyncrasies that creep into a work of art are not essential; in fact, the more we have to cope with these peculiarities, the less is it a question of art. What is essential in a work of art is that it should rise far above the realm of personal life and speak from the spirit and heart of the poet as man to the spirit and heart of mankind. The personal aspect is a limitation—and even a sin—in the realm of art. When a form of "art" is primarily personal it deserves to be treated as if it were a neurosis. There may be some validity in the idea held by the Freudian school that artists without exception are narcissistic —by which is meant that they are undeveloped persons with infantile and autoerotic traits. The statement is only valid, however, for the artist as a person, and has nothing to do with the man as an artist. In his capacity of artist he is neither auto-erotic, nor hetero-erotic, nor erotic in any sense. He is objective and impersonal—even inhuman—for as an artist he is his work, and not a human being.

Every creative person is a duality or a synthesis of contradictory aptitudes. On the one side he is a human being with a personal life, while on the other side he is an impersonal, creative process. Since as a human being he may be sound or morbid, we must look at his psychic make-up to find the determinants of his personality. But we can only understand him in his capacity of artist by looking at his creative achievement. We should make a sad mistake if we tried to explain the mode of life of an English gentleman, a Prussian officer, or a cardinal in terms of personal factors. The gentleman, the officer and the cleric function as such in an impersonal role, and their psychic make-up is qualified by a peculiar objectivity. We must grant that the artist does not function in an official capacity—the very opposite is nearer the truth. He nevertheless resembles the types I have named in one respect, for the specifically artistic disposition involves an overweight of collective psychic life as against the personal. Art is a kind of innate drive that seizes a human being and makes him its instrument. The artist is not a person endowed with free will who seeks his own ends, but one who allows art to realize its purposes through him. As a human being he may have moods and a will and personal aims, but as an artist he is "man" in a higher sense—he is "collective man"—one who carries and shapes the unconscious, psychic life of mankind. To perform this difficult office it is sometimes necessary for him to sacrifice happiness and everything that makes life worth living for the ordinary human being.

All this being so, it is not strange that the artist is an especially interesting case for the psychologist who uses an analytical method. The artist's life cannot be otherwise than full of conflicts, for two forces are at war within him—on the one hand the common human longing for happiness, satisfaction and security in life, and on the other a ruthless passion for creation which may go so far as to override every personal desire. The lives of artists are as a rule so highly unsatisfactory—not to say tragic—because of their inferiority on the human and personal side, and not because of a sinister dispensation. There are hardly any exceptions to the rule that a person must pay dearly for the divine gift of the creative fire. It is as though each of us were endowed at birth with a certain capital of energy. The strongest force in our make-up will seize and all but monopolize this energy, leaving so little over that nothing of value can come of it. In this way the creative force can drain the human impulses to such a degree that the personal ego must develop all sorts of bad qualities—ruthlessnes, selfishness and vanity (so-called "auto-erotism")—and even every kind of vice, in order to maintain the spark of life and to keep itself from being wholly bereft. The auto-erotism of artists resembles that of illegitimate or neglected children who from their tenderest years must protect themselves from the destructive influence of people who have no love to give them—who develop bad qualities for that very purpose and later maintain an invincible egocentrism by remaining all their lives infantile and helpless or by actively offending against the moral code or the law. How can we doubt that it is his art that explains the artist, and not the insufficiencies and conflicts of his personal life? These are nothing but the regrettable results of the fact that he is an artist—that is to say, a man who from his very birth has been called to a greater task than the ordinary mortal. A special ability means a heavy expenditure of energy in a particular direction, with a consequent drain from some other side of life.

It makes no difference whether the poet knows that his work is begotten, grows and matures with him, or whether he supposes that by taking thought he produces it out of the void. His opinion of the matter does not change the fact that his own work outgrows him as a child its mother. The creative process has feminine quality, and the creative work arises from unconscious depths—we might say, from the realm of the mothers. Whenever the creative force predominates, human life is ruled and moulded by the unconscious as against the active will, and the conscious ego is swept along on a subterranean current, being nothing more than a helpless observer of events. The work in process becomes the poet's fate and determines his psychic development. It is not Goethe who creates *Faust*, but *Faust* which creates Goethe. And what is *Faust* but a symbol? By this I do not mean an allegory that points to something all too familiar, but an expression that stands for something not clearly known and yet profoundly alive. Here it is something that lives in the soul of every German, and that Goethe has helped to bring to birth. Could we conceive of anyone but a German writing *Faust* or *Also sprach Zarathustra*? Both play upon something that reverberates in the German soul—a "primordial image," as Jacob Burckhardt once called it—the figure of a physician or teacher of mankind. The archetypal image of the wise man, the saviour or redeemer, lies buried and dormant in man's unconscious since the dawn of culture; it is awakened whenever the times are out of joint and a human society is committed to a serious error. When people go astray they feel the need of a guide or teacher or even of the physician.

These primordial images are numerous, but do not appear in the dreams of individuals or in works of art until they are called into being by the waywardness of the general outlook. When conscious life is characterized by one-sidedness and by a false attitude, then they are activated— one might say, "instinctively"—and come to light in the dreams of individuals and the visions of artists and seers, thus restoring the psychic equilibrium of the epoch.

In this way the work of the poet comes to meet the spiritual need of the society in which he lives, and for this reason his work means more to him than his personal fate, whether he is aware of this or not. Being essentially the instrument for his work, he is subordinate to it, and we have no reason for expecting him to interpret it for us. He has done the best that in him lies in giving it form, and he must leave the interpretation to others and to the future. A great work of art is like a dream; for all its apparent obviousness it does not explain itself and is never unequivocal. A dream never says: "You ought," or: "This is the truth." It presents an image in much the same way as nature allows a plant to grow, and we must draw our own conclusions. If a person has a nightmare, it means either that he is too much given to fear, or else that he is too exempt from it; and if he dreams of the old wise man it may mean that he is too pedagogical, as also that he stands in need of a teacher. In a subtle way both meanings come to the same thing, as we perceive when we are able to let the work of art act upon us as it acted upon the artist. To grasp its meaning, we must allow it to shape us as it once shaped him. Then we understand the nature of his experience. We see that he has drawn upon the healing and redeeming forces of the collective psyche that underlies consciousness with its isolation and its painful errors; that he has penetrated to that matrix of life in which all men are embedded, which imparts a common rhythm to all human existence, and allows the individual to communicate his feeling and his striving to mankind as a whole.

The secret of artistic creation and of the effectiveness of art is to be found in a return to the state of *participation mystique*—to that level of experience at which it is man who lives, and not the individual, and at which the weal or woe of the single human being does not count, but only human existence. This is why every great work of art is objective and impersonal, but none the less profoundly moves us each and all. And this is also why the personal life of the poet cannot be held essential to his art —but at most a help or a hindrance to his creative task. He may go the way of a Philistine, a good citizen, a neurotic, a fool or a criminal. His personal career may be inevitable and interesting, but it does not explain the poet.

1946

THE READER

1. *Jung makes a distinction between the "human being with a personal life" and the "impersonal, creative process." What is the importance of this distinction? How does it help to shape the rest of Jung's argument?*
2. *Consider the following stanzas (69–72) from Byron's "Childe Harold's Pilgrimage." To what extent would Jung feel that psychological considerations were helpful in analyzing these lines?*

> To fly from, need not be to hate, mankind:
> All are not fit with them to stir and toil,
> Nor is it discontent to keep the mind
> Deep in its fountain, lest it overboil
> In the hot throng, where we become the spoil
> Of our infection, till too late and long
> We may deplore and struggle with the coil,
> In wretched interchange of wrong for wrong
> Midst a contentious world, striving where none are strong.
>
> There, in a moment we may plunge our years
> In fatal penitence, and in the blight
> Of our own Soul turn all our blood to tears,
> And colour things to come with hues of Night;
> The race of life becomes a hopeless flight
> To those that walk in darkness: on the sea
> The boldest steer but where their ports invite—
> But there are wanderers o'er Eternity
> Whose bark drives on and on, and anchored ne'er shall be.
>
> Is it not better, then, to be alone,
> And love Earth only for its earthly sake?
> By the blue rushing of the arrowy Rhone,
> Or the pure bosom of its nursing Lake,
> Which feeds it as a mother who doth make
> A fair but froward infant her own care,
> Kissing its cries away as these awake;—
> Is it not better thus our lives to wear,
> Than join the rushing crowd, doomed to inflict or bear?
>
> I live not in myself, but I become
> Portion of that around me; and to me
> High mountains are a feeling, but the hum
> Of human cities torture: I can see
> Nothing to loathe in Nature, save to be
> A link reluctant in a fleshly chain,
> Classed among creatures, when the soul can flee,
> And with the sky—the peak—the heaving plain
> Of ocean, or the stars, mingle—and not in vain.

THE WRITER

1. Jung says that the "personal idiosyncracies that creep into a work of art are not essential," since art "should rise far above the realm of personal life and speak from the spirit and heart of the poet as man to the spirit and heart of mankind." Is a contradiction involved here? Can a poet speak from the heart without being personal? Are "personal idiosyncracies" desirable in a work to give it the flavor of a distinctive style?

2. In a brief essay, compare Jung's view of creativity with that of Bronowski in "The Reach of Imagination" (p. 133).

Robert Frost

EDUCATION BY POETRY: A MEDITATIVE MONOLOGUE[1]

I am going to urge nothing in my talk. I am not an advocate. I am going to consider a matter, and commit a description. And I am going to describe other colleges than Amherst. Or, rather say all that is good can be taken as about Amherst; all that is bad will be about other colleges.

I know whole colleges where all American poetry is barred—whole colleges. I know whole colleges where all contemporary poetry is barred.

I once heard of a minister who turned his daughter—his poetry-writing daughter—out on the street to earn a living, because he said there should be no more books written; God wrote one book, and that was enough. (My friend George Russell, "Æ", has read no literature, he protests, since just before Chaucer.)

That all seems sufficiently safe, and you can say one thing for it. It takes the onus off the poetry of having to be used to teach children anything. It comes pretty hard on poetry, I sometimes think, what it has to bear in the teaching process.

Then I know whole colleges where, though they let in older poetry, they manage to bar all that is poetical in it by treating it as something other than poetry. It is not so hard to do that. Their reason I have often hunted for. It may be that these people act from a kind of modesty. Who are professors that they should attempt to deal with a thing as high and as fine as poetry? Who are *they*? There is a certain manly modesty in that.

That is the best general way of settling the problem; treat all poetry as if it were something else than poetry, as if it were syntax, language, science. Then you can even come down into the American and into the

1. An address given at Amherst College in 1930.

contemporary without any special risk.

There is another reason they have, and that is that they are, first and foremost in life, markers. They have the marking problem to consider. Now, I stand here a teacher of many years' experience and I have never complained of having had to mark. I had rather mark anyone for anything —for his looks, carriage, his ideas, his correctness, his exactness, anything you please—I would rather give him a mark in terms of letters, A, B, C, D, than have to use adjectives on him. We are all being marked by each other all the time, classified, ranked, put in our place, and I see no escape from that. I am no sentimentalist. You have got to mark, and you have got to mark, first of all, for accuracy, for correctness. But if I am going to give a mark, that is the least part of my marking. The hard part is the part beyond that, the part where the adventure begins.

One other way to rid the curriculum of the poetry nuisance has been considered. More merciful than the others it would neither abolish nor denature the poetry, but only turn it out to disport itself, with the plays and games—in no wise discredited, though given no credit for. Any one who liked to teach poetically could take his subject, whether English, Latin, Greek or French, out into the nowhere along with the poetry. One side of a sharp line would be left to the rigorous and righteous; the other side would be assigned to the flowery where they would know what could be expected of them. Grade marks were more easily given, of course, in the courses concentrating on correctness and exactness as the only forms of honesty recognized by plain people; a general indefinite mark of X in the courses that scatter brains over taste and opinion. On inquiry I have found no teacher willing to take position on either side of the line, either among the rigors or among the flowers. No one is willing to admit that his discipline is not partly in exactness. No one is willing to admit that his discipline is not partly in taste and enthusiasm.

How shall a man go through college without having been marked for taste and judgment? What will become of him? What will his end be? He will have to take continuation courses for college graduates. He will have to go to night schools. They are having night schools now, you know, for college graduates. Why? Because they have not been educated enough to find their way around in contemporary literature. They don't know what they may safely like in the libraries and galleries. They don't know how to judge an editorial when they see one. They don't know how to judge a political campaign. They don't know when they are being fooled by a metaphor, an analogy, a parable. And metaphor is, of course, what we are talking about. Education by poetry is education by metaphor.

Suppose we stop short of imagination, initiative, enthusiasm, inspiration and originality—dread words. Suppose we don't mark in such things at all. There are still two minimal things, that we have got to take care of, taste and judgment. Americans are supposed to have more judgment than taste, but taste is there to be dealt with. That is what poetry, the only art in the colleges of arts, is there for. I for my part would not be afraid to go in for enthusiasm. There is the enthusiasm like a blinding light, or the enthusiasm of the deafening shout, the crude enthusiasm that you get uneducated by poetry, outside of poetry. It is exemplified in what I might call "sunset raving." You look westward toward the sunset, or if you get up early enough, eastward toward the sunrise, and you rave. It is oh's and ah's with you and no more.

But the enthusiasm I mean is taken through the prism of the intellect and spread on the screen in a color, all the way from hyperbole at one end —or overstatement, at one end—to understatement at the other end. It is a long strip of dark lines and many colors. Such enthusiasm is one object of all teaching in poetry. I heard wonderful things said about Virgil yesterday, and many of them seemed to me crude enthusiasm, more like a deafening shout, many of them. But one speech had range, something of overstatement, something of statement, and something of understatement. It had all the colors of an enthusiasm passed through an idea.

I would be willing to throw away everything else but that: enthusiasm tamed by metaphor. Let me rest the case there. Enthusiasm tamed to metaphor, tamed to that much of it. I do not think anybody ever knows the discreet use of metaphor, his own and other people's, the discreet handling of metaphor, unless he has been properly educated in poetry.

Poetry begins in trivial metaphors, petty metaphors, "grace" metaphors, and goes on to the profoundest thinking that we have. Poetry provides the one permissible way of saying one thing and meaning another. People say, "Why don't you say what you mean?" We never do that, do we, being all of us too much poets. We like to talk in parables and in hints and in indirections—whether from diffidence or some other instinct.

I have wanted in late years to go further and further in making metaphor the whole of thinking. I find some one now and then to agree with me that all thinking, except mathematical thinking, is metaphorical, or all thinking except scientific thinking. The mathematical might be difficult for me to bring in, but the scientific is easy enough.

Once on a time all the Greeks were busy telling each other what the All was—or was like unto. All was three elements, air, earth, and water (we once thought it was ninety elements; now we think it is only one). All was substance, said another. All was change, said a third. But best and most fruitful was Pythagoras' comparison of the universe with number. Number of what? Number of feet, pounds, and seconds was the answer, and we had science and all that has followed in science. The metaphor has held and held, breaking down only when it came to the spiritual and psychological or the out of the way places of the physical.

The other day we had a visitor here, a noted scientist, whose latest word to the world has been that the more accurately you know where a thing is, the less accurately you are able to state how fast it is moving. You can see why that would be so, without going back to Zeno's problem of the arrow's flight. In carrying numbers into the realm of space and at the same time into the realm of time you are mixing metaphors, that is all, and you are in trouble. They won't mix. The two don't go together.

Let's take two or three more of the metaphors now in use to live by. I have just spoken of one of the new ones, a charming mixed metaphor right in the realm of higher mathematics and higher physics: that the more accurately you state where a thing is, the less accurately you will be able to tell how fast it is moving. And, of course everything is moving. Everything is an event now. Another metaphor. A thing, they say, is an event. Do you believe it is? Not quite. I believe it is almost an event. But I like the comparison of a thing with an event.

I notice another from the same quarter. "In the neighborhood of matter space is something like curved." Isn't that a good one! It seems to me that that is simply and utterly charming—to say that space is something like curved in the neighborhood of matter. "Something like."

Another amusing one is from—what is the book?—I can't say it now; but here is the metaphor. Its aim is to restore you to your ideas of free will. It wants to give you back your freedom of will. All right, here it is on a platter. You know that you can't tell by name what persons in a certain class will be dead ten years after graduation, but you can tell actuarially how many will be dead. Now, just so this scientist says of the particles of matter flying at a screen, striking a screen; you can't tell what individual particles will come, but you can say in general that a certain number will strike in a given time. It shows, you see, that the individual particle can come freely. I asked Bohr about that particularly, and he said, "Yes, it is so. It can come when it wills and as it wills; and the action of the individual particle is unpredictable. But it is not so of the action of the mass. There you can predict." He says, "That gives the individual atom its freedom, but the mass its necessity."

Another metaphor that has interested us in our time and has done all our thinking for us is the metaphor of evolution. Never mind going into the Latin word. The metaphor is simply the metaphor of the growing plant or of the growing thing. And somebody very brilliantly, quite a while ago, said that the whole universe, the whole of everything, was like unto a growing thing. That is all. I know the metaphor will break down at some point, but it has not failed everywhere. It is a very brilliant metaphor, I acknowledge, though I myself get too tired of the kind of essay that talks about the evolution of candy, we will say, or the evolution of elevators—the evolution of this, that, and the other. Everything is evolution. I emancipate myself by simply saying that I didn't get up the metaphor and so am not much interested in it.

What I am pointing out is that unless you are at home in the metaphor, unless you have had your proper poetical education in the metaphor, you are not safe anywhere. Because you are not at ease with figurative values: you don't know the metaphor in its strength and its weakness. You don't know how far you may expect to ride it and when it may break down with you. You are not safe in science; you are not safe in history. In history, for instance—to show that is the same in history as elsewhere—I heard somebody say yesterday that Aeneas was to be likened unto (those words, "likened unto"!) George Washington. He was that type of national hero, the middle-class man, not thinking of being a hero at all, bent on building the future, bent on his children, his descendants. A good metaphor, as far as it goes, and you must know how far. And then he added that Odysseus should be likened unto Theodore Roosevelt. I don't think that is so good. Someone visiting Gibbon at the point of death, said he was the same Gibbon as of old; still at his parallels.

Take the way we have been led into our present position morally, the world over. It is by a sort of metaphorical gradient. There is a kind of thinking—to speak metaphorically—there is a kind of thinking you might say was endemic in the brothel. It is always there. And every now and then in some mysterious way it becomes epidemic in the world. And how does it do so? By using all the good words that virtue has invented to maintain virtue. It uses honesty, first—frankness, sincerity—those words; picks them up, uses them. "In the name of honesty, let us see what we are." You know. And then it picks up the word joy. "Let us in the name of joy, which is the enemy of our ancestors, the Puritans . . . Let us in the name of joy, which is the enemy of the kill-joy Puritan . . ." You see. "Let us," and so on. And then, "In the name of health . . ." Health is another good word. And that is the metaphor Freudianism trades on, mental health. And the first thing we know, it has us all in up to the top knot. I suppose we may blame the artists a good deal, because they are great people to spread by metaphor. The stage too—the stage is always a good intermediary between the two worlds, the under and the upper, if I may say so without personal prejudice to the stage.

In all this, I have only been saying that the devil can quote Scripture, which simply means that the good words you have lying around the devil can use for his purposes as well as anybody else. Never mind about my morality. I am not here to urge anything. I don't care whether the world is good or bad—not on any particular day.

Let me ask you to watch a metaphor breaking down here before you.

Somebody said to me a little while ago, "It is easy enough for me to think of the universe as a machine, as a mechanism."

I said, "You mean the universe is like a machine?"

He said, "No. I think it is one . . . Well, it is like . . ."

"I think you mean the universe is like a machine."

"All right. Let it go at that."

I asked him, "Did you ever see a machine without a pedal for the foot, or a lever for the hand, or a button for the finger?"

He said "No—no."

I said, "All right. Is the universe like that?"

And he said, "No. I mean it is like a machine, only . . ."

". . . it is different from a machine," I said.

He wanted to go just that far with that metaphor and no further. And so do we all. All metaphor breaks down somewhere. That is the beauty of it. It is touch and go with the metaphor, and until you have lived with it long enough you don't know when it is going. You don't know how much you can get out of it and when it will cease to yield. It is a very living thing. It is as life itself.

I have heard this ever since I can remember, and ever since I have taught: the teacher must teach the pupil to think. I saw a teacher once going around in a great school and snapping pupils' heads with thumb and finger and saying, "Think." That was when thinking was becoming the fashion. The fashion hasn't yet quite gone out.

We still ask boys in college to think, as in the nineties, but we seldom tell them what thinking means; we seldom tell them it is just putting this and that together; it is saying one thing in terms of another. To tell them is to set their feet on the first rung of a ladder the top of which sticks through the sky.

Greatest of all attempts to say one thing in terms of another is the philosophical attempt to say matter in terms of spirit, or spirit in terms of matter, to make the final unity. That is the greatest attempt that ever failed. We stop just short there. But it is the height of poetry, the height of all thinking, the height of all poetic thinking, that attempt to say matter in terms of spirit and spirit in terms of matter. It is wrong to call anybody a materialist simply because he tries to say spirit in terms of matter, as if that were a sin. Materialism is not the attempt to say all in terms of matter. The only materialist—be he poet, teacher, scientist, politician, or statesman—is the man who gets lost in his material without a gathering metaphor to throw it into shape and order. He is the lost soul.

We ask people to think, and we don't show them what thinking is. Somebody says we don't need to show them how to think; bye and bye they will think. We will give them the forms of sentences and, if they have any ideas, then they will know how to write them. But that is preposterous. All there is to writing is having ideas. To learn to write is to learn to have ideas.

The first little metaphor . . . Take some of the trivial ones. I would rather have trivial ones of my own to live by than the big ones of other people.

I remember a boy saying, "He is the kind of person that wounds with his shield." That may be a slender one, of course. It goes a good way in character description. It has poetic grace. "He is the kind that wounds with his shield."

The shield reminds me—just to linger a minute—the shield reminds me of the inverted shield spoken of in one of the books of the *Odyssey*, the book that tells about the longest swim on record. I forget how long it lasted—several days, was it?—but at last as Odysseus came near the coast of Phoenicia, he saw it on the horizon "like an inverted shield."

There is a better metaphor in the same book. In the end Odysseus comes ashore and crawls up the beach to spend the night under a double olive tree, and it says, as in a lonely farmhouse where it is hard to get fire —I am not quoting exactly—where it is hard to start the fire again if it goes out, they cover the seeds of fire with ashes to preserve it for the night, so Odysseus covered himself with the leaves around him and went to sleep. There you have something that gives you character, something of Odysseus himself. "Seeds of fire." So Odysseus covered the seeds of fire in himself. You get the greatness of his nature.

But these are slighter metaphors than the ones we live by. They have their charm, their passing charm. They are as it were the first steps toward the great thoughts, grave thoughts, thoughts lasting to the end.

The metaphor whose manage we are best taught in poetry—that is all there is of thinking. It may not seem far for the mind to go but it is the mind's furthest. The richest accumulation of the ages is the noble metaphors we have rolled up.

I want to add one thing more that the experience of poetry is to anyone who comes close to poetry. There are two ways of coming close to poetry. One is by writing poetry. And some people think I want people to write poetry, but I don't; that is, I don't necessarily. I only want people to write poetry if they want to write poetry. I have never encouraged anybody to write poetry that did not want to write it, and I have not always encouraged those who did want to write it. That ought to be one's own funeral. It is a hard, hard life, as they say.

(I have just been to a city in the West, a city full of poets, a city they have made safe for poets. The whole city is so lovely that you do not have to write it up to make it poetry; it is ready-made for you. But, I don't know —the poetry written in that city might not seem like poetry if read outside of the city. It would be like the jokes made when you were drunk; you have to get drunk again to appreciate them.)

But as I say, there is another way to come close to poetry, fortunately, and that is in the reading of it, not as linguistics, not as history, not as anything but poetry. It is one of the hard things for a teacher to know how close a man has come in reading poetry. How do I know whether a man has come close to Keats in reading Keats? It is hard for me to know. I have lived with some boys a whole year over some of the poets and I have not

felt sure whether they have come near what it was all about. One remark
sometimes told me. One remark was their mark for the year; had to be—
it was all I got that told me what I wanted to know. And that is enough, if
it was the right remark, if it came close enough. I think a man might make
twenty fool remarks if he made one good one some time in the year. His
mark would depend on that good remark.

The closeness—everything depends on the closeness with which you
come, and you ought to be marked for the closeness, for nothing else. And
that will have to be estimated by chance remarks, not by question and
answer. It is only by accident that you know some day how near a person
has come.

The person who gets close enough to poetry, he is going to know more
about the word *belief* than anybody else knows, even in religion nowadays. There are two or three places where we know belief outside of
religion. One of them is at the age of fifteen to twenty, in our self-belief. A
young man knows more about himself than he is able to prove to anybody. He has no knowledge that anybody else will accept as knowledge.
In his foreknowledge he has something that is going to believe itself into
fulfilment, into acceptance.

There is another belief like that, the belief in someone else, a relationship of two that is going to be believed into fulfilment. That is what we
are talking about in our novels, the belief of love. And disillusionment
that the novels are full of is simply the disillusionment from disappointment in that belief. That belief can fail, of course.

Then there is a literary belief. Every time a poem is written, every
time a short story is written, it is written not by cunning, but by belief.
The beauty, the something, the little charm of the thing to be, is more
felt than known. There is a common jest, one that always annoys me, on
the writers, that they write the last end first, and then work up to it; that
they lay a train toward one sentence that they think is pretty nice and
have all fixed up to set like a trap to close with. No, it should not be that
way at all. No one who has ever come close to the arts has failed to see the
difference between things written that way, with cunning and device,
and the kind that are believed into existence, that begin in something
more felt than known. This you can realize quite as well—not quite as
well, perhaps, but nearly as well—in reading as you can in writing. I
would undertake to separate short stories on that principle; stories that
have been believed into existence and stories that have been cunningly
devised. And I could separate the poems still more easily.

Now I think—I happen to think—that those three beliefs that I speak
of, the self-belief, the love-belief, and the art-belief, are all closely related
to the God-belief, that the belief in God is a relationship you enter into
with Him to bring about the future.

There is a national belief like that, too. One feels it. I have been where

I came near getting up and walking out on the people who thought that they had to talk against nations, against nationalism, in order to curry favor with internationalism. Their metaphors are all mixed up. They think that because a Frenchman and an American and an Englishman can all sit down on the same platform and receive honors together, it must be that there is no such thing as nations. That kind of bad thinking springs from a source we all know. I should want to say to anyone like that: "Look! First I want to be a person. And I want you to be a person, and then we can be as interpersonal as you please. We can pull each other's noses—do all sorts of things. But, first of all, you have got to have the personality. First of all, you have got to have the nations and then they can be as international as they please with each other."

I should like to use another metaphor on them. I want my palette, if I am a painter, I want my palette on my thumb or on my chair, all clean, pure, separate colors. Then I will do the mixing on the canvas. The canvas is where the work of art is, where we make the conquest. But we want the nations all separate, pure, distinct, things as separate as we can make them; and then in our thoughts, in our arts, and so on, we can do what we please about it.

But I go back. There are four beliefs that I know more about from having lived with poetry. One is the personal belief, which is a knowledge that you don't want to tell other people about because you cannot prove that you know. You are saying nothing about it till you see. The love belief, just the same, has that same shyness. It knows it cannot tell; only the outcome can tell. And the national belief we enter into socially with each other, all together, party of the first part, party of the second part, we enter into that to bring the future of the country. We cannot tell some people what it is we believe, partly, because they are too stupid to understand and partly because we are too proudly vague to explain. And anyway it has got to be fulfilled, and we are not talking until we know more, until we have something to show. And then the literary one in every work of art, not of cunning and craft, mind you, but of real art; that believing the thing into existence, saying as you go more than you even hoped you were going to be able to say, and coming with surprise to an end that you foreknew only with some sort of emotion. And then finally the relationship we enter into with God to believe the future in—to believe the hereafter in.

1930

THE READER

1. How can the "poetry nuisance" be gotten out of the curriculum? Does Frost think it ought to stay in? Why?
2. What is meant by "enthusiasm passed through an idea" and "enthusiasm tamed to metaphor" (p. 632)? What sort of metaphors does Frost

use in those phrases, and what do they imply?

3. *What does Frost mean when he says "unless you have had your proper poetical education in the metaphor, you are not safe anywhere" (p. 634)? Indicate some of the metaphors Frost examines in this essay. From what fields are they drawn? What does he say about each? Nominate some further metaphors—from politics, science, sociology, or anything else—and analyze them. To what extent are they useful? Do they have a breaking point? How might they mislead beyond the breaking point?*

THE WRITER

1. *In what way does the subtitle describe this essay? Is it rambling? Is it unified?*
2. *Frost admires a speech that has "range, something of overstatement, something of statement, and something of understatement." Is this spectrum visible in Frost's own speech? Show where and how.*
3. *Choose two metaphors from different fields (like literature and science, politics and biology, etc.), and write a brief essay comparing the use and usefulness of the metaphors in each field.*

Margaret Atwood

WRITING THE MALE CHARACTER

"Why do men feel threatened by women?" I asked a male friend of mine. (I love that wonderful rhetorical device, "a male friend of mine." It's often used by female journalists when they want to say something particularly bitchy but don't want to be held responsible for it themselves. It also lets people know that you *do* have male friends, that you aren't one of those fire-breathing mythical monsters, The Radical Feminists, who walk around with little pairs of scissors and kick men in the shins if they open doors for you. "A male friend of mine" also gives—let us admit it—a certain weight to the opinions expressed.) So this male friend of mine, who does by the way exist, conveniently entered into the following dialogue. "I mean," I said, "men are bigger, most of the time, they can run faster, strangle better, and they have on the average a lot more money and power." "They're afraid women will laugh at them," he said. "Undercut their world view." Then I asked some women students in a quickie poetry seminar I was giving, "Why do women feel threatened by men?" "They're afraid of being killed," they said.

From this I concluded that men and women are indeed different, if only in the range and scope of their threatenability. A man is not just a woman in funny clothes and a jock strap. *They don't think the same,* except about things like higher math. But neither are they an alien or inferior form of life. From the point of view of the novelist, this discovery has wide-ranging implications; and you can see that we are approaching this evening's topic, albeit in a crabwise, scuttling, devious and feminine manner; nevertheless, approaching. But first, a small digression, partly to demonstrate that when people ask you if you hate men, the proper reply is "which ones?"—because, of course, the other big revelation of the evening is that *not all men are the same.* Some of them have beards. Apart from that, I have never been among those who would speak slightingly of men by lumping them all in together; I would never say, for instance—as some have—"Put a paper bag over their bodies and they're all the same." I give you Albert Schweitzer in one corner, Hitler in another.

But think of what civilization would be today without the contributions of men. No electric floor polishers, no neutron bomb, no Freudian psychology, no heavy metal rock groups, no pornography, no repatriated Canadian Consitution[1] . . . the list could go on and on. And they're fun to play Scrabble with and handy for eating up the leftovers. I have heard some rather tired women express the opinion that the only good man is a dead man, but this is far from correct. They may be hard to find, but think of it this way: like diamonds, in the rough or not, their rarity makes them all the more appreciated. Treat them like human beings! This may surprise them at first, but sooner or later their good qualities will emerge, most of the time. Well, in view of the statistics . . . some of the time.

That wasn't the digression . . . this is the digression. I grew up in a family of scientists. My father was a forest entomologist and fond of children, and incidentally not threatened by women, and many were the happy hours we spent listening to his explanations of the ways of the wood-boring beetle, or picking forest tent caterpillars out of the soup because he had forgotten to feed them and they had gone crawling all over the house in search of leaves. One of the results of my upbringing was that I had a big advantage in the schoolyard when little boys tried to frighten me with worms, snakes and the like; the other was that I developed, slightly later, an affection for the writings of the great nineteenth century naturalist and father of modern entomology, Henri Fabre.[2] Fabre was, like Charles Darwin, one of those gifted and obsessive amateur naturalists which the nineteenth century produced in such abundance. He pursued his investigations for the love of the subject, and unlike many biologists today, whose language tends to be composed of numbers rather than words, he was an enthusiastic and delightful writer. I read with pleasure his account of the life of the spider, and of his

---

1. Until 1982, Canada's constitution was the British North America Act, with ultimate authority maintained in England. In 1982, Canada "returned" that power to itself in an independent constitution.

2. Jean Henri Fabre: distinguished French naturalist (1823–1915).

experiments with ant-lions, by which he tried to prove that they could reason. But it was not only Fabre's subject matter that intrigued me; it was the character of the man himself, so full of energy, so pleased with everything, so resourceful, so willing to follow his line of study wherever it might lead. Received opinion he would take into account, but would believe nothing until he had put it to the test himself. It pleases me to think of him, spade in hand, setting forth to a field full of sheep droppings, in search of the Sacred Dung Beetle and the secrets of her egg-laying ritual. "I am all eyes," he exclaimed, as he brought to light a little object, not round like the Sacred Beetle's usual edible dung-ball, but cunningly pear-shaped! "Oh blessed joys of truth suddenly shining forth," he wrote. "What others are there to compare with you!"

And it is in this spirit, it seems to me, that we should approach all subjects. If a dung-beetle is worthy of it, why not that somewhat more complex object, the human male? Admittedly the analogy has certain drawbacks. For instance, one dung-beetle is much like another, whereas, as we've noted, there's quite a range in men. Also, we are supposed to be talking about novels here, and, to belabor the obvious, a novel is not a scientific treatise; that is, it can make no claim to present the kind of factual truth which can be demonstrated by repeatable experiments. Although the novelist presents observations and reaches conclusions, they are not of the same order as the observations of Fabre on the behavior of the mating practices of the female scorpion, although some critics react as though they are.

Note that we have landed in the middle of a swamp, that is, at the crux of the problem: if a novel is not a scientific treatise, what is it? Our evaluation of the role of the male character within the novel will of course depend on what kind of beast we think we're dealing with. I'm sure you've all heard the one about the four blind philosophers and the elephant. Substitute "critics" for "philosophers" and "Novel" for "elephant" and you'll have the picture. One critic gets hold of the novelist's life and decides that novels are disguised spiritual autobiographies, or disguised personal sexual phobias, or something of the kind. Another gets hold of the *Zeitgeist* (or Spirit of the Times, for those unlucky enough never to have had to pass a Ph.D. language exam in German) and writes about the Restoration Novel or the Novel of Sensibility or The Rise of the Political Novel or The Novel of Twentieth Century Alienation; another figures out that the limitations of the language have something to do with what can be said, or that certain pieces of writing display similar patterns, and the air fills with mythopoeia, structuralism and similar delights; another goes to Harvard and gets hold of the Human Condition, a favorite of mine, and very handy to fall back on when you can't think of anything else to say. The elephant however remains an elephant, and sooner or later gets tired of having the blind philosophers feeling its parts, whereupon it stretches itself, rises to its feet and ambles away in another direction altogether. This is not to say that critical exercises are futile or trivial. From what I have said about dung-beetles—which also preserve their innermost secrets—you will know that I think the description of elephants is a worthwhile activity. But describing an elephant and giving birth to one are two different things, and the novelist and the critic approach the novel with quite different sets of preconceptions, problems and emotions.

"Whence comest thou?" says a well-known male character in a multi-faceted prose narrative with which I am sure you are all familiar. "From going to and fro in the earth, and from walking up and down in it," answers his adversary.[3] Thus the novelist. One would of course not want to continue with this analogy—a critic is not God, contrary to some opinions, and a novelist is not the Devil, although one could remark, with Blake, that creative energies are more likely to emerge from the under-world than from the upper world of rational order. Let us say only that the going to and fro and the walking up and down in the earth are things that all novelists seem to have done in some way or another, and that the novel proper, as distinguished from the romance and its variants, is one of the points in human civilization at which the human world as it is collides with language and imagination. This is not to limit the novel to a Zola-like naturalism (though Zola himself was not a narrow Zola-like natural-ist, as anyone who has read the triumphant final passage of *Germinal* will testify); but it is to state that some of the things that get into novels get into them because they are there in the world. There would have been no flogging scene in *Moby Dick* if there had been none on nineteenth century whaling ships, and its inclusion is not mere sado-masochism on the part of Melville. However, if the book consisted of nothing but, one might have cause to wonder.

Thus one must conclude that the less than commendable behavior of male characters in certain novels by women is not necessarily due to a warped view of the opposite sex on behalf of the authors. Could it be . . . I say it hesitantly, in a whisper, since like most women I cringe at the very thought of being called—how can I even say it— a *man-hater* . . . could it be that the behavior of some men in what we are fond of considering real life . . . could it be that not every man always behaves well? Could it be that some emperors have no clothes on?

* * *

Let me take you back a few years, to the days of Kate Millett's *Sexual Politics*, which was preceded ancestrally by Leslie Fiedler's *Love and Death in the American Novel*. Both were criticisms based on an analysis of the relations, within novels, of men and women, and both gave black marks to certain male authors for simplistic and stereotyped negative depictions of women. Well, that was interesting, but the worm has

---

3. God addresses the question to His adversary, Satan (see Job 1:7).

turned. Now we're handing out black marks for what male critics (and, to be fair, some female ones) consider to be unfavorable depictions of men by female authors. I base this conclusion mainly on reviews of my own books, naturally, since that's what I see most of, but I've noted it elsewhere too.

Now, we know there's no such thing as value-free novel writing. Creation does not happen in a vacuum, and a novelist is either depicting or exposing some of the values of the society in which he or she lives. Novelists from Defoe through Dickens and Faulkner have always done that. But it sometimes escapes us that the same is true of criticism. We are all organisms within environments, and we interpret what we read in the light of how we live and how we would like to live, which are almost never the same thing, at least for most novel readers. I think that political interpretations of novels have a place in the body of criticism, as long as we recognize them for what they are; but total polarization can only be a disservice to literature. For instance, a male friend of mine—just to let you know I have more than one—wrote a novel which has a scene in it in which men are depicted urinating outdoors standing up. Now, so far as I know, this is something men have been doing for many years, and they are still doing it, judging from the handwriting in the snow; it is merely one of those things that happens. But a female poet took my friend to task in print. She found this piece of writing not only unforgivably Central Canadian—you can tell she was from British Columbia—she also found it unforgivably *macho*. I'm not sure what novelistic solution she had in mind. Possibly she wanted my friend to leave out the subject of urination altogether, thus avoiding the upsetting problem of physiological differences; maybe she wanted the men to demonstrate equality of attitude by sitting on toilets to perform this function. Or maybe she wanted them to urinate outdoors standing up but also to feel guilty about it. Or maybe it would have been all right if they had been urinating into the Pacific Ocean, regionalism being what it is today. You may think this kind of criticism is silly, but it happens all the time on New Grub Street,[4] which is where I live.

For the female novelist, it means that certain men will find it objectionable if she depicts men behaving the way they do behave a lot of the time. Not enough that she may avoid making them rapists and murderers, child molesters, warmongers, sadists, power-hungry, callous, domineering, pompous, foolish or immoral, though I'm sure we will all agree that such men do exist. Even if she makes them sensitive and kind she's open to the charge of having depicted them as "weak." What this kind of critic wants is Captain Marvel,[5] without the Billy Batson *alter ego*; nothing less will do.

4. A metaphor for a kind of Bohemia, where young, struggling writers and artists cluster; derives from George Gissings's novel New Grub Street (1891).

5. Captain Marvel: the comic-strip hero with superhuman capacities; when he is ordinarily human, he is Billy Batson.

Excuse me for underlining the obvious, but it seems to me that a good, that is, a successfully-written, character in a novel is not at all the same as a "good," that is, a morally good, character in real life. In fact, a character in a book who is consistently well-behaved probably spells disaster for the book. There's a lot of public pressure on the novelist to write such characters, however, and it isn't new. I take you back to Samuel Richardson, author of such running-away-from-rape classics as *Pamela* and *Clarissa*. Both contain relatively virtuous women and relatively lecherous and nasty-minded men, who also happen to be English gentlemen. No one accused Richardson of being mean to men, but some English gentlemen felt that dirt had been done to them; in other words, the insecurities were primarily class ones rather than sex ones. Obligingly, Richardson came up with *Sir Charles Grandison*, a novel in which he set out to do right by the image of the English gentleman. It starts out promisingly enough, with an abduction with intent to rape by a villain after that priceless pot of gold, the heroine's virginity. Unfortunately Sir Charles Grandison enters the picture, saves the heroine from a fate worse than death, and invites her to his country residence; after which most readers kiss the novel goodbye. I however always sit to the end, even of bad movies, and since I'm the only person I've ever met who has actually made it through to page 900 of this novel I can tell you what happens. Sir Charles Grandison displays his virtues; the heroine admires them. That's it. Oh, and then there's a proposal. Feel like reading it? You bet you don't, and neither do all those male critics who complain about the image of men in books by women. A friend of mine—not a male one this time, but a perceptive reader and critic—says that her essential criterion for evaluating literature is, "Does it live or does it die?" A novel based on other people's needs for having their egos stroked, their images shored up, or their sensitivities pandered to is unlikely to live.

* * * Is *Hamlet*, for instance, a slur on men? Is *Macbeth*? Is *Faust*, in any version? How about the behavior of the men in *Moll Flanders*? Or *Tom Jones*? Is *A Sentimental Journey* about the quintessential wimp? Because Dickens created Orlick, Gradgrind, Dotheboys Hall, Fagin, Uriah Heep, Steerforth, and Bill Sykes, must we conclude that he's a man-hater? * * * Captain Ahab, although a forceful literary creation, is hardly anybody's idea of an acceptable role model. Please note that all these characters and novels were the creations of men, not women; but nobody, to my knowledge, has accused these male authors of being mean to men, although they've been accused of all sorts of other things. Possibly the principle involved is the same one involved in the telling of ethnic jokes: it's all right within the group, but coming from outside it's racism, though the joke may be exactly the same. If a man depicts a male character unfavorably, it's The Human Condition; if a woman does it, she's being mean to men. * * *

Incidentally, you could make a case—if you wanted to—for concluding that women authors have historically been easier on men in their books than male authors have.

* * * One of the questions people have been asking me most frequently is, "Do you write women's novels?" You have to watch this question, since, like many other questions, its meaning varies according to who's asking it and of whom. "Women's novels" can mean pop genre novels, such as the kind with nurses and doctors on the covers or the kind with rolling-eyed heroines in period costumes and windblown hair in front of gothic castles or Southern mansions or other locales where villainy may threaten and Heathcliff[6] is still lurking around in the Spanish moss. Or it may mean novels for whom the main audience is assumed to be women, which would take in quite a lot, since the main audience for novels of all kinds, with the exception of Louis L'amour western romances and certain kinds of porn, is also women. Or it can mean feminist propaganda novels. Or it can mean novels depicting male-female relationships, which again covers quite a lot of ground. Is *War and Peace* a women's novel? Is *Gone With The Wind*, even though it's got a war in it? Is *Middlemarch*, even though it's got The Human Condition in it? Could it be that women aren't afraid to be caught reading books that might be considered "men's novels," whereas men still think something they need will fall off them if they look too hard at certain supposedly malevolent combinations of words put together by women? Judging from my recent walking to and fro in the earth and going up and down in bookstores for the purpose of signing my name on a lot of fly-leafs, I can tell you that this attitude is on the fade. More and more men are willing to stand in the line and be seen; fewer and fewer of them say, "It's for my wife's birthday."

But I almost put the boots to my old friend and cohort, the redoubtable Pierre Berton,[7] when he asked me on television why all the men in my recent book *Bodily Harm* were wimps. Displaying the celebrated female compassion, not to be confused with feeble-mindedness, I merely dribbled aimlessly for a few minutes. "Pierre," I should have said, "who do you think is likely to have had more experience of men in sexual relationships: you, or me?" This is not quite so mean as it sounds, and there's even something to it. Women as people have a relatively large pool of experiences from which to draw. They have their own experiences with men, of course, but they also have their friends', since, yes, girls do discuss men more than men—beyond the dirty anecdote syndrome—discuss women. Women are willing to talk about their weaknesses and fears to other women; men are not willing to talk about theirs to men, since it's still a dog-eat-dog world out there for them and no man wants to reveal his underbelly to a pack of fang-toothed potential rivals. If men are

6. Heathcliff: the brooding, passionate hero of Emily Brontë's *Wuthering Heights* (1847).
7. Pierre Berton: distinguished Canadian journalist, writer, broadcaster, and popular historian.

going to talk about their problems with women to anybody, it's usually either to a shrink or—guess what? to another woman. In both reading and writing, women are likely to know more about how men actually behave with women than men are; so that what a man finds a slur on his self-image, a woman may find merely realistic or indeed unduly soft.

But to go back to Pierre Berton's assertion. I thought quite carefully about my male characters in *Bodily Harm*. There are three of them with whom the heroine actually sleeps, and the fourth main male character with whom she doesn't. A female novelist and critic noted that there is one good man in the book and no good women, and she's quite right. The other men are not "bad"—in fact they are quite nice and attractive as male characters in literature go, a sight better than Mr. Kurtz and Iago—but the *good* man is *black*, which is perhaps why the "mean-to-menners" overlooked him. When playing the role-model game, you have to read carefully; otherwise you may be caught in an embarrassing position, like that one.

Now, back to the practical concerns of New Grub Street. Let us suppose that I am writing a novel. First: how many points of view will this novel have? If it has only one point of view, will it be that of a man, a woman or a seagull? Let us suppose that my novel will have one point of view and that the eyes through which we see the world of the novel unfolding will be those of a woman. Immediately it follows that the perceptions of all male characters in the book will have to pass through the perceiving apparatus of this central character. Nor will the central character necessarily be accurate or just. It also follows that all the other characters will be, of necessity, secondary. If I'm skillful I will be able to bounce another set of perceptions off those of the central character, through dialogue and between-the-lines innuendo, but there will be a strong bias toward A as truth-teller and we will never get to hear what Characters B and C really think when they're by themselves, urinating outdoors perhaps or doing other male things. However, the picture changes if I use a multiple point of view. Now I can have Characters B and C think for themselves, and what they think won't always be what Character A thinks of *them*. If I like, I can add in yet another point of view, that of the omniscient author (who is of course not "me," the same me that had bran muffins for breakfast this morning and is right now giving this speech) but yet another voice within the novel. The omniscient author can claim to know things about the characters that even they don't know, thus letting the reader know these things as well.

The next thing I have to decide is what tone I'm taking, what mode I'm writing in. A careful study of *Wuthering Heights* will reveal that Heathcliff is never to be observed picking his nose, or indeed even blowing it, and you can search through Walter Scott in vain for any mention of bathrooms. Leopold Bloom on the other hand is preoccupied with the mundane wants of the body on almost every page, and we find him sympathetic, yes, and comic and also pathetic, but he is not exactly love's young dream. Leopold Bloom[8] climbing in through Cathy's window would probably slip. Which is the more accurate portrayal of Man with a capital M? Or, like Walter Mitty, does each man contain within him both an ordinary, limited and trivial self and a heroic concept, and if so, which should we be writing about? I carry no brief for either, except to remark that serious novelists in the twentieth century usually opt for Leopold, and poor Heathcliff has been relegated to the Gothic romance. If a given serious novelist of the twentieth century is female, she too will probably go for Leopold, with all his habits, daydreams and wants. This doens't mean she hates men; merely that she's interested in what they look like without the cloak.

All right. Suppose I've chosen to have in my novel at least one male character as a narrator or protagonist (not necessarily the same thing). I do not want to make my male character unnaturally evil, like Mr. Hyde; instead I'm trying for Dr. Jekyll, an essentially good man with certain flaws. That's a problem right there; because, as Stevenson knew, evil is a lot easier to write about and make interesting than goodness. What, these days, is a believable notion of a good man? Let us suppose that I'm talking about a man who is merely unbad; that is, one who obeys the major laws, pays his bills, helps with the dishes, doesn't beat up his wife or molest his kids, and so forth. Let's suppose that I want him to have some actual good qualities, good in the active, positive sense. What is he to do? And how can I make him—unlike Sir Charles Grandison—interesting in a novel?

This I suspect is the point at which the concerns of the novelist coincide with those of society. Once upon a time, when we defined people—much more that we do now—by how far they lived up or failed to live up to certain pre-defined sexual role models, it was a lot easier to tell what was meant by "a good man" or "a good woman." "A good woman" was one that fulfilled our notions of what a woman should be and how she should behave. Likewise "a good man." There were certain concepts about what constituted manliness and how you got it—most authorities agreed that you weren't just born with it, you somehow had to earn, acquire or be initiated into it; acts of courage and heroism counted for something, ability to endure pain without flinching, or drink a lot without passing out, or whatever. In any case there were rules, and you could cross a line that separated the men from the boys.

It's true that the male sexual role model had a lot of drawbacks, even for men—not everybody could be Superman, many were stuck with Clark Kent—but there were certain positive and, at that time, useful

8. Leopold Bloom: the protagonist of James Joyce's novel *Ulysses* (1922); Cathy: the tempestuous heroine of Emily Brontë's *Wuthering Heights* (1847); Walter Mitty: the henpecked husband in James Thurber's short story "The Secret Life of Walter Mitty" (1939).

features. What have we replaced this package with? We know that women have been in a state of upheaval and ferment for some time now, and movement generates energy; many things can be said by women now that were once not possible, many things can be thought that were once unthinkable. But what are we offering men? Their territory, though still large, is shrinking. The confusion and desperation and anger and conflicts that we find in male characters in novels don't exist only in novels. They're out there in the real world. "Be a person, my son," doesn't yet have the same ring to it as "Be a man," though it is indeed a worthy goal. The novelist *qua* novelist, as opposed to the utopian romancer, takes *what is there* as a point of departure. What is there, when we're talking about men, is a state of change, new attitudes overlapping with old ones, no simple rules any more. Some exciting form of life may emerge from all this.

Meanwhile, I think women have to take the concerns of men as seriously as they expect men to take theirs, both as novelists and as inhabitants of this earth. One encounters, too often, the attitude that only the pain felt by persons of the female sex is real pain, that only female fears are real fears. That for me is the equivalent of the notion that only working-class peole are real, that middle-class people are not, and so forth. Of course there's a distinction between earned pain and mere childish self-pity, and yes, women's fear of being killed by men is grounded in authenticity, not to mention statistics, to a greater extent than men's fear of being laughed at. Damage to one's self-image is not quite the same as damage to one's neck, though not to be underestimated: men have been known to murder and kill themselves because of it.

I'm not advocating a return to door-mat status for women, or even to the arrangement whereby women prop up and nurture and stroke and feed the egos of men without having men do at least some of the same for them. To understand is not necessarily to condone; and it could be pointed out that women have been "understanding" men for centuries, partly because it was necessary for survival. If the other fellow has the heavy artillery, it's best to be able to anticipate his probable moves. Women, like guerrilla fighters, developed infiltration rather than frontal attack as their favored strategy. But "understanding" as a manipulative tool—which is really a form of contempt for the thing understood—isn't the kind I would like to see. * * * But one cannot deprive any part of humanity of the definition "human" without grievous risk to one's own soul. And for women to define themselves as powerless and men as all-powerful is to fall into an ancient trap, to shirk responsibility as well as to warp reality. The opposite also is true; to depict a world in which women are already equal to men, in power, opportunities and freedom of movement, is a similar abdication.

I know I haven't given any specific directions for writing the male character; how can I? They're all different, remember. All I've given are a few warnings, an indication of what you're up against from the real world and from critics. But just because it's difficult is no reason not to try.

When I was young and reading a lot of comic books and fairy tales, I used to wish for two things: the cloak of invisibility, so I could follow people around and listen to what they were saying when I wasn't there, and the ability to teleport my mind into somebody else's mind, still retaining my own perceptions and memory. You can see that I was cut out to be a novelist, because these are the two fantasies novelists act out every time they write a page. Throwing your mind is easier to do if you're throwing it into a character who has a few things in common with you, which may be why I've written more pages from a female character's point of view than from a male's. But male characters are more of a challenge, and now that I'm middle-aged and less lazy I'll undoubtedly try a few more of them. If writing novels—and reading them—have any redeeming social value, it's probably that they force you to imagine what it's like to be somebody else.

Which, increasingly, is something we all need to know.

1982

THE READER

1. *Clearly Atwood believes that novels reflect reality (e.g., p. 641). But when she talks about point of view (p. 646), she offers a complicated differentiation of voices in a novel, including that of the omniscient author. What is the point of that complexity? Is she forgetting her conviction that novels reflect reality?*
2. *The essay is full of allusions. Some are explained (e.g., Fabre on p. 640); some are not presumably because Atwood thinks they are familiar (e.g., Darwin in the same paragraph); and some are not presumably because she thinks you can get the idea without an explanation (e.g., Heathcliff on p. 646: New Grub Street on p. 643). Ignoring the editors' footnotes, select some allusions, and distribute them on a scale running from those you understood because she explained them to those you couldn't understand because she didn't explain them or didn't explain them enough. What is the function of all these allusions? Are they part of her "crabwise, scuttling, devious and feminine manner" (p. 640)?*

THE WRITER

1. *Write a paragraph to explain how Atwood's two fantasies (p. 649) imply a basic conviction about what matters to a novelist.*
2. *At various points, Atwood dissociates herself from man-hating. What are her strategies for doing this? Is she witty, or "cute," or something else? What concerns her in these passages?*
3. *Is the gender barrier a particular part of a general writing problem— how to get things right—or is the writing problem part of the gender barrier? Does it matter?*

Virginia Woolf

IN SEARCH OF A ROOM OF ONE'S OWN[1]

It was disappointing not to have brought back in the evening some important statement, some authentic fact. Women are poorer than men because—this or that. Perhaps now it would be better to give up seeking for the truth, and receiving on one's head an avalanche of opinion hot as lava, discoloured as dish-water. It would be better to draw the curtains; to shut out distractions; to light the lamp; to narrow the enquiry and to ask the historian, who records not opinions but facts, to describe under what conditions women lived, not throughout the ages, but in England, say in the time of Elizabeth.

For it is a perennial puzzle why no woman wrote a word of that extraordinary literature when every other man, it seemed, was capable of song or sonnet. What were the conditions in which women lived, I asked myself; for fiction, imaginative work that is, is not dropped like a pebble upon the ground, as science may be; fiction is like a spider's web, attached ever so lightly perhaps, but still attached to life at all four corners. Often the attachment is scarcely perceptible; Shakespeare's plays, for instance, seem to hang there complete by themselves. But when the web is pulled askew, hooked up at the edge, torn in the middle, one remembers that these webs are not spun in midair by incorporeal creatures, but are the work of suffering human beings, and are attached to grossly material things, like health and money and the houses we live in.

I went, therefore, to the shelf where the histories stand and took down one of the latest, Professor Trevelyan's *History of England*. Once more I looked up Women, found "position of," and turned to the pages indicated. "Wife-beating," I read, "was a recognised right of man, and was practised without shame by high as well as low.... Similarly," the historian goes on, "the daughter who refused to marry the gentleman of her parents' choice was liable to be locked up, beaten and flung about the room, without any shock being inflicted on public opinion. Marriage was not an affair of personal affection, but of family avarice, particularly in the 'chivalrous' upper classes.... Betrothal often took place while one or both of the parties was in the cradle, and marriage when they were scarcely out of the nurses' charge." That was about 1470, soon after

1. This selection is Chapter 3 of Woolf's *A Room of One's Own*, a long essay that began as two lectures on women and fiction given at Newnham College and Girton College, women's colleges at Cambridge University, in 1928. In Chapter 1, Woolf advances the proposition that "a woman must have money and a room of her own if she is to write fiction." In Chapter 2, she describes a day spent at the British Museum (now the British Library) looking for information about the lives of women.

Chaucer's time. The next reference to the position of women is some two hundred years later, in the time of the Stuarts. "It was still the exception for women of the upper and middle class to choose their own husbands, and when the husband had been assigned, he was lord and master, so far at least as law and custom could make him. Yet even so," Professor Trevelyan concludes, "neither Shakespeare's women nor those of authentic seventeenth-century memoirs, like the Verneys and the Hutchinsons, seem wanting in personality and character." Certainly, if we consider it, Cleopatra must have had a way with her; Lady Macbeth, one would suppose, had a will of her own; Rosalind, one might conclude, was an attractive girl. Professor Trevelyan is speaking no more than the truth when he remarks that Shakespeare's women do not seem wanting in personality and character. Not being a historian, one might go even further and say that women have burnt like beacons in all the works of all the poets from the beginning of time—Clytemnestra, Antigone, Cleopatra, Lady Macbeth, Phèdre, Cressida, Rosalind, Desdemona, the Duchess of Malfi, among the dramatists; then among the prose writers: Millamant, Clarissa, Becky Sharp, Anna Karenina, Emma Bovary, Madame de Guermantes—the names flock to mind, nor do they recall women "lacking in personality and character." Indeed, if woman had no existence save in the fiction written by men, one would imagine her a person of the utmost importance; very various; heroic and mean; splendid and sordid; infinitely beautiful and hideous in the extreme; as great as a man, some think even greater.[2] But this is woman in fiction. In fact, as Professor Trevelyan points out, she was locked up, beaten and flung about the room.

A very queer, composite being thus emerges. Imaginatively she is of the highest importance; practically she is completely insignificant. She pervades poetry from cover to cover; she is all but absent from history. She dominates the lives of kings and conquerors in fiction; in fact she was the slave of any boy whose parents forced a ring upon her finger. Some of the most inspired words, some of the most profound thoughts in literature fall from her lips; in real life she could hardly read, could scarcely

2. "It remains a strange and almost inexplicable fact that in Athena's city, where women were kept in almost Oriental suppression as odalisques or drudges, the stage should yet have produced figures like Clytemnestra and Cassandra, Atossa and Antigone, Phèdre and Medea, and all the other heroines who dominate play after play of the 'misogynist' Euripides. But the paradox of this world where in real life a respectable woman could hardly show her face alone in the street, and yet on the stage woman equals or surpasses man, has never been satisfactorily explained. In modern tragedy the same predominance exists. At all events, a very cursory survey of Shakespeare's work (similarly with Webster, though not with Marlowe or Jonson) suffices to reveal how this dominance, this initiative of women, persists from Rosalind to Lady Macbeth. So too in Racine; six of his tragedies bear their heroines' names; and what male characters of his shall we set against Hermione and Andromaque, Bérénice and Roxane, Phèdre and Athalie? So again with Ibsen; what men shall we match with Solveig and Nora, Hedda and Hilda Wangel and Rebecca West?"—F. L. LUCAS, Tragedy, pp. 114–15 [Woolf's note].

spell, and was the property of her husband.

It was certainly an odd monster that one made up by reading the historians first and the poets afterwards—a worm winged like an eagle; the spirit of life and beauty in a kitchen chopping up suet. But these monsters, however amusing to the imagination, have no existence in fact. What one must do to bring her to life was to think poetically and prosaically at one and the same moment, thus keeping in touch with fact —that she is Mrs. Martin, aged thirty-six, dressed in blue, wearing a black hat and brown shoes; but not losing sight of fiction either—that she is a vessel in which all sorts of spirits and forces are coursing and flashing perpetually. The moment, however, that one tries this method with the Elizabethan woman, one branch of illumination fails; one is held up by the scarcity of facts. One knows nothing detailed, nothing perfectly true and substantial about her. History scarcely mentions her. And I turned to Professor Trevelyan again to see what history meant to him. I found by looking at his chapter headings that it meant—

"The Manor Court and the Methods of Open-field Agriculture . . . The Cistercians and Sheep-farming . . . The Crusades . . . The University . . . The House of Commons . . . The Hundred Years' War . . . The Wars of the Roses . . . The Renaissance Scholars . . . The Dissolution of the Monasteries . . . Agrarian and Religious Strife . . . The Origin of English Sea-power . . . The Armada . . ." and so on. Occasionally an individual woman is mentioned, an Elizabeth, or a Mary; a queen or a great lady. But by no possible means could middle-class women with nothing but brains and character at their command have taken part in any one of the great movements which, brought together, constitute the historian's view of the past. Nor shall we find her in any collection of anecdotes. Aubrey[3] hardly mentions her. She never writes her own life and scarcely keeps a diary; there are only a handful of her letters in existence. She left no plays or poems by which we can judge her. What one wants, I thought—and why does not some brilliant student at Newnham or Girton supply it?—is a mass of information; at what age did she marry; how many children had she as a rule; what was her house like; had she a room to herself; did she do the cooking; would she be likely to have a servant? All these facts lie somewhere, presumably, in parish registers and account books; the life of the average Elizabethan woman must be scattered about somewhere, could one collect it and make a book of it. It would be ambitious beyond my daring, I thought, looking about the shelves for books that were not there, to suggest to the students of those famous colleges that they should re-write history, though I own that it often seems a little queer as it is, unreal, lop-sided; but why should they not add a supplement to history? calling it, of course, by some inconspicu-

3. John Aubrey (1626–97), whose biographical writings were published posthumously as *Brief Lives*.

ous name so that women might figure there without impropriety? For one often catches a glimpse of them in the lives of the great, whisking away into the background, concealing, I sometimes think, a wink, a laugh, perhaps a tear. And, after all, we have lives enough of Jane Austen; it scarcely seems necessary to consider again the influence of the tragedies of Joanna Baillie upon the poetry of Edgar Allan Poe; as for myself, I should not mind if the homes and haunts of Mary Russell Mitford were closed to the public for a century at least.[4] But what I find deplorable, I continued, looking about the bookshelves again, is that nothing is known about women before the eighteenth century. I have no model in my mind to turn about this way and that. Here am I asking why women did not write poetry in the Elizabethan age, and I am not sure how they were educated; whether they were taught to write; whether they had sitting-rooms to themselves; how many women had children before they were twenty-one; what, in short, they did from eight in the morning till eight at night. They had no money evidently; according to Professor Treve-lyan they were married whether they liked it or not before they were out of the nursery, at fifteen or sixteen very likely. It would have been extremely odd, even upon this showing, had one of them suddenly written the plays of Shakespeare, I concluded, and I thought of that old gentleman, who is dead now, but was a bishop, I think, who declared that it was impossible for any woman, past, present, or to come, to have the genius of Shakespeare. He wrote to the papers about it. He also told a lady who applied to him for information that cats do not as a matter of fact go to heaven, though they have, he added, souls of a sort. How much thinking those old gentlemen used to save one! How the borders of ignorance shrank back at their approach! Cats do not go to heaven. Women cannot write the plays of Shakespeare.

Be that as it may, I could not help thinking, as I looked at the works of Shakespeare on the shelf, that the bishop was right at least in this; it would have been impossible, completely and entirely, for any woman to have written the plays of Shakespeare in the age of Shakespeare. Let me imagine, since facts are so hard to come by, what would have happened had Shakespeare had a wonderfully gifted sister, called Judith, let us say. Shakespeare himself went, very probably—his mother was an heiress—to the grammar school, where he may have learnt Latin—Ovid, Virgil and Horace—and the elements of grammar and logic. He was, it is well known, a wild boy who poached rabbits, perhaps shot a deer, and had, rather sooner than he should have done, to marry a woman in the neighbourhood, who bore him a child rather quicker than was right. That escapade sent him to seek his fortune in London. He had, it seemed, a taste for the theatre; he began by holding horses at the stage door. Very

4. Jane Austen (1775–1817), English novel-ist; Joanna Baillie (1762–1851), Scottish dramatist and poet; Mary Russell Mitford (1787–1855), English novelist and dramatist.

soon he got work in the theatre, became a successful actor, and lived at the hub of the universe, meeting everybody, knowing everybody, practising his art on the boards, exercising his wits in the streets, and even getting access to the palace of the queen. Meanwhile his extraordinarily gifted sister, let us suppose, remained at home. She was as adventurous, as imaginative, as agog to see the world as he was. But she was not sent to school. She had no chance of learning grammar and logic, let alone of reading Horace and Virgil. She picked up a book now and then, one of her brother's perhaps, and read a few pages. But then her parents came in and told her to mend the stockings or mind the stew and not moon about with books and papers. They would have spoken sharply but kindly, for they were substantial people who knew the conditions of life for a woman and loved their daughter—indeed, more likely than not she was the apple of her father's eye. Perhaps she scribbled some pages up in an apple loft on the sly, but was careful to hide them or set fire to them. Soon, however, before she was out of her teens, she was to be betrothed to the son of a neighbouring wool-stapler. She cried out that marriage was hateful to her, and for that she was severely beaten by her father. Then he ceased to scold her. He begged her instead not to hurt him, not to shame him in this matter of her marriage. He would give her a chain of beads or a fine petticoat, he said; and there were tears in his eyes. How could she disobey him? How could she break his heart? The force of her own gift alone drove her to it. She made up a small parcel of her belongings, let herself down by a rope one summer's night and took the road to London. She was not seventeen. The birds that sang in the hedge were not more musical than she was. She had the quickest fancy, a gift like her brother's, for the tune of words. Like him, she had a taste for the theatre. She stood at the stage door; she wanted to act, she said. Men laughed in her face. The manager—a fat, loose-lipped man—guffawed. He bellowed something about poodles dancing and women acting—no woman, he said, could possibly be an actress.[5] He hinted—you can imagine what. She could get no training in her craft. Could she even seek her dinner in a tavern or roam the streets at midnight? Yet her genius was for fiction and lusted to feed abundantly upon the lives of men and women and the study of their ways. At last—for she was very young, oddly like Shakespeare the poet in her face, with the same grey eyes and rounded brows—at last Nick Greene the actor-manager took pity on her; she found herself with child by that gentleman and so—who shall measure the heat and violence of the poet's heart when caught and tangled in a woman's body?—killed herself one winter's night and lies buried at some cross-roads where the omnibuses now stop outside the Elephant and Castle.

That, more or less, is how the story would run, I think, if a woman in

5. Boys played women's parts in the Elizabethan theater.

Shakespeare's day had had Shakespeare's genius. But for my part, I agree with the deceased bishop, if such he was—it is unthinkable that any woman in Shakespeare's day should have had Shakespeare's genius. For genius like Shakespeare's is not born among labouring, uneducated, servile people. It was not born in England among the Saxons and the Britons. It is not born today among the working classes. How, then, could it have been born among women whose work began, according to Professor Trevelyan, almost before they were out of the nursery, who were forced to it by their parents and held to it by all the power of law and custom? Yet genius of a sort must have existed among women as it must have existed among the working classes. Now and again an Emily Brontë or a Robert Burns blazes out and proves its presence.[6] But certainly it never got itself on to paper. When, however, one reads of a witch being ducked, of a woman possessed by devils, of a wise woman selling herbs, or even of a very remarkable man who had a mother, then I think we are on the track of a lost novelist, a suppressed poet, of some mute and inglorious Jane Austen,[7] some Emily Brontë who dashed her brains out on the moor or mopped and mowed about the highways crazed with the torture that her gift had put her to. Indeed, I would venture to guess that Anon, who wrote so many poems without signing them, was often a woman. It was a woman Edward Fitzgerald,[8] I think, suggested who made the ballads and the folk-songs, crooning them to her children, beguiling her spinning with them, or the length of the winter's night.

This may be true or it may be false—who can say?—but what is true in it, so it seemed to me, reviewing the story of Shakespeare's sister as I had made it, is that any woman born with a great gift in the sixteenth century would certainly have gone crazed, shot herself, or ended her days in some lonely cottage outside the village, half witch, half wizard, feared and mocked at. For it needs little skill in psychology to be sure that a highly gifted girl who had tried to use her gift for poetry would have been so thwarted and hindered by other people, so tortured and pulled asunder by her own contrary instincts, that she must have lost her health and sanity to a certainty. No girl could have walked to London and stood at a stage door and forced her way into the presence of actor-managers without doing herself a violence and suffering an anguish which may have been irrational—for chastity may be a fetish invented by certain societies for unknown reasons—but were none the less inevitable. Chastity had then, it has even now, a religious importance in a woman's life, and has so wrapped itself round with nerves and instincts that to cut it free and bring it to the light of day demands courage of the rarest. To

6. Woolf's examples are Emily Brontë (1818–48), the English novelist, and Robert Burns (1759–96), the Scottish poet.
7. Woolf alludes to Thomas Gray's "Elegy Written in a Country Churchyard": "Some mute inglorious Milton here may rest."
8. Edward FitzGerald (1809–83), poet and translator.

have lived a free life in London in the sixteenth century would have meant for a woman who was poet and playwright a nervous stress and dilemma which might well have killed her. Had she survived, whatever she had written would have been twisted and deformed, issuing from a strained and morbid imagination. And undoubtedly, I thought, looking at the shelf where there are no plays by women, her work would have gone unsigned. That refuge she would have sought certainly. It was the relic of the sense of chastity that dictated anonymity to women even so late as the nineteenth century. Currer Bell, George Eliot, George Sand, all the victims of inner strife as their writings prove, sought ineffectively to veil themselves by using the name of a man.[9] Thus they did homage to the convention, which if not implanted by the other sex was liberally encouraged by them (the chief glory of a woman is not to be talked of, said Pericles,[1] himself a much-talked-of man), that publicity in women is detestable. Anonymity runs in their blood. The desire to be veiled still possesses them. They are not even now as concerned about the health of their fame as men are, and, speaking generally, will pass a tombstone or a signpost without feeling an irresistible desire to cut their names on it, as Alf, Bert or Chas. must do in obedience to their instinct, which murmurs if it sees a fine woman go by, or even a dog, Ce chien est à moi.[2] And, of course, it may not be a dog, I thought, remembering Parliament Square, the Sieges Allee and other avenues; it may be a piece of land or a man with curly black hair. It is one of the great advantages of being a woman that one can pass even a very fine negress without wishing to make an Englishwoman of her.

    That woman, then, who was born with a gift of poetry in the sixteenth century, was an unhappy woman, a woman at strife against herself. All the conditions of her life, all her own instincts, were hostile to the state of mind which is needed to set free whatever is in the brain. But what is the state of mind that is most propitious to the act of creation, I asked. Can one come by any notion of the state that furthers and makes possible that strange activity? Here I opened the volume containing the Tragedies of Shakespeare. What was Shakespeare's state of mind, for instance, when he wrote Lear and Antony and Cleopatra? It was certainly the state of mind most favourable to poetry that there has ever existed. But Shakespeare himself said nothing about it. We only know casually and by chance that he "never blotted a line."[3] Nothing indeed was ever said by the artist himself about his state of mind until the eighteenth century perhaps. Rousseau perhaps began it.[4] At any rate, by the nineteenth

9. The pseudonyms of Charlotte Brontë (1816–55), English novelist; Mary Ann Evans (1819–80), English novelist; and Amandine Aurore Lucie Dupin, Baronne Dudevant (1804–76), French novelist.
1. Pericles (d. 429 B.C.), Athenian statesman.

2. That dog is mine.
3. As recorded by his contemporary Ben Jonson (Timber: Or Discoveries Made Upon Men and Matter).
4. Jean-Jacques Rousseau (1712–78), whose Confessions were published posthumously.

century self-consciousness had developed so far that it was the habit for men of letters to describe their minds in confessions and autobiographies. Their lives also were written, and their letters were printed after their deaths. Thus, though we do not know what Shakespeare went through when he wrote *Lear*, we do know what Carlyle went through when he wrote the *French Revolution*; what Flaubert went through when he wrote *Madame Bovary*; what Keats was going through when he tried to write poetry against the coming of death and the indifference of the world.

And one gathers from this enormous modern literature of confession and self-analysis that to write a work of genius is almost always a feat of prodigious difficulty. Everything is against the likelihood that it will come from the writer's mind whole and entire. Generally material circumstances are against it. Dogs will bark; people will interrupt; money must be made; health will break down. Further, accentuating all these difficulties and making them harder to bear is the world's notorious indifference. It does not ask people to write poems and novels and histories; it does not need them. It does not care whether Flaubert finds the right word or whether Carlyle scrupulously verifies this or that fact. Naturally, it will not pay for what it does not want. And so the writer, Keats, Flaubert, Carlyle, suffers, especially in the creative years of youth, every form of distraction and discouragement. A curse, a cry of agony, rises from those books of analysis and confession. "Mighty poets in their misery dead"[5]—that is the burden of their song. If anything comes through in spite of all this, it is a miracle, and probably no book is born entire and uncrippled as it was conceived.

But for women, I thought, looking at the empty shelves, these difficulties were infinitely more formidable. In the first place, to have a room of her own, let alone a quiet room or a sound-proof room, was out of the question, unless her parents were exceptionally rich or very noble, even up to the beginning of the nineteenth century. Since her pin money, which depended on the good will of her father, was only enough to keep her clothed, she was debarred from such alleviations as came even to Keats or Tennyson or Carlyle, all poor men, from a walking tour, a little journey to France, from the separate lodging which, even if it were miserable enough, sheltered them from the claims and tyrannies of their families. Such material difficulties were formidable; but much worse were the immaterial. The indifference of the world which Keats and Flaubert and other men of genius have found so hard to bear was in her case not indifference but hostility. The world did not say to her as it said to them, Write if you choose; it makes no difference to me. The world said with a guffaw, Write? What's the good of your writing? Here the

5. From William Wordsworth's poem "Resolution and Independence."

psychologists of Newnham and Girton might come to our help, I
thought, looking again at the blank spaces on the shelves. For surely it is
time that the effect of discouragement upon the mind of the artist should
be measured, as I have seen a dairy company measure the effect of
ordinary milk and Grade A milk upon the body of the rat. They set two
rats in cages side by side, and of the two one was furtive, timid and small,
and the other was glossy, bold and big. Now what food do we feed women
as artists upon? I asked, remembering, I suppose, that dinner of prunes
and custard.[6] To answer that question I had only to open the evening
paper and to read that Lord Birkenhead is of opinion—but really I am not
going to trouble to copy out Lord Birkenhead's opinion upon the writing
of women. What Dean Inge says I will leave in peace. The Harley Street
specialist may be allowed to rouse the echoes of Harley Street with his
vociferations without raising a hair on my head. I will quote, however,
Mr. Oscar Browning, because Mr. Oscar Browning was a great figure in
Cambridge at one time, and used to examine the students at Girton and
Newnham.[7] Mr. Oscar Browning was wont to declare "that the impression left on his mind, after looking over any set of examination papers,
was that, irrespective of the marks he might give, the best woman was
intellectually the inferior of the worst man." After saying that Mr.
Browning went back to his rooms—and it is this sequel that endears him
and makes him a human figure of some bulk and majesty—he went back
to his rooms and found a stable-boy lying on the sofa—"a mere skeleton,
his cheeks were cavernous and sallow, his teeth were black, and he did
not appear to have the full use of his limbs. . . . 'That's Arthur' [said Mr.
Browning]. 'He's a dear boy really and most high-minded.'" The two
pictures always seem to me to complete each other. And happily in this
age of biography the two pictures often do complete each other, so that
we are able to interpret the opinions of great men not only by what they
say, but by what they do.

But though this is possible now, such opinions coming from the lips of
important people must have been formidable enough even fifty years
ago. Let us suppose that a father from the highest motives did not wish
his daughter to leave home and become writer, painter or scholar. "See
what Mr. Oscar Browning says," he would say; and there was not only
Mr. Oscar Browning; there was the *Saturday Review*; there was Mr.
Greg[8]—the "essentials of a woman's being," said Mr. Greg emphatically,
"are that *they are supported by, and they minister to, men*"—there was an

6. In Chapter 1, Woolf contrasts the lavish
dinner—partridge and wine—she ate as a
guest in a men's college at Cambridge University with the plain fare—prunes and custard—served in a women's college.
7. In Chapter 2, Woolf lists the fruits of her
day's research on the lives of women, which

include Lord Birkenhead's, Dean Inge's, and
Mr. Oscar Browning's opinions of women;
she does not, however, quote them. Harley
Street is where fashionable medical doctors
in London have their offices.
8. Mr. Greg does not appear on Woolf's list
(see preceding note).

enormous body of masculine opinion to the effect that nothing could be expected of women intellectually. Even if her father did not read out loud these opinions, any girl could read them for herself; and the reading, even in the nineteenth century, must have lowered her vitality, and told profoundly upon her work. There would always have been that assertion —you cannot do this, you are incapable of doing that—to protest against, to overcome. Probably for a novelist this germ is no longer of much effect; for there have been women novelists of merit. But for painters it must still have some sting in it; and for musicians, I imagine, is even now active and poisonous in the extreme. The woman composer stands where the actress stood in the time of Shakespeare. Nick Greene, I thought, remembering the story I had made about Shakespeare's sister, said that a woman acting put him in mind of a dog dancing. Johnson repeated the phrase two hundred years later of women preaching.[9] And here, I said, opening a book about music, we have the very words used again in this year of grace, 1928, of women who try to write music. "Of Mlle. Germaine Tailleferre one can only repeat Dr. Johnson's dictum concerning a woman preacher, transposed into terms of music. 'Sir, a woman's composing is like a dog's walking on his hind legs. It is not done well, but you are surprised to find it done at all.'"[1] So accurately does history repeat itself.

Thus, I concluded, shutting Mr. Oscar Browning's life and pushing away the rest, it is fairly evident that even in the nineteenth century a woman was not encouraged to be an artist. On the contrary, she was snubbed, slapped, lectured and exhorted. Her mind must have been strained and her vitality lowered by the need of opposing this, of disproving that. For here again we come within range of that very interesting and obscure masculine complex which has had so much influence upon the woman's movement; that deep-seated desire, not so much that *she* shall be inferior as that *he* shall be superior, which plants him wherever one looks, not only in front of the arts, but barring the way to politics too, even when the risk to himself seems infinitesimal and the suppliant humble and devoted. Even Lady Bessborough, I remembered, with all her passion for politics, must humbly bow herself and write to Lord Granville Leveson-Gower:[2] "... notwithstanding all my violence in politics and talking so much on that subject, I perfectly agree with you that no woman has any business to meddle with that or any other serious business, farther than giving her opinion (if she is ask'd)." And so she goes on to spend her enthusiasm where it meets with no obstacle whatsoever

9. The quotation is from James Boswell's *The Life of Samuel Johnson, L.L.D.* Woolf, in her tale of Judith Shakespeare, imagines the manager bellowing "something about poodles dancing and women acting."
1. *A Survey of Contemporary Music*, Cecil Gray, p. 246 [Woolf's note].

2. Henrietta, Countess of Bessborough (1761–1821) and Lord Granville Leveson Gower, first Earl Granville (1773–1846). Their correspondence, edited by Castalia Countess Granville, was published as his *Private Correspondence, 1781 to 1821*, in 1916.

upon that immensely important subject, Lord Granville's maiden speech in the House of Commons. The spectacle is certainly a strange one, I thought. The history of men's opposition to women's emancipation is more interesting perhaps than the story of that emancipation itself. An amusing book might be made of it if some young student at Girton or Newnham would collect examples and deduce a theory—but she would need thick gloves on her hands, and bars to protect her of solid gold.

But what is amusing now, I recollected, shutting Lady Bessborough, had to be taken in desperate earnest once. Opinions that one now pastes in a book labelled cock-a-doodle-dum and keeps for reading to select audiences on summer nights once drew tears, I can assure you. Among your grandmothers and great-grandmothers there were many that wept their eyes out. Florence Nightingale[3] shrieked aloud in her agony.[4] Moreover, it is all very well for you, who have got yourselves to college and enjoy sitting-rooms—or is it only bed-sitting-rooms?—of your own to say that genius should disregard such opinions; that genius should be above caring what is said of it. Unfortunately, it is precisely the men or women of genius who mind most what is said of them. Remember Keats. Remember the words he had cut on his tombstone. Think of Tennyson;[5] think—but I need hardly multiply instances of the undeniable, if very unfortunate, fact that it is the nature of the artist to mind excessively what is said about him. Literature is strewn with the wreckage of men who have minded beyond reason the opinions of others.

And this susceptibility of theirs is doubly unfortunate, I thought, returning again to my original enquiry into what state of mind is most propitious for creative work, because the mind of an artist, in order to achieve the prodigious effort of freeing whole and entire the work that is in him, must be incandescent, like Shakespeare's mind, I conjectured, looking at the book which lay open at *Antony and Cleopatra*. There must be no obstacle in it, no foreign matter unconsumed.

For though we say that we know nothing about Shakespeare's state of mind, even as we say that, we are saying something about Shakespeare's state of mind. The reason perhaps why we know so little of Shakespeare —compared with Donne or Ben Jonson or Milton—is that his grudges and spites and antipathies are hidden from us. We are not held up by some "revelation" which reminds us of the writer. All desire to protest, to preach, to proclaim an injury, to pay off a score, to make the world the witness of some hardship or grievance was fired out of him and consumed. Therefore his poetry flows from him free and unimpeded. If ever

3. Florence Nightingale (1820–1910), English nurse and philanthropist.
4. See *Cassandra*, by Florence Nightingale, printed in *The Cause*, by R. Strachey [Woolf's note].
5. Keats's epitaph reads "Here lies one whose name was writ in water." Tennyson was notably sensitive to reviews of his poetry.

a human being got his work expressed completely, it was Shakespeare. If ever a mind was incandescent, unimpeded, I thought, turning again to the bookcase, it was Shakespeare's mind.

1929

S. I. Hayakawa

SEX IS NOT A SPECTATOR SPORT

In current discussions of pornography and obscenity, there is widespread confusion about two matters. First there is sexual behavior and what it means to the participants. Secondly there is the outside observer of sexual behavior and what it means to him. When a man and a woman make love, enjoying themselves and each other unself-consciously, a rich relationship is reaffirmed and made richer by their lovemaking. However beautiful or sacred that love relationship may be to that man and woman, it would have an entirely different significance to a Peeping Tom, secretly watching the proceedings from outside the window. The sexual behavior is not itself obscene. Obscenity is peculiarly the evaluation of the outside observer. Theoretically the actors may themselves be made the observers. If, for example, unknown to the man and woman, a movie were to be made of their lovemaking, and that movie were to be shown to them later, that lovemaking might take on an entirely different significance. What was performed unself-consciously and spontaneously might be viewed later by the actors themselves with giggling or shame or shock. They might even insist that the film be destroyed—which is entirely different from saying that they would stop making love.

What I am saying is that obscenity and pornography can happen only when sexual events are seen from the outside, from a spectator's point of view. This is the crux of the pornography problem. Pornography is sexual behvior made public through symbolization—by representation in literature, by simulation or enactment in a nightclub act or on stage, by arts such as painting, photography, or the movies. To object to pornographic movies or art is not, as some would have us believe, a result of hang-ups about sex. One may be completely healthy and still object to many of the current representations of sexual acts in the movies and on the stage.

Standards of morality are one thing. Standards of decorum are another. There is nothing immoral about changing one's clothes or evacuating one's bowels. But in our culture people as a rule do not change their clothing in the presence of the other sex, excepting their spouses. Men and women have separate public lavatories, and within them each toilet is in a separate compartment for privacy. Love too needs privacy. Human beings normally make love in private, whether that love is socially sanctioned, as in marriage, or unsanctioned, as in a house of prostitution.

The trouble with sexual intercourse as an object of artistic or literary representation is that its meaning is not apparent in the behavior. Hence serious writers have historically been reticent in their description of sex. In Dante's *Divine Comedy* Francesca tells of her tragic love for Paolo. They were reading an ancient romance, and as they read, their passions suddenly overcame them. What happened? Dante simply has Francesca say, "That day we read no further." The rest is left to the reader's imagination—and the reader cannot help feeling the power of that on-rushing, fatal passion.

Men and women couple with each other for a wide variety of reasons. Sometimes the sexual encounter is the fulfillment of true love and respect for each other. Sometimes one of the partners is using sex as an instrument of exploitation or aggression against the other. Sometimes sex is a commercial transaction, with either party being the prostitute. Sometimes sex is the expression of neurosis. Sometimes it is evidence of people getting over their neuroses. However, to the movie camera, as to a Peeping Tom, they are all "doing the same thing." To concentrate on the mechanics of sex is to ignore altogether its human significance.

Today movies do not stop at exhibiting copulation. Every kind of aberrant sexual behavior and sadomasochistic perversion is being shown. The advertisements in the newspaper before me announce such titles as *Nude Encounter, Too Hot to Handle, Deep Throat, The Devil in Miss Jones, The Passion Parlor, Hot Kitten,* and *Honeymoon Suite,* as well as "16 hours of hard-core male stag." The only purpose of movies such as these, from all I can tell from advertisements and reviews, is, as D. H. Lawrence expressed it, "to do dirt on sex." Let the American Civil Liberties Union fight for the right of these movies to be shown. I will not.

1979

THE READER

1. This is a short essay. What is the functional relation of its six paragraphs?
2. What is the function of Hayakawa's idea of decorum? How does he establish it?
3. What is the argumentative function of Hayakawa's distinction between meaning and behavior? Would behavior be obscene if it didn't have the right meaning?

THE WRITER

1. Is Hayakawa refuting an argument directed against the opponents of pornography, or is he asserting an argument opposing pornography?

Does it matter? What is the position he takes at the end?
2. Rewrite Hayakawa's conclusion so that it asserts a stronger position.
Can you do this without changing his argument?

E. B. White

SOME REMARKS ON HUMOR

Analysts have had their go at humor, and I have read some of this interpretative literature, but without being greatly instructed. Humor can be dissected, as a frog can, but the thing dies in the process and the innards are discouraging to any but the pure scientific mind.

In a newsreel theatre the other day I saw a picture of a man who had developed the soap bubble to a higher point than it had ever before reached. He had become the ace soap bubble blower of America, had perfected the business of blowing bubbles, refined it, doubled it, squared it, and had even worked himself up into a convenient lather. The effect was not pretty. Some of the bubbles were too big to be beautiful, and the blower was always jumping into them or out of them, or playing some sort of unattractive trick with them. It was, if anything, a rather repulsive sight. Humor is a little like that: it won't stand much blowing up, and it won't stand much poking. It has a certain fragility, an evasiveness, which one had best respect. Essentially, it is a complete mystery. A human frame convulsed with laughter, and the laughter becoming hysterical and uncontrollable, is as far out of balance as one shaken with the hiccoughs or in the throes of a sneezing fit.

One of the things commonly said about humorists is that they are really very sad people—clowns with a breaking heart. There is some truth in it, but it is badly stated. It would be more accurate, I think, to say that there is a deep vein of melancholy running through everyone's life and that the humorist, perhaps more sensible of it than some others, compensates for it actively and positively. Humorists fatten on trouble. They have always made trouble pay. They struggle along with a good will and endure pain cheerfully, knowing how well it will serve them in the sweet by and by. You find them wrestling with foreign languages, fighting folding ironing boards and swollen drainpipes, suffering the terrible discomfort of tight boots (or as Josh Billings[1] wittily called them, "tite" boots). They pour out their sorrows profitably, in a form that is not

1. Pseudonym of Henry Wheeler Shaw, nineteenth-century American humorist whose sketches often depended on an exag- gerated imitation of the dialect of rural New England or New York.

quite fiction nor quite fact either. Beneath the sparkling surface of these dilemmas flows the strong tide of human woe.

Practically everyone is a manic depressive of sorts, with his up moments and his down moments, and you certainly don't have to be a humorist to taste the sadness of situation and mood. But there is often a rather fine line between laughing and crying, and if a humorous piece of writing brings a person to the point where his emotional responses are untrustworthy and seem likely to break over into the opposite realm, it is because humor, like poetry, has an extra content. It plays close to the big hot fire which is Truth, and sometimes the reader feels the heat.

1954

THE READER

White uses a number of concrete details (dissected frog, soap bubbles and bubble blower, clowns with a breaking heart, fighting folding ironing boards and swollen drain pipes, suffering the terrible discomfort of tight boots, big hot fire which is Truth). Which of these are metaphors or analogies (comparisons with a different kind of thing), and which are concrete examples of general statements? Why does White use so many metaphors or analogies in his definition?

THE WRITER

1. Compare White's definition of humor with his definition of democracy (p. 514). Is there a recognizable similarity in language or style? In devices used?

2. Rewrite White's definition in abstract or general language, leaving out the analogies or metaphors and the concrete examples. Then compare the rewritten version with the original. Which is clearer? Which is more interesting to read?

X. J. Kennedy

WHO KILLED KING KONG?

The ordeal and spectacular death of King Kong, the giant ape, undoubtedly have been witnessed by more Americans than have ever seen a performance of *Hamlet*, *Iphigenia at Aulis*, or even *Tobacco Road*. Since RKO-Radio Pictures first released *King Kong*, a quarter-century has gone by; yet year after year, from prints that grow more rain-beaten, from sound tracks that grow more tinny, ticket-buyers by thousands still pursue Kong's luckless fight against the forces of technology, tabloid journalism, and the DAR. They see him chloroformed to sleep, see him whisked from his jungle isle to New York and placed on show, see him burst his chains to roam the city (lugging a frightened blonde), at last to plunge from the spire of the Empire State Building, machine-gunned by model airplanes.

Though Kong may die, one begins to think his legend unkillable. No clearer proof of his hold upon the popular imagination may be seen than what emerged one catastrophic week in March 1955, when New York WOR-TV programmed *Kong* for seven evenings in a row (a total of sixteen showings). Many a rival network vice-president must have scowled when surveys showed that *Kong*—the 1933 B-picture—had lured away fat segments of the viewing populace from such powerful competitors as Ed Sullivan, Groucho Marx and Bishop Sheen.

But even television has failed to run *King Kong* into oblivion. Coffee-in-the-lobby cinemas still show the old hunk of hokum, with the apology that in its use of composite shots and animated models the film remains technically interesting. And no other monster in movie history has won so devoted a popular audience. None of the plodding mummies, the stultified draculas, the whitecoated Lugosis[1] with their shiny pinball-machine laboratories, none of the invisible stranglers, berserk robots, or menaces from Mars has ever enjoyed so many resurrections.

Why does the American public refuse to let King Kong rest in peace? It is true, I'll admit, that *Kong* outdid every monster movie before or since in sheer carnage. Producers Cooper and Schoedsack crammed into it dinosaurs, headhunters, riots, aerial battles, bullets, bombs, bloodletting. Heroine Fay Wray, whose function is mainly to scream, shuts her mouth for hardly one uninterrupted minute from first reel to last. It is also true that *Kong* is larded with good healthy sadism, for those whose joy it is to see the frantic girl dangled from cliffs and harried by pterodactyls. But it seems to me that the abiding appeal of the giant ape rests on other foundations.

Kong has, first of all, the attraction of being manlike. His simian nature gives him one huge advantage over giant ants and walking vegetables in that an audience may conceivably identify with him. Kong's appeal has the quality that established the Tarzan series as American myth—for what man doesn't secretly image himself a huge hairy howler against whom no other monster has a chance? If Tarzan recalls the ape in us, then Kong may well appeal to that great-granddaddy primordial brute from whose tribe we have all deteriorated.

Intentionally or not, the producers of *King Kong* encourage this identification by etching the character of Kong with keen sympathy. For the ape is a figure in a tradition familiar to moviegoers: the tradition of the pitiable monster. We think of Lon Chaney in the role of Quasimodo,[2] of

1. Bela Lugosi, an actor in many horror movies.

2. The title character of Victor Hugo's novel *The Hunchback of Notre Dame*.

Karloff in the original *Frankenstein*. As we watch the Frankenstein monster's fumbling and disastrous attempts to befriend a flower-picking
child, our sympathies are enlisted with the monster in his impenetrable
loneliness. And so with Kong. As he roars in his chains, while barkers sell
tickets to boobs who gape at him, we perhaps feel something more deep
than pathos. We begin to sense something of the problem that engaged
Eugene O'Neill in *The Hairy Ape:* the dilemma of a displaced animal
spirit forced to live in a jungle built by machines.

King Kong, it is true, had special relevance in 1933. Landscapes of the
depression are glimpsed early in the film when an impresario, seeking
some desperate pretty girl to play the lead in a jungle movie, visits
souplines and a Woman's Home Mission. In Fay Wray—who's been
caught snitching an apple from a fruitstand—his search is ended. When
he gives her a big feed and a movie contract, the girl is magic-carpeted
out of the world of the National Recovery Act.[3] And when, in the film's
climax, Kong smashes that very Third Avenue landscape in which Fay
had wandered hungry, audiences of 1933 may well have felt a personal
satisfaction.

What is curious is that audiences of 1960 remain hooked. For in the
heart of urban man, one suspects, lurks the impulse to fling a bomb.
Though machines speed him to the scene of his daily grind, though IBM
comptometers ("freeing the human mind from drudgery") enable him to
drudge more efficiently once he arrives, there comes a moment when he
wishes to turn upon his machines and kick hell out of them. He wants to
hurl his combination radioalarmclock out the bedroom window and
listen to its smash. What subway commuter wouldn't love—just for once
—to see the downtown express smack head-on into the uptown local?
Such a wish is gratified in that memorable scene in Kong that opens with
a wideangle shot: interior of a railway car on the Third Avenue El.
Straphangers are nodding, the literate refold their newspapers. Unknown
to them, Kong has torn away a section of trestle toward which the train
now speeds. The motorman spies Kong up ahead, jams on the brakes.
Passengers hurtle together like so many peas in a pail. In a window of the
car appear Kong's bloodshot eyes. Women shriek. Kong picks up the
railway car as if it were a rat, flips it to the street and ties knots in it, or
something. To any commuter the scene must appear one of the most
satisfactory pieces of celluloid ever exposed.

Yet however violent his acts, Kong remains a gentleman. Remarkable
is his sense of chivalry. Whenever a fresh boa constrictor threatens Fay,
Kong first sees that the lady is safely parked, then manfully thrashes her
attacker. (And she, the ingrate, runs away every time his back is turned.)
Atop the Empire State Building, ignoring his pursuers, Kong places Fay

---

3. Legislation intended to bring an end to the Great Depression of the 1930s.

on a ledge as tenderly as if she were a dozen eggs. He fondles her, then turns to face the Army Air Force. And Kong is perhaps the most disinterested lover since Cyrano:[4] his attentions to the lady are utterly without hope of reward. After all, between a five-foot blonde and a fifty-foot ape, love can hardly be more than an intellectual flirtation. In his simian way King Kong is the hopelessly yearning lover of Petrarchan convention.[5] His forced exit from his jungle, in chains, results directly from his single-minded pursuit of Fay. He smashes a Broadway theater when the notion enters his dull brain that the flashbulbs of photographers somehow endanger the lady. His perilous shinnying up a skyscraper to pluck Fay from her boudoir is an act of the kindliest of hearts. He's impossible to discourage even though the love of his life can't lay eyes on him without shrieking murder.

The tragedy of King Kong then, is to be the beast who at the end of the fable fails to turn into the handsome prince. This is the conviction that the scriptwriters would leave with us in the film's closing line. As Kong's corpse lies blocking traffic in the street, the enterpreneur who brought Kong to New York turns to the assembled reporters and proclaims: "That's your story, boys—it was Beauty killed the Beast!" But greater forces than those of the screaming Lady have combined to lay Kong low, if you ask me. Kong lives for a time as one of those persecuted near-animal souls bewildered in the middle of an industrial order, whose simple desires are thwarted at every turn. He climbs the Empire State Building because in all New York it's the closest thing he can find to the clifftop of his jungle isle. He dies, a pitiful dolt, and the army brass and publicity-men cackle over him. His death is the only possible outcome to as neat a tragic dilemma as you can ask for. The machine-guns do him in, while the manicured human hero (a nice clean Dartmouth boy) carries away Kong's sweetheart to the altar. O, the misery of it all. There's far more truth about upper-middle-class American life in King Kong than in the last seven dozen novels of John P. Marquand.[6]

A Negro friend from Atlanta tells me that in movie houses in colored neighborhoods throughout the South, Kong does a constant business. They show the thing in Atlanta at least every year, presumably to the same audiences. Perhaps this popularity may simply be due to the fact that Kong is one of the most watchable movies ever constructed, but I wonder whether Negro audiences may not find some archetypical appeal in this serio-comic tale of a huge black powerful free spirit whom all the hardworking white policemen are out to kill.

4. Hero of the romantic drama Cyrano de Bergerac, whose extreme sensitivity about his large nose keeps him from professing his love.
5. The attitude of the lover in the sonnets of the fourteenth-century Italian poet Francis Petrarch and his followers.
6. Popular American author of novels of society.

Every day in the week on a screen somewhere in the world, King Kong relives his agony. Again and again he expires on the Empire State Building, as audiences of the devout assist his sacrifice. We watch him die, and by extension kill the ape within our bones, but these little deaths of ours occur in prosaic surroundings. We do not die on a tower, New York before our feet, nor do we give our lives to smash a few flying machines. It is not for us to bring to a momentary standstill the civilization in which we move. King Kong does this for us. And so we kill him again and again, in much-spliced celluloid, while the ape in us expires from day to day, obscure, in desperation.

1960

Aaron Copland

HOW WE LISTEN

We all listen to music according to our separate capacities. But, for the sake of analysis, the whole listening process may become clearer if we break it up into its component parts, so to speak. In a certain sense we all listen to music on three separate planes. For lack of a better terminology, one might name these: (1) the sensuous plane, (2) the expressive plane, (3) the sheerly musical plane. The only advantage to be gained from mechanically splitting up the listening process into these hypothetical planes is the clearer view to be had of the way in which we listen.

The simplest way of listening to music is to listen for the sheer pleasure of the musical sound itself. That is the sensuous plane. It is the plane on which we hear music without thinking, without considering it in any way. One turns on the radio while doing something else and absentmindedly bathes in the sound. A kind of brainless but attractive state of mind is engendered by the mere sound appeal of the music.

You may be sitting in a room reading this book. Imagine one note struck on the piano. Immediately that one note is enough to change the atmosphere of the room—proving that the sound element in music is a powerful and mysterious agent, which it would be foolish to deride or belittle.

The surprising thing is that many people who consider themselves qualified music lovers abuse that plane in listening. They go to concerts in order to lose themselves. They use music as a consolation or an escape. They enter an ideal world where one doesn't have to think of the realities of everyday life. Of course they aren't thinking about the music either. Music allows them to leave it, and they go off to a place to dream, dreaming because of and apropos of the music yet never quite listening to it.

Yes, the sound appeal of music is a potent and primitive force, but you must not allow it to usurp a disproportionate share of your interest. The sensuous plane is an important one in music, a very important one, but it does not constitute the whole story.

There is no need to digress further on the sensuous plane. Its appeal to every normal human being is self-evident. There is, however, such a thing as becoming more sensitive to the different kinds of sound stuff as used by various composers. For all composers do not use that sound stuff in the same way. Don't get the idea that the value of music is commensurate with its sensuous appeal or that the loveliest sounding music is made by the greatest composer. If that were so, Ravel would be a greater creator than Beethoven. The point is that the sound element varies with each composer, that his usage of sound forms an integral part of his style and must be taken into account when listening. The reader can see, therefore, that a more conscious approach is valuable even on this primary plane of music listening.

The second plane on which music exists is what I have called the expressive one. Here, immediately, we tread on controversial ground. Composers have a way of shying away from any discussion of music's expressive side. Did not Stravinsky himself proclaim that his music was an "object," a "thing," with a life of its own, and with no other meaning than its own purely musical existence? This intransigent attitude of Stravinsky's may be due to the fact that so many people have tried to read different meanings into so many pieces. Heaven knows it is difficult enough to say precisely what it is that a piece of music means, to say it definitely, to say it finally so that everyone is satisfied with your explanation. But that should not lead one to the other extreme of denying to music the right to be "expressive."

My own belief is that all music has an expressive power, some more and some less, but that all music has a certain meaning behind the notes and that that meaning behind the note constitutes, after all, what the piece is saying, what the piece is about. This whole problem can be stated quite simply by asking, "Is there a meaning to music?" My answer to that would be. "Yes." And "Can you state in so many words what the meaning is?" My answer to that would be, "No." Therein lies the difficulty.

Simple-minded souls will never be satisfied with the answer to the second of these questions. They always want music to have a meaning, and the more concrete it is the better they like it. The more the music reminds them of a train, a storm, a funeral, or any other familiar conception the more expressive it appears to be to them. This popular idea of music's meaning—stimulated and abetted by the usual run of musical commentator—should be discouraged wherever and whenever it is met. One timid lady once confessed to me that she suspected something seriously lacking in her appreciation of music because of her inability to connect it with anything definite. That is getting the whole thing backward, of course.

Still, the question remains, How close should the intelligent music lover wish to come to pinning a definite meaning to any particular work? No closer than a general concept, I should say. Music expresses, at different moments, serenity or exuberance, regret or triumph, fury or delight. It expresses each of these moods, and many others, in a numberless variety of subtle shadings and differences. It may even express a state of meaning for which there exists no adequate word in any language. In that case, musicians often like to say that it has only a purely musical meaning. They sometimes go farther and say that all music has only a purely musical meaning. What they really mean is that no appropriate word can be found to express the music's meaning and that, even if it could, they do not feel the need of finding it.

But whatever the professional musician may hold, most musical novices still search for specific words with which to pin down their musical reactions. That is why they always find Tchaikovsky easier to "understand" than Beethoven. In the first place, it is easier to pin a meaningword on a Tchaikovsky piece than on a Beethoven one. Much easier. Moreover, with the Russian composer, every time you come back to a piece of his it almost always says the same thing to you, whereas with Beethoven it is often quite difficult to put your finger right on what he is saying. And any musician will tell you that that is why Beethoven is the greater composer. Because music which always says the same thing to you will necessarily soon become dull music, but music whose meaning is slightly different with each hearing has a greater chance of remaining alive.

Listen, if you can, to the forty-eight fugue themes of Bach's *Well Tempered Clavichord*. Listen to each theme, one after another. You will soon realize that each theme mirrors a different world of feeling. You will also soon realize that the more beautiful a theme seems to you the harder it is to find any word that will describe it to your complete satisfaction. Yes, you will certainly know whether it is a gay theme or a sad one. You will be able, in other words, in your own mind, to draw a frame of emotional feeling around your theme. Now study the sad one a little closer. Try to pin down the exact quality of its sadness. Is it pessimistically sad or resignedly sad; is it fatefully sad or smilingly sad?

Let us suppose that you are fortunate and can describe to your own satisfaction in so many words the exact meaning of your chosen theme. There is still no guarantee that anyone else will be satisfied. Nor need they be. The important thing is that each one feel for himself the specific expressive quality of a theme or, similarly, an entire piece of music. And if it is a great work of art, don't expect it to mean exactly the same thing to you each time you return to it.

Themes or pieces need not express only one emotion, of course. Take such a theme as the first main one of the Ninth Symphony, for example. It is clearly made up of different elements. It does not say only one thing. Yet anyone hearing it immediately gets a feeling of strength, a feeling of power. It isn't a power that comes simply because the theme is played loudly. It is a power inherent in the theme itself. The extraordinary strength and vigor of the theme results in the listener's receiving an impression that a forceful statement has been made. But one should never try to boil it down to "the fateful hammer of life," etc. That is where the trouble begins. The musician, in his exasperation, says it means nothing but the notes themselves, whereas the nonprofessional is only too anxious to hang on to any explanation that gives him the illusion of getting closer to the music's meaning.

Now, perhaps, the reader will know better what I mean when I say that music does have an expressive meaning but that we cannot say in so many words what that meaning is.

The third plane on which music exists is the sheerly musical plane. Besides the pleasurable sound of music and the expressive feeling that it gives off, music does exist in terms of the notes themselves and of their manipulation. Most listeners are not sufficiently conscious of this third plane. . . .

Professional musicians, on the other hand, are, if anything, too conscious of the mere notes themselves. They often fall into the error of becoming so engrossed with their arpeggios and staccatos that they forget the deeper aspects of the music they are performing. But from the layman's standpoint, it is not so much a matter of getting over bad habits on the sheerly musical plane as of increasing one's awareness of what is going on, in so far as the notes are concerned.

When the man in the street listens to the "notes themselves" with any degree of concentration, he is most likely to make some mention of the melody. Either he hears a pretty melody or he does not, and he generally lets it go at that. Rhythm is likely to gain his attention next, particularly if it seems exciting. But harmony and tone color are generally taken for granted, if they are thought of consciously at all. As for music's having a definite form of some kind, that idea seems never to have occurred to him.

It is very important for all of us to become more alive to music on its sheerly musical plane. After all, an actual musical material is being used. The intelligent listener must be prepared to increase his awareness of the musical material and what happens to it. He must hear the melodies, the rhythms, the harmonies, the tone colors in a more conscious fashion. But above all he must, in order to follow the line of the composer's thought, know something of the principles of musical form. Listening to all of these elements is listening on the sheerly musical plane.

Let me repeat that I have split up mechanically the three separate planes on which we listen merely for the sake of greater clarity. Actually, we never listen on one or the other of these planes. What we do is to correlate them—listening in all three ways at the same time. It takes no mental effort, for we do it instinctively.

Perhaps an analogy with what happens to us when we visit the theater will make this instinctive correlation clearer. In the theater, you are aware of the actors and actresses, costumes and sets, sounds and movements. All these give one the sense that the theater is a pleasant place to be in. They constitute the sensuous plane in our theatrical reactions.

The expressive plane in the theater would be derived from the feeling that you get from what is happening on the stage. You are moved to pity, excitement, or gayety. It is this general feeling, generated aside from the particular words being spoken, a certain emotional something which exists on the stage, that is analogous to the expressive quality in music.

The plot and plot development is equivalent to our sheerly musical plane. The playwright creates and develops a character in just the same way that a composer creates and develops a theme. According to the degree of your awareness of the way in which the artist in either field handles his material will you become a more intelligent listener.

It is easy enough to see that the theatergoer never is conscious of any of these elements separately. He is aware of them all at the same time. The same is true of music listening. We simultaneously and without thinking listen on all three planes.

In a sense, the ideal listener is both inside and outside the music at the same moment, judging it and enjoying it, wishing it would go one way and watching it go another—almost like the composer at the moment he composes it; because in order to write his music, the composer must also be inside and outside his music, carried away by it and yet coldly critical of it. A subjective and objective attitude is implied in both creating and listening to music.

What the reader should strive for, then, is a more *active* kind of listening. Whether you listen to Mozart or Duke Ellington, you can deepen your understanding of music only by being a more conscious and aware listener—not someone who is just listening, but someone who is listening *for* something.

1957

Joan Didion

GEORGIA O'KEEFFE

"Where I was born and where and how I have lived is unimportant," Georgia O'Keeffe told us in the book of paintings and words published in her ninetieth year on earth. She seemed to be advising us to forget the beautiful face in the Stieglitz photographs. She appeared to be dismissing the rather condescending romance that had attached to her by then, the romance of extreme good looks and advanced age and deliberate isolation. "It is what I have done with where I have been that should be of interest." I recall an August afternoon in Chicago in 1973 when I took my daughter, then seven, to see what Georgia O'Keeffe had done with where she had been. One of the vast O'Keeffe "Sky Above Clouds" canvases floated over the back stairs in the Chicago Art Institute that day, dominating what seemed to be several stories of empty light, and my daughter looked at it once, ran to the landing, and kept on looking. "Who drew it," she whispered after a while. I told her. "I need to talk to her," she said finally.

My daughter was making, that day in Chicago, an entirely unconscious but quite basic assumption about people and the work they do. She was assuming that the glory she saw in the work reflected a glory in its maker, that the painting was the painter as the poem is the poet, that every choice one made alone—every word chosen or rejected, every brush stroke laid or not laid down—betrayed one's character. *Style is character.* It seemed to me that afternoon that I had rarely seen so instinctive an application of this familiar principle, and I recall being pleased not only that my daughter responded to style as character but that it was Georgia O'Keeffe's particular style to which she responded: this was a hard woman who had imposed her 192 square feet of clouds on Chicago.

"Hardness" has not been in our century a quality much admired in women, nor in the past twenty years has it even been in official favor for men. When hardness surfaces in the very old we tend to transform it into "crustiness" or eccentricity, some tonic pepperiness to be indulged at a distance. On the evidence of her work and what she has said about it, Georgia O'Keeffe is neither "crusty" nor eccentric. She is simply hard, a straight shooter, a woman clean of received wisdom and open to what she sees. This is a woman who could early on dismiss most of her contemporaries as "dreamy," and would later single out one she liked as "a very poor painter." (And then add, apparently by way of softening the judgment: "I guess he wasn't a painter at all. He had no courage and I believe that to create one's own world in any of the arts takes courage.") This is a woman who in 1939 could advise her admirers that they were missing her point, that their appreciation of her famous flowers was merely sentimental. "When I paint a red hill," she observed coolly in the catalogue for an exhibition that year, "you say it is too bad that I don't always paint flowers. A flower touches almost everyone's heart. A red hill doesn't touch everyone's heart." This is a woman who could describe the genesis of one of her most well-known paintings—the "Cow's Skull: Red, White and Blue" owned by the Metropolitan—as an act of quite deliberate and derisive orneriness. "I thought of the city men I had been seeing in the East," she wrote. "They talked so often of writing the Great American Novel—the Great American Play—the Great American Poetry.... So as I was painting my cow's head on blue I thought to myself, 'I'll make it an American painting. They will not think it great with the red stripes down the sides—Red, White and Blue—but they will notice it.'"

The city men. The men. They. The words crop up again and again as this astonishingly aggressive woman tells us what was on her mind when she was making her astonishingly aggressive paintings. It was those city men who stood accused of sentimentalizing her flowers: "I made you take time to look at what I saw and when you took time to really notice my flower you hung all your associations with flowers on my flower and you write about my flower as if I think and see what you think and see—and I don't." And I don't. Imagine those words spoken, and the sound you hear is don't tread on me. "The men" believed it impossible to paint New York, so Georgia O'Keeffe painted New York. "The men" didn't think much of her bright color, so she made it brighter. The men yearned toward Europe so she went to Texas, and then New Mexico. The men talked about Cézanne, "long involved remarks about the 'plastic quality' of his form and color," and took one another's long involved remarks, in the view of this angelic rattlesnake in their midst, altogether too seriously. "I can paint one of those dismal-colored paintings like the men," the woman who regarded herself always as an outsider remembers thinking one day in 1922, and she did: a painting of a shed "all low-toned and dreary with the tree beside the door." She called this act of rancor "The Shanty" and hung it in her next show. "The men seemed to approve of it," she reported fifty-four years later, her contempt undimmed. "They seemed to think that maybe I was beginning to paint. That was my only low-toned dismal-colored painting."

Some women fight and others do not. Like so many successful guerrillas in the war between the sexes, Georgia O'Keeffe seems to have been equipped early with an immutable sense of who she was and a fairly clear understanding that she would be required to prove it. On the surface her upbringing was conventional. She was a child on the Wisconsin prairie who played with china dolls and painted watercolors with cloudy skies because sunlight was too hard to paint and, with her brother and sisters, listened every night to her mother read stories of the Wild West, of Texas, of Kit Carson and Billy the Kid. She told adults that she wanted to be an artist and was embarrassed when they asked what kind of artist she wanted to be: she had no idea "what kind." She had no idea what artists did. She had never seen a picture that interested her, other than a pen-and-ink Maid of Athens in one of her mother's books, some Mother Goose illustrations printed on cloth, a tablet cover that showed a little girl with pink roses, and the painting of Arabs on horseback that hung in her grandmother's parlor. At thirteen, in a Dominican convent, she was mortified when the sister corrected her drawing. At Chatham Episcopal Institute in Virginia she painted lilacs and sneaked time alone to walk out to where she could see the line of the Blue Ridge Mountains on the horizon. At the Art Institute in Chicago she was shocked by the presence of live models and wanted to abandon anatomy lessons. At the Art Students League in New York one of her fellow students advised her that, since he would be a great painter and she would end up teaching painting in a girls' school, any work of hers was less important than modeling for him. Another painted over her work to show her how the Impressionists did trees. She had not before heard how the Impressionists did trees and she did not much care.

At twenty-four she left all those opinions behind and went for the first time to live in Texas, where there were no trees to paint and no one to tell her how not to paint them. In Texas there was only the horizon she craved. In Texas she had her sister Claudia with her for a while, and in the late afternoons they would walk away from town and toward the horizon and watch the evening star come out. "That evening star fascinated me," she wrote. "It was in some way very exciting to me. My sister had a gun, and as we walked she would throw bottles into the air and shoot as many as she could before they hit the ground. I had nothing but to walk into nowhere and the wide sunset space with the star. Ten watercolors were made from that star." In a way one's interest is compelled as much by the sister Claudia with the gun as by the painter Georgia with the star, but only the painter left us this shining record. Ten watercolors were made from that star.

1971

THE READER

1. What does Didion mean when she says her daughter assumed "that the painting was the painter as the poem is the poet"?
2. Didion records her daughter's assumption about "people and the work they do. . . . Style is character" (p. 673). Would Gaylin (p. 386) agree? Does Didion herself agree?
3. "Angelic rattlesnake" is an arresting phrase. Define it from the essay.
4. O'Keeffe used terms like "the city men," "the men," and "they" to

describe her audience. What does this show about her beliefs and practice as an artist?

5. How was O'Keeffe one of the "many successful guerrillas in the war between the sexes"?

6. What is the significance of the anecdote with which Didion ends her sketch?

THE WRITER

1. Didion talks about the "familiar principle" that "style is character." How much of Didion's character can you deduce from the style of her essay? Is that deduction confirmed in her other essays "On Going Home" (p. 40), "Salvador" (p. 302), and "On Keeping a Notebook" (p. 414)?

2. O'Keeffe put some distance between herself and the audience for her paintings because she felt the need to develop her own view of the things she painted. Does the writer need a similar distance to develop an original style? Is the process of communication different in painting than in writing?

3. Does Didion seem to have any principle for selecting the details about O'Keeffe's life and career that she does?

4. How can you tell that Didion admires O'Keeffe? How does she amplify her admiration? What does it show about Didion? Is what it shows about Didion confirmed in other essays by Didion?

5. Write a few sentences that would explain why "one's interest is compelled ... by the sister Claudia with the gun." Then write the logical transition from these sentences back to Didion's concluding point.

6. Write a brief biographical sketch, using Didion's as a model. First determine a dominant impression of the person that you wish to convey, and then choose your details to support that impression.

Philosophy and Religion

E. F. Schumacher

LEVELS OF BEING

Our task is to look at the world and see it whole.

We see what our ancestors have always seen: a great Chain of Being which seems to divide naturally into four sections—four "kingdoms," as they used to be called: mineral, plant, animal, and human. This "was, in fact, until not much more than a century ago, probably the most widely familiar conception of the general *scheme* of things, of the constitutive pattern of the universe."[1] The Chain of Being can be seen as extending downward from the Highest to the lowest, or it can be seen as extending upward from the lowest to the Highest. The ancient view begins with the Divine and sees the downward Chain of Being as moving an ever-increasing distance from the Center, with a progressive loss of qualities. The modern view, largely influenced by the doctrine of evolution, tends to start with inanimate matter and to consider man the last link of the chain, as having evolved the widest range of useful qualities. For our purposes here, the direction of looking—upward or downward—is unimportant, and, in line with modern habits of thought, we shall start at the lowest level, the mineral kingdom, and consider the successive gain of qualities or *powers* as we move to the higher levels.

No one has any difficulty recognizing the astonishing and mysterious difference between a living plant and one that has died and has thus fallen to the lowest Level of Being, inanimate matter. What is this *power* that has been lost? We call it "life." Scientists tell us that we must not talk of a "life force" because no such force has ever been found to exist. Yet the *difference* between alive and dead exists. We could call it "*x*," to indicate something that is there to be noticed and studied but that cannot be

---

1. Arthur O. Lovejoy, *The Great Chain of Being* (New York, 1960)[author's note].

explained. If we call the mineral level "m," we can call the plant level $m + x$. This factor x is obviously worthy of our closest attention, particularly since we are able to destroy it, although it is completely outside our ability to create it. Even if somebody could provide us with a recipe, a set of instructions, for creating life out of lifeless matter, the mysterious character of x would remain, and we would never cease to marvel that something that could do nothing is now able to extract nourishment from its environment, grow, and reproduce itself, "true to form," as it were. There is nothing in the laws, concepts, and formulae of physics and chemistry to explain or even to describe such powers. X is something quite new and additional, and the more deeply we contemplate it, the clearer it becomes that we are faced here with what might be called an *ontological discontinuity* or, more simply, a jump in the Level of Being.

From plant to animal, there is a similar jump, a similar addition of powers, which enable the typical, fully developed animal to do things that are totally outside the range of possibilities of the typical, fully developed plant. These powers, again, are mysterious and, strictly speaking, nameless. We can refer to them by the letter "y," which will be the safest course, because any word label we might attach to them could lead people to think that such a designation was not merely a hint as to their nature but an adequate description. However, since we cannot talk without words, I shall attach to these mysterious powers the label *consciousness*. It is easy to recognize consciousness in a dog, a cat, or a horse, if only because they can be knocked unconscious: the processes of life continue as in a plant, although the animal has lost its peculiar powers.

If the plant, in our terminology, can be called $m + x$, the animal has to be described as $m + x + y$. Again, the new factor "y" is worthy of our closest attention; we are able to destroy but not to create it. Anything that we can destroy but are unable to make is, in a sense, sacred, and all our "explanations" of it do not really explain anything. Again we can say that y is something quite new and additional when compared with the level "plant"—another *ontological discontinuity*, another jump in the Level of Being.

Moving from the animal to the human level, who would seriously deny the addition, again, of new powers? What precisely they are has become a matter of controversy in modern times, but the fact that man is able to do—and is doing—innumerable things which lie totally outside the range of possibilities of even the most highly developed animals cannot be disputed and has never been denied. Man has powers of life like the plant, powers of consciousness like the animal, and evidently something more: the mysterious power "z." What is it? How can it be defined? What can it be called? This power z has undoubtedly a great deal to do with the fact that man is not only able to think but is also *able to be aware of his thinking*. Consciousness and intelligence, as it were, recoil upon themselves. There is not merely a conscious being, but a being capable of being conscious of its consciousness; not merely a thinker, but a thinker capable of watching and studying his own thinking. There is something able to say "I" and to direct consciousness in accordance with its own purposes, a master or controller, a power at a higher level than consciousness itself. This power z, consciousness recoiling upon itself, opens up unlimited possibilities of purposeful learning, investigating, exploring, and of formulating and accumulating knowledge. What shall we call it? As it is necessary to have word labels, I shall call it self-awareness. We must, however, take great care always to remember that such a word label is merely (to use a Buddhist phrase) "a finger pointing to the moon." The "moon" itself remains highly mysterious and needs to be studied with the greatest patience and perseverance if we want to understand anything about man's position in the Universe.

Our initial review of the four great Levels of Being can be summed up as follows:

Man can be written	$m + x + y + z$
Animal can be written	$m + x + y$
Plant can be written	$m + x$
Mineral can be written	m

Only m is visible; x, y, and z are invisible, and they are extremely difficult to grasp, although their effects are matters of everyday experience.

If, instead of taking "minerals" as our base line and reaching the higher Levels of Being by the addition of powers, we start with the highest level directly known to us—man—we can reach the lower Levels of Being by the progressive subtraction of powers. We can then say:

Man can be written	M
Animal can be written	$M - z$
Plant can be written	$M - z - y$
Mineral can be written	$M - z - y - x$

Such a downward scheme is easier for us to understand than the upward one, simply because it is closer to our practical experience. We know that all three factors—x, y, and z—can weaken and die away; we can in fact deliberately destroy them. Self-awareness can disappear while consciousness continues; consciousness can disappear while life continues; and life can disappear leaving an inanimate body behind. We can observe, and in a sense feel, the process of diminution to the point of the apparently total disappearance of self-awareness, consciousness, and life. But it is outside our power to give life to inanimate matter, to give consciousness to living matter, and finally to add the power of self-awareness to conscious beings.

What we can do ourselves, we can, in a sense, understand; what we cannot do at all, we cannot understand—not even "in a sense." Evolution as a process of the spontaneous, accidental emergence of the powers of life, consciousness, and self-awareness, out of inanimate matter, is totally incomprehensible.

For our purposes, however, there is no need to enter into such speculations at this stage. We hold fast to what we can see and experience: the Universe is as a great hierarchic structure of four markedly different Levels of Being. Each level is obviously a broad band, allowing for higher and lower beings within each band, and the precise determination of where a lower band ends and a higher band begins may sometimes be a matter of difficulty and dispute. The existence of the four kingdoms, however, is not put into question by the fact that some of the frontiers are occasionally disputed.

Physics and chemistry deal with the lowest level, "minerals." At this level, x, y, and z—life, consciousness, and self-awareness—do not exist, (or, in any case, are totally inoperative and therefore cannot be noticed). Physics and chemistry can tell us nothing, *absolutely nothing*, about them. These sciences possess no concepts relating to such powers and are incapable of describing their effects. Where there is life, there is form, *Gestalt*, which reproduces itself over and over again from seed or similar beginnings which do not possess this *Gestalt* but develop it in the process of growth. Nothing comparable is to be found in physics or chemistry.

To say that life is nothing but a property of certain peculiar combinations of atoms is like saying that Shakespeare's *Hamlet* is nothing but a property of a peculiar combination of letters. The truth is that the peculiar combination of letters is nothing but a property of Shakespeare's *Hamlet*. The French or German versions of the play "own" different combinations of letters.

The extraordinary thing about the modern "life sciences" is that they hardly ever deal with *life as such*, the factor x, but devote infinite attention to the study and analysis of the physicochemical body that is life's carrier. It may well be that modern science has no method for coming to grips with *life as such*. If this is so, let it be frankly admitted; there is no excuse for the pretense that life is nothing but physics and chemistry.

Nor is there any excuse for the pretense that consciousness is nothing but a property of life. To describe an animal as a physicochemical system of extreme complexity is no doubt perfectly correct, except that it misses out on the "animalness" of the animal. Some zoologists, at least, have advanced beyond this level of erudite absurdity and have developed an ability to see in animals more than complex machines. Their influence, however, is as yet deplorably small, and with the increasing "rationalization" of the modern life-style, more and more animals are being treated as if they really were nothing but "animal machines." (This is a very telling example of how philosophical theories, no matter how absurd and offensive to common sense, tend to become, after a while, "normal practice" in everyday life.)

All the "humanities," as distinct from the natural sciences, deal in one way or another with factor y—consciousness. But a distinction between consciousness (y) and self-awareness (z) is seldom drawn. As a result, modern thinking has become increasingly uncertain whether or not there is any "real" difference between animal and man. A great deal of study of the behavior of animals is being undertaken for the purpose of understanding the nature of man. This is analogous to studying physics with the hope of learning something about life (x). Naturally, since man, as it were, *contains* the three lower Levels of Being, certain things about him can be elucidated by studying minerals, plants, and animals—in fact, everything can be learned about him *except that which makes him human*. All the four constituent elements of the human person—m, x, y, and z—deserve study, but there can be little doubt about their relative importance in terms of *knowledge for the conduct of our lives*.

This importance increases in the order given above, and so do the difficulty and uncertainty experienced by modern humanity. Is there really anything beyond the world of matter, of molecules and atoms and electrons and innumerable other small particles, the ever more complex combinations of which allegedly account for simply everything, from the crudest to the most sublime? Why talk about fundamental differences, "jumps" in the Chain of Being, or "ontological discontinuities" when all we can be really sure of are *differences in degree*? It is not necessary for us to battle over the question whether the palpable and overwhelmingly obvious differences between the four great Levels of Being are better seen as differences in kind or differences in degree. What has to be fully understood is that there are differences in kind, and not simply in degree, between the *powers* of life, consciousness, and self-awareness. Traces of these powers may already exist at the lower levels, although not noticeable (or not yet noticed) by man. Or maybe they are infused, so to speak, on appropriate occasions from "another world." It is not essential for us to have theories about their origin, provided we recognize their quality and, in so doing, never fail to remember that they are beyond anything our own intelligence enables us to create.

It is not unduly difficult to appreciate the difference between what is alive and what is lifeless; it is more difficult to distinguish consciousness from life; and to realize, experience, and appreciate the difference between self-awareness and consciousness (that is, between z and y) is hard indeed. The reason for the difficulty is not far to seek: While the higher comprises and therefore in a sense understands the lower, no being can understand anything higher than itself. A human being can indeed strain and stretch toward the higher and induce a process of growth through adoration, awe, wonder, admiration, and imitation, and by attaining a higher level expand its understanding * * *. But people within whom the power of self-awareness (z) is poorly developed cannot grasp it as a separate power and tend to take it as *nothing but* a slight extension of consciousness (y). Hence we are given a large number of definitions of man which make him out to be *nothing but* an exceptionally intelligent animal with a measurably larger brain, or a tool-making animal, or a political animal, or an unfinished animal, or simply a naked ape.

No doubt, people who use these terms cheerfully include themselves in their definitions—and may have some reason for doing so. For others, they sound merely inane, like defining a dog as a barking plant or a running cabbage. Nothing is more conducive to the brutalization of the modern world than the launching, in the name of science, of wrongful and degrading definitions of man, such as "the naked ape." What could one expect of such a creature, of other "naked apes," or, indeed, of oneself? When people speak of animals as "animal machines," they soon start treating them accordingly, and when they think of people as naked apes, all doors are opened to the free entry of bestiality.

"What a piece of work is a man! how noble in reason! how infinite in faculty!"[2] Because of the power of self-awareness (z), his faculties are indeed infinite; they are not narrowly determined, confined, or "programmed" as one says today. Werner Jaeger[3] expressed a profound truth in the statement that once a human potentiality is realized, it exists. It is the greatest human achievements that define man, not any average behavior or performance, and certainly not anything that can be derived from the observation of animals. "All men cannot be outstanding," says Catherine Roberts. "Yet all men, through knowledge of superior humanness, could know what it means to be a human being and that, as such, they too have a contribution to make. It is magnificent to become as human as one is able. And it requires no help from science. In addition, the very act of realising one's potentialities might constitute an advance over what has gone before."[4]

This "open-endedness" is the wonderful result of the specifically human powers of self-awareness (z), which, as distinct from the powers of life and consciousness, have nothing automatic or mechanical about them. The powers of self-awareness are *essentially* a limitless potentiality rather than an actuality. They have to be developed and "realized" by each human individual if he is to become truly human, that is to say, a *person*.

I said earlier on that man can be written

$$m + x + y + z.$$

These four elements form a sequence of increasing rarity and vulnerabil-

2. *Hamlet* II.ii.303–304.
3. Werner Jaeger (1888–1961): German-born scholar of literature, theology, and philosophy.
4. Catherine Roberts, *The Scientific Conscience* (Fontwell, Sussex, 1974) [author's note].

ity. Matter (m) cannot be destroyed; to kill a body means to deprive it of x, y, and z, and the inanimate matter remains; it "returns" to the earth. Compared with inanimate matter, life is rare and precarious; in turn, compared with the ubiquitousness and tenacity of life, consciousness is even rarer and more vulnerable. Self-awareness is the rarest power of all, precious and vulnerable to the highest degree, the supreme and generally fleeting achievement of a person, present one moment and all too easily gone the next. The study of this factor z has in all ages—except the present—been the primary concern of mankind. How is it possible to study something so vulnerable and fleeting? How is it possible to study that which does the studying? How, indeed, can I study the "I" that employs the very consciousness needed for the study? * * *. Before we can turn to [these questions] directly, we shall do well to take a closer look at the four great Levels of Being: how the intervention of additional powers introduces essential changes, even though similarities and "correspondences" remain.

Matter (m), life (x), consciousness (y), self-awareness (z)—these four elements are ontologically—that is, in their fundamental nature—different, incomparable, incommensurable, and discontinuous. Only one of them is directly accessible to objective, scientific observation by means of our five senses. The other three are none the less known to us because we ourselves, every one of us, can verify their existence from our own inner experience.

We never find life except as living matter; we never find consciousness except as conscious living matter; and we never find self-awareness except as self-aware, conscious, living matter. The ontological differences between these four elements are analogous to the discontinuity of dimensions. A line is one-dimensional, and no elaboration of a line, no subtlety in its construction, and no complexity can ever turn it into a surface. Equally, no elaboration of a two-dimensional surface, no increase in complexity, subtlety, or size, can ever turn it into a solid. Existence in the physical world we know is attained only by three-dimensional beings. One- or two-dimensional things exist only in our minds. Analogically speaking, it might be said that only man has "real" existence in this world insofar as he alone possesses the "three dimensions" of life, consciousness, and self-awareness. In this sense, animals, with only two dimensions —life and consciousness—have but a shadowy existence, and plants, lacking the dimensions of self-awareness and consciousness, relate to a human being as a line relates to a solid. In terms of this analogy, matter, lacking the three "invisible dimensions," has no more reality than a geometrical point.

This analogy, which may seem farfetched from a logical point of view, points to an inescapable existential truth: The most "real" world we live in is that of our fellow human beings. Without them we should experi-

ence a sense of enormous emptiness; we could hardly be human ourselves, for we are made or marred by our relations with other people. The
company of animals could console us only because, and to the extent to
which, they were reminders, even caricatures, of human beings. A world
without fellow human beings would be an eerie and unreal place of
banishment; with neither fellow humans nor animals the world would be
a dreadful wasteland, no matter how luscious its vegetation. To call it
one-dimensional would not seem to be an exaggeration. Human existence in a totally inanimate environment, if it were possible, would be
total emptiness, total despair. It may seem absurd to pursue such a line of
thought, but it is surely not so absurd as a view which counts as "real"
only inanimate matter and treats as "unreal," "subjective," and therefore
scientifically nonexistent the invisible dimensions of life, consciousness,
and self-awareness.

A simple inspection of the four great Levels of Being has led us to the
recognition of their four "elements"—matter, life, consciousness, and
self-awareness. It is this recognition that matters, not the precise association of the four elements with the four Levels of Being. If the natural
scientists should come and tell us that there are some beings they call
animals in whom no trace of consciousness can be detected, it would not
be for us to argue with them. Recognition is one thing; identification
quite another. For us, only recognition is important, and we are entitled
to choose for our purpose typical and fully developed specimens from
each Level of Being. If they manifest and demonstrate most clearly the
"invisible dimensions" of life, consciousness, and self-awareness, this
demonstration is not nullified or invalidated by any difficulty of classification in other cases.

Once we have recognized the ontological gaps and discontinuities that
separate the four "elements"—m,x,y,z— from one another, we know also
that there can exist no "links" or "transitional forms": Life is either
present or absent; there cannot be a half-presence; and the same goes for
consciousness and self-awareness. Difficulties of identification are often
increased by the fact that the lower level appears to present a kind of
mimicry or counterfeit of the higher, just as an animated puppet can at
times be mistaken for a living person, or a two-dimensional picture can
look like three-dimensional reality. But neither difficulties of identification and demarcation nor possibilities of deception and error can be used
as arguments against the existence of the four great Levels of Being,
exhibiting the four "elements" we have called Matter, Life, Consciousness, and Self-awareness. These four "elements" are four irreducible
mysteries, which need to be most carefully observed and studied, but
which cannot be explained, let alone "explained away."

In a hierarchic structure, the higher does not merely possess powers
that are additional to and exceed those possessed by the lower; it also has

power over the lower: it has the power to organize the lower and use it for its own purposes. Living beings can organize and utilize inanimate matter, conscious beings can utilize life, and self-aware beings can utilize consciousness. Are there powers that are higher than self-awareness? Are there Levels of Being above the human? At this stage in our investigation we need do no more than register the fact that the great majority of mankind throughout its known history, until very recently, has been unshakenly convinced that the Chain of Being extends upward beyond man. This universal conviction of mankind is impressive for both its duration and its intensity. Those individuals of the past whom we still consider the wisest and greatest not only shared this belief but considered it of all truths the most important and the most profound.

1977

Plato

THE ALLEGORY OF THE CAVE

And now, I said, let me show in a figure how far our nature is enlightened or unenlightened: Behold! human beings living in an underground den, which has a mouth open towards the light and reaching all along the den; here they have been from their childhood, and have their legs and necks chained so that they cannot move, and can only see before them, being prevented by the chains from turning round their heads. Above and behind them a fire is blazing at a distance, and between the fire and the prisoners there is a raised way; and you will see, if you look, a low wall built along the way, like the screen which marionette players have in front of them, over which they show the puppets.

I see.

And do you see, I said, men passing along the wall carrying all sorts of vessels, and statues and figures of animals made of wood and stone and various materials, which appear over the wall? Some of them are talking, others silent.

You have shown me a strange image, and they are strange prisoners.

Like ourselves, I replied; and they see only their own shadows, or the shadows of one another, which the fire throws on the opposite wall of the cave?

True, he said; how could they see anything but the shadows if they were never allowed to move their heads?

And of the objects which are being carried in like manner they would only see the shadows?

Yes, he said.

And if they were able to converse with one another, would they not suppose that they were naming what was actually before them?

Very true.

And suppose further that the prison had an echo which came from the other side, would they not be sure to fancy when one of the passers-by spoke that the voice which they heard came from the passing shadow?

No question, he replied.

To them, I said, the truth would be literally nothing but the shadows of the images.

That is certain.

And now look again, and see what will naturally follow if the prisoners are released and disabused of their error. At first, when any of them is liberated and compelled suddenly to stand up and turn his neck round and walk and look towards the light, he will suffer sharp pains; the glare will distress him and he will be unable to see the realities of which in his former state he had seen the shadows; and then conceive some one saying to him, that what he saw before was an illusion, but that now, when he is approaching nearer to being and his eye is turned towards more real existence, he has a clearer vision—what will be his reply? And you may further imagine that his instructor is pointing to the objects as they pass and requiring him to name them—will he not be perplexed? Will he not fancy that the shadows which he formerly saw are truer than the objects which are now shown to him?

Far truer.

And if he is compelled to look straight at the light, will he not have a pain in his eyes which will make him turn away to take refuge in the objects of vision which he can see, and which he will conceive to be in reality clearer than the things which are now being shown to him?

True, he said.

And suppose once more, that he is reluctantly dragged up a steep and rugged ascent, and held fast until he is forced into the presence of the sun himself, is he not likely to be pained and irritated? When he approaches the light his eyes will be dazzled and he will not be able to see anything at all of what are now called realities.

Not all in a moment, he said.

He will require to grow accustomed to the sight of the upper world. And first he will see the shadows best, next the reflections of men and other objects in the water, and then the objects themselves; then he will gaze upon the light of the moon and the stars and the spangled heaven; and he will see the sky and the stars by night better than the sun or the light of the sun by day?

Certainly.

Last of all he will be able to see the sun, and not mere reflections of him in the water, but he will see him in his own proper place, and not in another; and he will contemplate him as he is.

Certainly.

He will then proceed to argue that this is he who gives the season and the years, and is the guardian of all that is in the visible world, and in a certain way the cause of all things which he and his fellows have been accustomed to behold?

Clearly, he said, he would first see the sun and then reason about him.

And when he remembered his old habitation, and the wisdom of the den and his fellow-prisoners, do you not suppose that he would felicitate himself on the change, and pity them?

Certainly, he would.

And if they were in the habit of conferring honors among themselves on those who were quickest to observe the passing shadows and to remark which of them went before, and which followed after, and which were together; and who were therefore best able to draw conclusions as to the future, do you think that he would care for such honors and glories, or envy the possessors of them? Would he not say with Homer,

Better to be the poor servant of a poor master,

and to endure anything, rather than think as they do and live after their manner?

Yes, he said, I think that he would rather suffer anything than entertain these false notions and live in this miserable manner.

Imagine once more, I said, such an one coming suddenly out of the sun to be replaced in his old situation; would he not be certain to have his eyes full of darkness?

To be sure, he said.

And if there were a contest, and he had to compete in measuring the shadows with the prisoners who had never moved out of the den, while his sight was still weak, and before his eyes had become steady (and the time which would be needed to acquire this new habit of sight might be very considerable) would he not be ridiculous? Men would say of him that up he went and down he came without his eyes; and that it was better not even to think of ascending; and if any one tried to loose another and lead him up to the light, let them only catch the offender, and they would put him to death.

No question, he said.

This entire allegory, I said, you may now append, dear Glaucon, to the previous argument, the prison-house is the world of sight, the light of the fire is the sun, and you will not misapprehend me if you interpret the journey upwards to be the ascent of the soul into the intellectual world according to my poor belief, which, at your desire, I have expressed— whether rightly or wrongly God knows. But, whether true or false, my opinion is that in the world of knowledge the idea of good appears last of all, and is seen only with an effort; and, when seen, is also inferred to be the universal author of all things beautiful and right, parent of light and of the lord of light in this visible world, and the immediate source of reason and truth in the intellectual; and that this is the power upon which he who would act rationally either in public or private life must have his eye fixed.

I agree, he said, as far as I am able to understand you.

Moreover, I said, you must not wonder that those who attain to this beatific vision are unwilling to descend to human affairs; for their souls are ever hastening into the upper world where they desire to dwell; which desire of theirs is very natural, if our allegory may be trusted.

Yes, very natural.

And is there anything surprising in one who passes from divine contemplations to the evil state of man, misbehaving himself in a ridiculous manner; if, while his eyes are blinking and before he has become accustomed to the surrounding darkness, he is compelled to fight in courts of law, or in other places, about the images or the shadows of images of justice, and is endeavouring to meet the conceptions of those who have never yet seen absolute justice?

Anything but surprising, he replied.

Any one who has common sense will remember that the bewilderments of the eyes are of two kinds, and arise from two causes, either from coming out of the light or from going into the light, which is true of the mind's eye, quite as much as of the bodily eye; and he who remembers this when he sees any one whose vision is perplexed and weak, will not be too ready to laugh; he will first ask whether that soul of man has come out of the brighter life, and is unable to see because unaccustomed to the dark, or having turned from darkness to the day is dazzled by excess of light. And he will count the one happy in his condition and state of being, and he will pity the other; or, if he have a mind to laugh at the soul which comes from below into the light, there will be more reason in this than in the laugh which greets him who returns from above out of the light into the den.

That, he said, is a very just distinction.

4th century B.C.

Paul Tillich

THE RIDDLE OF INEQUALITY

For to him who has will more be given; and from him
who has not, even what he has will be taken away.

—MARK iv. 25

One day a learned colleague called me up and said to me with angry
excitement: "There is a saying in the New Testament which I consider to
be one of the most immoral and unjust statements ever made!" And then
he started quoting our text: "To him who has will more be given," and
his anger increased when he continued: "and from him who has not, even
what he has will be taken away." We all, I think, feel offended with him.
And we cannot easily ignore the offense by suggesting what *he* suggested
—that the words may be due to a misunderstanding of the disciples. It
appears at least four times in the gospels with great emphasis. And even
more, we can clearly see that the writers of the gospels felt exactly as we
do. For them it was a stumbling block, which they tried to interpret in
different ways. Probably none of these explanations satisfied them fully,
for with this saying of Jesus, we are confronted immediately with the
greatest and perhaps most painful riddle of life, that of the inequality of
all beings. We certainly cannot hope to solve it when neither the Bible
nor any other of the great religions and philosophies was able to do so.
But we can do two things: We can show the breadth and the depth of the
riddle of inequality and we can try to find a way to live with it, even if it is
unsolved.

I

If we hear the words, "to him who has will more be given," we ask
ourselves: What *do* we have? And then we may find that much is given to
us in terms of external goods, of friends, of intellectual gifts and even of a
comparatively high moral level of action. So we can expect that more will
be given to us, while we must expect that those who are lacking in all that
will lose the little they already have. Even further, according to Jesus'
parable, the one talent[1] they have will be given to us who have five or ten
talents. We shall be richer because they will be poorer. We may cry out
against such an injustice. But we cannot deny that life confirms it abundantly. We cannot deny it, but we can ask the question, do we *really* have
what we believe we have so that it cannot be taken from us? It is a
question full of anxiety, confirmed by a version of our text rendered by
Luke. "From him who has not, even what he *thinks* that he has will be
taken away." Perhaps our having of those many things is not the kind of

1. A Middle Eastern coin at the time of Christ.

689

having which is increased. Perhaps the having of few things by the poor ones is the kind of having which makes them grow. In the parable of the talents, Jesus confirms this. Those talents which are used, even with a risk of losing them, are those which we really have; those which we try to preserve without using them for growth are those which we do not really have and which are being taken away from us. They slowly disappear, and suddenly we feel that we have lost these talents, perhaps forever.

Let us apply this to our own life, whether it is long or short. In the memory of all of us many things appear which we had without having them and which were taken away from us. Some of them became lost because of the tragic limitations of life; we had to sacrifice them in order to make other things grow. We all were given childish innocence; but innocence cannot be used and increased. The growth of our lives is possible only because we have sacrificed the original gift of innocence. Nevertheless, sometimes there arises in us a melancholy longing for a purity which has been taken from us. We all were given youthful enthusiasm for many things and aims. But this also cannot be used and increased. Most of the objects of our early enthusiasm must be sacrificed for a few, and the few must be approached with soberness. No maturity is possible without this sacrifice. Yet often a melancholy longing for the lost possibilities and enthusiasm takes hold of us. Innocence and youthful enthusiasm: we had them and had them not. Life itself demanded that they were taken from us.

But there are other things which we had and which were taken from us, because we let them go through our own guilt. Some of us had a deep sensitivity for the wonder of life as it is revealed in nature. Slowly under the pressure of work and social life and the lure of cheap pleasures, we lose the wonder of our earlier years when we felt intense joy and the presence of the mystery of life through the freshness of the young day or the glory of the dying day, the majesty of the mountains or the infinity of the sea, a flower breaking through the soil or a young animal in the perfection of its movements. Perhaps we try to produce such feelings again, but we are empty and do not succeed. We had it and had it not, and it has been taken from us.

Others had the same experience with music, poetry, the great novels and plays. One wanted to devour all of them, one lived in them and created for oneself a life above the daily life. We had all this and did not have it; we did not let it grow; our love towards it was not strong enough and so it was taken from us.

Many, especially in this group, remember a time in which the desire to learn to solve the riddles of the universe, to find truth has been the driving force in their lives. They came to college and university, not in order to buy their entrance ticket into the upper middle classes or in order to provide for the preconditions of social and economic success, but they came, driven by the desire for knowledge. They had something and more could have been given to them. But in reality they did not have it. They did not make it grow and so it was taken from them and they finished their academic work in terms of expendiency and indifference towards truth. Their love for truth has left them and in some moments they are sick in their hearts because they realize that what they have lost they may never get back.

We all know that any deeper relation to a human being needs watchfulness and growth, otherwise it is taken away from us. And we cannot get it back. This is a form of having and not having which is the root of innumerable human tragedies. We all know about them. And there is another, the most fundamental kind of having and not having—our having and losing God. Perhaps we were rich towards God in our childhood and beyond it. We may remember the moments in which we felt his ultimate presence. We may remember prayers with an overflowing heart, the encounter with the holy in word and music and holy places. We had communication with God; but it was taken from us because we had it and had it not. We did not let it grow, and so it slowly disappeared leaving an empty space. We became unconcerned, cynical, indifferent, not because we doubted about our religious traditions—such doubt belongs to being rich towards God—but because we turned away from that which once concerned us infinitely.

Such thoughts are a first step in approaching the riddle of inequality. Those who have, receive more if they really have it, if they use it and make it grow. And those who have not, lose what they have because they never had it really.

II

But the question of inequality is not yet answered. For one now asks: Why do some receive more than others in the very beginning, before there is even the possibility of using or wasting our talents? Why does the one servant receive five talents and the other two and the third one? Why is the one born in the slums and the other in a well-to-do suburban family? It does not help to answer that of those to whom much is given much is demanded and little of those to whom little is given. For it is just this inequality of original gifts, internal and external, which arouses our question. Why is it given to one human being to gain so much more out of his being human than to another one? Why is so much given to the one that much *can* be asked of him, while to the other one little is given and little *can* be asked? If this question is asked, not only about individual men but also about classes, races and nations, the everlasting question of political inequality arises, and with it the many ways appear in which men have tried to abolish inequality. In every revolution and in every war, the will to solve the riddle of inequality is a driving force. But neither war nor revolution can remove it. Even if we imagine that in an indefinite future most social inequalities are conquered, three things remain: the inequality of talents in body and mind, the inequality created by freedom and destiny, and the fact that all generations before the time of such equality would be excluded from its blessings. This would be the greatest possible inequality! No! In face of one of the deepest and most torturing problems of life, it is unpermittably shallow and foolish to escape into a social dreamland. We have to live now; we have to live this our life, and we must face today the riddle of inequality.

Let us not confuse the riddle of inequality with the fact that each of us is a unique incomparable self. Certainly our being individuals belongs to our dignity as men. It is given to us and must be used and intensified and not drowned in the gray waters of conformity which threaten us today. One should defend every individuality and the uniqueness of every human self. But one should not believe that this is a way of solving the riddle of inequality. Unfortunately, there are social and political reaction-aries who use this confusion in order to justify social injustice. They are at least as foolish as the dreamers of a future removal of inequality. Who-ever has seen hospitals, prisons, sweatshops, battlefields, houses for the insane, starvation, family tragedies, moral aberrations should be cured from any confusion of the gift of individuality with the riddle of inequal-ity. He should be cured from any feelings of easy consolation.

III

And now we must make the third step in our attempt to penetrate the riddle of inequality and ask: Why do some use and increase what was given to them, while others do not, so that it is taken from them? Why does God say to the prophet in our Old Testament lesson that the ears and eyes of a nation are made insensible for the divine message?

Is it enough to answer: Because some use their freedom responsibly and do what they ought to do while others fail through their own guilt? Is this answer, which seems so obvious, sufficient? Now let me first say that it is sufficient if we apply it to ourselves. Each of us must consider the increase or the loss of what is given to him as a matter of his own responsibility. Our conscience tells us that we cannot put the blame for our losses on anybody or anything else than ourselves.

But if we look at others, this answer is not sufficient. On the contrary: If we applied the judgment which we must apply to anyone else we would be like the Pharisee in Jesus' parable.[2] You cannot tell somebody who comes to you in distress about himself: Use what has been given to you; for he may come to you just because he is unable to do so! And you cannot tell those who are in despair about what they are: Be something else; for this is just what despair means—the inability of getting rid of oneself. You cannot tell those who did not conquer the destructive influences of

2. Praying in the temple, the Pharisee said, "God, I thank thee, that I am not as other men are, extortioners, unjust, adulterers . . ." (Luke xviii. 11).

their surroundings and were driven into crime and misery that they should have been stronger; for it was just of this strength they had been deprived by heritage or environment. Certainly they all are men, and to all of them freedom is given; but they all are also subject to destiny. It is not up to us to condemn them because they were free, as it is not up to us to excuse them because they were under their destiny. We cannot judge them. And when we judge ourselves, we must be conscious that even this is not the last word, but that we like them are under an ultimate judgment. In it the riddle of inequality is eternally answered. But this answer is not ours. It is our predicament that we must ask. And we ask with an uneasy conscience. Why are they in misery, why not we? Thinking of some who are near to us, we can ask: Are we partly responsible? But even if we are, it does not solve the riddle of inequality. The uneasy conscience asks about the farthest as well as about the nearest: Why they, why not we?

Why has my child, or any of millions and millions of children, died before even having a chance to grow out of infancy? Why is my child, or any child, born feeble-minded or crippled? Why has my friend or relative, or anybody's friend or relative, disintegrated in his mind and lost both his freedom and his destiny? Why has my son or daughter, gifted as I believe with many talents, wasted them and been deprived of them? And why does this happen to any parent at all? Why have this boy's or this girl's creative powers been broken by a tyrannical father or by a possessive mother?

In all these questions it is not the question of our own misery which we ask. It is not the question: Why has this happened to me?

It is not the question of Job which God answers by humiliating him and then by elevating him into communion with him.[3] It is not the old and urgent question: Where is the divine justice, where is the divine love towards me? But it is almost the opposite question: Why has this not happened to me, why has it happened to the other one, to the innumerable other ones to whom not even the power of Job is given to accept the divine answer? Why—and Jesus has asked the same question—are many called and few elected?

He does not answer; he only states that this is the human predicament. Shall we therefore cease to ask and humbly accept the fact of a divine judgment which condemns most human beings away from the community with him into despair and self-destruction? Can we accept the eternal victory of judgment over love? We cannot; and nobody ever could, even if he preached and threatened in these terms. As long as he

3. Job, one of God's favored servants, was stricken with afflictions. His question, very briefly, was "Why?" God's answer was to remind Job of how powerless man was in comparison with God, and to refuse to explain His actions. After accepting this pronouncement, Job was elevated again into God's favor.

could not see himself with complete certainty as eternally rejected, his preaching and threatening would be self-deceiving. And who could see himself eternally rejected?

But if this is not the solution of the riddle of inequality at its deepest level, can we trespass the boundaries of the Christian tradition and listen to those who tell us that this life does not decide about our eternal destiny? There will be occasions in other lives, as our present life is determined by previous ones and what we have achieved or wasted in them. It is a serious doctrine and not completely strange to Christianity. But if we don't know and never will know what each of us has been in the previous or future lives, then it is not really our destiny which develops from life to life, but in each life it is the destiny of someone else. This answer also does not solve the riddle of inequality.

There is no answer at all if we ask about the temporal and eternal destiny of the single being separated from the destiny of the whole. Only in the unity of all beings in time and eternity can a humanly possible answer to the riddle of inequality be found. *Humanly* possible does not mean an answer which removes the riddle of inequality, but an answer with which we can live.

There is an ultimate unity of all beings, rooted in the divine life from which they come and to which they go. All beings, nonhuman as well as human, participate in it. And therefore they all participate in each other. We participate in each other's having and we participate in each other's not-having. If we become aware of this unity of all beings, something happens. The fact that others have-not changes in every moment the character of my having: It undercuts its security, it drives me beyond myself, to understand, to give, to share, to help. The fact that others fall into sin, crime and misery changes the character of the grace which is given to me: It makes me realize my own hidden guilt, it shows to me that those who suffer for their sin and crime, suffer also for me; for I am guilty of their guilt—at least in the desire of my heart—and ought to suffer as they do. The awareness that others who *could* have become fully developed human beings and never *have*, changes my state of full humanity. Their early death, their early or late disintegration, makes my life and my health a continuous risk, a dying which is not yet death, a disintegration which is not yet destruction. In every death which we encounter, something of us dies; in every disease which we encounter, something of us tends to disintegrate.

Can we live with this answer? We can to the degree in which we are liberated from the seclusion within ourselves. But nobody can be liberated from himself unless he is grasped by the power of that which is present in everyone and everything—the eternal from which we come and to which we go, which gives us to ourselves and which liberates us *from* ourselves. It is the greatness and the heart of the Christian message that God—as manifest in the Cross of the Christ—participates totally in the dying child, in the condemned criminal, in the disintegrating mind, in the starving one and in him who rejects him. There is no extreme human condition into which the divine presence would not reach. This is what the Cross, the most extreme of all human conditions, tells us. The riddle of inequality cannot be solved on the level of our separation from each other. It is eternally solved in the divine participation in all of us and every being. The certainty of the divine participation gives us the courage to stand the riddle of inequality, though finite minds cannot solve it. Amen.

1963

Langston Hughes

SALVATION

I was saved from sin when I was going on thirteen. But not really saved. It happened like this. There was a big revival at my Auntie Reed's church. Every night for weeks there had been much preaching, singing, praying, and shouting, and some very hardened sinners had been brought to Christ, and the membership of the church had grown by leaps and bounds. Then just before the revival ended, they held a special meeting for children, "to bring the young lambs to the fold." My aunt spoke of it for days ahead. That night I was escorted to the front row and placed on the mourners' bench with all the other young sinners, who had not yet been brought to Jesus.

My aunt told me that when you were saved you saw a light, and something happened to you inside! And Jesus came into your life! And God was with you from then on! She said you could see and hear and feel Jesus in your soul. I believed her. I had heard a great many old people say the same thing and it seemed to me they ought to know. So I sat there calmly in the hot, crowded church, waiting for Jesus to come to me.

The preacher preached a wonderful rhythmical sermon, all moans and shouts and lonely cries and dire pictures of hell, and then he sang a song about the ninety and nine safe in the fold, but one little lamb was left out in the cold. Then he said: "Won't you come? Won't you come to Jesus? Young lambs, won't you come?" And he held out his arms to all us young sinners there on the mourners' bench. And the little girls cried. And some of them jumped up and went to Jesus right away. But most of us just sat there.

A great many old people came and knelt around us and prayed, old women with jet-black faces and braided hair, old men with work-gnarled hands. And the church sang a song about the lower lights are burning, some poor sinners to be saved. And the whole building rocked with prayer and song.

Still I kept waiting to see Jesus.

Finally all the young people had gone to the altar and were saved, but one boy and me. He was a rounder's[1] son named Westley. Westley and I were surrounded by sisters and deacons praying. It was very hot in the church, and getting late now. Finally Westley said to me in a whisper: "God damn! I'm tired o' sitting here. Let's get up and be saved." So he got up and was saved.

Then I was left all alone on the mourners' bench. My aunt came and knelt at my knees and cried, while prayers and songs swirled all around me in the little church. The whole congregation prayed for me alone, in a mightly wail of moans and voices. And I kept waiting serenely for Jesus, waiting, waiting—but he didn't come. I wanted to see him, but nothing happened to me. Nothing! I wanted something to happen to me, but nothing happened.

I heard the songs and the minister saying: "Why don't you come? My dear child, why don't you come to Jesus? Jesus is waiting for you. He wants you. Why don't you come? Sister Reed, what is this child's name?"

"Langston," my aunt sobbed.

"Langston, why don't you come? Why don't you come and be saved? Oh, Lamb of God! Why don't you come?"

Now it was really getting late. I began to be ashamed of myself, holding everything up so long. I began to wonder what God thought about Westley, who certainly hadn't seen Jesus either, but who was now sitting proudly on the platform, swinging his knickerbockered legs and grinning down at me, surrounded by deacons and old women on their knees praying. God had not struck Westley dead for taking his name in vain or for lying in the temple. So I decided that maybe to save further trouble, I'd better lie, too, and say that Jesus had come, and get up and be saved.

So I got up.

Suddenly the whole room broke into a sea of shouting, as they saw me rise. Waves of rejoicing swept the place. Women leaped in the air. My aunt threw her arms around me. The minister took me by the hand and led me to the platform.

When things quieted down, in a hushed silence, punctuated by a few ecstatic "Amens," all the new young lambs were blessed in the name of God. Then joyous singing filled the room.

That night, for the last time in my life but one—for I was a big boy twelve years old—I cried. I cried, in bed alone, and couldn't stop. I buried

1. Loafer's, bum's.

my head under the quilts, but my aunt heard me. She woke up and told my uncle I was crying because the Holy Ghost had come into my life, and because I had seen Jesus. But I was really crying because I couldn't bear to tell her that I had lied, that I had deceived everybody in the church, and I hadn't seen Jesus, and that now I didn't believe there was a Jesus any more, since he didn't come to help me.

1940

THE READER

1. *When the preacher held out his arms to the young sinners, Hughes says, the little girls cried and some of them jumped up and went to Jesus right away. Is this a sexist observation? Does the fact that this was published in 1940 affect your answer?*
2. *Hughes obviously does not accept his Auntie Reed's explanation for his behavior. It is pretty hard to get around his explanation of why he cried, but when it comes to his salvation at the meeting, can her explanation be disproved?*

THE WRITER

1. *What are the signs in the first two paragraphs that point to the outcome?*
2. *What is Hughes's attitude toward Westley? Toward Auntie Reed?*
3. *This essay is written simply, with a careful regard for the facts. Replace Hughes's last paragraph with a plausible alternative that presents a different conclusion.*

E. M. Forster

WHAT I BELIEVE

I do not believe in Belief. But this is an age of faith, and there are so many militant creeds that, in self-defence, one has to formulate a creed of one's own. Tolerance, good temper and sympathy are no longer enough in a world which is rent by religious and racial persecution, in a world where ignorance rules, and science, who ought to have ruled, plays the subservient pimp. Tolerance, good temper and sympathy—they are what matter really, and if the human race is not to collapse they must come to the front before long. But for the moment they are not enough, their action is no stronger than a flower, battered beneath a military jackboot. They want stiffening, even if the process coarsens them. Faith, to my mind, is a stiffening process, a sort of mental starch, which ought to be applied as sparingly as possible. I dislike the stuff. I do not believe in it, for its own sake, at all. Herein I probably differ from most people, who believe in Belief, and are only sorry they cannot swallow even more than they do. My law-givers are Erasmus and Montaigne, not Moses and St. Paul. My temple stands not upon Mount Moriah[1] but in that Elysian Field[2] where even the immoral are admitted. My motto is: "Lord, I disbelieve—help thou my unbelief."

I have, however, to live in an Age of Faith—the sort of epoch I used to hear praised when I was a boy. It is extremely unpleasant really. It is bloody in every sense of the word. And I have to keep my end up in it. Where do I start?

With personal relationships. Here is something comparatively solid in a world full of violence and cruelty. Not absolutely solid, for Psychology has split and shattered the idea of a "Person," and has shown that there is something incalculable in each of us, which may at any moment rise to the surface and destroy our normal balance. We don't know what we are like. We can't know what other people are like. How, then, can we put any trust in personal relationships, or cling to them in the gathering political storm? In theory we cannot. But in practice we can and do. Though A is not unchangeably A or B unchangeably B, there can still be love and loyalty between the two. For the purpose of living one has to assume that the personality is solid, and the "self" is an entity, and to ignore all contrary evidence. And since to ignore evidence is one of the characteristics of faith, I certainly can proclaim that I believe in personal relationships.

Starting from them, I get a little order into the contemporary chaos. One must be fond of people and trust them if one is not to make a mess of life, and it is therefore essential that they should not let one down. They often do. The moral of which is that I must, myself, be as reliable as possible, and this I try to be. But reliability is not a matter of contract— that is the main difference between the world of personal relationships and the world of business relationships. It is a matter for the heart, which signs no documents. In other words, reliability is impossible unless there is a natural warmth. Most men possess this warmth, though they often have bad luck and get chilled. Most of them, even when they are politicians, want to keep faith. And one can, at all events, show one's own little light here, one's own poor little trembling flame, with the knowledge that it is not the only light that is shining in the darkness, and not the only one which the darkness does not comprehend. Personal relations are despised today. They are regarded as bourgeois luxuries, as products of a time of fair weather which is now past, and we are urged to get rid of them, and to dedicate ourselves to some movement or cause instead. I hate the idea of causes, and if I had to choose between betraying my country and be-

---

1. Biblical name for a hill in East Jerusalem, the site of Solomon's Temple. 2. In Greek religion, a happy otherworld for heroes favored by the gods.

traying my friend, I hope I should have the guts to betray my country. Such a choice may scandalise the modern reader, and he may stretch out his patriotic hand to the telephone at once and ring up the police. It would not have shocked Dante, though. Dante places Brutus and Cassius in the lowest circle of Hell because they had chosen to betray their friend Julius Caesar rather than their country Rome. Probably one will not be asked to make such an agonising choice. Still, there lies at the back of every creed something terrible and hard for which the worshipper may one day be required to suffer, and there is even a terror and a hardness in this creed of personal relationships, urbane and mild though it sounds. Love and loyalty to an individual can run counter to the claims of the State. When they do—down with the State, say I, which means that the State would down me.

This brings me along to Democracy, "even Love, the Beloved Republic, which feeds upon Freedom and lives." Democracy is not a Beloved Republic really, and never will be. But it is less hateful than other contemporary forms of government, and to that extent it deserves our support. It does start from the assumption that the individual is important, and that all types are needed to make a civilisation. It does not divide its citizens into the bossers and the bossed—as an efficiency-regime tends to do. The people I admire most are those who are sensitive and want to create something or discover something, and do not see life in terms of power, and such people get more of a chance under a democracy than elsewhere. They found religions, great or small, or they produce literature and art, or they do disinterested scientific research, or they may be what is called "ordinary people," who are creative in their private lives, bring up their children decently, for instance, or help their neighbours. All these people need to express themselves; they cannot do so unless society allows them liberty to do so, and the society which allows them most liberty is a democracy.

Democracy has another merit. It allows criticism, and if there is not public criticism there are bound to be hushed-up scandals. That is why I believe in the Press, despite all its lies and vulgarity, and why I believe in Parliament. Parliament is often sneered at because it is a Talking Shop. I believe in it *because* it is a talking shop. I believe in the Private Member who makes himself a nuisance. He gets snubbed and is told that he is cranky or ill-informed, but he does expose abuses which would otherwise never have been mentioned, and very often an abuse gets put right just by being mentioned. Occasionally, too, a well-meaning public official starts losing his head in the cause of efficiency, and thinks himself God Almighty. Such officials are particularly frequent in the Home Office.[3] Well, there will be questions about them in Parliament sooner or later,

3. A department of government in Great Britain corresponding to the Department of the Interior in the United States.

and then they will have to mind their steps. Whether Parliament is either a representative body or an efficient one is questionable, but I value it because it criticises and talks, and because its chatter gets widely reported.

So Two Cheers for Democracy: one because it admits variety and two because it permits criticism. Two cheers are quite enough: there is no occasion to give three. Only Love the Beloved Republic deserves that.

What about Force, though? While we are trying to be sensitive and advanced and affectionate and tolerant, an unpleasant question pops up: does not all society rest upon force? If a government cannot count upon the police and the army, how can it hope to rule? And if an individual gets knocked on the head or sent to a labour camp, of what significance are his opinions?

This dilemma does not worry me as much as it does some. I realise that all society rests upon force. But all the great creative actions, all the decent human relations, occur during the intervals when force has not managed to come to the front. These intervals are what matter. I want them to be as frequent and as lengthy as possible, and I call them "civilisation." Some people idealise force and pull it into the foreground and worship it, instead of keeping it in the background as long as possible. I think they make a mistake, and I think that their opposites, the mystics, err even more when they declare that force does not exist. I believe that it exists, and that one of our jobs is to prevent it from getting out of its box. It gets out sooner or later, and then it destroys us and all the lovely things which we have made. But it is not out all the time, for the fortunate reason that the strong are so stupid. Consider their conduct for a moment in the Niebelung's Ring.[4] The giants there have the guns, or in other words the gold; but they do nothing with it, they do not realise that they are all-powerful, with the result that the catastrophe is delayed and the castle of Walhalla, insecure but glorious, fronts the storms. Fafnir, coiled round his hoard, grumbles and grunts; we can hear him under Europe today; the leaves of the wood already tremble, and the Bird calls its warnings uselessly. Fafnir will destroy us, but by a blessed dispensation he is stupid and slow, and creation goes on just outside the poisonous blast of his breath. The Nietzschean would hurry the monster up, the mystic would say he did not exist, but Wotan, wiser than either, hastens to create warriors before doom declares itself. The Valkyries are symbols not only of courage but of intelligence; they represent the human spirit snatching its opportunity while the going is good, and one of them even finds time to love. Brünnhilde's last song hymns the recurrence of love, and since it is the privilege of art to exaggerate, she goes even further, and proclaims the love which is eternally triumphant and feeds upon

4. Four operas by Richard Wagner, based on a Middle High German legend of the thirteenth century.

freedom, and lives.

So that is what I feel about force and violence. It is, alas! the ultimate reality on this earth, but it does not always get to the front. Some people call its absences "decadence"; I call them "civilisation" and find in such interludes the chief justification for the human experiment. I look the other way until fate strikes me. Whether this is due to courage or to cowardice in my own case I cannot be sure. But I know that if men had not looked the other way in the past, nothing of any value would survive. The people I respect most behave as if they were immortal and as if society was eternal. Both assumptions are false: both of them must be accepted as true if we are to go on eating and working and loving, and are to keep open a few breathing holes for the human spirit. No millennium seems likely to descend upon humanity; no better and stronger League of Nations will be instituted; no form of Christianity and no alternative to Christianity will bring peace to the world or integrity to the individual; no "change of heart" will occur. And yet we need not despair, indeed, we cannot despair; the evidence of history shows us that men have always insisted on behaving creatively under the shadow of the sword; that they have done their artistic and scientific and domestic stuff for the sake of doing it, and that we had better follow their example under the shadow of the aeroplanes. Others, with more vision or courage than myself, see the salvation of humanity ahead, and will dismiss my conception of civilisation as paltry, a sort of tip-and-run[5] game. Certainly it is presumptuous to say that we *cannot* improve, and that Man, who has only been in power for a few thousand years, will never learn to make use of his power. All I mean is that, if people continue to kill one another as they do, the world cannot get better than it is, and that since there are more people than formerly, and their means for destroying one another superior, the world may well get worse. What is good in people—and consequently in the world—is their insistence on creation, their belief in friendship and loyalty for their own sakes; and though Violence remains and is, indeed, the major partner in this muddled establishment, I believe that creativeness remains too, and will always assume direction when violence sleeps. So, though I am not an optimist, I cannot agree with Sophocles that it were better never to have been born. And although, like Horace, I see no evidence that each batch of births is superior to the last, I leave the field open for the more complacent view. This is such a difficult moment to live in, one cannot help getting gloomy and also a bit rattled, and perhaps short-sighted.

In search of a refuge, we may perhaps turn to hero-worship. But here we shall get no help, in my opinion. Hero-worship is a dangerous vice, and one of the minor merits of a democracy is that it does not encourage

5. A game similar to cricket in which a batsman is required to run each time he touches a bowled ball with his bat.

702 E. M. FORSTER

it, or produce that unmanageable type of citizen known as the Great Man. It produces instead different kinds of small men—a much finer achievement. But people who cannot get interested in the variety of life, and cannot make up their own minds, get discontented over this, and they long for a hero to bow down before and to follow blindly. It is significant that a hero is an integral part of the authoritarian stock-in-trade today. An efficiency-regime cannot be run without a few heroes stuck about it to carry off the dullness—much as plums have to be put into a bad pudding to make it palatable. One hero at the top and a smaller one each side of him is a favourite arrangement, and the timid and the bored are comforted by the trinity, and, bowing down, feel exalted and strengthened.

No, I distrust Great Men. They produce a desert of uniformity around them and often a pool of blood too, and I always feel a little man's pleasure when they come a cropper. Every now and then one reads in the newspapers some such statement as: "The coup d'état appears to have failed, and Admiral Toma's whereabouts is at present unknown." Admiral Toma had probably every qualification for being a Great Man—an iron will, personal magnetism, dash, flair, sexlessness—but fate was against him, so he retires to unknown whereabouts instead of parading history with his peers. He fails with a completeness which no artist and no lover can experience, because with them the process of creation is itself an achievement, whereas with him the only possible achievement is success.

I believe in aristocracy, though—if that is the right word, and if a democrat may use it. Not an aristocracy of power, based upon rank and influence, but an aristocracy of the sensitive, the considerate and the plucky. Its members are to be found in all nations and classes, and all through the ages, and there is a secret understanding between them when they meet. They represent the true human tradition, the one permanent victory of our queer race over cruelty and chaos. Thousands of them perish in obscurity, a few are great names. They are sensitive for others as well as for themselves, they are considerate without being fussy, their pluck is not swankiness but the power to endure, and they can take a joke. I give no examples—it is risky to do that—but the reader may as well consider whether this is the type of person he would like to meet and to be, and whether (going farther with me) he would prefer that this type should *not* be an ascetic one. I am against asceticism myself. I am with the old Scotsman who wanted less chastity and more delicacy. I do not feel that my aristocrats are a real aristocracy if they thwart their bodies, since bodies are the instruments through which we register and enjoy the world. Still, I do not insist. This is not a major point. It is clearly possible to be sensitive, considerate and plucky and yet be an ascetic too, if anyone possesses the first three qualities, I will let him in! On they go—

an invincible army, yet not a victorious one. The aristocrats, the elect, the chosen, the Best People—all the words that describe them are false, and all attempts to organise them fail. Again and again Authority, seeing their value, has tried to net them and to utilise them as the Egyptian Priesthood or the Christian Church or the Chinese Civil Service or the Group Movement, or some other worthy stunt. But they slip through the net and are gone; when the door is shut, they are no longer in the room; their temple, as one of them remarked, is the Holiness of the Heart's Affection, and their kingdom, though they never possess it, is the wide-open world.

With this type of person knocking about, and constantly crossing one's path if one has eyes to see or hands to feel, the experiment of earthly life cannot be dismissed as a failure. But it may well be hailed as a tragedy, the tragedy being that no device has been found by which these private decencies can be transmitted to public affairs. As soon as people have power they go crooked and sometimes dotty as well, because the possession of power lifts them into a region where normal honesty never pays. For instance, the man who is selling newspapers outside the Houses of Parliament can safely leave his papers to go for a drink and his cap beside them: anyone who takes a paper is sure to drop a copper into the cap. But the men who are inside the Houses of Parliament—they cannot trust one another like that, still less can the Government they compose trust other governments. No caps upon the pavement here, but suspicion, treachery and armaments. The more highly public life is organised the lower does its morality sink; the nations of today behave to each other worse than they ever did in the past, they cheat, rob, bully and bluff, make war without notice, and kill as many women and children as possible; whereas primitive tribes were at all events restrained by taboos. It is a humiliating outlook—though the greater the darkness, the brighter shine the little lights, reassuring one another, signalling: "Well, at all events, I'm still here. I don't like it very much, but how are you?" Unquenchable lights of my aristocracy! Signals of the invincible army! "Come along—anyway, let's have a good time while we can." I think they signal that too.

The Saviour of the future—if ever he comes—will not preach a new Gospel. He will merely utilise my aristocracy, he will make effective the good will and the good temper which are already existing. In other words, he will introduce a new technique. In economics, we are told that if there was a new technique of distribution, there need be no poverty, and people would not starve in one place while crops were being ploughed under in another. A similar change is needed in the sphere of morals and politics. The desire for it is by no means new; it was expressed, for example, in theological terms by Jacopone da Todi over six hundred years ago. "Ordina questo amore, O tu che m'ami," he said; "O thou who lovest me—set this love in order." His prayer was not granted, and I do not myself believe that it ever will be, but here, and not through a change of heart, is our probable route. Not by becoming better, but by ordering and distributing his native goodness, will Man shut up Force into its box, and so gain time to explore the universe and to set his mark upon it worthily. At present he only explores it at odd moments, when Force is looking the other way, and his divine creativeness appears as a trivial byproduct, to be scrapped as soon as the drums beat and the bombers hum.

Such a change, claim the orthodox, can only be made by Christianity, and will be made by it in God's good time: man always has failed and always will fail to organise his own goodness, and it is presumptuous of him to try. This claim—solemn as it is—leaves me cold. I cannot believe that Christianity will ever cope with the present world-wide mess, and I think that such influence as it retains in modern society is due to the money behind it, rather than to its spiritual appeal. It was a spiritual force once, but the indwelling spirit will have to be restated if it is to calm the waters again, and probably restated in a non-Christian form. Naturally a lot of people, and people who are not only good but able and intelligent, will disagree here; they will vehemently deny that Christianity has failed, or they will argue that its failure proceeds from the wickedness of men, and really proves its ultimate success. They have Faith, with a large F. My faith has a very small one, and I only intrude it because these are strenuous and serious days, and one likes to say what one thinks while speech is comparatively free: it may not be free much longer.

The above are the reflections of an individualist and a liberal who has found liberalism crumbling beneath him and at first felt ashamed. Then, looking around, he decided there was no special reason for shame, since other people, whatever they felt, were equally insecure. And as for individualism—there seems no way of getting off this, even if one wanted to. The dictator-hero can grind down his citizens till they are all alike, but he cannot melt them into a single man. That is beyond his power. He can order them to merge, he can incite them to mass-antics, but they are obliged to be born separately, and to die separately, and, owing to these unavoidable termini, will always be running off the totalitarian rails. The memory of birth and the expectation of death always lurk within the human being, making him separate from his fellows and consequently capable of intercourse with them. Naked I came into the world, naked I shall go out of it! And a very good thing too, for it reminds me that I am naked under my shirt, whatever its colour.

1939

Gilbert Highet

THE MYSTERY OF ZEN

The mind need never stop growing. Indeed, one of the few experiences which never pall is the experience of watching one's own mind, and observing how it produces new interests, responds to new stimuli, and develops new thoughts, apparently without effort and almost independently of one's own conscious control. I have seen this happen to myself a hundred times; and every time it happens again, I am equally fascinated and astonished.

Some years ago a publisher sent me a little book for review. I read it, and decided it was too remote from my main interests and too highly specialized. It was a brief account of how a young German philosopher living in Japan had learned how to shoot with a bow and arrow, and how this training had made it possible for him to understand the esoteric doctrines of the Zen sect of Buddhism. Really, what could be more alien to my own life, and to that of everyone I knew, than Zen Buddhism and Japanese archery? So I thought, and put the book away.

Yet I did not forget it. It was well written, and translated into good English. It was delightfully short, and implied much more than it said. Although its theme was extremely odd, it was at least highly individual; I had never read anything like it before or since. It remained in my mind. Its name was *Zen in the Art of Archery*, its author Eugen Herrigel, its publisher Pantheon of New York. One day I took it off the shelf and read it again; this time it seemed even stranger than before and even more unforgettable. Now it began to cohere with other interests of mine. Something I had read of the Japanese art of flower arrangement seemed to connect with it; and then, when I wrote an essay on the peculiar Japanese poems called *haiku*, other links began to grow. Finally I had to read the book once more with care, and to go through some other works which illuminated the same subject. I am still grappling with the theme; I have not got anywhere near understanding it fully; but I have learned a good deal, and I am grateful to the little book which refused to be forgotten.

The author, a German philosopher, got a job teaching philosophy at the University of Tokyo (apparently between the wars), and he did what Germans in foreign countries do not usually do: he determined to adapt himself and to learn from his hosts. In particular, he had always been interested in mysticism—which, for every earnest philosopher, poses a problem that is all the more inescapable because it is virtually insoluble. Zen Buddhism is not the only mystical doctrine to be found in the East,

705

but it is one of the most highly developed and certainly one of the most difficult to approach. Herrigel knew that there were scarcely any books which did more than skirt the edge of the subject, and that the best of all books on Zen (those by the philosopher D. T. Suzuki) constantly emphasize that Zen can never be learned from books, can never be studied as we can study other disciplines such as logic or mathematics. Therefore he began to look for a Japanese thinker who could teach him directly.

At once he met with embarrassed refusals. His Japanese friends explained that he would gain nothing from trying to discuss Zen as a philosopher, that its theories could not be spread out for analysis by a detached mind, and in fact that the normal relationship of teacher and pupil simply did not exist within the sect, because the Zen masters felt it useless to explain things stage by stage and to argue about the various possible interpretations of their doctrine. Herrigel had read enough to be prepared for this. He replied that he did not want to dissect the teachings of the school, because he knew that would be useless. He wanted to become a Zen mystic himself. (This was highly intelligent of him. No one could really penetrate into Christian mysticism without being a devout Christian; no one could appreciate Hindu mystical doctrine without accepting the Hindu view of the universe.) At this, Herrigel's Japanese friends were more forthcoming. They told him that the best way, indeed the only way, for a European to approach Zen mysticism was to learn one of the arts which exemplified it. He was a fairly good rifle shot, so he determined to learn archery; and his wife co-operated with him by taking lessons in painting and flower arrangement. How any philosopher could investigate a mystical doctrine by learning to shoot with a bow and arrow and watching his wife arrange flowers, Herrigel did not ask. He had good sense.

A Zen master who was a teacher of archery agreed to take him as a pupil. The lessons lasted six years, during which he practiced every single day. There are many difficult courses of instruction in the world: the Jesuits, violin virtuosi, Talmudic scholars, all have long and hard training, which in one sense never comes to an end; but Herrigel's training in archery equaled them all in intensity. If I were trying to learn archery, I should expect to begin by looking at a target and shooting arrows at it. He was not even allowed to aim at a target for the first four years. He had to begin by learning how to hold the bow and arrow, and then how to release the arrow; this took ages. The Japanese bow is not like our sporting bow, and the stance of the archer in Japan is different from ours. We hold the bow at shoulder level, stretch our left arm out ahead, pull the string and the nocked arrow to a point either below the chin or sometimes past the right ear, and then shoot. The Japanese hold the bow above the head, and then pull the hands apart to left and right until the left hand comes down to eye level and the right hand comes to

learned more quickly than he, and reached the final point together with him. All their effort had not been in vain: Herrigel and his wife had really acquired a new and valuable kind of wisdom. Only at this point, when he was about to abandon his lessons forever, did his Master treat him almost as an equal and hint at the innermost doctrines of Zen Buddhism. Only hints he gave; and yet, for the young philosopher who had now become a mystic, they were enough. Herrigel understood the doctrine, not with his logical mind, but with his entire being. He at any rate had solved the mystery of Zen.

Without going through a course of training as absorbing and as complete as Herrigel's, we can probably never penetrate the mystery. The doctrine of Zen cannot be analyzed from without: it must be lived.

But although it cannot be analyzed, it can be hinted at. All the hints that the adherents of this creed give us are interesting. Many are fantastic; some are practically incomprehensible, and yet unforgettable. Put together, they take us toward a way of life which is utterly impossible for westerners living in a western world, and nevertheless has a deep fascination and contains some values which we must respect.

The word Zen means "meditation." (It is the Japanese word, corresponding to the Chinese Ch'an and the Hindu Dhyana.) It is the central idea of a special sect of Buddhism which flourished in China during the Sung period (between a.d. 1000 and 1300) and entered Japan in the twelfth century. Without knowing much about it, we might be certain that the Zen sect was a worthy and noble one, because it produced a quantity of highly distinguished art, specifically painting. And if we knew anything about Buddhism itself, we might say that Zen goes closer than other sects to the heart of Buddha's teaching: because Buddha was trying to found, not a religion with temples and rituals, but a way of life based on meditation. However, there is something eccentric about the Zen life which is hard to trace in Buddha's teaching; there is an active energy which he did not admire, there is a rough grasp on reality which he himself eschewed, there is something like a sense of humor, which he rarely displayed. The gravity and serenity of the Indian preacher are transformed, in Zen, to the earthy liveliness of Chinese and Japanese sages. The lotus brooding calmly on the water has turned into a knotted tree covered with spring blossoms.

In this sense, "meditation" does not mean what we usually think of when we say a philosopher meditates: analysis of reality, a longsustained effort to solve problems of religion and ethics, the logical dissection of the universe. It means something not divisive, but whole; not schematic, but organic; not long-drawn-out, but immediate. It means something more like our words "intuition" and "realization." It means a way of life in which there is no division between thought and action; none of the painful gulf, so well known to all of us, between the unconscious and the conscious mind; and no absolute distinction between the self and the external world, even between the various parts of the external world and the whole.

When the German philosopher took six years of lessons in archery in order to approach the mystical significance of Zen, he was not given direct philosophical instruction. He was merely shown how to breathe, how to hold and loose the bowstring, and finally how to shoot in such a way that the bow and arrow used him as an instrument. There are many such stories about Zen teachers. The strangest I know is one about a fencing master who undertook to train a young man in the art of the sword. The relationship of teacher and pupil is very important, almost sacred, in the Far East; and the pupil hardly ever thinks of leaving a master or objecting to his methods, however extraordinary they may seem. Therefore this young fellow did not at first object when he was made to act as a servant, drawing water, sweeping floors, gathering wood for the fire, and cooking. But after some time he asked for more direct instruction. The master agreed to give it, but produced no swords. The routine went on just as before, except that every now and then the master would strike the young man with a stick. No matter what he was doing, sweeping the floor or weeding in the garden, a blow would descend on him apparently out of nowhere; he had always to be on the alert, and yet he was constantly receiving unexpected cracks on the head or shoulders. After some months of this, he saw his master stooping over a boiling pot full of vegetables; and he thought he would have his revenge. Silently he lifted a stick and brought it down; but without any effort, without even a glance in his direction, his master parried the blow with the lid of the cooking pot. At last, the pupil began to understand the instinctive alert-ness, the effortless perception and avoidance of danger, in which his master had been training him. As soon as he had achieved it, it was child's play for him to learn the management of the sword: he could parry every cut and turn every slash without anxiety, until his opponent, exhausted, left an opening for his counterattack. (The same principle was used by the elderly samurai for selecting his comrades in the Japanese motion picture *The Magnificent Seven*.)

These stories show that Zen meditation does not mean sitting and thinking. On the contrary, it means acting with as little thought as possible. The fencing master trained his pupil to guard against every attack with the same immediate, instinctive rapidity with which our eyelid closes over our eye when something threatens it. His work was aimed at breaking down the wall between thought and act, at completely fusing body and senses and mind so that they might all work together rapidly and effortlessly. When a Zen artist draws a picture, he does it in a rhythm almost the exact reverse of that which is followed by a Western artist. We begin by blocking out the design and then filling in the details, usually working more and more slowly as we approach the completion of the picture. The Zen artist sits down very calmly; examines his brush carefully; prepares his own ink; smooths out the paper on which he will work; falls into a profound silent ecstasy of contemplation—during which he does not think anxiously of various details, composition, brushwork, shades of tone, but rather attempts to become the vehicle through which the subject can express itself in painting; and then, very quickly and almost unconsciously, with sure effortless strokes, draws a picture containing the fewest and most effective lines. Most of the paper is left blank; only the essential is depicted, and that not completely. One long curving line will be enough to show a mountainside; seven streaks will become a group of bamboos bending in the wind; and yet, though technically incomplete, such pictures are unforgettably clear. They show the heart of reality.

All this we can sympathize with, because we can see the results. The young swordsman learns how to fence. The intuitional painter produces a fine picture. But the hardest thing for us to appreciate is that the Zen masters refuse to teach philosophy or religion directly, and deny logic. In fact, they despise logic as an artificial distortion of reality. Many philosophical teachers are difficult to understand because they analyze profound problems with subtle intricacy: such is Aristotle in his *Metaphysics*. Many mystical writers are difficult to understand because, as they themselves admit, they are attempting to use words to describe experiences which are too abstruse for words, so that they have to fall back on imagery and analogy, which they themselves recognize to be poor media, far coarser than the realities with which they have been in contact. But the Zen teachers seem to deny the power of language and thought altogether. For example, if you ask a Zen master what is the ultimate reality, he will answer, without the slightest hesitation, "The bamboo grove at the foot of the hill" or "A branch of plum blossom." Apparently he means that these things, which we can see instantly without effort, or imagine in the flash of a second, are real with the ultimate reality; that nothing is more real than these; and that we ought to grasp ultimates as we grasp simple immediates. A Chinese master was once asked the central question, "What is the Buddha?" He said nothing whatever, but held out his index finger. What did he mean? It is hard to explain; but apparently he meant "Here. Now. Look and realize with the effortlessness of seeing. Do not try to use words. Do not think. Make no efforts toward withdrawal from the world. Expect no sublime ecstasies. Live. All *that* is the ultimate reality, and it can be understood from the motion of a finger as well as from the execution of any complex ritual, from any subtle argument, or from the circling of the starry universe."

In making that gesture, the master was copying the Buddha himself, who once delivered a sermon which is famous, but was hardly understood by his pupils at the time. Without saying a word, he held up a flower and showed it to the gathering. One man, one alone, knew what he meant. The gesture became renowned as the Flower Sermon.

In the annals of Zen there are many cryptic answers to the final question, "What is the Buddha?"—which in our terms means "What is the meaning of life? What is truly real?" For example, one master, when asked "What is the Buddha?" replied, "Your name is Yecho." Another said, "Even the finest artist cannot paint him." Another said, "No nonsense here." And another answered, "The mouth is the gate of woe." My favorite story is about the monk who said to a Master, "Has a dog Buddha-nature too?" The Master replied, "Wu"—which is what the dog himself would have said.

Now, some critics might attack Zen by saying that this is the creed of a savage or an animal. The adherents of Zen would deny that—or more probably they would ignore the criticism, or make some cryptic remark which meant that it was pointless. Their position—if they could ever be persuaded to put in into words—would be this. An animal is instinctively in touch with reality, and so far is living rightly, but it has never had a mind and so cannot perceive the Whole, only that part with which it is in touch. The philosopher sees both the Whole and the parts, and enjoys them all. As for the savage, he exists only through the group; he feels himself as part of a war party or a ceremonial dance team or a ploughing-and-sowing group or the Snake clan; he is not truly an individual at all, and therefore is less than fully human. Zen has at its heart an inner solitude; its aim is to teach us to live, as in the last resort we do all have to live, alone.

A more dangerous criticism of Zen would be that it is nihilism, that its purpose is to abolish thought altogether. (This criticism is handled, but not fully met, by the great Zen authority Suzuki in his *Introduction to Zen Buddhism.*) It can hardly be completely confuted, for after all the central doctrine of Buddhism is—Nothingness. And many of the sayings of Zen masters are truly nihilistic. The first patriarch of the sect in China was asked by the emperor what was the ultimate and holiest principle of Buddhism. He replied, "Vast emptiness, and nothing holy in it." Another who was asked the searching question "Where is the abiding-place for the mind?" answered, "Not in this dualism of good and evil, being and non-being, thought and matter." In fact, thought is an activity which divides. It analyzes, it makes distinctions, it criticizes, it judges, it breaks reality into groups and classes and individuals. The aim of Zen is to abolish that kind of thinking, and to substitute—not unconsciousness, which would be death, but a consciousness that does not analyze but experiences life directly. Although it has no prescribed prayers, no sacred scriptures, no ceremonial rites, no personal god, and no interest in the soul's future destination, Zen is a religion rather than a philosophy. Jung points out that its aim is to produce a religious conversion, a "transformation": and he adds, "The transformation process is incommensurable with intellect." Thought is always interesting, but often painful; Zen is calm and painless. Thought is incomplete; Zen enlightenment brings a sense of completeness. Thought is a process; Zen illumination is a state. But it is a state which cannot be defined. In the Buddhist scriptures there is a dialogue between a master and a pupil in which the pupil tries to discover the exact meaning of such a state. The master says to him, 'If a fire were blazing in front of you, would you know that it was blazing?'

"Yes, master."

"And would you know the reason for its blazing?"

"Yes, because it had a supply of grass and sticks."

"And would you know if it were to go out?"

"Yes, master."

"And on its going out, would you know where the fire had gone? To the east, to the west, to the north, or to the south?"

"The question does not apply, master. For the fire blazed because it had a supply of grass and sticks. When it had consumed this and had no other fuel, then it went out."

"In the same way," replies the master, "no question will apply to the meaning of Nirvana, and no statement will explain it."

Such, then, neither happy nor unhappy but beyond all divisive description, is the condition which students of Zen strive to attain. Small wonder that they can scarcely explain it to us, the unilluminated.

1957

THE READER

1. On p. 712, Highet says that "Zen is a religion rather than a philosophy." How has he led up to this conclusion? What definitions of "religion" and "philosophy" does he imply?

2. To what extent is Zen "the creed of a savage or an animal"? How does Highet go about refuting this charge?

THE WRITER

1. What difficulties does Highet face in discussing Zen? How does he manage to give a definition in spite of his statement that Zen "cannot be analyzed"?

2. Why does Highet describe the training in archery in such detail?

3. By what means does Highet define "meditation"? Would other means have worked as well? Explain. Write a brief definition of a similar term (perhaps intuition or realization), using an approach similar to Highet's.

Virginia Woolf

THE DEATH OF THE MOTH

Moths that fly by day are not properly to be called moths; they do not excite that pleasant sense of dark autumn nights and ivy-blossom which the commonest yellow-underwing asleep in the shadow of the curtain never fails to rouse in us. They are hybrid creatures, neither gay like butterflies nor sombre like their own species. Nevertheless the present specimen, with his narrow hay-coloured wings, fringed with a tassel of the same colour, seemed to be content with life. It was a pleasant morning, mid-September, mild, benignant, yet with a keener breath than that of the summer months. The plough was already scoring the field opposite the window, and where the share had been, the earth was pressed flat and gleamed with moisture. Such vigour came rolling in from the fields and the down beyond that it was difficult to keep the eyes strictly turned upon the book. The rooks too were keeping one of their annual festivities; soaring round the tree tops until it looked as if a vast net with thousands of black knots in it had been cast up into the air; which, after a few moments sank slowly down upon the trees until every twig seemed to have a knot at the end of it. Then, suddenly, the net would be thrown into the air again in a wider circle this time, with the utmost clamour and vociferation, as though to be thrown into the air and settle slowly down upon the tree tops were a tremendously exciting experience.

The same energy which inspired the rooks, the ploughmen, the horses, and even, it seemed, the lean bare-backed downs, sent the moth fluttering from side to side of his square of the window-pane. One could not help watching him. One was, indeed, conscious of a queer feeling of pity for him. The possibilities of pleasure seemed that morning so enormous and so various that to have only a moth's part in life, and a day moth's at that, appeared a hard fate, and his zest in enjoying his meagre opportunities to the full, pathetic. He flew vigorously to one corner of his compartment, and, after waiting there a second, flew across to the other. What remained for him but to fly to a third corner and then to a fourth? That was all he could do, in spite of the size of the downs, the width of the sky, the far-off smoke of houses, and the romantic voice, now and then, of a steamer out at sea. What he could do he did. Watching him, it seemed as if a fibre, very thin but pure, of the enormous energy of the world had been thrust into his frail and diminutive body. As often as he crossed the pane, I could fancy that a thread of vital light became visible. He was little or nothing but life.

Yet, because he was so small, and so simple a form of the energy that was rolling in at the open window and driving its way through so many narrow and intricate corridors in my own brain and in those of other human beings, there was something marvellous as well as pathetic about him. It was as if someone had taken a tiny bead of pure life and decking it as lightly as possible with down and feathers, had set it dancing and zig-zagging to show us the true nature of life. Thus displayed one could not get over the strangeness of it. One is apt to forget all about life, seeing it humped and bossed and garnished and cumbered so that it has to move with the greatest circumspection and dignity. Again, the thought of all that life might have been had he been born in any other shape caused one to view his simple activities with a kind of pity.

After a time, tired by his dancing apparently, he settled on the window ledge in the sun, and, the queer spectacle being at an end, I forgot about him. Then, looking up, my eye was caught by him. He was trying to resume his dancing, but seemed either so stiff or so awkward that he could only flutter to the bottom of the window-pane; and when he tried to fly across it he failed. Being intent on other matters I watched these futile attempts for a time without thinking, unconsciously waiting for him to resume his flight, as one waits for a machine, that has stopped momenta-rily, to start again without considering the reason of its failure. After perhaps a seventh attempt he slipped from the wooden ledge and fell, fluttering his wings, on to his back on the window sill. The helplessness of his attitude roused me. It flashed upon me that he was in difficulties; he could no longer raise himself; his legs struggled vainly. But, as I stretched out a pencil, meaning to help him to right himself, it came over me that the failure and awkwardness were the approach of death. I laid the pencil down again.

The legs agitated themselves once more. I looked as if for the enemy against which he struggled. I looked out of doors. What had happened there? Presumably it was midday, and work in the fields had stopped. Stillness and quiet had replaced the previous animation. The birds had taken themselves off to feed in the brooks. The horses stood still. Yet the power was there all the same, massed outside indifferent, impersonal, not attending to anything in particular. Somehow it was opposed to the little hay-coloured moth. It was useless to try to do anything. One could only watch the extraordinary efforts made by those tiny legs against an oncom-ing doom which could, had it chosen, have submerged an entire city, not merely a city, but masses of human beings; nothing, I knew, had any chance against death. Nevertheless after a pause of exhaustion the legs fluttered again. It was superb this last protest, and so frantic that he succeeded at last in righting himself. One's sympathies, of course, were all on the side of life. Also, when there was nobody to care or to know, this gigantic effort on the part of an insignificant little moth, against a power of such magnitude, to retain what no one else valued or desired to keep, moved one strangely. Again, somehow, one saw life, a pure bead. I lifted the pencil again, useless though I knew it to be. But even as I did so, the unmistakable tokens of death showed themselves. The body relaxed, and instantly grew stiff. The struggle was over. The insignificant little creature now knew death. As I looked at the dead moth, this minute wayside triumph of so great a force over so mean an antagonist filled me with wonder. Just as life had been strange a few minutes before, so death was now as strange. The moth having righted himself now lay most decently and uncomplainingly composed. O yes, he seemed to say, death is stronger than I am.

1947

THE READER

1. Why does Woolf describe the rooks in some detail, but not the ploughmen?
2. Does Woolf see any resemblances between the moth and human beings? How do you know?
3. In "The New Biography" (p. 420), Woolf speaks of the kind of biography written by Harold Nicolson, in which the biographer uses devices of fiction. Are there any devices of fiction in "The Death of the Moth"? Has she written a biography of the moth? She represents Nicolson as laughing at eminent men; she is very respectful of the insect. What does this suggest about her?

THE WRITER

1. Observe an insect, and describe it from two points of view—one objective and one subjective, or as a scientist might describe it and as a poet or a novelist might describe it.
2. Read Frost's poem "To a Moth Seen in Winter," printed below. Does Frost feel the same way about his moth that Woolf does about hers? Does one author identify with the moth more than the other? Woolf's piece takes place in the fall, Frost's in winter. What is the significance of the difference in seasons? Embody some of your conclusions in a brief essay of comparison.

TO A MOTH SEEN IN WINTER

Here's first a gloveless hand warm from my pocket,
A perch and resting place 'twixt wood and wood,
Bright-black-eyed silvery creature, brushed with brown,
The wings not folded in repose, but spread.
(Who would you be, I wonder, by those marks
If I had moths to friend as I have flowers?)
And now pray tell what lured you with false hope
To make the venture of eternity

And seek the love of kind in wintertime?
But stay and hear me out. I surely think
You make a labor of flight for one so airy
Spending yourself too much in self-support.
Nor will you find love either nor love you.
And what I pity in you is something human,
The old incurable untimeliness,
Only begetter of all ills that are.
But go. You are right. My pity cannot help.
Go till you wet your pinions and are quenched.
You must be made more simply wise than I
To know the hand I stretch impulsively
Across the gulf of well nigh everything
May reach to you, but cannot touch your fate.
I cannot touch your life, much less can save,
Who am tasked to save my own a little while.

Jean-Paul Sartre

EXISTENTIALISM

Man is nothing else but what he makes of himself. Such is the first principle of existentialism. It is also what is called subjectivity, the name we are labeled with when charges are brought against us. But what do we mean by this, if not that man has a greater dignity than a stone or table? For we mean that man first exists, that is, that man first of all is the being who hurls himself toward a future and who is conscious of imagining himself as being in the future. Man is at the start a plan which is aware of itself, rather than a patch of moss, a piece of garbage, or a cauliflower; nothing exists prior to this plan; there is nothing in heaven; man will be what he will have planned to be. Not what he will want to be. Because by the word "will" we generally mean a conscious decision, which is subsequent to what we have already made of ourselves. I may want to belong to a political party, write a book, get married; but all that is only a manifestation of an earlier, more spontaneous choice that is called "will." But if existence really does precede essence, man is responsible for what he is. Thus, existentialism's first move is to make every man aware of what he is and to make the full responsibility of his existence rest on him. And when we say that a man is responsible for himself, we do not only mean that he is responsible for his own individuality, but that he is responsible for all men.

The word "subjectivism" has two meanings, and our opponents play on the two. Subjectivism means, on the one hand, that an individual chooses and makes himself; and, on the other, that it is impossible for man to transcend human subjectivity. The second of these is the essential meaning of existentialism. When we say that man chooses his own self, we mean that every one of us does likewise; but we also mean by that that in making this choice he also chooses all men. In fact, in creating the man that we want to be, there is not a single one of our acts which does not at the same time create an image of man as we think he ought to be. To choose to be this or that is to affirm at the same time the value of what we choose, because we can never choose evil. We always choose the good, and nothing can be good for us without being good for all.

If, on the other hand, existence precedes essence, and if we grant that we exist and fashion our image at one and the same time, the image is valid for everybody and for our whole age. Thus, our responsibility is much greater than we might have supposed, because it involves all mankind. If I am a workingman and choose to join a Christian trade union rather than be a Communist, and if by being a member, I want to show that the best thing for man is resignation, that the kingdom of man is not of this world, I am not only involving my own case—I want to be resigned for everyone. As a result, my action has involved all humanity. To take a more individual matter, if I want to marry, to have children, even if this marriage depends solely on my own circumstances or passion or wish, I am involving all humanity in monogamy and not merely myself. There- fore, I am responsible for myself and for everyone else. I am creating a certain image of man of my own choosing. In choosing myself, I choose man.

This helps us understand what the actual content is of such rather grandiloquent words as anguish, forlornness, despair. As you will see, it's all quite simple.

First, what is meant by anguish? The existentialists say at once that man is anguish. What that means is this: the man who involves himself and who realizes that he is not only the person he chooses to be, but also a lawmaker who is, at the same time, choosing all mankind as well as himself, cannot help escape the feeling of his total and deep responsibil- ity. Of course, there are many people who are not anxious; but we claim that they are hiding their anxiety, that they are fleeing from it. Certainly, many people believe that when they do something, they themselves are the only ones involved, and when someone says to them, "What if everyone acted that way?" they shrug their shoulders and answer, "Everyone doesn't act that way." But really, one should always ask himself, "What would happen if everybody looked at things that way?" There is no escaping this disturbing thought except by a kind of double-dealing. A man who lies and makes excuses for himself by saying "not everybody does that," is someone with an uneasy conscience, because the act of lying implies that a universal value is conferred upon the lie.

Anguish is evident even when it conceals itself. This is the anguish that Kierkegaard called the anguish of Abraham. You know the story: an angel has ordered Abraham to sacrifice his son; if it really were an angel who has come and said, "You are Abraham, you shall sacrifice your son," everything would be all right. But everyone might first wonder, "Is it really an angel, and am I really Abraham? What proof do I have?"

There was a madwoman who had hallucinations; someone used to speak to her on the telephone and give her orders. Her doctor asked her, "Who is it who talks to you?" She answered, "He says it's God." What proof did she really have that it was God? If an angel comes to me, what proof is there that it's an angel? And if I hear voices, what proof is there that they come from heaven and not from hell, or from the subconscious, or a pathological condition? What proves that they are addressed to me? What proof is there that I have been appointed to impose my choice and my conception of man on humanity? I'll never find any proof or sign to convince me of that. If a voice addresses me, it is always for me to decide that this is the angel's voice; if I consider that such an act is a good one, it is I who will choose to say that it is good rather than bad.

Now, I'm not being singled out as an Abraham, and yet at every moment I'm obliged to perform exemplary acts. For every man, everything happens as if all mankind had its eyes fixed on him and were guiding itself by what he does. And every man ought to say to himself, "Am I really the kind of man who has the right to act in such a way that humanity might guide itself by my actions?" And if he does not say that to himself, he is masking his anguish.

There is no question here of the kind of anguish which would lead to quietism, to inaction. It is a matter of a simple sort of anguish that anybody who has had responsibilities is familiar with. For example, when a military officer takes the responsibility for an attack and sends a certain number of men to death, he chooses to do so, and in the main he alone makes the choice. Doubtless, orders come from above, but they are too broad; he interprets them, and on this interpretation depend the lives of ten or fourteen or twenty men. In making a decision he cannot help having a certain anguish. All leaders know this anguish. That doesn't keep them from acting; on the contrary, it is the very condition of their action. For it implies that they envisage a number of possibilities, and when they choose one, they realize that it has value only because it is chosen. We shall see that this kind of anguish, which is the kind that existentialism describes, is explained, in addition, by a direct responsibility to the other men whom it involves. It is not a curtain separating us from action, but is part of action itself.

When we speak of forlornness, a term Heidegger was fond of, we mean only that God does not exist and that we have to face all the consequences of this. This existentialist is strongly opposed to a certain kind of secular ethics which would like to abolish God with the least possible expense. About 1880, some French teachers tried to set up a secular ethics which went something like this: God is a useless and costly hypothesis; we are discarding it; but, meanwhile, in order for there to be an ethics, a society, a civilization, it is essential that certain values be taken seriously and that they be considered as having an *a priori* existence. It must be obligatory, *a priori*, to be honest, not to lie, not to beat your wife, to have children, etc., etc. So we're going to try a little device which will make it possible to show that values exist all the same, inscribed in a heaven of ideas, though otherwise God does not exist. In other words—and this, I believe, is the tendency of everything called reformism in France—nothing will be changed if God does not exist. We shall find ourselves with the same norms of honesty, progress, and humanism, and we shall have made of God an outdated hypothesis which will peacefully die off by itself.

The existentialist, on the contrary, thinks it very distressing that God does not exist, because all possibility of finding values in a heaven of ideas disappears along with Him; there can no longer be an *a priori* Good, since there is no infinite and perfect consciousness to think it. Nowhere is it written that the Good exists, that we must be honest, that we must not lie; because the fact is we are on a plane where there are only men. Dostoievsky said, "If God didn't exist, everything would be possible." That is the very starting point of existentialism. Indeed, everything is permissible if God does not exist, and as a result man is forlorn, because neither within him nor without does he find anything to cling to. He can't start making excuses for himself.

If existence really does precede essence, there is no explaining things away by reference to a fixed and given human nature. In other words, there is no determinism, man is free, man is freedom. On the other hand, if God does not exist, we find no values or commands to turn to which legitimize our conduct. So, in the bright realm of values, we have no excuse behind us, nor justification before us. We are alone, with no excuses.

That is the idea I shall try to convey when I say that man is condemned to be free. Condemned, because he did not create himself, yet, in other respects is free; because, once thrown into the world, he is responsible for everything he does. The existentialist does not believe in the power of passion. He will never agree that a sweeping passion is a ravaging torrent which fatally leads a man to certain acts and is therefore an excuse. He thinks that man is responsible for his passion.

The existentialist does not think that man is going to help himself by finding in the world some omen by which to orient himself. Because he thinks that man will interpret the omen to suit himself. Therefore, he thinks that man, with no support and no aid, is condemned every moment to invent man. Ponge, in a very fine article, has said, "Man is the future of man." That's exactly it. But if it is taken to mean that this future is recorded in heaven, that God sees it, then it is false, because it would really no longer be a future. If it is taken to mean that, whatever a man may be, there is a future to be forged, a virgin future before him, then this remark is sound. But then we are forlorn.

To give you an example which will enable you to understand forlornness better, I shall cite the case of one of my students who came to see me under the following circumstances: his father was on bad terms with his mother, and, moreover, was inclined to be a collaborationist,[1] his older brother had been killed in the German offensive of 1940, and the young man, with somewhat immature but generous feelings, wanted to avenge him. His mother lived alone with him, very much upset by the half-treason of her husband and the death of her older son; the boy was her only consolation.

The boy was faced with the choice of leaving for England and joining the Free French forces—that is, leaving his mother behind—or remaining with his mother and helping her to carry on. He was fully aware that the woman lived only for him and that his going off—and perhaps his death—would plunge her into despair. He was also aware that every act that he did for his mother's sake was a sure thing, in the sense that it was helping her to carry on, whereas every effort he made toward going off and fighting was an uncertain move which might run aground and prove completely useless; for example, on his way to England he might, while passing through Spain, be detained indefinitely in a Spanish camp; he might reach England or Algiers and be stuck in an office at a desk job. As a result, he was faced with two very different kinds of action: one, concrete, immediate, but concerning only one individual; the other concerned an incomparably vaster group, a national collectivity, but for that very reason was dubious, and might be interrupted en route. And, at the same time, he was wavering between two kinds of ethics. On the one hand, an ethics of sympathy, of personal devotion; on the other, a broader ethics, but one whose efficacy was more dubious. He had to choose between the two.

Who could help him choose? Christian doctrine? No. Christian doctrine says, "Be charitable, love your neighbor, take the more rugged path, etc., etc." But which is the more rugged path? Whom should he love as a brother? The fighting man or his mother? Which does the greater good, the vague act of fighting in a group, or the concrete one of helping a

1. With the occupying German army, or its puppet government in Vichy.

particular human being to go on living? Who can decide a *priori*? Nobody. No book of ethics can tell him. The Kantian ethics says, "Never treat any person as a means, but as an end." Very well, if I stay with my mother, I'll treat her as an end and not as a means; but by virtue of this very fact, I'm running the risk of treating the people around me who are fighting, as means; and, conversely, if I go to join those who are fighting, I'll be treating them as an end, and, by doing that, I run the risk of treating my mother as a means.

If values are vague, and if they are always too broad for the concrete and specific case that we are considering, the only thing left for us is to trust our instincts. That's what this young man tried to do; and when I saw him, he said, "In the end, feeling is what counts. I ought to choose whichever pushes me in one direction. If I feel that I love my mother enough to sacrifice everything else for her—my desire for vengeance, for action, for adventure—then I'll stay with her. If, on the contrary, I feel that my love for my mother isn't enough, I'll leave."

But how is the value of a feeling determined? What gives his feeling for his mother value? Precisely the fact that he remained with her. I may say that I like so-and-so well enough to sacrifice a certain amount of money for him, but I may say so only if I've done it. I may say "I love my mother well enough to remain with her" if I have remained with her. The only way to determine the value of this affection is, precisely, to perform an act which confirms and defines it. But, since I require this affection to justify my act, I find myself caught in a vicious circle.

On the other hand, Gide has well said that a mock feeling and a true feeling are almost indistinguishable; to decide that I love my mother and will remain with her, or to remain with her by putting on an act, amount somewhat to the same thing. In other words, the feeling is formed by the acts one performs; so, I cannot refer to it in order to act upon it. Which means that I can neither seek within myself the true condition which will impel me to act, nor apply to a system of ethics for concepts which will permit me to act. You will say, "At least, he did go to a teacher for advice." But if you seek advice from a priest, for example, you have chosen this priest; you already knew, more or less, just about what advice he was going to give you. In other words, choosing your adviser is involving yourself. The proof of this is that if you are a Christian, you will say, "Consult a priest." But some priests are collaborating, some are just marking time, some are resisting. Which to choose? If the young man chooses a priest who is resisting or collaborating, he has already decided on the kind of advice he's going to get. Therefore, in coming to see me he knew the answer I was going to give him, and I had only one answer to give: "You're free, choose, that is, invent." No general ethics can show you what is to be done; there are no omens in the world. The Catholics will reply, "But there are." Granted—but, in any case, I myself choose the meaning they have.

When I was a prisoner, I knew a rather remarkable young man who was a Jesuit. He had entered the Jesuit order in the following way: he had had a number of very bad breaks; in childhood, his father died, leaving him in poverty, and he was a scholarship student at a religious institution where he was constantly made to feel that he was being kept out of charity; then, he failed to get any of the honors and distinctions that children like; later on, at about eighteen, he bungled a love affair; finally, at twenty-two, he failed in military training, a childish enough matter, but it was the last straw.

This young fellow might well have felt that he had botched everything. It was a sign of something, but of what? He might have taken refuge in bitterness or despair. But he very wisely looked upon all this as a sign that he was not made for secular triumphs, and that only the triumphs of religion, holiness, and faith were open to him. He saw the hand of God in all this, and so he entered the order. Who can help seeing that he alone decided what the sign meant?

Some other interpretation might have been drawn from this series of setbacks; for example, that he might have done better to turn carpenter or revolutionist. Therefore, he is fully responsible for the interpretation. Forlornness implies that we ourselves choose our being. Forlornness and anguish go together.

As for despair, the term has a very simple meaning. It means that we shall confine ourselves to reckoning only with what depends upon our will, or on the ensemble of probabilities which make our action possible. When we want something, we always have to reckon with probabilities. I may be counting on the arrival of a friend. The friend is coming by rail or streetcar; this supposes that the train will arrive on schedule, or that the streetcar will not jump the track. I am left in the realm of possibility; but possibilities are to be reckoned with only to the point where my action comports with the ensemble of these possibilities, and no further. The moment the possibilities I am considering are not rigorously involved by my action, I ought to disengage myself from them, because no God, no scheme, can adapt the world and its possibilities to my will. When Descartes said, "Conquer yourself rather than the world," he meant essentially the same thing.

The Marxists to whom I have spoken reply, "You can rely on the support of others in your action, which obviously has certain limits because you're not going to live forever. That means: rely on both what others are doing elsewhere to help you, in China, in Russia, and what they will do later on, after your death, to carry on the action and lead it to its fulfillment, which will be the revolution. You even have to rely upon that, otherwise you're immoral." I reply at once that I will always rely on fellow-fighters insofar as these comrades are involved with me in a common struggle, in the unity of a party or a group in which I can more or less make my weight felt; that is, one whose ranks I am in as a fighter and whose movements I am aware of at every moment. In such a situation, relying on the unity and will of the party is exactly like counting on the fact that the train will arrive on time or that the car won't jump the track. But, given that man is free and that there is no human nature for me to depend on, I cannot count on men whom I do not know by relying on human goodness or man's concern for the good of society. I don't know what will become of the Russian revolution; I may make an example of it to the extent that at the present time it is apparent that the proletariat plays a part in Russia that it plays in no other nation. But I can't swear that this will inevitably lead to a triumph of the proletariat. I've got to limit myself to what I see.

Given that men are free and that tomorrow they will freely decide what man will be, I cannot be sure that, after my death, fellow-fighters will carry on my work to bring it to its maximum perfection. Tomorrow, after my death, some men may decide to set up Fascism, and the others may be cowardly and muddled enough to let them do it. Fascism will then be the human reality, so much the worse for us.

Actually, things will be as man will have decided they are to be. Does that mean that I should abandon myself to quietism? No. First, I should involve myself; then, act on the old saw, "Nothing ventured, nothing gained." Nor does it mean that I shouldn't belong to a party, but rather that I shall have no illusions and shall do what I can. For example, suppose I ask myself, "Will socialization, as such, ever come about?" I know nothing about it. All I know is that I'm going to do everything in my power to bring it about. Beyond that, I can't count on anything. Quietism is the attitude of people who say, "Let others do what I can't do." The doctrine I am presenting is the very opposite of quietism, since it declares, "There is no reality except in action." Moreover, it goes further, since it adds, "Man is nothing else than his plan; he exists only to the extent that he fulfills himself; he is therefore nothing else than the ensemble of his acts, nothing else than his life."

According to this, we can understand why our doctrine horrifies certain people. Because often the only way they can bear their wretchedness is to think, "Circumstances have been against me. What I've been and done doesn't show my true worth. To be sure, I've had no great love, no great friendship, but that's because I haven't met a man or woman who was worthy. The books I've written haven't been very good because I haven't had the proper leisure. I haven't had children to devote myself to because I didn't find a man with whom I could have spent my life. So there remains within me, unused and quite viable, a host of propensities, inclinations, possibilities, that one wouldn't guess from the mere series of things I've done."

Now, for the existentialist there is really no love other than one which manifests itself in a person's being in love. There is no genius other than one which is expressed in works of art; the genius of Proust is the sum of Proust's works; the genius of Racine is his series of tragedies. Outside of that, there is nothing. Why say that Racine could have written another tragedy, when he didn't write it? A man is involved in life, leaves his impress on it, and outside of that there is nothing. To be sure, this may seem a harsh thought to someone whose life hasn't been a success. But, on the other hand, it prompts people to understand that reality alone is what counts, that dreams, expectations, and hopes warrant no more than to define a man as a disappointed dream, as miscarried hopes, as vain expectations. In other words, to define him negatively and not positively. However, when we say, "You are nothing else than your life," that does not imply that the artist will be judged solely on the basis of his works of art; a thousand other things will contribute toward summing him up. What we mean is that a man is nothing else than a series of undertakings, that he is the sum, the organization, the ensemble of the relationships which make up these undertakings.

When all is said and done, what we are accused of, at bottom, is not our pessimism, but an optimistic toughness. If people throw up to us our works of fiction in which we write about people who are soft, weak, cowardly, and sometimes even downright bad, it's not because these people are soft, weak, cowardly, or bad; because if we were to say, as Zola did, that they are that way because of heredity, the workings of environment, society, because of biological or psychological determinism, people would be reassured. They would say, "Well, that's what we're like, no one can do anything about it." But when the existentialist writes about a coward, he says that this coward is responsible for his cowardice. He's not like that because he has a cowardly heart or lung or brain; he's not like that on account of his physiological make-up; but he's like that because he has made himself a coward by his acts. There's no such thing as a cowardly constitution; there are nervous constitutions; there is poor blood, as the common people say, or strong constitutions. But the man whose blood is poor is not a coward on that account, for what makes cowardice is the act of renouncing or yielding. A constitution is not an act; the coward is defined on the basis of the acts he performs. People feel, in a vague sort of way, that this coward we're talking about is guilty of being a coward, and the thought frightens them. What people would like is that a coward or a hero be born that way. . . .

From these few reflections it is evident that nothing is more unjust than the objections that have been raised against us. Existentialism is nothing else than an attempt to draw all the consequences of a coherent atheistic position. It isn't trying to plunge man into despair at all. But if one calls every attitude of unbelief despair, like the Christians, then the word is not being used in its original sense. Existentialism isn't so atheistic that it wears itself out showing that God doesn't exist. Rather, it declares that even if God did exist, that would change nothing. There you've got our point of view. Not that we believe that God exists, but we think that the problem of His existence is not the issue. In this sense existentialism is optimistic, a doctrine of action, and it is plain dishonesty for Christians to make no distinction between their own despair and ours and then to call us despairing.

1947

THE READER

1. *What is the significance of the words "if existence really does precede essence"? What does this mean? What is the force of "if"? Why does Sartre repeat the words later in the essay?*
2. *Why does Sartre use three separate terms—"anguish," "forlornness," "despair"? What, if any, are the differences among them?*
3. *Sartre makes a distinction between treating "any person as a means . . . [and] as an end" (p. 722). What are the implications of this distinction?*

THE WRITER

1. *What are some of the methods or devices Sartre uses to define existentialism? Why does he use more than one method or device? Compare the techniques that Sartre uses with those that Highet uses in defining Zen (p. 705).*
2. *Sartre says that "when we say that a man is responsible for himself, we do not only mean that he is responsible for his own individuality, but that he is responsible for all men." Write a brief essay explaining how, in the existentialist view, this is possible.*

Authors

Maya Angelou (1928–   )
American author, playwright, actress, poet, and singer. Born in St. Louis, Angelou attended public schools in Arkansas and California before studying music and dance. In a richly varied career, she has been a cook, streetcar conductor, singer, actress, dancer, and teacher. Author of several volumes of poetry and ten plays (stage, screen, and television), Angelou may be best known for her autobiography, a work-in-progress of which five volumes have been published so far. "Graduation" originally appeared in *I Know Why the Caged Bird Sings* (1970), the first volume of that autobiography.

Hannah Arendt (1906–1975)
German-American political scientist and philosopher. Born in Hanover, Germany, and educated at the University of Heidelberg, Arendt began her academic career in Germany but was forced to flee when Hitler came to power. Arriving in the United States in 1940, she became chief editor for a major publisher and a frequent lecturer on college campuses. Arendt taught at a number of American colleges and universities, finishing her career at the New School for Social Research in New York City. Of the dozen or so major books she wrote, three received greatest attention: *Eichmann in Jerusalem: A Report on the Banality of Evil* (1963); *On Revolution* (1963); and *The Origins of Totalitarianism* (1968). "Denmark and the Jews" comes from *Eichmann in Jerusalem*; in slightly different form, it first appeared in *The New Yorker*.

Michael Arlen (1930–   )
American journalist and writer. After receiving his undergraduate degree from Harvard in 1952, Arlen became a reporter for *Life* magazine. Since 1957, he has been a staff writer and television critic for *The New Yorker*. Many of his critical essays have been collected and published in book form: *Living-Room War* (1969); *The View from Highway 1* (1976); *Thirty Seconds* (1980); and *The Camera Age: Essays on Television* (1981). "Griefspeak" first appeared in *Living-Room War*.

Isaac Asimov (1920–   )
American biochemist and science writer. Born in Russia, Asimov was educated in the United States and received a Ph.D. in biochemistry from Columbia. He became a member of the faculty at the School of Medicine, Boston University, in 1949, and he is currently professor of biochemistry there. An extraordinarily prolific author, Asimov has published over 250 books on topics as diverse as mathematics, astronomy, physics, chemistry, biology, mythology, Shakespeare, the Bible, and geography; he also writes science fiction. Among his works: *The Stars, Like the Dust* (1951); *Science, Numbers and I* (1968); *ABC's of the Earth* (1971); *The Road to Infinity* (1979); and *The Exploding Suns: The Secrets of Supernovas* (1985). "The Eureka Phenomenon" comes from *The Left Hand of the Electron* (1972).

Margaret Atwood (1939–   )
Canadian poet, novelist, and critic. After study at Victoria College, University of Toronto, and Radcliffe, Atwood became a film-script writer and worked for a marketing-research firm. Though her first book of poems, *Double Persephone*, was published in 1961, it was not until the second, *The Circle Game* (1966), that she began to be recognized. In all, she has published ten volumes of poetry. In the late 1960s, Atwood began writing novels; among them, *Surfacing* (1972; 1973), *Bodily Harm* (1981), and *The Handmaid's Tale* (1985)

stand out. She has also written short stories, criticism, and works for children. "Writing the Male Character" comes from *Second Words* (1982), a collection of Atwood's critical essays.

Francis Bacon (1561-1626)

English politician, statesman, and philosopher. Trained as a lawyer, Bacon served as a member of Parliament during the reign of Queen Elizabeth I. After her death, he found favor with King James I and advanced in government service. His career was cut short in 1621 when he was convicted of accepting bribes. Retired, he devoted the rest of his life to study and writing texts, among them *The Advancement of Learning* (1605), *Novum Organum* (1620), and *Essays* (various editions, 1597-1625), from which "Of Revenge" comes.

Tom Bethell (1940-   )

American journalist and writer. Born in London, Bethell attended the Royal Naval College and Trinity College, Oxford. He came to the United States in 1962 and taught mathematics at a private preparatory school in Virginia until 1965. He then became managing editor of *New Orleans* magazine and did free-lance writing and research. Bethell served as editor of the *New Orleans Courier* (1972-1974) and of the *Washington Monthly* (1975-1976) before joining the staff of *Harper's*, where he is now a contributing editor. "Agnostic Evolutionists" originally appeared in *Harper's* (February 1985).

Bruno Bettelheim (1903-1990)

American child psychologist, educator, and writer. Born and educated in Vienna, Bettelheim came to the United States in 1939 and joined the faculty of the University of Chicago in 1944, beginning a long and distinguished teaching career there (1944-1973). He has written several dozen books, including *Love Is Not Enough: The Treatment of Emotionally Disturbed Children* (1950); *The Informed Heart: Autonomy in a Mass Age* (1960); *The Children of the Dream* (1969); *The Uses of Enchantment: The Meaning and Importance of Fairy Tales* (1976); and *A Good Enough Parent* (1987). "A Victim" originally appeared in *The Informed Heart*.

Wayne C. Booth (1921-   )

American writer, literary critic, and teacher. After receiving a Ph.D. from the University of Chicago in 1950, Booth began a teaching career that has taken him to Haverford College, Earlham College, and back to the University of Chicago, where he is now professor of English. Among Booth's books are *The Rhetoric of Fiction* (1961; revised edition, 1983); *A Rhetoric of Irony* (1974); *Modern Dogma and the Rhetoric of Assent* (1974); and *Critical Understanding: The Powers and Limits of Pluralism* (1979). "Is There Any Knowledge That a Man Must Have?" originally appeared in *The Knowledge Most Worth Having* (1967); "Boring from Within: The Art of the Freshman Essay" was an address given to the Illinois Council of College Teachers (1963).

Jacob Bronowski (1908-1974)

English mathematician, scientist, and writer. Born in Poland, educated in England, where he received a Ph.D. in mathematics from Cambridge in 1933, Bronowski served as a university lecturer before entering government service during World War II. From 1950 until 1963, he was head of research for Britain's National Coal Board; from 1964 until his death, he was a resident fellow at the Salk Institute, La Jolla, California. The author of many books, among them *Science and Human Values* (1956; 1965), *Nature and Knowledge* (1969), *Magic, Science, and Civilization* (published posthumously, 1978), Bronowski achieved fame with the thirteen-part television series "The Ascent of Man" (1973-1974). "The Nature of Scientific Reasoning" comes from *Science and Human Values*, "The Reach of Imagination" from *Proceedings of the American Academy of Arts and Letters and National Institute of Arts and Letters, Second Series*, No. 17 (1976).

Anthony Burgess (1917-   )

[John] Anthony Burgess [Wilson], English novelist, playwright, editor, and writer. Born in Manchester, England, and a graduate of Manchester University, Burgess was a lecturer and teacher of English until 1954. He then became an education officer in the Colonial Service, stationed in Malaya. His writing career began there. In 1959, when he was told that he had a year to live, Burgess returned to England and wrote five novels in one year. Since then he has written several dozen more, including *A Clockwork Orange* (1962), *Enderby Outside* (1968), and *Earthly Powers* (1980). In addition, Burgess has written critical studies, giving special attention to James Joyce and D. H. Lawrence. "Is America

Falling Apart?" originally appeared in *The New York Times* in 1971.

Nigel Calder (1931–   )
English research physicist and writer. After earning two degrees at Cambridge, Calder was a research physicist for two years before he joined the staff of the *New Scientist*. In 1966, he left his position as editor to become a free-lance writer. He has published over two dozen books and has adapted a number of them for television. His in-depth knowledge of complex subject matter coupled with his ability to communicate with a broad audience have made his books popular, including *Restless Earth* (1972), *Einstein's Universe* (1979), *Time-Scale* (1983), and *The Green Machines* (1986). "Heads and Tails" is Chapter 4 from *The Comet Is Coming!* (1980).

Edward Hallett Carr (1892–1982)
English historian, journalist, and statesman. After studying classics at Trinity College, Cambridge, Carr spent twenty years in the diplomatic service. In 1936, he became professor of international relations at University College in Wales and began to write about diplomatic history. In 1941, he became assistant editor of *The Times* (London). In 1946, he left teaching and journalism to begin work on his major opus: a fourteen-volume study, *A History of Russia*, completed in 1978. "The Historian and His Facts" comes from Carr's *What Is History?* (1961).

Samuel L. Clemens (1835–1910)
American novelist, journalist, humorist, and writer. First apprenticed as a printer, Clemens was by turns a river-boat pilot, gold prospector, and journalist. Under his nom de plume of Mark Twain, he became famous when his short story "The Celebrated Jumping Frog of Calaveras County" was published in 1867. Clemens wrote a good deal and lectured widely after that. At least two of his novels, *The Adventures of Tom Sawyer* (1876) and *Adventures of Huckleberry Finn* (1885), rank as American classics. "Advice to Youth" is the text of a lecture delivered by Clemens.

Ralph W. Conant (1926–   )
American political scientist and writer. Educated at the University of Vermont and the University of Chicago, Conant has pursued interests in public planning, social violence, and politics. He has taught at a number of American schools, including the University of Denver, MIT, Harvard,

and Rice. Conant is now president of Public Research, Inc. He has written and edited many books, among them *Problems in Research on Community Violence* (1969) and *The Conant Report: A Study of the Education of Librarians* (1980). While Conant was associate director of the Lemberg Center for the Study of Violence at Brandeis University, he wrote "The Justification of Civil Protest, Nonviolent and Violent"; it originally appeared as "Rioting, Insurrection and Civil Disobedience" in *The American Scholar* 37, no. 3 (Summer 1968).

Aaron Copland (1900–   )
American composer and writer. Copland studied music theory and practice in Paris (1921–1924), then returned to New York. After some experimentation with adapting jazz to classical composition, Copland developed a distinctly American style, incorporating American folk songs and legends into three ballet scores: *Billy the Kid* (1938), *Rodeo* (1942), and *Appalachian Spring* (1944); poetry into *Twelve Poems of Emily Dickinson*, songs for voice and piano (1950); and historical material into *Lincoln Portrait* (1942), for narrator and orchestra. Copland has also written about music. "How We Listen" comes from a collection of his essays, *What to Listen for in Music* (1939).

Robertson Davies (1913–   )
Canadian novelist, playwright, and critic. Educated in Canada and at Balliol College, Oxford, Davies joined the Old Vic Company, one of England's most prestigious acting troupes, for two seasons. From 1940 to 1962, he worked as a journalist and then became involved in writing and directing for the theater. On his return to Canada, he joined the faculty of the University of Toronto; from 1962 until 1981, he was master of Massey College there. Davies's fiction is generally deemed more important than his journalism and drama. He has written two trilogies—*The Salterton Trilogy* (1951–1958) and *The Deptford Trilogy* (1970–1975)—and four major novels, the most recent of which is *What's Bred in the Bone* (1985). "A Few Kind Words for Superstition" comes from *One Half of Robertson Davies* (1978), a collection of essays. It first appeared in *Newsweek*.

Joan Didion (1934–   )
American novelist, essayist, and screenwriter. A native Californian, Didion stud-

ied at the University of California, Berkeley. After winning Vogue magazine's Prix de Paris contest for excellence in writing, she went to work for the magazine. Didion rose from promotional copywriter to associate feature editor before leaving Vogue in 1963, the year her first novel, Run River, was published. Since then, she has written three more novels (Play It As It Lays, 1971; A Book of Common Prayer, 1977: Democracy, 1984). A frequent contributor to magazines like Vogue and Harper's Bazaar, Didion has published two collections of essays (Slouching towards Bethlehem, 1969; The White Album, 1979). Salvador, a work of fiction based on her visit to El Salvador in 1983, marked Didion's growing concern with politics. She is currently working on a novel, Angel Visits, and a collection of childhood reminiscences, Fairytales. "On Going Home" and "On Keeping a Notebook" originally appeared in Slouching towards Bethlehem; "Salvador" comes from Salvador; "Georgia O'Keeffe" was written for The Saturday Evening Post in 1976, then reprinted in The White Album.

Kildare Dobbs (1923–   )

Canadian writer. Born in India and educated at Cambridge, Dobbs spent time in the British foreign service before becoming a journalist and an editor; he is now a free-lance writer. He has written autobiographical sketches (Running to Paradise, 1962), short stories (Pride and Fall, 1981), and essays, some of which were collected in Reading the Time (1968). "The Shatterer of Worlds" originally appeared in that collection.

John Donne (1572–1631)

English poet, essayist, and cleric. Born into an old Roman Catholic family, Donne attended Oxford and Cambridge but could not receive a degree because of his religion. He studied, though never practiced, law and, after quietly abandoning Catholicism some time during the 1590s, entered government service. In 1615, he was received into the Anglican Church. One of the greatest religious orators of his age, Donne becamse dean of St. Paul's Cathedral in 1621. Donne's literary reputation rests on his poetry as well as on his sermons and devotions (e.g., "Men Are Sleeping Prisoners").

Barbara Ehrenreich (1941–   )

American writer. Educated at Reed College and Rockefeller University, where she earned a Ph.D. in biology, Ehrenreich taught at New York University and the State University of New York before becoming a full-time writer and lecturer on women's issues and social policy. A regular contributor to Ms., Vogue, and The New York Times, she has written several important feminist studies: For Her Own Good: 150 Years of the Experts' Advice to Women (co-author, 1978); The Hearts of Men: American Dreams and the Flight from Commitment (1984); and Re-making Love: The Feminization of Sex (co-author, 1986). Her most recent work appears in Mean Season: The Attack on the Welfare State, by Fred Block and others (1987). "College Today: Tune In, Drop Out, and Take the Cash" originally appeared as a "Hers" column in The New York Times (March 7, 1985).

Loren Eiseley (1907–1977)

American anthropologist, historian of science, and poet. Educated at the University of Nebraska and the University of Pennsylvania, Eiseley taught at the University of Kansas, Oberlin, and finally back at the University of Pennsylvania, where he remained for thirty years. A humanist deeply concerned with major ethical issues, he established a national reputation with his writings: The Immense Journey (1957); Darwin's Century (1958); The Firmament of Time (revised edition, 1960); The Night Country (1971), in which "The Brown Wasps" originally appeared; and The Unexpected Universe (1972). A collection of Eiseley's poems, Another Kind of Autumn, was published posthumously in 1977.

Ralph Waldo Emerson (1803–1882)

American poet, philosopher, and essayist. One of the most influential writers of the American tradition, Emerson entered Harvard at the age of fourteen. After graduation in 1821, he taught school for several years before beginning theological studies in 1825. In 1829, he was ordained a Unitarian minister. In 1832, he resigned his pastorate, retiring to Concord, Massachusetts, to a life of study and reflection. With the publication of his first book, Nature, in 1836, Emerson became an important force in the development of American Transcendentalism. Emerson's occasional lectures at Harvard and the publication of his Essays (1841) enhanced his reputation. "The Language of the Street" is from The Journals and Miscellaneous Notebooks of Ralph Waldo Emerson, edited by George Clark and others (1960–1978).

Daniel Mark Epstein (1948–   )
American poet and playwright. Educated at Kenyon College, Epstein is the author of four books of poetry (*No Vacancies in Hell*, 1973; *The Follies*, 1977; *Young Men's Gold*, 1978; *The Book of Fortune*, 1982), two plays (*Jenny and the Phoenix*, 1977; *The Gayety Burlesque*, 1978), and a collection of essays (*Star of Wonder*, 1986). He is much concerned with myth and ritual, both political and religious, and with the American character. Epstein is a frequent contributor to *The Atlantic*, *The New Yorker*, and *The New Criterion*, where "The Case of Houdini" originally appeared (October 1986).

William Faulkner (1897–1962)
American novelist. A native of Mississippi, Faulkner lived his whole life there. He attended the University of Mississippi in the town of Oxford. With the help of Sherwood Anderson, he published his first novel, *Soldier's Pay*, in 1926. His work, which won him a Nobel Prize in 1949, often depicts life in fictional Yoknapatawpha County, an imaginative reconstruction of the area adjacent to Oxford. Faulkner's major novels include *The Sound and the Fury* (1929), *As I Lay Dying* (1930), *Sanctuary* (1931), *Light in August* (1932), and *Absalom! Absalom!* (1936). His short stories are included in the collections *These Thirteen* (1931), *Go Down, Moses and Other Stories* (1942), and *The Collected Stories of William Faulkner* (1950).

Robert Finch (1943–   )
American writer. Finch combines a keen interest in the world of the naturalist with a concern for the craft of writing. He has published three books: *Common Ground: A Naturalist's Cape Cod* (1981); *The Primal Place* (1983); and *Outlands: Journeys to the Outer Edges of Cape Cod* (1986). Publicity director for the Cape Cod Museum of Natural History, he also serves on the staff of the Bread Loaf Writers' Conference at Middlebury College. "Very Like a Whale" comes from *Common Ground*, a collection of essays on the natural environment.

Frances FitzGerald (1940–   )
American journalist and writer. A freelance journalist since her graduation from Radcliffe in 1962, FitzGerald achieved critical success with her first book, *Fire in the Lake: The Vietnamese and Americans in Vietnam* (1972); it won four major awards, including a Pulitzer Prize and a National Book Award. Since then, she has written two other books: *America Revised: History Schoolbooks in the Twentieth Century* (1979) and *Cities on a Hill: Journeys through American Cultures* (1986). Although FitzGerald regularly contributes to several American periodicals, she is most closely associated with *The New Yorker*, where "Rewriting American History" appeared before being published in *America Revised*.

E. M. Forster (1879–1970)
British novelist, critic, and essayist. Educated at King's College, Cambridge, Forster was closely associated with the Bloomsbury set, a group of literary and artistic figures that included Virginia Woolf. Forster's literary reputation rests on four novels: *Where Angels Fear to Tread* (1905); *A Room with a View* (1908); *Howard's End* (1910); and *A Passage to India* (1924). Some of his essays on life and literature were gathered in *Aspects of the Novel* (1927) and *Two Cheers for Democracy* (1951), where "What I Believe" originally appeared.

Benjamin Franklin (1706–1790)
American statesman, inventor, writer, and diplomat. Apprenticed at the age of twelve to his brother, a Philadelphia printer, Franklin learned all aspects of the trade, from setting type to writing editorials. At the age of twenty-four, he was editor and publisher of the *Pennsylvania Gazette*. In 1733, he began writing *Poor Richard's Almanack*, a collection of aphorisms and advice. He retired from business at the age of forty-two to devote himself to study and research but soon found himself involved in colonial politics. From 1757 until 1763, he was diplomatic representative for the colonies in England. He served as a member of the committee appointed to draft the Declaration of Independence and later as minister to France and delegate to the Paris peace conference that officially concluded the Revolutionary War. "The Convenience of Being 'Reasonable'" comes from Franklin's *Autobiography*, written between 1771 and 1788.

Ian Frazier (1951–   )
American writer and satirist. A graduate of Harvard, where he wrote for the *Harvard Lampoon*, Frazier has been on the staff of *The New Yorker* since 1975. He

contributes humorous sketches as well as factual essays and profiles. He has published two books, both substantially taken from material previously published in *The New Yorker: Dating Your Mom* (1986), a collection of humorous pieces, and *Nobody Better, Better Than Nobody* (1987), a volume of five character portraits. "Just a Country Boy" comes from *Dating Your Mom.*

Robert Frost (1874–1963)

American poet, teacher, and lecturer. This quintessential "New England" poet was born in California and spent his childhood there. He studied briefly at Dartmouth and Harvard, married, and tried farming for a while. In 1912, he moved to England, where his first book of poems, *A Boy's Will*, was published. In 1914, his second collection, *North of Boston*, received favorable reviews, and the poet returned to the United States. For the next fifty years, Frost was a respected and successful poet, writing about the people and landscape of New England in a voice sometimes lyric, sometimes humorous, sometimes desolate. During the last part of his life, Frost held a number of teaching appointments and lectured widely on poetry and the role of the poet. "Education by Poetry: A Meditative Monologue," an address delivered at Amherst College in 1930, comes from *Selected Prose of Robert Frost*, edited by Hyde Cox and Edward Connery Latham (1966).

Northrop Frye (1912–)

Canadian literary critic and teacher. Educated at the University of Toronto and at Merton College, Oxford, he has been a member of the faculty at Victoria College, University of Toronto, since 1939. Although Frye specializes in Renaissance and Romantic literature, he has also written on Milton, the Bible, and Canadian literature. He has published more than forty books, including *Fearful Symmetry: A Study of William Blake* (1947); *Anatomy of Criticism* (1957); *The Educated Imagination* (1964), from which "The Motive for Metaphor" comes; *The Secular Scripture: A Study of the Structure of Romance* (1976); and *The Great Code: The Bible and Literature* (1982).

John Gardner (1933–1982)

American poet, novelist, critic, and teacher. Educated at Washington University and the State University of Iowa, Gardner wrote poetry and nearly all kinds of prose (novels, short stories, children's books, fairy tales, critical essays) in a distinguished career cut short by his death at age forty-nine in a motorcycle accident. Gardner came to popular attention with his novel *Grendel* (1971), a retelling of the *Beowulf* legend from the monster's point of view. Another novel, *October Light*, won the National Book Critics' Award in 1976. His critical powers were at their sharpest in *On Moral Fiction* (1978), an indictment of much modern writing. "What Writers Do" originally appeared in *Antaeus*, no. 40/41 (Winter/Spring 1981).

Barbara Garson (1941–)

American playwright, social critic, and writer. Garson achieved prominence with *MacBird!*, a two-act play produced in 1967, a parody of *Macbeth* based on the administration of President Lyndon B. Johnson. She has written two other plays: *The Co-op* (co-authored with Fred Gardner, 1972) and *The Dinosaur Door* (1976). "Whistle While You Work" comes from *All the Livelong Day: The Meaning and Demeaning of Routine* (1975).

Willard Gaylin (1925–)

American psychiatrist and psychoanalyst. After receiving an M.D. degree from Case Western Reserve University, Gaylin did advanced work in psychoanalytic medicine at Columbia and opened a private practice in psychiatry. In 1970, he co-founded the Hastings Center, Institute of Society, Ethics and the Life Sciences at Hastings-on-Hudson, New York. His writings reflect a broad range of interests: *In the Service of Their Country: War Resisters in Prison* (1970); *Partial Justice: A Study of Bias in Sentencing* (1974); and *Feelings: Our Vital Signs* (1979). Gaylin's study of the use of the insanity defense, *The Killing of Bonnie Garland: A Question of Justice* (1982), received considerable attention. "What You See Is the Real You" originally appeared in *The New York Times* (October 7, 1977).

Herb Goldberg (1937–)

American psychologist and writer. Professor of psychology at California State University, Los Angeles, since 1965, Goldberg is a practicing psychotherapist as well. A frequent contributor to professional journals, he has also written five books, one of which *The Hazards of Being Male* (1976), is the source of "In Harness: The Male Condition."

William Golding (1911–   )

English novelist. Educated at Oxford, Golding was a schoolmaster at Bishop Wordsworth's School, Salisbury, before becoming a novelist at the age of forty-three. Golding's novels are strikingly original, characterized by their darkly poetic tone and dense symbolism. His most famous work is *Lord of the Flies* (1954), a story of schoolboys marooned on an island who revert to savagery. Other novels include *Pincher Martin* (1956), *The Spire* (1964), *The Pyramid* (1967), *Rites of Passage* (1980), and *Close Quarters* (1987). In 1983, Golding received the Nobel Prize for literature. "Thinking as a Hobby" originally appeared in *Holiday Magazine* (August 1961).

Stephen Jay Gould (1941–   )

American paleontologist, writer, and teacher. Gould grew up in New York City, graduated from Antioch College, and received his Ph.D. from Columbia in 1967, joining Harvard the same year. Now professor of geology and zoology at Harvard, Gould teaches paleontology, biology, and history of science. Witty and fluent, Gould demystifies science for lay readers in essays written for a regular column in *Natural History* magazine and collected in *Ever since Darwin* (1977); *The Panda's Thumb* (1980); *Hen's Teeth and Horse's Toes* (1983); and *The Flamingo's Smile* (1985). His books include *Ontogeny and Phylogeny* (1977) and, most recently, *Time's Arrow, Time's Cycle: Myth and Metaphor in the Discovery of Geological Time* (1987). "Our Allotted Lifetimes" originally appeared in *Natural History*, no. 7 (1977); "Darwin's Middle Road" comes from *The Panda's Thumb*; "The Terrifying Normalcy of AIDS" first appeared in *The New York Times Magazine* (April 19, 1987).

Barbara Grizzuti Harrison (1934–   )

American writer. Since 1960, Harrison has been a free-lance writer. Although she has published a novel, *Foreign Bodies* (1984), she has concentrated on works of nonfiction: *Unlearning the Lie: Sexism in School* (1971); *Visions of Glory: A History and a Memory of Jehovah's Witnesses* (1975). A frequent contributor to the *Village Voice*, the *New Republic*, and several other American periodicals, Harrison wrote "Abortion" for *The New York Times* (May 8, 1980).

S. I. Hayakawa (1906–   )

Samuel Ichiye Hayakawa, Japanese-American writer, educator, and politician. Before becoming president of San Francisco State College, Hayakawa established himself as a scholar and pioneer in language and semantics with books like *Language in Action* (1941; revised as *Language in Thought and Action*, 1949), *Our Language and Our World* (1959), and *Symbol, Status and Personality* (1963). His tenure as college president (1969–1973) was marked by student demonstrations and protests against authority. Throughout, Hayakawa asserted a firm belief in authority, traditional values, and the rule of law and order. With the same ideas as a campaign platform, he was elected to the United States Senate, where he served from 1977 until 1982. "Sex Is Not a Spectator Sport" comes from a collection of Hayakawa's essays, *Through the Communication Barrier* (1979).

Ernest Hemingway (1899–1961)

American novelist and short-story writer. Hemingway began his professional writing career as a journalist, reporting for newspapers in Kansas City and Toronto. In the 1920s, he lived in Paris, a part of the American expatriate community that included Gertrude Stein and Ezra Pound. Hemingway's literary reputation rests on his short stories, collected in volumes like *In Our Time* (1925) and *Men without Women* (1927), and his novels, including *The Sun Also Rises* (1926), *A Farewell to Arms* (1929), and *For Whom the Bell Tolls* (1940). *The Old Man and the Sea* (1952) was the last work published during his lifetime. Hemingway received the Nobel Prize for literature in 1954.

Michael Herr (1940–   )

American writer and historian of popular culture. In 1977, Herr published *Dispatches*, a nonfiction account of American involvement in the war in Vietnam; ten years before, he had gone there to cover the story for *Esquire*. Herr earned substantial praise for the book and for the narration he wrote for Francis Ford Coppola's film about the war, *Apocalypse Now*. "'How Bad Do You Want to Get to Danang?'" comes from *Dispatches*. A regular contributor to *Esquire*, *The New American Review*, and *Rolling Stone*, Herr recently collaborated on *The Big Room* (1986), a popular history of celebrities in twentieth-century American art.

Gilbert Highet (1906–1978)

American scholar of classical literature, poet, writer, and teacher. Born in Glasgow, Scotland, Highet was educated at the University of Glasgow and Oxford University. From 1932 until 1936, he taught at St. John's College, Oxford, then accepted an appointment at Columbia University, where he taught Greek and Latin literature for thirty years. Considered a master teacher, Highet communicated his enthusiasm for classical literature not only in the classroom, but also in a number of books. Of the fourteen books he wrote, perhaps the most famous are *The Classical Tradition* (1949), *The Art of Teaching* (1950), and *The Anatomy of Satire* (1962). "The Mystery of Zen" comes from *Talents and Geniuses* (1957), a collection of essays by Highet.

John Holt (1923–1985)

American educator and author. After ten years as a teacher, Holt wrote *How Children Fail* (1964), a highly critical analysis of the American educational process. From 1965 until 1967, he taught English at a high school in Boston. Following teaching appointments at Harvard and the University of California, Berkeley, Holt founded Holt Associates, a consulting firm concerned with education and social issues. Among his books are *Freedom and Beyond* (1972) and *Instead of Education* (1976). "How Teachers Make Children Hate Reading" originally appeared in *Redbook* (November 1967).

Jane Howard (1935–   )

American writer. After receiving her undergraduate degree from the University of Michigan, Howard joined *Life* magazine, serving as associate editor and staff writer. Combining the skills of a reporter with the curiosity of a social scientist, Howard has written four books: *Please Touch: A Guided Tour of the Human Potential Movement* (1970); *A Different Woman* (1973; revised edition, 1982); *Families* (1978); and *Margaret Mead: A Life* (1984). "Pomp and Circumstance in Groundhog Hollow" comes from *A Different Woman*.

Langston Hughes (1902–1967)

American poet, playwright, and writer. An extraordinarily prolific writer, Hughes published seventeen volumes of poetry, two novels, seven collections of short stories, and twenty-six plays. Hughes emerged as a key figure in the Harlem Renaissance of the 1920s and 1930s, an awakening of black artists centered in New York City. Encouraged by his fellow artists, Hughes published his first collection of poems, *The Weary Blues* (1926). Although critical response was mixed, the degree of public acceptance achieved by Hughes with this and subsequent works enabled him to become the first black American writer to support himself from his writing and lecturing. "Salvation" is a chapter from Hughes's autobiography *The Big Sea* (1940).

Richard Hugo (1923–1982)

American poet and teacher. Hugo was educated at the University of Washington, and then worked for Boeing (1951–1963), writing poetry in his spare time. In 1964, he joined the Department of English at the University of Montana, eventually becoming professor of English there. From 1977 until his death, Hugo served as judge of the Yale Younger Poets Series. He published nine volumes of poetry, including *The Lady in Kicking Horse Reservoir* (1973) and *White Center* (1980), the novel *Death and the Good Life* (1981), a collection of essays entitled *The Triggering Town* (1979), and the memoir *The Real West Marginal Way: A Poet's Autobiography* (published posthumously, 1986). "How I Never Met Eudora Welty" is a chapter in Hugo's autobiography.

Thomas Jefferson (1743–1826)

Third president of the United States, lawyer, architect, and writer. An educated man of significant accomplishments in many fields, Jefferson entered politics in his native state of Virginia, serving in the House of Burgesses and eventually becoming governor (1779–1781). He founded the University of Virginia (1809) and designed both the buildings and curriculum. Jefferson served as secretary of state to Washington (1789–1793), vice-president to John Adams (1797–1801), and president (1801–1809). A fluent stylist, Jefferson wrote books on science, religion, architecture, even Anglo-Saxon grammar, but is probably best known for writing the final draft of the Declaration of Independence. Preliminary drafts were done by committee, but it was to Jefferson that the members turned for the last revision.

Carl Gustav Jung (1875–1961)

Swiss psychiatrist and founder of analytic psychology. Jung was educated at the University of Basel and began practice in 1900 at a mental hospital in Zürich. From 1907 to 1913, he and Sigmund Freud collaborated in research on psychiatry and psychoanalysis. In 1914, after the two had severed connections, Jung devoted himself to private practice and writing. A prolific writer, whose Collected Works consist of eighteen volumes, Jung did pioneering work on schizophrenia and related personality disorders, and, in the process of classifying personality types, introduced terms like "extrovert," "complex," and "introvert" into the vocabulary of psychiatry. Jung's interest in human creativity led him to posit the existence of a "collective unconscious," a part of the human mind to which human beings relegate unpleasant experiences and from which creativity springs. Among Jung's major books are The Psychology of Dementia (1906), The Psychology of the Unconscious (1912), and Psychological Types (1921). "The Poet" comes from his Modern Man in Search of a Soul (1933).

Michael J. Katz (1950–   )
American physician and teacher. Katz received his M.D. and Ph.D. degrees from Case Western School. He is a philosopher at Case Western Medical School. "On the Wings of an Angel: An Exploration of the Limits of Biological Enterprise" first appeared in Harvard Magazine (September–October 1985).

Garrison Keillor (1942–   )
American humorist, writer, and broadcaster. While still an undergraduate at the University of Minnesota, Keillor became a staff announcer at a Minneapolis radio station. He continued to work for KUOM-Radio until 1968. In 1971, he went to work for Minnesota Public Radio in St. Paul, producing and announcing shows. In 1974, as host and principal writer, Keillor started a weekly program, "A Prairie Home Companion." This two-hour mix of music, monologue, and conversation attained a cult following in its thirteen-year run; Keillor broadcast his last show on June 13, 1987. He now lives in Denmark. "The Tower Project" comes from Happy to Be Here: Stories and Comic Pieces (1982). A number of these pieces first appeared in The New Yorker and the Atlantic Monthly. Keillor has also written Lake Wobegon Days (1985), a collection of stories set in the mythical town of Lake Wobegon, Minnesota.

X. J. Kennedy (1929–   )
Pseudonym of Joseph C. Kennedy, American poet, critic, and teacher. Since the publication of Nude Descending a Staircase (1961), an award-winning collection of poems, Kennedy has published novels and essays as well as poetry. A distinguished teacher, he has written several well-known textbooks, including Introduction to Poetry, now in its sixth edition, and Introduction to Fiction (1976, 1986). "Who Killed King Kong?" originally appeared in the spring-1960 issue of Dissent, a quarterly review of politics and the arts.

Martin Luther King, Jr. (1929–1968)
American clergyman and civil-rights leader. By the age of twenty-six, King had completed his undergraduate education, finished divinity school, and received a Ph.D. in religion from Boston University. The Montgomery bus boycott (1956) marked King's entry into public politics; blacks in Montgomery, Alabama, boycotted segregated buses, and King took a public stand in their support. Drawing upon the New Testament teachings of Jesus and the principles of passive resistance of Mahatma Gandhi, King advocated nonviolent protest to effect significant social change. In the years following the boycott, he became a major figure in the civil-rights movement, uniting small groups of blacks in their struggle. In 1963, Birmingham, Alabama, the most segregated city in the South, became the focal point for violent confrontations between blacks and whites; 2,400 civil-rights workers, King among them, went to jail. It was then that he wrote his now-famous "Letter from Birmingham Jail." In 1964, at the age of thirty-five, Martin Luther King, Jr. became the youngest person to receive the Nobel Peace Prize. He was assassinated on April 4, 1968, in Memphis, Tennessee.

Arthur Koestler (1905–1983)
British writer. Born in Hungary and educated at the University of Vienna, Koestler worked as an editor of a Cairo newspaper, then as foreign correspondent for several other papers before settling in England in 1941, when his novel, Darkness at Noon, appeared. That novel, an indictment of the Communist party, mapped the territory for Koestler's next ten years of work. In the 1950s, however, he turned to writing about a wide range of topics: psychology, religion, philosophy, evolution, among others. Koestler wrote over forty books, among them The God That Failed (1950), The Ghost in the Machine

(1967), and *The Lion and the Ostrich* (1973). "Gravity and the Holy Ghost" originally appeared in *The Act of Creation* (1964).

Elisabeth Kübler-Ross (1926–)
Swiss-American psychologist. Born and educated in Switzerland, Kübler-Ross has come to prominence in the United States, where she has lived since 1958. Her work is largely a response to what she calls "the horrifying experience of the [postwar European] concentration camps." She has given seminars and written about death and dying not only in order to understand the process better, but also to learn how to care for the terminally ill. "On the Fear of Death" comes from Kübler-Ross's best-selling book *On Death and Dying* (1969). Other books on the subject have followed, including most recently *AIDS: The Ultimate Challenge* (1987).

John Leo (1935–)
American journalist and writer. Leo has been a staff writer for the *Village Voice* and *The New York Times*, and associate editor for *Commonweal*, a biweekly journal of public affairs, literature, and the arts. Until recently a senior writer for *Time*, Leo is now a contributor to that magazine, where "Journalese for the Lay Reader" originally appeared (March 18, 1985).

Doris Lessing (1919–)
British novelist and political activist. Lessing was born in Persia but grew up in Southern Rhodesia, where she was largely responsible for her own education. She married and divorced twice before leaving Africa for London in 1949. There, her career as a professional writer of more than thirty books began with the publication of her first novel, *The Grass Is Singing* (1950). The central theme of Lessing's work has been women's quest for identity in a world fragmented by prejudice, ideology, and violence (the *Children of Violence* Series, 1952–1969; *The Golden Notebook*, 1962). In the *Canopus in Argos: Archives* Series (1979–1983), she has turned to science fiction. Her latest work includes two novels about the stages of women's lives (*The Diary of a Good Neighbor*, 1983; *If the Old Could . . .* , 1984) and three political novels (*The Good Terrorist*, 1985; *African Tale*, 1987; *The Wind Blows Away Our Words*, 1987). "My Father" first appeared in the London *Sunday Telegraph* (September 1, 1963); it was reprinted in the collection of essays, reviews, and interviews entitled *A Small Personal Voice* (1975).

Michael Levin (1943–)
American philosopher. Educated at Michigan State University and Columbia, Levin was a member of the Department of Philosophy at Columbia from 1968 until 1980. He is currently professor of philosophy at City College of the City University of New York. His research interests include ethics, philosophy, and the mind. The author of a number of scholarly articles, Levin has published *Metaphysics and the Mind-Body Problem* (1979). "The Case for Torture" originally appeared in *Newsweek* (June 7, 1982).

Abraham Lincoln (1809–1865)
Lawyer, orator, and sixteenth president of the United States (1861–1865). Born in Kentucky, Lincoln was a self-made and self-taught man. His family moved to Illinois in 1830, where Lincoln prepared himself for a career in law. In 1834, he was elected to the first of four terms in the Illinois state legislature and, in 1847, to the U.S. Congress. Elected president in 1860, Lincoln sought to preserve the Union amid the strife of the Civil War while he worked for the passage of the Thirteenth Amendment, which would outlaw slavery everywhere and forever in the United States. Lincoln was assassinated by actor John Wilkes Booth on April 15, 1865. During his first term, Lincoln delivered the Gettysburg Address (1863). Reelected in 1864, he gave his Second Inaugural Address, an eloquent appeal for reconciliation and peace.

Konrad Z. Lorenz (1903–)
Austrian-German scientist. Although he studied medicine at the University of Vienna, Lorenz's early interests lay in the field of animal behavior. *King Solomon's Ring* (1952), from which "The Taming of the Shrew" comes, deals with the behavior of jackdaws, geese, and other animals. *On Aggression* (1963) and *Civilized Man's Eight Deadly Sins* (1974) detail Lorenz's beliefs about humankind's behavior and civilization's harmful effects on people and the environment. With Niko Tinbergen and Karl von Frisch, Lorenz won the Nobel Prize for Physiology or Medicine in 1973.

Niccolò Machiavelli (1469–1527)
Florentine statesman and political philosopher. An aristocrat who held office while

Florence was a republic, Machiavelli fell from favor when the Medicis returned to power in 1512. Briefly imprisoned, he was restored to an office of some influence, but he never regained his former importance. Machiavelli's most famous work, *The Prince* (1513), from which "The Morals of the Prince" comes, has exerted considerable literary and political influence.

Hugh MacLennan (1907–)

Canadian novelist, essayist, and teacher. Educated at Dalhousie University and Oxford, MacLennan received a Ph.D. in classics from Princeton. He began writing fiction while at Princeton, although it was not until 1941 that his first novel, *Barometer Rising*, was published. With the commercial success of his second novel, *Two Solitudes* (1945), MacLennan left college teaching to become a free-lance journalist and broadcaster. In 1951, he returned to academic life as a member of the Department of English at McGill University in Montreal, where he taught until 1979. "On Living in a Cold Country" comes from *The Other Side of Hugh MacLennan*, a collection of essays edited by Elspeth Cameron.

John McMurtry (1939–)

Canadian athlete, writer, and teacher. Educated at the University of Toronto, McMurtry became a professional football player before earning his Ph.D. in philosophy at the University of London. A member of the Department of Philosophy at the University of Guelph since 1970, he has written two books: *The Dimensions of English: A Concise Compendium* (1970) and *The Structure of Marx's World View* (1978). "Kill 'Em! Crush 'Em! Eat 'Em Raw!" originally appeared in the October 1971 issue of the Canadian news magazine *Maclean's*.

Joyce Maynard (1953–)

American writer. While she was a freshman at Yale, Maynard attracted considerable attention when she wrote "An Eighteen-Year-Old Looks Back at Life" for *The New York Times Magazine* (April 23, 1972). Since then, she has published two books: *Looking Back: A Chronicle of Growing Up Old in the Sixties* (1973), based on that article, and *Baby Love* (1981), a novel. "Four Generations" originally appeared as a "Hers" column in *The New York Times* (April 12, 1979).

Margaret Mead (1901–1978)

American anthropologist, writer, and social critic. After receiving her undergraduate degree from Barnard, Mead did graduate work in anthropology under the direction of Franz Boas at Columbia. Her first book, *Coming of Age in Samoa* (1928), was a groundbreaking study of adolescence. Her suggestion that the relaxed sexual mores of that culture might well be applied to American society generated controversy. Mead became a popular lecturer but found time to write two other important studies: *And Keep Your Powder Dry: An Anthropologist Looks at America* (1942) and *Male and Female* (1949). An outspoken feminist, Mead worked diligently to increase opportunities for women. "Home and Travel" comes from Mead's memoir, *Blackberry Winter* (1972).

Charles R. Morris

American investment banker and writer. A graduate of the University of Pennsylvania and its law school, Morris has worked in the public and private sectors, serving as assistant budget director for New York City, secretary of social and health services for the state of Washington, and a vice-president of Chase Manhattan Bank. He has written two books: *The Cost of Good Intentions: New York City and the Liberal Experiment—1960-1975* (1980) and *A Time of Passion: America 1960-1980* (1984), from which "Civil Disobedience" comes.

Desmond Morris (1928–)

British zoologist and writer. After receiving a Ph.D. in zoology from Oxford, Morris remained there to do research. In 1959, he became curator of mammals at the London Zoo. During the next eight years, he wrote five books on animals. In 1968, he returned to research at Oxford and began writing books on human and animal behavior: *The Naked Ape* (1967); *The Human Zoo* (1969); *Intimate Behavior* (1971); *Manwatching* (1977); and *Bodywatching* (1985). "Territorial Behavior" comes from *Manwatching*.

Thomas Murray (1946–)

American social psychologist. Educated at Temple University, Murray did graduate work in psychology at Princeton. Although he was trained as an empirical scientist, he is most interested in ethical issues. Until recently, Murray was professor of ethics and public policy at the Institute for Medical Humanities, the

University of Texas Medical Branch, Gal-
veston, Texas. While he was there, he
founded and edited the *Medical Humanities Review*. He is now director of and
professor at Case Western Reserve Medical School. "The Growing Danger" originally appeared in *Discover* (February
1987).

Ngũgĩ wa Thiong'o (1936–   )
Formerly known as James T. Ngugi, African novelist and essayist. Educated in Af-
rica and at Leeds University in England,
Ngũgĩ wrote his first novel, *The River be-
tween Us*, in 1963–1964, but it was not
published until 1965, after his *Weep Not
Child* (1964). He continues to write novels
(*Devil on the Cross*, 1982), but his memoir,
Detained: A Prisoner Writer's Diary
(1981), an account of his arrest and deten-
tion for teaching his native Gĩkũyũ lan-
guage, has attracted most attention.
"Decolonizing the Mind" is part of the
Introduction to Ngũgĩ's *Decolonising the
Mind: The Politics of Language in African
Literature* (1986), the last book he wrote in
English.

George Orwell (1903–1950)
Pen name of Eric Blair, English journalist,
essayist, novelist, and critic. Born in India
and educated in England, Orwell became
an officer in the Indian Imperial Police in
Burma (1922–1927), a part of his life that
he later recounted in a novel, *Burmese
Days* (1934). In 1927, he went to Europe to
develop his writing talents. His first book,
Down and Out in Paris and London (1933),
depicts his years of poverty and struggle
while working as a dishwasher and day
laborer. Orwell's experiences fighting in
the Spanish Civil War are the subject of
his memoir, *Homage to Catalonia* (1938).
Of his seven novels, *Animal Farm* (1945)
and *Nineteen Eighty-Four* (1949), satires
directed at totalitarian government, have
become twentieth-century classics. Orwell published five collections of essays,
including *Shooting an Elephant* (1950),
from which both "Politics and the English
Language" and "Shooting an Elephant"
come.

S. J. Perelman (1904–1979)
American humorist, playwright, screenwriter, and journalist. After graduating
from Brown University in 1925, Perelman
took a job as a cartoonist. Soon afterward,
he wrote the screenplays for *Monkey Business* and *Horse Feathers*, two of the Marx
Brothers' most successful films. Although

he wrote a number of stage plays as well,
Perelman was most closely associated with
The New Yorker, writing stories, articles,
and even cartoon captions from 1931 until
1979. A prolific writer, Perelman is the
author of over 450 essays, 10 screenplays, 8
stage plays, and more than a dozen books.
"The Machismo Mystique" comes from
Vinegar Puss (1975), a collection of Perelman's short stories and essays.

William G. Perry, Jr. (1913–   )
American educator. Born in Paris and educated at Harvard, Perry taught at Williams College from 1941 to 1945 before
moving to Harvard, where he has been
director of the Bureau of Study Counsel
since 1948 and professor of education
since 1964. With C. P. Whitelock, he
wrote the *Harvard Reading Course* (1948).
His *Forms of Intellectual and Ethical Development* was published in 1968. "Examsmanship and the Liberal Arts: A Study
in Educational Epistemology" originally
appeared in *Examining in Harvard College:
A Collection of Essays*, by members of the
Harvard faculty (1964).

Plato (c. 428–c. 348 B.C.)
Greek philosopher and teacher. When
Socrates died in 339 B.C., Plato went into
exile. He returned in the 380s and founded
a school, the Academy. He adopted the
Socratic method of teaching, a technique
of asking, rather than answering, questions. Although many of Plato's writings
take the form of dialogues, he does occasionally, as in the case of "The Allegory of
the Cave," use the parable.

Neil Postman
American writer and critic, with major interests in linguistics and teaching. Postman's first book, *Television and the
Teaching of English* (1961), began a career
that has produced nearly two dozen books
and many articles, particularly for *Atlantic*
and *The Nation*. With the appearance of
his *Teaching as a Subversive Activity*
(1969), written with Charles Weingart-
ner, Postman emerged as a spokesman for
radical educational reform. In 1979, he
wrote *Teaching as a Conserving Activity*,
in which he asserts that schools must act
as conserving agents during times of accel-
erated social change. Postman is currently
professor of media ecology at New York
University. "Confusing Levels of Abstraction" originally appeared in *Crazy Talk,
Stupid Talk: How We Defeat Ourselves by*

the *Way We Talk and What to Do about It* (1976).

James C. Rettie (1904–1969)
American economist and conservationist. Rettie worked for the National Forest Service, Department of Agriculture. His long career in government service culminated in his appointment as an economic adviser for the Department of the Interior during the Kennedy and Johnson administrations. " 'But a Watch in the Night': A Scientific Fable" was written while he was a conservationist at the Upper Darby, Pennsylvania, field station, and first appeared in a collection of essays, *Forever the Land* (1950), edited by Russell Lord and Kate Lord.

Betty Rollin (1936–   )
American writer, journalist, and television reporter. Rollin spent several years as a stage and television actress before beginning a career in journalism, first at *Vogue* (1964), then at *Look* (1965–1971). Since 1971, she has worked as a network correspondent, chiefly for NBC. Rollin is the author of five books, including *First, You Cry* (1976); *Am I Getting Paid for This?: A Romance about Work* (1982); and *Last Wish* (1985). "Motherhood: Who Needs It?" originally appeared in *Look* (September 22, 1970).

Phyllis Rose (1942–   )
American writer and teacher. Educated at Radcliffe, Yale, and Harvard, Rose has been a member of the Department of English at Wesleyan University since 1969. Her major publications include *Woman of Letters: A Life of Virginia Woolf* (1978), *Parallel Lives: Five Victorian Marriages* (1983), and *Writing of Women* (1985). She is a regular contributor to *Vogue*, *The Nation*, *The Atlantic*, and *The New York Times*. "Shopping and Other Spiritual Adventures" originally appeared in a "Hers" column in *The New York Times* (April 12, 1984).

Carl Sagan (1934–   )
American astronomer and writer. Sagan received a Ph.D. in astronomy and astrophysics from the University of Chicago in 1960. He taught at the University of California, Berkeley, and at Harvard before joining the faculty of Cornell, where he is currently professor of astronomy and director of the Laboratory for Planetary Studies. While Sagan's early writing concerns his work as an astronomer, *The Dragons of Eden* (1977) delves into the subject of human intelligence. Like *Broca's Brain* (1979) and his television series "Cosmos," it extended Sagan's audience considerably. His novel *Contact* (1985) became a best seller. "The Abstractions of Beasts" originally appeared in Sagan's Pulitzer Prize–winning book *The Dragons of Eden*.

Jean-Paul Sartre (1905–1980)
French playwright, novelist, critic, philosopher, and left-wing activist. After earning an advanced degree in philosophy, Sartre became a provincial schoolmaster, then a playwright and writer of philosophical essays. Described by *The New York Times* as "a rebel of a thousand causes, a modern Don Quixote," Sartre was a major force in the intellectual life of post-World War II France. His philosophy of existentialism influenced generations of artists and thinkers. Steadfastly independent, Sartre refused both the Nobel Prize for Literature (1964) and the Legion of Honor. He died having completed only three volumes of a four-volume study of Gustave Flaubert. A sampling of his major works includes *The Flies* (1943), *Being and Nothingness* (1943), *No Exit* (1944), and *Life Situations* (1977). "Existentialism" is taken from *Existentialism* (1947).

Jonathan Schell (1943–   )
American writer and editor. While he was a graduate student in Far Eastern history at Harvard, Schell, returning from study in Japan, accompanied American forces on their evacuation of the South Vietnamese village of Ben Suc (January 1967) and wrote a series of articles on the operation for *The New Yorker*. A contributing editor to that magazine since 1967, Schell has written four books, the contents of which first appeared in *The New Yorker*: two books on the American war in Vietnam— *The Village of Ben Suc* (1967) and *The Military Half: An Account of Destruction in Quang Ngai and Quang Tin* (1968); a chronicle of Richard Nixon's presidency —*The Time of Illusion* (1975); and a detailed consideration of the consequences of nuclear war,— *The Fate of the Earth* (1982). "The Destructive Power of a One-Megaton Bomb on New York City" comes from *The Fate of the Earth*.

Hans A. Schmitt (1921–   )
American historian with special interests in French intellectual history and German constitutional history. Born in Frankfurt, Germany, he and his family fled to the

United States to escape Hitler. After receiving a Ph.D. from the University of Chicago, Schmitt began a college teaching career that culminated in his appointment as professor of history at the University of Virginia. He has written a number of books, including *The Path to European Union* (1962), *Charles Peguy* (1967), and *Historians of Modern Europe* (ed., 1971). "January 30, 1933: A Memoir" originally appeared in the *Virginia Quarterly Review* (Winter 1983).

E. F. Schumacher (1911–1977)

British economist and writer. Born in Bonn, Schumacher studied abroad in the 1930s and returned to Germany under Hitler only to flee to England in 1937. Schumacher worked for the British government during World War II, drafting theories for a welfare state. After the war, he became economic adviser to Britain's National Coal Board (1950–1970). His *Small Is Beautiful* (1973), an economic study that advocates small-scale use of technology, became an international best seller. "Levels of Being" is the second chapter in Schumacher's last book, *A Guide for the Perplexed* (1977).

Nancy Sommers (1951–   )

American teacher and writer. A specialist in the theory and practice of composition, Sommers has taught writing at Boston University, the Harvard Graduate School of Business Administration, New York University, and the University of Oklahoma, where she served as director of composition. At the Rutgers Graduate School of Education, she did her research on the role of revision in the writing process. She is currently associate director of expository writing at Harvard. "Revision Strategies of Student Writers and Experienced Adult Writers" originally appeared in *College Composition and Communication* 31 (December 1980).

Brent Staples (1951–   )

American journalist and writer. Born in Chester, Pennsylvania, Staples holds a Ph.D. in psychology from the University of Chicago. He is Assistant Metropolitan Editor of *The New York Times*. His essay "Just Walk On By" appeared in *Ms.* magazine in September 1986. An excerpt, entitled "Black Men and Public Space," was published in *Harper's* (December 1986).

Wallace Stegner (1909–   )

American essayist, novelist, and teacher. Influenced by Twain, Cather, and Conrad, Stegner writes of the development of individuals within particular landscapes. Stegner's landscapes are often those of the American West, for he is a serious naturalist with special interest in that area. In a long career, he has written and edited more than forty books, among them the novels *Remembering Laughter* (1937), *The Big Rock Candy Mountain* (1943), and *Recapitulation* (1979), as well as historical narratives like *Mormon Country* (1941) and *The Gathering of Zion: The Story of the Mormon Trail* (1964). Stegner is a member of the Department of English at Stanford University. "The Town Dump" originally appeared in *Wolf Willow: A History, a Story, and a Memory of the Last Plains Frontier* (1963, 1980). "Goodbye to All T--t" comes from the book of the same name, published in 1965.

Benjamin Stein (1944–   )

American novelist, scriptwriter, and writer. After undergraduate study at Columbia, Stein earned his degree in law at Yale, then went to work for the Federal Trade Commission before becoming a speechwriter for Presidents Nixon (1973–1974) and Ford (1974). In 1974, he moved to the West Coast and became a scriptwriter for Norman Lear (1976–1977), a free-lance writer, and a columnist for the *Los Angeles Herald-Examiner*. Stein has written over a dozen books, including fiction (*On the Brink*, 1977; *The Croesus Conspiracy*, 1978) as well as nonfiction (*Dreemz*, 1978; *The View from Sunset Boulevard: America as Brought to You by the People Who Make Television*, 1979). "Whatever Happened to Small-Town America?" originally appeared in *The Public Interest* no. 44 (Summer 1976). It was subsequently reprinted in *The View from Sunset Boulevard*.

Michael Stone (1948–   )

American journalist. "Should Testing for the AIDS Virus Be Mandatory?" is Part III of "Q. and A. on AIDS," which appeared in *New York Magazine* (March 23, 1987).

Jonathan Swift (1667–1745)

Anglo-Irish poet, satirist, and cleric. Born to English parents who resided in Ireland, Swift studied at Trinity College, Dublin, then departed for London (1689). There he became part of the literary and political worlds, beginning his career by writing political pamphlets in support of the Tory cause. Ordained in the Church of Ireland

(1695), Swift was appointed dean of St. Patrick's Cathedral, Dublin, in 1713 and held the post until his death. One of the master satirists of the English language, he wrote several scathing attacks on extremism, including *The Tale of a Tub* (1704), *The Battle of the Books* (1704), and *A Modest Proposal* (1729), as well as poetry, but he is probably best known for his novel *Gulliver's Travels* (1726).

Dylan Thomas (1914–1953)

Welsh poet and writer. Born and raised in the coal-mining district of Wales, Thomas lived a turbulent life marked by chronic alcoholism that helped bring about his early death. His writing, though, particularly his recollections of childhood, reveals an awareness of the sweetness of living that is expressed in bold, inventive, often playful language. Although he is perhaps best known for his poetry, particularly the verse drama *Under Milk Wood* (1954), Thomas also wrote short stories, plays, and film scripts. *Quite Early One Morning* (1954), a collection of his reminiscences of a Welsh childhood, and especially *A Child's Christmas in Wales* (1954) have become classics. "Memories of Christmas" first appeared in *The Listener* (December 20, 1945). It was later reprinted in *Quite Early One Morning*.

Lewis Thomas (1913–   )

American physician, teacher, writer, and humanist. Educated at Princeton and Harvard Medical School, Thomas has specialized in pediatrics, public health, and cancer research. From 1973 until 1980, he served as president of Memorial Sloan-Kettering Cancer Center in New York City; he is currently Emeritus President there. In 1970, Thomas began writing occasional essays for the *New England Journal of Medicine*. A number of these, gathered in *The Lives of a Cell* (1974), established Thomas's reputation as a writer. Since then, three more collections have been published: *The Medusa and the Snail* (1979), *The Youngest Science* (1983), and *Late Night Thoughts on Listening to Mahler's Ninth Symphony* (1983). His most recent work, *The Lasker Awards: Four Decades of Scientific Medical Progress* (1986), traces developments in cancer research. "Humanities and Science" was first published in *Late Night Thoughts*; "Notes on Punctuation" and "On Magic in Medicine" originally appeared in the *New England Journal of Medicine* before publication in *The Medusa and the Snail*;

"The Long Habit" appeared in *The Lives of a Cell* after having been published in the *New England Journal of Medicine*.

James Thurber (1894–1961)

American humorist, cartoonist, and writer. Born in Columbus, Ohio, Thurber attended Ohio State University. He started his career as a professional writer working for the *Columbus Dispatch* (1920–1924), then moved on to the *Chicago Tribune* and the *New York Evening Post*. In 1927, encouraged by E. B. White, he became managing editor of and staff writer for *The New Yorker*. Throughout his career he contributed stories, essays, and cartoons to the magazine. Thurber wrote more than thirty books, including *The Owl in the Attic and Other Perplexities* (1931), *The Beast in Me and Other Animals* (1948), and *The Secret Life of Walter Mitty* (1939). "University Days" comes from Thurber's *My Life and Hard Times* (1933), "A Dog's Eye View of Man" comes from his *Thurber's Dogs* (1955); and "The Rabbits Who Caused All the Trouble" comes from Thurber's *Fables for Our Time* (1940).

Paul Tillich (1886–1965)

German-American philosopher and theologian. Born into a German Lutheran family and educated at several German universities, Tillich served as an army chaplain in World War I. Afterward, he joined the theology faculty of the University of Berlin. When Hitler came to power, Tillich was dismissed from the Chair of Philosophy at Frankfurt University. He fled to the United States, where he spent over twenty years on the faculty of the Union Theological Seminary in New York City. Upon retirement, he became University Professor at Harvard. Tillich's most important work, the three-volume *Systematic Theology*, was published in 1963. Among other important works are *The Eternal Now* (1963) and *A History of Christian Thought* (revised edition, 1968). "The Riddle of Inequality" comes from *The Eternal Now*, a collection of Tillich's sermons.

John Updike (1932–   )

American poet, fiction writer, and critic. After attending Harvard and Oxford, Updike joined the staff of *The New Yorker*, beginning an association that continues today. He has written over thirty books, including collections of poetry (*The Carpentered Hen and Other Tame Crea-*

tures, 1958; *Seventy Poems*, 1972), short stories (some collected in *The Music School*, 1966; *Trust Me*, 1987), and novels (*The Centaur*, 1963; *The Witches of Eastwick*, 1984; *Roger's Version*, 1986). Today, Updike writes occasional essays, short stories, and poems for *The New Yorker*, while serving as a regular book reviewer for that magazine. "Beer Can" originally appeared in the "Talk of the Town" section of *The New Yorker* (January 18, 1964).

Judith Viorst (1931–)
American poet, writer, and editor. Viorst began writing poetry as a child and published her first book of poems, *The Village Square*, in 1965. But it was not until her second book, *It's Hard to Be Hip over Thirty and Other Tragedies of Married Life* (1968), that she became well known as a writer of humorous verse. Two more volumes, *How Did I Get to Be Forty and Other Atrocities* (1976) and *When Did I Stop Being Twenty and Other Injustices* (1987), followed. A writer of fiction and nonfiction for children, Viorst has also contributed a regular column to *Redbook* magazine since 1972. "Good as Guilt" is taken from *Necessary Losses* (1986), her study of confronting loss and separation as part of emotional and psychological growth.

Eudora Welty (1909–)
American writer, critic, amateur painter, and photographer. Born and brought up in Jackson, Mississippi, Welty has retained her deep attachment to the people and places of the South. After graduating from the University of Wisconsin in 1929 and a year's study at Columbia University's School of Business, she returned to Jackson and eventually found work as a publicity agent for the Works Progress Administration, a New Deal social agency. With the help of Robert Penn Warren and Cleanth Brooks, she had several short stories published, and her literary career was launched. Welty has published four collections of short stories, three novellas, two novels (*The Optimist's Daughter* [1972] won a Pulitzer Prize), two volumes of photographs, and an acclaimed collection of critical essays, *The Eye of the Story* (1978). "One Writer's Beginnings" is taken from her memoir, *One Writer's Beginnings* (1985).

E. B. White (1899–1985)
American poet, journalist, editor, and essayist. After graduating from Cornell in

1921, White became a reporter, then an advertising copywriter before beginning a sixty-year career on the staff of *The New Yorker*. With Harold Ross, the magazine's founding editor, and Katharine Angell, its literary editor, White made *The New Yorker* the most important publication of its kind in the United States. He wrote poems and articles for the magazine and served as a discreet and helpful editor. Among his many books, three written for children earned him lasting fame: *Stuart Little* (1945), *Charlotte's Web* (1952), and *The Trumpet of the Swan* (1970). White revised and edited William Strunk's text *The Elements of Style*, a classic guide. "Once More to the Lake" originally appeared in "One Man's Meat," White's column for *Harper's Magazine* (October 1941); it was reprinted in *The Essays of E. B. White* (1977). "Progress and Change" also appeared in "One Man's Meat" (December 1938); it was reprinted in a collection of the same title (1942). "Democracy" first appeared in *The New Yorker* (July 3, 1944); it was reprinted in *The Wild Flag* (1946). "Some Remarks on Humor" is adapted from the Preface to *Subtreasury of American Humor*, edited by Katharine S. White and E. B. White (1941).

Walt Whitman (1819–1892)
American poet and writer. Born on Long Island and raised in Brooklyn, New York, Whitman received scant formal education before going to work at age eleven in a newspaper office. Even though he taught school from 1835 to 1840 and worked at several government posts during his lifetime, Whitman considered himself a writer, publishing poetry, stories, and newspaper articles from the age of nineteen. In 1855, he published *Leaves of Grass*, a series of twelve poems that most scholars consider his finest work. As it evolved through a number of editions, *Leaves of Grass* came to include well over 100 poems, including "Calamus," "Crossing Brooklyn Ferry," and "Out of the Cradle Endlessly Rocking." In his poetry and prose, Whitman celebrates the landscape and people of the United States. Although he was an ardent Democrat, he supported Lincoln; indeed, Lincoln was one of the subjects of Whitman's moving elegy "When Lilacs Last in the Dooryard Bloom'd" (1865). "Death of Abraham Lincoln" comes from Whitman's *Specimen Days* (1882), which partly consists of diary

entries and newspaper articles written during the previous two decades.

Edward O. Wilson (1929–)
American biologist, writer, and teacher. After receiving a Ph.D. in biology from Harvard, Wilson remained there and is now Frank B. Baird, Jr. Professor of Science. Early in his career, Wilson became an expert on ants and social insects. In 1975, his focus shifted to sociobiology. His book *Sociobiology: The New Synthesis* (1975) sets forth the principles of this new science, which interprets behavior in biological terms. Wilson's central thesis, that all human behavior is determined by genetic structures, ignited controversy. Subsequent books—*On Human Nature* (1978); *Genes, Mind and Culture* (with Charles Lumsden, 1981); *Promethean Fire* (1983) —present Wilson's further explorations of the subject. His most recent book, *Biophilia: The Human Bond to Other Species* (1984), from which "The Superorganism" comes, is an ethical appeal for the conservation of all life.

Virginia Woolf (1882–1941)
English novelist, critic, and essayist. The daughter of respected philosopher and writer Sir Leslie Stephen, Woolf educated herself by unrestricted reading in her father's library. She lived at the center of the "Bloomsbury Group," a celebrated gathering of artists, scholars, and writers. Woolf, together with her husband socialist writer Leonard Woolf, founded the Hogarth Press. Her work, whether it be nonfiction or fiction, is marked by a resonant autobiographical voice. *A Room of One's Own* (1929), an historical investigation of women and creativity; *Mrs. Dalloway* (1925), *To the Lighthouse* (1927), and *The Waves* (1931), novels about artis-

tic consciousness and the development of personality; *The Common Reader* (1925, 1932), collections of essays on topics as diverse as literature and automobiles, reveal penetrating intelligence as well as innovations in narrative technique. "My Father: Leslie Stephen," originally entitled "Leslie Stephen, the Philosopher at Home: A Daughter's Memories," was first published in the London *Times* (November 28, 1932), on the centenary of his birth; it was later reprinted in *Atlantic Monthly* (March 1950) and in a collection of Woolf's essays, *The Captain's Death Bed* (1950). "The Death of the Moth" first appeared in a collection of essays bearing that title (1942). "What the Novelist Gives Us" comes from the essay "How Should One Read a Book?" in *The Second Common Reader* (1932). "In Search of a Room of One's Own" comes from *A Room of One's Own*. "The New Biography" comes from *Granite and Rainbow*, © 1958 by Leonard Woolf.

William Zinsser (1922–)
American journalist, writer, and teacher. After graduating from Princeton in 1944 and serving in the army for two years, Zinsser joined the staff of the *New York Herald Tribune* (1946–1959), first as a features editor, then as a drama editor and film critic, and finally as an editorial writer. In 1959, he became a free-lance writer, joining the English faculty at Yale University from 1971 until 1979. Zinsser is the author of more than a dozen books, among them the well-known *On Writing Well: An Informal Guide to Writing Non-Fiction* (1976; revised edition, 1980). "College Pressures" originally appeared in *Blair and Ketchum's Country Journal* (April 1979).

Index

746 INDEX

Murray: "The Growing Danger" from *Discover Magazine*, February 1987. © 1978 Family Media Inc. Reprinted by permission.

Ngũgĩ: "Decolonizing the Mind" from *Decolonising the Mind: The Politics of Language in African Literature*. Copyright © 1986 by Ngũgĩ wa Thiong'o. Reprinted by permission of Heineman Educational Books, Inc.

Orwell: "Politics and the English Language" copyright 1946 by Sonia Brownell Orwell; renewed 1974 by Sonia Orwell. "Shooting an Elephant" copyright 1950 by Sonia Brownell Orwell; renewed 1978 by Sonia Pitt-Rivers. Both selections from *Shooting an Elephant and Other Essays* by George Orwell. Both selections reprinted by permission of Harcourt Brace Jovanovich, Inc. and the estate of the late Sonia Brownell Orwell and Martin Secker & Warburg, Ltd.

Perelman: "The Machismo Mystique" from *Vinegar Puss* by S. J. Perelman. Copyright © 1942, 1970, 1971, 1973, 1974, 1975 by S. J. Perelman. Reprinted by permission of the estate of S. J. Perelman.

Perry: "Examsmanship and the Liberal Arts: A Study in Educational Epistemology" reprinted by permission of the publishers from *Examining in Harvard College: A Collection of Essays* by Members of the Harvard Faculty, Cambridge, Mass.: Harvard University Press, 1963.

Postman: "Confusing Levels of Abstraction" from *Crazy Talk, Stupid Talk* by Neil Postman. © 1976 by Neil Postman. Reprinted by permission of the author.

Rettie: "'But a Watch in the Night'" by James C. Rettie in *Forever the Land* edited by Russell and Kate Lord. Copyright 1950 by Harper & Row, Publishers, Inc. By permission of Harper & Row, Publishers, Inc.

Rollin: "Motherhood: Who Needs It?" from *Look*, Sept. 22, 1970. © 1970 by WESH-TV Broadcasting Co.

Rose: "Shopping and Other Spiritual Adventures" from *The New York Times*, April 12, 1984. Reprinted by permission of the author. Copyright © 1984 by Phyllis Rose.

Sagan: "The Abstractions of Beasts" from *The Dragons of Eden*, by Carl Sagan. Copyright © 1977 by Carl Sagan. Reprinted by permission of the author.

Sartre: "Existentialism" from *Existentialism*. Reproduced by permission of Philosophical Library Publishers.

Schell: "The Destructive Power of a One-Megaton Bomb on New York City" from *The Fate of the Earth*, by Jonathan Schell. Copyright © 1982 by Jonathan Schell. Reprinted by permission of Alfred A. Knopf, Inc. Originally appeared in *The New Yorker*.

Schmitt: "January 30, 1933: A Memoir" by Hans Schmitt from the *Virginia Quarterly Review*, Vol. 59, No. 1, Winter 1983. Reprinted by permission.

Schumacher: "Levels of Being," Chapter 2 from *A Guide for the Perplexed* by E. F. Schumacher. Copyright © 1977 by E. F. Schumacher. Reprinted by permission of Harper & Row, Publishers, Inc.

Sommers: "Revision Strategies of Student Writers and Experienced Adult Writers" reprinted from *College Composition and Communication*, December 1980. Copyright © 1980 National Council of Teachers of English. Reprinted with permission.

Staples: "Black Men and Public Space" first appeared as "Just Walk on By," in *Ms.*, September, 1986. Copyright © 1986 by Brent Staples. Reprinted by permission.

Stegner: "The Town Dump" from *Wolf Willow* by Wallace Stegner. Copyright © 1959 by Wallace Stegner. Reprinted by permission of Brandt & Brandt Literary Agents, Inc. "Good-Bye to All T--t!" by Wallace Stegner. Copyright © 1965 by Wallace Stegner. Reprinted by permission of Brandt & Brandt Literary Agents, Inc.

Stein: "Whatever Happened to Small-Town America?" Reprinted with permission of the author from: *The Public Interest*, No. 44 (Summer, 1976), pp. 17–26. © 1976 by National Affairs, Inc.

Stone: "Should Testing for the AIDS Virus Be Mandatory?" from *New York Magazine*, March 23, 1987. Copyright © 1988 by New America Publishing, Inc. Reprinted by permission of *New York Magazine*.

Thomas, Dylan: "Memories of Christmas," from *Quite Early One Morning*, by Dylan Thomas. Copyright 1954 by New Directions Publishing Corporation. Reprinted by permission of New Directions. Also published by J. M. Dent & Sons Ltd. and reprinted by permission of David Higham Associates Limited.

Thomas, Lewis: "Notes on Punctuation" from *The Medusa and the Snail: More Notes of a Biology Watcher* by Lewis Thomas. Copyright © 1979 by Lewis Thomas. Originally published in the *New England Journal of Medicine*. "On Magic in Medicine" from *The Medusa and the Snail* by Lewis Thomas. Copyright © 1978 by Lewis Thomas. "The Long